The Australian Federal Judicial System

The Australian Federal Judicial System

EDITED BY

Brian Opeskin and Fiona Wheeler

MELBOURNE UNIVERSITY PRESS

MELBOURNE UNIVERSITY PRESS
PO Box 278, Carlton South, Victoria 3053, Australia
info@mup.unimelb.edu.au
www.mup.com.au

First published 2000

Designed by Lauren Statham, Alice Graphics
Typeset by Syarikat Seng Teik Sdn. Bhd., Malaysia, in 11/13 pt Sabon
Printed in Australia by Brown Prior Anderson, Burwood

National Library of Australia Cataloguing-in-Publication entry

The Australian federal judicial system.
  Bibliography.
  Includes index.
  ISBN 0 522 84889 3.
  1. Judicial power—Australia. 2. Jurisdiction—Australia. 3. Courts—Australia. I. Opeskin, Brian. II. Wheeler, Fiona, 1966– .
347.94012

Foreword

FROM TIME TO TIME, it becomes fashionable to decry the complexities which attend the operation of the system of federal jurisdiction which is mandated by Chapter III of the Constitution. Phrases such as 'arid jurisdictional dispute' are, once again, pressed into service.

The structure imposed by the Constitution tends to be blamed, even by those professing a knowledge of constitutional law, for situations disclosing mischiefs, an answer for which in truth is placed by the Constitution in the legislators themselves.

But what, after all, is so strange in those branches of government, which enact and execute the laws of the Commonwealth, preferring, at least in some instances, to entrust the adjudication of matters arising under those laws to courts created and funded by the Parliament of the Commonwealth, whose judges are appointed under s 72 of the Constitution and whose forum is Australia as a whole?

If there is cause for dissatisfaction with fragmentation of the judicial structure it is with the unending fascination of state governments in the creation of new 'specialist' courts and tribunals. To achieve this, state legislatures contract the jurisdiction of the Supreme Courts, including their supervisory powers over inferior courts and tribunals. The significance which this, in turn, may have for the ultimate authority of the High Court is yet fully to be appreciated. The point was made by the Constitutional Commission, where in its *Final Report* in 1988 it stated that 'no part of the law of this country, whether State or federal, should be shielded from review by the High Court'.[1]

In some measure, the conscription, by s 77(iii) of the Constitution, of state courts for the exercise of federal jurisdiction has the consequence of investing them with a measure of protection from pressures against which Chapter III of the Constitution insulates federal courts. The significance in this respect for state (and territorial) courts of the reasoning in *Kable v Director of Public Prosecutions (NSW)* may be yet to be fully appreciated.[2] In some of the papers in this collection there is a tone of complaint that in this and other respects the exposition of constitutional principle by the High Court may be hedged with uncertainty as to its application in cases which are yet to arrive. To the contrary, reflection may suggest that in this may lie some of the strength and wisdom of the decisions in question.

There remains a great deal of ignorance in the legal profession concerning federal jurisdiction, both in its constitutional outlines and its detailed application. This is so even among those whose legal practices oblige them to know better. How can it still be, in the face of the exclusion of the Supreme Courts by s 38 of the *Judiciary Act 1903* (Cth), which has been amended only once in nearly a century,[3] that counsel commence in a state Supreme Court actions for mandamus against Ministers for the Commonwealth, apparently relying on the general investment of federal jurisdiction by s 39 of that Act? In an action brought in a state court between residents of different states, even on a common law cause of action, the jurisdiction exercised is federal and ss 79 and 80 of the *Judiciary Act* pick up the law of that state (not just its procedural law) as surrogate federal law.

---

[1] Australian Constitutional Commission (1988) vol. 1, 386.

[2] (1996) 189 CLR 51.

[3] By s 5 of the *Judiciary Amendment Act (No 2) 1984 (Cth)* to include a reference to the power of remitter under s 44.

However, one gets the impression from time to time that federal jurisdiction is exercised without those doing so appreciating it.

The Honourable Peter Nygh points out the importance of ss 79 and 80 (and much else) in his chapter. Professor Zines, with good reason, continues to ponder the significance for s 75(v) of the Constitution of Sir Owen Dixon's reasoning in *R v Hickman; Ex parte Fox and Clinton*.[4] Henry Burmester QC draws attention, not previously remarked upon to any extent in Australia, to the stricter approach taken by the United States Supreme Court over the last decade to questions of standing and contrasts it to the tendency in High Court decisions. Justice French rightly observes that had it not been for the creation of the Federal Court, for which Sir Nigel Bowen and R. J. Ellicott QC will be well remembered, the development over the last years of a substantial body of Australian administrative law would not have been possible. I mention these contributions not to be in any way exhaustive but to indicate some of the benefits to the reader of the collection.

The contributors and the editors are to be congratulated. The importance and dynamism of the subjects tackled in this volume suggest we may hope for further collections to follow.

W. M. C. Gummow
High Court of Australia
Canberra
1 July 1999

---

[4] (1945) 70 CLR 598, 615.

Contents

Preface

IN THE UNITED STATES, the intricacies of the federal judicial system have long attracted the attention of law students, scholars and practitioners alike. There, the importance of the subject matter is attested by the weight and influence of successive editions of works such as Charles Wright's *The Law of Federal Courts*, and Erwin Chemerinsky's *Federal Jurisdiction*.[1] Yet, while some might take the view that in the United States too much has been written on the subject, in Australia the converse is true. In some ways this is surprising. The hypnotic fascination of Australia's constitutional drafters with the United States model is nowhere more clearly evident than in Chapter III of the Australian Constitution, which finds close parallels with Article III of its American counterpart.

Despite some early Australian interest in the topic,[2] and a steady stream of cases defining the legal framework for the exercise of federal judicial power, Chapter III has long been a neglected subject of legal scholarship. Geoffrey Sawer published a number of influential essays on aspects of the federal judicial system, and Zelman Cowen

---

[1] Wright (1994); Chemerinsky (1994).

[2] Quick and Groom (1904).

and Leslie Zines made an outstanding contribution with *Federal Jurisdiction in Australia*.[3] But beyond these pockets of scholarship little else was written. Even within them, federal jurisdiction received bad press at the hands of these doyens of constitutional law. Sir Owen Dixon had once famously remarked that the subtleties and refinements of federal jurisdiction formed a 'special and peculiarly arid study' that few undertake.[4] To this Zelman Cowen added his own epithets, claiming the Australian law of federal jurisdiction was 'technical, complicated, difficult and not infrequently absurd'. Indeed, the Introduction to the first edition of his book ended with the pious hope that 'its most satisfying achievement would be its own relegation to the shelves of legal history'.[5]

Far from fulfilling this wish, history has demonstrated the vitality and dynamism of Chapter III of the Constitution in shaping the contours of the Australian judicial system. It is now impossible to ignore the sway of Chapter III. Under the direction of an innovative High Court, its ten modest sections have taken on the complexion of a charter for the protection of individual liberty, as well as a means for shaping the state judicial systems. The pages of the law reports now abound with cases invoking—sometimes successfully, sometimes not—the express provisions of Chapter III or the implications to be derived from them.

The federal legislature has also added to the current interest and relevance of Chapter III. When the second edition of *Federal Jurisdiction in Australia* was published in 1978, the federal judicial system was at the dawn of a new age. Two new federal courts—the Federal Court and the Family Court—had just been created with highly limited jurisdiction, and the jurisdiction of the High Court was in the midst of a long overdue rationalisation. In the years that followed we have seen the gradual expansion of the legislative jurisdiction of the federal courts, the creation and abolition of a specialist federal labour court, the enactment of co-operative legislation for

---

[3] Sawer (1961a), (1961b) and (1967); Cowen (1959); Cowen and Zines (1978).
[4] Sir Owen Dixon (1935) 608.
[5] Cowen (1959) ix, xv.

the cross-vesting of jurisdiction, a realignment of the relationship between federal tribunals and federal courts, the establishment of a federal magistracy, and the evolution of the High Court into an institution specialising in constitutional matters and the resolution of appeals on legal questions of public importance.

The variety and pace of change in the federal judicial system demonstrated to us the need for a fresh examination of the subject from a broad perspective—one that examined the founding principles, institutions, jurisdiction and personnel at the heart of the federal judicial system. The four parts of this book reflect these concerns. Specifically, Part I examines three themes that recur in complex patterns throughout the book—the separation of powers, federalism, and the independence of the judiciary. Part II examines the evolution of the federal courts, the way in which they conduct their business and their relationship to federal tribunals. Part III analyses aspects of federal jurisdiction, including issues of standing and justiciability, accrued jurisdiction, cross-vesting and choice of law. Finally, Part IV discusses the federal judges themselves—who they are, how they are appointed and removed, and their role as holders of non-judicial office. From this brief outline it should be apparent that we have sought to be comprehensive in our treatment of the subject matter, without attempting to be exhaustive. Indeed, the pace of developments in this field make futile any attempt to be exhaustive. As additional cases are decided over the next few years, two topics that are likely to call for particular attention beyond that found in this volume are the position of territorial courts and the impact of Chapter III on the judicial systems of the states.

The compilation and editing of this book could not have been achieved without the support and assistance of many organisations and individuals. We are grateful for the financial support received from the Australian National University's Publications Committee. Ben McGuire was tireless in his efforts to reduce fourteen individually authored chapters into a coherent manuscript, and managed to do so with constant good humour. Sally Nicholls provided excellent support as copy-editor. The publishers were generous in their forbearance in the face of an oft-delayed manuscript. But most especially, we are grateful for the perseverance of the contributors themselves, who generously gave advice during the project's conception, waited patiently during its long gestation, and willingly updated their chapters during a sometimes troubled labour. For them, and for others who may find this book of interest, we are delighted at last to signify its delivery.

Brian Opeskin and Fiona Wheeler
January 2000

Notes on Contributors

Margaret Allars holds a personal chair in the Faculty of Law, University of Sydney, where she teaches undergraduate and postgraduate courses in Administrative Law, Constitutional Law and Health Law. She is the author of *Introduction to Australian Administrative Law* (1990); the administrative law title in *Halsbury's Laws of Australia* (1991); *Administrative Law: Cases and Commentary* (1997); and many articles and book chapters.

Bryan Beaumont has been a Judge of the Federal Court of Australia since 1983 and is a member of that Court's Practice and Procedure Committee. In 1990–92 he was Chairman of the Australian Institute of Judicial Administration. In 1990 he was involved in the implementation of the Closer Economic Relations Protocol with New Zealand. He is a Foreign Member of the American Law Institute and an adviser on its Transnational Rules of Procedure project. Before his appointment to the Federal Court, he practised at the Australian bar.

A. R. Blackshield, LLM (Sydney), is Emeritus Professor of Law at Macquarie University; Adjunct Professor of Law at the Australian National University and the University of New South Wales; and Honorary Professor of the Indian Law Institute, New Delhi. After teaching jurisprudence and international law at the University of Sydney Law School through the 1960s, he joined the University of New South Wales Law School in 1971 as one of its six foundation members. From 1979 to 1988 he was Professor of Legal Studies at La Trobe University, and from 1988 to 1999 Professor of Law at Macquarie University. In 1983 he was a member of the Commonwealth Attorney-General's Task Force on Human Rights.

Henry Burmester QC is Chief General Counsel in the Australian Government Solicitor. He has acted as Commonwealth Solicitor-General. He has a BA, LLB (ANU) and an LLM (Virginia). Apart from a period at the Law Faculty of the Australian National University (1981–85), he has been a Commonwealth government legal adviser since 1972, principally in the fields of constitutional and international law. As adviser, he has appeared as Counsel in the International Court, the High Court, and other federal courts.

Robert French was appointed as a Judge of the Federal Court of Australia in November 1986. In 1994 he was appointed as President of the National Native Title Tribunal, an office he occupied until December 1998. He is a Council Member of the Judicial Conference of Australia and of the Australian Association of Constitutional Law. He is a former member of the Council and Board of Management of the Australian Institute of Judicial Administration.

Andrew Goldsmith was appointed to the Foundation Chair of Legal Studies, Flinders University, Adelaide, in January 1997. Previously, he taught at Monash University, Melbourne. His background is in criminology as well as law. He holds degrees in these areas from Adelaide University, London School of Economics and the University of Toronto. His earlier work includes an empirical study of the costs of litigation, as well as contributions on criminal justice, legal education and legal ethics. His published work includes *Complaints Against the Police: The Trend to External Review* (1991).

Gavan Griffith QC, of Counsel. Solicitor-General of Australia 1984–97.

Geoffrey Kennett practises as a barrister in Sydney. He grew up in Canberra and studied at the Australian National University. His public service career included stints as a legal adviser in the Office of General Counsel in the Commonwealth Attorney-General's Department (1991–96) and as Counsel Assisting the Commonwealth Solicitor-General (1997–98). He appeared in some of the leading constitutional cases of the 1990s and has published articles on constitutional law and insurance law.

Sir Anthony Mason AC KBE is a former Chief Justice of the High Court of Australia. He is a National Fellow at the Research School of Social Sciences, Australian National University, the President of the Solomon Islands Court of Appeal, a Judge of the Supreme Court of Fiji, and a member of the panel of foreign judges of the Hong Kong Court of Final Appeal. Sir Anthony was Arthur Goodhart Professor in Legal Science at the University of Cambridge and holds honorary doctorates from a number of universities.

Peter Nygh, LLD (Sydney), SJD (Michigan), has been Adjunct Professor of Law at the University of New South Wales since 1998. He was Professor of Law at the University of Sydney (1969–74), Foundation Professor and Head of the School of Law at Macquarie University (1974–79), a Judge of the Family Court of Australia assigned to the appellate division (1979–93), and a Member of the Australian Delegation to the Hague Conference on Private International Law (1976 and 1996–99). He was also a Principal Member of the Refugee Review Tribunal (1998–99). His publications include *Conflict of Laws in Australia* (6th edn 1995); McLachlan and Nygh (eds), *Transnational Torts Litigation* (1996); and *Autonomy in International Contracts* (1999).

Brian Opeskin is a Senior Lecturer in the Faculty of Law at the University of Sydney, where he has taught since 1989. His main research and teaching interests are in the field of public law, and he has published widely in the areas of constitutional law, public international law, and private international law as they affect Australia's federal system of government. He is a consultant to the Australian Law Reform Commission in its reference on the *Judiciary Act 1903* (Cth). His published work includes Opeskin and Rothwell (eds), *International Law and Australian Federalism* (1997).

Stephen Parker is Professor of Law and Dean at Monash University. He previously held positions at Griffith University, the Australian National University, and University College, Cardiff. Professor Parker's research interests include legal ethics, the court system, judicial independence, civil procedure and family law. He has been the Honorary Secretary and Treasurer of The Judicial Conference of Australia since 1996.

Cheryl Saunders holds a personal chair in law at the University of Melbourne and is Director of the University's Centre for Comparative Constitutional Studies. She has specialist research interests in comparative constitutional law and theory, constitution-making and design, and intergovernmental relations. She is joint editor of the *Public Law Review* and a member of the Executive Committee of the International Association of Constitutional Law.

Fiona Wheeler is a Senior Lecturer in the Faculty of Law, Australian National University, where she teaches constitutional law and introduction to law. She has written a doctoral thesis on the separation of federal judicial power and has published a number of articles in the area. She is Comments Editor of the *Public Law Review* and Treasurer of the Australian Association of Constitutional Law.

Leslie Zines AO, LLB (Sydney), LLM (Harvard), LLD (honoris causa) (ANU), FASSA, is Emeritus Professor and Visiting Fellow in the Law Program, Research School of Social Sciences at the Australian National University. He was formerly Robert Garran Professor at that University and Arthur Goodhart Professor of Legal Science at the University of Cambridge. His published works include Zines and Cowen, *Federal Jurisdiction in Australia* (2nd edn 1978); *Sawer's Australian Constitutional Cases* (4th edn 1982); *Constitutional Change in the Commonwealth* (1991); and *The High Court and the Constitution* (4th edn 1997).

PART I

Recurrent Themes

1

The Separation of Powers

Cheryl Saunders

1 History and Theory

The idea of limiting power by dividing or sharing it is an old one, which has taken different forms. One was the technique of mixed government,[1] given effect in England from at least the thirteenth century, through a Parliament in which power was shared between three main estates: the Monarch, the Lords, and the Commons.[2] The influence of mixed government continues today, through the constitution of Parliaments in both England and Australia. The balance on which its efficacy depended[3] has been transformed, however, through major internal shifts in power.

The doctrine generally referred to as the separation of powers represents a different approach, dividing public power within a single level of government along functional lines.[4] It gained some currency

---

[1] Wood (1972) 197; Casper (1997) 9.

[2] Wood (1972) 20.

[3] Blackstone (1765) 44.

[4] 'Functional' is used here to distinguish a separation of powers from other forms of dispersing power. Compare its use by justices of the High Court to describe the technique by which particular functions take their character from the context in which they are exercised: *Nicholas v The Queen* (1998) 193 CLR 173.

in England during the interregnum, in the absence of two of the three estates on which the mixed constitution depended.[5] It continued to attract the attention of political theorists in the aftermath of the Restoration and the revolution of 1688: most famously John Locke canvassed the merits of the separation of legislative, executive and 'federative' powers in his Second Treatise of Civil Government in 1690.[6] The modern conception of a separation of legislative, executive and judicial power, however, generally is attributed to the French theorist, Montesquieu.[7] While Montesquieu himself may have been surprised at the results,[8] his ideas in turn influenced the Constitution of the newly independent United States of America and, in the more muted guise of separation of functions, successive constitutions in post-revolutionary France.[9] At the end of the twentieth century, most modern western democracies claimed a system of government based on a functional separation of powers of some kind.

The core concept of a separation of powers, as it has developed in western constitutionalism, involves the conferral of legislative, executive and judicial power on corresponding institutions of government. There is no blueprint, however. Complete segregation of institutions, each exercising its allotted power exclusively of others, is impracticable. Ironically, as experience of some early American state constitutions showed, effective separation demands a degree of interaction.[10] One model for a system of checks and balances was popularised in the Constitution of the United States of America. Many variations are conceivable, however: in the degree of autonomy of institutions; in the nature of the checks and balances; and in the potential for admixture of powers across institutional borders. Options for

---

[5] Wood (1972) 151; Vile (1967) 47.

[6] Locke (1690) 190–2.

[7] Montesquieu (1748) 433–8. For an evaluation of the significance of Montesquieu's writings on the evolution of the doctrine, see Wood (1972) 152; compare Vile (1967) 62.

[8] The nuances in Montesquieu's work are often ignored by those who claim him as authority: in particular, his reference to the 'power of judging' rather than to judicial power and his admiration for the exercise of the power by juries, rather than by judges: see Stoner Jr (1992) 156.

[9] Zoller (1999) 311.

[10] Wood (1972) 451.

a separation of legislative and executive power range between presidential models at one end of a broad spectrum and parliamentary systems at the other. Approaches to the separation of judicial power are also diverse. In large part, this is due to different conceptions of the judicial role in different systems. In England, the course of history created a judiciary whose role in subjecting the executive to law was accepted and whose independence thus became all the more important. In France, on the other hand, mistrust of the judiciary from pre-revolutionary times left it with a more limited function.[11]

In both cases, the course of the judiciary was set independently of separation of powers theory.[12] Reformulation of the theory to include the judiciary resulted in two distinct approaches to the separation of judicial power. In common law systems, separation of judicial power was construed not only to tolerate review of executive action but to protect judicial independence, put at greater risk by the scope of judicial power. In civilian systems in the French tradition,[13] by contrast, more closely following Montesquieu in this respect, the separation of judicial power was understood to prevent the judiciary impinging upon actions of the executive at all.[14]

With the creation of the United States Constitution, a third approach emerged. In *Marbury v Madison*[15] the Supreme Court affirmed what Alexander Hamilton had cautiously foreshadowed, that the judicial power extended to review of the validity of legislation itself.[16] The justification lay in the status of the Constitution as fundamental law. It differed from ordinary law because it drew its authority from the people. It established norms, including a federal division of power, which could not be left to the legislature of a single level of government to enforce. The task fell to the courts, reinforcing the argument for judicial independence. The separation of judicial power, ready to hand as a component of a wider system

---

[11] Bell (1992) 20.

[12] Locke (1690) 160–1; Montesquieu (1748) 434–5.

[13] Compare the Kelsenian approach: Ohlinger (1998).

[14] Zoller (1999) 187.

[15] 5 US 137 (1803).

[16] Hamilton, Jay and Madison (1787) No 78. For a brief summary of the debate on whether the Court intended to go so far, see Stoner Jr (1992) 4.

of checks and balances, was one mechanism through which independence could be secured.

The Australian Constitution drew on the constitutional traditions of both England and the United States. Each offered a different approach to relations between the three branches of government, while accepting a need for judicial independence. Whether those who framed the Australian Constitution intended to embody a separation of powers and, if so, of what kind, is far from clear. Silences in the conventions[17] and in some early constitutional texts[18] suggest that the framers may not have thought about it much at all. Quick and Garran's contemporary commentary shows that they, at least, attached significance to the similarity of the structure of the Australian Constitution with that of the United States.[19] It may be, however, that most of the delegates assumed the value of judicial independence, with which they were already familiar, but did not necessarily link it to a separation of powers.

In fact, as early as 1931, it was settled that the Australian Constitution embodied a three-way separation of powers between the legislature, the executive and the judiciary.[20] The nature of the separation was complicated, however, by the combination of parliamentary responsible government and federalism. The former necessitates an overlapping in the membership of the legislative and executive branches.[21] In the British tradition, it involves some intermixture of power as well.[22] Federalism, on the other hand, was for a long time advanced as the principal justification for a strict separation of judicial power from the other branches, in order to maintain the

---

[17] Fiona Wheeler has identified the relatively few instances in which the concept of separation of powers was mentioned, explicitly or implicitly: Wheeler (1996a).

[18] Ibid 98–9.

[19] Quick and Garran (1901) 720.

[20] *Victorian Stevedoring & General Contracting Co Pty Ltd v Dignan* (1931) 46 CLR 73. It had been stated much earlier, in the context of the separation of judicial power: see *New South Wales v Commonwealth (Wheat Case)* (1915) 20 CLR 54.

[21] Constitution s 64.

[22] The legislature can override executive power, and the executive can exercise delegated legislative power: see *Victorian Stevedoring & General Contracting Co Pty Ltd v Dignan* (1931) 46 CLR 73.

independent judiciary that the federal compact required.[23] These competing pressures were reconciled pragmatically by accepting the 'asymmetry' of the doctrine of separation of powers, Australian-style.[24] The asymmetry has become more pronounced, as the role played by the separation of judicial power in the Australian constitutional system has evolved beyond the demands of federalism.

While it takes a substantially weaker form, the separation of legislative and executive power is not insignificant in Australia. In particular, a powerful Senate in which the government generally lacks a majority forces attention to be paid to the distinction between matters that need legislative approval and those that can be done by the government alone.[25] The focus here, however, is the separation of judicial power. Part two examines and explains the extent and nature of the separation, under the law as it presently exists. Parts three, four and five respectively identify the institutional and doctrinal implications of the Australian separation of judicial power and its relevance for relations between people and the state. In part six, I briefly evaluate the contribution of the separation of judicial power to Australian constitutional arrangements. Finally, I conclude with some observations on the role of the High Court in the evolution of the doctrine that now is accepted in Australia.

2 Separation of Judicial Power

(a) Constitutional construction

Few older constitutions explicitly state the principles on which they are based and the Australian Constitution is no exception. Rather, the conclusion that the Constitution embodies a separation of powers is attributed to the terms and structure of the Constitution itself. In the words of the Privy Council: 'But, first and last, the question is one of construction and they [the Privy Council] doubt whether, had Locke and Montesquieu never lived nor the Constitution of the

---

[23] *Attorney-General of the Commonwealth of Australia v The Queen* (1957) 95 CLR 529; [1957] AC 288 (PC).

[24] *Victorian Stevedoring & General Contracting Co Pty Ltd v Dignan* (1931) 46 CLR 73, 101 (Dixon J).

[25] *Brown v West* (1990) 169 CLR 195 is an example of a failure accurately to make the distinction.

United States ever been framed, a different interpretation of the Constitution of the Commonwealth could validly have been reached'.[26]

The principal textual indication of a three-way separation of powers in the Australian Constitution is the focus of its first three chapters on the legislature, the executive and the judicature respectively. In addition, the first section of each of these three chapters— ss 1, 61, and 71—makes a statement about the disposition of legislative, executive and judicial power conferring it, apparently exclusively, on its corresponding institution.

While these features suggest a separation of some kind, they cannot themselves explain the form that the doctrine came to take in Australia. Contrary to the conclusions that principles of statutory interpretation normally would draw from the almost identical vesting provisions in ss 1, 61 and 71,[27] the degree of separation between legislative and executive power on the one hand and judicial power on the other is substantially different, prompting the acknowledgement of 'asymmetry' noted in the preceding part. The textual explanation for the difference lies elsewhere, in the substance of the chapters themselves. In particular, Chapter II expressly precludes an institutional separation of the legislature and the executive, by requiring Ministers to be members of Parliament.[28] By implication it accepts some commingling of powers as well, to the extent normally associated with the system of responsible government. By contrast, the judicature chapter, Chapter III, recognises no such intermixture, either of institutions or of powers. It imposes no qualification, of the kind found in Chapter II, on a separation of judicial power.

The nature and degree of the Australian separation of judicial power has been attributed to the 'detailed and exhaustive' character of the judicature chapter, Chapter III.[29] The relevant provisions of

---

[26] *Attorney-General of the Commonwealth of Australia v The Queen* (1957) 95 CLR 529, 540; see also *R v Kirby; Ex parte Boilermakers' Society of Australia* (1956) 94 CLR 254, 275 (Dixon CJ, McTiernan, Fullagar and Kitto JJ).

[27] Section 61 vests executive power in the Queen; ss 1 and 71 require power to be vested in the Parliament and the courts respectively, once those institutions are established.

[28] Constitution s 64.

[29] *Attorney-General of the Commonwealth of Australia v The Queen* (1957) 95 CLR 529, 538.

Chapter III for this purpose are as follows. Section 71 identifies the High Court, other federal courts, and courts of the states as the three categories of courts in which the 'judicial power of the Commonwealth' may be vested. Sections 75 and 76 list the nine heads of jurisdiction that are vested in the High Court or that may be vested by the Parliament in other Chapter III courts. Section 73 describes the courts from which appeals may lie to the High Court. Section 72 protects the independence of the two categories of courts which lie within the Commonwealth sphere through the traditional procedures for appointment and removal, guaranteed levels of remuneration and tenure until retirement.

Nowhere does the Constitution say that courts may not exercise other powers properly conferred on them or that judicial power may not be vested elsewhere. These are 'negative' implications, drawn from the affirmative provisions of Chapter III, with the assistance of the assumption that the chapter is exhaustive.[30] The implications are persuasive, but not necessarily compelling.[31] And nor, on its face, is Chapter III truly exhaustive. Section 51(xxxix) confers power on the Commonwealth Parliament to legislate for 'matters incidental to the execution of any power vested by this Constitution in the Parliament ... or in the Government of the Commonwealth or in the Federal Judicature'. While the limited nature of this power is said to affirm the authority of Chapter III,[32] it nevertheless lies outside it. The constitutional terms of reference of the Inter-State Commission in Chapter IV include 'powers of adjudication' which, potentially, invoke judicial power.[33] Judicial power may be exercised by military tribunals in relation to members of the defence forces[34]

---

[30] *Gould v Brown* (1998) 193 CLR 346, 418–19 (McHugh J), 448–9 (Gummow J).

[31] For one alternative explanation, see Finnis (1968).

[32] *Attorney-General of the Commonwealth of Australia v The Queen* (1957) 95 CLR 529, 538.

[33] Constitution s 101.

[34] *Re Tracey; Ex parte Ryan* (1989) 166 CLR 518; *Re Nolan; Ex parte Young* (1991) 172 CLR 460, 474–5 (Mason CJ and Dawson J), 481 (Brennan and Toohey JJ); and compare 489 (Deane J), 498 (Gaudron J), and 499 (McHugh J), who would have limited the exception to more peculiarly service offences.

and by the Parliament itself in contempt proceedings,[35] under the authority of relevant provisions in Chapter I of the Constitution. The apparently unrestricted power of the Commonwealth Parliament to make laws 'for the government of any territory' under s 122 in Chapter VI enables it to establish territory courts and to invest them with jurisdiction or to authorise a territory government and legislature to do so. Through the course of constitutional interpretation, each of these contra-indications has been reconciled with the core doctrine of the separation of judicial power in different ways. In the case of the territories power, as will be seen, that accommodation is under review.

The text of the Constitution alone has not determined the Australian doctrine of separation of judicial power. The perceived purposes of a separation of judicial power have also played a part in shaping the doctrine. These purposes have been, above all, to protect judicial independence and to maintain public confidence in the judiciary. Judicial independence is not viewed as an end in itself, but as a necessary prerequisite for the impartial adjudication of disputes. While early justifications of the need for impartiality focused on federalism, it is assumed now without question that judicial independence serves all spheres of adjudication and is both crucial and peculiarly at risk where government is a party or is likely to be interested in the outcome. Perceptions of the purpose served by the doctrine have evolved in other ways as well. In particular, in recent years the High Court has emphasised its importance for individuals as well as for the system as a whole and has begun to explore the ramifications of the impartial adjudication of disputes for the maintenance of the rule of law more broadly.

(b) The emergence of the Australian doctrine

The discrete character of Chapter III of the Constitution, on which the current doctrine of the separation of judicial power relies, was recognised by the High Court within the first two decades after federation. Its implications were established more gradually, however.

---

[35] *R v Richards; Ex parte Fitzpatrick and Browne* (1955) 92 CLR 157. See generally Twomey (1997).

The dual effect of the doctrine, on the power of courts as well as that of non-judicial bodies, did not emerge clearly until the decision in *R v Kirby; Ex parte Boilermakers' Society of Australia* (*Boilermakers' Case*) in 1956.[36]

The exclusive authority of Chapter III courts to exercise federal judicial power was settled by 1918. *New South Wales v Commonwealth* (*Wheat Case*)[37] removed the principal textual obstacle to it by interpreting the terms of reference of the Inter-State Commission to authorise the exercise of quasi-judicial, but not judicial, power. The difficulty could not be overcome by establishing the Commission as a court, because the tenure of its members was set by s 103 of the Constitution and did not comply with Chapter III. The same principle was applied in *Waterside Workers' Federation of Australia v J W Alexander Ltd* (*Alexander's Case*) [38] in the less obvious context of the Commonwealth Court of Conciliation and Arbitration. The 'Court' was established to deal with industrial disputes by way of conciliation and arbitration and, also, to enforce its own awards, thus exercising a mix of judicial and non-judicial power. It was constituted by a justice of the High Court of Australia for a period of seven years. The conferral of judicial power was held to be invalid, but severable.[39] The flaw, apparently, was the conferral of judicial power on a body that was not established in accordance with the tenure requirements of Chapter III.[40] The first limb of the doctrine was settled.

Three years later, the seeds of the second were sown. In *Re Judiciary and Navigation Acts* the issue was whether an advisory jurisdiction could be validly conferred on the High Court. It was held that it could not.[41] The Court accepted that the function was

---

[36] (1956) 94 CLR 254.

[37] (1915) 20 CLR 54.

[38] (1918) 25 CLR 434 (Griffith CJ, Barton, Isaacs, Powers and Rich JJ).

[39] In *Alexander's Case*, Barton, Isaacs, Powers and Rich JJ held the conferral of judicial power to be invalid. Barton J did not agree that it was severable; Higgins J joined the others to form a majority on this point.

[40] Ibid 457, 462 (Barton J), 469 (Isaacs and Rich JJ), 489 (Powers J).

[41] (1921) 29 CLR 257 (Knox CJ, Gavan Duffy, Powers, Rich and Starke JJ; Higgins J dissenting).

judicial in this case, because it involved 'an authoritative declaration of the law'.[42] It was not the kind of judicial power contemplated by Chapter III, however. Abstract determination of questions of law did not constitute a 'matter' within the meaning of ss 75 and 76. The exhaustive character of those sections operated 'as a necessary exclusion of any other exercise of original jurisdiction'.[43]

Strictly speaking, *Re Judiciary and Navigation Acts* decided only that the judicial power that could be conferred on the High Court by the Commonwealth must be federal judicial power. Its wider ramifications were less clear, however. With hindsight it is easy to see how the decision supports the view that Chapter III is an exhaustive statement of the power that may be vested in federal courts. But at the time it was less obvious. An alternative view, drawing on the British, rather than the American antecedents of the Australian judicature and encouraged by the absence of specific prohibition, might have accepted that the Parliament could confer non-judicial power on federal courts under s 51 subject, perhaps, to limits to protect the integrity of the judicial function. After inconclusive skirmishes,[44] the issue finally was joined, in the *Boilermakers' Case*, in another challenge to the validity of proceedings before the Commonwealth Court of Conciliation and Arbitration, again exercising both arbitral and enforcement functions, but with its members now appointed for life.

The combination of powers was held to be unconstitutional, both in the High Court, by a majority,[45] and in the Privy Council. With characteristic pragmatism, the end result was that the conferral of judicial power failed. Despite formal compliance with s 72 of the Constitution, the Court of Conciliation and Arbitration was not

---

[42] Ibid 264. It has since been doubted whether the power was judicial. In particular, see *Attorney-General of the Commonwealth of Australia v The Queen* (1957) 95 CLR 529, 541.

[43] *Re Judiciary and Navigation Acts* (1921) 29 CLR 257, 265.

[44] See, for example, *R v Federal Court of Bankruptcy; Ex parte Lowenstein* (1938) 59 CLR 556, 566 (Latham CJ), 577 (Starke J); compare 585 (Dixon and Evatt JJ).

[45] *R v Kirby; Ex parte Boilermakers' Society of Australia* (1956) 94 CLR 254 (Dixon CJ, McTiernan, Fullagar, and Kitto JJ; Williams, Webb and Taylor JJ dissenting).

a Chapter III court, because the preponderance of its power was non-judicial.[46] At a more general level, however, the case stands for the proposition that a federal court can exercise non-judicial power only when it is incidental to judicial power. Alternative formulations were rejected which would have allowed courts to exercise non-judicial power unless it were 'inconsistent' with judicial power judged by the standards of natural justice[47] or the demands of the judicial process[48] or unless a power were 'essentially legislative or executive' in character.[49] The outcome was justified by the need to preserve judicial independence, especially under a regime in which courts interpret and apply a federal constitution as fundamental law.[50]

There was occasional speculation after the *Boilermakers' Case* was decided, fuelled by observations from the bench, that the doctrine might be modified to enable federal courts to exercise a limited degree of non-judicial power.[51] The moment has passed, however, and the two limbs of the *Boilermakers' Case* are now firmly entrenched, by precedent and by institutional practices and doctrines to which the precedents have given rise.

(c) The definition of judicial power

Taken at face value, the version of the separation of powers that emerged from the *Boilermakers' Case* made rigid distinctions between courts and other institutions and between judicial and other powers. In fact, however, several features give it a degree of flexibility. The most significant of these features is the definition of judicial power.

A separation of judicial power, in an entrenched constitution, demands the ability to determine whether functions are judicial or

---

[46] Ibid 289; *Attorney-General of the Commonwealth of Australia v The Queen* (1957) 95 CLR 529, 535.

[47] *Attorney-General of the Commonwealth of Australia v The Queen* (1957) 95 CLR 529, 542.

[48] *R v Kirby; Ex parte Boilermakers' Society of Australia* (1956) 94 CLR 254, 315 (Williams J).

[49] Ibid 340–1 (Taylor J).

[50] Ibid 269, 276.

[51] *R v Joske; Ex parte Australian Building Construction Employees & Builders' Labourers' Federation* (1974) 130 CLR 87, 90 (Barwick CJ).

non-judicial in character.[52] The Constitution itself provides no guidance beyond the use of the word 'matter' to preface the nine heads of federal jurisdiction. The High Court consistently has emphasised that no exhaustive definition is possible. In *Brandy v Human Rights and Equal Opportunity Commission* (*Brandy's Case*) four justices admitted to a temptation to define judicial power as 'the power exercised by courts ... [which] can only be defined by reference to what courts do and the way in which they do it'.[53] Nevertheless, within the first decade after federation, a working definition had begun to emerge,[54] based on experience and the traditional functions of courts in a system of common law.[55] Key elements of this definition identified judicial power as a binding and authoritative determination of rights, duties and other justiciable claims, by reference to law. Applying this definition, the arbitral function that was in issue in both *Alexander's Case* and the *Boilermakers' Case* was non-judicial: determination of a new award or alteration of an old one was 'ancillary to the legislative function'.[56] The determination and punishment of criminal guilt[57] and the trial of actions for breach of contract[58] and civil wrongs,[59] by contrast, have long since been accepted as judicial.

Notoriously, however, the identification of judicial power is difficult at the margin and the margin may be broad. Courts themselves make new law in deciding cases.[60] Bodies other than courts properly

---

[52] *R v Kirby; Ex parte Boilermakers' Society of Australia* (1956) 94 CLR 254, 333 (Taylor J).

[53] (1995) 183 CLR 245, 267. For a more recent analysis see *Nicholas v The Queen* (1998) 193 CLR 173.

[54] *Huddart, Parker & Co Pty Ltd v Moorehead* (1909) 8 CLR 330, 357 (Griffith CJ).

[55] *Waterside Workers' Federation of Australia v J W Alexander Ltd* (1918) 25 CLR 434, 442 (Griffith CJ).

[56] Ibid 464; *R v Kirby; Ex parte Boilermakers' Society of Australia* (1956) 94 CLR 254, 281–2.

[57] *Chu Kheng Lim v Minister for Immigration* (1992) 176 CLR 1, 27; *Polyukhovich v Commonwealth* (1991) 172 CLR 501, 536–9, 608–10, 613–14, 632, 647, 649, 685, 705–7, 721.

[58] *Brandy v Human Rights and Equal Opportunity Commission* (1995) 183 CLR 245, 258.

[59] *H A Bachrach Pty Ltd v Queensland* (1998) 156 ALR 563, 567.

[60] For a recent analysis see McHugh (1999).

make decisions by reference to law. Long usage has made acceptable the exercise of powers that are ostensibly judicial by bodies other than courts and the exercise by courts of powers that do not neatly fit the classic definition. Additional criteria therefore have been developed for use in appropriate cases.

A broad discretion, exercisable by reference to policy considerations the nature or substance of which are not normally associated with the judiciary, is unlikely to constitute judicial power.[61] A power that historically was exercised by courts or by a body other than a court may take its character from that fact.[62] Legislative context may affect characterisation of a power as well.[63] These last two considerations have caused a further distinction to be drawn within the category of power exercisable by courts. Some powers are 'inalienable'.[64] Others, however, may take their character from the context and be conferred on non-judicial bodies;[65] or be regulated by Parliament;[66] or be exercised by court officers, under judicial supervision.[67] The distinction between 'core' and other functions may not be the same in all cases.

One further criterion, which generally is determinative, is the binding quality of a decision. Decisions of courts are final in the sense that, subject to appeal processes, they are immediately enforceable. Other bodies may engage in dispute settlement, may adopt adjudicatory procedures and may evaluate claims by reference to law. All this may be consistent with the separation of judicial power, in the absence of a power of enforcement.[68] So, when first established, the

---

[61] *Queen Victoria Memorial Hospital v Thornton* (1953) 87 CLR 144; *R v Trade Practices Tribunal; Ex parte Tasmanian Breweries Pty Ltd* (1970) 123 CLR 361; *Precision Data Holdings Ltd v Wills* (1991) 173 CLR 167.

[62] *R v Davison* (1954) 90 CLR 353; *R v Quinn; Ex parte Consolidated Food Corporation* (1977) 138 CLR 1.

[63] *R v Davison* (1954) 90 CLR 353, 370 (Dixon CJ and McTiernan J).

[64] *Brandy v Human Rights and Equal Opportunity Commission* (1995) 183 CLR 245, 258.

[65] *H A Bachrach Pty Ltd v Queensland* (1998) 156 ALR 563, 567.

[66] *Nicholas v The Queen* (1998) 193 CLR 173, 208.

[67] *Harris v Caladine* (1991) 172 CLR 84, 95.

[68] *Shell Co of Australia Ltd v Federal Commissioner of Taxation* [1931] AC 275.

Human Rights and Equal Opportunity Commission (HREOC) was able to conduct inquiries into complaints about breaches of specified human rights and to issue determinations, as long as enforcement of the Commission's determinations lay with the Federal Court. Once the legislation was amended to require determinations to be lodged with the Court and to give them effect as an order of the Court, in the absence of an application for review, the line was crossed. The new procedure was invalid because, in effect, it made the determinations of the HREOC directly enforceable.[69]

(d) Institutional flexibility

The Australian doctrine of the separation of powers assumes the institutional separation of courts, as the forum for the exercise of judicial power. As the doctrine has evolved, however, a degree of institutional flexibility has been accepted. The common characteristic of the two principal examples is that control of the nature and extent of the departure from a strict separation lies with the judges themselves.

The first example offers some internal flexibility to courts. It accepts that federal courts may be authorised to delegate certain functions of a judicial character to registrars and other non-judicial officers of the court, without infringing the separation of judicial power.[70] Delegations must be limited; they may authorise non-judicial officers to make consent orders[71] but not to deal with 'the more important aspects of contested matters'.[72] And they must be subject to effective supervision and control by the judges themselves, preferably through the availability of a hearing de novo.[73]

The second example concerns the extra-curial activities of judges. This is the subject of Chapter 14 and only its essential features need be noted here. Within limits that are continuing to evolve,

---

[69] *Brandy v Human Rights and Equal Opportunity Commission* (1995) 183 CLR 245.

[70] *Harris v Caladine* (1991) 172 CLR 84.

[71] Ibid (Mason CJ, Deane, Dawson, Gaudron and McHugh JJ; Brennan and Toohey JJ dissenting).

[72] Ibid 95 (Mason CJ and Deane J).

[73] Ibid 95 (Mason CJ and Deane J), 122–3 (Dawson J), 151–2 (Gaudron J), 164 (McHugh J). See also *Harrington v Lowe* (1997) 190 CLR 311.

federal judges may be appointed to exercise non-judicial functions, individually, or as a member of another body. The present limits to the practice have been set by reference to what is described as 'the principle underlying the *Boilermakers' Case*'[74] which, in this context, is treated as coextensive with the purpose of the constitutional separation of judicial power.[75] While formulations vary, the broad goal has been described as 'the guarantee of liberty' through a system of checks and balances, to which judicial independence is a means, drawing on a reading of Montesquieu suitably anglicised by Blackstone.[76] A subsidiary but related goal is the maintenance of public confidence in adjudication.

The conditions that apply are twofold. Non-judicial functions must be conferred on a judge personally, detached from the court of which he or she is a member. At the very least, this condition means that a judge must be able to choose whether to accept appointment or not.[77] Second, the function must not be incompatible with the judicial function. Incompatibility may be of a practical nature, if a new commitment precludes proper attention to judicial duties. Consistently with principle, a function that compromises the performance of judicial functions, or that diminishes public confidence in a particular judge or in the integrity of the judiciary as a whole, is likely to be incompatible as well.[78]

Future evolution of this aspect of the separation of powers is likely to see further limits on the circumstances in which federal judges can be used to perform non-judicial functions. Powerful dissenting judgments revealed unease about this practice within the High Court from the outset. The difficulty of applying the limits that have been set are demonstrated by inconsistencies in two recent cases—*Grollo v Palmer* and *Wilson v Minister for Aboriginal and Torres Strait Islander Affairs* (*Wilson's Case*)[79]—in which public

---

[74] *Hilton v Wells* (1985) 157 CLR 57, 74 (Gibbs CJ, Wilson, and Dawson JJ).

[75] *Wilson v Minister for Aboriginal and Torres Strait Islander Affairs* (1996) 189 CLR 1, 15.

[76] Ibid 11.

[77] *Hilton v Wells* (1985) 157 CLR 57.

[78] *Grollo v Palmer* (1995) 184 CLR 348, 365 (Brennan CJ, Deane, Dawson and Toohey JJ).

[79] (1995) 184 CLR 348 and (1996) 189 CLR 1 respectively. See also Walker (1997).

confidence in the administration of justice was an issue. Significantly, in *Wilson's Case*, the Court found that the limits of the practice had been exceeded.[80] Quite apart from its relevance as precedent, the case provides a warning that governments are unlikely to ignore.

(e) State courts

There is no binding separation of judicial power under the constitutions of the Australian states.[81] However, two states have constitutional procedures that apply to courts and help to underpin their independence. Part 3 of the Victorian Constitution entrenches the Supreme Court and provides a mandatory procedure that must be followed in ousting its jurisdiction.[82] Part 9 of the Constitution of New South Wales provides some protection for judicial tenure.[83] Otherwise, while the states have inherited the common law tradition of respect for judicial independence and while state systems assume that judicial power normally will be exercised by courts, this is not a requirement of state constitutions. Bodies that are not or may not be courts exercise judicial power. State courts can be given non-judicial power.[84]

The Commonwealth Parliament may confer jurisdiction on state courts.[85] Beyond its constitutional power to prescribe the number of justices who must exercise the jurisdiction,[86] however, it is limited in its capacity to regulate them. It must accept the terms and conditions

---

[80] *Wilson v Minister for Aboriginal and Torres Strait Islander Affairs* (1996) 189 CLR 1 (Brennan CJ, Dawson, Toohey, Gaudron, McHugh and Gummow JJ; Kirby J dissenting).

[81] *Kable v Director of Public Prosecutions (NSW)* (1996) 189 CLR 51, 65 (Brennan CJ), 78 (Dawson J), 93 (Toohey J), 109 (McHugh J).

[82] *Constitution Act 1975* (Vic) s 85. The entrenchment procedure in s 18 requires absolute majorities in each House of Parliament for the second and third readings of an alteration Bill.

[83] *Constitution Act 1902* (NSW). Under s 7B, the procedures are entrenched by referendum.

[84] *Kable v Director of Public Prosecutions (NSW)* (1996) 189 CLR 51, 117 (McHugh J).

[85] Constitution ss 71 and 77(iii).

[86] Constitution s 79.

of appointment of state judges[87] and 'the structure, organisation and jurisdictional limits' of state courts,[88] although some procedural matters fall within the incidental power.[89] It may not itself confer non-judicial power on state courts.[90] Evidently it is possible, however, that a state court might exercise federal jurisdiction side-by-side with a non-judicial power validly conferred on it by the state.

Nevertheless, it is now established that the separation of federal judicial power prescribed by the Australian Constitution affects state court systems as well. The emergence of this doctrine, almost one hundred years after federation, was prompted by extreme circumstance.[91] Under the *Community Protection Act 1994* (NSW), the New South Wales Parliament had conferred power on the Supreme Court to make an order to detain in custody a particular person who was considered dangerous but who had served his sentence for a previous offence and had not, as yet, committed another. In *Kable v Director of Public Prosecutions (NSW) (Kable's Case)* justices variously characterised the function as 'purely executive in nature' and the 'antithesis of the judicial process', the defects of which were compounded, from the standpoint of courts, by its focus on a single, named person.[92]

The High Court rejected arguments, however, that the New South Wales legislation was invalid either because there was a separation of judicial power under the New South Wales Constitution[93] or because there was some general standard of propriety with which legislation of New South Wales must comply.[94] Instead, a majority held the legislation invalid by reference to the federal separation of

---

[87] It is not clear whether *Kable v Director of Public Prosecutions (NSW)* (1996) 189 CLR 51 requires this proposition to be qualified in extreme cases.

[88] Ibid 102 (Gaudron J).

[89] *Kotsis v Kotsis* (1970) 122 CLR 69.

[90] *Queen Victoria Memorial Hospital v Thornton* (1953) 87 CLR 144.

[91] Comparable legislation had already been enacted in Victoria without challenge: see *Community Protection Act 1990* (Vic).

[92] (1996) 189 CLR 51, 122 (McHugh J), 106 (Gaudron J), 98 (Toohey J).

[93] Ibid 65 (Brennan CJ), 78 (Dawson J), 93 (Toohey J), 109 (McHugh J).

[94] Ibid 65 (Brennan CJ), 76 (Dawson J), 91 (Toohey J), 109 (McHugh J). Gaudron and Gummow JJ decided the case on other grounds.

judicial power.[95] These justices pointed to the creation, by Chapter
III of the Constitution, of an integrated Australian judicial system,
in which federal jurisdiction might be exercised by state courts and
in which the High Court was the sole court of final appeal. For them,
Chapter III itself placed some limits on the power of state Parliaments in relation to state courts. Most obviously, there must be state
courts.[96] In addition, by extension, such courts must meet the same
broad standards of integrity and perceived integrity that the separation of judicial power was designed to secure for federal courts. This
did not require a separation of judicial power at the state level.[97] It
meant, however, that no functions might be conferred on state courts
or state judges that are incompatible with the exercise of judicial
power.[98] The concept of incompatibility was broadly similar to the
doctrine used to evaluate the validity of the conferral of non-judicial
functions on federal judges.[99]

(f) Adjudication in the territories

The position in the territories is different. The Commonwealth
Parliament derives power to legislate for its territories from s 122 of
the Constitution. Judicial interpretation of its meaning has ranged
between two broad views. One accepts the power as plenary, largely
unrestricted by the rest of the Constitution. The other views the
power as an integral part of the Constitution, subject to the same
checks and limitations that apply to Commonwealth action in the
states, unless the Constitution suggests otherwise, expressly or by
implication. The concept of the territories power as 'disparate'[100] is
consistent with an inherited tradition that makes Australians reluctant constitutionalists, accepting the overriding authority of a

---

[95] Toohey, Gaudron, McHugh and Gummow JJ formed the majority; Brennan CJ and
Dawson J dissented.
[96] *Kable v Director of Public Prosecution (NSW)* (1996) 189 CLR 51, 103 (Gaudron
J), 110 (McHugh J), 140 (Gummow J).
[97] Ibid 117 (McHugh).
[98] Ibid 99 (Toohey J), who confined the proposition to circumstances where the judicial
power of the Commonwealth is involved. This will normally be the case where the
Australian Constitution is invoked.
[99] For critical comment, see Campbell (1997).
[100] *Attorney-General of the Commonwealth of Australia v The Queen* (1957) 95 CLR
529, 545; Zines (1966) 73–4.

normative Constitution only to the extent necessary to secure the federation. The greater willingness of the High Court to subject the territories power to other constitutional constraints has broadly co-incided with growing awareness of the significance of the Constitution for other purposes.

The tensions have been evident in judicial consideration of the relevance of the separation of federal judicial power in the territories. Their resolution has been complicated by practical considerations. Section 122 of the Constitution applies to all territories, in all circumstances: internal and external; populated and uninhabited; dependent, partly autonomous or administered as a trust.[101] In addition to its national role, Commonwealth law in a territory provides for matters that elsewhere in the country would be matters of state concern, either directly or through self-governing institutions. Section 122 must be interpreted with these varied applications in mind.

The view that Chapter III has limited or no effect on the exercise of the territories power was endorsed in the *Boilermakers' Case*.[102] It was consistent with the link made there between the need for an independent judiciary and the federal division of power. As subsequently explained in *Spratt v Hermes* the basis for this view is that

> the first five Chapters of the Constitution belong to a special universe of discourse, namely that of the creation and the working of a federation of States, with all the safeguards, inducements, checks and balances that had to be negotiated and carefully expressed in order to secure the assent of the peoples of the several Colonies.[103]

In doctrinal terms, it led to a distinction between a power that is 'plenary' and one that is directed to a subject matter.[104] It required a definition of the 'judicial power of the Commonwealth' in s 71,

---

[101] *Berwick Ltd v Gray* (1976) 133 CLR 603.

[102] *Attorney-General of the Commonwealth of Australia v The Queen* (1957) 95 CLR 529, 545.

[103] (1965) 114 CLR 226, 250.

[104] See *Kruger v Commonwealth* (1997) 190 CLR 1, 53–7 (Dawson J) and the authorities there cited.

which excluded judicial power exercised in the territories; an interpretation of the references to 'other courts' in ss 71 and 72, to
exclude territory courts;[105] and, until recently, a denial that a law
made under s 122 was a law 'made by the Parliament', for the purposes of s 76(ii), capable of creating federal jurisdiction.[106] Thus
construed, s 73 makes no provision for appeals to the High Court
from territory courts, requiring a concession that Chapter III is not
exhaustive, at least to this extent. This has been under challenge in
the cross-vesting litigation.[107] In mid-1999, it remained the law that
the separation of judicial power for which Chapter III provides has
limited if any application in the territories.[108] Signs of change are
evident, however, in cases dealing both with judicial power[109] and
with the application of other constitutional provisions in the territories,[110] all of which undermine a prima facie assumption that s 122
is separate and apart.

3 Institutional Effects

(a) Relations between courts

The view that Chapter III is exclusive, on which the separation of
judicial power partly depends, has implications for the relationship
of Commonwealth courts with state courts and, potentially, with
courts of other countries as well.

---

[105] *Capital TV & Appliances Pty Ltd v Falconer* (1971) 125 CLR 591.

[106] *Kruger v Commonwealth* (1997) 190 CLR 1, 62 (Dawson J); *Northern Territory v GPAO* (1999) 161 ALR 318, 339–41 (Gleeson CJ and Gummow J), 345–6 (Gaudron), 387–8 (Hayne J); contrast 360–2 (McHugh and Callinan JJ).

[107] *Gould v Brown* (1998) 193 CLR 346, 426–7 (McHugh J).

[108] Subject to the possible implications of *Kable v Director of Public Prosecutions (NSW)* (1996) 189 CLR 51.

[109] *Kruger v Commonwealth* (1997) 190 CLR 1, 84 (Toohey J), 107 (Gaudron J), 162 (Gummow J); see also the cautious observations of Gleeson CJ and Gummow J in *Northern Territory v GPAO* (1999) 161 ALR 318, 338–42.

[110] *Capital Duplicators Pty Ltd v Australian Capital Territory (No 1)* (1992) 177 CLR 248 (discussing s 90); *Newcrest Mining (WA) Ltd v Commonwealth* (1997) 190 CLR 513 (discussing s 51(xxxi)).

As noted earlier, Chapter III specifically authorises the Commonwealth Parliament to confer federal jurisdiction on state courts.[111] The absence of a reciprocal power caused no inconvenience and attracted no attention, as long as a more or less single system of courts was maintained, combining federal and state jurisdiction in state court systems, with the High Court at the apex. (The avenues of appeal to the Queen in Council, until 1986, are unimportant for this purpose.) The establishment of other federal courts below the level of the High Court from the mid-1970s (in particular, the Family Court of Australia in 1975 and the Federal Court of Australia in 1976), made jurisdictional limits more significant and presented the possibility, soon realised, that some cases might lie beyond the authority of a single court. A pragmatic, if complex, solution was found in the enactment of complementary cross-vesting legislation by all Australian Parliaments.[112] With some exceptions, which are unimportant for present purposes, the effect of the scheme was to authorise a court properly seized of proceedings to determine all legal issues raised before it.

From the outset it was known that the scheme might be constitutionally insecure. The competing arguments were canvassed in *Gould v Brown*, and the validity of the scheme was upheld by a technical majority of a High Court of six.[113] The majority construed the *Boilermakers' Case* narrowly, determining that it controlled only powers conferred by the Commonwealth Parliament on federal courts. For the dissentients, the affirmative provisions of Chapter III exhausted, by implication, the jurisdiction that might be conferred on federal courts,[114] an implication that for McHugh J was confirmed by *Re Judiciary and Navigation Acts*.[115] On this reasoning, the Commonwealth Parliament could not validly authorise the

---

[111] Constitution ss 71 and 77(iii).

[112] *Jurisdiction of Courts (Cross-vesting) Act 1987* (Cth). See Mason and Crawford (1988); Moloney and McMaster (1992); Johnson (1993).

[113] (1998) 193 CLR 346 (Brennan CJ, Toohey and Kirby JJ; Gaudron, McHugh and Gummow JJ dissenting).

[114] Ibid 423 (McHugh J), 443–7 (Gummow J), 410 (Gaudron J).

[115] Ibid 420–1.

conferral of state jurisdiction on federal courts; nor could the problem be resolved by a reference of powers under s 51(xxxvii). The issues were canvassed again in a further challenge to the scheme in *Re Wakim; Ex parte McNally* in December 1998. The decision has established that the cross-vesting scheme is, to this extent, ineffective.[116]

Similar reasoning is assumed to inhibit the establishment of a trans-Tasman court with New Zealand or, for that matter, institutional judicial co-operation with any other neighbouring country with which Australia might seek to enter into arrangements of a domestic nature. The question was canvassed most seriously in connection with the implementation of trans-Tasman competition policy, which replaced the anti-dumping arrangements between Australia and New Zealand.[117] Obviously it was desirable to ensure the consistency of adjudication under the harmonised legislation. One possibility may have been a joint Commerce Court. This possibility was precluded by the need for justices of a court that exercises federal jurisdiction to be appointed and to hold office on terms that comply with s 72 of the Constitution, unless the court is a state court. Similarly, it probably was not possible for New Zealand to confer jurisdiction on a court established by the Commonwealth for the purpose, because of the exclusive character of Chapter III; and s 73 presented impediments to appropriate appeal provisions as well. In the event, an arrangement of a different kind facilitated co-operation and co-ordination between the two court systems, avoiding the constitutional problem, at least for the time being.[118]

(b) Operations of the Commonwealth government

The constitutional separation of judicial power affects the practical operations of Commonwealth government in a variety of ways. Two that are directly attributable to the doctrine are considered here. The doctrine also is a factor in the important contemporary debate on

---

[116] *Re Wakim; Ex parte McNally* (1999) 163 ALR 270.

[117] *Trade Practices (Misuse of Trans-Tasman Market Power) Act 1990* (Cth) and corresponding amendments to the *Commerce Act 1986* (NZ), putting into effect Article 4 of the 1988 Protocol on Acceleration of Free Trade in Goods.

[118] Barker and Beaumont (1992).

the extent to which the Commonwealth Parliament can oust the jurisdiction of the High Court and other federal courts (see Chapters 7 and 9).[119]

The separation of judicial power, as interpreted and applied in Australia, has both encouraged the establishment of tribunals and restricted the scope of the jurisdiction that can be conferred on them. The encouragement stems from the limits that the doctrine places on the powers of courts. Its effects were manifested initially in successive industrial relations tribunals and subsequently in the sophisticated procedures for merits review offered by the Administrative Appeals Tribunal (AAT), as an integral part of a reformed administrative law system.[120] Understood in this way, the separation of powers left a discrete niche in the system of government which only tribunals could occupy. The potential of this opportunity has not fully been realised.

At the same time, the doctrine has prevented the conferral on tribunals of the power to issue binding decisions, necessitating the relitigation of disputes before courts, where tribunal decisions have failed to persuade. This is not an issue for the AAT, which assumes the function of the primary decision-maker.[121] It has been a continuing difficulty for adjudicative tribunals, however, as the saga of *Brandy's Case* shows.[122]

An institutional effect of a different kind concerns the absence of an advisory jurisdiction. The main textual justification for denying this jurisdiction to federal courts is the prefatory requirement of a 'matter', in ss 75 and 76, which is assumed to be limiting. The argument is underpinned by the interpretation of Chapter III as an exhaustive prescription of the power the Commonwealth Parliament might confer on Chapter III courts.[123] The point of principle said to be served is judicial independence from executive government, actual and perceived. Its importance was endorsed again recently, in the

---

[119] *R v Hickman; Ex parte Fox and Clinton* (1945) 70 CLR 598, 615–16.

[120] Saunders (1993).

[121] *Turner v Minister for Immigration and Ethnic Affairs* (1981) 35 ALR 388, 390.

[122] *Brandy v Human Rights and Equal Opportunity Commission* (1995) 183 CLR 245.

[123] *Re Judiciary and Navigation Acts* (1921) 29 CLR 257.

different context of the circumstances in which judges might hold non-judicial office.[124]

In so far as the defect in an advisory jurisdiction lies in its abstract nature and the absence of a real issue to be tried, this textual analysis has other implications as well (see Chapter 8). It justifies refusal on the part of a court to answer hypothetical questions raised in a matter before it.[125] A distinction is drawn, however, between determination of an 'abstract question of law' and 'a declaration of law divorced or dissociated from any attempt to administer it'.[126] Thus, in *Croome v Tasmania*[127] the High Court accepted jurisdiction in a challenge to the validity of a Tasmanian Act, clearly inconsistent with a Commonwealth Act, notwithstanding the absence of any attempt on the part of Tasmania to enforce it. Relying on the same distinction, the Court also has accepted jurisdiction in challenges to the constitutionality of legislation that has been enacted but not yet proclaimed.[128]

4 Doctrinal Effects

The constraint on the power that constitutionally can be conferred on federal courts inhibits expansion of their role beyond what they themselves consider the exercise of judicial power. While there is no constitutional separation of powers at the state level,[129] the position of the High Court as a final court of appeal in matters of both state and federal jurisdiction ensures that indirect doctrinal effects of the federal separation of powers are felt at the state level as well.

Most common law courts observe self-imposed limits on their own authority to make new law or to usurp decisions properly made by the other branches of government. These limits are not necessarily attributable to the constitutional separation of powers and are

---

[124] *Wilson v Minister for Aboriginal and Torres Strait Islander Affairs* (1996) 189 CLR 1.

[125] *North Ganalanja Aboriginal Corporation v Queensland* (1996) 185 CLR 595.

[126] *Mellifont v Attorney-General (Q)* (1991) 173 CLR 289, 303.

[127] (1997) 191 CLR 119.

[128] *New South Wales v Commonwealth (Incorporation Case)* (1990) 169 CLR 482.

[129] *Kable v Director of Public Prosecutions (NSW)* (1996) 189 CLR 51.

not exclusively the consequences of it. They developed as part of the corpus of the common law. They are a prudent response by the courts to their position of relative weakness *vis-à-vis* the executive and the Parliament, captured by Hamilton in his assessment of the judiciary as the 'least dangerous branch'.[130] They may also symbolise a degree of deference by the appointed branch of government towards others that are directly or indirectly elected.

Logically, however, limits of this kind are connected with the concept of separation of powers as well. A doctrine that precludes the exercise of non-judicial power by the courts helps to explain why courts hesitate to supply the deficiencies of statutes,[131] review decisions on the merits,[132] overturn previously established decisions,[133] invalidate legislation prospectively,[134] or apply unincorporated international treaties.[135] Occasionally the influence of the separation of judicial power is explicitly acknowledged in cases of this kind.[136] The dividing line between an impermissible exercise of power, rendered non-judicial by its creativity, and the proper exercise of judicial power within the common law tradition, adapting the law as cases arise, necessarily is a fine one. The precise location of that line is not always clear.

Other practices, familiar in Australia and elsewhere,[137] may be explained by reference to the separation of powers more generally. These include deference to executive judgment, particularly in matters of foreign affairs,[138] the presumption of constitutionality,[139] and the principle of justiciability to the extent to which it inhibits

---

[130] Hamilton, Jay and Madison (1787) No 78, 504.

[131] *Strickland v Rocla Concrete Pipes Ltd* (1971) 124 CLR 468.

[132] *Minister for Aboriginal Affairs v Peko-Wallsend Ltd* (1986) 162 CLR 24.

[133] *Queensland v Commonwealth* (1977) 139 CLR 585; *John v Federal Commissioner of Taxation* (1989) 166 CLR 417, 451–2.

[134] *Ha v New South Wales* (1997) 189 CLR 465. For an analysis of a range of other considerations relevant to the technique, see K. Mason (1989).

[135] *Minister for Immigration and Ethnic Affairs v Teoh* (1995) 183 CLR 273, 287 (Mason CJ and Deane J).

[136] *Minister for Aboriginal Affairs v Peko-Wallsend Ltd* (1986) 162 CLR 24.

[137] See, for example, the practices grouped under the heading of 'prudentialism': Kommers and Finn (1998) 38–9.

[138] *Horta v Commonwealth* (1994) 181 CLR 183.

[139] D. Williams (1996) 203–4.

courts from dealing with matters which are still before Parliament
or which raise political questions.[140] However, the dividing line is
also indistinct in these instances, reflecting the delicate balance of
authority between courts and the other branches of government,
which varies between jurisdictions and over time.

5 People and the State

Most of the effects of the separation of judicial power discussed so
far are systemic. From the standpoint of the system of government,
the doctrine diffuses power, protects judicial independence and
encourages public confidence in judges and courts. The ultimate
beneficiary is the Australian people for whom government exists.
The initial focus, however, is the system of government itself.

More recent decisions, however, have begun to explore the
direct implications of the doctrine for individuals affected by an
exercise of public power.[141] These cases are consistent with the growing acceptance of the relevance of the Constitution for relations
between individuals and the state as well as for relations between
governments. In the absence of a Bill of Rights, there is a sphere
within which the separation of judicial power can assume an important role. It has particular relevance for limits on power that in
other constitutional settings are classed under the headings of freedom and security of the person, and of procedural due process.[142] In
1989, Deane J observed that 'the guarantee that the citizen can be
subjected to the exercise of Commonwealth judicial power only by
the "courts" designated by Ch. III' is the 'most important' of the
guarantees of rights and immunities, express or implied, under the
Australian Constitution.[143]

Three broad bases on which the doctrine might directly benefit
individuals have begun to emerge. First and most obviously, prohibition of the exercise of judicial power by a body other than a

---

[140] *Cormack v Cope* (1974) 131 CLR 432.

[141] By contrast with earlier 'less fastidious' times: Winterton (1994) 190.

[142] See, for example, *Constitution of the Republic of South Africa*, Articles 12(1)(a) and
(b) and aspects of Article 35.

[143] *Street v Queensland Bar Association* (1989) 168 CLR 461, 521.

Chapter III court prevents its exercise by the legislature, or by the executive under legislative authority. In a series of recent cases, the High Court has grappled with the point at which a proper exercise of legislative power becomes a legislative usurpation of judicial power.[144] In general, the line has left considerable latitude to the Parliament, while protecting what has been identified as the essential core of judicial power. Most central of all is 'the adjudgment and punishment of criminal guilt',[145] but 'inalienable' functions include 'the trial of actions for breach of contract and for civil wrongs' as well.[146] Outside this core, there are functions that, while taking on the character of judicial power when exercised by courts, might properly be exercised by the other branches.[147] Clearly, the Parliament must be able to provide the law by reference to which the courts exercise judicial power.[148] The Parliament may also provide the framework within which adjudication takes place in the form of, for example, the law of evidence and other procedural rules.[149]

Applying this analysis, a legislative judgment in the form of a bill of attainder,[150] or along the slightly more subtle lines held invalid in *Liyanage v The Queen*,[151] would offend the Australian separation of judicial power.[152] Going a significant step further, in *Chu Kheng Lim v Minister for Immigration* (*Lim's Case*), three of the majority justices relied on the separation of powers to limit the authority of the other branches of government to detain in custody a citizen who was not in breach of the law, as determined by a court.[153] The future

---

[144] *Chu Kheng Lim v Minister for Immigration* (*Lim's Case*) (1992) 176 CLR 1.

[145] Ibid 27 (Brennan, Deane and Dawson JJ).

[146] *H A Bachrach Pty Ltd v Queensland* (1998) 156 ALR 563, 567.

[147] Ibid 567. Gaudron J described these powers as 'ancillary' to the judicial power when exercised by courts: see *Nicholas v The Queen* (1998) 193 CLR 173, 207–8.

[148] *Polyukhovich v Commonwealth* (1991) 172 CLR 501; *H A Bachrach Pty Ltd v Queensland* (1998) 156 ALR 563.

[149] *Nicholas v The Queen* (1998) 193 CLR 173, 188 (Brennan CJ).

[150] *Polyukhovich v Commonwealth* (1991) 172 CLR 501 (Mason CJ, Dawson, Toohey and McHugh JJ). Mason CJ described such a bill as 'a legislative enactment adjudging a specific person . . . guilty of an offence constituted by past conduct and imposing punishment in respect of that offence': 535.

[151] [1967] 1 AC 259.

[152] *Nicholas v The Queen* (1998) 193 CLR 173, 221–2, 256.

[153] (1992) 176 CLR 1, 27 (Brennan, Deane and Dawson JJ).

of this line of development is uncertain. The number of exceptions to the principle, which the joint judgment acknowledged, influenced the fourth member of the majority to reach a similar conclusion by other means.[154]

Few of the cases that provoke argument about legislative usurpation of judicial power provide such obvious targets as these, involving, as they do, detention without judicial determination of guilt. More difficult are cases in which pending litigation is affected by legislation that is retrospective, or alters the rights in issue, or is directed to specific persons. On the law as it presently stands, none of these factors in isolation necessarily will render the legislation invalid. Retrospective legislation alone does not offend the separation of judicial power as long, at least, as a court is left to determine issues that arise at a trial.[155] Alteration of statutory entitlements does not involve a usurpation of judicial power, although legislation concerning the guilt of persons charged with criminal offences may do so.[156] Legislation that is ad hominem, that is, directed to an individual, is more likely than general legislation to be invalid.[157] Even this is not conclusive, however;[158] and the appearance of specificity is easy enough to avoid, despite the willingness of courts to look beyond form to the substance. Whether such factors transgress the separation of judicial power, alone or in combination, will depend in each case on the threat presented by the challenged legislation to the values that the doctrine is designed to protect.

The second manifestation of this aspect of the doctrine is an extension of the first.[159] Just as the legislature may not itself exercise

---

[154] Ibid 57 (Gaudron J, by reference to the scope of the power to legislate with respect to 'aliens').

[155] *Nicholas v The Queen* (1998) 193 CLR 173, 234 (Gummow J, drawing on *Polyukhovich v Commonwealth* (1991) 172 CLR 501, 539, 643–4, 690, 719).

[156] *H A Bachrach Pty Ltd v Queensland* (1998) 156 ALR 563, 567–8; *Australian Building Construction Employees' and Builders Labourers' Federation v Commonwealth* (1986) 161 CLR 88.

[157] *Leeth v Commonwealth* (1992) 174 CLR 455, 469–70 (Mason CJ, Dawson and McHugh JJ); *Nicholas v The Queen* (1998) 193 CLR 173, 257 (Kirby J).

[158] *Nicholas v The Queen* (1998) 193 CLR 173, 212 (Gaudron J); *Liyanage v The Queen* [1967] 1 AC 259.

[159] *Nicholas v The Queen* (1998) 193 CLR 173, 220 (McHugh J).

judicial power or authorise the executive to do so, so it may not direct the courts in the manner in which they exercise judicial power. Again, the decision in *Lim's Case* provides an example. In that case, the majority invalidated a provision that they interpreted as a direction from the Parliament not to release specified persons from custody, even if they were unlawfully held.[160]

Here, also, marginal cases cause considerable difficulty, as shown by the divisions in the High Court in *Nicholas v The Queen*.[161] At issue was the validity of new s 15X of the *Crimes Act 1914* (Cth). The section directed a court to disregard the illegality of the importation of narcotics by customs officers in a 'controlled' operation, in exercising the court's discretion to admit evidence of the importation. For the majority, the section was a proper exercise of legislative power to prescribe the law of evidence as long, at least, as the ultimate discretion whether to admit evidence were left to the court.[162] For the two minority justices, the direction to the court was invalid, although for reasons that went rather to the responsibility of the court to protect the judicial process than to arguments based on usurpation or direction.[163] In joining the majority, Hayne J drew attention to the fine but significant line between the proper legislative prescription of rules of evidence or procedure and 'changes . . . which would be so radical and so pointed . . . that they could be seen, in substance, to deal with ultimate issues of guilt or innocence'.[164]

Finally, the separation of judicial power limits the power of the Parliament to alter the context in which courts exercise judicial power in ways that would reduce the protection of the doctrine to one of mere form.[165] The focus here is on the process of the courts,[166]

---

[160] *Chu Kheng Lim v Minister for Immigration* (1992) 176 CLR 1, 36–7 (Brennan, Deane and Dawson JJ), 53 (Gaudron J).

[161] (1998) 193 CLR 173.

[162] Brennan CJ, Toohey, Gaudron, Gummow and Hayne JJ.

[163] *Nicholas v The Queen* (1998) 193 CLR 173, 226 (McHugh J), 264–5 (Kirby J).

[164] Ibid 278.

[165] *Chu Kheng Lim v Minister for Immigration* (1992) 176 CLR 1, 27 (Brennan, Deane and Dawson JJ); *Leeth v Commonwealth* (1992) 174 CLR 455, 470, 487.

[166] This aspect of the doctrine has variously been described as protective of 'due process', 'judicial process', and 'curial due process': see Wheeler (1997) 249–50 and references there cited.

as the feature that distinguishes the exercise of judicial power. So important is this consideration for Gaudron J, that she includes judicial process within her definition of judicial power itself.[167] To understand the meaning and extent of these limits, it is necessary to identify those aspects of the judicial process central to its nature, from which it takes its special character. A starting point is the judicial method itself: 'the quelling of . . . controversies by ascertainment of the facts, by application of the law and by exercise, where appropriate, of judicial discretion'.[168] Judicial process involves a duty to act impartially and to be seen to do so.[169] Other features identified by Gaudron J include:

> The right of a party to meet the case made . . . the independent determination of the matter . . . by application of the law to facts determined in accordance with rules and procedures which truly permit the facts to be ascertained and, in the case of criminal proceedings, the determination of guilt or innocence by means of a fair trial according to law . . . [A] court cannot be required or authorised to proceed in any manner which involves an abuse of process, which would render its proceedings inefficacious, or which brings or tends to bring the administration of justice into disrepute.[170]

The evolution of this aspect of the separation of powers is still in its early stages. Progress is likely to be difficult and contested. There is potential for conflict between the notion that parts of the judicial process are indispensable and moves by governments to streamline the operations of the court.[171] Opposition can be expected also, if the penumbra of the judicial process that is protected by the doctrine intrudes too far into areas generally considered the province of a Bill of Rights. The skirmish that has already taken

---

[167] See, for example, *Nicholas v The Queen* (1998) 193 CLR 173, 207–8.

[168] *Fencott v Muller* (1983) 152 CLR 570, 608.

[169] *Nicholas v The Queen* (1998) 193 CLR 173, 188 (Brennan CJ).

[170] Ibid 208–9 (Gaudron J). See also the various characteristics of the judicial process identified in *Kable v Director of Public Prosecutions (NSW)* (1996) 189 CLR 51. See, generally, Wheeler (1997).

[171] Sir Anthony Mason (1996); McKillop (1997).

place, over the extent to which the judicial process requires equal treatment of litigants, procedurally or in substance, may fore-shadow battles to come.[172]

6 Conclusions

(a) Evaluation

A principal purpose of a division of power between institutions or arms of government on functional or other lines is to protect liberty by checking a concentration of authority that is likely to be harmful to it. Depending on design, a separation of powers is also conducive to institutional efficiency and effectiveness: to the performance of public functions in a way best suited to their nature, understood in the light of constitutional principle. A separation of judicial power, in a common law context, has the additional effect of protecting judicial independence, shielding courts from undue interference by the legislature or executive. It protects the perception of judicial independence as well, thus encouraging public confidence in the integrity and impartiality of judicial decisions. Institutionally, these purposes are ends in themselves. But they also serve a wider good, structuring a system of government to meet the needs of the people, for whom, in a democracy, government is deemed to exist.

The separation of judicial power serves all these purposes in Australia, as elsewhere. In addition, it now protects aspects of civil liberties associated with freedom of the person and due process. This development is peculiarly Australian. In most other compar-able countries, these and other civil rights derive protection from a Bill of Rights. There is no need and no incentive to probe the impli-cations for individuals of a constitutional separation of powers. One principal argument against a Bill of Rights is that Parliaments and courts, in their different ways, already provide sufficient safeguards. Ironically, by securing the position of the courts, the separation of judicial power, as it has evolved in Australia, may have strengthened this argument.

---

[172] *Leeth v Commonwealth* (1992) 174 CLR 455, 486–7 (Deane and Toohey JJ), 502 (Gaudron J); *Nicholas v The Queen* (1998) 193 CLR 173, 208–9 (Gaudron J).

Whatever its merits in principle, the practical effects of the Australian doctrine have been criticised from time to time. Most obviously, it forces institutional duplication. To comply with constitutional requirements, the Commonwealth provides separately for non-judicial and judicial adjudication in key areas of its responsibility including industrial relations, trade practices, human rights, and the determination of native title. Duplication is expensive and an inconvenience to parties who must present their arguments again, if enforcement is required. Further inconvenience can be expected from the partial demise of the cross-vesting legislation. The constraints of Chapter III have undoubtedly affected the design of federal magistrates' courts as well.[173]

As with every other aspect of constitutional design, these disadvantages must be balanced against the significant if less tangible advantages that the separation of judicial power brings to Australian governance. These include a system of justice whose integrity is rarely doubted and on which litigants can depend. Ironically, the parties with greatest cause for complaint are the state partners to the federation in whose interests the separation of judicial power originally was invoked.[174]

Moreover, the significance of the practical drawbacks of the separation of judicial power may be exaggerated. They have been ameliorated to a degree by some flexibility in the definition of judicial power, the appointment of judges to tribunals under the persona designata doctrine, and the exercise of judicial functions by non-judicial court officials under delegation. Some of the effects of the doctrine are irritating in the short term but may be for the best in the end. The fallout from *Brandy's Case*[175] may be an example, if it forces human rights cases into a judicial forum that is appropriately

---

[173] Commonwealth Attorney-General, Press Release, 20 October 1998.

[174] The decision in *Amalgamated Society of Engineers v Adelaide Steamship Co Ltd* (*Engineers' Case*) (1920) 28 CLR 129 is one cause of the steady expansion of Commonwealth power. Judicial decisions also have been instrumental in the consolidation of Commonwealth financial control.

[175] *Brandy v Human Rights and Equal Opportunity Commission* (1995) 183 CLR 245.

constituted.[176] On the other hand, in the wake of the failure of the cross-vesting legislation, the only solution may be constitutional change, either to authorise the conferral of state jurisdiction on federal courts, with appropriate safeguards, or to redesign the Australian judicature so as to constitute a single, integrated system.[177]

In some respects it is an anomaly that the strict separation of judicial power, with its advantages for the judicial system, is available at the Commonwealth but not at state levels in Australia. The gap has been narrowed through the recent development of the incompatibility doctrine in *Kable's Case*.[178] Other changes to state constitutions themselves, reacting to controversies within individual states, have provided a degree of protection for state judicatures as well. And it may be that this is adequate. The strict separation of judicial power may work as well as it does in the Commonwealth sphere because federal courts are courts of limited jurisdiction,[179] in which functions are more readily distinguished. Its effects on the more general jurisdiction of state court systems would be difficult to predict and, possibly, unwelcome.[180]

(b) Judicial interpretation

The Australian Constitution necessarily rests upon two broad principles or doctrines. One is federalism, without which the six Australian colonies would not have agreed to unite in 1901. The second is representative democracy, which provided the underlying organising principle for the new national system of government that the Constitution created. Since the Constitution came into effect, the course of judicial interpretation has identified the separation of powers as a third doctrine underpinning the Constitution. It is manifested most prominently in the separation of judicial power. It had some link to federalism, in the early stages of its development, but has long since assumed significance in its own right.

---

[176] But compare Nand (1997) 19.

[177] For the earlier debate on this issue see Australian Constitutional Commission Advisory Committee on the Australian Judicial System (1987).

[178] *Kable v Director of Public Prosecutions (NSW)* (1996) 189 CLR 51.

[179] *Gould v Brown* (1998) 193 CLR 346, 422 (McHugh J).

[180] See Hope (1996).

There was nothing inevitable about the form that the separation of judicial power came to take under the Australian Constitution. The doctrine did not loom large in the public debates at the original Conventions. It is supportable by the text and structure of the Constitution, but the text and structure have never been conclusive. There are counter-indications in the text, on which reliance might have been placed to justify a different course. The history of the evolution of the doctrine has been marked by eloquent and persuasive dissenting views.

In many ways, the Australian doctrine of the separation of judicial power is a typical product of the interpretation of a liberal democratic constitution, in a common law environment, over the second half of the twentieth century. The text of the Constitution has provided the base on which the doctrine has developed incrementally. Successive courts have been guided, implicitly or explicitly, by a view of the purpose served by this part of the Constitution. Over time that view has changed, also by degrees, with changes to the context in which the Constitution applies. Courts have responded to disputes brought before them. Novel issues have been resolved by reference to the existing text, to the extent deemed to be consistent with precedent, legal reasoning, and the currently accepted bounds of the responsibility of a court of final appeal.

While the *Boilermakers' Case* identified the two main facets of the separation of judicial power, other key aspects of the doctrine remained unsettled. One has been resolved: the extent to which Chapter III is exclusive of state judicial power, as well as of other forms of federal power. A second, the relevance of Chapter III in the territories, is presently under review. The larger question, of the extent of the limits placed on legislative and executive power by the exclusive conferral of judicial power on courts and constitutional protection of the context in which the power is exercised, will be worked out only over time.

2

Judicial Federalism

Gavan Griffith and Geoffrey Kennett

1 Introduction

It will be practicable under this section, should the Parliament so desire, to dispense altogether, at the outset, with the creation of any federal courts other than the High Court, and to assign to the courts of the States such federal jurisdiction as may be necessary in order to secure the proper administration of the judicial business of the Commonwealth. In this way it will be possible to dispense with unduly cumbersome judicial machinery in the early years of the Commonwealth, and only develop and extend the national judicial system to meet the gradually increasing requirements of the people. But whilst federal functions may thus be exercised under federal authority, by State tribunals, the Federal Parliament can at any time revoke the authority, and transfer the whole of this subsidiary jurisdiction to courts of its own creation.

It is noteworthy that in this section, as elsewhere in the Constitution, the judicial department of the Commonwealth is more national, and less distinctively federal, in character, than either the legislative or executive departments.[1]

---

[1] Quick and Garran (1901) 803–4 (discussing s 77).

If 'judicial federalism' is defined as the working out of the consequences of a federal system of government in the judicial sphere, it
is a large field of operations and one that in a work of limited com-
pass must be discussed thematically rather than comprehensively.
The focus here is on the recent approach of the High Court to the
role of federal courts. We suggest that at least some justices have
sought to entrench the purity of judicial power in the federal sphere
at a level that, paradoxically, may tend to inhibit the provision at
state level of the protections that flow from entrenchment of judicial
independence.

Broadly, the phrase 'judicial federalism' encompasses the accommodation of the judicial branch to the requirements of a federal
system. That settlement was foreshadowed in the provisions of
Chapter III of the Constitution and accomplished in outline by Sir
Samuel Griffith's summer exercise in drafting the *Judiciary Act 1903*
(Cth).[2] The basic structure erected by Griffith remains intact today.
But Griffith's ingenuity did much to obscure the complexity which
has only recently become apparent with the rise of federal courts
and the exercise of their federal jurisdiction. In its Australian version
judicial federalism includes at least the following:

1 The principle in *Marbury v Madison*,[3] which established the
   duty of the United States Supreme Court to pronounce on the
   constitutionality of actions of the other branches of government when such issues arose before it, has always been accepted
   as applicable in Australia[4] (with some exceptions),[5] with the
   High Court given ultimate responsibility for policing the federal division of power and other constitutional limitations on
   government power.

---

[2] Griffith produced the first draft in February 1901: see Joyce (1984) 257.

[3] 5 US 137 (1803).

[4] See *Australian Communist Party v Commonwealth* (1951) 83 CLR 1, 262 (Fullagar J); *Commonwealth v Mewett* (1997) 191 CLR 471, 497 (Dawson J), 547
(Gummow and Kirby JJ; Brennan CJ and Gaudron J agreeing).

[5] See Thomson (1997) 56–67.

2 The Constitution defines and provides for the conferral of a body of jurisdiction that is distinctively 'federal'.[6]

3 Principles are required for determining the boundaries of federal jurisdiction in any particular matter where there is a question as to the scope of a federal court's jurisdiction or whether a state court is exercising federal jurisdiction (which may determine, for example, where an appeal lies from that court). These principles find expression in the development of the concept of a 'matter' and the 'accrued jurisdiction' (see Chapters 8 and 9).

4 Federal courts are established by legislation for the exercise of that federal jurisdiction: ss 71 and 72 of the Constitution assume (or perhaps require) the establishment of the High Court, and implicitly empower the Parliament to establish other federal courts.

5 Rules are established, both at the constitutional level[7] and in federal statute,[8] for determining which bodies exercise federal jurisdiction. In Australia these rules have historically centred upon the 'autochthonous expedient'[9] of vesting federal jurisdiction in state courts—a process whose constitutional mandate necessarily draws state courts into the maelstrom of judicial federalism.[10]

6 Courts exercising federal jurisdiction require rules for ascertaining the procedural law to be applied, as well as the substantive law to the extent that it is not provided by federal law. These are legislatively prescribed.[11]

---

[6] Federal jurisdiction comprises the exercise of judicial power in respect of matters of the kinds mentioned in ss 75 and 76, conferred directly by the Constitution (s 75) or by federal law (under s 76 or s 77). We leave aside the question of whether territory courts are federal courts or their jurisdiction is 'federal' in character.

[7] Constitution ss 71, 73, 76, and 77.

[8] Principally the *Judiciary Act 1903* (Cth) Parts IV–VI. Jurisdiction in particular classes of matter is conferred by other Acts, such as the *Trade Practices Act 1974* (Cth) s 86 and the *Family Law Act 1975* (Cth) Part V.

[9] *R v Kirby; Ex parte Boilermakers' Society of Australia* (1956) 94 CLR 254, 268.

[10] See *Kable v Director of Public Prosecutions (NSW)* (1996) 189 CLR 51.

[11] *Judiciary Act 1903* (Cth) ss 79 and 80.

7 The High Court was installed by the Constitution as a court of
appeal from both state and federal courts on all issues, not
merely matters arising in original federal jurisdiction,[12] with
the result that a single Australian common law could develop.
Rather too recently, the removal of the final avenues to the Privy
Council has confirmed the High Court as the ultimate court of
appeal for Australia.[13]

8 Rules and practices have developed governing the relationship
between federal and state courts and between the courts of the
various states. This is the case, for example, with respect to
enforcement of judgments and orders,[14] and the extent to which
prerogative writs run against courts in other hierarchies.[15]

9 Courts are required for the administration of justice in the territories, which are governed solely under the authority of the
Commonwealth (whether directly or by polities established by
legislation under s 122). The constitutional position of territory
courts, the nature of their jurisdiction, and the extent to which
the provisions of Chapter III apply to them are sometimes
matters of controversy.[16]

Australian judicial federalism as practised since 1987 has also
included statutory provisions for the vesting of the jurisdiction of
each state and territory in the courts of each other state and territory
and in the Federal Court of Australia and the Family Court, as well
as for the vesting of the Federal and Family Courts' jurisdiction
(save for a few areas of exclusive jurisdiction) in state and territory
courts.[17] However, in 1999 an important element of that scheme—

---

[12] Constitution s 73.

[13] *Australia Acts 1986* (Cth) (UK) s 11.

[14] *Service and Execution of Process Act 1992* (Cth).

[15] See *R v Murray and Cormie; Ex parte Commonwealth* (1916) 22 CLR 437. A recent
example is *Slater v Miles* (unreported, Federal Court, Finn J, 16 October 1998).

[16] See *Kruger v Commonwealth* (1997) 190 CLR 1, 43–4 (Brennan CJ), 62 (Dawson J),
81–4 (Toohey J), 108–9 (Gaudron J), 162, 167–76 (Gummow J); *Gould v Brown*
(1998) 193 CLR 346, 401–3 (Gaudron J), 426–7 (McHugh J), 493 (Kirby J); *Re
Governor, Goulburn Correctional Centre, Goulburn; Ex parte Eastman* (1999)
165 ALR 171.

[17] *Jurisdiction of Courts (Cross-vesting) Act 1987* of the Commonwealth and of each
state and the Northern Territory, and the Act of the same name enacted by the
Australian Capital Territory in 1993. A parallel regime relating specifically to corporations law matters is included in the *Corporations Act 1989* (Cth) and the *Corporations Act 1990* of each state and the Northern Territory.

the vesting of state jurisdiction in federal courts—was held invalid.[18] Detailed analysis of the cross-vesting scheme is unlikely to be rewarding, in advance of a complete legislative response to the invalidity. However, in what follows we discuss the scheme briefly in order to take issue with the approach of the High Court to it—an approach based on what we suggest may be excessive purity at the federal level.

Our remarks concern judicial conceptions of the nature of federal judicial power and the special position of federal courts, and their implications in a federal system. First we discuss the unified judicial system for which the Constitution and the *Judiciary Act* provide. Second, we discuss the position of federal courts in that system and the problems that arise if their jurisdictions are limited strictly to federal matters. Third, we discuss the position of state courts, and particularly the extent to which the Constitution protects the independent exercise of judicial power in the states. We argue that a purist approach to the conferral of powers on federal courts and the separation of federal judicial power may tend to inhibit the implication of appropriate protections at the state level by imposing standards that are too high for translation to that sphere.

2 The Unified Judicial System

The Australian framers departed from United States precedent by providing for both the creation of federal courts other than the High Court (implicitly in ss 71, 72, 73(ii), and 77(i) and (ii)), and the vesting of federal jurisdiction in state courts (s 77(iii) and implicitly in s 71). In the United States Constitution, Article III s 1 provides for the vesting of judicial power only in the Supreme Court and courts established by Congress (state courts may be called on to enforce rights under federal law where their jurisdiction is adequate in terms of territorial nexus and subject matter, but they cannot be invested with jurisdiction by Congress and therefore do not exercise federal judicial power in the sense in which that expression is understood in Australia).[19] Although the issue was keenly argued among the

---

[18] *Re Wakim, Ex parte McNally* (1999) 163 ALR 270.

[19] See Cowen and Zines (1978) 174–5.

founders of the United States, the view which prevailed was that
the new federal government ought to be complete in all three arms.
The Australian Constitution's framers appear not to have shared the
concerns of their United States counterparts that vesting federal
judicial power in state courts would expose the nation to state rival-
ries and local partialities; they were therefore ready to adopt the
economical course of using existing state courts.[20]

Another significant departure from the United States precedent
which promoted the unity of the Australian judicial system was the
establishment of the High Court as a general court of appeal from
both federal and state courts. The United States Supreme Court
hears only federal matters and therefore exercises supervisory jurisdiction over the state courts only in limited circumstances. In Australia, on the other hand, the High Court both symbolically links
all of the courts from which it hears appeals, and settles a single
common law which applies throughout the country.

The 'Federal Supreme Court' envisaged by s 71 of the Constitution was not established until the commencement of the *Judiciary
Act* in August 1903. Jurisdiction had earlier been vested in state
courts in respect of offences, penalties and condemnation under the
Customs Act 1901 (Cth), offences under other Acts and civil claims
against the Commonwealth.[21] The basic plan of the *Judiciary Act*
survives to this day. Section 30 conferred on the High Court original
jurisdiction in respect of matters arising under the Constitution or
involving its interpretation (this was in addition to the matters in
which jurisdiction is conferred directly by s 75 of the Constitution).[22]
Section 38 made the jurisdiction of the High Court exclusive in
respect of matters arising under any treaty, suits between states, suits
between the Commonwealth and a state, and matters in which writs
of mandamus or prohibition were sought against Commonwealth
officers or courts. Section 39 relevantly provided as follows:

---

[20] Ibid 105–6, 175.

[21] See Quick and Groom (1904) 9.

[22] See s 76 of the Constitution. Section 30 was amended in 1914 and 1915 so as to
confer jurisdiction in three classes of matter within s 76 but by further amendment in
1939 this was reduced to two such classes—constitutional matters and trials of
indictable offences against laws of the Commonwealth.

39 (1) The jurisdiction of the High Court in matters not mentioned in the last preceding section shall be exclusive of the jurisdiction of the several Courts of the States, except as provided in this section. (2) The several Courts of the States shall within the limits of their several jurisdictions, whether such limits are as to locality, subject-matter, or otherwise, be invested with federal jurisdiction, in all matters in which the High Court has original jurisdiction or in which original jurisdiction can be conferred upon it, except as provided in the last preceding section, and subject to the following conditions and restrictions:

(a) Every decision of the Supreme Court of a State, or any other court of a State from which at the establishment of the Commonwealth an appeal lay to the Queen in Council, shall be final and conclusive except so far as an appeal may be brought to the High Court.

The curious form of s 39, which remains substantially the same today, had two important effects. First, it rendered largely academic the question whether state courts had their 'own' jurisdiction, that is, jurisdiction other than that conferred by the Commonwealth, in matters within the classes specified in ss 75 and 76 of the Constitution. Section 39(1) excluded any jurisdiction the state courts would otherwise have had in matters that were within the High Court's original jurisdiction under s 75 of the Constitution or s 30 of the *Judiciary Act*. Section 39(2) then conferred jurisdiction on the state courts in respect of the whole range of ss 75 and 76 matters except for those specifically excluded by s 38. The jurisdiction exercised by state courts in such matters as were covered by s 39(1) was therefore undoubtedly federal.

As there was not complete correspondence between s 76 of the Constitution and the jurisdiction actually conferred on the High Court (since s 30 has never conferred jurisdiction on the High Court in terms matching s 76(iv) or the full breadth of s 76(ii), and only conferred jurisdiction in s 76(iii) matters for a relatively short period), questions did remain as to whether state courts had jurisdiction other than that conferred by s 39 in particular s 76 matters. However, those questions were resolved by Dixon J in *Ffrost v Stevenson*,[23] who held that the conferral of federal jurisdiction in a

---

[23] (1937) 58 CLR 528, 573.

matter covered by s 39 overrides and excludes, by virtue of s 109 of the Constitution, any remaining non-federal jurisdiction a state court might have had in that matter.[24]

The second and related effect of the terms of s 39(1) and (2) was to bring all of the matters listed in ss 75 and 76 within Commonwealth control as regards appeals to the Privy Council. Section 39(2) then proceeded, in the first of the 'conditions and restrictions', to prohibit direct appeals to the Privy Council in such matters. Thus, for all matters in federal jurisdiction, the only route to the Privy Council lay through the High Court (under s 74 of the Constitution —a route capable of closure by Commonwealth legislation).[25] Given the capacity of 'matters' in federal jurisdiction to encompass issues arising under the general law, this enhanced the High Court's status as a general court of appeal and a unifying force in Australian law.

For a long period the regime erected by the *Judiciary Act* provided for the relatively seamless administration of justice. Matters in which the Commonwealth was a party or which arose under Commonwealth laws were routinely disposed of in the state courts. The exceptions were the matters reserved to the exclusive jurisdiction of the High Court (notably constitutional issues and matters in which judicial review of decisions by Commonwealth officers was sought) and the specialised areas of bankruptcy and industrial relations, where federal courts were established, as discussed in Chapter 5. Complications arose in some cases where it became necessary to determine whether a state court was exercising jurisdiction under s 39 of the *Judiciary Act* or not,[26] but these did not intrude upon the ability of the court in which proceedings were commenced to dispose of the controversy.

---

[24] See also *Felton v Mulligan* (1971) 124 CLR 367; *Moorgate Tobacco Co Ltd v Philip Morris Ltd* (1980) 145 CLR 457, 471 (Gibbs J), 479 (Stephen, Mason, Aickin and Wilson JJ; Murphy J agreeing).

[25] See *Privy Council (Limitation of Appeals) Act 1968* (Cth), *Privy Council (Appeals from the High Court) Act 1975* (Cth) and *Australia Act 1986* (Cth) s 11(1).

[26] See *Felton v Mulligan* (1971) 124 CLR 367, where the question whether an appeal could be taken to the Privy Council depended on the source of the jurisdiction being exercised.

Thus the federal and state judicatures were enmeshed in a composite system. Given its federal nature that system had idiosyncrasies. In conformity with the general presumption that the Constitution is predicated upon the continued existence and institutional autonomy of the states,[27] it was established early that the Commonwealth took state courts as it found them[28] and could not alter their structure or organisation for the purpose of exercising federal jurisdiction. For example, registrars in bankruptcy holding office under a Commonwealth Act could not be designated by that Act officers of state courts and empowered to exercise powers and functions of those courts.[29] However, the federal and state judicatures were firmly locked together. State courts dealt with federal matters with exactly the same degree of finality as would a federal court subordinate to the High Court. In the 1950s it was established that federal courts could not be vested with non-judicial powers,[30] and that the Commonwealth had no power to vest non-judicial powers in state courts.[31] Meanwhile, the work of the High Court as a court of appeal from all the states brought the common law of Australia together into a single stream. The position of the High Court was enhanced by the limitation and then abolition of appeals from its decisions to the Privy Council,[32] although appeals from state courts to the Privy Council in non-federal matters were not finally abolished until the commencement of the *Australia Acts 1986* (Cth) and (UK).

The decision of the High Court in *Kable v Director of Public Prosecutions (NSW) (Kable's Case)*[33] affirms the essential unity of

---

[27] The best-known expression of which is the implied limitation on Commonwealth legislative power which prevents discrimination against the states or measures which compromise their ability to exist as elements of the federal structure. See, for example, *Queensland Electricity Commission v Commonwealth* (1985) 159 CLR 192, 217 (Mason J).

[28] *Federated Sawmill, Timberyard and General Woodworkers' Employees' Association (Adelaide Branch) v Alexander* (1912) 15 CLR 308, 313 (Griffith CJ).

[29] *Le Mesurier v Connor* (1929) 42 CLR 481.

[30] *R v Kirby; Ex parte Boilermakers' Society of Australia* (1956) 94 CLR 254.

[31] *Queen Victoria Memorial Hospital v Thornton* (1953) 87 CLR 144.

[32] *Privy Council (Limitation of Appeals) Act 1968* (Cth); *Privy Council (Appeals from the High Court) Act 1975* (Cth); see also *Kirmani v Captain Cook Cruises Pty Ltd (No 2)* (1985) 159 CLR 461.

[33] (1996) 189 CLR 51.

the federal judicial system provided for by Chapter III and brought into existence by the *Judiciary Act*. That decision is an important one in that it establishes for the first time that the requirements of that system and its underpinnings in Chapter III have an impact on the states' organisation of their courts.

In *Kable's Case* the Court considered the validity of the *Community Protection Act 1994* (NSW) which was aimed specifically at Mr Kable, who was then serving a sentence for manslaughter. The Act was intended to 'protect the community by providing for the preventive detention' (s 3) of Mr Kable, and empowered the Supreme Court to make an order for an additional term of imprisonment dependent on an assessment of whether he was likely to commit serious acts of violence (s 5). The Court accepted that there was no principle of the separation of powers entrenched in the New South Wales Constitution.[34] The impugned legislation therefore did not fall foul of any prohibition on the conferral of non-judicial functions on state courts by the state legislature. However, a majority held that the function conferred on the Supreme Court (which was seen as tending to undermine public confidence in that Court by involving it in the imposition of further terms of imprisonment on a person without further findings of criminal guilt) was 'incompatible' with that Court's exercise of federal jurisdiction.[35] The concept of 'incompatibility' was borrowed from cases on the persona designata doctrine (see Chapter 14), under which federal judicial officers may undertake non-judicial functions in an individual capacity. In the context of that doctrine the notion of incompatibility prevents the undertaking of functions which would tend to compromise the functions of the court to which the judicial officer belongs.

State courts are state institutions, able to be vested with powers by the Commonwealth but axiomatically to be taken by the Commonwealth as it finds them. It might therefore be thought that the result, if any, of vesting of an 'incompatible' function in a state Supreme Court would be that that body would cease to answer the description of a 'court' for the purposes of ss 71 and 77 and that

---

[34] Ibid 65 (Brennan CJ), 77–80 (Dawson J), 92–4 (Toohey J), 109 (McHugh J).
[35] Ibid 98 (Toohey J), 104–7 (Gaudron J), 119–24 (McHugh J), 134–5 (Gummow J).

the vesting of that federal jurisdiction in it would therefore fail. However, the view of the majority was that the conferral of the incompatible function must fail, because Chapter III mandated a unified federal judicial system and thus required the states to maintain a system of courts available for the vesting of federal jurisdiction.[36] The unity of the system was therefore the basis for holding that a form of the separation of powers—albeit an attenuated one— was entrenched at state level by implication from the Australian Constitution. Members of the majority emphasised that state courts invested with federal jurisdiction exercise a jurisdiction of the same quality as the federal courts, not a second-class federal jurisdiction.[37]

The conceptual unity of the federal judicial system was given practical effect by the cross-vesting legislation. The effect of that legislation was to allow the courts of each state and territory and the federal courts to exercise jurisdiction conferred by the other polities in the federation. Thus, as a general rule it became unnecessary to determine as a point of law whether a matter was in federal jurisdiction or whether it was within the general but territorially based jurisdiction of a state Supreme Court.[38] Apart from the limited exclusive jurisdiction reserved to the Federal Court, the choice of forum became a matter of appropriateness rather than technicality.

3 The Federal Courts in the Unified System

The establishment of the Federal Court and the Family Court in the 1970s created new challenges for the federal judicial system which had been established by the *Judiciary Act*. Both were federal superior courts exercising jurisdiction in large classes of matters which were likely to intersect with controversies arising under state laws (such as family law and state property laws; claims under the *Trade Practices Act 1974* (Cth) and under the general law of contract). However, the establishment of federal courts exercising broad (albeit not general) jurisdiction, including areas of exclusive jurisdiction,

---

[36] Ibid 100–3 (Gaudron J), 110–16 (McHugh J), 137–43 (Gummow J).

[37] Ibid 103 (Gaudron J), 114–15 (McHugh J), 142 (Gummow J).

[38] See, for example, the *Supreme Court Act 1970* (NSW) s 23.

created new requirements to draw the boundaries of federal jurisdiction and new classes of cases in which that boundary assumed
critical importance.

(a) The *Boilermakers'* principle

As Geoffrey Sawer has pointed out, the allocation of governmental
functions within elements of a federation can have federal significance if the internal separation of powers in the different elements is
dissimilar.[39] It is therefore appropriate to consider the current application of the separation of powers principle established by *R v Kirby;
Ex parte Boilermakers' Society of Australia (Boilermakers' Case),*[40]
since the discrepancy between that principle (which applies to federal judicial power) and the position under the state constitutions
creates an imbalance that may have undesirable consequences.

The two negatives of the principle established in the *Boilermakers' Case* provide for a rigorous separation of judicial and other
powers at the federal level. A federal court may not be made the
repository of powers other than judicial power and powers ancillary
thereto. And only courts may exercise the judicial power of the
Commonwealth. Some commentators have criticised this separation
as being too restrictive.[41] Others have seen in the case law since the
1970s a 'decline' of the separation of powers.[42] This period does
seem to have been characterised by the Commonwealth's improved
success rate in vesting decision-making powers without infringing
the *Boilermakers'* principle. However, that success rate probably has
more to do with increasingly sophisticated drafting and attention to
the underlying concepts of judicial power than any retreat by the
courts from the *Boilermakers'* principles.

So far as the courts' monopoly on the exercise of judicial power
is concerned, the powers whose conferral on non-judicial bodies has

---

[39] Sawer (1967) 152.
[40] (1956) 94 CLR 254.
[41] See Zines (1997) 167–70, 212–14; see also Sir Anthony Mason (1996).
[42] P. H. Lane (1997) 455–7, 471–2, 477–8; de Meyrick (1995a).

been upheld have involved the creation of new rights rather than the conclusive determination of existing ones,[43] or the application of broad policy factors unsuitable for judicial determination,[44] or have allowed determinations without the conclusive character of a judicial decision.[45] In such decisions the substance of the separation of powers is retained: the task of conclusively determining whether a legal standard has been breached, and imposing a penalty, always remains one for the courts. It has always been open to Parliament (subject to s 51(xxxi) of the Constitution) to alter rights as between persons or to make such alteration dependent on the opinion of a statutory body; the formation of that opinion remains necessarily subject to judicial review. Nor has the success of the Commonwealth in avoiding infringement of the *Boilermakers'* principles been complete. An attempt to give determinations of the Human Rights and Equal Opportunity Commission the status of court orders, where they were not objected to within a prescribed time limit, was held invalid in *Brandy v Human Rights and Equal Opportunity Commission*.[46]

The only real relaxation of the courts' monopoly on the exercise of federal judicial power has been the upholding in *Harris v Caladine*[47] of a power conferred on a court to delegate some of its judicial functions to non-judicial officers. Even that delegation is closely circumscribed. It was upheld on the basis that the delegation was effected by, and revocable by, the court (that is, the judges); the officers to whom power was delegated were within the administrative structure of the court; and the officers' decisions were subject to

---

[43] See, for example, *R v Trade Practices Tribunal; Ex parte Tasmanian Breweries Pty Ltd* (1970) 123 CLR 361; *R v Quinn; Ex parte Consolidated Food Corporation* (1977) 138 CLR 1; *Precision Data Holdings Ltd v Wills* (1991) 173 CLR 167.

[44] See, for example, *R v Trade Practices Tribunal; Ex parte Tasmanian Breweries Pty Ltd* (1970) 123 CLR 361; *Re Dingjan; Ex parte Wagner* (1995) 183 CLR 323, 361. Contrast *Finch v Herald & Weekly Times Ltd* (1996) 65 IR 239.

[45] *Attorney-General (Cth) v Breckler* (1999) 163 ALR 576.

[46] (1995) 183 CLR 245.

[47] (1991) 172 CLR 84.

review de novo by a judge on the application of a party.[48] According
to Mason CJ and Deane J, the power to delegate was also subject to
the limitation that 'judges must continue to bear the major responsibility for the exercise of judicial power at least in relation to the
more important aspects of contested matters'.[49]

As to the principle that courts may exercise only judicial power,
it is possible to point to cases in which the application of seemingly
amorphous standards has been held to be a judicial function when
performed by a court.[50] However, this is by no means a new development: in at least three cases decided before the *Boilermakers'
Case*, decisions on the basis of 'good cause' or 'equity and good con-
science' were held to be acceptable for s 71 courts.[51] Furthermore,
these standards, while vague (or in some cases no express standard
at all), call for an assessment of justice between individual parties—
an issue which has long been the province of the courts and on
which substantial latitude is often found in the general law. It is not
so much the vagueness of criteria that makes a power non-judicial—
courts will eventually develop principles for the decision of any issue
through layers of precedent—but the introduction of factors going
beyond individual justice, such as 'administrative and industrial
considerations',[52] the 'public interest',[53] or industrial or commercial
'policy'.[54]

---

[48] See also *Cheesman v Waters* (1997) 148 ALR 21. An application for special leave to
appeal to the High Court was refused.

[49] *Harris v Caladine* (1991) 172 CLR 84, 95.

[50] See the cases cited in P. H. Lane (1997) 478, n. 1 and 3; see also *Finch v Herald &
Weekly Times Ltd* (1996) 65 IR 239.

[51] *British Medical Association v Commonwealth* (1949) 79 CLR 201; *Peacock v New-
town Marrickville and General Cooperative Building Society No 4 Ltd* (1943) 67
CLR 25; *British Imperial Oil Co Ltd v Federal Commissioner of Taxation* (1925) 35
CLR 422.

[52] *R v Spicer; Ex parte Waterside Workers' Federation of Australia* (1957) 100 CLR
312, 321.

[53] *R v Trade Practices Tribunal; Ex parte Tasmanian Breweries Pty Ltd* (1970) 123 CLR
361, 377, 384, 399–400, 409, 411.

[54] *Precision Data Holdings Ltd v Wills* (1991) 173 CLR 167, 190–1; *Re Dingjan; Ex
parte Wagner* (1995) 183 CLR 323, 361.

The only real relaxation of this limb of the *Boilermakers'* rule has been the acceptance of individual federal judicial officers holding non-judicial appointments as designated persons. This is by no means a new development: members of the High Court undertook various assignments (of considerable duration) for the executive during World War II.[55] More recently, the performance of extra-judicial functions has been held to be acceptable where a judge is appointed as a designated person—that is, the function is performed by the judge as an individual and not by the court to which he or she belongs nor by the judge in his or her capacity as a member of that court (even if holding a commission as a judge is a prerequisite for appointment).[56] The conferral of non-judicial functions on a judge is subject to the consent of the judge and to the function not being 'incompatible' with the judge's normal judicial role.[57] Incompatibility arises where the non-judicial role tends to interfere with the functioning of the court to which the judge belongs or to undermine public confidence in the impartiality of that court.

The 'incompatibility' condition has assumed some importance. In *Wilson v Minister for Aboriginal and Torres Strait Islander Affairs* (*Wilson's Case*)[58] the appointment of the Hon. Justice Jane Mathews, who was a judge of the Federal Court, to inquire into and report to the Minister on a claim for protection under Aboriginal heritage protection legislation was held to be 'incompatible' with the judge's judicial duties and therefore invalid. The majority judgments in *Wilson's Case*[59] take a restrictive approach to the incompatibility test. Incompatibility arose mainly from the nature of the non-judicial role as adviser to the executive; yet there was nothing new in a judge taking on a role of inquiry and report, or for that matter a role of

---

[55] Sir John Latham as envoy to Japan 1940–41 (64 CLR iv), Sir Owen Dixon as envoy to the United States 1942–44 (69 CLR iv) and Sir Edward McTiernan on an inquiry into the National Security Regulations (66 CLR iv). Dixon also undertook other tasks: 80 CLR iv; J. D. Holmes (1955) 272. See also *Wilson v Minister for Aboriginal and Torres Strait Islander Affairs* (1996) 189 CLR 1, 45–6 (Kirby J).

[56] *Hilton v Wells* (1985) 157 CLR 57.

[57] *Grollo v Palmer* (1995) 184 CLR 348, 365.

[58] (1996) 189 CLR 1.

[59] Brennan CJ, Dawson, Toohey, Gaudron, McHugh and Gummow JJ; Kirby J dissenting.

involvement in executive decision-making. Although the majority in *Wilson's Case* was at pains to emphasise that judges could safely be appointed to conduct Royal Commissions and as presidential members of the Administrative Appeals Tribunal (AAT),[60] that reassurance may owe more to the practical impossibility of 'unwinding' years of judicial involvement than to principled distinction. The AAT does operate independently but it is, in fundamental terms, an agency of the executive: it makes decisions which stand as decisions of various executive officers and bodies, and those decisions are predicated on general compliance with government policy. Furthermore, the presidency of the AAT is effectively a full time position and judges appointed to that office[61] are able to do very little work in the court to which they belong.[62] The logic of the decision in *Wilson's Case* is thus difficult to reconcile with some functions that have hitherto been performed by federal judges with minimal controversy and generally beneficial results.[63]

Recent decisions on both limbs of the rule in the *Boilermakers' Case* therefore show little or no relaxation in the determination of the courts to protect the exercise of federal judicial power from contamination by contact with legislative or executive power. Of more immediate relevance is the interface between federal judicial power and powers derived from state law.

(b) The problem of jurisdictional limits

The Federal Court and the Family Court were both established in the 1970s. The Family Court had jurisdiction in matters arising under the *Family Law Act 1975* (Cth), which covered the full range of family law—dissolutions, custody and access, property settlements and declarations of nullity. These areas had until then been within the jurisdiction of state courts (albeit as federal jurisdiction following the enactment of the *Matrimonial Causes Act 1959* (Cth)).

---

[60] (1996) 189 CLR 1, 17–18.

[61] Ironically, Justice Mathews was President of the AAT when appointed to the reporting role which gave rise to the litigation in *Wilson's Case*.

[62] Compare *Grollo v Palmer* (1995) 184 CLR 348, 365, quoted by the majority in *Wilson's Case* (1996) 189 CLR 1, 14.

[63] On these functions see *Wilson's Case* (1996) 189 CLR 1, 42 (Kirby J).

The Federal Court had, or later acquired, jurisdiction in matters arising under a range of Commonwealth statutes, notably the *Trade Practices Act 1974* (Cth) (which included both consumer protection and restrictive trade practices matters) and the *Administrative Decisions (Judicial Review) Act 1977* (Cth). The Federal Court acquired jurisdiction in federal tax matters, and in taxation and other areas it hears 'appeals' from decisions of the Administrative Appeals Tribunal.

Both of the new federal courts had within their jurisdictions matters which could give rise to claims under state Acts and the general law as well as under federal statute. A transaction might give rise to claims under ordinary contract law or state fair trading legislation as well as the *Trade Practices Act*.[64] A matrimonial property dispute might give rise to issues under state law as to the nature and priority of the interests in the property. In such situations it became necessary to ascertain the limits of federal jurisdiction so as to determine which claims the court was able to hear. (The need could arise to ascertain the boundaries of federal jurisdiction exercised by a state court, but only for the purpose of determining where an appeal lay— not as an issue going to the competence of the court at first instance.)

The position was complicated by the exclusivity of some areas of the new courts' jurisdictions. Parliament decided as a matter of policy that only the Federal Court should hear claims under the *Trade Practices Act*,[65] and that only the Family Court (in the absence of state family courts approved under the *Family Law Act*) should hear most family law matters. This exclusivity meant that the boundary of federal jurisdiction could become an issue in a state court, if it was argued that some or all of the issues in respect of which the court's jurisdiction had been invoked lay within the exclusive jurisdiction of a federal court.

These jurisdictional issues produced a series of complicated cases which hold great interest for students of the federal judicial

---

[64] See *Adamson v Western Australian National Football League (Inc)* (1978) 38 FLR 237.

[65] See s 86 of the Act as originally enacted. The position has been softened by s 86(2) of the Act (but see s 86(4) of the same Act, and ss 4(4)(d) and 6 of the *Jurisdiction of Courts (Cross-vesting) Act 1987* (Cth)).

system but have little to do with the merits of any claim.[66] The concept of 'accrued jurisdiction'—by which the 'matter' in federal jurisdiction was taken to include the whole of the justiciable controversy and thus all the legal claims arising from a single substratum of facts —was developed and went some way to avoiding multiplicity of proceedings. For example, where proceedings on a *Trade Practices Act* claim were commenced in the Federal Court, the concept of accrued jurisdiction allowed that Court also to deal with a contract claim that arose out of the same transaction.[67]

As accrued jurisdiction is addressed in Chapter 9, only three remarks will be made here. First, the concept of accrued jurisdiction does not remove the inherent difficulty in identifying where one class of jurisdiction ends and another begins. Whether a claim that is not in itself federal comes within the accrued jurisdiction, and thus within a federal 'matter', depends on whether the various claims can be said to arise from the same factual substratum. This will sometimes be obvious but, equally, will sometimes be a matter of impression and degree. In the complex web of modern commercial transactions the limits of the factual substratum may sometimes need to be arbitrarily drawn. Second, taking federal jurisdiction out to the limits of the 'matter' can only ever be a partial solution to the problem of multiplicity of actions. Third, the task of the courts in deciding how far the jurisdiction of the Federal Court should extend beyond purely 'federal' issues was further complicated by the clash between the desirability of allowing the Federal Court to dispose of entire controversies and the (arguably legitimate) institutional interests of the state courts.[68]

Thus there arose both complex arid jurisdictional disputes and real injustice. For example, in *Re F; Ex parte F*,[69] the Family Court had in January 1984 awarded Mr F custody of a young child believed

---

[66] Two well-known examples are *Stack v Coast Securities (No 9) Pty Ltd* (1983) 154 CLR 261 and *Philip Morris Inc v Adam P Brown Male Fashions Pty Ltd* (1981) 148 CLR 457.

[67] *Adamson v Western Australian National Football League (Inc)* (1978) 38 FLR 237.

[68] Compare *Philip Morris Inc v Adam P Brown Male Fashions Pty Ltd* (1981) 148 CLR 457, 513 (Mason J).

[69] (1986) 161 CLR 376.

to be the child of his marriage to Mrs F. The marriage was dissolved in February 1985 and in July of that year blood samples were taken which established that the child could not be the child of Mr F. Mrs F wished to obtain custody of the child. Since the child was not a 'child of the marriage' in a biological sense, and Commonwealth power (and hence the Family Court's jurisdiction) was limited to 'matrimonial causes',[70] she applied both to the Family Court for custody and to the Supreme Court of New South Wales for a declaration and custody. The former court expressed doubts about its jurisdiction, while the latter would not entertain the proceedings in the face of the original Family Court order which remained in force. Mrs F then applied for prerogative writs in the High Court. By majority,[71] the High Court held in 1986 that the provision of the *Family Law Act* deeming an ex-nuptial child to be a 'child of the marriage' was beyond power. It followed that the Family Court had no jurisdiction in respect of the child and the original custody order was quashed. Thus Mr F through a constitutional quirk lost the benefit of the original custody order in respect of the child he had brought up as his, while Mrs F needed to apply to three different courts to have her claim heard. Gibbs CJ described the case as 'another example of the lamentable results that can ensue when the limits of the respective jurisdictions of state and federal courts are not clearly defined'.[72] The specific problem that arose in *Re F; Ex parte F* was eventually addressed by references of power to the Commonwealth in five states.[73]

(c) Cross-vesting

The more general problem of jurisdictional limits was addressed by the cross-vesting scheme enacted in 1987. That scheme, which involves complementary legislation of the Commonwealth, each

---

[70] Constitution s 51(xxii).

[71] Gibbs CJ, Wilson, Brennan and Dawson JJ; Mason and Deane JJ dissenting.

[72] *Re F; Ex parte F* (1986) 161 CLR 376, 386.

[73] *Commonwealth Powers (Family Law—Children) Act 1986* (NSW); *Commonwealth Powers (Family Law—Children) Act 1990* (Qld); *Commonwealth Powers (Family Law) Act 1986* (SA); *Commonwealth Powers (Family Law) Act 1987* (Tas); *Commonwealth Powers (Family Law—Children) Act 1986* (Vic).

state and the Northern Territory,[74] comprises the following basic elements:

1 The jurisdiction of the Federal and Family Courts (to the extent not otherwise conferred) is conferred on the Supreme Court of each state and territory, apart from certain specific matters which remain exclusive.[75]

2 The civil jurisdiction of the Supreme Court of each state[76] and territory[77] is conferred on the Supreme Court of each other state and territory.

3 The jurisdiction of the Supreme Court of each state[78] and territory[79] is conferred on the Federal and Family Courts, with the consent of the Commonwealth Parliament,[80] though the conferral of state jurisdiction on federal courts has subsequently been held invalid.

4 A proceeding may be transferred from the court in which it is commenced to another which is more appropriate to hear it[81] (and in the case of 'special federal matters'—some matters under the *Trade Practices Act* and the *Family Law Act*, federal administrative law matters, and matters under s 32 of the *National Crime Authority Act 1984* (Cth)—a proceeding must be transferred unless there are 'special reasons' not to do so).[82]

The purpose and effect of the cross-vesting legislation was to make it normally unnecessary to consider whether a particular proceeding or part of a proceeding was within federal jurisdiction or

---

[74] *Jurisdiction of Courts (Cross-vesting) Act 1987* (Cth) (Commonwealth Act); *Jurisdiction of Courts (Cross-vesting) Act 1987* of each state and Northern Territory (which are substantially identical) and *Jurisdiction of Courts (Cross-vesting) Act 1993* (ACT) (State Acts).

[75] Commonwealth Act s 4(1) and (4).

[76] State Acts s 4(3) (jurisdiction is also conferred on state Family Courts by s 4(4)). The ACT and Northern Territory are 'States', not 'Territories', for the purposes of the scheme: see s 3 of each Act.

[77] Commonwealth Act s 4(2).

[78] State Acts s 4(1) and (2).

[79] Commonwealth Act s 4(2).

[80] Commonwealth Act s 9(2).

[81] Commonwealth Act and State Acts s 5.

[82] Commonwealth Act and State Acts s 6 and definition in s 3(1).

not. The precise source of jurisdiction was irrelevant to the court's power to hear the proceeding, the procedural and substantive law to be applied, and the available avenues of appeal. This was the vision of the original *Judiciary Act*, freed of the complicating factor of the Privy Council and expanded to encompass the new federal courts. The cross-vesting legislation is examined in Chapter 10.

The jurisdiction conferred on the Federal and Family Courts by the cross-vesting legislation was jurisdiction with respect to 'State matters'. There are good grounds for construing such a conferral as limited to matters the disposition of which involves the exercise of judicial power of the same character as that involved in the exercise of federal jurisdiction. The expression 'matter' is clearly borrowed from ss 75 to 77 of the Constitution and, although there is no necessary correspondence between any of the classes of matter mentioned there and a 'State matter', it seems reasonably clear that the latter expression was meant to connote a justiciable controversy. The jurisdiction conferred was thus, in a real sense, parallel to that identified in *Re Judiciary and Navigation Acts* as proper for exercise by Chapter III courts.[83] This conclusion is reinforced by s 15 of each of the cross-vesting Acts, which requires them to be read so as not to exceed constitutional limits.

The cross-vesting scheme therefore respected the basic separation between judicial and other powers which is embodied in Chapter III. However, in *Gould v Brown* the vesting of state jurisdiction in the Federal Court under the parallel cross-vesting scheme which is contained in the Corporations Law scheme (which is in relevant respects the same) was barely upheld following a 3:3 split in the High Court.[84] In *Re Wakim; Ex parte McNally* that aspect of the scheme was held invalid by a majority of the Court.[85]

It is not possible here to analyse all the arguments in *Gould v Brown* and *Re Wakim; Ex parte McNally*. Fundamentally, those justices who held invalid the vesting of state jurisdiction in the Federal Court (Gleeson CJ, Gaudron, McHugh, Gummow, Hayne

---

[83] (1921) 29 CLR 257.

[84] (1998) 193 CLR 346. The decision of the Full Court of the Federal Court upholding the provisions was therefore upheld by operation of s 23(2) of the *Judiciary Act 1903* (Cth).

[85] (1999) 163 ALR 270.

and Callinan JJ) took the view that ss 75 and 76 of the Constitution are exhaustive not merely as to the powers that may be conferred by the Commonwealth on federal courts, but also as to the jurisdiction those courts are permitted to exercise.[86] While this position can be supported on textual grounds, it does represent a very strict approach to the separation of powers in Chapter III. The approach arguably goes beyond the separation of powers established in the *Boilermakers' Case*, as well as the strictures flowing from the definition of federal judicial power established in *Re Judiciary and Navigation Acts*.[87] This result seems particularly harsh in the light of the decision in *Northern Territory v GPAO*, where it was held that the jurisdiction that may be conferred on federal courts includes matters arising under territory laws even though territory courts administering such laws do not exercise the judicial power of the Commonwealth.[88] On this approach the purity of federal judicial power must prevail over the manifest practical advantages of allowing co-operative action by the Australian Parliaments to vest other judicial powers in federal courts.

4 State Courts in the Unified System

It is essential to the proper operation of the unified judicial system contemplated by Chapter III that the proper operation of the state courts is protected by an appropriate degree of judicial independence. Not only must state courts be free of interference in their actual exercise of federal jurisdiction; they must also retain a high degree of institutional integrity to be suited to that task, and to that end must not be compromised by being drawn into the executive process or required to act in a non-judicial manner. This is the logic behind the majority judgments in *Kable's Case*, and on that reason-

---

[86] *Gould v Brown* (1998) 193 CLR 346, 420–2 (McHugh J), 443–6 (Gummow J, Gaudron J agreeing); *Re Wakim; Ex parte McNally* (1999) 163 ALR 270, 289–91 (McHugh J, Callinan J agreeing), 303–4 (Gummow and Hayne JJ, Gleeson CJ and Gaudron J agreeing).

[87] (1921) 29 CLR 257.

[88] (1999) 161 ALR 318. See also *Spratt v Hermes* (1965) 114 CLR 226; *Capital TV & Appliances Pty Ltd v Falconer* (1971) 125 CLR 591; *Re Governor, Goulburn Correctional Centre, Goulburn; Ex parte Eastman* (1999) 165 ALR 171.

ing there must be in each state a court of general jurisdiction available and suitable for the vesting of federal jurisdiction.

It is also arguable that a federal system embodying the rule of law and representative government requires a more general protection of judicial power at the state level. It seems somewhat unreal for those values to have been embodied in the Constitution of the new Commonwealth but not so as to impose any requirements on the states. The High Court has held that the implied freedom of political communication extends to communications concerning political matters at the state, local, and federal government levels. The rationale has been simply that political discourse is so integrated that it is impossible to draw real distinctions.[89] The same observation might be made of a judicial system in which most state courts are repositories of federal jurisdiction and Commonwealth legislation is so far-reaching that almost any proceeding might, perhaps unexpectedly, take on a federal aspect.

An alternative rationale for the extension of free political communication to state matters, advanced in the most recent implied freedoms cases but not pronounced upon by the High Court, was that the Constitution independently requires each state to maintain a 'Parliament' in which at least the more powerful chamber is popularly elected. That argument was based on provisions referring to state Parliaments and electors, but also finds support in the inherent unlikelihood of a constitutional system that entrenched democratic values in the federal sphere while allowing pocket boroughs to determine the government of constituent elements of the federation. Similar considerations can be pointed to in relation to the values of Chapter III. The regime of Chapter III depends in part on the existence of state 'courts', by which must be meant institutions capable of the independent exercise of judicial power; and it would be incongruous for the Constitution to envisage the pure regime of federal jurisdiction existing alongside corrupt or partial state courts. Such considerations are the basis for the reasonable argument that Chapter III by implication requires a reasonably strict separation of powers at state as well as federal level.

---

[89] *Lange v Australian Broadcasting Corporation* (1997) 189 CLR 520.

The High Court has so far not been attracted to these arguments. In *Kable's Case* all members of the Court who addressed the
issue agreed that no strict separation of powers was entrenched in
the New South Wales Constitution. Instead, the majority used the
Supreme Court's status as a repository of federal jurisdiction, together with the concept of incompatibility, to exclude the conferral
of a function on the Supreme Court. That analysis provides a degree
of protection to state judicial power which is somewhat indetermi-
nate, convoluted in its reasoning, and much weaker than a genuine
separation of powers.[90] It appears to have been fashioned to meet
the conferral of powers which the majority considered particularly
unsuitable for performance by a court.

Certainly there are sound historical reasons for holding that the
state constitutions do not entrench any separation of powers. However, as some recent decisions show, the long-term acceptance of a
proposition is not an insurmountable barrier to its displacement by
new understandings of what the Constitution requires.[91]

One reason why there can be no shift towards the acceptance
of a real separation of powers at the state level is that the stringency
of the concept as expounded in the *Boilermakers' Case* and more
recent decisions would make it unworkable in the state sphere. States
are accustomed to creating and empowering courts in accordance
with considerations of practicality, and the result is that the co-
existence of judicial and non-judicial powers in the one body is
commonplace, as are other breaches of *Boilermakers'* standards such
as the appointment of acting judges and the appointment of Chief
Justices as Lieutenant-Governors. The imposition of a strict *Boilermakers'* standard would be cataclysmic.

5 Conclusion

The separation of judicial power entrenched by Chapter III has been
noted as a potentially significant source of 'due process' rights.[92]

---

[90] *Kable v Director of Public Prosecutions (NSW)* (1996) 189 CLR 51, 103 (Gaudron J).

[91] See, for example, *Theophanous v Herald & Weekly Times Ltd* (1994) 182 CLR 104;
Commonwealth v Mewett (1997) 191 CLR 471, 545–51 (Gummow and Kirby JJ;
Brennan CJ and Gaudron J agreeing), holding that the doctrine of Crown immunity
from suit in tort did not apply to the Commonwealth.

[92] See, for example, Winterton (1994).

Implications from Chapter III not only protect the general independence of the courts and prevent the power to punish for breaches of the law from being allocated to non-judicial bodies, but also prevent Chapter III courts from being required to act inconsistently with judicial method. In this they go some way to guaranteeing freedoms which are arguably as important to a free society as any right to democratic participation.

Paradoxically, however, the stricter the approach to the separation of powers at the federal level, the greater the obstacles facing the implication of a similar standard at the state level. So long as such standards exist only in the federal sphere, citizens are left without the guarantees of due process that ought to be the hallmark of a society such as Australia's.

The purist approach evident in the majority judgments in *Re Wakim; Ex parte McNally* could conceivably rebound to the detriment of the system as a whole. One possible method of overcoming the invalidity of a central element of the cross-vesting scheme might be to abandon the Federal and Family Courts and vest all original federal jurisdiction (except perhaps for some specialised areas) in state and territory courts. In that case, the advantages that were perceived in having Commonwealth laws interpreted consistently throughout Australia by a single court would be lost. Furthermore, federal jurisdiction would be administered in courts whose independence was protected by the doctrine in *Kable's Case* rather than by a true separation of powers.

The High Court would be wise to look beyond the narrow horizons of the protection of federal courts and to seek principles of universal application to enhance the exercise of jurisdiction, federal or state, in all courts. The current approach of the High Court to the constitutional role of federal courts—applying principles which are based merely on inference and implication from Chapter III—is one which, while founded on high principle, is capable of leading to real damage to the federal framework and the overall ability of Australians to be confident in the proper adjudication of their legal rights.

3

The Independence of the Judiciary

Stephen Parker

1 Introduction

This chapter has three purposes. First, it discusses independence of the judiciary as a recurrent theme underlying the federal judicial system. Alongside the doctrine of the separation of powers and the expedient of judicial federalism in Australia, the general policy of protecting judicial independence provides an essential context within which to understand federal courts, federal jurisdiction and the federal judiciary. It helps to explain the relevant constitutional and legislative provisions, the organisational and institutional arrangements concerning courts, and at least some of the issues concerning the role of the judiciary at federal level. Second, the chapter examines a number of topical issues that show how protecting the independence of the judiciary is not simply a question of providing security of tenure and guaranteed terms and conditions. Third, the chapter seeks to identify the core social value promoted by judicial independence and suggests a design or model for promoting it in modern conditions.

Australia is currently ill-equipped to discuss judicial independence in an informed way. As a society, we have not grappled sufficiently in theoretical terms with the nature and purpose of judicial independence, and consequently we lack a conceptual model that will help us to formulate policies, explain them, and know how to respond to issues as they arise. This may seem paradoxical. Generally, judicial independence commands almost universal approval. How can its purpose and manifestation be little understood? A cynic might say that the approval stems partly from the very lack of understanding. There is indeed a respectable argument that human relationships and institutions endure despite people's fundamental differences in values precisely because they are thought about only to the extent necessary for them to be put into day-to-day operation. 'Incompletely theorised agreements',[1] as Cass Sunstein calls them, help the world go round.

This may be true to some extent in relation to judicial independence but it does not fit all the facts. The evidence is that when people in a liberal democracy are asked to consider judicial independence carefully, support for it remains strong, and possibly even grows. When in March 1995 the people of New South Wales were asked in a referendum whether they approved proposals to entrench certain constitutional provisions concerning judicial independence, just under 66 per cent agreed. In October 1996, 3 per cent of the Belgian population marched peacefully in the streets of Brussels (the equivalent of 540 000 Australians marching through Canberra) in support of judicial independence from the government of the day. It followed the dismissal of an investigating magistrate who was following a trail that led from a child murderer to government officials and onwards to government ministers. Members of the government had apparently leaned on the Supreme Court to dismiss the magistrate in an effort to stop his investigation.

Perhaps the true position is that people intuitively know that the core value protected by judicial independence—perceived impartiality in adjudication—is vital for the survival and cohesion of social groups. The arrangements for protecting that value are, however, a matter for specialist judgment in the light of the circumstances of the group. In complex, differentiated societies like Australia and the other liberal democracies, the arrangements comprise interlocking sets of constitutional provisions, other laws, conventions, and institutional practices. Unsurprisingly, these have limited interest for the

---

[1] Sunstein (1996) viii.

lay person. One might go further and suggest that those who seek to promote and explain the importance of judicial independence might be taking the wrong tack, despite the best of intentions. Rather than attempting to define 'judicial independence' in relation to other political values we believe people understand and adhere to, such as the rule of law, the separation of powers, and the protection of individual rights, we should be tapping into people's deeper sense of the social importance of impartiality in adjudication.

Judicial independence should be seen as the sum of arrangements that exist from time to time and place to place to protect perceived judicial impartiality. Recent attempts to defend the judiciary may have started at the wrong end, by focusing on today's legal and institutional arrangements as if they were timeless and universal ends in themselves, rather than focusing on the core value of impartiality and then determining what, in modern conditions, is desirable for its protection. The present tack may be engendering in the community a sense that a comfortably placed judiciary is looking after its own interests.

While the focus here is naturally on issues relating to the federal judiciary, it has not been possible to confine it to them. This is particularly so where a matter that has arisen in the states might yet arise in the federal sphere. In addition, much of the theoretical and conceptual discussion is equally applicable to all Australian courts. Speaking generally, judicial independence is better protected in the federal sphere than in the states and territories. This is largely due to the entrenched protections in the Australian Constitution as interpreted by a High Court which has been keenly aware of the need to safeguard the independence of the courts. It should also be said that successive Commonwealth governments have tended to show caution and restraint in matters pertaining to the judiciary. In contrast, none of the constitutions elsewhere has the same degree of entrenched protection, and most have none at all.

2 The Meaning and Rationale of Judicial Independence

The last decade has seen a surge in the amount of writing about, and inquiries into, judicial independence in the common law liberal democracies. Serving and retired senior judges have adopted it as a central theme in articles and addresses. Inquiries have been set up to assess its current state of health. Bodies have been formed to promote and protect it. Declarations have been made by Chief Justices at home and abroad. The reasons for this surge at this time would repay attention, but the point of noting it here is that it means the definitions and rationales put forward by today's leading thinkers on the subject are readily available for inspection.

The initial impression is of considerable diversity in approach and formulation of these definitions and rationales, but it is difficult to identify whether the differences are merely linguistic, in that different words have been chosen to express the same idea, or semantic, in the strict sense that a different meaning is intended. The very uncertainty over whether substantive differences are intended illustrates the relative lack of theoretical and conceptual attention to what judicial independence is, and how it relates to other political and social values. Even a small selection from what has been described as 'an immense international literature'[2] on the subject is sufficient to convey the impression of diversity.

Sir Ninian Stephen approached the subject with greater confidence about what judicial independence is not, than about what it is:

> Like most concepts that mankind debates, judicial independence conveys different shades of meanings to different minds. But what it can never mean is some privileged position for judges, some special advantage given them for their benefit. What its precise meaning must always include is a state of affairs in which judges are free to do justice in their communities, protected from the power and influence of the State and also made as immune as humanly possible from all other influences that may affect their impartiality.[3]

Some connection between impartiality of judging—the 'supreme judicial virtue'[4]—and the independence of judges is made by almost all commentators. Sir Gerard Brennan uses the idea of the rule of law to describe the relationship:

---

[2] Friedland (1995) 18.
[3] Stephen (1989) 6.
[4] Brennan (1998) 34.

The reason why judicial independence is of such public importance is that a free society exists only so long as it is governed by the rule of law—the rule which binds the governors and the governed, administered impartially and treating equally all those who seek its remedies or against whom its remedies are sought. However vaguely it may be perceived, however unarticulated may be the thought, there is an aspiration in the hearts of all men and women for the rule of law.[5]

The Report of the Commission on Separation of Powers and Judicial Independence for the American Bar Association emphasises the rights of the subject:

Judicial independence makes a system of impartial justice possible by enabling judges to protect and enforce the rights of the people, and by allowing them without fear of reprisal to strike down actions of the legislative and executive branches of government which run afoul of the Constitution. Independence is not for the personal benefit of the judges but rather for the protection of the people, whose rights only an independent judge can preserve.[6]

In addition to the rule of law and the protection of rights, the separation of powers features in many statements of the meaning and rationale of judicial independence. This might involve the normal usage of separation of powers, as indicating a separation of the judicature from the executive and the legislature, but it might also involve federal systems where there is a separation between federal powers on the one hand and state or provincial powers on the other. Constitutional courts in federations are aware of the tensions that can arise between governments and the function of their decisions in preserving the distribution of powers envisaged by the founders.[7]

---

[5] Brennan (1996) 2.

[6] American Bar Association (1997) iii.

[7] In Australia see, for example, *Waterside Workers' Federation of Australia v J W Alexander Ltd* (1918) 25 CLR 434, 469–70 (Isaacs and Rich JJ); *R v Kirby; Ex parte Boilermakers' Society of Australia* (1956) 94 CLR 254, 276 (Dixon CJ, McTiernan, Fullagar and Kitto JJ); *Wilson v Minister for Aboriginal and Torres Strait Islander Affairs* (1996) 189 CLR 1, 12–13 (Brennan CJ, Dawson, Toohey, McHugh and Gummow JJ). In Canada, see *R v Beauregard* (1987) 30 DLR (4th) 481, 493 (Dickson CJ).

Other statements of the rationale of judicial independence go beyond the regulation and limitation of governmental power and recognise the presence of other powerful groups in society that might sway or corrupt a judge: 'Judicial independence requires that judges be protected from governments *and other pressures* in order that they may try cases fairly and impartially'.[8]

Perhaps recognising the difficulty of ranking hierarchically the values protected by judicial independence, Archibald Cox (who, as the first Watergate Special Prosecutor, dismissed by President Nixon, could speak from experience) stated some as co-equals:

> The ideal of an independent judiciary is deeply rooted in the American tradition. Senator Sam Ervin, of Watergate fame, wrote just a few years before Watergate: '[t]o my mind, an independent judiciary is perhaps the most essential characteristic of a free society.' I agree. Yet even though the ideal is traditional, it is worth recalling the reasons which led men to fight for the ideal through the centuries and which equally support it today. The reasons fall into three categories: (1) protection against executive oppression; (2) protection against violations of fundamental human rights; and (3) assurances of upright and impartial justices.[9]

All of these formulations, impliedly at least, connect judicial independence with democratic liberalism of the kind forged out of constitutional struggles that began in about the seventeenth century. True, 'the rule of law', 'the protection of rights', 'constitutionality', 'justice', and 'the separation of powers' are stated in somewhat bewildering inter-relationships, but this might only reflect deeper differences in the understanding of liberalism one finds in political theory in general. To note a tendency impliedly to connect judicial independence with the dominant political ideology in the Western world is hardly to criticise the authors. There may, however, be a deeper anthropological truth about judicial independence that is partially obscured by such accounts. If we can identify this, we may have the basis for a stronger theoretical understanding.

---

[8] Justice Society Committee on the Judiciary (1992) 4 (emphasis added).

[9] Cox (1996) 567.

Social groups need procedures and institutions to resolve conflicts and disputes if they are to maintain a reasonable degree of internal order and protect themselves from external threats. Dispute resolution is most effective when the loser in any dispute has no reason to suppose afterwards that the procedure amounted to two against one. This not only helps truly to resolve the particular dispute, it also channels other disputes in the direction of the procedure. Acceptance of the outcome by the loser is highly dependent upon a belief in the impartiality of the decision-maker. Even where the decision-maker uses a wholly irrational process, such as an ordeal or tossing a coin,[10] it is important that the procedure is administered impartially. This is the 'logic of the triad', which, in Martin Shapiro's words, is 'the root concept of courtness'.[11] Assuming only two disputants, 'courtness' involves three equidistant points. It is abrogated when two points (the adjudicator and the winner) are closer to each other than they are to the third (the loser).

This takes us to the idea that the core value really under discussion is the perception of judicial impartiality—the maintenance of the logic of the triad. This must always be interpreted in a contextual way according to prevailing conditions and ideologies. In less-organised or less-developed societies without a state apparatus, the value is seen in terms of preservation of the group, family stability and collective harmony in the face of internal disputes. In more organised societies with differentiated power structures, the value is seen in terms of institutions, balances, and political systems. In specifically liberal societies, the language of individual rights, legality and the separation of powers may resonate better.

This proposition deliberately emphasises the perception of judicial impartiality and may seem to dwell upon the ephemeral. Surely, one might counter, the actuality of impartial decision-making is what really matters. However, perceptions are fundamentally important because actual impartiality is so difficult to identify and define satisfactorily. Impartiality is a problematic concept and the ability to convey at least a perception of impartiality deflects the disappointed loser from probing it too deeply. We are guided away

---

[10] For an argument that tossing a coin can be rational, see Elster (1989).
[11] Shapiro (1981) 1.

from very tricky philosophical territory regarding the possibility that any mortal can be wholly neutral; very tricky psychological territory regarding the possibility of excluding subconscious predispositions; and very tricky political territory regarding the possibility of being even-handed when a rule or constitutional arrangement is not regarded as right by the whole community. Perceptions of impartiality enable us to arrive at incompletely theorised agreements about what is just. Such perceptions steer us away from taking on insoluble problems about the meaning of impartiality so that we can get on with our lives, and they have always done so.

If one accepts the social importance of perceived impartiality, as a form of anthropological truth long pre-dating liberalism, one might take a different approach to conceptualising judicial independence in modern conditions. The central question is not: do we think that judges of the calibre usually appointed really would be partial? It becomes: would a normal litigant, with no reason to know much about the law or judges, have reasonable fears about partiality? When directed to this question, we become much more sensitive to the need for rules, conventions, and practices to guard against perceptions that a litigant may have, but which lawyers themselves are unlikely to entertain.

Most extended discussions of judicial independence mention public confidence. Sir Anthony Mason, for example, refers to the role of public confidence in the practical operation of the courts:

> The preservation of public confidence in the impartial and independent administration of justice is a vital element in the judicial function. Loss of confidence in the system whether due to its inefficiency or, more particularly, due to perceptions of a want of independence or impartiality on the part of the judiciary is extremely damaging to the effective working of the justice system.[12]

Just as judicial impartiality is interpreted and explained in a contextual way according to the times and the society, so too must the role of perception and its collective modern counterpart, public confidence in the administration of justice. Hence, modern discussions in liberal societies often focus on the supposedly consensual

---

[12] Sir Anthony Mason (1997) 7.

basis of those societies and the need in particular for legal institutions to be obeyed voluntarily. As Justice Felix Frankfurter put
it: 'The Court's authority, consisting of neither the purse nor the
sword, rests ultimately on substantial public confidence in its moral
sanction'.[13]

In the absence of a civil militia or religious fundamentalism,
courts in liberal societies must continually build respect if their decisions are to be followed. This is particularly so with a supreme
constitutional court, such as the High Court of Australia. The whole
federal polity could be jeopardised if the constituent states in the federation had a perception that the judges of that court were not
impartial in constitutional matters. Just as the individual litigant
must have a perception of impartial adjudication, so must the community at large if other litigants are to use the procedures and if the
polity and society are to seem legitimate. The stakes are very high;
and nowhere more so than in liberal societies, which assume voluntary obedience.

The following propositions, therefore, can be advanced about
the rationale of judicial independence:

1 All organised societies depend for their survival and well-being
   upon the existence of institutions to handle disputes and
   conflicts.

2 The institutions can perform their functions effectively only if
   there is a perception, sufficiently widely shared, that those who
   adjudicate are impartial.

3 It is ultimately the perception that matters, but this is not such
   an alarming proposition as may first appear. Adjudicators who
   approach their task with preconceptions about the particular
   litigants, or the class to which the litigants belong, or who are
   'got at' by one party, or who are unduly influenced by the prospective reaction of others to a particular finding, or who are
   motivated in their characterisation of facts or interpretation of
   the law by a desire to bring about particular social ends, may
   soon lose the perception of impartiality. Once that happens,

---

[13] Quoted in Ministry of Attorney-General (Ontario) (1995) 6. See also McGarvie
(1996).

their function begins to fail. Aside from this, however, the perception of impartiality has an independent importance in legitimating the social order and defusing conflict. In societies we recognise as having a legal system, most judges are biased at one level. They must be. They are ultimately an arm of government. They must uphold the values of the society as enshrined in its laws. Where those laws operate to the benefit of some and the detriment of others, as happens in all legal systems, they must favour the beneficiary. The perception of impartiality in the individual case, however, preserves the logic of the triad while maintaining the judges' ultimate role as an arm of government and control.[14]

4 The interpretation and description of these truths are very much conditioned by the nature of the society. In liberal democracies, judicial independence is expressed through the language of the rule of law, rights, constitutionality and so forth. Perception is expressed through the language of public confidence in the courts.

5 'Judicial independence' describes a set of arrangements designed to promote and protect the perception of impartial adjudication. The arrangements will differ according to the age and the society, and they may be more or less effective in achieving the ends to which they are directed. The core concept with which we should be concerned, however, is perceived impartial adjudication. Judicial independence is only a derivative concept which describes the conditions designed to preserve such adjudication.

3 Constitutional Provisions Regarding Judicial Independence

Any analysis of judicial independence in Australia must acknowledge the influence of constitutional provisions at the federal level. This influence is the major point of contrast between the Commonwealth and the states, although we might now be witnessing the start of a process whereby the Australian Constitution reaches into the

---

[14] This is a version of a thesis advanced by certain historians of eighteenth-century England. See Hay et al. (1977) ch. 1.

state courts, as a result of the High Court's decision in *Kable v Director of Public Prosecutions (NSW)* (*Kable's Case*).[15]

The central relevant provision in the Australian Constitution is s 72, which provides:

> The Justices of the High Court and of the other courts created by the Parliament—
> (i) Shall be appointed by the Governor-General in Council:
> (ii) Shall not be removed except by the Governor-General in Council, on an address from both Houses of the Parliament in the same session, praying for such removal on the ground of proved misbehaviour or incapacity:
> (iii) Shall receive such remuneration as the Parliament may fix; but the remuneration shall not be diminished during their continuance in office.

The section then goes on to deal with questions of age and retirement as they apply since amendments to the Constitution in 1977. Justices of the High Court cannot be appointed after they reach the age of seventy and they must be appointed for a term expiring upon reaching that age. The same applies to justices of other courts created by the Parliament unless the Parliament makes a law fixing an earlier age.

Provisions similar, although by no means identical, to s 72 exist elsewhere in relation to security of tenure and remuneration. The English *Act of Settlement 1701*[16] provided that judges' commissions were to be made during good behaviour 'and their salaries ascertained and established; but upon the address of both houses of Parliament it may be lawful to remove them'. Under Article III s 1 of the United States Constitution 'the Judges, both of the supreme and inferior Courts, shall hold their Offices during good Behaviour, and shall, at stated Times, receive for their Services, a Compensation, which shall not be diminished during their Continuance in Office'. By virtue of s 99 of the Constitution Act of Canada the judges of the superior courts hold office 'during good behaviour, but shall

---

[15] (1996) 189 CLR 51.
[16] 12 & 13 Will III, c 2, s 3.

be removable by the Governor General on address of the Senate and House of Commons'. Section 100 provides that 'The Salaries, Allowances, and Pensions of the Judges of the Superior, District and County Courts . . . shall be fixed and provided by the Parliament of Canada'.

Section 72 was designed to protect the independence of federal judges by insulating them from the possible threat of removal from office, except under the specified circumstances of proved misbehaviour or incapacity, and from the diminution of their remuneration. Section 72 operates in tandem with s 71 which, as interpreted in various decisions of the High Court,[17] effectively reserves the exercise of the federal judicial power to justices who have these protections (allowing for a degree of permissible delegation of powers),[18] and to judicial officers of state courts invested with federal jurisdiction. The argument has not yet been tackled whether the particular tenure and conditions of a state judicial officer render her or him unsuitable to exercise the judicial power of the Commonwealth. That is, it remains to be seen whether s 72, in the light of the approach taken by the High Court in *Kable's Case*, will have some effect outside federal courts. As a result of s 72, concerns that have been expressed in the states about the appointment there of acting judges and the conferral of judicial powers upon tribunals which lack these protections do not seem to arise at the federal level.

The protections conferred in s 72 are obviously designed in part to promote impartiality of adjudication in cases when the government itself is a litigant. The Commonwealth government is not only a litigant in constitutional cases before the High Court, it is regularly a party in the Federal Court. In a small pilot study carried out by the Australian Law Reform Commission, a sample of 'general files' (excluding winding up cases) was taken. The government was the respondent in two-thirds of the cases where the respondent was

---

[17] See in particular *Waterside Workers' Federation of Australia v J W Alexander Ltd* (1918) 25 CLR 434; *R v Kirby; Ex parte Boilermakers' Society of Australia* (1956) 94 CLR 254; *Brandy v Human Rights and Equal Opportunity Commission* (1995) 183 CLR 245.

[18] In relation to registrars, see *Harris v Caladine* (1991) 172 CLR 84.

a large organisation.[19] Section 72 has the further function of insulating federal judges against the possibility that powerful non-
governmental groups might lobby the government or Parliament to
commence proceedings for their removal. In addition, the protections
in s 72 promote confidence amongst litigants who are opposed to
the government or a perceived ally of the government, by reassuring
them that the court cannot be threatened directly or indirectly by
their opponent. In effect, as has been the intention since the English
Act of Settlement, these protections promote both the actuality and
perception of impartiality. It is important, however, not to focus only
on s 72. As mentioned earlier, much of the case law on the judicial
power and s 71 has been dominated by the policy of channelling the
exercise of the federal judicial power into courts where the judicial
officers have the protection of s 72. This is buttressed by the rule
in *R v Kirby; Ex parte Boilermakers' Society of Australia* (*Boilermakers' Case*)[20] that non-judicial functions cannot validly be conferred on federal courts other than functions incidental to the exercise
of judicial functions. In turn, conventions and practices bolster and
supplement the constitutional rules. Some of these arise below.

4 Topical Issues

(a) The abolition of courts or the removal of their jurisdiction

One practical way for a government to rid itself of judges whose
decisions it does not like is to abolish the court in which they sit, or
effectively to deprive it of any jurisdiction. The jurisdiction can then
be conferred upon a court with judges more to the government's
liking. It could be argued that this was what occurred in 1988, with
the abolition of the Arbitration Commission, its replacement with
the Australian Industrial Relations Commission, and the non-
appointment of Justice Staples to the new body. Other examples are
the reorganisation of the magistracy in New South Wales and the
failure to appoint six magistrates of the Courts of Petty Sessions to
the new Local Courts; and the abolition of the Accident Compen-

---

[19] Australian Law Reform Commission (1997a) 35.
[20] (1956) 94 CLR 254.

sation Tribunal in Victoria (whose members had the rank, status, and precedence of a County Court judge) and the failure to appoint nine members elsewhere.

Litigation about such practices has been limited and many issues remain unresolved. Where examples involved tribunals, they were complicated by the question of whether the bodies should be regarded as courts for these purposes. With the possible exception of the Staples affair, in no case is it completely clear that the dominant purpose of abolition was to remove a particular judge or group of judges. As Sir Anthony Mason has said: 'the abolition of a court usually takes place as part of a planned re-organisation of the court structure, in circumstances where the legislature and the executive claim that the re-organisation is being undertaken in the public interest in order to provide a better or more efficient court system'.[21]

If a clear case of abolishing a court to remove a particular judge or judges did arise, there is a widespread belief that it would violate a constitutional convention, but it is not obvious what legal proceedings, if any, could be taken.[22] In principle, provided the judicial officer continues to receive the remuneration he or she would have received until reaching the stipulated retirement age, there is seemingly no limit on a government's ability to abolish federal courts, except in the case of the High Court (the existence of which is provided for in s 71 of the Constitution). There might conceivably be a constitutional convention, based on past practice, that the judge should be appointed to any new court created to take the place of the old one or to a court of similar status, and that only if no such appointment is available is it appropriate simply to continue the remuneration, but such a convention is not free from doubt.[23] There is no doubt, however, that the judiciary would regard this as the appropriate way of protecting judicial independence,[24] but the legal status of the idea is uncertain. In the states, provided one did not

---

[21] Sir Anthony Mason (1997) 26.

[22] Zeitz (1998).

[23] Justice Kirby is the principal proponent of this idea. See, particularly, Kirby (1995).

[24] See, for example, Article 29 of the Beijing Statement of Principles of the Independence of the Judiciary, affirmed by the Chief Justices of the Lawasia Region. See also Judicial Conference of Australia (1996).

reach the unknown point at which there was an insufficient court system for the investment of federal jurisdiction anticipated by s 77(iii), there is no obvious impediment to abolition in the Australian Constitution.[25]

Even though a federal judicial officer has security of remuneration, the threat of abolition of the court may still be a potent one. Judges are drawn from among the most talented lawyers and they wish to make use of their skills in the public interest and for their personal satisfaction. They may have taken an overall drop in remuneration to become a judge. The threat of having the work removed from them, and the public odium that might follow from being seen to be paid for doing nothing, could play on the mind of a judicial officer. Being offered a commission in another court without loss of status may be suitable compensation to some, but not, for example, where the work in the abolished court was of a specialist nature and the judge had accepted appointment because of the opportunity it provided to develop the specialism. No concept of 'constructive removal' akin to constructive dismissal in employment law has been developed.

(b) Remuneration

The fact that the remuneration of federal judges may not be reduced during their continuance in office is certainly seen as an essential pillar of judicial independence in modern times. In Hamilton's words, 'in the general course of human nature, a power over a man's subsistence amounts to a power over his will'.[26] The possibility of judges being tempted to favour government or to seek financial advantage elsewhere should be avoided, as should any perception by a party appearing before the court that the judge is in this position. The salaries of judges of the Supreme Court of Canada during the 1880s were said to be so low that all but one of the judges was

---

[25] In *Kable v Director of Public Prosecutions (NSW)* (1996) 189 CLR 51, three judges indicated that the integrated judicial system contemplated by the Constitution requires the continuation of a system of state courts: 103 (Gaudron J), 110–11 (McHugh J) and 140 (Gummow J). Two judges specified that a state legislature cannot abolish its Supreme Court: 111 (McHugh J), 139 (Gummow J).

[26] Hamilton, Jay and Madison (1787) No 79, 512.

heavily indebted to their banks.[27] Similarly, in the sixteenth and seventeenth centuries various English judges felt it necessary to supplement their income by accepting gifts or bribes from litigants.[28] Such situations must be avoided.

Contemporary issues include determining what amounts to remuneration, what is a reduction and what is the effect of the words 'during their continuance in office'. Questions arising from these issues that relate to judicial independence can become entangled with other questions relating to equity with other groups, government wages policies, and the need to attract appropriate talent to the bench.

Space does not permit an account of the turbulent history of the setting of federal judicial salaries,[29] but it is fair to say that in recent times the story has not been a happy one for the judiciary. The salaries of federal judges are determined by the Remuneration Tribunal established by the *Remuneration Tribunal Act 1973* (Cth),[30] subject to disallowance of the determination by either House or, in any event, to being overridden by statute. Section 5(1) provides that the Remuneration Tribunal must have regard to the Principles of Wage Determination established from time to time by the Australian Industrial Relations Commission and decisions by the Commission from time to time in National Wage Cases. These requirements are widely thought to be inappropriate to judicial remuneration and have had the effect of severely limiting increases in judicial remuneration.[31] As a consequence of this, during periods of high inflation in the 1980s the remuneration of federal judges declined in real terms, giving rise at least to speculation that s 72(iii) of the Constitution had been infringed. In Canada one constitutional decision held that judicial salaries must be adjusted upwards from time to time to maintain their real value constitutionally.[32] This has not been the

---

[27] Friedland (1995) 53.
[28] Brooke (1997) 99–100.
[29] Winterton (1995) 43–58.
[30] Sections 5(1) and 7(5B).
[31] Commonwealth Remuneration Tribunal (1989).
[32] *R v Campbell; R v Ekmecic; R v Wickman* [1995] 2 WWR 469.

case in the United States where, in Article III s 1, words identical to those in s 72 of the Australian Constitution are used.[33]

Attractive pension or superannuation arrangements are understood in many countries to be important means of protecting judicial independence by removing or reducing the financial worries of judges as they approach retirement age, and thus shielding them from influences and temptations. 'Remuneration' is assumed to include judicial pensions, and the Remuneration Tribunal in determining salaries takes into account the non-contributory pensions provided under the *Judicial Pensions Act 1968* (Cth). The Commonwealth government in 1997 conceded that remuneration includes post-retirement pensions when exempting serving federal judges from the superannuation contributions surcharge tax. Nevertheless, this has not been established by judicial decision, nor has the argument been tested that a reduction in pension, which only takes effect following retirement, is not a diminution of remuneration 'during their continuance in office'. The deletion of these words from s 72 would seem desirable.

One question which may become prominent in relation to judicial salaries is whether 'packaging' or some degree of individual negotiation can be permitted. At first sight, the idea that an individual judge might negotiate a form and level of remuneration that differs from other judges in the same court gives rise to the possibility that the judge's attitude to the government might be affected by the negotiations, particularly if there is some continuing possibility of renegotiation, for example, in relation to a motor vehicle, overseas travel for study purposes, and so on. The role of the Commonwealth Remuneration Tribunal would seem to confine the possibilities for salary packaging at federal level, although it seems to be starting to occur in the states and territories.

Indirect methods of differentiating the remuneration levels of judges may be available, such as by creating positions within courts to which appointments effectively are made by governments. If these positions carry higher levels of remuneration than those of the judges of that court generally, they could be used for the purposes of

---

[33] *United States v Will*, 449 US 200 (1980).

inducement. This could become a backdoor way of introducing performance-based pay. In April 1997, the eight Chief Justices of the states and territories released a Declaration of Principles on Judicial Independence which seems to contemplate these dangers. Article 5 states:

> It should not be within the power of Executive Government to appoint a holder of judicial office to any position of seniority or administrative responsibility or of increased status or emoluments within the judiciary for a limited renewable term or on the basis that the appointment is revocable by Executive Government, subject only to the need, if provided for by statute, to appoint acting judicial heads of Courts during the absence of a judicial head or during the inability of a judicial head for the time being to perform the duties of the office.[34]

This statement presumably does not refer to federal courts, and constitutional objections might arise at the Commonwealth level to any such attempts by the federal government. In the Family Court, Judge Administrators may be appointed from among the judges of the Court,[35] but the tenure of the appointment is not made clear. We know that a Judge Administrator may resign from that position without resigning as a judge.[36] There is also an unspecific reference to a commission of appointment terminating through expiration of the term.[37] The substantial workload of Judge Administrators seems to make it an unlikely form of inducement, but this office may, in theory, be an example of the indirect methods being discussed.

(c) The financing and administration of courts

Any modern democracy is likely to leave to the elected legislature the ultimate power of appropriating public money. There seems to be little realistic alternative to decisions about the level of financing of courts being made directly by the Parliament or indirectly by an appropriation to a government department which then allocates a budget to a court. There is no constitutional provision preventing

---

[34] Chief Justices of the States and Territories (1997) 114.

[35] *Family Law Act 1975* (Cth) s 21(3)(c).

[36] See s 22(2AFA).

[37] See s 23(11).

the reduction of allocations to courts. Such a provision could be undesirable in that it might prevent transfers of jurisdiction where there are good grounds, or lock money into jurisdictions that are declining. Nevertheless, the power to decide a court's budget has some potential to be used to undermine judicial independence because declining resources and working conditions are bound to concern dedicated professional people. Similarly, the failure to increase the number of judges proportionate to the increase in caseload can make the judges of a court, collectively, supplicants to government. Like most borderline matters being discussed here, motive is important. It may be reprehensible to refuse to appoint more judges because a government does not like the decisions of a court or the behaviour of the Chief Justice. However, refusing to appoint more judges because the work practices of the court are thought to be inefficient might be supportable on the facts.

Questions of court governance and who should have the responsibility for administering a court have vexed many Australian and overseas jurisdictions. In the United States the federal and most state judicial systems are run by the judiciary. This is much less the case in Canada and England. Various governance models can be found in the Australian states and territories.[38] In Canada the Supreme Court has held that while the executive must not interfere with, or attempt to influence, the adjudicative functions of courts, the same is not the case with administrative matters. In the leading case of *Valente v The Queen*[39] the Supreme Court upheld the decision of Howland CJO in the Ontario Court of Appeal that direct administration by a government department did not infringe the requirement in the Charter of Rights and Freedoms that a person must not be convicted of an offence unless proven guilty according to law in a fair and public hearing by an independent and impartial tribunal.

It may be relevant to consider some of the changes that are taking place in modern courts when evaluating this issue. With the arrival of expectations of judicial case management, pro-active and interventionist judging, and the routine use of information

---

[38] See Parker (1998) 12.
[39] (1985) 24 DLR (4th) 161.

technology, judges may become more dependent upon administrative support than in earlier times. To the extent that a government department administering the court can regulate such support it might seek to exercise its powers for an improper purpose, such as bringing to heel a judge or Chief Justice it regards as errant rather than invoking removal procedures.

In Australia today there is a considerable degree of administrative autonomy and 'one-line budgeting' within the federal courts, although this does not extend to deciding the number of judicial officers nor, of course, to deciding the budget to be allocated. The High Court obtained administrative autonomy in 1979. Section 17(1) of the *High Court of Australia Act 1979* (Cth) provides that 'The High Court shall administer its own affairs subject to, and in accordance with, this Act'. It is given capacity to enter into contracts and take other steps necessary to administer its affairs, and may appoint committees of justices to exercise the powers of the court and to make Rules of Court. Section 18 provides for a 'Chief Executive and Principal Registrar' who shall be appointed by the Governor-General upon the nomination of the Court, and whose function it is to assist the justices in the administration of the affairs of the Court. The *Courts and Tribunals Administration Amendment Act 1989* (Cth) amended the *Family Law Act 1975* (Cth) and the *Federal Court of Australia Act 1976* (Cth) to give similar, although not identical, administrative autonomy to the Family and Federal Courts.

From the point of view of judicial independence these seem desirable steps, although as former Chief Justice of the High Court, Sir Harry Gibbs, pointed out in 1983, the power of appropriation remains the key issue:

> The Court must still depend on Parliament for its annual budget, and that means that in practice the Executive can still effectively influence the decision of important matters of administration affecting the Court ... It is an illusion to think that legislation such as the High Court of Australia Act has more than a symbolic significance so far as the independence of the Court is concerned.[40]

---

[40] Gibbs (1983) 3–4.

(d) Who defends the judges?

The traditional position is said to be that the Commonwealth Attorney-General, as the first Law Officer of the Crown, is the defender of the federal judiciary.[41] This ensured, in the Westminster system as applied in Australia, that there was some form of representation of the judicial arm of government with the political arms. Furthermore, a defence by the Attorney-General was thought likely to attract some media attention and be more effective than the alternatives. In 1998, the Attorney-General, the Honourable Daryl Williams QC, having foreshadowed as much while in Opposition, openly sought to depart from the supposed tradition. He attracted criticism from former Chief Justice, Sir Anthony Mason, senior serving judges and the legal profession. Comments he made in April 1998 serve to summarise his position:

> Attorneys General, as members of governments, are politicians. An Attorney General cannot simply abandon this role and expect to stand as an entirely independent defender of the judiciary. In fact, it has never been clearly articulated or accepted that Australian Attorneys General do have such a duty.
>
> Argument that an Attorney General should defend the judiciary and has an obligation to do so is an outmoded notion which derives from a different British tradition.
>
> Unlike the situation in Australia, the Attorney in the United Kingdom is invariably a barrister of high standing, does not administer a department, is not responsible for administration of justice and has no formal role in relation to the appointment of judges and magistrates.
>
> Justice Kirby recently suggested that such a responsibility derives from the assertion that the Attorney General is the traditional leader of the legal profession. Yet this categorisation is at odds with the realities of the profession in Australia in the 1990s where leadership of the profession includes the heads of the various law societies, bar associations and councils. The members of these bodies elect the lawyers who head the legal profession.

---

[41] There are assumptions in the states and territories that Attorneys-General have this role but their actual practice provides less support for the assumption, particularly in jurisdictions in which they have often not been lawyers.

These fundamental differences highlight the frailty of the notion that there is a tradition that Australian Attorneys General always defend the judiciary. Each arm of government has its place in the constitutional framework with distinct responsibilities, and is expected to refrain from interference in the roles properly designated for the other institutions of government.

As I have consistently stated, it would seem to me more in keeping with the independence of the judiciary from the executive arm of government that the judiciary should not ordinarily rely on an Attorney General to represent or defend it in public debate.

It is the courts or judges, either individually or collectively, who are most suited to speak in their own defence. Such an approach sits well with the concept of the courts as the third arm of government.[42]

This stance creates organisational difficulties for the judiciary. It also jeopardises one of the balances in the separation of powers and democratic theory and, perhaps ironically, poses problems for judicial independence. One of the conventions that has long existed, known variously as judicial restraint or judicial reticence, has limited what judges can prudently say extra-curially. The tradition of reticence has certainly had the support of politicians, some of whom are quick to seize on comments that might do them electoral damage as evidence of judges overstepping the line, becoming involved in political matters, and infringing the separation of powers. If judges— individually, collectively, or through their head of court—are now supposed to defend themselves, they are exposed to political retaliation by those who have readier access to, and perhaps greater facility with, the media. This might seem alarmist but many matters on which past Attorneys-General have defended the judiciary, if only behind the scenes, have involved mixed issues of politics, administration, misunderstanding, reasonable differences of view, and so on. It is now quite likely that the political dimensions of an issue will emerge in unpredictable ways.

A contemporary example can be found in the seeming unwillingness of Daryl Williams, as Attorney-General, to defend future-appointed members of the judiciary from the application of the

---

[42] D. Williams (1998) 50–1.

superannuation surcharge contributions tax in 1997/98. In general terms, this legislation was designed to impose a 15 per cent surcharge on the contributions that employers of high income earners make to superannuation funds. It apparently aims to catch arrangements whereby employees agree to 'salary sacrifices' in return for superannuation contributions by their employers. Judges, however, are not members of a superannuation scheme and there are no contributions as such. Their pensions are funded at the point of payment out of consolidated revenue. Separate legislation was therefore enacted by the Commonwealth government so that what it believed was an equivalent tax would be applied to the pensions of those judges appointed after the commencement date. It seems, however, that the legislation has a disproportionate effect on judges caught by the tax and, in any event, it unsettles an assumption on which judicial salaries are fixed by the Remuneration Tribunal. In the absence of a public defence by the Attorney-General, The Judicial Conference of Australia entered the debate, and this may in turn have led to a politicisation of the issue.[43] The government behaved as if a key plank of its legislative program was under attack and the media portrayed the matter as supposed evidence of poor relations between the judiciary and the government of the day.

This example is proffered not by way of discussion of the merits of the surcharge legislation but as an illustration of how an issue can develop a life of its own and soon give rise to perceptions that judges collectively may be for or against a particular law or government. Because the government is a regular litigant it is possible that decisions that go against it will lead to grumblings about a judge's motives. This is certainly the view of a few judicial officers who indicated concern about hearing any case involving the government while the superannuation surcharge matter remained controversial. However ill-founded the grumblings, given the argument that it is

---

[43] The Judicial Conference of Australia is a voluntary association of judges and magistrates, formed in 1994. Among its other functions, it has assumed the role of a representative and defensive body, but its resources are limited and its members dispersed among many jurisdictions.

perceptions of impartiality that ultimately matter, one can see how a seemingly innocuous decision of an Attorney-General to retreat from the role of defender of the judiciary can have untold implications when a messy issue arises (and many public issues are messy in some way).

(e) Attacks on judges

The last two decades have seen mounting concern within the judiciary about public attacks on their decisions, their approach to adjudication, or even them personally. This has been the experience in the United Kingdom, United States, and Australia.[44] The reactions of some political leaders to the decisions of the High Court in *Mabo v Queensland [No 2]*[45] and *Wik Peoples v Queensland*[46] are often cited as clear examples of a recent trend in Australia. There is certainly a view that the *Wik* decision and some of the judges who decided it were attacked publicly so that the decision could be discredited, thereby shoring up support for legislative plans to limit its supposed consequences. The matter was discussed carefully in an article by Justice Michael Kirby, where he acknowledged the benefits of critical public scrutiny:

> The principle of public justice and open courts is designed constantly to submit the judges themselves to public scrutiny. Incompetent, dilatory, ill-tempered, prejudiced judges may deserve to be exposed so long as the object is truth not just entertainment at the behest of a disgruntled litigant whose views are given currency at the expense of a judge who cannot effectively answer back.[47]

Daryl Williams has conceded that the Attorney-General still has a role in defending the judiciary from 'sustained political attacks capable of undermining public confidence in the judiciary', although it is not clear what he would regard as a deserving case:

---

[44] See, respectively, Stevens (1993) 173–7; American Bar Association (1997) 46, Bright (1997); Kirby (1998).

[45] (1992) 175 CLR 1.

[46] (1996) 187 CLR 1.

[47] Kirby (1998) 604.

I agree with the President of the Law Council, Mr Bret Walker SC, who responded to Justice Kirby's comments by rejecting the assertion that the High Court has been undermined in the eyes of the community by any of the recent debate. I acknowledge that where sustained political attacks occur that are capable of undermining public confidence in the judiciary it would be proper and may be incumbent upon an Attorney General to intervene.

The recent debate has fallen well short of undermining public confidence in the ability of the judiciary to deal with cases impartially, on their merits and according to law.[48]

Some of the problems posed for judicial independence by attacks on judges are fairly clear. It must be possible that at the margins some judges actually are affected by the anticipated reaction of the media or political figures when making difficult decisions. Even a minor adjustment in approach can lead to a major difference in outcome. Impartiality can be imperilled, albeit unconsciously. Given the traditions from which judges come, it is unlikely that this is a significant or widespread problem. More alarming is the perception that an unpopular litigant or criminal defendant might have. If it is reasonable to suppose that a decision favourable to the litigant or defendant will result in the public vilification of the judge, then the litigant may worry about irrelevant extraneous considerations being taken into account in the case. From there an expectation of partiality is engendered. Public confidence in the impartiality of the courts may be undermined not only if a section of the public is persuaded that the attacks are warranted, but also if people feel that the judiciary will act to avoid unwarranted attacks.

This is probably a larger potential problem in criminal jurisdictions—and hence in the states and territories—because of the possibility that politicians will stir up public feelings about sentencing practices as a way of securing electoral favour. Nevertheless, a topical instance in a non-criminal area is the criticism by a government minister in December 1998 of some (unnamed) Federal Court judges who were said to be taking their own, presumably unwarranted, line in immigration cases. On one interpretation this is a claim that those judges are breaching their judicial oaths and it must have the poten-

---

[48] D. Williams (1998) 51.

tial to raise in a litigant's mind the possibility that a judge will favour the government to avoid repetition of the criticism.

To be added to the modern picture is the changing reach and function of law in countries like Australia. As law is used to regulate affairs that were previously dealt with by government policy, other institutions, or were left unregulated, all courts increasingly become drawn into deciding matters over which there is clear dissensus in society. As legislatures confer increasing amounts of discretion upon judges, a decision can be made by one judge that would not have been made by a different judge in the adjoining court and yet no one can say who was wrong. For this reason, among others, appellate courts decline to intervene. As superior courts feel the need to modernise the law in fast-changing times, because legislatures cannot (or will not) do so, such courts invite charges of excessive activism. Furthermore, what seems to have happened in recent times is that specific sections of the community have identified themselves as groups affected by certain kinds of judicial decisions, whereas previously people's reactions were more individualised. Thus, for example, men's rights groups in family law and rural landowners and indigenous communities in native title law have group-related responses to particular decisions. It is elementary political science that groups are more effective in lobbying than are individuals and that politicians respond to lobbying. If, as cause or effect, politicians are less restrained in their comments about cases, we have the conditions for an extremely unhealthy fuelling of organised attacks on judges.

(f) Judicial restraint

The tradition is that judges speak only in their courtrooms and through their judgments. They do not comment on criticisms or media reports of their judgments, nor do they speak extra-curially about any changes in the law that might be politically controversial. In particular, they do not speak to the media. In 1955 the then Lord Chancellor, Lord Kilmuir, informed the British Broadcasting Corporation that he and his colleagues had agreed that as a general rule it was undesirable for members of the judiciary to broadcast on the 'wireless' or television. One reason was that 'so long as a judge keeps silent his reputation for wisdom and impartiality remains unassailable'.

The so-called Kilmuir Rules were observed in all courts until quite recently. They have been abandoned in the United Kingdom[49] and by the end of the 1980s some senior Australian judges who had hitherto been opposed to any direct contact between the judiciary and the media signalled a shift in position. There are some judges, including Chief Justices, who now feature quite regularly in radio or television programs or who give interviews with print journalists. The Federal and Family Courts have their own media liaison officers, and the High Court has sought funding from the federal government to employ one. The Chief Justice of the Family Court has explicitly defended the role of judges, and particularly a head of jurisdiction, in drawing to public attention matters concerning the administration of justice that might be affected by government proposals.[50] While there remain many arguments in favour of a large measure of judicial reticence, the consideration coming to the fore is the need to ensure that the public is provided with a balanced and accurate account of what courts do (and do not do).[51]

From the point of view of judicial independence, as distinct from promoting mutual understanding between the courts and the public, extra-curial comment has a number of risks, particularly if it disturbs the reciprocal restraint between politicians and judges. One danger is that a remark by a judge may be taken the wrong way by a public figure, who then reacts to it inadvisedly. This being meat and drink to the media, the headlines will duly talk of 'showdown', 'confrontation', and relations sinking 'to an all-time low'. Fate will then arrange for a case to come before the judge involving the same subject matter, and the perception of impartiality is considerably threatened.

5 A Design for Judicial Independence

The remainder of the chapter examines the components of a system that seems to be desirable for the preservation of perceived impar-

---

[49] Mackay (1994) 26.
[50] See Family Court of Australia (1997) 23. The Chief Justice gave legal aid and counselling as examples.
[51] See generally Doyle (1997) and Davies (1997).

tiality. This discussion draws on the earlier conceptual analysis that the perception of impartial adjudication is essential for the survival and well-being of social groups, and upon the discussion of topical cases. In some respects, elements of the system are to be found more in the federal sphere than in the Australian states and territories. The list below progresses from protections for individual judges towards institutional considerations. It is followed by a brief discussion of correlative obligations that arguably fall upon judges.

1 *Appointment procedures for judicial officers based on merit.* In relation to judicial independence, as distinct from the need to ensure adjudicators of the highest quality, the main point is that appointment for any reason other than merit raises questions about whether the appointee will owe favours to those responsible for the appointment. There is no serious move towards the election of judicial officers in Australia, but there is some concern that the power of executive governments to appoint them is currently too vulnerable to political considerations. That is, if left undefined, the concept of 'merit' can be used to justify too many decisions. One possibility is the establishment of a judicial appointments commission, at least to act as a preliminary filter of candidates and to provide some consistency of detailed criteria (see Chapter 13).[52]

2 *Security of tenure.* On the assumption that the proposed federal magistracy will have the protections in s 72 of the Constitution, the most pressing concerns in Australia are in the states and territories, where most of the protections are contained in ordinary legislation or in constitutional legislation that is not entrenched. Only in New South Wales does the judiciary and magistracy have entrenched[53] constitutional protection.

3 *Security of terms and conditions.* It would clearly be desirable for the understanding of the concept of 'remuneration' to be brought up to date in the light of modern forms of reward

---

[52] The idea has had a number of supporters, including Sir Garfield Barwick: (1995) 230.

[53] Under s 7B of the *Constitution Act 1902* (NSW), amendments to Part 9 concerning the judiciary require the approval of the electors of New South Wales before being presented to the Governor for Royal Assent.

systems and for there to be a guarantee of remuneration in real terms.

4 *Immunity from suit.* Such immunity would protect actions undertaken or words spoken in the course of carrying out judicial duties, and would include related privileges against discovery of documents and compulsion to testify. The immediate reasons for this are obvious, if not all traceable back to policies of judicial independence. They were reaffirmed by the High Court in *Mann v O'Neill*, which emphasised that it was a matter of 'necessity' that persons involved in judicial proceedings should be able to discharge their duties freely and without fear of civil action.[54] If a judicial officer fears legal retaliation for certain remarks, decisions, or reasoning processes, impartial adjudication according to law and evidence might be inhibited.

5 *An ethic of independence.* This means a collective tradition of an individual cast of mind and is sometimes referred to as 'internal independence'. This is the hardest element of the system to define. It lives in court conventions such as not being swayed by the perceived views of other judicial officers when making a decision, and in limits on the powers of heads of jurisdiction. Occasionally, it surfaces in appellate courts, such as in the Privy Council decision in *Rees v Crane*[55] that the Chief Justice of Trinidad and Tobago had no power to exclude a judge from hearing cases pending the resolution of complaints against the judge. In many respects, the other elements in this list exist partly to bolster this ethic of independence. With the trend in modern societies towards larger organisations, corporate cultures, and co-operative work practices, the climate is not hospitable to robust individualism within the courts.

6 *Separation of powers.* Such a separation requires at least the separation of judicial power from other governmental power, even if, as in Australia, the executive government is drawn from the legislative arm in the Westminster tradition. At the state level this separation is particularly indistinct, with no state consti-

---

[54] (1997) 191 CLR 204, 213.
[55] [1994] 2 AC 173.

tution providing a separation of powers equivalent to that in Chapter III of the Australian Constitution.

7 *Institutional separation.* This is necessary to ensure that the court is seen as a discrete entity to which judicial officers belong. Even though a court might be administered generally by a department of state, as occurs in Queensland or New South Wales, decisions over the assignment of judges, court listings, and sittings must remain with the judiciary.

8 *Institutional support.* This term implies the provision of sufficient resources to do the job, and certainly at a level sufficient to avoid the appearance and actuality of judges being supplicants to executive governments.

9 *Institutionalised respect.* Conventions and perhaps legal rules are needed to govern permissible levels of, and occasions for, criticism of judicial comments and decisions. Laws on contempt and abuse of process serve in particular to protect respect for the judicature as an institution. The majority decision in *Mann v O'Neill* was that complaints against a judicial officer are not necessarily protected by absolute privilege, so that the judge or magistrate might be able to sue a complainant for defamation. In that case, as with most decisions concerning privilege, there was some complex weighing of competing considerations. Not all of these related to judicial independence, but the result is a small fragment in the mosaic that protects respect for the judiciary.

Three important correlative obligations that complete the system are ethics, reticence and accountability. The Australian Institute of Judicial Administration has a project to develop a code of judicial ethics, and a serving superior court judge is the author of a major text on the subject.[56] The extent of reticence that should be expected has also been the subject of judicial debate.[57] The question of accountability, and in particular whether there should be disciplinary mechanisms for conduct that falls short of grounds for removal, is a

---

[56] Thomas (1997).

[57] This featured in a session at the Judicial Conference's Annual Symposium in 1997 and is the subject of draft guidelines.

common topic for discussion both at conferences involving judges, and whenever a Judicial Commission similar to that which operates in New South Wales is proposed.

None of the elements in this design is novel but its structure and arrangement may help advance the debate. We can see that judicial independence ideally should be protected by more than Act of Settlement-type provisions concerning removal and remuneration. Also, specifying clearly some correlative obligations upon judges is a way of giving substance to the point that is repeatedly made by them that judicial independence is there for the benefit of the public and not for judges personally. Considerably more conceptual work and policy formulation needs to be done on each of the items. In time, however, we could arrive at the optimal system for protecting judicial independence, one on which most reasonable people could agree, and against which existing arrangements in a particular juris-diction could be evaluated.

What may be more novel and more controversial is the analysis of the value of perceived impartiality of adjudication in any organ-ised society and the reasons offered here for its importance. The per-ception of impartiality helps reconcile the loser to the outcome. In the guise of public confidence, it channels dispute resolution towards the prescribed procedures and helps legitimate the social order in the face of real conceptual difficulties in defining actual impartiality. If this analysis is accepted, it justifies considerable sensitivity to rules, institutions, and practices designed to promote public confidence and the perception of impartiality. It suggests that the central judg-ment is not whether informed observers of the legal system, knowing the kinds of people who are appointed as judges, would think that a judge is likely to be swayed improperly by a certain state of affairs. Rather, the central judgment is whether ordinary but fair-minded citizens, with no particular knowledge of lawyers and legal pro-cedures, might doubt the impartiality of decision-making in the courts. If the conclusion is that they might have these doubts, urgent action is needed. Otherwise one of the fundamental requirements for the well-being of a social group is in jeopardy.

PART II
Federal Courts

4

The Evolving Role and Function of the High Court

Sir Anthony Mason

1 Introduction

The purpose of this chapter is to trace the evolution of the jurisdiction of the High Court of Australia, more particularly with respect to the role which it undertakes and the nature of the judicial work in which it is engaged. The chapter begins with the early vision of the High Court in the eyes of the framers of the Constitution and then examines the various jurisdictional changes made over the years, and their impact. The chapter concludes by noting the Court's present position and its contribution to various areas of the law by identifying some questions for the future.

2 The Early Vision of the Court

Dissatisfaction with the appeal to the Privy Council from the courts of the Australian colonies was a factor in the early days of the federal movement. Professor Harrison Moore stated: 'in the early history of the Federal movement in Australia, there were few matters which were more frequently referred to as demonstrating the need for union than the hardships and inconvenience of "a distant and expensive system of appeal"'.[1]

---

[1] Harrison Moore (1910) 220.

While the goal of establishing a general constitutional and appellate court for the Australian colonies remained constant throughout the history of the federal movement, it was not an important political factor in winning support for the movement. Other considerations, such as economic goals and improvement of communications, were more significant in that respect.[2]

Dissatisfaction with the appeal to the Privy Council was considerable. In 1870 a commission in Victoria recommended the creation of an Intercolonial Court of Appeal.[3] In 1901, at a conference held in London, Mr Justice Hodges, with the concurrence of Alfred Deakin, then Attorney-General, protested against a decision that the House of Lords and the Privy Council should continue as separate tribunals and advocated that they should give way to one Imperial Court of Appeal.[4] In 1903, in his second-reading speech on the Judiciary Bill 1903 (Cth), Deakin referred in detail to the stringent criticisms made of Privy Council decisions by the Chief Justice of New Zealand, Sir Robert Stout, and his colleagues. The Reuter's report from which the Attorney-General quoted said: 'The Chief Justice then, in proof of the Privy Council's ignorance of our laws, gives a series of blunders they have made, most of them in recent years, in deciding other New Zealand appeals'.[5]

To these concerns, Deakin added his own criticism of the landmark Privy Council decision in *Macleod v Attorney-General for New South Wales*.[6] The point of the criticism was to draw attention to the risks to which litigants exposed themselves 'when dealing at such a distance with intricate questions of purely local law, or determining any right under purely local law'.[7]

The draft Constitution submitted to the Imperial Government had substantially excluded the appeal to the Privy Council from the High Court. That exclusion was unacceptable to the Imperial Government which was concerned that the High Court would

---

[2] Ibid 220–1.
[3] *Commonwealth Parliamentary Debates*, House of Representatives, 9 June 1903, 592.
[4] Ibid 593–4.
[5] Ibid 595.
[6] [1891] AC 455.
[7] *Commonwealth Parliamentary Debates*, House of Representatives, 9 June 1903, 595.

become the final arbiter on matters of Imperial interest. The provisions of ss 73 and 74 of the Constitution reflect the compromise that was reached. It has been said that s 74 was accepted on the basis that it constituted the High Court as a paramount court of appeal on matters of Australian interest and enabled an appeal to be taken to the Privy Council on matters of Imperial interest.[8]

Under s 74 of the Constitution, the appeal from the High Court took the form of the exercise of the prerogative power to grant special leave to appeal, though this appeal was subject to the prohibition that no appeal from the High Court should be permitted upon any question as to the limits inter se of the constitutional powers of the Commonwealth and those of any state or states, or as to the limits inter se of the constitutional powers of two or more states, unless the High Court should certify that the question is one that ought to be determined by the Privy Council. The Constitution contains no provision relating to appeals from state courts to the Privy Council.

The last sentence in the third and final paragraph of s 74 of the Constitution provided that the Parliament 'may make laws limiting the matters in which such leave may be asked' of the Privy Council. In 1903, Deakin had little doubt that it would be exercised after practical experience of the working of the High Court had accumulated, though he acknowledged the great capacity and record of the Privy Council in matters of mercantile law.[9] There was, at that time, and for a long time thereafter, some support for the view that the continuance of the Privy Council appeal would play an important part in ensuring the uniformity of the common law throughout the Empire.[10]

The High Court was seen by its founders as a court to rank with the leading courts of the common law world. Deakin's grand

---

[8] Deakin (1944) ch. XXII.

[9] *Commonwealth Parliamentary Debates*, House of Representatives, 9 June 1903, 596, 599.

[10] Justice Inglis Clark strongly disagreed with this view except in the case of the interpretation of Imperial statutes such as the *Merchant Shipping Act*. See Inglis Clark (1901) app. 3.

vision of the High Court as a constitutional court stemmed from his recognition that the Constitution contained 'merely the framework of government'[11] and that it was necessarily limited 'by the ideas and circumstances which obtained in the year 1900'.[12] Because the nation grows and it alters, it was the responsibility of the High Court to enable the Constitution 'to grow and to be adapted to the changeful necessities and circumstances of generation after generation ... Amendments achieve direct and sweeping changes, but the court moves by gradual, often indirect, cautious, well considered steps, that enable the past to join the future, without undue collision and strife in the present'.[13]

Deakin's conception of the constitutional role of the High Court has much in common with the 'living force' approach to constitutional interpretation expounded by Justice Andrew Inglis Clark[14] who was described by Deane J as the 'principal architect of our Constitution'.[15]

Those who established the High Court contemplated it becoming a final court of appeal, subject only to an appeal to the Privy Council in exceptional cases. However, appeals could be brought to the Privy Council from state courts. Indeed, Orders in Council applying to state Supreme Courts permitted appeals as of right subject to pecuniary qualifications.

One object of the establishment of the High Court as a general court of appeal was the achievement of greater uniformity in Australian law. It was thought that High Court decisions would bring about greater uniformity in the common law and in the interpretation of statutes which were expressed in like terms. That expectation has been realised. As we approach the centenary of federation, we can say that, unlike the United States—where the Supreme Court

---

[11] A letter to the London *Morning Post* written in 1900, reproduced in La Nauze (1968) 7.

[12] *Commonwealth Parliamentary Debates*, House of Representatives, 18 March 1902, 10 967.

[13] Ibid 10 967–8.

[14] Inglis Clark (1901) 19–22.

[15] *Theophanous v Herald & Weekly Times Ltd* (1994) 182 CLR 104, 171–2, adopting Inglis Clark's 'living force' approach.

is principally a constitutional court, not a general court of appeal—Australia possesses a common law which exhibits marked uniformity.

3 The Appeal to the Privy Council

The distinction made by s 74 of the Constitution between inter se questions and non inter se questions endeavoured to give effect to the division between Imperial and Australian interests. Inter se questions could not be taken to the Privy Council except pursuant to a certificate granted by the High Court. Other decisions could be taken by special leave, not as of right. What was important for the future was the power given by the section to Parliament to limit the matters in which leave may be sought to appeal to the Privy Council. It was then thought that limitation did not extend to abrogation.[16]

Australia's early determination to confine appeals to the Privy Council both from the High Court and the state Supreme Courts gave rise to a conflict between the High Court and the Privy Council. In only one case, in 1912, has the High Court ever granted a certificate that an inter se question ought to be determined by the Privy Council.[17] Since then all applications have been refused.

Section 39 of the *Judiciary Act 1903* (Cth) was a key element in limiting appeals to the Privy Council. This section, which invested state courts with federal jurisdiction, deprived those courts of non-federal jurisdiction in the matters in respect of which federal jurisdiction was invested. The section then made the exercise of that federal jurisdiction by a Supreme Court final and conclusive except for an appeal to the High Court. The operation of s 39 became the source of conflict. In *Webb v Outtrim*[18] the Privy Council held that the section did not block an appeal from a state court to the Privy Council in the exercise of invested federal jurisdiction. Because the case involved an inter se question, a matter the Privy Council failed to recognise, the High Court subsequently refused to follow it,

---

[16] *Commonwealth Parliamentary Debates*, House of Representatives, 23 June 1903, 1199–205 (Higgins and Deakin).

[17] *Colonial Sugar Refining Co Ltd v Attorney-General for the Commonwealth* (*Royal Commissions Case*) (1912) 15 CLR 183.

[18] (1906) 4 CLR 356.

holding that s 39(2)(a) of the *Judiciary Act* validly eliminated the
appeal as of right from state courts to the Privy Council in matters
of federal jurisdiction.[19] The impediments to an appeal from state
courts were strengthened by the introduction of s 40A of the *Judiciary Act* which provided for the automatic removal to the High
Court of a cause pending in a state Supreme Court involving an inter
se question. Section 40A played an important part in removing cases
to the High Court in the decades in which it was in operation.

The validity of s 39(2)(a) was reinforced by decisions in later
cases arising by way of appeal to the High Court from orders made
by state Supreme Courts granting leave to appeal to the Privy Council
under Orders in Council regulating appeals as of right to the Privy
Council.[20]

By these means the determination of inter se questions was
restricted to the High Court. Other constitutional questions could
be taken or were taken on appeal from the High Court to the Privy
Council, pursuant to the grant of special leave. They included a
number of cases on s 92 and other provisions of the Constitution.
In addition, appeals were taken in many cases involving statutory
interpretation and the general law. As Privy Council decisions were
binding on Australian courts and those decisions were largely a
reflection of English law, Australian judge-made law was a reflection
of English law. There was little disposition on the part of the High
Court to develop a jurisprudence that was in any sense either distinctively Australian or different from English law.

It was not until 1968 that the first step was taken to limit
the appeal from the High Court to the Privy Council. In that year,
s 3(1) of the *Privy Council (Limitation of Appeals) Act 1968* (Cth)
confined the matters in which special leave to appeal to the Privy
Council could be sought.[21] The broad effect of the Act was to limit
the appeal to the Privy Council from the High Court to matters of

---

[19] *Baxter v Commissioners of Taxation (NSW)* (1907) 4 CLR 1087, 1137–40.

[20] *Commonwealth v Limerick Steamship Co Ltd* (1924) 35 CLR 69; *Commonwealth v
Kreglinger & Fernau Ltd* (1926) 37 CLR 393.

[21] The validity of the 1968 Act was recognised by the Privy Council in *Kitano v
Commonwealth* (1975) 132 CLR 231 and by the High Court in *Attorney-General
(Cth) v Finch (No 2)* (1984) 155 CLR 107.

non-federal jurisdiction. The High Court thereby became the final arbiter in all constitutional cases and other matters of federal jurisdiction. Appeals from the Supreme Court of a state to the Privy Council in matters of federal jurisdiction had effectively been blocked by s 39(2) of the *Judiciary Act*.

The final step in the elimination of the appeal to the Privy Council from the High Court was the enactment of the *Privy Council (Appeals from the High Court) Act 1975* (Cth), which came into operation on 8 July 1975. Section 3 of that Act effectively eliminated the appeal. In *Attorney-General (Cth) v T & G Mutual Life Society Ltd*,[22] the High Court held that the phrase 'limiting the matters in which such leave may be asked', which appears in s 74 of the Constitution, was sufficient to support the abolition of all appeals to the Privy Council from the High Court, save for the theoretical possibility of appeals upon the certificate of the High Court upon inter se questions. That is the present situation.

The fact that appeals in non-federal jurisdictions could still be brought from state Supreme Courts to the Privy Council was a source of conflict. An unsuccessful party could appeal either to the High Court or the Privy Council. The potentiality for conflict arose in a series of cases in which the High Court asserted its obligation to proceed with an appeal duly instituted in the High Court, notwithstanding endeavours by the opposing party subsequently to invoke the jurisdiction of the Privy Council.[23] But the duality of appeal systems led to confusion and complexity as well as a problem of precedent and authority which could only be solved, if at all, by a doctrine of mutual respect.

The complexities arising from the dual systems of appeal from state Supreme Courts were finally eliminated by the *Australia Acts 1986* (Cth) and (UK) by which the appeals from state Supreme Courts to the Privy Council were abolished. From that time onwards, the High Court was in a position authoritatively to declare the law

---

[22] (1978) 144 CLR 161.
[23] See *Southern Centre of Theosophy Inc v South Australia* (1979) 145 CLR 246; *Caltex Oil (Aust) Pty Ltd v XL Petroleum (NSW) Pty Ltd* (1984) 155 CLR 72; *Attorney-General (Cth) v Finch (No 1)* (1984) 155 CLR 102; *Attorney-General (Cth) v Finch (No 2)* (1984) 155 CLR 107.

for Australia, without being bound by Privy Council decisions. The Court could fashion the common law to be appropriate to Australian conditions and circumstances. In doing so, it would look upon English authorities as providing valuable assistance but would not be constrained by them. Since 1986, the High Court has delivered a number of judgments in which it has declined to follow particular English decisions and has reformulated the principles as enunciated by English courts. It would be a mistake to regard what has happened as amounting to a significant reform of the general law. Viewed in context, the changes are no more than refinements designed, for the most part, to give greater symmetry and coherence to Australian law.

The elimination of the Privy Council appeal on its own might not have enabled the Court to achieve such a result. Two reforms to the Court's jurisdiction were necessary. One was to relieve the Court from the heavy burden of work in its original jurisdiction, thereby enabling it to concentrate on its constitutional and appellate work. The other was to reform the Court's appellate jurisdiction, eliminate appeals as of right and condition all appeals on the grant of special leave, thereby ensuring that appeals mainly presented questions of important principle.

4 The Jurisdiction of the High Court Under the Constitution

The Constitution conferred both appellate and original jurisdiction on the High Court (ss 73 and 75 respectively). It also provided that Parliament could make laws conferring original jurisdiction on the High Court in certain matters (s 76). Section 77 enables Parliament to make laws: (i) defining the jurisdiction of any federal court other than the High Court; (ii) defining the extent to which the jurisdiction of any federal court shall be exclusive of that which belongs to or is invested in the courts of the states; and (iii) investing any court of a state with federal jurisdiction (see Appendix 1). The scope of these provisions is examined in Chapter 9.

The Report of the Royal Commission on the Constitution in 1929 drew attention to the unsatisfactory character of the list of heads of original jurisdiction set out in ss 75 and 76 of the Constitution. Despite the emphasis given to the High Court's role as a constitutional and appellate court, ss 75 and 76 armed the Court with an extensive original jurisdiction. In considering the magnitude of that jurisdiction, one has to bear in mind that much of the original jurisdiction is exercised by a Full Bench, a matter to be discussed later.

Whether original jurisdiction can be given to the High Court beyond the matters mentioned in ss 75 and 76 has been the subject of debate. Statements to the effect that ss 75 and 76 are exhaustive[24] were treated as if they were directed to the effect of Chapter III alone, leaving the Parliament at liberty to confer additional jurisdiction under other powers it may have,[25] such as s 122 of the Constitution. On this question now, see Chapter 10.

Section 73 conferred upon the High Court jurisdiction to hear and determine appeals from judgments, decrees, orders and sentences: (i) of any justice exercising the original jurisdiction of the High Court; (ii) of any other federal court or court exercising federal jurisdiction, or of the Supreme Court of a state, or of any other court of a state from which, at the time of the establishment of the Commonwealth, an appeal lay to the Privy Council; and (iii) of the Inter-State Commission but only as to questions of law. This grant of appellate jurisdiction was expressed to be subject to 'such exceptions and subject to such regulations as the Parliament prescribes'. It was, however, specifically provided that no such exception or regulation should prevent the High Court from hearing and determining any appeal from the Supreme Court of a state in any matter in which at the establishment of the Commonwealth an appeal lay from such Supreme Court to the Privy Council.

---

[24] *Ah Yick v Lehmert* (1905) 2 CLR 593, 603 (Griffith CJ); *R v Maryborough Licensing Court; Ex parte Webster & Co Ltd* (1919) 27 CLR 249, 253 (Knox CJ); *Re Judiciary and Navigation Acts* (1921) 29 CLR 257, 265; see also *Porter v The King; Ex parte Yee* (1926) 37 CLR 432, 447.

[25] See *Federal Capital Commission v Laristan Building & Investment Co Pty Ltd* (1929) 42 CLR 582, 584–5 (Dixon J); *Spratt v Hermes* (1965) 114 CLR 226, 240 (Barwick CJ), see also 254–7, 264–5, 268, 269, 279–80; *Capital TV & Appliances Pty Ltd v Falconer* (1971) 125 CLR 591, 604 (Menzies J); but compare *Re Judiciary and Navigation Acts* (1921) 29 CLR 257, 265.

5 The Nature and Extent of the Original Jurisdiction

Of the matters in which original jurisdiction was conferred on the High Court by s 75, some have generated little, if any, litigation. Matters arising under a treaty (s 75(i)) and matters affecting consuls or other representatives of other countries (s 75(ii)) fall into this category. Two other heads of jurisdiction mentioned in s 75 have always generated substantial High Court litigation. They are matters in which the Commonwealth, or a person suing or being sued on behalf of the Commonwealth, is a party (s 75(iii)) and matters in which a writ of mandamus or prohibition or an injunction is sought against an officer of the Commonwealth (s 75(v)).

The remaining head of original jurisdiction conferred by s 75, that is, matters between states, or between residents of different states, or between a state and a resident of another state (s 75(iv)), did not generate as much work as might have been expected, even in the early days of the High Court. One reason, which applied to s 75(iii) as well, was that the High Court's original jurisdiction was not exclusive; state courts also had jurisdiction in these matters. Indeed, the *Judiciary Act* invested state courts with federal jurisdiction in relation to some, but not all, matters in which s 75 conferred jurisdiction on the High Court. Another reason was the restricted interpretation given to the expressions 'residents of different States' and 'resident' in s 75(iv). They were held to refer to natural persons, not artificial persons or corporations.[26]

Of the heads of jurisdiction listed in s 76 and vested in the High Court by s 30 of the *Judiciary Act*, matters arising under the Constitution or involving its interpretation (s 76(i)) and matters arising under any laws made by the Parliament (s 76(ii)) have been fertile sources of litigation in the High Court. Matters of admiralty and maritime jurisdiction (s 76(iii)), notwithstanding its uncertain content,[27] also engaged the attention of the High Court to a significant

---

[26] *Australasian Temperance and General Mutual Life Assurance Society Ltd v Howe* (1922) 31 CLR 290; *Cox v Journeaux* (1934) 52 CLR 282.

[27] As to which, see *John Sharp & Sons Ltd v The Katharine Mackall* (1924) 34 CLR 420, 426–33 (Isaacs J); *McIlwraith McEachern Ltd v Shell Co of Australia Ltd* (1945) 70 CLR 175, 207–9 (Dixon J).

extent. That was largely because the High Court was a colonial court of admiralty under the *Colonial Courts of Admiralty Act 1890* (Imp).[28] The jurisdiction of the High Court under that Act may not have been co-extensive with the jurisdiction which Parliament can confer on the High Court under s 76(iii).[29] On the other hand, the High Court has had no occasion to consider matters relating to the same subject matter claimed under the laws of different states.

The great bulk of the Court's original jurisdiction work has consisted of matters within ss 75(v) and 76(i) and (ii). There has been a constant flow of work under these heads of jurisdiction. It is important to note that the exercise of the original jurisdiction is not to be equated to the exercise of jurisdiction by a single justice. Applications under s 75(v) for a prerogative writ against an officer of the Commonwealth, though initially made to a single justice, if successful, have resulted in an order nisi returnable before a Full Court or an order directing argument before a Full Court.

Section 75(v) has been a prolific source of work, particularly in industrial cases, where it led to continued supervision by judicial review of proceedings in the old Commonwealth Court of Conciliation and Arbitration and its successor, the Conciliation and Arbitration Commission (later known as the Australian Industrial Relations Commission). Applications under s 75(v) were made in relation to proceedings before Deputy Presidents and Commissioners as well as proceedings before a Full Bench of the Commission. Although occasionally an application would generate a case of great importance—industrial cases have played a very large part in our constitutional jurisprudence—many of these applications raised minor questions unworthy of the High Court's attention. Yet they made a significant contribution to the Court's workload.

Such was the political power of the industrial 'club' that no government was willing to enact legislation that would enable another court to exercise the jurisdiction. It was thought that the grant of prerogative relief by another court would derogate from

---

[28] *Judiciary Act 1903* (Cth) s 30A; *Colonial Courts of Admiralty Act 1890* (Imp) ss 2 and 15.

[29] *McIlwraith McEachern Ltd v Shell Co of Australia Ltd* (1945) 70 CLR 175, 208 (Dixon J).

the status of the Commission. Even when the Court was given an express power to remit matters to other courts, matters relating to the Commission were excluded. Only later was the express power extended to these applications, thereby substantially reducing the number of applications determined by the High Court.

Likewise, most constitutional cases under s 76, though initially listed before a single justice, ultimately have been determined by a Full Court as an exercise of original jurisdiction. That is because in most such cases a question of law has been stated or reserved by the Chief Justice or a single justice for the consideration of a Full Court. Similarly, some constitutional cases have reached the High Court by way of a case stated or question reserved by another court, for example, under s 18 of the *Judiciary Act*. Again, these cases are instances of original jurisdiction. A constitutional case has infrequently reached a Full Court by way of appeal from the decision of a single justice. The constitutional cases heard by the Court in its appellate jurisdiction sometimes have been appeals from the decisions of other courts.

Other constitutional cases have reached the High Court as a result of automatic removal pursuant to the old s 40A of the *Judiciary Act* (when an inter se question arose in another court) or an order for removal under s 40 of that Act (where the cause is one arising under the Constitution or involving its interpretation). Cases reaching the High Court by these means again result in an exercise of its original jurisdiction, even if they are removed from a court which is itself exercising appellate jurisdiction.[30]

Much the same point can be made about some of the matters arising under a law made by the Parliament in which jurisdiction was conferred upon the High Court under s 76(ii). Under the *Income Tax Assessment and Social Services Contribution Act 1936* (Cth), the High Court was given jurisdiction in appeals in relation to objections against assessments (s 197) and on questions of law from Taxation Boards of Review (s 196). In each case the appeal was an exercise of original jurisdiction by the single justice who heard the case.[31] The

---

[30] *Attorney-General (NSW) v Commonwealth Savings Bank* (1986) 160 CLR 315, 323.

[31] As to an appeal under s 196, see *Watson v Federal Commissioner of Taxation* (1953) 87 CLR 353.

High Court also exercised original jurisdiction in appeals concerning estate duty and gift duty.[32] Likewise, the High Court heard and determined appeals from the Commissioner of Patents and the Registrar of Trade Marks.[33] Other instances can be given.[34] Petitions for the revocation of a patent[35] and applications for the extension of the term of a patent were also heard and determined by the High Court.[36] Even applications for the appointment of a controller of enemy property were made to the High Court.[37]

Thus, in the absence of a federal court below the level of the High Court,[38] jurisdiction was conferred upon the High Court in a wide variety of matters, in preference to investing jurisdiction in state superior courts under particular statutes. The exercise of jurisdiction by the High Court offered uniformity of interpretation by a court in which the Commonwealth would naturally have confidence as well as offering determination by a court which was linked to political responsibility on the part of the Commonwealth. In a number of instances the statute conferring jurisdiction conferred jurisdiction on Supreme Courts of the states as well as the High Court. In many cases the moving party elected to invoke the jurisdiction of the High Court rather than that of a Supreme Court.

The exercise of original jurisdiction constituted a large part of the Court's work. Quite apart from constitutional cases, which were estimated to amount to less than one-fifth of the Court's work[39] and were mainly heard in the original jurisdiction, there was a host of matters arising under a miscellany of statutes in which the Court

---

[32] *Estate Duty Assessment Act 1914* (Cth) and *Gift Duty Assessment Act 1941* (Cth) respectively.

[33] *Patents Act 1952* (Cth) and *Trade Marks Act 1955* (Cth) respectively.

[34] *Defence Forces Retirement Benefits Act 1948* (Cth); *Commonwealth Employees Compensation Act 1930* (Cth); *Seamen's Compensation Act 1911* (Cth). The latter two statutes conferred jurisdiction on the High Court to determine appeals from inferior state courts invested with federal jurisdiction.

[35] *Patents Act 1952* (Cth) Pt X; see, for example, *Rose Holdings Pty Ltd v Carlton Shuttlecocks Ltd* (1957) 98 CLR 444.

[36] See, for example, *Re Usines de Melle's Patent* (1954) 91 CLR 42.

[37] *Trading with the Enemy Act 1939* (Cth) s 13; see *Attorney-General (Cth) v Schmidt* (1961) 105 CLR 361.

[38] See later as to the Commonwealth Industrial Court.

[39] Sawer (1961a) 71.

exercised original jurisdiction. The extent and scope of these matters is exhibited in the Commonwealth Law Reports which show that the High Court was the principal court dealing with matters of taxation, gift duty, estate duty and intellectual property as well as other matters arising under federal law.

6 The Decline of the High Court's Non-Constitutional Original Jurisdiction

After the establishment in 1956 of the Commonwealth Industrial Court (renamed the Australian Industrial Court in 1973) in consequence of the decision in *R v Kirby; Ex parte Boilermakers' Society of Australia (Boilermakers' Case)*,[40] the Court was given an industrial jurisdiction and also a non-industrial jurisdiction under some particular statutes. In earlier times, that non-industrial jurisdiction might have been given to the High Court or the Supreme Courts of the states. The new Court was not given the non-constitutional original jurisdiction of the High Court.

The High Court's growing volume of work led to proposals to establish a Commonwealth Superior Court to relieve the High Court of the major part of its non-constitutional jurisdiction.[41] Bills to establish such a court, introduced in 1968, 1973, 1974 and 1975, were either abandoned or rejected by the Senate. In 1976, however, the Federal Court of Australia was created by the *Federal Court of Australia Act 1976* (Cth). The Court had two divisions: an Industrial and a General Division.

The Industrial Division was to exercise the jurisdiction formerly exercised by the Australian Industrial Court, while the General Division was to deal with other matters, including non-constitutional matters previously dealt with by the High Court, and non-industrial matters formerly dealt with by the Australian Industrial Court. The matters formerly dealt with by that Court included restrictive trade practices, consumer protection, insurance law and administrative appeals.

---

[40] (1956) 94 CLR 254; *Attorney-General of the Commonwealth of Australia v The Queen* (1957) 95 CLR 529.

[41] Barwick (1964).

Section 24 of the *Federal Court of Australia Act* included in the appellate jurisdiction of the Court appeals from judgments of a court of a state, other than a Full Court of a Supreme Court, exercising federal jurisdiction. By amendments made to s 96 of the *Income Tax Assessment Act 1936* (Cth), s 48 of the *Patents Act 1952* (Cth), and s 14 of the *Trade Marks Act 1955* (Cth), jurisdiction was given to the Federal Court to hear appeals from state courts exercising federal jurisdiction under these Acts. In each of these cases, initial jurisdiction was to be exercised by the Supreme Court of a state with no appeal from the determination by a state judge to the Full Court or the Court of Appeal of the state. Subsequently, the Federal Court was given original jurisdiction in these and other matters.[42]

The legislative dispositions which enabled the Federal Court and the Supreme Courts of the states to exercise jurisdiction in matters falling within the High Court's original jurisdiction did not deprive the Court of the jurisdiction given to it by s 75 of the Constitution. Only a constitutional amendment could achieve that result. As a litigant could invoke the jurisdiction, it was desirable, if not necessary, to arm the Court with an express power of remitter so that a case commenced in the original jurisdiction could, if the Court thought fit, be remitted to another court for hearing and determination.

Section 44 of the *Judiciary Act* confers on the High Court extensive powers of remitter to any federal court, or court of a state or territory. The powers extend to a matter, or part of a matter, that is pending in the Court. Specific provision is made enabling remitter to the Federal Court of a matter in which the Commonwealth or a person suing or being sued on behalf of the Commonwealth is a party (s 44(2A)). Where the High Court remits a matter falling within certain categories of federal jurisdiction, the remitter operates to confer jurisdiction on the court to which the matter is remitted (s 44(3)).

The arrangements with respect to the original jurisdiction do not extend to the Court's jurisdiction when sitting as the Court of Disputed Returns under the *Commonwealth Electoral Act 1918* (Cth). The jurisdiction relates to the election of senators and members of the House of Representatives. Over the years, the High

---

[42] *Federal Court of Australia Act 1976* (Cth) s 26.

Court, sitting as the Court of Disputed Returns, has decided many cases, including important questions concerning the qualifications of members of Parliament under the Constitution.[43]

7 The Appellate Jurisdiction

The early operation of s 73 was to confer appellate jurisdiction on the High Court from decisions of justices in the exercise of the Court's original jurisdiction, courts exercising federal jurisdiction, and the Supreme Courts of the states. Apart from the old Commonwealth Court of Conciliation and Arbitration, the Commonwealth Industrial Court, and the Federal Court of Bankruptcy, Parliament did not establish any federal court, pursuant to the power conferred by s 71 of the Constitution, until 1975 when the Family Court of Australia was established, to be followed by the Federal Court of Australia in 1977. The appeal from the Inter-State Commission has been virtually a dead letter.[44]

Section 35(1) of the *Judiciary Act* as enacted in 1903, using the existing Privy Council appeals as a model, provided for appeals as of right and appeals by leave and special leave.[45] The class of appeals as of right extended to final judgments of the Supreme Court of a state or other court of a state from which, at the establishment of the Commonwealth, an appeal lay to the Privy Council, so long as the judgment related to a claim to the value of £300 or affecting the status of any person under the laws relating to aliens, marriage, divorce, bankruptcy or insolvency. If such a judgment was interlocutory, an appeal could not be brought except by leave of the Supreme Court or the High Court. Under s 35(1)(b), an appeal also lay to the High Court from any judgment, whether final or interlocutory, with respect to which the High Court granted special leave to appeal. In

---

[43] See, for example, *Sykes v Cleary* (1992) 176 CLR 77.

[44] An appeal, at least in form, was brought from an order of the Commission in *New South Wales v Commonwealth* (1915) 20 CLR 54, 59 (Griffith CJ). It was held that Parliament had no power to constitute the Commission as a court, a decision which limited the Commission's functions.

[45] In order to obtain leave, it must appear that the judgment appealed from is arguably wrong. In order to obtain special leave it must also be shown that the appeal involves a question of public importance.

the result, an appeal could be brought to the High Court, either as of right or by leave, from every judgment, decree, or order from which an appeal could be brought to the Privy Council under the Imperial Order in Council of 13 November 1850.

In 1955, s 35(1) was amended by substituting the amount of £1500 for £300.[46] In 1973, s 35(1) was amended by omitting the reference to the judgments of any other court of a state from which, at the establishment of the Commonwealth, an appeal could be brought to the Privy Council.[47] In 1976, a new s 35 was introduced.[48] The thrust of the new section was to confine an appeal as of right to an appeal from a final judgment of the Full Court of the Supreme Court of a state, the pecuniary limit being increased to $20 000. An appeal on a ground that related to the quantum of damages in respect of death or personal injury could not be brought as of right and could only be brought by special leave. Other appeals from judgments, whether final or interlocutory, could only be brought by special leave, subject to the qualification that an appeal could be brought as of right from the judgment of the Full Court of a Supreme Court of a state where a ground of appeal involved the interpretation of the Constitution.[49]

Section 33 of the *Federal Court of Australia Act* as initially enacted, made similar provision for appeals to the High Court from judgments of the Federal Court as was then made by s 35 of the *Judiciary Act* for appeals to the High Court from judgments of the Supreme Court of a state. Under s 33(2) of the *Federal Court of Australia Act*, no appeal lay from a judgment of a single judge of the Federal Court to the High Court, except as provided by another Act.

Under s 95 of the *Family Law Act 1975* (Cth), an appeal also lay and still lies to the High Court from a judgment of the Full Court of the Family Court of Australia by special leave or pursuant to a certificate granted by the Full Court of the Family Court that an important question of law in the public interest is involved. The Family Court has rarely issued such a certificate, preferring to leave

---

[46] *Judiciary Act 1955* (Cth) s 2.
[47] *Statute Law Revision Act 1973* (Cth) s 3, Sch 1.
[48] *Judiciary Amendment Act 1976* (Cth) s 6.
[49] *Judiciary Act 1903* (Cth) s 35(6).

the unsuccessful appellant to make application to the High Court for special leave to appeal.

In 1984, important amendments were made to the *Judiciary Act*[50] and the *Federal Court of Australia Act*.[51] The effect of these amendments was to abolish appeals as of right to the High Court and to require the grant of special leave to appeal as a condition of an appeal to the High Court. Appeals from the Full Court of a Supreme Court of a state and the Federal Court were placed on the same footing as appeals from the Full Court of the Family Court. In considering applications for special leave, the Court was required to consider whether there is a question of law of public importance, whether a High Court decision is necessary to resolve differences of opinion in courts or a court below, and whether the interests of the administration of justice, either generally or in the particular case, require reconsideration of the judgment.[52] The validity of the 1984 amendments was unanimously upheld by the High Court.[53]

8 The Consequences of the 1984 Amendments

The 1984 amendments were the final step in relieving the High Court of its oppressive workload and enabling it to devote itself to its responsibilities as a constitutional court and as an ultimate court of appeal. The earlier steps—elimination of the appeal to the Privy Council and the provision made for the exercise by other courts of the High Court's original jurisdiction—left the Court with a large volume of appeals of which many were appeals as of right. Of those appeals as of right, a significant proportion raised no important question of law. Indeed, some of them turned upon an issue of fact. That was the consequence of allowing appeals as of right, subject only to a pecuniary qualification. The 1984 amendments marked a move away from the notion that the magnitude of the amount in issue or the value of what was in issue was a very important consider-

---

[50] *Judiciary Amendment Act (No 2) 1984* (Cth) s 3, introducing a new s 35 and s 35A.

[51] *Federal Court of Australia Amendment Act 1984* (Cth) s 3(1).

[52] *Judiciary Act 1903* (Cth) s 35A.

[53] *Smith Kline & French Laboratories (Aust) Ltd v Commonwealth* (1991) 173 CLR 194.

ation. It had been a significant factor taken into account by the Court in granting special leave applications.

(a) Civil appeals

The principal consequence of the 1984 amendments was that, by reason of the criteria applied in granting or refusing special leave applications, civil appeals have been largely restricted to those cases in which an important question of general principle arises for consideration. In civil cases, the considerations mentioned in s 35A of the *Judiciary Act* generally translate into the criterion whether an important question of principle is involved and, in a relatively small number of cases, whether there has been a departure from the rules governing procedural regularity, such as a departure from the rules of procedural fairness.

It was only to be expected that the 1984 amendments brought about a marked change in the nature of the High Court's work. There was a sharp decline in the number of appeals in 'run of the mill' personal injury cases which had formerly satisfied the pecuniary qualifications governing appeals as of right.

Other casualties of the 1984 amendments were appeals in contract cases which had previously often satisfied the pecuniary qualifications governing appeals as of right. Once they were excluded from that category, they fell foul of the criteria applicable to the grant of special leave. Many contract cases turn not on any great point of principle but on the interpretation of the particular contract and whether it has been breached. Hence, it is not easy to show that a case in contract, particularly commercial contract, involves a question of general principle.

The leading contract cases in the High Court in recent times have been equity cases where an equitable principle or doctrine has been in question. Cases such as *Taylor v Johnson, Legione v Hateley, Commercial Bank of Australia Ltd v Amadio* and *Stern v McArthur* illustrate the point.[54]

---

[54] See, respectively, (1983) 151 CLR 422 (unilateral mistake); (1983) 152 CLR 406 (relief against forfeiture and specific performance of a contract terminated for breach of an essential time stipulation); (1983) 151 CLR 447 (unconscionable conduct); and (1988) 165 CLR 489 (relief against forfeiture and specific performance of a contract for the sale of land terminated by the vendor).

The criteria governing the grant of special leave tend to favour cases involving questions of statutory interpretation because the answer to the question is likely to have general significance and satisfy the public or general importance test. It has even been suggested that the High Court's concern with matters of statutory interpretation has transformed it into an administrative court rather than a court which enunciates general principles of common law and equity. The High Court's constant exposition of general principles in the last decade or so rebuts this suggestion.

Nonetheless, there is some force in the related comment that the criteria favour public law questions over private law questions. It is difficult to determine whether this is so. Certainly the High Court has been able to develop the principles of administrative law, not least in the area of procedural fairness, but that may be no more than a reflection of the need for such development. The principles of administrative law have been expounded mainly in appeals from the Federal Court. A fairly high proportion of the High Court's work has come by way of appeal from the Federal Court, no doubt because the Federal Court has been invested with jurisdiction under Commonwealth statutes which have broken new ground.

The absence of an entrenched or statutory Bill of Rights has meant that the High Court has not been called upon to deal with as many questions relating to fundamental rights as might otherwise have been the case. However, the Court has dealt with a variety of human rights questions arising under Commonwealth and state legislation, or under the general law, including questions affecting the rights of indigenous peoples, most notably the land rights cases of *Mabo v Queensland [No 2]* and *Wik Peoples v Queensland*.[55] The constitutional cases, rarely arising by way of appeal, include not only those concerning the implied freedom of communication as to matters of government and politics as an incident of the system of representative government established by the Constitution, but also the privileges and protections which have been derived from Chapter III of the Constitution.

---

[55] (1992) 175 CLR 1; (1996) 187 CLR 1.

Although the Federal Court has been a fertile source of work for the High Court, as have been the Supreme Courts of the states and, to a much lesser extent, the territories, the Family Court has provided comparatively little work. Much of the Family Court's work calls for the exercise of a judicial discretion which does not often give rise to an important question of general principle. A significant proportion of the family law cases that have come to the High Court since 1975 have been constitutional cases concerning the jurisdiction and powers of the Family Court.

(b) Criminal appeals

In criminal law, there was an expansion in the volume of cases attracting the grant of special leave. This came about because the Court had traditionally taken the view that it was not a court of criminal appeal and would not grant special leave to appeal in criminal cases unless some point of general importance was involved. That principle was endorsed in 1985 by the majority decision in *Liberato v The Queen*,[56] a case in which a court of criminal appeal had held that there were defects in the trial judge's directions to the jury, but concluded there was no substantial miscarriage of justice within the meaning of the statutory proviso.

Although the case has not been overruled, the High Court subsequently granted special leave to appeal in cases where there has been a reasonably arguable case that there was a miscarriage of justice. In particular, special leave has been granted and an appeal allowed in cases where it appears that a court of criminal appeal has not comprehensively reviewed the evidence with a view to ascertaining whether a verdict is unsafe and unsatisfactory.[57] The grant of special leave in such cases derives from the requirement in s 35A of the *Judiciary Act* that the Court take account of the interests of the administration of justice, even in the particular case.

In sentencing cases, although the Court has maintained the rule that a question of principle must arise, the Court has granted special leave more frequently than it had done in the past.

---

[56] (1985) 159 CLR 507.

[57] *Morris v The Queen* (1987) 163 CLR 454; *Chidiac v The Queen* (1991) 171 CLR 432; see also *M v The Queen* (1994) 181 CLR 487.

As a result of a more liberal approach to the grant of special leave in criminal cases, the volume of criminal work that came to the High Court was greater than at any time in the past. The consequence was to be seen in the extensive number of important judgments which elaborated the principles, procedure, and practice in that area of the law.[58] Indeed, in the past fifteen to twenty years, the High Court has, perhaps, made a greater contribution to criminal law than to any other branch of the law.

9 The Australianisation of Our Law

The demise of the appeal to the Privy Council, the new arrangements made for the disposition of the original jurisdiction work, and the introduction of the requirement for special leave as a condition of all appeals have enabled the High Court to formulate principles of general law appropriate to Australia's conditions and circumstances. In *Cook v Cook*,[59] the Court stated that the principle that Australian courts below the level of the High Court should, as a general rule, follow decisions of the English Court of Appeal no longer applied. The High Court noted that, subject, perhaps, to the special position of decisions of the House of Lords given in the period in which appeals lay to the Privy Council, the precedents of other legal systems are not binding and are useful only in so far as their reasoning is persuasive.

Thus, the Court has adopted an independent approach to the construction of exclusion and limitation clauses in contracts, without deferring to the House of Lords.[60] However, the more striking illustrations of the Australianisation of our law are to be found in

---

[58] See, for example, *Zecevic v Director of Public Prosecutions (Vict)* (1987) 162 CLR 645 (intoxication as a defence); *Williams v The Queen* (1986) 161 CLR 278 (detention of a suspect for the purpose of interrogation); *Walton v The Queen* (1989) 166 CLR 283 and *Benz v The Queen* (1989) 168 CLR 110 (exceptions to the hearsay rule); *Chidiac v The Queen* (1991) 171 CLR 432 (unsafe and unsatisfactory verdicts); *McKinney v The Queen* (1991) 171 CLR 468 (trial judge's duty to warn the jury of the danger of convicting on an uncorroborated confession to a police officer).

[59] (1986) 162 CLR 376, 390.

[60] *Darlington Futures Ltd v Delco Australia Pty Ltd* (1986) 161 CLR 500, 507–10.

the array of leading decisions in criminal law, tort law (especially negligence), equity, restitution and administrative law. Developments in administrative law have been associated with the *Administrative Decisions (Judicial Review) Act 1975* (Cth) but the judicial development of criminal and tort law has not been materially influenced by statute. Much of the judicial development of the general law, notably in the law of negligence, has had as its object greater unity, coherence, and symmetry in principle and doctrine,[61] rather than the adjustment of principle to suit Australian conditions and circumstances. Indeed, some significant departures from English principle are doctrinally based, as with the duty of care, exemplified in the different approaches taken to the liability of a public authority for negligence.[62]

10 The High Court's Increasingly Prominent Role as a Constitutional Court

There is a general impression abroad that the High Court's role as a constitutional court is more prominent than it was. Whether this impression is accurate is by no means clear. The High Court's public profile as a constitutional court has fluctuated over the years, depending upon the nature of the issues it has been called upon to decide. When a government, more often a Labor government, embarks upon a legislative program that skirts the margins of Commonwealth powers, the challenges to that legislation naturally project the Court into a position of prominence. Constitutional cases by their very nature attract more political and media attention and lead to more controversy than do other cases.

---

[61] See, for example, *Australian Safeway Stores Pty Ltd v Zaluzna* (1987) 162 CLR 479 (subsuming the liability of occupiers into liability for breach of the general duty of care); *Burnie Port Authority v General Jones Pty Ltd* (1994) 179 CLR 520 (subsuming liability under the rule in *Rylands v Fletcher* (1868) LR 3 HL 330 into liability in negligence).

[62] Compare *Sutherland Shire Council v Heyman* (1985) 157 CLR 424; *Nagle v Rottnest Island Authority* (1993) 177 CLR 423; *Pyrenees Shire Council v Day* (1998) 192 CLR 330; *Romeo v Conservation Commission (NT)* (1998) 192 CLR 431; *Murphy v Brentwood District Council* [1991] 1 AC 398; *Stovin v Wise* [1996] AC 923.

The Court's decisions on the external affairs power[63] enabling the Commonwealth Parliament to enact legislation to implement a treaty to which the Commonwealth is a party, even though the legislation is not on a subject within the heads of Commonwealth legislative power under the Constitution, attracted very considerable controversy. The same can be said of the Court's decisions on the implied freedom of communication with respect to matters of government and politics[64] and the decisions on excise duties.[65] These decisions, along with other constitutional decisions, certainly placed the Court in a prominent position and focused attention on its constitutional role.

Yet the Court's decisions on Aboriginal land rights in *Mabo v Queensland [No 2]* and *Wik Peoples v Queensland* attracted longer-lasting controversy and critical comment and they were not constitutional cases.[66] As they were decisions that related to an extraordinarily controversial issue, they do not detract from the statement that the High Court's predominant role is as a constitutional court.

In terms of the volume of cases determined by the Court, constitutional cases constitute a minority. However, they tend to occupy a disproportionate amount of judicial time. In the estimation of the community and of the justices, it is probably correct to say that the Court's constitutional role is its primary one.

11 The Changing Methodology of the Court

Much has been written of the methodology of the High Court. It has been said that its legalistic technique, emphasised by Sir Owen Dixon, and its legalism have given way to a species of legal realism and to a form of interpretation sometimes called moderate original-

---

[63] See *Koowarta v Bjelke-Petersen* (1982) 153 CLR 168; *Commonwealth v Tasmania (Tasmanian Dam Case)* (1983) 158 CLR 1; *Richardson v Forestry Commission* (1988) 164 CLR 261.

[64] *Nationwide News Pty Ltd v Wills* (1992) 177 CLR 1; *Australian Capital Television Pty Ltd v Commonwealth* (1992) 177 CLR 106; *Theophanous v Herald & Weekly Times Ltd* (1994) 182 CLR 104; *McGinty v Western Australia* (1996) 186 CLR 140; *Lange v Australian Broadcasting Corporation* (1997) 189 CLR 520.

[65] See *Ha v New South Wales* (1997) 189 CLR 465.

[66] (1992) 175 CLR 1; (1996) 187 CLR 1.

ism. These comments are very much a matter of subjective judgment. It is true to say, however, that in more recent times the Court has been more willing to examine policy issues and expose its reasoning on such matters rather than bury the reasoning beneath an overburden of authority and doctrine. There are signs that this approach may be waning. The Court may be returning to a methodology that places great store by doctrinal discussion ostensibly little influenced by discussion of policy considerations. Here again, impressions may be largely subjective and more time is needed in which a clear pattern may develop. Some cases like *Lange v Australian Broadcasting Corporation* and *McGinty v Western Australia* call for discussion of policy issues; others do not.[67]

A notable feature of High Court judgments is the use made of comparative law and decisions in other jurisdictions, apart from England. Frequent use of United States authorities in the interpretation of the Australian Constitution was made by the justices in the early days of the High Court. The doctrine of implied intergovernmental immunity was based on American authority. But thereafter until the 1970s there was comparatively little reference to non-English authorities. Since the early 1970s there have been constant and growing references to authorities in other common law jurisdictions, especially Canada, New Zealand and the United States, as well as the United Kingdom and Ireland. This trend has not been confined to Australia. It is a characteristic of the judgments in Canada and New Zealand and to a lesser extent in the United Kingdom. Use of transnational law is the result of its accessibility and of the great upsurge in legal publications.

Much the same comment can be made about the High Court's use of academic writings, except that their extensive use can be traced back to Windeyer J. Again, it is a use that can be seen in the judgments of other common law courts. Reference to comparative and academic writings, when allied with lengthy discussion of the decided cases, gives the modern judgment the appearance of an academic essay. United States judgments, written in the 'telegrammatic' style, are an exception to this generalisation.

---

[67] (1997) 189 CLR 520; (1996) 186 CLR 140.

Use has also been made by the High Court and courts in other common law jurisdictions of international conventions, both in the interpretation of statutes and in the formulation of common law principles. Mention should be made here of the controversial decision in *Minister for Immigration and Ethnic Affairs v Teoh*,[68] where the High Court held that it was legitimate to formulate common law principle by reference to the provisions of a convention ratified but not implemented by Australia. Earlier, the Court had stated that international conventions, particularly those declaring fundamental rights, were a legitimate influence on the development of the common law.[69]

12 High Court Procedures

The introduction of special leave as a prerequisite for an appeal had the effect of reducing the number of substantive matters in which the Full Court is called upon to deliver a reserved judgment from 90 to approximately 60 per annum. However, as a percentage of the previous appeals as of right were relatively uncomplicated, the smaller number of matters does not mean that there is a lesser burden of work, as now virtually all appeals involve important questions of principle. At the same time the number of special leave applications has continued to increase. They presently number over 350 per annum.

These developments have led to the Court giving more emphasis to written argument. A skeletal argument is presented to the Court by each party and, from time to time, the parties are directed to file and serve comprehensive written arguments. Except in special leave applications, there is no time limit on oral argument. On the other hand, cases are set down on the footing that certain time is allocated to a case and the time allotted is infrequently exceeded. Oral argument is more succinct and shorter than it used to be, a characteristic greatly encouraged by Sir Garfield Barwick, who as Chief Justice discouraged the reading of lengthy passages from judgments.

---

[68] (1995) 183 CLR 273.
[69] *Mabo v Queensland [No 2]* (1992) 175 CLR 1, 42; see also *Dietrich v The Queen* (1992) 177 CLR 92.

Time limits of twenty minutes and a reply for each side have been imposed upon special leave applications, both civil and criminal. As well, each party is required to file and serve an outline of argument which can be considered by the Court in advance of the oral argument. Although this procedure has been a success, the consideration of special leave applications, including reading the voluminous papers, takes up a great deal of a justice's time.

13 Interventions

In constitutional cases, s 78A of the *Judiciary Act* confers upon the Attorneys-General of the Commonwealth and states a right to intervene. In the case of other parties, whatever the nature of the case, the Court has power to grant leave to intervene. The power has been granted sparingly. The traditional view was that a party should not be granted leave to intervene unless the party seeking such leave had at stake a right or interest which would be affected by the outcome of the litigation.[70] More recently, in *Kruger v Commonwealth*,[71] the Court, in refusing an application by the International Commission of Jurists, said 'Applicants for leave to intervene must ordinarily show an interest in the subject of litigation greater than a mere desire to have the law declared in particular terms'.[72] Subsequently, in *Levy v Victoria*, Brennan CJ stated that: 'Jurisdiction to grant leave to intervene to persons whose legal interests are likely to be substantially affected by a judgment exists in order to avoid a judicial affection of such a person's legal interests without that person being given the opportunity to be heard'.[73] In the same case, the granting of amicus curiae status was discussed.[74] In *Project Blue Sky Inc v Australian Broadcasting Authority*,[75] amicus curiae status was granted to eleven persons.

---

[70] *Australian Railways Union v Victorian Railways Commissioners* (1930) 44 CLR 319.

[71] (1997) 190 CLR 1.

[72] Transcript of Proceedings, 12 February 1996, 12.

[73] (1997) 189 CLR 579, 603.

[74] Ibid 604–5 (Brennan CJ).

[75] (1998) 153 ALR 490.

As Kirby J noted in *Levy v Victoria*,[76] although a tight rein needs to be kept on interventions, there is a case for granting applications to intervene rather more liberally than in the past: the Court would benefit from more assistance in discharging its function in declaring the law, particularly in cases where the intervener will present an argument which differs from those to be presented by the parties.

14 Future Directions

Further thought needs to be given to the bases on which intervener status and amicus curiae status are to be granted and to the procedures to be followed as well as to the entitlements that arise from the grant of such status. The problems have been discussed elsewhere.[77]

The burden of work is likely to increase, not least in a greater volume of special leave applications. That may mean that such applications will be dealt with ultimately on written materials, subject to the Court having a power to list a case for oral argument, when that course is considered appropriate. It may even be that in time oral argument will be limited in substantive appeals, though that seems not to be an immediate prospect.

Another expedient would be to increase the number of justices from seven to nine, though it is doubtful that this course would significantly reduce the workload on the individual justice, unless the Court adopted the practice of publishing a single majority and a single minority judgment, a practice which has not commended itself to the Court so far. In any case, it is by no means certain that such a practice would lessen the workload of an individual justice because the practice calls for extensive judicial conferencing and consultation. In one respect, an increase in the number of justices would have a beneficial effect; it would provide a larger judicial pool to share the special leave applications.

One other matter may require attention and that is the identification of a procedure for receiving evidence and determining facts in constitutional cases. This is an important matter which has not been settled by the High Court.

---

[76] (1997) 189 CLR 579, 650–1.
[77] Kenny (1998); Sir Anthony Mason (1998).

5

Federal Courts Created by Parliament

Robert French

FEDERAL COURTS were for many years the poor relations in Australia's judicial system, which was dominated by the High Court and the Supreme Courts of the states. The latter were inheritors of the traditions and authority of English courts of general jurisdiction. Their standing at federation favoured the option of investing them with federal jurisdiction rather than creating a system of federal courts.

With the passage of the years the level of legislative and administrative activity by the Commonwealth rose to heights undreamed of by the drafters of the Constitution. With that activity came increasing pressure for a federal judicature, manifested initially in narrowly based specialist courts in industrial and bankruptcy law. But after a convoluted political history the federal judicature found its expression in the creation of two major national courts. The largest of these, the Family Court of Australia, administers highly contentious law created by the *Family Law Act 1975* (Cth). The other, the Federal Court of Australia, began in 1977 with twenty members and a narrow band of statutory jurisdictions. It has evolved to a fifty-member court exercising jurisdiction under 125 federal statutes covering a field so wide as to justify its description as 'a superior court of general jurisdiction in Australia'.[1]

---

[1] Crawford (1993) 168; also described as a 'world class civil court', in Australian Law Reform Commission (1999b) 87.

The development of Australia's federal judicature differs in its origins and outcomes from that of the federal courts of the United States and Canada. Its story carries with it substantial elements of the political and social history of Australia as well as constitutional exegesis of the judicial power of the Commonwealth. This chapter reviews the history of each federal court that has been created by Parliament under Chapter III of the Australian Constitution.

1 Constitutional Origins and Framework

By virtue of s 71 of the Constitution, the judicial power of the Commonwealth vests in the High Court of Australia, 'such other federal courts as the Parliament creates', and such other courts as it invests with federal jurisdiction.

The appellate jurisdiction of the High Court is defined by s 73 of the Constitution and specific original jurisdiction conferred directly by s 75. The latter may be extended by legislation under s 76 in any matter arising under the Constitution or involving its interpretation, arising under any laws made by the Parliament, of admiralty or maritime jurisdiction, or relating to the same subject matter claimed under the laws of different states. For any of the matters referred to in ss 75 and 76 the Parliament may, under s 77, define the jurisdiction of 'any federal court other than the High Court', define the extent of its exclusivity of jurisdiction which belongs to or is invested in the courts of the states and invest any court of a state with federal jurisdiction. The jurisdiction so invested or defined, like that of the High Court, carries with it an 'accrued jurisdiction' to determine all claims comprising the matter[2] which may include claims under state law.[3] The scope of the jurisdiction thus defined is a matter of 'impression and of practical judgment'.[4]

The appointment and tenure of federal judges and the protection of their remuneration are provided for in s 72. Since the 1977

---

[2] *R v Bevan; Ex parte Elias and Gordon* (1942) 66 CLR 452; *Moorgate Tobacco Co Ltd v Philip Morris Ltd* (1980) 145 CLR 457; *Philip Morris Inc v Adam P Brown Male Fashions Pty Ltd* (1981) 148 CLR 457.

[3] *Fencott v Muller* (1983) 152 CLR 570, 606; *Stack v Coast Securities (No 9) Pty Ltd* (1983) 154 CLR 261, 293.

[4] *Fencott v Muller* (1983) 152 CLR 570, 608.

amendment to the Constitution the appointment of justices of federal courts expires when the appointee reaches seventy years of age, or such lesser age as is fixed by Parliament.

There is no express power to create subordinate federal courts.[5] As Quick and Garran wrote in 1901 of the phrase 'such other federal courts as the Parliament creates': 'These words impliedly give the Federal Parliament a power to create other federal courts besides the High Court'.[6] Express power was 'thought unnecessary by the framers of the Australian Constitution who adopted so definitely the general pattern of Art. III [of the US Constitution] but in their variations and departures from its detailed provisions evidenced a discriminating appreciation of American experience'.[7]

Discussion of s 71 at the constitutional Convention Debates focused upon the High Court. Delegates were concerned about economies and the possibility that the Court might be underworked. The people were thought not to care 'about a large expenditure on law and lawyers'.[8] It was undesirable to 'overload the Federal Constitution with judicial machinery'.[9] The rationale for using existing state courts rather than requiring the creation of 'other federal courts' was stated by J. H. Symon QC:

> The method adopted in the United States of having circuit courts, and so on, all over the country has been wiped out here, so that the Federal Parliament may save that expense, and the Parliament has been given power to vest the judicial control of matters not to be dealt with by the High Court in the state courts.[10]

In *R v Kirby; Ex parte Boilermakers' Society of Australia* (*Boilermakers' Case*), the High Court dubbed this the 'autochthonous expedient'.[11]

---

[5] By contrast, see the Constitution of the United States, Article I, s 8.

[6] Quick and Garran (1901) 725.

[7] *R v Kirby; Ex parte Boilermakers' Society of Australia* (1956) 94 CLR 254, 268.

[8] Craven (1986) (1897 Convention, Adelaide) 9387.

[9] Craven (1986) (1898 Convention, Melbourne) 268.

[10] Ibid 298.

[11] (1956) 94 CLR 254, 268. This has been said not to be an accurate description as state courts in the United States can exercise concurrent federal and state jurisdiction. See *Felton v Mulligan* (1971) 124 CLR 367, 393 (Windeyer J); Opeskin (1995) 766. By contrast, see Byers and Toose (1963) 329.

It was an expedient rejected by the framers of the United States Constitution. Reasons for its rejection included the parochialism and lack of independence of some state courts. It would be impossible, according to Alexander Hamilton, to foresee 'how far the prevalency of a local spirit [might] be found to disqualify the local tribunals for the jurisdiction of national causes'. The constitution of some state courts would render them 'improper channels of the judicial authority of the Union'. Those in which judges held office at pleasure or from year to year would be 'too little independent to be relied upon for an inflexible execution of the national laws'.[12] The Supreme Courts of the states of Australia, on the other hand, were seen as being of uniformly high standard, a situation which was 'in marked contrast with that which obtained in the United States shortly after its establishment'.[13]

The risk of legislative erosion of the independence of state courts in Australia, including the Supreme Courts, was always present under state constitutions and their colonial predecessors. With limited exceptions in New South Wales and Victoria, those constitutions do not entrench the independence of the courts or protect the tenure or remuneration of state judges.[14] State constitutional protection would involve manner and form requirements for the alteration of courts' structures, composition and independence.[15]

The Australian Constitution and its designation of the state courts as instruments for the exercise of the judicial power of the Commonwealth provides some protective umbrella. Since federation the state courts have had a status and role that by virtue of the Australian Constitution extends beyond the state judicial systems: 'They are part of an integrated system of State and federal courts and organs for the exercise of federal judicial power as well as State judicial power'.[16]

---

[12] Hamilton, Jay and Madison (1787) No 81, 528.

[13] Sawer (1967) 20–1; Barwick (1977) 482.

[14] *McCawley v The King* [1920] AC 691, 713. See also *Constitution Act 1902* (NSW) s 7B and *Constitution Act 1975* (Vic) s 18.

[15] Handsley (1998) 184–5; French (1993).

[16] *Kable v Director of Public Prosecutions (NSW)* (1996) 189 CLR 51, 114–15 (McHugh J) and see also 102 (Gaudron J) and 143 (Gummow J).

The Supreme Courts of the states, at least, cannot be invested with jurisdiction incompatible with their integrity, independence and impartiality as courts in which federal jurisdiction has also been vested under Chapter III of the Australian Constitution. It is not a large step from that principle to the proposition that state Parliaments cannot erode their independence in ways that would make them 'improper channels' of the judicial power of the Commonwealth: 'In the case of State courts, this means they must be independent and appear to be independent of their own State's legislature and executive government as well as the federal legislature and government'.[17]

The United States constitutional convention of 1787 debated whether to establish inferior federal courts at all. Issues of expense, necessity and state rights were canvassed. In the event, creation of such courts by force of the Constitution was rejected in favour of the compromise under which the judicial power of the United States was vested in the Supreme Court 'and in such inferior Courts as the Congress may from time to time ordain and establish'.[18] Nevertheless, state courts are required to exercise federal judicial power where necessary to enforce federal rights.

The power to establish inferior federal courts was intended 'to obviate the necessity of having recourse to the Supreme Court in every case of federal cognizance'.[19] Congress could not vest any portion of the judicial power of the United States except in federal courts. It was bound therefore to create inferior federal courts in which to vest that jurisdiction which under the Constitution was exclusively vested in the United States and of which the Supreme Court could not take original cognisance.[20]

This reasoning did not apply to the Constitution of the Commonwealth. The federal Parliament had power to extend the original

---

[17] Ibid 116 (McHugh J).

[18] Constitution of the United States, Article III, s 1. See also Cowen and Zines (1978) 105.

[19] Hamilton, Jay and Madison (1787) No 81, 527.

[20] The jurisdiction of the Supreme Court is defined by Article III, s 2. Its original jurisdiction is limited to 'all Cases affecting Ambassadors, other public Ministers and Consuls, and those in which a State shall be a Party'. See also Story (1891) 411–12.

jurisdiction of the High Court 'to any case to which original cognizance under the judicial power of the Commonwealth can extend'.[21] The Parliament could invest any court of a state with federal jurisdiction. It was envisaged that for some time there would be no need to create any inferior federal courts.[22]

Indeed, in the early stages of the federation there was a view propounded by Henry Higgins, among others, that establishing the High Court could be deferred and the supervision of the Constitution be left to the state Supreme Courts. They were, after all, bound by the Constitution by virtue of its covering clause 5. In the event the Parliament passed the *Judiciary Act 1903* (Cth) which provided for a High Court comprising a Chief Justice and two other justices.[23]

Investiture of state courts with federal jurisdiction pursuant to s 71 of the Constitution was effected by s 39 of the *Judiciary Act*. The power so to invest them was exercised 'almost to its fullest extent'. The scheme of s 39 was:

> to embrace the whole of the matters of federal jurisdiction which it is not intended to give to the High Court exclusively, and to declare, first, that the State Courts shall according to their nature and degree have jurisdiction in all of them, whether they are matters of which the Court would have jurisdiction under the State law or not; secondly, that no jurisdiction shall be exercised by the State Courts in any of such matters, except as federal jurisdiction.[24]

Exclusive elements of the High Court's jurisdiction were expressed in ss 38 and 38A (the latter section has now been repealed).

Chapter III of the Constitution specifies exhaustively the vehicles through which federal judicial power can be exercised: 'There is a mandate to create a High Court; there is a discretionary power to create other federal Courts; and there is a discretionary power to invest with federal jurisdiction such Courts as Parliament finds already in existence, that is, State Courts. But that exhausts the judi-

---

[21] Quick and Garran (1901) 726.
[22] Ibid.
[23] Sawer (1967) 21.
[24] Harrison Moore (1910) 217.

cature'.[25] Hence, the Inter-State Commission for which s 101 of the Constitution provides, with 'such power of adjudication . . . as the Parliament deems necessary for the execution and maintenance, within the Commonwealth, of the provisions of [the] Constitution relating to trade and commerce, and of all laws made thereunder', was held in *New South Wales v Commonwealth* (*Wheat Case*) not to be validly invested with judicial powers by the *Inter-State Commission Act 1912* (Cth).[26]

In spite of the sweeping proposition in the *Wheat Case* of the universal application of Chapter III to the exercise of federal judicial power, not every court created by the Commonwealth is the repository of such power. So, in 1915, the Court in *R v Bernasconi* held that Chapter III was limited in its application to the judicial power of the Commonwealth in respect of functions of government in which the Commonwealth stands in place of the states. It had no application to the territories.[27] The question was revisited in 1965 in relation to the Court of Petty Sessions of the Australian Capital Territory. In *Spratt v Hermes*, the High Court held that laws made under s 122 could create courts that did not comply with the requirements of s 72 in relation to the appointment of their judicial officers. These were not 'federal' courts. However, the wider proposition advanced in *R v Bernasconi* that no part of Chapter III had any application to the territories was rejected.[28]

The subject matter of laws made under s 122 had attracted the designation 'disparate non-federal matter', coined by the Privy Council on appeal from the High Court in the *Boilermakers' Case*.[29] It was a characterisation adopted by Kitto and Taylor JJ in *Spratt v Hermes*.[30] But this constitutional duality did not attract universal approval. It was described as 'artificial and unreal' by Barwick CJ. Nevertheless, in *Capital TV & Appliances Pty Ltd v Falconer* the

---

[25] *New South Wales v Commonwealth* (1915) 20 CLR 54, 89.

[26] Ibid.

[27] (1915) 19 CLR 629, 635 (Griffith CJ, Gavan Duffy and Rich JJ agreeing).

[28] (1965) 114 CLR 226, 242–5, 253, 257, 280.

[29] *Attorney-General of the Commonwealth of Australia v The Queen* [1957] AC 288, 320.

[30] (1965) 114 CLR 226, 251 (Kitto J), 263 (Taylor J).

former Chief Justice, in common with other justices of the Court, applied *Spratt v Hermes* and held that the Supreme Court of the Australian Capital Territory was not a federal court.[31] The doctrine was also reflected in *Teori Tau v Commonwealth*, which decided that s 51(xxxi) did not apply in the territories to require acquisition of property by the Commonwealth to be on just terms.[32] Other decisions, however, reflected an integrationist philosophy.[33]

Two recent decisions of the High Court have reflected further on this question. In *Newcrest Mining (WA) Ltd v Commonwealth*,[34] a 4:3 majority declined to overrule *Teori Tau v Commonwealth* in relation to the application of the just terms limitation. The disparate powers doctrine was restated.[35] Brennan CJ took as an illustration the absence of any jurisdiction in the High Court under s 73 to entertain appeals from the courts of the territories, the jurisdiction being conferred by laws enacted under s 122: 'Courts of the Territories are not "federal" courts, even though they are created by the Parliament, since those Courts are not created in exercise of a federal legislative power but in exercise of the non-federal power conferred on the Parliament by s 122'.[36] In *Kruger v Commonwealth* somewhat divergent views were expressed.[37] None of these cases on the face of it prevents the creation by the Parliament of federal courts to exercise jurisdiction within the territories of Australia.

The existence of state and federal judicial systems has been criticised as unnecessary and expensive and numerous proposals for

[31] (1971) 125 CLR 591, 600.

[32] (1969) 119 CLR 564.

[33] For example, *Lamshed v Lake* (1958) 99 CLR 132 upheld the applicability of laws made under s 122 in the states.

[34] (1997) 190 CLR 513.

[35] Ibid 535, 538 (Brennan CJ), 550 (Dawson J) and 577–8 (McHugh J). By contrast, see 591–607 (Gummow J, supported generally, save as to the force of *Teori Tau*, by Toohey J), 656–7 (Kirby J).

[36] Ibid 538.

[37] (1997) 190 CLR 1, 43–4 (Brennan CJ), 62 (Dawson J), 84 (Toohey J, who found the argument that Chapter III is applicable to the territories to be 'very persuasive'), 107 and 109 (Gaudron J). See generally Zines (1998). Most recently, the High Court, in *Re Governor, Goulburn Correctional Centre, Goulburn; Ex parte Eastman* (1999) 165 ALR 171, held the courts of the internal territories not to be courts created by the Parliament under s 72 of the Constitution.

rationalisation of the Australian judicature have been advanced.[38] Sir Owen Dixon was a strong proponent of a unified national system, observing that 'it would not have been beyond the wit of man to devise machinery which would have placed the Courts, so to speak, upon neutral territory where they administered the whole law irrespective of its source'.[39] The fact remains that the Constitution gave the Parliament a choice of vehicle for the exercise of federal jurisdiction and: 'There is no indication in Ch. III that the making of this choice was to be strongly weighted against the creation of federal courts in favour of investing federal jurisdiction in State courts'.[40]

Today an array of state and federal courts cover between them the exercise of all federal jurisdiction in Australia. Accrued jurisdiction over claims arising under state law may be exercised by federal courts as an incident of the exercise of federal jurisdiction derived from its constitutional expression. A cross-vesting scheme for the exercise by federal courts of state jurisdiction, by state courts of federal jurisdiction, and by state courts of the jurisdiction of each other was enacted in 1987 and came into force on 1 July 1988 to reduce the incidence of jurisdictional debate. The validity of the scheme in so far as it vested state jurisdiction in federal courts, however, was under a shadow for some time and it has now been found to be invalid (see Chapter 10).[41] Further exegesis of the constitutional framework of judicial power can be traced through the history of the federal courts.

---

[38] Else-Mitchell (1969); Burt (1982); Street (1982); Australian Constitutional Convention (1983) vol. I, 317; vol. II, 12–18; Australian Constitutional Convention Judicature Sub-Committee (1984); Australian Constitutional Convention (1985) vol. II, 14; Australian Institute of Judicial Administration (1983).

[39] Sir Owen Dixon (1935) 607.

[40] *Stack v Coast Securities (No 9) Pty Ltd* (1983) 154 CLR 261, 293.

[41] Even before the legislation was passed, the shadow was cast. See Australian Constitutional Commission Advisory Committee on the Australian Judicial System (1987) 44. It lengthened in *West Australian Psychiatric Nurses' Association (Union of Workers) v Australian Nursing Federation* (1991) 102 ALR 265 and in *Gould v Brown* (1998) 193 CLR 346 the scheme barely survived on an evenly split decision of six justices of the High Court. In *Re Wakim; Ex parte McNally* (1999) 163 ALR 270 the High Court by a 6:1 majority held the scheme to be invalid in so far as it invested state jurisdiction in the Federal and Family Courts.

2 Federal Industrial Courts—Lessons in Judicial Power and Politics

The first attempt to create a statutory federal court brought into existence the Commonwealth Court of Conciliation and Arbitration under the *Conciliation and Arbitration Act 1904* (Cth). Its President was appointed from among the justices of the High Court for a term of seven years. He could appoint any justice of the High Court or a judge of a state Supreme Court to be his deputy to exercise such of the President's powers as he thought fit to assign.

The first President, from 1905 to 1907, was Justice O'Connor of the High Court. The second was Justice Higgins. In 1908 Higgins dismissed an appeal from a decision of an Industrial Registrar. His decision was appealed to the High Court. The Industrial Registrar objected that the Commonwealth Court of Conciliation and Arbitration was not a federal court within the meaning of s 73 of the Constitution. The High Court dismissed the objection summarily. Section 73 of the Constitution gave an appeal to the High Court from the orders of any other federal court and, it was said, 'the Court appealed from is such a Court'.[42]

The question whether the Court could exercise judicial powers having regard to the limited tenure of its members was stated and resolved in the negative in 1918 in *Waterside Workers' Federation of Australia v J W Alexander Ltd.*[43] The *Conciliation and Arbitration Act* was amended in 1926 to provide for appointments to be made in accordance with Chapter III, namely by the Governor-General in Council and for life. The functions of the Court continued to be predominantly arbitral. Amendments in 1947 and subsequently conferred further arbitral and judicial functions on the Court. The constitutional propriety of this combination was not addressed directly until 1956.

---

[42] *Jumbunna Coal Mine, No Liability v Victorian Coal Miners' Association* (1908) 6 CLR 309, 324. See also *Federated Amalgamated Government Railway and Tramway Service Association v New South Wales Railway Traffic Employees Association* (1906) 4 CLR 488, in which it was held that in hearing an appeal under the Act from the decision of a Registrar, the President was acting as the Court.

[43] (1918) 25 CLR 434.

Eventually the doctrine of separation of powers overtook the Court in the *Boilermakers' Case*.[44] It had already been established that judicial power could be exercised only by 'a court created pursuant to s. 71 and constituted in accordance with s. 72 or a court brought into existence by a State'.[45] The question whether a federal court could exercise judicial and non-judicial functions had not previously been considered. Nevertheless, the High Court found it:

> impossible to escape the conviction that Chap. III does not allow the exercise of a jurisdiction which of its very nature belongs to the judicial power of the Commonwealth by a body established for purposes foreign to the judicial power, notwithstanding that it is organized as a court and in a manner which might otherwise satisfy ss. 71 and 72, and that Chap. III does not allow a combination with judicial power of functions which are not ancillary or incidental to its exercise but are foreign to it.[46]

The Court had become a kind of economic legislature. In the prosperous post-war era its role involved 'dividing up . . . economic gains'. It was perhaps to be expected that the High Court in 1956 would hold 'that this type of economic arbitration could not be undertaken by a court possessing federal judicial power'.[47]

The *Boilermakers' Case* led to the division of judicial and arbitral functions previously carried out by the Conciliation and Arbitration Court between a court and a commission respectively. In 1956 a new federal court, the Commonwealth Industrial Court, was established. It was renamed the Australian Industrial Court in 1973. The Conciliation and Arbitration Commission was created as an arbitral body.

An early contention that the Court was the repository of an impermissible mix of judicial and non-judicial powers was rejected. The High Court held that the amending Act provided 'abundant evidence of the intention to establish a Commonwealth Industrial Court

---

[44] *R v Kirby; Ex parte Boilermakers' Society of Australia* (1956) 94 CLR 254.
[45] Ibid 270.
[46] Ibid 296.
[47] McCallum (1992) 404; Hawke (1956).

for the purpose of exercising judicial power even if some of the functions conferred upon it may in truth go outside Chap III of the
Constitution'. If there were impermissible non-judicial authorities
conferred these would be severable.[48]

Because the *Boilermakers' Case* has produced inconvenience
and difficulty in application, its doctrine has been eroded.[49] Despite
broad definitions such as that of Griffith CJ in *Huddart, Parker &
Co Pty Ltd v Moorehead*,[50] the elusiveness of the concept of judicial
power and the difficulty of its definition remains.[51] Its correctness
has been questioned[52] although it has recently been reaffirmed.[53]

In considering the federal courts' jurisdiction, it is wise to bear
in mind the words of Sir Hayden Starke about the High Court which
are equally applicable to each subordinate federal court: 'To the Constitution and the laws made under the Constitution it owes its existence and all its powers, and whatever jurisdiction is not found there
either expressly or by necessary implication does not exist'.[54]

The Australian Industrial Court was invested with a number of
non-industrial jurisdictions including exclusive jurisdiction under
the *Trade Practices Act 1974* (Cth).[55] It had been intended that those
jurisdictions would be conferred on a proposed Superior Court of
Australia. The Bill to create that court was rejected by the Senate in

---

[48] *Seamen's Union of Australia v Matthews* (1957) 96 CLR 529, 534, 535.

[49] *R v Davison* (1954) 90 CLR 353, 366; *Harris v Caladine* (1991) 172 CLR 84, 122.

[50] (1909) 8 CLR 330.

[51] *R v Davison* (1954) 90 CLR 353, 366; *Harris v Caladine* (1991) 172 CLR 84, 122;
Polyukhovich v Commonwealth (1991) 172 CLR 501, 532.

[52] *R v Joske; Ex parte Australian Building Construction Employees & Builders'
Labourers' Federation* (1974) 130 CLR 87 and *R v Joske; Ex parte Shop Distributive
and Allied Employees' Association* (1976) 135 CLR 194; de Meyrick (1995a) and
(1995b); Gibbs (1987); Winterton (1983) 61–4; Sawer (1961b).

[53] *Western Australia v Commonwealth* (*Native Title Act Case*) (1995) 183 CLR 373,
485–6.

[54] *R v Bevan; Ex parte Elias and Gordon* (1942) 66 CLR 452, 464–5.

[55] Other jurisdictions exercised by the Australian Industrial Court include those under
the *Administrative Appeals Tribunal Act 1975* (Cth), *National Health Act 1953*
(Cth), *Health Insurance Act 1973* (Cth), *Commonwealth Employees Compensation
Act 1930* (Cth), *Navigation Act 1912* (Cth), *Prices Justification Act 1973* (Cth), and
the *Stevedoring Industry Act 1956* (Cth).

1974. The Court retained its jurisdiction until the Federal Court of Australia, created in 1976, took it over and began operating on 1 February 1977.[56]

Legislation ancillary to that creating the Federal Court provided for the abolition of the Industrial Court on a date to be fixed, 'being a day on which no person holds office as a Judge of the Australian Industrial Court'.[57] This avoided setting a precedent for the abolition of a court while its judges remained in office albeit with no jurisdiction. At the time of the transfer of its jurisdiction the Court comprised a Chief Judge and eleven other justices. From 1977 until 1993 the Federal Court of Australia was the only national industrial court.

In 1985 the Committee of Review of Australian Industrial Relations Law and Systems (the Hancock Committee) recommended changes to Australia's industrial law including the creation of an Australian Labour Court. The Committee recommended that each judge hold a separate concurrent appointment as a designated person on the Australian Industrial Relations Commission. The Committee found dissatisfaction with institutional arrangements flowing from the division of arbitral and judicial powers. The existing system involved unnecessary complexity and legalism. Moreover, there could be a 'better appreciation and awareness of industrial relations considerations by persons who specialise in industrial relations'.[58] It recommended the creation of a new Labour Court with all appointments from suitably qualified members of the Commission. Its general argument included the need to have 'expert knowledge of industrial relations ... available to the Court'.[59]

The *Industrial Relations Act 1988* (Cth) was enacted pursuant to the Committee's report. The Labour Court proposal did not go forward because of opposition from employer interests, the withdrawal of a compliance package, and the imminence of a federal

---

[56] *Federal Court of Australia (Consequential Provisions) Act 1976* (Cth).

[57] *Conciliation and Arbitration Amendment Act (No 3) 1976* (Cth) s 4.

[58] Committee of Review into Australian Industrial Relations Law and Systems (1985) 382–3.

[59] Ibid 388.

election.[60] So the Federal Court continued to deal with the matters that would otherwise have been transferred to the Labour Court.

In 1993 an Industrial Relations Reform Bill was introduced to amend the 1988 Act. It included the establishment of 'a new specialist federal court, the Industrial Relations Court of Australia', to take over the industrial relations jurisdiction of the Federal Court.[61] The then Opposition Leader, John Howard, described it as unnecessary, adding that: 'Specialist courts are always a little suspect because the concern is that they will do special deals for special groups'.[62] The Shadow Attorney-General, Daryl Williams, criticised its establishment for want of any justification. In a partly self-fulfilling prophecy he pointed to the dangers of creating 'small specialist courts' to serve particular social purposes. Such courts could be vulnerable to abolition following a change of government. They had a tendency to develop a limited outlook which would not affect courts of broader jurisdiction.[63] The Law Council of Australia had expressed concern that the Court would have a 'less independent legal culture'.

In the event the Court was established. No provision was made for the concurrent appointment of the judges of the Court as members of the Commission. Nine of the initial ten judges were appointed from existing members of the Federal Court. The tenth judge, Justice Michael Moore, a Vice-President of the Australian Industrial Relations Commission, was appointed concurrently to the Industrial Relations Court and to the Federal Court. All the judges sat from time to time on both Courts.[64] In 1995 three new appointees were also appointed to the Federal Court.

Following a change of government in 1996 the *Industrial Relations Act* was amended and renamed the *Workplace Relations and Other Legislation Amendment Act 1996* (Cth). The jurisdiction of the Industrial Relations Court was reinvested in the Federal Court

---

[60] *Commonwealth Parliamentary Debates*, House of Representatives, 28 April 1998, 2334–5. Note also the reference to the decision of the High Court in *Re Ranger Uranium Mines Pty Ltd; Ex parte Federated Miscellaneous Workers' Union of Australia* (1987) 163 CLR 656, with respect to which see Ludeke (1994) 142.

[61] *Commonwealth Parliamentary Debates*, House of Representatives, 28 October 1993, 2783.

[62] Ibid 17 November 1993, 3046.

[63] Ibid 22 November 1993, 3293–6.

[64] Industrial Relations Court of Australia (1995) 5.

with effect from 25 May 1997. In his second reading speech the new Attorney-General, Daryl Williams, explained this aspect of the legislation in terms of a pre-election commitment. Nevertheless, he accepted that the Court had, from the outset, carried out its responsibilities 'with the high level of skill and dedication which the community has come to expect from the Federal Court'. Its innovative user-friendly practices and procedures were being examined by the Federal Court.[65] Consistent with the transfer of Australian Industrial Court jurisdiction to the Federal Court in 1976, the 1996 Act did not abolish the Industrial Relations Court. The appointments, remuneration, and terms and conditions of the judges as judges of the Federal Court were unaffected. The remuneration and position of the Chief Justice of the Industrial Relations Court was maintained.

Debate about specialist courts tends to be intense and more so in politically sensitive areas such as industrial relations and family law. Of the Australian Industrial Court it was said by one commentator that 'its judges were mentally hemmed in by the narrowness of their industrial relations jurisdiction'. While an industrial court with limited powers was tolerated in the 1950s and 1960s it 'would not find favour in the harsh economic climate of an Australia in the 1990s'. Moreover, appointees would be vulnerable to the charge that they were members of an industrial relations club.[66] On the other hand it was argued that the creation of a specialist industrial relations court should be likened to the creation of the Family Court to bring a national approach to matrimonial dissolution and the creation of the Federal Court as a national superior court of record hearing federal legal controversies.[67]

A substantial part of the Hancock Committee's rationale for the creation of a specialist court was lost when its proposal to appoint members of the court from among members of the Commission was rejected. Indeed, given the predominance of appointments from among serving members of the Federal Court, it could fairly be asked what rationale had remained for its establishment.

---

[65] *Commonwealth Parliamentary Debates*, House of Representatives, 30 May 1996, 1848–9.
[66] McCallum (1992) 430–1.
[67] Shaw (1994) 17–24.

Federal Courts

The appointment profile of the Industrial Relations Court of Australia suggests that there was governmental sensitivity to the possibility that appointments might be seen as being of a lesser calibre than those made to the Federal Court of Australia, a criticism that had been advanced in relation to the Family Court.[68]

3 The Federal Court of Bankruptcy

The *Bankruptcy Act 1924* (Cth) supplanted state bankruptcy laws, which conferred jurisdiction on their Supreme Courts and specialist bankruptcy or insolvency courts. Section 18 of the Act provided that the courts having jurisdiction in bankruptcy should be state and territory courts 'specially authorized by the Governor-General by proclamation to exercise that jurisdiction'. Section 12 designated the Registrar and Deputy Registrars in Bankruptcy, who were officers of the Commonwealth, as officers of the relevant state courts to have such duties as directed by the Attorney-General. Section 24 provided that the Registrar could also exercise power delegated by the court.

The provisions for investing state courts with federal jurisdiction by executive proclamation failed in the High Court in *Le Mesurier v Connor*.[69] It was not a 'law investing' federal jurisdiction under s 77 of the Constitution: 'the natural meaning of the words of sec. 77 requires that the law made by the Parliament should not only define the jurisdiction to be invested but identify the State Court in which the jurisdiction is thereby invested'.[70]

Moreover, the Parliament could not make a Commonwealth officer a functionary of a state court authorising the officer to act on its behalf and to administer its jurisdiction. The power conferred by s 77(iii) of the Constitution is to confer additional judicial authority upon a court fully established by or under another legislature:

> To affect or alter the constitution of the Court itself or of the organization through which its jurisdiction and powers are exercised is to go outside the limits of the power conferred and to seek to achieve a

---

[68] See Gibbs (1985) 522; Evatt (1985) vi.
[69] (1929) 42 CLR 481.
[70] Ibid 500 (Knox CJ, Rich and Dixon JJ).

further object, namely, the regulation or establishment of the instrument or organ of Government in which judicial power is invested, an object for which the Constitution provides another means, the creation of Federal Courts.[71]

Section 18 of the *Bankruptcy Act* was amended in 1929 to invest federal bankruptcy jurisdiction in the Supreme Courts of all states and territories save for Victoria and South Australia, where the jurisdiction was invested in the Courts of Insolvency of those states. Pursuant to s 18(1)(a) of the Act, jurisdiction could also be vested in 'such Federal Courts as the Parliament creates to be Courts of Bankruptcy'. The federal Registrars in Bankruptcy were not to be officers of the Court but could be 'controlled' by the Court and have such duties as the Attorney-General directed or as were prescribed (s 12(5)). They could exercise such of the administrative powers of the Court as the Court directed or authorised. These amendments survived challenge.[72]

The Federal Court of Bankruptcy was created in 1930 by further amendment (s 18A). It was to consist of not more than two judges. It only sat in New South Wales and Victoria where state courts could not cope with the increased workload resulting from the Great Depression. The Supreme Courts of Queensland, Western Australia and Tasmania and the Court of Insolvency of South Australia continued to exercise jurisdiction.

The purity of the judicial power was considered in respect of a provision of the Act authorising the Court to charge a bankrupt with an offence and to try him summarily for it. The provisions were held to be valid in *R v Federal Court of Bankruptcy; Ex parte Lowenstein* (*Lowenstein's Case*).[73] In dissent, Dixon and Evatt JJ observed that if 'the inherent character of the function reposed in the courts is at variance with the conception of judicial power, then . . . it must fail'.[74] Here the concept of a function incompatible with

---

[71] Ibid 496.
[72] *Bond v George A Bond & Co Ltd* (1930) 44 CLR 11.
[73] (1938) 59 CLR 556.
[74] Ibid 588.

the exercise of the judicial power was adumbrated other than in terms of the separation of powers. Subsequently the High Court declined to reconsider *Lowenstein's Case*.[75]

In *R v Davison* the High Court held that Chapter III prevented a Registrar in Bankruptcy from making a sequestration order which would operate as an order of the Federal Court of Bankruptcy.[76] It accepted nevertheless that judicial functions can be executed, subject to judicial confirmation or review, by an officer of the court such as a master. No High Court decision under Chapter III prevented a statute from providing for the discharge of the duties of a federal court in this way.[77] This issue was to be revisited in relation to the Family Court of Australia in a series of cases resulting in acceptance of the delegation of powers to court officers subject to their supervision and control by Chapter III judges.[78]

In early proposals for a national federal court it was thought undesirable that jurisdiction in bankruptcy should continue to be exercised by such a wide variety of tribunals as under the combined federal and state arrangements. If a new federal court were to take over all the original jurisdiction in bankruptcy, appeals in the first instance could go to the appellate side of that court.[79] In the event the jurisdiction of the Bankruptcy Court was transferred to the newly established Federal Court of Australia in 1977. The Federal Court of Bankruptcy was to be abolished 'upon a day to be fixed by Proclamation, being a day on which no person holds office as a Judge of the Federal Court of Bankruptcy'.[80] That proclamation took effect on 30 September 1995, following the retirement in June 1995 of Justice Sweeney, the last judge of the Federal Court of Bankruptcy.

---

[75] *Sachter v Attorney-General (Commonwealth)* (1954) 94 CLR 86.

[76] (1954) 90 CLR 353.

[77] Ibid 365 (Dixon CJ and McTiernan J).

[78] See *Harris v Caladine* (1991) 172 CLR 84 and *Commonwealth v Hospital Contribution Fund* (1982) 150 CLR 49.

[79] Byers and Toose (1963) 316; Barwick (1964) 17.

[80] *Bankruptcy Amendment Act 1976* (Cth) s 8.

4 The Family Court of Australia

The Commonwealth Parliament has power to make laws with respect to marriage (s 51(xxi)), divorce and matrimonial causes and, in relation thereto, parental rights and the custody and guardianship of infants (s 51(xxii)). Until 1961 each state had its own laws based broadly upon, but variously differing from, the *Matrimonial Causes Act 1857* (UK). The earliest Commonwealth law on the topic, the *Matrimonial Causes Act 1945* (Cth), was of limited application to spouses of overseas servicemen.[81] In 1951–52 the Law Council of Australia drafted a Uniform Divorce Bill including provision for a Federal Divorce Court.[82] However, a federal court to deal with family law matters was still nearly twenty-five years away. The *Matrimonial Causes Act 1959* (Cth) and the *Marriage Act 1961* (Cth) represented the first full exercise of the Commonwealth's constitutional power over marriage and divorce. The *Matrimonial Causes Act* established a uniform law throughout Australia for divorce and related property, maintenance and custody issues. It was largely a consolidation of existing law. Jurisdiction under both Acts was vested in state and territory Supreme Courts.

Pressure for law reform built up in the 1960s and early 1970s with proposals for the creation of a Federal Family Court.[83] A review of the *Matrimonial Causes Act* was commenced in 1972 by the Senate Standing Committee on Constitutional and Legal Affairs. Following the election of the Whitlam Labor government in 1972 a Family Law Bill was presented in the Senate late in 1973. It was envisaged that jurisdiction would be exercised by a Family Law Division of the proposed Superior Court (the progenitor of the Federal Court of Australia).[84] But the Senate Standing Committee supported the establishment of a specialist court on the basis that this measure together with the simplified substantive provisions of the Bill would reduce the scope for legal dispute.[85] After vicissitudes connected to

---

[81] See Star (1996) and Crawford (1993) ch. 10.

[82] Law Council of Australia (1951) 381; Harry Woolf (1952).

[83] Star (1996) 51–74.

[84] Ibid 81.

[85] Senate Standing Committee on Constitutional and Legal Affairs (1974) 29.

the want of a Labor majority in the Senate and the double dissolution of the Commonwealth Parliament in April 1974, the revised Bill passed through both Houses in May 1975 and received Royal Assent on 12 June 1975. It came into force on 5 January 1976.

The *Family Law Act 1975* (Cth) establishes the Family Court of Australia as a superior court of record. Section 31 provides that its jurisdiction includes matters arising under the Act and the *Marriage Act 1961* (Cth), and s 33 vests it with jurisdiction in matters 'associated with matters ... in which [its] jurisdiction ... is invoked'. Sitting as a Full Court it has appellate jurisdiction (s 94). Federal jurisdiction can be invested in state Family Courts under the Act, but pursuant to s 41, they must comply with requirements of the federal Act. Only Western Australia entered into such an arrangement. Each of its judges also holds a commission on the Family Court of Australia and participates in the appeal work of that Court.

The *Family Law Act* initially conferred jurisdiction upon the Court in relation to maintenance, property, and custody of children which extended to parties to a marriage. In this respect its provisions relied upon the marriage power in s 51(xxi). For the most part they survived challenge subject to reading down the custody jurisdiction to cases involving disputes between parents, and the property jurisdiction to cases involving proceedings for principal relief.[86] The artificiality of constitutionally derived distinctions based upon the reservation to state legislatures of powers in relation to child custody, guardianship, access and maintenance was overcome by all states except Western Australia referring power over these issues to the Commonwealth.[87] The Family Court in Western Australia was always able to exercise both federal and state jurisdiction. Jurisdictional issues with respect to property disputes remain. There has been no referral of power on that matter.[88]

---

[86] *Russell v Russell* (1976) 134 CLR 495, 529 (Stephen J), 542 (Mason J). Jacobs J held all relevant provisions to be valid.

[87] Reference of power was recommended by the Joint Select Committee on the Family Law Act (1980) and effected by the following state legislation: *Commonwealth Powers (Family Law—Children) Act 1986* (NSW), (Vic); *Commonwealth Powers (Family Law—Children) Act 1990* (Qld); *Commonwealth Powers (Family Law) Act 1986* (SA) and *Commonwealth Powers (Family Law) Act 1987* (Tas).

[88] See generally Crawford (1993) 224–6.

Like the Federal Court, the Family Court has accrued jurisdiction over causes of action arising under state and federal law
attached to and not severable from the primary federal claim. Its
associated jurisdiction covers related federal claims and will attract
its own accrued jurisdiction as part of the associated matter. It has
been suggested that the accrued jurisdiction of the Family Court is
limited because of the character and limits of the Court's property
jurisdiction, especially in relation to third parties.[89] In one case the
Court was found to have no accrued jurisdiction to approve a maintenance agreement for the purposes of the *Family Provision Act
1982* (NSW).[90] But that did not define an inherent limit. The Constitutional Commission's Advisory Committee on the Australian
Judicial System reported that the doctrine of accrued jurisdiction
had not been helpful in solving the jurisdictional difficulties of the
Family Court although 'it may yet become so'. The Committee saw
no reason why the Family Court could not have accrued jurisdiction
in appropriate cases.[91] This was a curiously worded observation.
The accrued jurisdiction comes with the federal territory, notwithstanding that its exercise may be discretionary with respect to non-
federal claims. That is not to say, in the light of recent jurisprudence
on privative provisions in the *Migration Act 1958* (Cth), that the
accrued jurisdiction could not be expressly excluded by statute.[92]

In 1983 the *Family Law Act* was amended so that the jurisdiction of the Court was expressly conferred in terms of 'matters',
although whether such an amendment could make any substantive
difference to the scope of the Court's jurisdiction is questionable.[93]
Jurisdiction of federal courts under the Constitution is arguably to
be defined either in terms of 'matters' or nothing.

The Family Court has had perhaps the most difficult history of
any of Australia's federal courts. The *Family Law Act* has been 'with
the exception of the Income Tax Assessment Act . . . the most heavily

---

[89] Ibid 226–7.

[90] *Smith v Smith* (1986) 161 CLR 217.

[91] Australian Constitutional Commission Advisory Committee on the Australian
Judicial System (1987) 29.

[92] *Abebe v Commonwealth* (1999) 162 ALR 1.

[93] *Family Law Amendment Act 1983* (Cth) substituting a new s 31.

scrutinised, picked over and amended piece of legislation in Australian history'.[94] The Court has been the subject of intense social and political debate, in large part because of the nature of its jurisdiction and the law it must administer. One of its members, Judge David Opas, was shot dead at the front door of his home in 1980. In March 1984 a bomb was detonated on the front steps of the home of his replacement, Judge Richard Gee. The Parramatta Registry was bombed in April 1984, and the wife of the senior judge at that Registry was killed by a bomb left at the front door of their home in July 1984. There have been many threats directed to the Court from time to time.

In addition to violence and threats, there have been disparities between the salaries paid to Family Court and Federal Court judges, as well as suggestions that the former are of a lesser calibre than those appointed to the Federal or Supreme Courts. In 1985 the Chief Justice of the High Court, Sir Harry Gibbs, suggested that the creation of the Court as a separate court had made it difficult to maintain the highest standards of judicial appointment.[95] The Chief Judge of the Family Court responded that the High Court appeared to be unaware of the objectives of the legislation and had shown insensitivity to the needs of a fully developed family law. To this had been added 'the further sting of gratuitous insults'.[96] Her successor, however, called the establishment of a separate court 'a disastrous mistake' and said it should have been a division of the Federal Court.[97]

The 1987 Report of the Constitutional Commission's Advisory Committee on the Australian Judicial System referred to the 'isolation of Judges of the Family Court from the "mainstream" of the judiciary' and 'an undesirable lack of variety' in their work. In retrospect there was much to be said for vesting federal family law jurisdiction in state Family Courts based on the Western Australian model.[98] But that was unlikely to be accepted. There remained 'a

[94] Star (1996) 119–20.
[95] Gibbs (1985) 522.
[96] Evatt (1985) vi.
[97] Nicholson (1988) 20. See also Star (1996) 144 and Crawford (1993) 232.
[98] Australian Constitutional Commission Advisory Committee on the Australian Judicial System (1987) 48–9.

strongly held view that family law is of national concern and that it should be dealt with uniformly, both as to substance and procedure'.[99]

The *Family Law Act* was amended in 1988 to create the office of Judicial Registrar to exercise delegated powers in a wide range of the Court's work. The same amendment authorised the Federal Court to transfer proceedings within its own jurisdiction to the Family Court.[100] This was to implement the recommendation of the Constitutional Commission Advisory Committee 'that the jurisdiction of the Family Court be extended so as to broaden the work of the Family Court judges'. It was designed to give judges 'some relief from the burdens of the highly emotive family law jurisdiction'.[101]

The new Judicial Registrars and existing Registrars could exercise wide powers including the determination of certain contested applications and the making of interim orders. The validity of these delegations was challenged and upheld in *Harris v Caladine*.[102] But the High Court held that delegation of judicial power to officers of a Chapter III court must be consistent with control by the judges of the court's jurisdiction. Moreover, the decisions of such officers must be subject to review by a judge to be consistent with the obligation of the court to act judicially.[103] Importantly, the High Court recognised organisational flexibility for Chapter III courts: 'a court may be organized or structured in a wide variety of ways for the purpose of exercising its jurisdiction'.[104]

The salaries of Family Court judges were fixed at the same level as those of judges of the Federal Court in 1989.[105] Previously there

---

[99] Ibid 49.

[100] *Family Court of Australia (Additional Jurisdiction and Exercise of Powers) Act 1988* (Cth).

[101] *Commonwealth Parliamentary Debates*, House of Representatives, 28 October 1987, 1613–14 (Lionel Bowen QC, Attorney-General).

[102] (1991) 172 CLR 84.

[103] Ibid 95 (Mason CJ and Deane J), 121–2 (Dawson J), 151–2 (Gaudron J), and 164 (McHugh J). The judgment involved argument by analogy from the decision in *Commonwealth v Hospital Contribution Fund* (1982) 150 CLR 49 that state courts could exercise invested federal jurisdiction through a non-judicial officer of the court, overruling *Kotsis v Kotsis* (1970) 122 CLR 69 and *Knight v Knight* (1971) 122 CLR 114.

[104] *Harris v Caladine* (1991) 172 CLR 84, 91.

[105] *Judicial and Statutory Officers Remuneration Legislation Amendment Act 1989* (Cth).

was pressure from elements in the Attorney-General's Department, the legal profession and the Family Court for its restructuring as a division of the Federal Court. That pressure subsequently diminished. The additional jurisdiction has been little exercised.

In 1990 the Chief Justices of both the Family Court and the Federal Court were given statutory responsibility for the administrative management of their Courts. With self-administration came increased scrutiny and criticism of the management and structure of the Family Court. In 1991 a Joint Select Committee was established by the Commonwealth Parliament to undertake a comprehensive review of the *Family Law Act*. It expressed scepticism in its report about complaints by the Court that it had never been adequately funded in respect of its statutory responsibilities.[106] It decided to conduct an administrative review of the Court, presumably as an extension of its general review of the Act. That review was not completed but was re-established by a new committee in May 1993. It also covered a proposal by the Chief Justice of the Court for the establishment of a two-tier structure of judges and magistrates instead of judges, judicial registrars and registrars. A similar proposal was advanced by the Family Law Council in July 1995.[107]

When the Committee reported in November 1995, it expressed concern at aspects of the Court's administration, including its forward financial planning and implementation of new programs without identification of sufficient funding to support them.[108] It proposed a significant change in the governance of the Court, vesting its administrative control in 'a collegiate system determined by the judicial officers of the Court and expressed in the Rules of Court'.[109] That system has not been implemented.

The Committee rejected as not viable a two-tier structure of judges and federal magistrates. It proposed instead a two-tier structure of judiciary and registrars with existing judicial registrars appointed under Chapter III as part of the judiciary. It also recommended that, in the longer term, consideration be given to the Fam-

---

[106] Joint Select Committee on Certain Aspects of the Operation and Interpretation of the Family Law Act (1992) 24–5.

[107] Family Law Council (1995).

[108] Joint Select Committee on Certain Family Law Issues (1995) 34.

[109] Ibid 109.

ily Court becoming a division of the Federal Court of Australia and that the establishment of a federal magistracy be considered at that time.[110]

The merger proposal was based on a paper by the Chief Justice of the Family Court which canvassed the following benefits: cessation of judicial apartheid of Family Court judges; rationalisation of judicial skills and resources in both Courts; avoidance of the duplication of facilities in Commonwealth court buildings; cross-flow of knowledge and expertise between members of the two Courts; freedom of judges from confinement to specialist jurisdictions; and an enhanced attractiveness of the Court to potential recruits.[111]

The question of a federal magistracy was considered in a joint report of the Australian Law Reform Commission and the Human Rights and Equal Opportunity Commission published in May 1997.[112] It was one option for resolving state and federal jurisdictional difficulties in relation to the care and protection of children. These included extending cross-vesting arrangements, a full referral of power to the Commonwealth, a limited transfer of power to the Commonwealth, a single national Court of Appeal for care and protection matters, specialist state and territorial magistrates, and a specialist Family Court magistracy.[113]

In December 1998 the Attorney-General announced approval in principle by Cabinet for the creation of a federal magistracy to be appointed under Chapter III of the Constitution to relieve burdens upon both the Family and Federal Courts. The magistracy would exercise both family law and other federal jurisdiction. Proposals by the Chief Justice of the Family Court that family law magistrates be appointed into the Family Court were not accepted. The magistrates to be appointed will do what their Federal Court and Family Court colleagues cannot do, namely exercise jurisdiction freely in areas covered by both Courts. The Act creating the Federal Magistrates Court—the *Federal Magistrates Act 1999* (Cth)—came into operation on 23 December 1999.

---

[110] Ibid 71, 72.
[111] Ibid 65–6.
[112] Australian Law Reform Commission (1997b).
[113] Ibid 368–84.

5 The Federal Court of Australia

In February 1963 the Solicitor-General for the Commonwealth, Sir
Kenneth Bailey, informed the Thirteenth Legal Convention of the
Law Council of Australia that the Attorney-General, Sir Garfield
Barwick QC, had been authorised by Cabinet to 'design a new federal Court with a view to consideration by Cabinet for approval for
legislative action'.[114] Its purpose was to ease the burden on the High
Court. The Solicitor-General was responding to a paper presented at
the Convention by M. H. Byers QC and P. B. Toose QC,[115] proposing
a more substantial change for a wider purpose and rested on what
might still be seen as some bold assumptions.

The first of these assumptions was that the original understanding of the federal bargain contemplated the eventual creation
of a complete structure of federal courts.[116] The second was that
there was no longer among members of the public the strong state
sentiment which had existed at the time of federation and supported
the use of state courts for the exercise of federal jurisdiction.[117] It
was proposed that the original jurisdiction of the Court consist of all
matters in respect of which original jurisdiction is given to the High
Court under s 75, all matters in respect of which original jurisdiction had been conferred on the High Court under s 76, and all
matters in respect of which the courts of the states (other than
Courts of Petty Sessions) had been invested with federal jurisdiction.
The jurisdiction of the Federal Court of Bankruptcy and the Commonwealth Industrial Court and of the territorial courts would all
be conferred on the new federal court. The conferring of Supreme
Court federal jurisdiction would also mean that the proposed federal
court would exercise original jurisdiction in matrimonial causes.

Criticism came immediately. F. T. P. Burt QC, a leading silk and
later Chief Justice of Western Australia, predicted that the 'two

---

[114] Byers and Toose (1963) 325.

[115] Ibid.

[116] For a rebuttal, see *Commonwealth Parliamentary Debates*, House of Representatives, 24 July 1974, 598 (R. J. Ellicott QC), and Rogers (1980) 632–3. The rebuttal goes too far in suggesting that the founding fathers saw the creation of federal
courts as unnecessary except in the last resort; see *Stack v Coast Securities (No 9) Pty
Ltd* (1983) 154 CLR 261, 293 discussed earlier.

[117] Byers and Toose (1963) 313.

channel system' would breed 'complexity—and black motor cars', seriously reducing the status of state Supreme Courts and accentuating an imbalance in the Australian judicial system under which too much inferior work was being done by superior courts.[118] Support for the proposal came from Gough Whitlam QC, then Deputy Leader of the Opposition, who argued that on principle federal judges should interpret and apply federal laws.

Garfield Barwick responded in an article published soon after his appointment as Chief Justice of the High Court.[119] His objective was to free the High Court for the discharge of its fundamental duties as interpreter of the Constitution and as the national court of appeal. The investiture of state courts with federal jurisdiction was a potentially permanent and desirable feature of the Australian judicial system.[120] The jurisdiction of the federal court would as a rule be limited to 'special' matters. Bankruptcy and industrial law were obvious examples, federal courts having been created to exercise those jurisdictions. Beyond these historical examples no coherent policy for selection of federal court jurisdiction was disclosed.

In May 1967 the then Attorney-General, Nigel Bowen QC, made a ministerial statement about the proposed Commonwealth Superior Court. He eschewed as uneconomic the provision of an entire system of federal courts. The government had decided that 'a relatively small new Federal court of quality and standing be established'.[121] Its initial jurisdiction was to be part of the original jurisdiction of the High Court. Wider jurisdiction could be conferred if experience demonstrated that it were desirable. The Commonwealth Superior Court Bill was introduced into the House of Representatives in November 1968. The Court was to incorporate both the Commonwealth Industrial Court and the Federal Bankruptcy Court. Its jurisdiction was more extensive than that described in the ministerial statement of May 1967.[122]

---

[118] Ibid 323–4.

[119] Barwick (1964).

[120] Ibid 2.

[121] *Commonwealth Parliamentary Debates*, House of Representatives, 18 May 1967, 2337.

[122] Ibid 21 November 1968, 3142–6.

The second reading speech was adjourned and the Bill allowed
to lapse. There was opposition to it.[123] In 1972 the Attorney-
General, Senator Ivor Greenwood, announced that the project was
being abandoned.[124] The government had decided to invest state
Supreme Courts and the Supreme Courts of mainland territories
with original jurisdiction in certain additional matters in respect of
which the High Court was exercising original jurisdiction. The project was reactivated by the Whitlam government. In December 1973
the new Attorney-General, Senator Lionel Murphy, introduced a
second Superior Court of Australia Bill. A federal court for federal
law seemed to be a theme of the second reading speech: 'It is proper
that the Australian Government should be able to be sued and to sue
in its own courts'.[125]

Judicial review of administrative action was foreshadowed as
a 'very significant part of the jurisdiction of the new court'.[126] This
was linked to proposals to establish an Administrative Appeals
Tribunal and to simplify and extend procedures for judicial review
of administrative decisions. It was also a concern of the Attorney-
General that the administration of federal law in state courts excluded the Parliament in practice from considering reforms in the
important area of practice and procedure.

The Bill was defeated in the Senate. Following the government's
dismissal by the Governor-General in 1975 and the election of
the Liberal–Country Party Coalition, the Federal Court of Australia
Bill was introduced in October 1976. The then Attorney-General,
R. J. Ellicott QC, criticised the previous proposal on the basis that it
'would have removed from State courts the bulk of the federal jurisdiction exercised by those courts and greatly weakened the status of
those courts and the quality of the work dealt with by them'.[127]

---

[123] See P. H. Lane (1969); Sawer (1965); Bowen (1967) 344 (commentary of Windeyer);
and see also Else-Mitchell (1969).

[124] *Commonwealth Parliamentary Debates*, Senate, 27 October 1972, 2086–8.

[125] Ibid 12 December 1973, 2725.

[126] Ibid 2725.

[127] *Commonwealth Parliamentary Debates*, House of Representatives, 21 October 1976,
2110.

The rationale then advanced for a Federal Court was twofold, namely, to put the existing federal court system on a more rational basis and to relieve the High Court of some of the workload it bore in matters of federal and territory law. The government believed that only where there were 'special policy or perhaps historical reasons for doing so should original federal jurisdiction be vested in a federal court'. Industrial law, bankruptcy, trade practices, and judicial review of administrative decisions answered these criteria. Moreover, the Court would act as an appellate court from state courts exercising federal jurisdiction 'in matters of special federal concern such as taxation, bankruptcy, industrial property and trade practices'.[128] The Bill was passed and the Federal Court of Australia began operating on 1 February 1977. The creation of the Court was not without continuing criticism. In 1981 the Chief Justice of the High Court, Sir Harry Gibbs, found it 'difficult to discover any valid reason in principle, or any practical necessity, for bringing into existence the new Federal Court and conferring upon it its present jurisdiction'.[129]

The *Federal Court of Australia Act 1976* (Cth) defines the jurisdiction of the Court in ambulatory terms—'the Court has such original jurisdiction as is vested in it by laws made by the Parliament'.[130] Initially, the principal components of its original jurisdiction were those transferred from the Federal Bankruptcy Court and the Australian Industrial Court. The latter had acquired some non-industrial jurisdiction which had been intended for the proposed Superior Court of Australia (discussed earlier). So the Court's initial original jurisdiction covered bankruptcy, industrial law, trade practices, appeals from the Administrative Appeals Tribunal, and compensation for Commonwealth government employees. By s 39B of the *Judiciary Act*, enacted in 1983, it was given jurisdiction over the

---

[128] Ibid 2111.

[129] Gibbs (1981) 677. See also Street (1978); Rogers (1980); Burt (1982).

[130] Section 19 in its original form limited that jurisdiction to 'matters arising under laws made by the Parliament'. The *Statute Law (Miscellaneous Provisions) Act 1983* (Cth) brought it to its present form to overcome remitter arguments advanced in *O'Reilly; Ex parte Bayford Wholesale Pty Ltd* (1983) 151 CLR 557. Section 39B of the *Judiciary Act 1903* (Cth) was enacted at the same time.

grant of prerogative and injunctive relief against officers of the Commonwealth essentially in the same terms that such jurisdiction was conferred on the High Court by s 75(v) of the Constitution. It did not extend in the case of the Federal Court to the grant of relief against judges of the Family Court or holders of office under the *Conciliation and Arbitration Act 1904* (Cth) or the *Coal Industry Act 1987* (Cth). A further important jurisdiction in judicial review was conferred by the *Administrative Decisions (Judicial Review) Act 1977* (Cth) (*ADJR Act*).

The administrative law jurisdiction gave the Court an important role in the construction of a wide range of Commonwealth statutes and supervision of the process of administrative decision-making under those statutes. The *ADJR Act* provided powerful tools for review of executive action untrammelled by the technicalities of prerogative remedies which were still at that time the principal vehicles of judicial review under state laws. In a way that neither the bankruptcy nor industrial jurisdictions could, its administrative law jurisdiction gave the Court a foundation for developing a stature and authority not ordinarily achievable by small specialist courts.

The jurisdiction conferred by the *Trade Practices Act* also played a large part in moving the Court away from the conception of a specialist tribunal concerned with a relatively narrow band of federal statutes. Through the provisions of Part V and, in particular, the prohibition in s 52 against misleading or deceptive conduct by corporations, the Court became involved in mainstream commercial litigation.[131] Its accrued jurisdiction enabled the Court in dealing with issues under Part V of the Act to deal with non-federal claims as part of the controversy in which the federal claim was embedded. There were jurisdictional debates in some of the cases but the development by the High Court of a 'practical judgment' test for the scope of the accrued jurisdiction meant that related non-federal claims in the Federal Court were not often defeated for want of jurisdiction. The cause of action for misleading or deceptive conduct was at the heart of the case in which the High Court authoritatively

---

[131] Pengilley (1987); French (1989b); French (1989a); French (1996).

defined the scope of the accrued jurisdiction.[132] The Court's exclusive jurisdiction under the anti-trust provisions of Part IV of the *Trade Practices Act* gave it a central role in the development of competition law in Australia. The number of cases decided under those provisions is considerably fewer than under Part V of the Act[133] but their significance and complexity has attracted considerable professional and academic interest and a sense of intellectual hierarchy.[134]

The Court's jurisdiction in matters arising under the *Trade Practices Act* was originally exclusive (s 86). This gave rise to possible difficulties between federal and state courts particularly in relation to the exercise of the accrued jurisdiction in common law claims. It was resolved in part by the High Court's determination that the accrued jurisdiction under the *Trade Practices Act* in relation to non-federal claims was non-exclusive and discretionary.[135] In the event, in 1987, the courts of the states were invested with federal jurisdiction under s 86(2) of the *Trade Practices Act* (not including Part IV). Section 86A gave the Federal Court authority to transfer proceedings under the Act to appropriate state courts. This foreshadowed a comprehensive cross-vesting scheme introduced the following year.

The jurisdiction of the Court expanded considerably in the two decades following its establishment. In 1987 it acquired exclusive jurisdiction in taxation and original civil jurisdiction under intellectual and industrial property laws. Appellate jurisdiction in these areas is exclusive. From 1 July 1988 it had direct jurisdiction conferred under state law pursuant to the cross-vesting scheme although this was later found to be invalid.[136] In January 1989 it was invested with civil admiralty jurisdiction to be exercised concurrently with state and territory Supreme Courts.[137] Its jurisdiction was further extended in 1991 to cover civil proceedings arising

---

[132] *Fencott v Muller* (1983) 152 CLR 570.

[133] The jurisdiction in relation to misleading or deceptive conduct is sometimes disparagingly known as the Federal Court's 'running down jurisdiction'.

[134] A leading Victorian barrister, now a member of the Court of Appeal in that state, remarked at a legal conference that when discussion turned to Part V the 'real lawyers' went out and played tennis.

[135] *Stack v Coast Securities (No 9) Pty Ltd* (1983) 154 CLR 261.

[136] *Re Wakim; Ex parte McNally* (1999) 163 ALR 270.

[137] *Admiralty Act 1988* (Cth).

under the Corporations Law, although this was in part dependent upon what was found to be the invalid vesting of jurisdiction under state laws (see Chapter 10). In January 1994 the Court acquired a new major and resource intensive jurisdiction under the *Native Title Act 1993* (Cth).

In April 1997 the enactment of s 39B(1A) of the *Judiciary Act* conferred on the Court jurisdiction in any matter: in which the Commonwealth is seeking an injunction or declaration; arising under the Constitution or involving its interpretation; and arising under any laws made by the Parliament. The Court does not have jurisdiction to hear and determine offences against federal laws although it may hear and determine prosecutions for the imposition of pecuniary penalties under the provisions of the *Trade Practices Act*. In 1998 the sources of the Court's jurisdiction were to be found in 125 federal statutes.

It has been said that the growth of Federal Court jurisdiction has adversely affected the status of state Supreme Courts. The Constitutional Commission's Advisory Committee on the Australian Judicial System in its 1987 report said:

> On each occasion when the Commonwealth vests jurisdiction in a federal court there is a corresponding decline in the role of the courts of the States and, if the areas of jurisdiction of the Federal Courts continue to expand, the courts (particularly the Supreme Courts) of the States will become more and more restricted in the scope of their jurisdiction.[138]

The Committee's view was that the trend was in favour of expanding the jurisdiction of federal courts and although the pace of that change might alter or be reversed from time to time, the probability was that overall it would continue if nothing further were done.

The growth in jurisdiction of the Court has been paralleled by a growth in its numbers from an initial twenty to fifty judges in 1998. Five former members of the Court—Justices Brennan, Deane, Toohey, Gummow and Kirby—have been appointed to the High

---

[138] Australian Constitutional Commission Advisory Committee on the Australian Judicial System (1987) 28.

Court. The early standing of the Court was enhanced by a number of its appointees, particularly the Chief Judge (later designated Chief Justice), Sir Nigel Bowen, who had served as Commonwealth Attorney-General and Minister for External Affairs as well as Chief Judge in Equity in the Supreme Court of New South Wales. He served as Chief Justice until 1990. Although the Federal Court was a national court from the outset, there was in the first fifteen years of its existence an imbalance between its standing in Sydney and Melbourne. Contributing to this imbalance was the fact that the principal registry of the Court was located in Sydney, as was the residence of the Chief Justice. The imbalance has been redressed by a significant number of new appointments, including a Chief Justice, resident in Melbourne.

Being able to construct its practices and procedures afresh, the Federal Court has established a distinctively modern judicial culture. Its rules provide for a single form of application to initiate most of the proceedings in which it has jurisdiction. Important in terms of its interface with the profession and litigants is the use of judicial case management so that judges are involved in pre-trial and interlocutory steps through the use of mandatory directions hearings from the time proceedings are initiated. That process has evolved into a 'docket' system in which one judge is allocated to take responsibility for the pre-trial management, and often the hearing, of a list of actions. The benefits gleaned from the expedited and commercial lists of the state courts have been generally available in the Federal Court for most of its existence. Following the High Court, the Federal Court abolished the wearing of wigs by its judges and recently announced that counsel appearing before it were no longer required to wear wigs.

The Court has at times been described as aggressive in the exercise of its jurisdiction and, more recently, in the way it discharges its judicial review function. This is particularly so in the area of judicial review of immigration decisions where judges of the Court have been accused of entering upon merits review rather than confining themselves to the issues of lawfulness, rationality and fairness reflected in the various grounds of review under the *ADJR Act* and now the *Migration Act 1958* (Cth). In 1996 the Chief General Counsel for the Attorney-General's Department referred to:

the aggressive and activist work, principally of the Federal Court, in curbing the excesses of the executive as they see it, by resort to reliance on the protection of individual rights, by the expansion of procedural safeguards, and by interference at the preliminary or investigative stage of the administrative process. The outcome has been to turn judicial review into a merits review exercise, to find a means, if at all possible, to overturn decisions that a judge does not like.[139]

Steps have been taken to limit the jurisdiction of the Court in the judicial review of decisions under the *Migration Act*.[140]

The history of the Court indicates a continuing trend from its initial conception as a specialist body dealing with a narrow band of federal statutes to one which is effectively a court of general jurisdiction. The trend will ebb and flow but it is notable that Professor James Crawford's 1993 prediction of the enactment of s 39B(1A) of the *Judiciary Act* has been realised, which change, he said, would complete the conversion of the Court 'into a superior court of general jurisdiction in Australia'.[141]

It is perhaps a measure of the strength of this trend that the Court has been perceived by particular interest groups as insufficiently specialised for specific areas of its jurisdiction. In 1991 and 1992 submissions were made to the federal government's Industrial Property Advisory Committee for the establishment of a specialist intellectual property court or a specialist division of the Federal Court for that purpose. The submission was rejected.[142] The Committee noted that the establishment of the United States Court of Appeals as a specialised court to hear patent appeals had led to improvement in consistency, certainty, conceptual integration and the industrial and commercial relevance of patent law. Nevertheless, it concluded that 'significantly, the criticism is made that with its narrowly specialized jurisdiction, the Court has failed to articulate a

---

[139] Burmester (1996) 387.
[140] *Migration Act 1958* (Cth) Part 8, especially ss 476 (2) and (3) and s 485, found to be valid in *Abebe v Commonwealth* (1999) 162 ALR 1. Further restrictions have been proposed in the Migration Legislation Amendment Bill (No 2) 2000 (Cth).
[141] Crawford (1993) 168.
[142] Industrial Property Advisory Committee (1992).

role in integrating patent and competition law'.[143] The Committee recommended that the allocation of appeal work to the Federal Court in intellectual property matters should not be disturbed.

Other proposals for judicial specialisation were put to the Hilmer Committee in its inquiry into a National Competition Policy, some of which suggested that there was dissatisfaction with Federal Court procedures for utilising economic material in judgments about economic facts. The establishment of a specialist division of the Federal Court was suggested. While the Committee considered that proposals for refinement of court processes were worthy of further consideration, it rejected proposals to create a specialist division or refer economic issues to the Trade Practices Tribunal.[144]

Proposals for specialisation have been made from time to time including the establishment of a specialist human rights court and a native title division. The quest for specialisation in relation to human rights matters was sparked by the decision of the High Court in *Brandy v Human Rights and Equal Opportunity Commission*.[145] That decision found invalid a legislative scheme under which administrative determinations of the Human Rights and Equal Opportunity Commission could be registered as judgments of the Federal Court subject to review in that Court.

An important question relating to judicial power has arisen through judges of the Court accepting appointments to non-judicial offices, such as the presidency or membership of administrative tribunals. In addition, judges have been asked to carry out administrative functions such as the issue of telephonic interception warrants, and the conduct of Royal Commissions and other statutory inquiries. There is a well-established principle that a judge of a Chapter III court can be appointed to a non-judicial body or office provided the appointment is in a personal capacity and with his or her consent.[146] But the nature of the office must not be incompatible with the

---

143 Ibid 62.
144 Independent Committee of Inquiry (1993) 172, 178–9.
145 (1995) 183 CLR 245.
146 *Drake v Minister for Immigration and Ethnic Affairs* (1979) 24 ALR 577.

discharge of the judicial function.[147] This doctrine, which is still developing, defines no clear boundary between what is compatible with the judicial function and what is not. It does suggest, however, that in future non-judicial appointments of federal judges will be somewhat constrained.

6 The Future

The history of statutory federal courts outlined in this chapter is not one of smooth progression to a comprehensive federal judicature. There have been and will be advances and retreats from the use of federal courts and the emphasis on specialist as distinct from generalist judges.

The creation of a federal magistracy exercising jurisdiction in both family law matters and other matters at the lower end of the Federal Court's jurisdiction is significant. The proposal for the magistracy was approved in principle by federal Cabinet in December 1998. Its stated rationale is to 'free up judges in the federal courts and allow them to focus more on complex matters requiring their attention'.[148] In relation to this proposal, the Attorney-General made the point that the 'magistrates would be appointed under Chapter III of the Constitution which means that they will be able to make final decisions, unlike judicial registrars'. There is an expectation by government that 'with a less formal judicial culture and more streamlined procedures than those of the existing federal courts a magistracy would ... reduce costs of litigants'.[149] This language suggests that the policy objective of establishing a federal magistracy is to reduce delays in the Family Court, although it is aimed at addressing the problem of judicial resources in both the Federal and Family Courts being tied up with less complex work.[150] The *Federal*

---

[147] *Wilson v Minister for Aboriginal and Torres Strait Islander Affairs* (1996) 189 CLR 1. Compare *Mistretta v United States*, 488 US 361 (1989) and *Morrison v Olson*, 487 US 654 (1988).

[148] Commonwealth Attorney-General, 'Federal Magistracy to be Established', News Release, 8 December 1998.

[149] Ibid 2.

[150] Ibid 4.

Magistrates Act 1999 (Cth) was passed and assented to on 23 December 1999 and came into operation on that date. The Act creates a self-administering court with its own head of jurisdiction although it will be provided with administrative support for the time being by the Federal and Family Courts. Although the new court will exercise the disparate jurisdiction of those two courts it will not have a divisional structure. The legislation has not been without its detractors. The Chief Justice of the Family Court has aired publicly his view that federal magistrates exercising jurisdiction in family law should be part of the Family Court. The Attorneys-General of Victoria, New South Wales and Queensland called for the relevant jurisdiction to be invested in state magistrates.[151] Editorial commentary in one newspaper made the point that with the potential collapse of the cross-vesting system the Attorney-General and the states 'may have to look at a fundamental restructuring of the whole court system'.[152] Given the outcome of the challenge to the cross-vesting scheme, the advent of a federal magistracy exercising a unified federal jurisdiction in Federal and Family Court matters may, in some minds, raise for consideration a more far-reaching rationalisation of federal jurisdiction in Australia.

The possibility of a National Court of Appeal in relation to federal jurisdiction remains open. If the three-tier state systems of Supreme, District or County and Magistrates Courts evolve into two tiers for trial work with Courts of Appeal in each state, the case for a National Court of Appeal incorporating state Appeal Courts may also be strengthened.

There are various permutations of and alternatives to these scenarios. It can be predicted with reasonable confidence, however, that Australia is firmly on the path to the development of an enduring national judicial system, whatever its ultimate shape. The Federal Court and the Family Court, individually or together, will continue to be its major components for the foreseeable future.

---

[151] 'Federal Court Plan Under New Attack', *Australian*, 18 January 1999, 5; Attorney-General (Queensland), 'Williams Plan for Federal Magistracy a Waste: Foley', Press Release, 9 December 1998.

[152] 'Magistrate to Join Federal Court System', *Courier Mail*, 11 December 1998, 22.

6

Managing Litigation in the Federal Court

Bryan Beaumont

*A court is a collegial system—unwieldy, hard to
direct, impossible to command.*[1]

1 Introduction

The causes of popular dissatisfaction with the administration of
justice in America identified by Roscoe Pound in his famous address
to the American Bar Association in 1906 included American exag-
gerations of the common law's 'contentious procedure'. Pound had
in mind Wigmore's 'sporting' theory of justice—the instinct of giving
the game fair play, where the judge should be a mere umpire, to
rule upon objections and hold counsel to the rules of the game, in
order that the parties might fight out their own game without judicial
interference. It led counsel, Pound complained, to forget that they
were officers of the court, and turned witnesses, especially experts,
into 'partisans pure and simple'. Yet, although the sporting theory
was so rooted in the American profession that most Americans took
it for a fundamental legal tenet, it was probably only a survival of
the days when a lawsuit was 'a fight between two clans in which
change of venue had been taken to the forum'. Pound pointed out
that the theory, far from being fundamental to jurisprudence, was
peculiar to Anglo-American law. But, significantly for our purposes,

---

[1] Wald (1983) 784.

he noted that the theory had been 'strongly curbed in modern English practice'.[2]

Pound did not describe modern English practice.[3] No doubt he had in mind the principle, consistently applied in England, Australia and New Zealand, that in the discharge of its duty to adjudicate disputes by administering justice in accordance with law, the court has the power, which must be fairly exercised, to control or manage the proceedings. The existence of this power has never been questioned in Anglo-Australasian jurisprudence,[4] and is central to an understanding of the ways in which the Federal Court copes with its growing, complex, and frequently novel caseload.

This chapter, in describing the principles that have been developed and the management skills that need to be applied by the Federal Court in the conduct of its business, will first consider the rationale of the concept of managerial judging. There will follow a description of the techniques and the technology employed by a national trial and appellate court across the broad spectrum of its (mainly civil) jurisdiction in order to control all aspects of the litigation, including its pace, in a way that is fair to both sides, at least relatively inexpensive, and efficient in the application of the parties' time and resources. Finally, some topical issues in judicial administration and possible future directions will be identified.

Given the dynamics of the litigious process, we must accept that there are limits to what can be achieved by scholarship in this area.[5] For 'it is only in watching business being conducted and in that alone, not through books, that the practice of the law and the

---

[2] Pound (1913) 7–8.

[3] Now itself reformed by Lord Woolf: (1996b). An Interim Report issued in 1995 was the subject of considerable discussion. See, for example, Zuckerman and Cranston (1995). In July 1996 Draft Civil Proceedings Rules (Lord Woolf 1996a) were issued to implement the judicial case management principles in the Final Report. See also Flanders (1998) 318. Pound's message was received in the United States: Wright has described the contemporary American federal judge as 'a puissant figure': see Wright (1994) 693.

[4] *R v Prosser* (1848) 50 ER 834, 837–8; Mathew (1902) 20; *Ashmore v Corporation of Lloyd's* [1992] 1 WLR 446, 448, 454; *Barton v The Queen* (1980) 147 CLR 75, 96; *Landsal Pty Ltd v Rei Building Society* (1993) 113 ALR 643, 649; Dockray (1997).

[5] Posner (1996) 69; Murphy (1998).

meaning of the law can be learned'.[6] This is not to deny the considerable benefits that can accrue from sound empirical studies, notably Martineau's recent illuminating analysis of the work of the English Court of Appeal.[7] On the contrary, there is an urgent need for an Australian work of this quality.

2 Managerial Judging—the Rationale

The Federal Court's power to control the parties' conduct of their litigation at trial level has been explained in this way:

> The Court always remains in overall control of the proceedings before it. Judges have power, until the hearing is concluded, to make, and to continue to make, such directions as seem to them best suited properly and adequately to manage and direct the cases in their lists. Obviously they will always pay due attention to what the parties themselves suggest and will usually accept consent timetables for procedural steps at their face value. But if an investigation of a matter at a directions hearing reveals that existing directions, whether made by consent or not, are not adequate for, or are not suited to, the needs of the case, the court has a duty to substitute appropriate directions for the existing ones, if necessary, against the will of the parties themselves.
>
> In complex cases it is usual for courts to hold extensive directions hearings with a view to finding out what the real issues are, what the extent of the evidence will be, what steps may usefully be taken to confine or compress evidence and how long the case will occupy the court's time. Holding directions hearings of this kind is not only of benefit to the parties themselves; it enables the court to administer its list in the best way.[8]

Thus, the court's responsibility to control proceedings in individual cases should also be viewed in the wider context of the court's inherent power to regulate its business overall.[9] This confers a broad

---

[6] Sullivan (1928) 368.

[7] Martineau (1990).

[8] *E I Du Pont de Nemours & Co v Commissioner of Patents* (1987) 16 FCR 423, 424 (Sheppard J). See also Bowen (1985) 197; Mathew (1902) 17.

[9] *Federal Court of Australia Act 1976* (Cth) s 15(1).

discretion, to be exercised so as to ensure that all cases may be heard in the order that justice and convenience require.[10] In practice, the court has accepted, from its establishment under Chief Justice Bowen in 1977, that there is no laissez-faire option: the size and complexity of litigation brought to the court for resolution is such that a fair, but firm, control of every stage of proceedings in each matter is essential if litigation is to be properly dealt with.

In the exercise of these powers, the Federal Court now regulates its business, mostly complicated litigation, by the case management method known in America as the individual assignment or docket system.[11] Under the docket method, cases are allocated to the docket of a particular judge as soon as they are commenced. Cases in certain areas (admiralty, human rights, industrial and intellectual property, taxation, restrictive trade practices, native title) are allocated to a judge who is a member of a panel in those special areas. Each case that is placed in the docket of a particular judge ordinarily stays with that judge from commencement until disposition. The judge's associate is the parties' sole point of contact. The docket judge is responsible for setting down all pre-trial hearings and, where applicable, for scheduling and hearing the trial of the matter. If any urgent matter arises which the docket judge is unable to deal with immediately, it is referred to the duty judge for that day. The number of pre-trial hearings is minimised, so as to maximise the benefits of each such hearing. Cases are actively managed from commencement to disposition; compliance with directions is monitored. At appropriate pre-trial stages, status or evaluation conferences are held. Shortly before the trial, a settlement conference may be arranged at which prospects of settlement can be explored. It is expected that final disposition of most cases should be achieved within eighteen months of commencement of proceedings.

The individual assignment system was introduced with the expectation that there would be several benefits: savings in time and

---

[10] *Bristol City Council v Lovell* [1998] 1 WLR 446, 454; *Bomanite Pty Limited v Slatex Corp Aust Pty Ltd* (1991) 32 FCR 379, 392 (French J).

[11] Schwarzer (1996) 143. However, the Australian Federal Court has always sought to maintain continuity of judicial involvement.

cost resulting from the docket judge's familiarity with the case, eliminating the need to explain the case afresh each time it came before the court, resulting in fewer formal pre-trial hearings; general efficiencies arising from more active case management; consistency of approach throughout the progress of each case; earlier focus by the parties on the real issues; better identification of cases suitable for mediation; greater efficiency and flexibility in setting dates for interlocutory applications, short hearings, and the trials themselves (particularly in cases where some urgency is involved); and a more efficient and cost-effective final disposition of the case.

The introduction of the individual assignment should not be viewed as radical reform. The court has always had a policy of continuity of judicial responsibility for a particular matter where practicable from its commencement to final judgment. Originally, a centralised 'master calendar' system was used, which also aimed to achieve continuity of management both prior to, and at the trial itself.[12] Reforms and refinements in procedures (such as the introduction of the single docket system) have originated periodically from recommendations by standing committees of judges in areas of practice and procedure, assisted by input from periodic strategic issues workshops in the court and advice from consultants. The court's practices, procedures and rules are continuously monitored, reviewed and revised in the light of changing conditions in order to introduce procedures for reducing the complexity of litigation and expediting its flow, and to devise strategies for creating additional capacity within the court. Adjectival law, as much as substantive law, must be stable; yet it cannot stand still.[13] And, where appropriate, account is taken of relevant developments in comparative jurisdictions.[14]

The operation of the single docket system is being evaluated by the Civil Justice Research Centre. Moreover, all the work of the court, its practices and procedures, its whole philosophy, and perhaps even its very raison d'être, are being scrutinised by the Australian Law Reform Commission as part of its wide-ranging review

---

[12] On the benefits of the continuity principle, see I. R. Scott (1995).

[13] Pound (1923) 1.

[14] See, for example, Cairns (1997); Law Council of Australia (1997).

of the advantages and disadvantages of the 'adversarial' system in federal courts. Initial signals from the Commission suggested that it might recommend that the court discard the common law method and adopt one of the continental 'inquisitorial' systems.[15] This now seems unlikely. For one thing, any legislation for an inquisitorial system in the federal judicial process might be unconstitutional unless basic procedural fairness is preserved.[16] For another, continental civil jurisdictions are not inquisitorial. In France, a plaintiff must still prove its case. Moreover, the court is confined to determining the case presented.[17] Emphasis on the dossier on the continent, and consequent loss of the benefits of the Socratic method, make it more difficult to provide individualised justice in complex cases.[18] This is not to say that we should ignore other systems—they can provide a mirror in which the strengths, and the weaknesses, of our procedures can be viewed and better understood.[19]

While the existence of the court's power to control the conduct of proceedings, both before and during the trial, and the existence of the judge's duty to do so fairly[20] are clearly established, contentious questions can occasionally arise as to the appropriate exercise of control in particular situations. The court must then weigh the relevant competing considerations, discarding a rigid or mechanical approach. In complex litigation, this discretionary evaluation process can be finely balanced and difficult to adjudge, especially where each side can claim significant potential prejudice if a suggested course is or is not followed. Occasionally, when the competing considerations

---

[15] In a review of the resources of the court an 'interventionist' rather than 'inquisitorial' method was preferred: Review of the Federal Court (1990) 38.

[16] Sir Anthony Mason (1996) 7; Mahoney (1996).

[17] New Code of Civil Procedure, Articles 5 and 9; Larivière (1996); Markesinis (1995) 268–9; Lasser (1995). German judges may be more active in civil proceedings: Baur (1976).

[18] McKillop (1997).

[19] Capra (1988) 174–5; Downes (1999); Abrahams, 'Review of "The Cartel" by E. Whitton', *Age*, 16 May 1998.

[20] 'Fairness' here includes not only the fair exercise of a discretion, but also the fundamental tenet of natural justice that a party has fair opportunity to present its case. Compare *Esso Australia Resources Ltd v Federal Commissioner of Taxation* (1997) 150 ALR 117, 125 (Foster J).

appear to be more or less evenly balanced, it may be appropriate for the court, in the interests of securing justice for all of its litigants, to have regard to the general state of its list and the condition and timely disposition of other cases.[21] Without 'rationing' justice,[22] certainty in listing arrangements for a trial date should be insisted upon, and faithfully adhered to, except for special reasons. An amendment may be allowed, and a consequential adjournment granted, by reason of a significant supervening event; but the nature of the possible final outcome of the whole proceedings, including (but not limited to) the amount of a potential verdict, should not be overlooked, and the distortion of the general list, and the elimination of a culture of certainty of a trial date (with its consequent impact on anticipated settlement rates) are also material factors.

Justice requires that some reasonable limit be placed upon the amount of public time and resources that are devoted to any particular dispute. So much is established by the decision of the High Court in *Sali v SPC Ltd*.[23] Brennan, Deane and McHugh JJ distinguished earlier decisions that an adjournment, which, if refused, would result in a serious injustice to an applicant for an adjournment, should be refused only if that is the sole way that justice can be done to another party in the action. Their Honours observed that this proposition was 'formulated when court lists were not as congested as they are today and the concept of case management had not developed into the sophisticated art that it has now become', adding:

> In determining whether to grant an adjournment, the judge of a busy court is entitled to consider the effect of an adjournment on court resources and the competing claims by litigants in other cases awaiting hearing in the court as well as the interests of the parties. As Deane J pointed out in *Squire v Rogers* this 'may require knowledge of the working of the listing system of the particular court or judge and the importance in the proper working of that system of adherence to

---

[21] The procedural or adjectival issues have a parallel in the substantive 'individualised justice' debate: Atiyah (1978); Stone (1981); Atiyah (1987).

[22] T. Baker (1994).

[23] (1993) 116 ALR 625.

dates fixed for hearing'. What might be perceived as an injustice to a party when considered only in the context of an action between parties may not be so when considered in a context which includes the claims of other litigants and the public interest in achieving the most efficient use of court resources.[24]

The subsequent decision of the High Court in *Queensland v J L Holdings Pty Ltd (J L's Case)*[25] illustrates the dilemma for a judge of not providing disproportionate public resources to a particular case (in order that the court may be in a position to deal with the whole of the court's list in an orderly but efficient manner), yet not disregarding the individual 'right' of a party to present its case adequately.

In *J L's Case*, the judge, managing a complicated case, in the exercise of her discretion, refused leave to amend a defence because it might raise substantial new issues of fact and could involve the joinder of another party, thus jeopardising the final hearing date proposed. Since the matter would be unlikely to be relisted for some time, there would be prejudice to the plaintiff.[26]

However, the High Court held that leave to amend should be granted. Dawson, Gaudron and McHugh JJ distinguished *Sali v SPC Ltd*, saying:

> *Sali v SPC Ltd* was a case concerning the refusal of an adjournment in relation to which the proper principles of case management may have a particular relevance. However, nothing in that case suggests that those principles might be employed, except perhaps in extreme circumstances, to shut a party out from litigating an issue which is fairly arguable. Case management is not an end in itself. It is an important and useful aid for ensuring the prompt and efficient disposal of litigation. But it ought always to be borne in mind, even in changing times, that the ultimate aim of a court is the attainment of justice and no principle of case management can be allowed to supplant that aim.[27]

---

[24] Ibid 629.
[25] (1997) 189 CLR 146.
[26] *J L Holdings Pty Ltd v Queensland* (unreported, Federal Court, Kiefel J, 28 August 1996).
[27] *Queensland v J L Holdings Pty Ltd* (1997) 189 CLR 146, 154.

Kirby J said:

> Efficient management . . . is now an essential feature of the adminis-
> tration of justice, the importance of which is likely to increase in the
> years ahead. But whilst it remains in judicial hands it is a function
> which must be performed with flexibility and with an undiminished
> commitment to afford to all who come to the courts a manifestly just
> trial of their disputes.[28]

It would be tempting, yet superficial, to treat *J L's Case* as deciding that overall efficiency, in the form of a general system of case
management, is somehow in competition with a concept of the provision of justice in individual cases. The power, and duty, of every
court in each case to administer justice in accordance with law was
never in question in *J L's Case*. Rather, the High Court's decision
should be seen as accepting that the court's power to control a case
must be exercised fairly, but as holding that, on balance, the managerial powers were not exercised fairly in the particular circumstances of that case.

That is to say, managerial judging must reflect the interests of
justice in every sense. The principal theme of Lord Woolf's reforms
is that dealing with a case justly is achieved, rather than denied, by
managerial procedures that embody the principles of equality, economy, proportionality and expedition.[29] These reforms parallel the
evolution of the Federal Court's case management philosophies and
methods. So viewed, *J L's Case* did not involve any departure from
the approach taken in *Sali v SPC Ltd*.

In its appellate jurisdiction, the Federal Court has a similar
power (of control) and the same duty (to act fairly) in the conduct of
appeals, both in individual cases and in the overall dimension. The
High Court's recent decision in *Jackamarra v Krakouer* illustrates
the difficulties that may be encountered in fairly regulating the
conduct of the appellate process when exceptional circumstances
arise.[30] Here, an appeal was lodged within time, but subsequent pro-

---

[28] Ibid 174.

[29] Scott (1996).

[30] (1998) 153 ALR 276, on appeal from a state Supreme Court. The principles are
equally applicable to the Federal Court.

cedural default by the appellant occurred. The appellant applied to the Full Supreme Court for an extension of time, but was refused. In refusing the extension, the Supreme Court embarked upon an examination of the prospects of success of the appeal itself. But it was held by a majority of the High Court that the extension should have been granted. Brennan CJ and McHugh J said:

> An appeal, honestly lodged by a suitor within time, 'must be investigated and decided in the manner appointed'. If the appeal is frivolous, it can be disposed of summarily. If there is gross delay in prosecuting the appeal, it may be dismissed for want of prosecution. If it fails to comply with a particular rule, the rules of court may entitle the respondent to strike it out. But the merits of the appeal are not a relevant consideration where the application concerns an extension of time for taking a step in prosecuting the appeal unless, unusually, the court can be satisfied that the appeal is so devoid of merit that it would be futile to extend time.[31]

3 Trial Management Techniques—the Process

The essential elements of the caseflow management system used by the court pre-trial include a commitment to caseflow management principles and leadership by the judiciary; the establishment of time goals within which cases will be disposed; the judicial control of the pace of litigation from commencement to disposition, so as not to leave the pace in the control of the parties or their practitioners; the minimisation of adjournments to those that are essential and that arise because of circumstances that could not have been foreseen when the matter was listed for final hearing; trial date certainty as a high priority; and the establishment of a comprehensive monitoring system to measure performance and avoid delay.

These objectives are achieved by 'collapsing' procedure into management at a series of directions hearings.[32] Accordingly, formal procedures are kept to a minimum. Where appropriate, pleadings may be supplemented by a statement of facts, issues and contentions.

---

[31] Ibid 279, citing *Cox v Journeaux (No 2)* (1935) 52 CLR 713, 720 (Dixon J).

[32] Scott (1995) 24–5; Bowen (1985).

Where pleadings are not ordered, as in tax litigation, or, if ordered, have failed to illuminate what is truly in dispute, the managing judge can direct that the parties amend their pleadings.[33] Alternatively, each party may be directed to file a statement of the facts, both primary and secondary, which the party contends the court should find; the issues which, in the party's view, arise for determination; and the contentions, including any points of law, made on behalf of the party. In factually complicated litigation, a statement of facts, issues and contentions such as this can provide, before the trial commences,[34] a more illuminating view of the real issues than would a formal pleading.

Discovery often requires intensive judicial management and so is often limited to documents that are 'directly relevant', instead of the traditional 'train of inquiry' test.[35] A party seeking discovery has the burden of showing that there is a real need for it.[36] Exceptionally, discovery will be dispensed with entirely if a final hearing is urgent.[37] Interrogatories, as a branch of discovery, are strictly limited to a few, if any.

For the trial itself, a written outline of an opening and a 'reading list' of significant material—such as a 'technical primer' if scientific issues arise[38]—are usually required in order that rulings on evidence may be readily made, and so that all parties involved may focus on only those issues which actually require resolution, thus avoiding unnecessary and collateral inquiries. Although lengthy written submissions,[39] like lengthy pleadings, are expensive and are usually not

---

[33] *The Ritz Hotel Ltd v Charles of the Ritz Ltd* (1988) 91 FLR 37.

[34] The trial management process needs first to identify the point in the progress of the action at which the initiating party must commit itself to a particular account of the facts which it avers and on which, as it has averred, it relies, and second, the degree of specificity with which it must give its account: MacCormick (1978) 49.

[35] *Compagnie Financiere du Pacifique v Peruvian Guano Co* (1882) 11 QBD 55, 62–3; Lindgren and Branson (1998) 75-021.

[36] *BT Australasia Pty Ltd v New South Wales* (unreported, Federal Court, Sackville J, 15 May 1998).

[37] *Trade Practices Commission v Rank Commercial Ltd* (1994) 53 FCR 303, 317–18.

[38] *Chiron Corp v Evans Medical Supplies Ltd, The Times,* 20 January 1998; *Hoechst Celanese Corp v BP Chemicals Ltd, The Times,* 2 April 1998.

[39] *Travel Compensation Fund v FAI General Insurance Co Ltd* (unreported, Federal Court, Lindgren J, 9 April 1998) 3.

helpful at the trial level, a reasoned written submission provided on an appeal can be useful, as Sir Anthony Mason has pointed out.[40] But the experience of trial judges is that at first instance lengthy written submissions tend to obscure the real issues.[41] Anecdotal evidence confirms this, but sound empirical research in this area is needed.[42] Accordingly, the parties are usually directed to provide no more than a skeleton or outline of their final address.

A primary object of pre-trial management is the early identification by the court of what is, and what is not, seriously in dispute. This will expedite the trial process by avoiding protracted collateral inquiries, for instance where a hearsay objection is taken and it later emerges that the underlying facts should not really have been disputed. Thus, objections to the form of particular evidence are discouraged in civil cases if there is no real contest about the facts sought to be established.

Forcing the parties to focus on the core issues also facilitates (and hopefully accelerates) the natural evolutionary process of settlement, something achieved by parties and advisers in most cases in the Federal Court.[43] The timing of a settlement process can be crucial: proper case management should facilitate, in an orderly way, the prospects of compromise of any dispute. We must accept that some 'test' cases will require adjudication. The great majority of other cases, if treated tactfully, will be identified by the managerial judge as having potential for private compromise: unsophisticated, heavy-handed exhortations to the parties to settle can be misunderstood, and rarely achieve a satisfactory outcome.

We should accept that directions hearings, status or evaluation conferences, and settlement conferences inevitably consume time and expense for the court and the parties. To this extent, managerial judging diverts a court from its main responsibilities—the conduct of a final hearing, followed by a timely yet adequately reasoned judgment. But on balance this diversion of resources ought to be

---

[40] Sir Anthony Mason (1984) 541.
[41] Forsyth (1998) 160, citing a complex trial where pleadings exceeded one thousand pages but 'obscured the issues'.
[42] Flanders (1998) 318.
[43] Cranston (1995) 44.

allowed in the hope and in the realistic expectation that this intervention by the court will achieve real benefits, particularly in facili-
tating an early yet fair settlement. Another practical advantage, and
a significant resource factor, is the working knowledge of a dispute
acquired in pre-trial management, to be used by the judge in assessing how much time should be allowed for a final hearing and what
the prospects of a settlement might be. The application of this knowledge encourages a more efficient allocation of final hearing times in
a judge's docket overall.[44] Knowledge acquired by a managing judge
before trial also reduces time at the final hearing—a better-informed
judge is well placed to assess the time that should reasonably be
allowed for cross-examination and for submissions.[45] Another benefit flowing from effective pre-trial management is that the judge is
able to identify, at an early stage, any preliminary question of law
that is sufficiently important and ripe for reference directly to a Full
Court for determination. If this is decisive of even part of a case, time
and expense may be saved that otherwise might have been wasted
at trial.[46]

A further advantage arising out of early court control of proceedings is the ability of the judge to direct the appropriate form of
evidence at the trial. Where it appears likely that most of the facts
will be seriously in dispute, there is much to be said for excluding
affidavits, as is the American practice.[47] A trial of complicated facts,
especially if what was actually said in discussions is in issue, may be
unable to proceed in an orderly and expeditious way if extensive
affidavit evidence is used. Another problem is that an affidavit that
narrates lengthy discussions between the parties can be difficult to
weigh if credit is in issue. This is not to devalue the utility of directing written evidence in either affidavit or statement form where most
of the main facts are not contentious, or where the principal facts
are documented. In those circumstances, such a direction should

---

[44] The average size of a docket at any time is now around fifty cases, so that some
judicious overlisting may need to occur in the reasonable anticipation of a high settlement rate.

[45] *Wakeley v The Queen* (1990) 93 ALR 79, 86.

[46] *Burgundy Royale Investments Pty Ltd v Westpac Banking Corporation* (1987) 18
FCR 212.

[47] Zuckerman (1994) 379.

simplify the process and may also assist the parties to achieve a better informed compromise.

4 Using Modern Technologies

Ironically, modern technology has created some problems for the court, especially in the areas of discovery (multiple and unnecessary copying by the parties of documents of little or no ultimate significance), interrogatories (attempts to use computers for the mechanical administration of multiple but unhelpful questions), and in the preparation of lengthy pleadings and submissions. If allowed to proceed unchecked, these tendencies could create situations which might threaten to make major litigation virtually unmanageable, or incapable of final resolution within reasonable parameters. Experience in American anti-trust litigation indicates that these concerns are not theoretical. The Federal Court is well aware that in complex cases a disciplined approach by the parties is essential if a timely yet reasoned judgment is to be delivered.

Tensions have been identified in the growth of information technology between the greater accuracy and detail of information and the difficulties associated with managing increasingly large amounts of data. This has led to what has been termed a 'technology lag', created by the lack of sophistication in knowledge-based systems to properly manage and analyse the vast amounts of data available.[48] Senior advocates and judges have attributed 'today's escalating costs and delays in the courtroom to the document analysis and management tasks which that technology seems to require of us'.[49]

Some areas need immediate attention if courts are to cope with the electronic age. Discovery rules will need to deal comprehensively with the electronic storage of information. Evidentiary rules of proof of this information must address the possibility that an electronic document may have been altered between the time of its creation and its production in evidence. Audit trail systems, back-up devices, and the documentation of conversion systems (on transfer from an

---

[48] Susskind (1996) 56–60.
[49] Ibid 59.

old to a new computer system) should be taken into account in assessing the technical reliability of electronic evidence.[50]

At the same time, technology has brought significant benefits in the conduct of complex litigation in the form of video-conferencing (available for the convenience of interstate and overseas witnesses); real-time transcript (instantly available where difficult credit issues arise in the trial); and electronic transcript analyser (for use in factually complicated cases to search comprehensively for references to particular topics in the evidence). The introduction of electronic filing is also being examined by the court.[51]

Although Sir Ninian Stephen, in an address to the Law Institute of Victoria (19 August 1998), advocated televising High Court proceedings to enhance public understanding of the issues dealt with, the use of television in the Federal Court has, to this point, proceeded on an ad hoc basis. Over the last three years, brief television coverage of aspects of proceedings has been permitted on twenty occasions, usually showing the delivery of a judgment. No witness has been exposed to television coverage.

There is a protocol for use where evidence is taken by video-conferencing (VCF)[52] under which provision is made for monitoring by a local court to ensure that the witness does not take direction or guidance from any other person in the room, or consult documents, without the leave of the presiding judge. The VCF protocol may be capable of adaptation for television purposes. The availability of a video-conference facility has assisted in reducing the inconvenience and cost in taking evidence from interstate and overseas witnesses, and in native title cases when the witness resides a long distance from the trial venue. A question as to the procedural fairness of this process could conceivably arise if the evidence taken by VCF is both significant and complex.

[50] Heard and Edwards (1998) 7–8; Electronic Commerce Framework Bill (Vic).

[51] Sherman and Stanfield (1998) 92. If the system is implemented, the disadvantaged position of unrepresented litigants will require specific measures. In practice, however, documents and pleadings can be faxed to the courts, somewhat obviating the need for electronic filing.

[52] CCH, *Australian High Court and Federal Court Practice*, vol. 2, 71501 (as at May 1997).

The court will need to develop policies for the use of other forensic technology, such as real-time transcript. Where the facts are complicated, parties may request that this facility be provided, as it offers instant retrieval of testimony. There are only a few suppliers of this specialist service. Issues addressed in framing court guidelines include: whether there should be only one transcript provider in those proceedings; whether modifications are required to the court's usual transcript format, including the designation of one paper version as the official version; training for the judge and staff for use with transcript analyser software; courtroom protocols; provision of back-up audio recording; and copyright questions.

Legislation and Rules of Court have authorised evidence to be taken and submissions to be received by VCF or telephone in trans-Tasman proceedings.[53] Under comprehensive reciprocal legislation enacted pursuant to the Closer Economic Relations Trade Agreement, the Federal Court may sit in New Zealand, counsel may practise in either country, and orders, including subpoenas, may be served in either country.[54]

5 Special Management Issues

(a) Remitters

Special management issues can arise in transferring cases to other courts (under s 86A of the *Trade Practices Act 1974* (Cth)) and on remitter from the High Court. Once remitted, a matter becomes a proceeding in the Federal Court for all purposes.[55] Unnecessary complexities and consequent increases in costs can occur where only part of a matter can be remitted because the Federal Court's jurisdiction is limited by statutes such as the *Migration Act 1958* (Cth). Then only some of the grounds for the issue of a prerogative writ are remitted, and the remaining grounds continue in the High Court.[56]

---

[53] See, for example, Federal Court Rules O 69A r 8.

[54] Barker and Beaumont (1992).

[55] *Dinnison v Commonwealth* (1997) 74 FCR 184.

[56] *Re Bedlington; Ex parte Chong* (1997) 149 ALR 266; *Re Bedlington; Ex parte Chong (No 2)* (1997) 151 ALR 575.

(b) Expert witnesses

A significant issue in judicial administration in every jurisdiction is the appropriate role of expert witnesses. For whatever reason, and whether consciously or unconsciously, expert witnesses instructed on behalf of parties to litigation, if called as witnesses at all, often tend, to a greater or lesser extent, to espouse the cause of those instructing them, and on occasion become more partisan than even the parties.[57] The Federal Court has now issued guidelines in the form of a Practice Direction aimed at a better understanding of the role of expert witnesses. The guidelines emphasise that an expert witness has an overriding duty to assist the court on matters relevant to his or her area of expertise and is not merely an advocate for a party.[58]

This theme is developed in the guidelines in several ways. First, an expert's written report must give details of the expert's qualifications, and of material or literature used in making the report; all assumptions made by the expert should be clearly and fully stated. The report should identify who carried out any tests or experiments upon which the expert relied in compiling the report, and give details of the qualifications of the person who carried out any such test or experiment. Where a number of opinions are provided in the report, the expert should summarise them. The expert should give reasons for each opinion. At the end of the report the expert should declare that '[the expert] has made all the inquiries which [the expert] believes are desirable and appropriate and that no matters of significance which [the expert] regards as relevant have, to [the expert's] knowledge, been withheld from the Court'.

Second, there should be attached to the report a copy of all written instructions (original and supplementary) given to the expert, as well as a note containing a summary of any oral instructions received. The expert witness should make it clear when a

---

[57] *Abbey National Mortgages Plc v Key Surveyors Ltd* [1996] 1 WLR 1534, 1542. Sheppard argues that unreliable experts have no more than three cases: one in which to learn the ropes, a second, having done so, in which to shine, and a third in which to be found out: see Sheppard (1999) 19.

[58] Lord Woolf (1996a) Part 32.1; Cooper (1998).

particular question or issue falls outside his or her expertise. If, after exchange of reports or at any other stage, an expert witness, having read another expert's report, or for any other reason, changes his or her view on a material matter, such change of view should be communicated in writing (through legal representatives) without delay to each party to whom the expert witness's report has been provided and, when appropriate, to the court. If an expert's opinion is not fully researched because he or she considers that insufficient data is available or for any other reason, this must be stated with an indication that the opinion is no more than a provisional one. Where an expert witness who has prepared a report believes that it may be incomplete or inaccurate without some qualification, that qualification must be stated in the report. Where expert evidence refers to photographs, plans, calculations, analyses, measurements, survey reports, or other extrinsic matter, these must be provided to the opposing party at the same time as the exchange of reports.[59]

Third, if experts retained by the parties meet at the direction of the court, it will be deemed improper conduct for an expert to be given or to accept instructions not to reach agreement. If the experts cannot reach agreement on matters of expert opinion, they should specify their reasons for being unable to do so.

Difficulties have arisen in the reception of expert evidence where a clear line cannot be drawn between the facts (proven or assumed) and the opinion. Order 10 r 1(2)(j) of the Rules of Court now empowers the court to direct that the opinion (or part thereof) of an expert be received by way of submission, in such manner and form as the court thinks fit, whether or not the opinion would be admissible as evidence.

The 'empanelment' procedure for expert evidence devised by Justice Lockhart for use in the Australian Competition Tribunal is being examined by the court with a view to its adoption.[60] Under the empanelment (or 'hot tub') method, before experts are called to give evidence, they are informed that they should feel free to modify

---

[59] *The 'Ikarian Reefer'* [1993] 20 FSR 563, 565–6; Ormrod (1968).
[60] *Re Queensland Independent Wholesalers Limited* (1995) 17 ATPR 40 914, 40 925.

the views expressed by them in their reports as little or as much as they wish, on the footing that the benefit of their present views is sought, since they have by then had access to all of the evidence. At the conclusion of all evidence other than that of the experts, and before the commencement of addresses, each expert is sworn, one immediately after the other. Each expert, in turn, gives an oral exposition of his or her opinion with respect to the relevant issues arising from the evidence, and in turn then expresses his or her opinion about the opinions expressed by the other experts. Counsel next cross-examines the experts, being at liberty to cross-examine on the basis either that questions could be put to each expert in the customary fashion, one after the other, completing the cross-examination of one before proceeding to the next; or that questions may be put to all or any of the experts, one after the other, in respect of a particular subject before proceeding to the next subject. Re-examination is conducted on the same basis. The court may intervene with its questions.

There are a number of advantages to the above procedure. First, experts are required to prepare written submissions which are set down as a connected argument so that when giving oral evidence the same thread runs through the evidence rather than examination being a series of disconnected responses to questions from counsel. Second, it achieves the result of the experts defining, for their purposes, points of agreement and disagreement. Third, it takes the expert as far away from the 'adversarial' field as possible.

(c) Court-appointed experts

Another, perhaps more controversial, proposal under consideration by the court is the appointment of a court expert to advise the court in technical and scientific cases. The idea is not novel. In a celebrated essay published in 1901, Learned Hand used historical, logical and practical arguments to attack the 'absurd' practice of parading experts hired by litigants before a lay jury in complex scientific cases.[61] Hand urged the introduction of an advisory panel of independent, court-appointed experts.[62]

---

[61] Gunther (1994) 60.
[62] Hand (1901) 56; Gunther (1994) 312.

Although Sir Owen Dixon suggested that more use be made of special referees,[63] he saw many objections to the use of scientific assessors:

> If the assessors are to be relied upon in substitution for the scientific witnesses, the parties to the litigation are deprived of an opportunity of putting adequately before the judge, who must in the end decide the case, their rival views of the scientific material upon which he relies, and of understanding on what basis his conclusion is reached. If they merely advise, and are additions to the evidence of experts, their utility is doubtful.[64]

Yet, in a patent action heard in the High Court's then original jurisdiction in *Adhesives Pty Ltd v Aktieselskabet Dansk Gaerings-Industri*,[65] Evatt J, with the consent of the parties, sought the aid of assessors. By the parties' consent Evatt J also freely availed himself of trade and technical writings.[66] Although these processes were undertaken in the exercise of federal jurisdiction, no problem seems to have arisen with regard to polluting the federal judicial process. Whatever these jurisprudential demons might be, there are practical benefits in managing scientific issues with such assistance.

The use of court-appointed scientific advisers was recommended in a Review of the Federal Court in 1990,[67] and in *Genetic Institute Inc v Kirin-Amgen Inc (No 2)*,[68] Heerey J held that since the function of an assessor appointed under s 217 of the *Patents Act 1990* (Cth) is purely to assist the judge in understanding technical evidence, it was not judicially determinative of any issues, and was not contrary to the rules of natural justice. Following the approach taken by Barker J in New Zealand in *Beecham Group Ltd v Bristol-Myers Co (No 2)*,[69] Heerey J observed:

---

[63] In federal jurisdiction, this would be subject to constitutional limits: *Harris v Caladine* (1991) 172 CLR 84.

[64] Sir Owen Dixon (1965) 19, 21–2.

[65] (1935) 55 CLR 523.

[66] Ibid 571–2.

[67] Review of the Federal Court (1990) 41–2 (citing *Genentech Inc v The Wellcome Foundation Ltd* (1988) 15 IPR 423, 429, 503, 539).

[68] (1997) 78 FCR 368.

[69] [1980] 1 NZLR 192; also raising complex scientific issues.

It can be said of many disciplines that the basic concepts can be readily explained to intelligent lay people, including [as counsel for the respondent, in opposing the appointment, had submitted] school-children, but that does not prevent disputes arising between experts, who can contest issues with the enormous advantage of a lifetime of experience in the discipline. The resolution of such disputes by a non-expert judge is likely to be aided by expert assistance such as that provided by an assessor. No doubt the judge could reach a decision without such assistance, but that is not the point; s 217 does not posit a criterion of total judicial inadequacy as a pre-condition of appoint-ment of an assessor. It is simply a question whether the judicial task can be better performed. Other practical problems were advanced by counsel for the respondent. It was said that more than one discipline was involved in the present case, and that there may be difficulty in finding experts who are not affected by 'personal animosities' or membership of one or other of rival schools of thought in this area. However, these are things which we will have to cope with if and when they arise.[70]

It has been suggested that courts have inherent power to obtain independent expert evidence, but that only limited use can be made of this evidence: the expert cannot determine any matter in issue between the parties. The duty of the court is to obtain from the ex-pert's report whatever assistance it can.[71]

Provision is already made by the *Federal Court Rules* for the appointment of a court expert to inquire into and report upon a question (O 34 r 2). The report of the expert is, unless the court otherwise orders, admissible in evidence on the question on which it is made, but is not binding on any party, except to the extent to which that party agrees to be bound by it (O 34 r 3(3)). Upon appli-cation, the court will order cross-examination of the court expert by all the parties either before the court (at the trial, or at some other time) or before an examiner (O 34 r 4). The remuneration of the expert is fixed by the court (O 34 r 5(1)). Unless the court otherwise

---

[70] *Genetic Institute Inc v Kirin-Amgen Inc (No 2)* (1997) 78 FCR 368, 373.
[71] *Minnesota Mining and Manufacturing Co v Beiersdorf (Australia) Ltd* (1980) 144 CLR 253, 269–70.

orders, the parties are jointly and severally liable to the court expert
to pay the amount fixed by the court for his or her remuneration
(O 34 r 5(2)). Where a court expert has made a report on any question, any party may adduce evidence of one other expert on the same
question, but only if he or she has, at a reasonable time before the
commencement of the trial, hearing or examination at which he or
she adduces the evidence, given to the other interested parties notice
of intention to do so (O 34 r 6(a)). However, subject to this, a party
cannot adduce evidence of any other expert on the same question,
except with leave of the court (O 34 r 6(b)).

Because it has proved to have serious limits in practice, the
O 34 procedure has not been as extensively used as it might have
been. In *Trade Practices Commission v Arnotts Limited (No 4)*[72] the
admissibility of a report by a court-appointed statistical expert was
challenged on the basis that the document did not satisfy the description of a 'report' in O 34 r 2(1) because, it was said, it addressed the
wrong questions as a matter of substance. The document was admitted on the basis that it is sufficient for the purposes of that order
that the findings made are a genuine attempt to address the questions referred. The fact that the findings made by the expert are tentative does not prevent the document from being characterised as a
'report'. But collateral inquiries of this kind should be avoided: they
consume significant time and incur significant expense and tend to
advance only peripherally the process of resolving the parties' real
dispute.

The court is now examining whether, apart from any inherent
powers in this area, the *Federal Court Rules* should provide for the
appointment of a scientific adviser of the kind in *Beecham Group
Ltd v Bristol-Myers Co (No 2)* and *Genetic Institute Inc v Kirin-
Amgen Inc (No 2)*. The adviser, who could not be cross-examined,
could advise the court on how the invention (or its equivalent) actually works, without expressing any opinion on the ultimate issues in
the litigation. The court adviser could also provide other fundamental but non-contentious assistance such as providing a dictionary or
other information of the kind found in a technical primer.[73] One

---

[72] (1989) 21 FCR 318.
[73] Lord Woolf (1997) 313.

practical consideration in favour of appointing such an adviser is that there must be at least a reasonable chance that the expert, with no axe to grind, but a clear obligation to act carefully and objectively, may prove to be a reliable source of expert opinion whose assistance should enhance settlement prospects.[74]

The proposal should not be confused with a practice adopted in France regarding 'lay' experts. Because French civil procedure is marked by a strong preference for written proof, there is a tendency among French judges to avoid factual determinations that must be based on evidence which is complex or otherwise difficult to evaluate. A French court will normally appoint a lay expert to carry out this fact-finding task.[75] This practice is unlikely to be adopted in other jurisdictions. Richard Posner has observed: 'When [American] Judges got busy, the first thing they delegated was opinion-writing; yet even today it would be considered a scandal if Judges delegated the hearing of testimony or argument, though actually there is growing delegation of these functions to magistrates and special masters'.[76]

Although special referees have been used in state courts,[77] there is no provision for references out in the *Federal Court of Australia Act* or the *Federal Court Rules*, presumably for constitutional reasons of the kind explained in *Brandy v Human Rights and Equal Opportunity Commission*.[78] Section 53A(1A) of the Act empowers the court to order arbitration with the consent of the parties. This power is rarely used.

6 Appellate Case Management—the Methods

Initially, an appeal is managed by a list judge at one of the periodic Full Court call-overs held to ascertain state of readiness. If ready, the

---

[74] *Abbey National Mortgages Plc v Key Surveyors Nationwide Ltd* [1996] 1 WLR 1534, 1542.

[75] Beardsley (1986) 459.

[76] Posner (1995) 130.

[77] Giles (1996); Byrne (1994) 207.

[78] (1995) 183 CLR 245; *Fourmile v Selpam Pty Ltd* (1998) 80 FCR 151. Earlier, the High Court had assumed the validity of s 33A of the *Judiciary Act 1903* (Cth): *Minister for Home and Territories v Smith* (1924) 35 CLR 120.

appeal will be fixed for hearing at the next Full Court sittings. (Urgent appeals need to be individually managed ad hoc.) At the call-over, directions will be given for the conduct of the appellate hearing, including the provision by the appellant of a chronology in suitable matters,[79] and the provision of summaries of argument. Lengthy written arguments in the nature of 'position papers' which do not address the opposition's stronger points in any focused way are discouraged. On the other hand, material that is not truly contentious, particularly factual or background information, should be reduced to written form even, and especially, if lengthy. The order usually made for written submissions directs that the appellant file and serve its written submissions not later than five working days before the date fixed for the hearing of the appeal; that the respondent file and serve its written submissions not later than two working days before the date fixed for the hearing of the appeal; and that the appellant file and serve any written submissions in reply on the last working day before the date fixed for the hearing of the appeal. Unless otherwise ordered, written submissions are not to exceed twenty-five pages. Oral argument is confined to the elaboration, where necessary, of points made in the written submissions. Counsel are at liberty to develop the critical points in oral argument, but should not feel obliged to advance oral argument if they feel that it is adequately covered in the written argument.[80]

At the call-over, the judge will ascertain whether the appellate format proposed by the parties is suitable, and in particular, if the case is large, whether electronic appeal books should be used. In one appeal, after a trial extending over one hundred and one days, a 7000-page transcript of the proceedings at trial was also available in electronic form. This was loaded on to laptop computers for use by the judges and counsel on the hearing of the appeal. All participants agreed to use the same transcript analyser software. On reference being made to a section of the transcript during the argument, the judges and counsel were able to navigate through the transcript using

---

[79] Federal Court Practice Note No 1, Paragraph E.

[80] CCH, *Australian High Court and Federal Court Practice*, vol. 2 (as at May 1997), 74 501.

a 'go to' facility. This provided full text searching capability over the entire transcript.[81]

Electronic appeal books have been found to be advantageous in factually complicated appeals. Early identification by the court of matters suitable for this format is essential, since preparation of appeal books commences upon lodgement of notice of appeal. In a complex appeal, there are many areas where electronic material can be used, including the transcript of the evidence at trial, the reasons for judgment or directions of the trial judge, and the transcript of the argument on the appeal itself. (Exhibits may need imaging treatment.) Appropriate electronic media could be used to prepare, distribute and use the electronic material. These include disc, CD-ROM and electronic communication (internet e-mail). In the courtroom, the electronic material/appeal book could be used in several ways, including on individual computers (usually laptop PCs); in a 'view only' mode, where the associate operates a computer to identify the references made by counsel, which are then displayed on monitors in the courtroom; or through use of a dedicated courtroom network (intranet).[82]

7 Future Directions—Appellate Case Management

How can an intermediate appellate court, such as the Full Federal Court, do its work better in the face of increasing demands on its time, but with resources now less than adequate? Judge Patricia Wald, a senior American judge of the United States Court of Appeals, has observed that, in order to deal with more cases, more complex subject matter, more judges and more staff, intermediate appellate courts need 'ordered collegiality' in order to assure relatively accurate, uniform and timely decision-making.[83] Her arguments are discussed below.

First, there is a need to reallocate judicial time in chambers by expanding the numbers of personal staff. On the premise that a

---

[81] Sherman and Stanfield (1998) 79.
[82] Ibid 40.
[83] Wald (1983) 776–81, 784.

judge researches and writes every opinion, he or she could write only a dozen or so opinions a term.[84] An Australian Federal Court judge, with substantial trial and appellate responsibilities, has the assistance of one associate only, compared with an American federal appellate judge with research and writing assistance from a team of law clerks.

Second, scheduling help from support staff is essential in handling appellate business. Ensuring that these staff efficiently schedule appeals assures both effective presentation and matching of interdependent cases. In the United States, the court's staff counsel meet with lawyers to plan the presentation of a case. Staff counsel aim to 'weight' a case, so that each day's 'package' of cases is roughly equivalent.[85] The Review of the English Court of Appeal (Civil Division)[86] recommends that appeals be more intensively case managed, both judicially and by the Civil Appeals Office; individual case management should be the responsibility of a number of casework teams within the office; and their work should be divided up to match the responsibilities of the supervising judges.[87]

Third, judges must make discriminating choices about how to allocate their time,[88] specifically in terms of summary or extended treatment of their decisions. Abridged memorandum treatment for cases where existing rules of law are applied to a standard fact situation could be adopted. The memorandum could identify the issues, the court's disposition and the 'principle bases' for the ruling, normally foregoing an exposition of the facts and procedural history. The memorandum approach should not be used when the court develops or modifies a rule of law, resolves a conflict between panels, faces an issue of special public interest, or is not unanimous.[89] Australian intermediate appellate courts will need to examine the

---

[84] Ibid 777.
[85] Ibid 779.
[86] Chaired by Sir Jeffery Bowman (1997); Jacob (1998).
[87] Bowman (1997) 79.
[88] Gleeson (1998).
[89] Wald (1983) 782; compare T. Baker (1994); Weis (1995).

memorandum option where the circumstances are suitable.[90] This is not to say that the Federal Court should move, as some have suggested, to the abbreviated continental style of judgment writing, resting as it does essentially in assertion, mainly for economic reasons. This approach is conceptually quite different from the Anglo-Australian method, and also departs from the American style.[91] The court is presently examining the scope and place, if any, of the summary form of reasons for judgment. In this review, Fuller's point that the fairness and the effectiveness of adjudication are both promoted by opinions that are well reasoned[92] must be given due weight, if we are to retain its professional credibility.

Fourth, the need for deadlines is demonstrable. Judges' output can slip because they spend much of their time working alone without external controls.[93] Delay has become particularly unacceptable in the dynamics of modern societies, and particularly unbearable for the party who is not economically strong enough to endure its burdens.[94] An expeditious hearing ought to be matched with an expedited judgment,[95] accepting always that 'it is easy to dispense injustice quickly and cheaply, but it is better to do justice even if it takes a little longer and costs a little more'.[96] The Federal Court has adopted a Full Court judgment protocol, to ensure that judgment will usually be given within three months of the hearing. A conference is held on the morning of the hearing to discuss the management of the hearing, including whether a short form judgment is likely to be appropriate. Immediately after the conclusion of the hearing, a date and time is fixed for a conference in no more than

---

[90] However, Lord Oliver has expressed the view that the present English and Australian 'informative' model of appellate judgment writing, with its step-by-step analysis, rather than the more 'telegrammatic' American style, is more helpful in isolating the ratio and in assessing the impact of the decision on other cases: Lord Oliver (1992) 75.

[91] McKillop (1995).

[92] Fuller (1978) 388; compare MacCormick (1978) 75.

[93] Wald (1983) 784. Undue delay in delivering judgment should be explained. See the observations of Sir Frederick Lawton in 1986, cited in Arthur Robinson & Hedderwicks (1998).

[94] Cappelletti (1989) 243.

[95] Supreme Court of New South Wales (1997) 26.

[96] *Gale v Superdrug Stores Plc* [1996] 1 WLR 1089, 1098 (Millet LJ).

five weeks' time (by video or phone hook-up where appropriate). If at least two members of the court tentatively agree on the result, one will be nominated to prepare a draft. The first draft is to be prepared within one month. A conference is held immediately after the production of the first draft, to discuss the draft. Any further draft is to be produced within twenty-one days. The associate to the presiding judge is responsible for arranging conferences and following up draft judgments.[97]

8 Other Issues

Other important issues of concern to the Federal Court in the area of judicial administration should be mentioned briefly.

1 There is a need to develop better court management information,[98] given the limit on the utility of raw judicial statistics.[99]

2 Attempts at the institutionalisation of Alternative Dispute Resolution (ADR) in a court setting should be pursued, notwithstanding the high proportion of cases in the court that already settle. We must ensure, as Deane J has urged, that court rules place sufficient emphasis upon the element of conciliation,[100] consistently with the established policy of the common law to encourage the compromise of doubtful claims. We should also heed the warning of Chief Justice Black that ADR should not be seen 'as a sort of dustbin into which you siphon off the cases that the system hasn't the resources to deal with'.[101] More empirical studies, analysing rates and patterns of settlement, are

---

[97] These are not only management issues; the integrity of the system, real and perceived, is involved: compare *Bruce v Cole* (1998) 45 NSWLR 163.

[98] Patricia Lane (1993). There is a real need for scholarship and judicial leadership in this area.

[99] Murphy (1991); Collins (1997) 63; Supreme Court of New South Wales (1997) 27.

[100] *Re Queensland Electricity Commission; Ex parte Electrical Trades Union of Australia* (1987) 72 ALR 1, 12; *Practice Statement (Commercial Cases: Alternative Dispute Resolution) (No 2)* [1996] 1 WLR 1024 dealing with early neutral evaluation. If appropriate—for example, if the costs of the litigation significantly outweigh the amount in dispute—there is a facility for mediation within the court by a registrar.

[101] Black, 'Seeking Greater Efficiency Aids Aim of Doing Justice', *Australian Financial Review*, 28 May 1997, 54.

needed.[102] Here, account should be taken of the dynamics of the whole of the litigious process and of the role of the managerial judge, as significant factors in altering incentives for a just settlement.[103] The real issue is the extent to which ADR, specifically mediation, should be court-annexed and institutionalised in that form. In examining this prospect, we should bear in mind always that the origins of mediation are ancient and eastern, and that the more formal techniques have been developed in the United States, rather than in Australia or in the United Kingdom, with a notable exception in the area of family disputes.[104] The *Federal Court of Australia Act 1976* (Cth) and *Federal Court Rules*[105] now empower a judge to order compulsory mediation, yet in the face of opposition, this power is sparingly exercised for both practical and principled reasons.[106] It appears that only in the United States has mandatory mediation received significant support.[107]

3 Procedures in representative proceedings were innovative when introduced and are proving to be complicated and uncertain. An assessment of their future directions is timely.[108]

4 Imaginative measures are required to cope with significant inefficiencies and delays arising from the sharp increase in the number of unrepresented parties.[109] This affects every level of the court's operations, especially the resources of the Registry (including transcript).[110] One measure would be to expand the scope of O 78 r 6, which provides that in native title matters,

---

[102] Black (1996); De Garis (1994); Scott (1997) 40.

[103] Scott (1995) 29; Cranston (1995) 44; Elliott (1986) 336.

[104] Gould and Cohen (1998).

[105] Section 53A(1), (1A); O 72 r 8, O 72 r 7(1)(a), O 72 r 2(2), O 10 r 1(2)(h).

[106] *Kilthistle No 6 Pty Ltd v Austwide Homes Pty Ltd* (unreported, Federal Court, Lehane J, 10 December 1997); *Carpentaria Land Council Aboriginal Corporation v Queensland* (1998) 83 FCR 483, 508.

[107] Clark and Mays (1997) 37.

[108] Wilcox (1997); *Australian Competition and Consumer Commission v Golden Sphere International Inc* (1998) 83 FCR 424, 442; *McMullin v ICI Australia Operations Pty Ltd* (1998) 84 FCR 1; *Ryan v Great Lakes Council* (1998) 154 ALR 584.

[109] *Cachia v Hanes* (1994) 179 CLR 403, 415.

[110] *W J D v T E K* (1998) 19(9) Leg Rep SL4 (McHugh, Kirby and Callinan JJ).

the court or a judge may direct the registrar to provide reasonable assistance to an unrepresented party to enable preparation of a case, and, if funds are available, to provide counsel to assist the party. Another measure, suggested in a thoughtful United States study,[111] is a protocol for judges to achieve a degree of judicial consistency in this area, so that the court's handling of a case is neither too active nor too restrained. A further proposal is pro bono representation from a practitioner as amicus on legal questions.[112] These are not only administrative problems, for they can raise important substantive, natural justice issues. There is also potential for an abuse of process by a litigant acting without the guidance of expert advice.[113] The court has recently commissioned a study of the impact of unrepresented parties on the management of litigation. It is a major issue in judicial administration, yet is largely ignored.

5 The development by judges of expertise in specialist areas,[114] an important feature of the court's work, raises management questions (in the form of a need for co-ordination in listing in such matters as native title cases), as well as a role for professional development programs and collegial 'knowledge coupling', such as in the form of benchbooks.

6 The court has a fundamental responsibility to provide reasonable access to justice and so contain the cost of litigation within reasonable parameters. Its primary duty is to insist that its procedures are efficient and thus proportionate cost-wise.[115] A particularly vulnerable area is the expense of providing discovery. Discovery costs have been measured in millions of dollars. This is unacceptable. Senior practitioners must accept responsibility by devoting more time to supervising discovery, so that the process is properly monitored. There are other avenues available to reduce costs overall. There is nothing unlawful at common

---

111 Goldschmidt et al. (1998).
112 Andrews (1988) 139.
113 *Gilham v Browning* [1998] 1 WLR 682, 690–1; *Dev Hurnam v SSV Paratian* [1998] 2 WLR 790.
114 Opeskin (1995) 778.
115 Zuckerman (1996).

law in a practitioner agreeing to forgo all or part of a fee if the party loses, provided there is no attempt to recover more than ordinary profit costs and disbursements if the party wins.[116] Consideration could also be given to the case for 'commuting' correct judgments for 'timely' judgments.[117] Both A. A. S. Zuckerman and Patrick Atiyah have suggested that there may be some litigants who, instead of conducting costly full-scale litigation to finality, would be prepared to accept interlocutory orders as dispositive of their dispute.[118] The prior informed consent of both parties to the adoption of such a regime would naturally be required. Another dimension in the issue of costs is the court's control over the scale of fees allowed on taxation. Work is being done by the court in this area, aiming to eliminate disincentives to settlement and to abolish incentives for wasteful expenditure in the proposed new scale of costs.[119] In addition, the German system of fixing lawyers' fees by reference to the amount of the claim, considered also by Lord Woolf,[120] could be examined.[121] This has meant less expense for German litigants, especially in simpler cases, but has regrettably led to a lower rate of settlements, and, consequentially, more litigation. There is an unfortunate perception of 'litigation mania' in that country.[122] If we are to claim to be truly civilised, our society must get this balance right.

---

[116] *Thai Trading Co v Taylor* [1998] 2 WLR 893.
[117] Zuckerman (1994).
[118] Ibid; Atiyah (1987).
[119] P. Williams et al. (1998).
[120] Brennan (1997) 142–3.
[121] Zuckerman (1996) 787.
[122] Markesinis (1990).

7

Federal Courts and Federal Tribunals: Pluralism and Democratic Values

Margaret Allars

1 Introduction

Tribunals have become such an established part of the Australian legal system that arguments for or against their continued existence seem misplaced. In this context, theories of legal pluralism, advocating a diversity of institutions and procedures for resolving disputes between the individual and the state, now appear merely descriptive of the current legal scene and therefore somewhat jaded. We have no apprehension that sustaining tribunals as well as courts may undermine the rule of law or democratic values. On the contrary, public lawyers regard these institutions as complementing the role of the courts. This is not to say that there are no apprehensions.

Legal pluralism appears to endorse tinkering with organisational and structural aspects of the current system in order to enhance the representation of different interests. Altering institutional arrangements may provide government with opportunities to undermine the independence of the personnel of these alternative institutions and diminish the quality of their decisions (see Chapter 3). This chapter argues that in some of its forms a commitment to legal pluralism may mask a retreat from democratic values.[1] Public

---

[1] No attempt is made here to distinguish between different versions of pluralism. For accounts of the leading theories, see Dunleavy and O'Leary (1987) and Craig (1990).

lawyers need to understand legal pluralism in a fresh way, engaging more closely with the relationships between institutions, addressing in particular how the appointment and qualities of their personnel affect those relationships. This should provide a foundation for the development of principles of constitutional and administrative law in the Federal Court and the High Court which mediate the relationships in a way that protects democratic values.

By studying the relationships between federal tribunals and federal courts, a view will emerge regarding the impact of the tribunals on those courts. The term 'tribunal' is used to refer to an administrative decision-maker with statutory powers distinct from those exercised within government departments. The two major types of federal tribunals are merits review tribunals and regulatory agencies.[2] Examples of federal merits review tribunals are the Administrative Appeals Tribunal (AAT), the Immigration Review Tribunal (IRT), the Refugee Review Tribunal (RRT), and the Commonwealth Ombudsman. Examples of regulatory agencies are the Australian Securities and Investment Commission and the Australian Competition and Consumer Commission.

2 Legal Pluralism

(a) Theory

According to conventional views, the legal system consists of one set of norms which is the source of answers to legal controversies. Legal pluralism argues that just as individuals live simultaneously in a number of contexts and belong to multiple social groups, so legal controversies are governed by multiple normative systems. A pluralist conception of democracy emphasises participation by individuals as members of groups, and the process by which groups are permitted to represent the interests of their members in adjudicative decisions affecting groups, in the making of delegated legislation,

---

[2] Where relevant, 'merits review tribunal' or 'regulatory agency' is used rather than 'tribunal'.

in government policy-making by agencies and departments, or in seeking judicial review pursuant to principles relating to standing.[3]

From an institutional perspective legal pluralism supports diversity in social and political arrangements.[4] In the public law sphere the pluralist answer to the issue of the kinds of legal institutions which should administer laws and monitor their faithful application is found in a variety of institutions with the function of resolving disputes. Differing in their jurisdiction and powers, each institution is responsive to the needs and internal dynamics of the constituencies it serves.[5] Effective dispute resolution is to be achieved through specialisation, the key indicator of pluralism. Institutional structure and decision-making is designed to respond to any needs for speedy outcomes and access to decision-making processes, the needs of the institution's clientele, the question of whether ongoing relationships are involved, and the nature of the facts to be proved.

In relation to the division of review functions between courts and tribunals, this institutional version of legal pluralism has had a powerful influence upon thinking in Australian public law. Its influence can be traced to practical considerations appreciated by the Kerr Committee as the architect of the federal system of administrative review.[6] Federal courts may provide judicial review, which is the inherent jurisdiction of superior courts to supervise administrative action, applying the doctrines of excess of power and procedural fairness. On the other hand, under the constitutional doctrine of separation of powers federal courts may not exercise merits review jurisdiction, re-hearing and determining questions of fact and law, and possibly reviewing government policy. Moreover, independent of the constraints flowing from federal constitutional law, a broad political doctrine of separation of powers found in the common law precludes a superior court in judicial review from trespassing upon the merits of the administrative decision challenged. If it is thought desirable to provide merits review of administrative decisions, these

---

[3] See generally Craig (1990) 116–36.
[4] This institutional aspect of pluralism is developed in particular by Arthurs (1985). See also Dunleavy and O'Leary (1987) 65; Dahl (1982).
[5] Abel (1982); Arthurs (1985) 201.
[6] Kerr Committee (1971).

constitutional and common law limitations necessitate creating institutions other than courts.

General theories of pluralism have had their critics. Decentralisation of power tends to promote corporatism—the domination and control of the participative process by major groups which comprise elites enjoying the support of government.[7] Such criticism needs to be addressed in any examination of principles governing participation in adjudicative decisions, rule-making or judicial review. The danger of corporatism is also present in the narrower realm of institutional design where government functions are corporatised, privatised or contracted out. This results in the handling of legal rights and obligations within the separate normative systems of smaller non-governmental units which may indeed place little importance upon participation and democratic values. Tribunals do not present this problem in such a stark form, for they are statutory authorities that belong to the executive branch of government rather than to the private sphere. Nevertheless, it is arguable that conflict between norms may occur. The retreat from democratic values which accompanies the creation of non-governmental units may also be seen as a looming danger for federal tribunals. Provisions for the appointment and removal of tribunal members and for the review of tribunal decisions are critical to maintaining an appropriate relationship with federal courts and hence to the protection of democratic values. Further questions arise about whether current and proposed structures for the federal tribunal system respect those values, and what task the structures present for federal courts.

(b) Federal merits review tribunals

Evaluating the relationship between tribunals and courts requires a preliminary examination of the design of each institution. Understanding institutional design begins with interrogating the reasons for creating the tribunals. The focus here is upon the reasons for the establishment of the most important of the federal merits review tribunals, the AAT. The reasons are very easily identified, yet have sometimes been misrepresented.

---

[7] See Craig (1990) 148–53.

The Kerr Committee's reasons for recommending the establishment of a general merits review tribunal were threefold. First, any comprehensive system of administrative review should provide not only for judicial review but also for merits review by an external tribunal. Second, because of the federal constitutional doctrine of separation of powers, such merits review jurisdiction cannot be conferred upon a federal court, and must be conferred upon an independent tribunal. Third, it is undesirable that there be a proliferation of specialist tribunals. In 1975 the AAT was established to implement these recommendations. Another tribunal, the office of Commonwealth Ombudsman, was also established in 1976 to implement other of the Kerr Committee's recommendations.

A close analysis of the reasoning of the Kerr Committee is important because it set a course for the federal system of tribunals for the next three decades. The first reason, that merits review must be provided by an independent decision-maker, laid the foundation for the other reasons. The second reason, relating to separation of powers, was integral to conferring the jurisdiction upon a body other than a federal court. The third reason was the principle of non-proliferation of tribunals, though some federal merits review tribunals were subsequently established for reasons different to those of the Kerr Committee. Their establishment involved either a justified qualification to the non-proliferation principle, or the rejection of the principle.

(c) The need for merits review

The Kerr Committee was established in 1968 by the federal Attorney-General with terms of reference oriented primarily towards reforming the procedure for obtaining judicial review of administrative action. At this time the only means for challenging most federal administrative decisions was confined to judicial review for legal error, using the prerogative writs, declaration or injunction in the High Court.[8] The terms of reference required the Committee to consider what jurisdiction should be conferred upon a proposed federal court, the procedures by which review was to be obtained, the

---

[8] Kerr Committee (1971) 5–6.

substantive grounds for review, and the desirability of introducing legislation along the lines of the *Tribunals and Inquiries Act 1958* (UK).

In response to the first three terms of reference the Committee recommended that there should be a Commonwealth superior court with jurisdiction by way of judicial review, a procedure statute to provide for a simple review procedure replacing the old technical prerogative remedies, codification of the grounds of review and a duty imposed on administrators to give reasons for their decisions.[9] The procedure statute was intended to facilitate judicial review of administrative action.[10] The Ellicott Committee was established with terms of reference confined to considering the jurisdiction, procedures and substantive grounds of review to be available in the specialist court proposed by the Kerr Committee. The Ellicott Committee endorsed the recommendation for a specialist court. In a passing comment on merits review, the Committee observed that review by a federal court on the merits 'would not constitute an exercise of judicial power'.[11]

The terms of reference of the Kerr Committee contained no explicit reference to merits review. Although the Committee was required to consider the desirability of legislation akin to the *Tribunals and Inquiries Act*, that Act contained no provision itself for merits review. The Kerr Committee had a deep conviction that it was a fundamental fault of the Australian system of review that many federal administrative decisions were not reviewable on the merits.[12] The Committee therefore interpreted broadly its first term of reference, concerning the jurisdiction of the proposed federal specialist court. It reasoned that if it was to formulate recommendations as to the jurisdiction of the court, it would be necessary to examine the review of administrative decisions 'in its entirety' and 'in the total context' to determine whether the court's function was complementary to a system of merits review by one or more

---

[9] Ibid 74–9.
[10] Ibid 74.
[11] Ellicott Committee (1973) 5.
[12] Kerr Committee (1971) 9–10, 20.

tribunals.[13] According to the Committee, 'it has been universally accepted that judicial review by the courts alone by [the existing method], cannot provide for an adequate review of administrative decisions'.[14]

The Committee was convinced, probably from the experience of the eminent lawyers who were its members, that merits review was usually the kind of review that aggrieved citizens were seeking and for which the system should provide. The Committee recognised that because of the federal constitutional doctrine of separation of powers, merits review jurisdiction could not be conferred upon the specialist federal court.[15]

The Kerr Committee was prepared to allow a greater diversity than a specialist court and a general merits review tribunal. It accepted that not all administrative decisions would be suitable for review on the merits by the proposed tribunal.[16] Some would not be suitable because they involved important policy considerations or were already reviewable by a specialist tribunal.[17] The jurisdiction of the general review tribunal would need to be developed carefully over a significant period of time. The proposed Administrative Review Council (ARC) would make recommendations regarding new jurisdiction for the tribunal, including transfer of jurisdiction from existing specialist tribunals.[18]

It is not surprising that a Committee with a brief to consider judicial review assumed that merits review would be performed by a body which, like a court, was external to the primary decision-maker. This assumption was buttressed by the more important tenet, which the Kerr Committee clearly thought needed no discussion, that merits review must be provided by an independent decision-maker. External review would secure independence. In later reports of the

---

[13] Ibid 1–2.

[14] Ibid 1–2. The assumption of universal acceptance was drawn from the Committee's review of the creation of tribunals to supplement the role of courts in the United Kingdom, the United States and New Zealand.

[15] Ibid 24, 74.

[16] Ibid 69–70.

[17] Ibid 105–6.

[18] Ibid 75.

ARC recommending conferral of new jurisdiction upon the AAT, the notion of independence is articulated more clearly.

The Kerr Committee made no reference to the need to examine procedures for maintaining the quality of primary decision-making and facilities for internal review as integral components of a system whose object is accountability of the executive branch. Its focus was on review for the purpose of detection of legal and factual error.[19] In contrast, the Coombs Report, written in 1976 by a public administrator, emphasised the need for improvement in administrative procedure.[20] But the Coombs Report did not dampen the impetus for external merits review provided by the Kerr Report.

Was the Kerr Committee's a pluralist approach? Arthurs would answer in the affirmative and in fact cites the AAT as an example of pluralism; a recognition that 'administrative legality should be adjudicated by a special body'.[21] However, the Kerr and Ellicott Committees proposed the new specialist court as the separate body which would provide review of the legality of administrative decisions. The Federal Court which was established to implement the recommendations of the Committees commenced with a specialist jurisdiction in administrative law but later acquired other major jurisdictions. Neither the AAT nor the Federal Court was created for the sake of diversity in institutional arrangements. While governmental and legislative intent is not conclusive of the question of pluralism it should be remembered that the AAT was created because of a perceived need for merits review and recognition that this could not be provided by the Federal Court because of the doctrine of separation of powers.

(d) Constitutional constraints

At first glance the Australian Constitution is not noted for its legal pluralism. While it contemplates the creation of federal courts in addition to the High Court and a structure of state and federal courts of which the High Court is the apex,[22] it does not mention any of the

---

[19] Ibid 3.

[20] Royal Commission on Australian Government Administration (1976).

[21] Arthurs (1985) 211.

[22] Constitution Chapter III; *Kable v Director of Public Prosecutions (NSW)* (1996) 189 CLR 51.

federal merits review tribunals. The evolution of the highly sophisticated federal system of tribunals from the 1970s to the 1990s may therefore appear somewhat surprising.

Explicit provision was made in the Constitution for one tribunal, the Inter-State Commission (ISC).[23] Despite its constitutional status, and later legislation establishing its powers, the tribunal no longer exists.[24] Had the ISC operated as envisaged in the early part of the century, federal regulatory agencies would have developed in Australia according to a model very different from that which is familiar today. However, the High Court decision in *New South Wales v Commonwealth* (*Wheat Case*)[25] in 1915 struck down as unconstitutional the part of the first statute for the ISC empowering it to adjudicate disputes and grant damages and injunctive relief in respect of contraventions of the provisions of the Constitution relating to trade and commerce. This precluded the possibility of an agency with combined adjudicative and enforcement functions as a central model for regulation in Australia.

Turning to merits review tribunals, the federal constitutional doctrine of separation of powers which accounts for the result in the *Wheat Case* has continued to play a critical role in restricting the models for these bodies. While departures from the separation of legislative and executive power were accepted within the Constitution[26] and by the High Court,[27] the separation of judicial and executive power was maintained more strictly.

Shortly after the *Wheat Case*, the High Court struck down the appointment of a judge of the High Court as President of the Arbitration Court to exercise judicial power as well as arbitral powers. His terms of appointment did not provide for tenure in accordance with Chapter III of the Australian Constitution.[28] The doctrine of

---

[23] Constitution ss 101–104.

[24] See generally Coper (1990).

[25] (1915) 20 CLR 54.

[26] Constitution s 64 (government ministers responsible for administering federal departments and members of the Executive Council must also be Members of Parliament within three months of their appointment to office).

[27] *Victorian Stevedoring & General Contracting Co Pty Ltd v Dignan* (1931) 46 CLR 73 (Parliament may delegate power to the executive branch to make subordinate legislation).

[28] *Waterside Workers' Federation of Australia v J W Alexander Ltd* (1918) 25 CLR 434.

separation of powers was more fully enunciated in 1956 in *R v Kirby; Ex parte Boilermakers' Society of Australia (Boilermakers' Case)*, where it was inferred by the High Court from the structure of the Constitution.[29] Provisions vesting both arbitral and judicial powers in the Commonwealth Court of Conciliation and Arbitration violated Chapter III.[30] By amending legislation the Court was replaced by a Conciliation and Arbitration Commission and a Commonwealth Industrial Court, removing a constitutional violation which had existed for thirty years.[31]

Although the High Court raised doubts about the *Boilermakers' Case* in the 1970s,[32] and has since conceded the lack of any precise definition of judicial power of the Commonwealth,[33] the doctrine remains good law. Not only in the case of the ISC, but more generally at the federal level, administrative and judicial functions could not and still cannot be combined in one body. Federal courts could not exercise administrative functions unless they were incidental to the exercise of judicial power of the Commonwealth. Federal tribunals could not exercise judicial power of the Commonwealth, which could only be exercised by federal courts.

---

[29] (1956) 94 CLR 254; affirmed by the Privy Council in *Attorney-General of the Commonwealth of Australia v The Queen* (1957) 95 CLR 529.

[30] Since arbitral power has the object of ascertaining what legal rights and obligations should exist in the future rather than ascertaining existing legal rights and obligations, it is not judicial power of the Commonwealth. See also *Re Ranger Uranium Mines Pty Ltd; Ex parte Federated Miscellaneous Workers' Union of Australia* (1987) 163 CLR 656, 665–6.

[31] Following *Waterside Workers' Federation of Australia v J W Alexander Ltd (Alexander's Case)* (1918) 25 CLR 434 the enforcement function was transferred to courts of petty sessions. Despite this case, the enforcement powers were restored to the Arbitration Court in 1926. Although its judges had life tenure, the combination of functions violated separation of powers as expounded by Isaacs and Rich JJ in *Alexander's Case*.

[32] The decision was questioned in obiter in 1974 and in argument in 1976 but not thereafter: *R v Joske; Ex parte Australian Building Construction Employees & Builders' Labourers' Federation* (1974) 130 CLR 87; *R v Joske; Ex parte Shop Distributive and Allied Employees' Association* (1976) 135 CLR 194.

[33] *Huddart, Parker & Co Pty Ltd v Moorehead* (1909) 8 CLR 330, 357 (Griffith CJ); *Federal Commissioner of Taxation v Munro* (1926) 38 CLR 153, 175–80 (Isaacs J), affirmed in *Shell Co of Australia Ltd v Federal Commissioner of Taxation* [1931] AC 275; *R v Trade Practices Tribunal; Ex parte Tasmanian Breweries Pty Ltd* (1970) 123 CLR 361, 373 (Kitto J).

Nonetheless, the separation of judicial from executive functions has not prevented conferral upon some regulatory agencies of extensive coercive powers and powers to regulate conduct in the future. This has resulted in the development of a model of federal regulatory agencies with differing manifestations. Agencies without power to regulate conduct in the future appear to be powerless. This is the case with respect to the Human Rights and Equal Opportunity Commission (HREOC), the enforcement powers of which were struck down in *Brandy v Human Rights and Equal Opportunity Commission* (*Brandy's Case*).[34] Agencies with power to regulate conduct in the future, such as the Corporations and Securities Panel of the Australian Securities and Investment Commission,[35] exercise an increasingly significant impact on individual rights and commercial activity.

While the doctrine in the *Boilermakers' Case* requires a separation of judicial personnel as well as functions from those of the executive branch,[36] it has not prevented the appointment of federal judges as members of federal tribunals.[37] As an exception to the strict separation of judicial from administrative personnel, the persona designata doctrine treats a judge's appointment to perform an executive function as being made in the judge's personal capacity, rather than as an exercise of administrative power by a federal judge. Thus, federal judges may be appointed as royal commissioners, as presidential members of the AAT[38] and the HREOC, or given authority to issue telephone tapping warrants.[39]

The Kerr Committee's recommendation that a judge should be president of the proposed new tribunal was based on early

---

[34] (1995) 183 CLR 245.

[35] *Precision Data Holdings Ltd v Wills* (1991) 173 CLR 167, 190.

[36] *R v Trade Practices Tribunal; Ex parte Tasmanian Breweries Pty Ltd* (1970) 123 CLR 361, 389–90 (Windeyer J).

[37] A second exception to the separation of powers doctrine permitted judicial power to be exercised by registrars and masters of federal courts, provided that exercise was subject to review and was under the real supervision and control of the judges of the court: *Harris v Caladine* (1991) 172 CLR 84.

[38] *Drake v Minister for Immigration and Ethnic Affairs* (1979) 24 ALR 577.

[39] *Hilton v Wells* (1985) 157 CLR 57; *Grollo v Palmer* (1995) 184 CLR 348.

case-law endorsing the persona designata doctrine.[40] The Committee acknowledged the argument that the involvement of judges in tribunals concerned with correct application of policy could threaten public confidence in the judiciary. The Committee described these fears as 'exaggerated' and found no difficulties had arisen so far in Australia through use of the doctrine. Indeed, judges would 'benefit from the experience gained in presiding over a Review Tribunal'.[41]

However, twenty years later a majority of High Court judges perceived a threat to public confidence in the judiciary which called for the enunciation of a limit to the persona designata doctrine. The test is whether performance of the administrative function is incompatible with the judge's performance of judicial functions or the proper discharge by the judiciary of its responsibility as an institution exercising judicial power.[42] The line set by this incompatibility test was overstepped in *Wilson v Minister for Aboriginal and Torres Strait Islander Affairs* (*Wilson's Case*)[43] when a federal judge was appointed to perform the statutory function of hearing submissions and providing a report on the significance to Aboriginal heritage of an area of land. The report was a precondition to a ministerial decision to make a permanent declaration protecting the site.

The incompatibility test is comprised of a loose set of criteria addressing the closeness of the connection of the administrative function with the functions of the executive branch, including the degree of independence of the decision-maker from executive or legislative 'instruction, advice or wish',[44] the presence of any requirement to exercise discretion upon political grounds, and the application of the principles of procedural fairness, in particular the appearance of impartiality.[45] In *Wilson's Case* the role played by the judge in pro-

---

[40] Kerr Committee (1971) 87–8, 109, 110.

[41] Ibid 87.

[42] *Grollo v Palmer* (1995) 184 CLR 348; *Wilson v Minister for Aboriginal and Torres Strait Islander Affairs* (1996) 189 CLR 1.

[43] (1996) 189 CLR 1.

[44] Ibid 17.

[45] Ibid 17–18. In contrast to the joint judgment of Brennan CJ, Dawson, Toohey, McHugh and Gummow JJ, where these four criteria are set out, Gaudron J in a separate judgment regarded the appearance of impartiality as the single criterion relevant to maintaining public confidence in the integrity and independence of federal courts. Kirby J dissented.

viding a report to the Minister as to whether the site should be protected placed her 'firmly in the echelons of administration, liable to removal by the Minister before the report is made and shorn of the usual judicial protections, in a position equivalent to that of a ministerial adviser'.[46] Her function was essentially political, with no immunity and no requirement that she disregard ministerial instruction, advice or wish in preparing the report.

The decision in *Wilson's Case* does not affect the performance of functions that had previously been understood to be constitutionally acceptable, such as appointment of a federal judge as a royal commissioner (provided the terms of reference did not depart from the normal independence of a commissioner), as a member of the AAT, as an Aboriginal Land Commissioner, or as an eligible person to issue telephone tapping warrants.[47] However, the High Court acknowledged that the incompatibility test was new and some judicial appointments in the past may not have conformed to it.[48] Perceiving the function of issuing telephone tapping warrants to have only narrowly passed the incompatibility test, the federal government amended the legislation to enable AAT members to be empowered to issue such warrants.[49] In future the function is likely to be performed exclusively by non-judicial AAT members acting in their individual capacities rather than by federal judges.

Wilson's Case has important implications for the role of federal judges in the administrative review process. If the structure of the federal merits review system is altered so that administrative review is conducted predominantly by way of a version of internal review, rather than by an independent external tribunal such as the AAT, federal judges would be precluded for constitutional reasons from holding appointments in that review process.

Along with federalism, a doctrine of separation of powers provides intersecting divisions of power which limit the possibility of tyranny by the majority. These political structures can be regarded

---

[46] Ibid 18–19.

[47] Ibid 17–19, 25–6.

[48] Ibid 20.

[49] *Telecommunications (Interception) and Listening Device Amendment Act 1997* (Cth), inserting s 6DA into the *Telecommunications (Interception) Act 1979* (Cth).

as pluralist in themselves.[50] However, legal pluralism from the institutional perspective is then a weak term encompassing any political arrangement more complex than unified and unchecked state power. If legal pluralism from an institutional perspective is to provide a compelling contribution to democracy it must protect and promote core democratic values of representation and faithful and equal application of legal norms. In seeking to protect the fundamental value of independence of the judiciary, *Wilson's Case* suggests how a deeper understanding of pluralism might be achieved.[51]

3 The Federal System of Merits Review Tribunals

(a) The non-proliferation principle

The Kerr Committee's third reason for recommending establishment of a general administrative review tribunal was that it is undesirable that there be a proliferation of specialist tribunals. It is difficult to categorise the non-proliferation principle as pluralist or not. Certainly the principle rejects a centralist and Diceyan trust in judicial review as the sole means for securing accountability of the executive branch. In recommending the creation of a specialist court to conduct judicial review and two major new tribunals, the Committee embraced a pluralism of institutions for resolving disputes between government and the governed.

On the other hand the Committee's non-proliferation principle could be seen to be a retreat from pluralism in rejecting the diversity of separate specialist tribunals. However, this would misrepresent the Committee's approach. It recognised the importance of expertise in external merits review decision-making, and hence of other normative systems, but thought the appropriate response was to appoint expert members to divisions of the AAT. Moreover, the Kerr Committee was not absolutist in its rejection of specialist tribunals. It recognised that there may in the future exist a 'real case' for estab-

---

[50] Dunleavy and O'Leary (1987) 14–15.

[51] For an argument that *Brandy v Human Rights and Equal Opportunity Commission* (1995) 183 CLR 245, while apparently reducing the effectiveness of the HREOC, also protects fundamental democratic values, see Allars (1996b).

lishing a specialist tribunal,[52] but did not indicate what circumstances might constitute such a case.

As a step towards implementing the recommendations of the Kerr Committee, the Bland Committee was appointed to examine existing administrative discretions under federal statutes and advise as to which should be reviewable on the merits by an external review tribunal.[53] The Bland Committee strongly supported the non-proliferation principle, stating that:

> to permit a continuing proliferation of tribunals would be wasteful of resources, inimical to the efficient functioning of government and calculated to cause public dissatisfaction . . . our society requires less and less the narrow compartmentation of issues. More and more is evident the inter-relationship of individual issues. Governmental machinery strives with varying degrees of success to attempt some co-ordination of decision making . . . tribunals reviewing administrative decisions are themselves but an extension of administration.[54]

Yet curiously, the Bland Committee recommended establishing three separate tribunals—a Valuation and Compensation Tribunal, a Medical Appeals Tribunal and a General Administrative Tribunal —each with its own divisional structure. The recommendation was not implemented. The Committee set an objective of economic use of resources and better and more even resolution of individual issues, where tribunal members would not be narrow in their jurisdictional range.[55]

Despite its recommendation for three separate tribunals, the Bland Committee found even less justification than did the Kerr Committee for separate tribunals with specialised jurisdiction:

> a separate tribunal is not to be justified solely on the grounds that, in some area of administration, the issues thrown up are so complex and the demand for review by a tribunal so great as to keep it fully

---

[52] Kerr Committee (1971) 70.

[53] Bland Committee (1973b) 1.

[54] Bland Committee (1973a) 24–5.

[55] Ibid 25.

occupied. This sort of problem could, in our view, be met if the same membership of one tribunal were assigned to deal with cases in the one area.[56]

The principle of non-proliferation dominated federal government's approach to transfer and conferral of jurisdiction upon federal merits review tribunals for almost two decades.[57] When the AAT was established the jurisdiction of several existing tribunals was transferred to it. Later the Taxation Boards of Review were abolished and their jurisdiction transferred to the AAT. Gradually the AAT acquired what is now an immense range of areas of jurisdiction conferred in over 300 different enactments.

(b) First-tier tribunals

However, this period did not pass without the establishment of new merits review tribunals with specialist jurisdictions. The Social Security Appeals Tribunal (SSAT) was established in 1975 by a ministerial instruction and in 1988 was placed on a statutory basis.[58] Social security decisions are potentially subject to internal review, then external review by the SSAT, and then by the AAT, with an appeal on questions of law lying to the Federal Court. In 1979 the two tribunals which heard appeals from the Repatriation Commission, criticised for a lack of independence,[59] were abolished and replaced by the Repatriation Review Tribunal. In 1985 this tribunal was replaced by the Veterans' Review Board (VRB) with the possibility of a second tier of merits review by the AAT.

The creation of these specialist tribunals raises the question whether the limited endorsement of pluralism reflected in the non-proliferation principle was being undermined by a more vigorous diversity asserting a full-blown form of pluralism. In both cases the ARC accepted that a departure from the non-proliferation principle is appropriate in high volume areas of decision-making where a

---

[56] Ibid 25.

[57] Until the early 1990s the AAT also provided a model for law reform recommendations in the states and territories.

[58] The Student Assistance Review Tribunal, which pre-dated the AAT, was incorporated into the SSAT in 1995.

[59] Toose (1975). See generally Creyke (1992).

first-tier tribunal can usefully handle the bulk of the case load.[60] More difficult cases requiring detailed consideration, or test cases requiring development of general principles should proceed to the AAT. These developments could thus be regarded as consistent with the non-proliferation principle, which is not intended to operate in an absolute manner, and tolerates a specialist tribunal where there is a real need for it. However, in the system that developed there was no leave requirement at any stage. It is therefore also arguable that, given the ever-increasing jurisdiction of the AAT and its role in some areas as a second tier of review, the creation of the new tribunals amounted to departures from the principle, made without extinguishing it.

(c) Tribunals of comparable status

From its establishment the AAT exercised jurisdiction to review criminal deportation decisions. It is curious then that two specialist tribunals were subsequently established to review migration decisions. In 1989 the Immigration Review Tribunal replaced the Immigration Review Panel. In 1993 the Refugee Review Tribunal replaced the Determination of Refugee Status Committee. Both of the abolished tribunals were partially constituted by departmental representatives and had been criticised for a lack of independence. Their replacement by external tribunals certainly endorsed the Kerr Committee's assumption of the value of independence in the merits review process and the tribunal as the pre-eminent means for achieving it.[61] Since the only possible further level of review was the Federal Court these new tribunals were of comparable status to the AAT.[62]

However, there can hardly have been a 'real case' in terms of the non-proliferation principle for the fragmentation of immigration review between one generalist and two specialist tribunals. To account for this structure in pluralist theory, it would be necessary to identify differences in specialised jurisdictional needs which could

---

[60] Administrative Review Council (1984); Administrative Review Council (1983).

[61] Administrative Review Council (1986) 25.

[62] A facility for referral of questions from the IRT and RRT to the AAT existed but it was never used: *Migration Act 1958* (Cth) ss 381 and 443.

only be met by the different structure, procedure and ethos of each tribunal. In addition, the managerialist ethos in public administration in the late 1980s would have reinforced the non-proliferation principle, given the greater efficiency and savings in resources achieved by conferring jurisdiction upon an existing tribunal. The explanation for not adopting this course lies in the highly sensitive political context in which migration review occurs in Australia.

The provision of more accessible forums responsive to particular vulnerable groups, such as migrants, could be regarded as enhancing pluralism. However, the early emphasis placed upon securing the independence of tribunals dwindled. Extremely negative sentiments towards the role of lawyers as members of tribunals or representatives of parties to tribunal proceedings were expressed by government in the second half of the 1980s and throughout the 1990s. This was pronounced in the context of migration review. Moreover, in a manner not encountered in the case of the AAT and first-tier tribunals, politicisation of appointment practices in the IRT attracted severe criticism in a minority report of a Senate Committee.[63] Further adjustments were made and planned for the structure of the system of migration review, providing further opportunities for removal and appointment of tribunal members.[64] A determination to exert executive control in this area was reflected not only in the establishment of new tribunals with the accompanying mandate to appoint their members, but also in the tightening of discretion in relation to onshore applications, a bewildering complexity and instability in the regime of regulations and visa classes, and negative governmental views towards the contribution lawyers might make to ensuring independence in decision-making.[65]

By the late 1980s Federal Court judges played a much reduced role as deputy presidents of the AAT. There is no basis upon which

---

[63] Joint Standing Committee on Migration (1994).

[64] These were a formal system of internal review by the Migration Internal Review Office (MIRO) as a precondition to review by the IRT, followed by amalgamation in 1998 of both these layers of review into a new external merits review tribunal called the Migration Review Tribunal (MRT): *Migration Legislation Amendment Act (No 1) 1998* (Cth). The MRT will have a life of only about a year before migration review is transferred to a division of the new Administrative Review Tribunal (ART) the government proposes to establish.

[65] Ruddock (1997).

federal courts could be called to scrutinise the general arrangements for securing the independence of these tribunals. While the incompatibility principle does not prevent federal judges from serving as members of external merits review tribunals its focus is upon protection of the independence of judges in performing their judicial functions. The constitutional doctrine of separation of powers has been concerned with preserving integrity in the application of legal norms by federal courts. The doctrine does not extend to protecting the independence of tribunal members in the application of legal and non-legal norms in merits review. If separation of powers also endorses pluralism in the fuller sense of diversity of tribunals, then arguably further development of constitutional principle should embrace protection of the independence of all institutions responsible for checking the proper application of legal norms.

(d) The *Better Decisions* Report

In a general review in 1995 of the peak federal merits review tribunals, the ARC recommended that the jurisdiction of the AAT, the SSAT, the VRB, the IRT and the RRT be amalgamated into one tribunal to be called the Administrative Review Tribunal (ART).[66] The Council's *Better Decisions* report recommended a divisional structure in the ART to permit specialisation, with appeals lying from the divisions to a review panel, but only by leave.[67] The ART proposal thus involved losing a layer of review in the social security and veterans' affairs areas. However, in the migration area the proposal introduced a second, strictly controlled, opportunity for external merits review prior to possible review by the Federal Court.

The ARC's objective in recommending this structural change was not expressed to be the restoration of the non-proliferation principle. Nor did the report explicitly relate the proposal for amalgamation to costs savings.[68] Nonetheless, in some ways the report reflected the continuing influence of the Kerr Committee's thinking. It did not question the proposition that merits review is valuable and tended to assume that it includes the power of the reviewing tribunal

---

[66] Administrative Review Council (1995).

[67] Ibid ch. 8.

[68] The method proposed for costs savings was the contracting out of various of the tribunals' corporate services: ibid 127.

to substitute its decision for that of the original decision-maker.[69] Moreover, the report did not question the proposition that such review should be conducted by a tribunal external to the primary decision-maker.[70]

In reaffirming the need for merits review by a tribunal in addition to judicial review and ensuring diversity by recommending a divisional structure reflecting the specialist jurisdictions of the tribunal, the ARC's approach may well be described as pluralist, in the sense in which legal pluralism is discussed here. However, at this point the qualifications and appointment process for tribunal members requires careful scrutiny in order to ascertain whether the Kerr Committee's foundation assumption of independence in external review has been maintained.

The *Better Decisions* report referred to the concept of independence. This was described not as an ultimate objective but as an attribute which can be achieved in a variety of ways and which contributes to the overall objective of correct and preferable decisions. Decisions are more likely to be 'correct or preferable' if they are fairer, more credible, and improve accountability.[71]

The rejection in the *Better Decisions* report of the argument that tribunal members ought to enjoy tenure will not be considered here, although this remains an issue of central importance to independence. Of more immediate significance in signalling a departure from the Kerr Committee approach and past practice in the AAT was the low value the report placed on the skills of lawyers in tribunal decision-making. It claimed that skills in statutory interpretation, understanding legal arguments and knowledge of the rules of evidence are 'not exclusively correlated with formal legal qualifications'.[72] The ARC appeared to condone the use by non-lawyer tribunal members of legal advice obtained from tribunal research staff and through informal liaison with members with legal training.[73] This was and remains a practice of the RRT.

---

[69] Ibid 9.

[70] Ibid 9–10.

[71] Ibid 11.

[72] Ibid 73.

[73] Ibid 73.

The ARC tended to treat the legal aspects of decision-making as a problem of avoiding legal error which may be detected if review is sought. Referral of an issue out of its case context for a quick legal opinion disregards the integration of legal, policy and factual issues in merits review. It ignores the particular legal problem of denial of procedural fairness to which it may give rise. By taking submissions on legal issues without the parties' knowledge, a tribunal denies them a fair hearing and potentially generates an appearance of bias.

After a period of inaction followed by rumours of proposals by an inter-departmental committee to remove the external nature of merits review—hence undermining its independence—the government responded to the *Better Decisions* report in February 1998. The amalgamation of the AAT, SSAT, RRT and IRT into the new ART would proceed, but the VRB would remain a separate specialist tribunal, with appeals lying to a division of the ART.[74] The divisional structure of the ART in the government's proposal differed slightly from that recommended by the ARC.[75] A second tier of review by a review panel would be available only by leave. It was also proposed that the ART would conduct merits review on the same basis as the AAT had done, with no statutory direction to apply government policy. However, a broad review of the nature and scope of merits review would be undertaken by the government.

4 The Relationship Between Federal Tribunals and Courts

Merits review takes a tribunal into the realm of adjudicating upon non-legal norms. Nonetheless, the normative systems of federal tribunals have much in common with the conventional system of legal

---

[74] Commonwealth Attorney-General, *Reform of Merits Review Tribunals*, News Release, 3 February 1998; Leon (1998). The Attorney-General claimed that the exclusion of the VRB from the amalgamation was due to its having achieved 'very specialised, low cost, non-legalistic' review. But it was clear that the veterans' constituency was simply a stronger lobbying force than were other interest groups with a stake in retaining their own specialist tribunal.

[75] There would be an Immigration and Refugee Division, an Income Support Division, a Taxation Division, a Compensation Division, a Veterans' Appeals Division, and a Commercial and General Division.

norms applied by federal courts. The empowering statute of the tribunal, the statutory regime of benefits and detriments administered
by the tribunal and the common law principles relating to excess of
power and procedural fairness are all shared norms.

This may not eliminate all normative conflict. An institution
that encounters conflict arising from administration of a different
normative system is not required to choose between the extremes of
deference or intolerance towards the other system. An approach
outlined for possible resolution of this conflict is to build solutions
upon fundamental democratic values with which each system must
comply while permitting systems to express their compliance in differing ways. To achieve this, a principle of comity should operate
requiring mutual respect.[76]

(a) Co-ordination of review

Federal and High Court decisions contain little reference to the
pluralist character of the system of review. The general absence of
reference in judicial review judgments to the federal scheme of
review of administrative action as a whole is in itself significant. It
indicates a judicial acceptance of the tribunal system. Investigative
tribunals have infrequently drawn disapproval from federal courts.[77]
No judicial hostility has been displayed towards federal merits
review tribunals. The critics of the system of merits review have
been politicians and senior public servants, not the Federal Court.
Indeed in the area of migration review the criticism by politicians
has been directed at the Federal Court as well as the tribunals. This
is particularly striking when comparisons are made with state jurisdictions. For example, in Victoria the expression by judges of anti-
tribunal sentiment has been pronounced.[78]

One notable instance of judicial acknowledgement of the complementary roles of the Federal Court and the AAT is the High

---

[76] Arthurs (1985) 210.

[77] There is a note of hostility in the High Court's decision in *Balog v Independent Commission Against Corruption* (1990) 169 CLR 625. This occurs more frequently and
in stronger terms in state court decisions. See *Greiner v Independent Commission
Against Corruption* (1992) 28 NSWLR 125.

[78] Supreme Court of Victoria (1988); Victorian Legal and Constitutional Committee
(1990) 13–14.

Court's decision in *Australian Broadcasting Tribunal v Bond*.[79] There, Mason CJ observed that the facility of merits review by the AAT indicates a legislative intention that the Federal Court was not to provide merits review under the *Administrative Decisions (Judicial Review) Act 1977* (Cth) (*ADJR Act*), for this would 'bring about a radical change in the relationship between the executive and judicial branches of government'.[80] Mason CJ returned to this theme later in his judgment, describing the *ADJR Act* as 'an element in the statutory scheme of review' which includes the AAT.[81] The sharp institutional basis for distinguishing between review of the facts and review for error of law assisted Mason CJ in moving towards a conclusion regarding the proper basis for the no evidence ground of review under the *ADJR Act*.[82]

The AAT and the other peak federal merits review tribunals are not 'court substitutes', exercising jurisdiction transferred to them from courts; theirs was a new role. Merits review was not novel, but the general nature of the AAT's jurisdiction was. The scale of this jurisdiction as it developed made the AAT a unique legal institution in the common law world. By contrast, at the state level the transfer of some jurisdiction from courts to tribunals, as in the fields of consumer claims and residential tenancy disputes, may have operated to reduce comity in their relationships. Transfer of jurisdiction from courts to tribunals is not a feature of the federal system, except in the industrial relations area. Here, as a result of the *Boilermakers' Case*, the functions of arbitration and adjudication of enforcement of awards had to be split between a tribunal and a court.

Indeed, federal judges are evidently concerned to ensure that merits review tribunals are permitted to perform their roles effectively and are accorded an appropriate status. A dramatic example is found in the warning of Toohey J in *Haoucher v Minister for Immigration and Ethnic Affairs*.[83] The Minister had published a policy containing a promise that he would only depart from an AAT

---

[79] (1990) 170 CLR 321.

[80] Ibid 341.

[81] Ibid 357.

[82] Ibid 344–5.

[83] (1990) 169 CLR 648.

recommendation that the deportation order be revoked where there were exceptional circumstances or strong evidence. The decision to deport Haoucher involved a denial of procedural fairness based upon a legitimate expectation that the Minister would not depart from his policy without giving the deportee a hearing as to what were the exceptional circumstances or strong evidence. Toohey J warned that if the Minister departed from his policy in this way it would make the AAT review 'an empty ritual and the policy statement mere rhetoric'.[84]

The Kerr Committee envisaged that the power of the proposed review tribunal to deal with issues of law as well as the merits, and the participation of federal judges as its members, would result in many cases being taken to the tribunal rather than to the proposed Commonwealth superior court. Use of the tribunal as a 'preferable alternative' would reduce the work of the court.[85]

The fact that an applicant is entitled to seek review by the AAT or has exercised that entitlement provides a basis for the Federal Court in its discretion to decline to exercise jurisdiction, even though the test of justiciability is satisfied (s 10(2)(b)(ii) of the *ADJR Act*). This discretionary power has been exercised by the Federal Court only occasionally. The onus lies on the respondent administrator to persuade the court to decline to exercise jurisdiction.[86] The issue appears to be infrequently argued. While the rate of use of the *ADJR Act* where AAT review was available is unclear, it is probably true to say that this occurs infrequently. Review on the merits is normally an 'adequate' alternative and in recent cases the Federal Court has indicated that it will fairly readily regard the onus as discharged.[87]

In judicial review at general law superior courts have exercised the discretion to refuse the remedy of mandamus where there is an

---

[84] Ibid 671. See also *Nikac v Minister for Immigration, Local Government and Ethnic Affairs* (1988) 92 ALR 167, 185 where Wilcox J observed that if AAT criminal deportation decisions are not customarily accepted by the Minister, the AAT's decisions will 'fall into disrepute'.

[85] Kerr Committee (1971) 75.

[86] *Kelly v Coats* (1981) 35 ALR 93.

[87] *Swan Portland Cement Ltd v Comptroller-General of Customs* (1989) 90 ALR 280, 286–7; *Hagedorn v Department of Social Security* (1996) 44 ALD 274, 281–2. Compare *Beale v Administrative Appeals Tribunal and Repatriation Commission* (1998) 50 ALD 895.

equally convenient, beneficial and effective remedy, such as merits review by an independent tribunal.[88] While the discretion with regard to relief is broader in review under the *ADJR Act* the issue of utilising tribunal review as an alternative is usually addressed as a jurisdictional one within the context of s 10(2)(b)(ii).

(b) Statutory appeals, the *ADJR Act* and migration review

The Kerr Committee envisaged that the proposed review tribunal would be subject to supervision by the proposed specialist court.[89] The volume of appeals from the AAT on questions of law to the Federal Court is not high and in the majority of cases the Court has upheld the AAT's decision.[90] The Court has adopted a careful approach to the difficult question of what constitutes a question of law.[91]

In review of tribunal decisions under the *ADJR Act* the Federal Court's approach is a balanced one. While prepared at times to take an activist approach, there are also many instances in which the Court has declined to intervene where invited to trespass upon the merits. The High Court's decision in *Minister for Immigration and Ethnic Affairs v Wu Shan Liang (Wu's Case)*[92] in 1996 was greeted by some commentators as indicative of a new restraint by the Court in review of tribunal and other administrative decisions. However, in *Wu's Case* the High Court simply restated the well-established principle that in scrutinising the reasons of a tribunal the Federal Court ought not to be overzealous in finding errors of law in unfortunate phraseology of the tribunal. Applying this principle, the High Court corrected a line of cases where the Federal Court had fallen into this error in review of decisions of the RRT. This does not detract from Federal Court case-law establishing that tribunals must meet a high but not unrealistic standard in preparing statements of reasons for their decisions. *Wu's Case* has certainly provided a

---

[88] *Adler v District Court of New South Wales* (1990) 19 NSWLR 317, 338.

[89] Kerr Committee (1971) 74.

[90] *Administrative Appeals Tribunal Act 1975* (Cth) s 44(1). See Hill (1998) 110.

[91] *Collector of Customs v Pozzolanic Enterprises Ltd* (1993) 115 ALR 1, 9. See Administrative Review Council (1997).

[92] (1996) 185 CLR 259.

handy authority for Federal Court judges to cite when restating the importance of not trespassing upon the merits, but that of itself does not amount to a new era of restraint.

(c) Defining and engaging in merits review

The Federal Court has displayed respect for the AAT with regard to institutional competence in defining the nature of merits review. The AAT's empowering Act gave no greater guidance concerning the nature of the AAT's role in review than to say that the AAT has 'all the powers and discretions' of the decision-maker whose decision is under review.[93] The scope of the AAT's merits review power was defined in *Drake v Minister for Immigration and Ethnic Affairs* *(Drake (No 1))* and *Re Drake and Minister for Immigration and Ethnic Affairs (No 2) (Drake (No 2))*.[94] The former was an appeal to the Full Federal Court from a decision of the AAT in its criminal deportation jurisdiction. The latter was a re-hearing of the matter by the AAT. The principles articulated in these cases provided the benchmark for other merits review tribunals in Australia.[95]

In *Drake (No 1)* the Full Federal Court enunciated well-established principles of administrative law applying to federal tribunals. An existing government policy applicable to the decision was one relevant consideration the AAT was bound to take into account.[96] Since the AAT was an independent statutory authority, having taken the policy into account, it was not bound to apply it. It was held that it should not abdicate its function of making an independent decision in which the propriety of the policy is considered.[97] The Court confined itself to stating the legal constraints upon the AAT and refrained from describing the nature of merits review, other than to say that the function of the AAT is to reach the correct

---

[93] *Administrative Appeals Tribunal Act 1975* (Cth) s 43(1).
[94] (1979) 24 ALR 577 and (1979) 2 ALD 634 respectively.
[95] Note that since the *Migration Reform Act 1992* (Cth) came into operation, s 499 of the *Migration Act 1958* (Cth) has provided for the Minister to issue policy directions which bind the IRT, removing the policy review aspect of merits review in certain areas of its jurisdiction.
[96] *Drake v Minister for Immigration and Ethnic Affairs* (1979) 24 ALR 577, 590–1.
[97] Ibid 590–1. See also *Minister for Immigration, Local Government and Ethnic Affairs v Gray* (1994) 50 FCR 189.

or preferable decision on the material before it.[98] This showed a respect for institutional boundaries. The Court held that it was appropriate for the AAT itself to determine the more precise aspects of its role in reviewing policy.

In *Drake (No 2)* Brennan J, constituting the AAT, provided this guidance. The AAT had the responsibility for developing a set of non-legal norms expressing the mutual comity with the Court and with the primary decision-makers in the executive branch whose decisions it reviewed. Brennan J held that departures from government policy should be 'cautious and sparing', and made only where there are 'cogent reasons' for doing so, such as where applying government policy would be unjust in the individual case.[99] Just as it would be wrong to describe *Drake (No 2)* as an example of deference to government, it is wrong to say that *Drake (No 1)* is an instance of deference by the Federal Court to the AAT.

(d) Judicial scrutiny of tribunal decision-making

The relationship between the Federal Court and federal tribunals is defined in the course of statutory appeals and judicial review at general law under s 39B of the *Judiciary Act 1903* (Cth), under the *ADJR Act* and under Part 8 of the *Migration Act 1958* (Cth). The common law principles applied in review at general law and the statutory limits to review set by statutory appeal provisions, the *ADJR Act* and *Migration Act* determine the scope for an approach of mutual comity on the part of the Federal Court towards tribunals. A vigorous approach to review of administrative decisions has been tempered by an appreciation of the dangers of overzealous scrutiny of the reasons of tribunals.

A major change in the relationship between federal courts and tribunals was quietly effected when the *ADJR Act* came into force in October 1980. Judicial review at general law at that time in Australia was limited to cases of jurisdictional error or non-jurisdictional error appearing on the face of the record. Now there was a new specialist federal court with jurisdiction under the *ADJR Act* to

---

[98] *Drake v Minister for Immigration and Ethnic Affairs* (1979) 24 ALR 577, 589.

[99] *Re Drake and Minister for Immigration and Ethnic Affairs (No 2)* (1979) 2 ALD 634, 644–5.

conduct review in respect of all errors of law, whether or not they appeared on the face of the record.[100]

The extent of this new exposure of tribunals to judicial scrutiny should not be over-estimated. The AAT and other merits review tribunals had duties to give reasons for their decisions.[101] The AAT had separately been made subject to appeals on questions of law to the Federal Court.[102] Decisions of the federal industrial tribunals were not justiciable by the Federal Court under the *ADJR Act* or the general law jurisdiction conferred on the Court in 1983.[103] High Court review of these federal industrial tribunals remained available and had in the past produced the leading cases on the relationship between courts and tribunals. The most important impact of the *ADJR Act* was in relation to primary decisions which were not reviewable by a tribunal, in particular those of ministers and regulatory agencies.

Migration proved to be an area of judicial review which was not only high in volume but was also the cutting edge for development by the Federal Court of common law principles. With the establishment of the IRT and RRT, appeals initially lay on questions of law to the Federal Court. However, in a powerful reflection of the resolve of the executive branch to regain control of this area, Federal Court review of decisions of these tribunals and other migration decisions, particularly primary decisions, was drastically restricted by the insertion of Part 8 into the *Migration Act*.[104] Henceforth, while the decisions of the IRT and RRT were 'judicially-reviewable', the grounds available for review were severely limited. There is some basis for arguing that as these restrictions began to preclude the Federal Court from holding that denial of procedural fairness or *Wednesbury* unreasonableness was established,[105] Federal Court judges took a more activist approach to interpretation of the common

---

[100] *Administrative Decisions (Judicial Review) Act 1977* (Cth) ss 5(1)(f) and 6(1)(f).

[101] See, for example, *Administrative Appeals Tribunal Act 1975* (Cth) s 44(2B).

[102] *Administrative Appeals Tribunal Act 1975* (Cth) s 44(1).

[103] *Administrative Decisions (Judicial Review) Act 1977* (Cth) Schedule 1(a) and (c); *Judiciary Act 1903* (Cth) s 39B(2)(a).

[104] These provisions, inserted by the *Migration Reform Act 1992* (Cth), came into force on 1 September 1994.

[105] *Associated Provincial Picture Houses Ltd v Wednesbury Corporation* [1948] 1 KB 223. See the *Migration Act 1958* (Cth) ss 476(2)(a) and (b).

law grounds of review available to them. However, that is an argument which requires careful analysis of a number of strands of case-law, a task which will not be attempted here.

In judicial review of tribunals at general law prior to 1995, whether in the High Court, Federal Court or state courts, a plaintiff had to establish the traditional grounds of review—jurisdictional error or error of law on the face of the record. In 1995 in *Craig v South Australia* (*Craig's Case*)[106] the High Court reaffirmed traditional principles and dramatically changed direction. Such principles were affirmed with respect to review of inferior courts, where there is a distinction between jurisdictional and non-jurisdictional questions and the record is to be understood in the narrow sense. The dramatic change of direction was the High Court's acceptance in obiter that the distinction between jurisdictional and non-jurisdictional errors is abolished for tribunals.[107] This also means that error of law on the face of the record is an obsolete ground of review of tribunal decisions. *Craig's Case* brought the position under general law into line with that applying under the *ADJR Act*. Henceforth, in the absence of an effective privative clause, judicial review of tribunal decisions would be equivalent to a statutory appeal on any question of law.

In restricting the change of direction to tribunals, the High Court made an awkward general distinction between inferior courts and tribunals, relying partly upon the federal doctrine of separation of powers. The Court also relied upon the broad generalisation that unlike judges of inferior courts, tribunal members are not lawyers and hence ought to be subject to review for all errors of law. This need not be interpreted as conveying a lack of respect for tribunals, but rather as reflecting the fact that the Court was compelled to justify its reluctance to abolish the distinction between jurisdictional and non-jurisdictional errors for inferior courts. There is a strong argument that the High Court would have done better simply to abolish the distinction for inferior courts as well as tribunals.

---

[106] (1995) 184 CLR 163.

[107] That is, that the House of Lords decision in *Anisminic Ltd v Foreign Compensation Commission* [1969] 2 AC 147 applies to tribunals in Australia: *Craig v South Australia* (1995) 184 CLR 163, 179. A more conservative interpretation could be placed upon the High Court's obiter dictum in *Craig v South Australia*. See Allars (1996a) 250.

Craig's Case exposed tribunals generally to closer scrutiny by the courts. In practical terms the major impact of the case was upon state tribunals. Most federal tribunals were either subject to statutory appeal or judicial review for any error of law under the *ADJR Act*. This strengthening of the courts' position in scrutinising tribunal decisions suggests a reduced tolerance of diversity in interpretation of shared legal norms, an adjustment of any mediating principle of comity in the midst of pluralism. Curiously, another decision of the High Court two years later appeared to offer the affected tribunals a compensating protection by renewing the effectiveness of the privative clause. This later decision suggested increased tolerance for the role of tribunals in administering other normative systems as intended by the legislature.

(e) The impact of privative clauses

Privative clauses existing at the date when the *ADJR Act* came into force became ineffective to oust the jurisdiction of the Federal Court to conduct judicial review under that Act.[108] In review at general law privative clauses could have effect, but only in limited situations. Their effectiveness depended upon their drafting and the nature of the error made by the tribunal. Privative clauses expressed in comprehensive terms, asserting that a tribunal's decision 'shall not be quashed or questioned in any court of law' or that 'no certiorari' and 'no prohibition' were available, were ineffective to exclude judicial review for jurisdictional error.[109] The courts' ingenious reasoning was that where a tribunal made a jurisdictional error its decision was void and there was no decision of the tribunal for the privative clause to protect. In one small area the comprehensive privative clause was effective. Where there was a non-jurisdictional error on the face of the record of the tribunal, the comprehensive privative clause protected the decision from judicial review.[110] However, a

---

[108] *Administrative Decisions (Judicial Review) Act 1977* (Cth) s 4.

[109] *Ex parte Wurth; Re Tully* (1954) 55 SR (NSW) 47.

[110] *Houssein v Under Secretary of Industrial Relations and Technology (NSW)* (1982) 148 CLR 88, 93; *Hockey v Yelland* (1984) 157 CLR 124, 130; *Public Service Association of South Australia v Federated Clerks' Union of Australia, South Australian Branch* (1991) 102 ALR 161.

court was able to intervene by characterising a tribunal's error as a case of the tribunal asking itself the wrong question or misconceiving its function. This was a jurisdictional error, not protected by any privative clause.

Craig's Case had nothing to say about privative clauses. The legislation did not provide for appeals from interlocutory decisions of the District Court of South Australia adjourning criminal trials indefinitely, nor did it contain a privative clause protecting decisions of the Court from judicial review. It was arguable that after *Craig's Case*, with all errors of law made by a tribunal going to its jurisdiction, no privative clause could protect its decisions.

That conclusion has been placed in doubt by the revival of a principle of interpretation set out by Dixon J in *R v Hickman; Ex parte Fox and Clinton (Hickman's Case)*.[111] According to the *Hickman* principle a tribunal's decision is not to be invalidated on the ground that it has not conformed to a procedural requirement or has not remained within the limits of its power, provided three conditions are met: 'that its decision is a bona fide attempt to exercise its power, that it relates to the subject matter of the legislation, and that it is reasonably capable of reference to the power given to the body'.[112]

From the time it was decided in 1945, *Hickman's Case* was frequently referred to in federal case-law on jurisdictional error, but infrequently in state cases. The settled law was that in a case of jurisdictional error a comprehensive privative clause was ineffective because there was no decision of the tribunal to protect. Authority was cited for this in state cases without reference to *Hickman's Case*. Even in the federal context the *Hickman* test was infrequently applied to determine an outcome.

The *Hickman* test was understood by many commentators to be a test confined to cases where the problem of the constitutional validity of privative clauses in federal legislation arose. Indeed, when *Hickman's Case* was cited it was usually as authority for the clear constitutional principle that no ordinary federal enactment can oust or affect the original jurisdiction of the High Court under

---

[111] (1945) 70 CLR 598.
[112] Ibid 615.

s 75(iii) or (v) of the Constitution or its jurisdiction to review decisions and orders that exceed constitutional limits. The High Court
affirmed this principle in *Hickman's Case* and in subsequent cases,
including *Darling Casino Ltd v NSW Casino Control Authority*
(*Darling Casino Case*).[113]

A dormant confusion between the established principle and the
Hickman principle erupted in *O'Toole v Charles David Pty Ltd* and
Deputy Commissioner of Taxation v Richard Walter Pty Ltd.[114] The
High Court's decision in the *Darling Casino Case* was awaited in the
hope that it would resolve the uncertainties regarding the scope of
operation of the *Hickman* principle, but at first glance it deepens the
confusion. The case raised the question whether the Supreme Court
of New South Wales had jurisdiction to review a decision to award
a casino licence to one tenderer and not to another (the plaintiff),
irrespective of a privative clause. The clause expressed decisions of
the Casino Control Authority to be final and not subject to appeal
or review, but provided for appeals on questions of law from decisions of the Authority to cancel, suspend or amend the conditions
of a licence. The High Court held, first, that the Authority had made
no errors of law in the tendering process, and, second, in obiter, that
in cases where a privative clause is inconsistent with other provisions in the empowering Act of a tribunal, resort may be made to
the *Hickman* principle in order to resolve the inconsistency.

It is not possible here to attempt to unravel the source of the
confusion or explore in detail the proper interpretation of dicta in the
Darling Casino Case. Suffice to say that the question emerging from
these cases is one of characterisation of statutory provisions which
impact upon the scope and basis for judicial review. According to
one view all of these kinds of provisions should be interpreted as
having been intended to restrict the jurisdiction of superior courts.
Then they are ineffective to oust judicial review for jurisdictional
error. The alternative view is that the statutory provisions are
intended to validate the decisions of a tribunal, thus expanding the
jurisdiction of the tribunal in respect of decisions it has already
made. Such provisions are inconsistent with others in the tribunal's

---

[113] (1997) 191 CLR 602, 631–2.
[114] (1990) 171 CLR 232 and (1995) 183 CLR 168 respectively.

empowering statute, but provided the *Hickman* test is satisfied, they effectively validate the tribunal's decision, making judicial review pointless. The label 'privative clause' may indeed be attached once the legislative intention has been ascertained, the key question being whether a provision is intended to restrict the jurisdiction of the superior court or to expand the jurisdiction of the tribunal.

In addressing this question of characterisation of statutory provisions amending or limiting the jurisdiction of federal courts, it should be remembered that Dixon J's fundamental assumption in *Hickman's Case* was made in a very different context of judicial review of federal tribunals, long before the Federal Court of Australia was established. While the *Hickman* test indicates how the inconsistency between the provisions of the empowering statute is to be resolved, it does not assist in determining how to identify a provision which falls into this category rather than the category of provision directed at the jurisdiction of courts. Provisions imposing new limitations upon the jurisdiction of courts of limited jurisdiction, such as the Federal Court, could well be described as privative clauses when they deprive the court of jurisdiction it formerly had. Part 8 of the *Migration Act* provides a good example, although the privative clause nomenclature was only begun with a Bill which is to repeal Part 8 and further restrict the Court's jurisdiction, again posing the question of the status of the *Hickman* principle.[115]

5 Conclusion

Like the Kerr Committee, the Federal Court and the High Court have implicitly endorsed a pluralism of legal institutions for resolving disputes between individuals and government. The doctrine of separation of powers has ensured that federal courts retain jurisdiction which at state level might be subject to transfer to a tribunal.

---

[115] Migration Legislation Amendment (Judicial Review) Bill 1998 (Cth). Compare *Abebe v Commonwealth* (1999) 162 ALR 1, 29 (Gaudron J) and 44 (Gummow and Hayne JJ), holding Part 8 of the *Migration Act 1958* (Cth) is not a privative clause, but belongs in a third category of provision which is jurisdiction-conferring or jurisdiction-limiting (although these judges held in dissent that Part 8 was invalid as contrary to Chapter III of the Constitution). See also *Minister for Immigration and Multicultural Affairs v Eshetu* (1999) 162 ALR 577, 594.

The doctrine thus promotes legal pluralism and at the same time reduces the potential for tension between courts and tribunals. However, *Craig's Case*, *Wilson's Case* and many others indicate that federal courts regard themselves as a last bastion for the protection of individual rights against executive excess, whether by primary decision-makers or tribunals.

Legal pluralism promises a diversity of institutions which is inimical to centralised and unchecked state power. Pluralism does not argue for a doctrine of deference by courts to tribunals. It argues for mutual respect, or comity, between them. The independence of both kinds of institutions from the central and primary decision-making processes of government is often too readily assumed. Without that independence pluralism provides little protection for democratic values. As government seeks to gain greater control of the tribunal system through appointment of tribunal members, structural change and privative clauses, the judicial role in maintaining that principle of comity by oversight of shared legal norms is weakened. Federal courts may seek further bases for the protection of democratic values. The beginnings of this are found in *Wilson's Case* where the incompatibility test turns largely on the key idea of preserving the independence of federal courts from the executive branch. The issue that looms for the Federal Court and High Court is whether the doctrine of separation of powers may protect the independence of tribunals in the way it protects the independence of federal courts. For without independence there is no legal pluralism of the kind that respects democratic values.

PART III
Federal Jurisdiction

8

Limitations on Federal Adjudication

Henry Burmester

1 Introduction

The jurisdiction of the High Court and other federal courts is defined in Chapter III of the Constitution. The fundamental doctrine of the separation of powers has led the High Court to interpret that jurisdiction in a way that ensures federal courts maintain their distance from the other arms of government (see Chapter 1). The principal way in which this has been achieved is through interpretation of the word 'matter', which is the key concept used by the Constitution to define the jurisdiction of federal courts. As part of this concept, the High Court has also developed particular approaches in relation to standing and justiciability, including advisory opinions. This chapter will examine the way in which these various issues have been dealt with to create either jurisdictional or discretionary barriers to the exercise of federal judicial power. The barriers or limitations are judicially created, rather than mandated by the express terms of the Constitution itself. They are also 'self-regarding' in the sense that they speak to the courts' own power and a study of them is, as Professor Tribe says, 'the description of an institutional psychology' of how the judges view their own role.[1]

---

[1] Tribe (1988) 68.

In the United States, the term 'justiciability' is often used to cover the full range of doctrines that determine which matters federal courts can hear and determine: standing, ripeness, mootness, the political questions doctrine, and the prohibition against advisory opinions.[2] Similar doctrines exist in Australia, but justiciability is generally used in a narrower sense that focuses on the subject matter of the claim, while standing focuses on the person bringing the claim. The approach adopted by the High Court demonstrates a relaxed attitude to the issue of standing and a broad view of what is justiciable, although there is continued resistance to any role that is too advisory or which would take the court into inappropriate areas, such as occurs when attempts are made to agitate issues directly involving Australia's obligations at international law.[3]

Recent judicial consideration indicates that the constitutional basis for the various limitations is receiving greater emphasis. But the precise demarcation between those limitations constitutionally mandated and those resulting from prudential discretion remains somewhat uncertain. This is, however, probably inevitable and even desirable.

Central to the debate over the appropriate scope of the various judicial limitations is the question of the appropriate judicial role. I support a restrained approach to issues like standing on the ground that the judicial role, particularly in constitutional interpretation, should be seen as properly limited to disputes that come before a court where the parties are directly and actually affected.[4] A private rights model of adjudication, suggested by such an approach, is criticised as outdated and inconsistent with maintaining the Constitution and the rule of law. The courts, in some cases, and certain commentators have argued for an expansive judicial role in order, they say, better to protect the rule of law against possible executive transgressions.[5] Against this, however, must be weighed other consider-

---

[2] Chemerinsky (1994) 42.

[3] *Lindon v Commonwealth (No 2)* (1996) 136 ALR 251; *Thorpe v Commonwealth (No 3)* (1997) 144 ALR 677.

[4] Burmester (1992).

[5] See, for example, Fisher and Kirk (1997). See also *Bateman's Bay Local Aboriginal Land Council v Aboriginal Community Benefit Fund Pty Ltd* (1998) 194 CLR 247.

ations, including a need to recognise the political process as the principal player in the resolution of generalised grievances. The precise balance to be struck in this area remains a matter for debate.

The High Court and other federal courts do continue to exercise a certain restraint in relation to the disputes they will adjudicate, founded in their recognition that the judicial arm of government is best able to perform its role not only if its purity is preserved (see Chapter 3) but also if there is continuing recognition by the judicial arm itself that there are certain issues that cannot be resolved in a judicial forum and which must be left to resolution through the general political process. The courts resist legislative and executive functions being conferred on them and at the same time use the various limitations on adjudication to ensure that the judiciary cannot and does not exercise inappropriate functions.

The underlying rationale for these self-denying limitations is the constitutional doctrine of separation of powers. This applies whether the limitations are seen as jurisdictional or discretionary. This constitutional doctrine is seen as important to the rule of law and the protection of individual rights by an independent judiciary.[6] Other justifications for the limitations are that they conserve judicial resources, improve judicial decision-making by guaranteeing the necessary concrete adversarial nature of a controversy, and ensure fairness by ensuring that the rights of those who are not parties are not determined.[7] However, the ultimate explanation is that the various limitations reflect and explain the judicial understanding of the proper role of the courts in our constitutional system. No discussion of the various limitations can ignore this normative question as it determines the view one takes as to whether the limitations have been too narrowly or broadly applied.[8] Unfortunately, the courts tend to assert what they see as their proper role with little explanation or analysis in response to the particular situations that come before them.

---

[6] See Allan (1993) chs 3 and 8; K. Mason (1995) 114, 120.

[7] Chemerinsky (1994) 43–4.

[8] Burmester (1992) 148; Bandes (1990).

2 The Meaning of 'Matter'

The starting point in the Australian federal context is the meaning of 'matter' in Chapter III of the Constitution. The simplicity of this word, as with the United States equivalent of 'cases and controversies', contains 'submerged complexities which go to the very heart of our constitutional form of government'.[9] The meaning of 'matter' and hence the nature of controversies that can be the subject of federal jurisdiction cannot be divorced from the circumstances of a particular case. The facts of a case will often dictate the particular limitation invoked in order to deny jurisdiction or to decline its exercise. The word 'matter' appears in ss 73, 74, 75, 76, 77 and 78 of the Constitution. It is relevant to defining both the original and appellate jurisdiction of the High Court. The original jurisdiction of the High Court is restricted by ss 75 and 76 of the Constitution to the 'matters' there set out. Those 'matters' are defined either by subject matter or by reference to the parties to a suit. But the critical ingredient is the requirement of a 'matter'. This requirement for a 'matter' has been interpreted as a limitation on the power of the High Court and other federal courts to provide, for instance, advisory opinions or to exercise what have been characterised as non-judicial powers. The meaning of the term is important, therefore, in understanding the scope of federal jurisdiction.

Quick and Groom, writing in 1904, said of the term:

> The term 'matters' used in this section differs from the terms 'cases' and 'controversies' used in the corresponding section of the Constitution of the United States. The word 'matters' is the widest, capable of embracing every possible kind of judicial procedure that could arise in the ambit of the section. 'Matters' must be understood as a technical term used in judicial procedure between parties; it is not synonymous with all 'disputed law points' which may be of a political nature subject to decision by the political authorities.[10]

In the United States, 'controversies' had been construed not to include, for instance, criminal jurisdiction. Hence, it was seen as a

---

[9] *Flast v Cohen*, 392 US 83, 94 (1967).
[10] Quick and Groom (1904) 27.

more limited concept by the drafters of the Australian Constitution. By using the word 'matters', however, it was not intended to embrace extra-judicial matters.[11]

The broad meaning of 'matters' was endorsed early in *South Australia v Victoria* where Griffith CJ said 'the word "matters" was in 1900 in common use as the widest term to denote controversies which might come before a Court of Justice'.[12] But it only embraced justiciable controversies requiring the application of judicial, and not political, considerations. O'Connor J said:

> The generality of the word 'matters' in this context [s 75] is restricted by sec. 71. Reading the sections together the power which is thus vested in the High Court is judicial power, and judicial power only. 'Matters' must therefore be read as meaning 'matters capable of judicial determination'. In other words it is only where the matter in controversy between States is 'justiciable' that the High Court can entertain it.[13]

Whatever might have been the position under the United States Constitution,[14] the High Court could only determine boundary disputes between states by the application of recognised legal principles.

The early interpretation of the meaning of 'matter' was confirmed in *Re Judiciary and Navigation Acts*.[15] In that case, the High Court, with Higgins J dissenting, held invalid Part XII of the *Judiciary Act 1903* (Cth) which purported to give the High Court jurisdiction to hear and determine any question referred to it by the Governor-General as to the validity of any enactment of the Parliament. The Court said:

> It was suggested in argument that 'matter' meant no more than legal proceeding, and that Parliament might at its discretion create or invent a legal proceeding in which this Court might be called on to interpret the Constitution by a declaration at large. We do not accept this contention; we do not think that the word 'matter' in sec. 76

---

[11] Quick and Garran (1901) 765–8.

[12] (1911) 12 CLR 667, 675.

[13] Ibid 708.

[14] Ibid 708–9.

[15] (1921) 29 CLR 257.

means a legal proceeding, but rather the subject matter for determination in a legal proceeding. In our opinion there can be no matter within the meaning of the section unless there is some immediate right, duty or liability to be established by the determination of the Court.[16]

Subsequent cases confirm that 'the subject matter' for determination in a legal proceeding is the 'settled prima facie meaning of the word in Chap. III of the Constitution',[17] but it is not to be narrowly construed.[18] In a much quoted passage, the Court went on to say:

> [The legislature] cannot authorize this Court to make a declaration of the law divorced from any attempt to administer that law . . . we can find nothing in Chapter III of the Constitution to lend colour to the view that Parliament can confer power or jurisdiction upon the High Court to determine abstract questions of law without the right or duty of any body or person being involved.[19]

'Matter', therefore, has two elements: the subject matter itself as defined by reference to the heads of jurisdiction set out in Chapter III, and the concrete or adequate adversarial nature of the dispute sufficient to give rise to a justiciable controversy.

At one time the meaning of 'matter' may have been considered by some judges to bear little relation to the different expression 'cases' and 'controversies' in the United States Constitution. However, Mason J said, in *Philip Morris Inc v Adam P Brown Male Fashions Pty Ltd*, that the meaning of 'matter', as formulated in *Re Judiciary and Navigation Acts*, 'does not depart from the American conception of "cases" and "controversies"'.[20] That view may no longer prevail.[21]

---

[16] Ibid 265.

[17] *Crouch v Commissioner for Railways (Q)* (1985) 159 CLR 22, 37.

[18] *Moorgate Tobacco Co Ltd v Philip Morris Ltd* (1980) 145 CLR 457. See also *Collins v Charles Marshall Pty Ltd* (1955) 92 CLR 529, 541–2, 556–7.

[19] *Re Judiciary and Navigation Acts* (1921) 29 CLR 257, 266–7.

[20] (1981) 148 CLR 457, 508 (Mason J).

[21] *Abebe v Commonwealth* (1999) 162 ALR 1, 37 (Gaudron J); *Truth About Motorways Pty Ltd v Macquarie Infrastructure Investment Management Ltd* [2000] HCA 11.

In the context of s 75 in particular, which defines the minimum original jurisdiction of the High Court, the result of this approach to the meaning of 'matter' is that the focus is on the 'substantial subject matter of the controversy' and not on the form in which the legal proceedings happen to be framed.[22] Hence, where a state instrumentality rather than the state itself is sued, this may still amount to a matter between 'a State' and a resident of another state for the purposes of s 75(iv) of the Constitution.[23] Nevertheless, the context in which the word 'matter' is used needs to be considered when determining whether jurisdiction exists. In relation to some 'matters' the nature of the claim is important. In other cases the nature of the party is important.[24]

In *Abebe v Commonwealth* the majority of the High Court considered that a 'matter' is concerned with rights, duties and liabilities identified by reference to 'some law or state of affairs described in s 75 or s 76, and which exists independently of the jurisdiction of a court or its procedures'.[25] However, that does not mean that Parliament can only define the jurisdiction of a federal court by reference to the totality of rights, privileges, powers and duties that arise under that law or state of affairs. This would be contrary to the express recognition in s 77 of the Australian Constitution that Parliament may define the extent to which the jurisdiction of a federal court shall be exclusive of the jurisdiction invested in state courts. Nevertheless, three judges strongly disagreed with this approach. Gummow and Hayne JJ considered that legislative provisions in the *Migration Act 1958* (Cth) by which the Federal Court could consider only certain grounds of attack on the lawfulness of certain executive decisions prevented the Federal Court from quelling the whole of the controversy. This has the consequence that the Federal Court was not conferred with jurisdiction over a 'matter'.[26] Gaudron J adopted a similar view.[27] For these judges, a matter

---

[22] *Crouch v Commissioner for Railways (Q)* (1985) 159 CLR 22, 37.

[23] Ibid 58.

[24] *Carter v Egg and Egg Pulp Marketing Board (Vict)* (1942) 66 CLR 557, 579.

[25] (1999) 162 ALR 1, 10 (Gleeson CJ and McHugh J); see also 61 (Kirby J), 73–4 (Callinan J).

[26] Ibid 45–9.

[27] Ibid 34.

represents the justiciable controversy and not the legal proceedings (a view supported by previous decisions). This meant that the limited statutory remedy in respect of which jurisdiction was given to the Federal Court could not define the 'matter'. By limiting the powers of a federal court in this way, it was being prevented from exercising judicial power. This decision demonstrates that the concept of a 'matter' is still a potent force in constitutional litigation.

Due to the descriptions in ss 75 and 76 of the particular matters in which the High Court has original jurisdiction or in relation to which original jurisdiction can be conferred, there are also issues which arise where subject matters not falling within the descriptions are linked with a subject matter falling within federal jurisdiction. The High Court has allowed accrued jurisdiction beyond that specifically conferred or authorised by the Constitution, but a real and substantial basis must exist for the federal jurisdiction to which the accrued jurisdiction is attached (see Chapter 9).[28]

In relation to appellate jurisdiction, s 73 confers jurisdiction on the High Court to hear appeals from 'all judgments, decrees, orders and sentences'. However, there is also a reference to 'matter' in the second paragraph of the section dealing with the power of Parliament to prevent the High Court from hearing appeals from a Supreme Court of a state in any 'matter' in which at the establishment of the Commonwealth an appeal lies from the Supreme Court to the Queen in Council. Numerous cases have established that the High Court can only hear appeals from judgments, decrees, orders and sentences related to determinations made by courts in exercise of judicial power, that is, in 'matters' as traditionally understood.[29] As will be discussed later, the Court will not hear appeals from advisory opinions.

The High Court's consideration of the meaning of 'matter' in *Croome v Tasmania*[30] points to a willingness not to impose too strict a requirement as to the necessary concrete adverseness for a 'matter' to exist. In that case, two homosexual men sought a declaration that certain provisions of the Tasmanian Criminal Code outlawing

---

[28] P. H. Lane (1997) 509–17.

[29] *Mellifont v Attorney-General (Q)* (1991) 173 CLR 289, 299; *Kable v Director of Public Prosecutions (NSW)* (1996) 189 CLR 51, 142 (Gummow J).

[30] (1997) 191 CLR 119.

homosexual conduct were invalid on the ground of inconsistency with the *Human Rights (Sexual Conduct) Act 1994* (Cth). The Act had been passed in response to a finding by the United Nations Human Rights Committee, established under the International Covenant on Civil and Political Rights, that the Tasmanian law was contrary to Article 17 of the Covenant, which provided for the right not to be subjected to arbitrary interference with privacy. Tasmania's principal argument was that no administration of the law was involved as no prosecution had been brought or was imminent under the provisions of the Criminal Code. In two separate judgments the six members of the High Court hearing the matter considered that the risk to the men of possible criminal prosecution was sufficient to give rise to a matter. As Gaudron, McHugh and Gummow JJ said:

> Their Honours in *In Re Judiciary and Navigation Acts* are not to be taken as lending support to the notion that, where the law of a State imposes a duty upon the citizen attended by liability to prosecution and punishment under the criminal law, and the citizen asserts that, by operation of s 109 of the Constitution, the law of the State is invalid, there can be no immediate right, duty or liability to be established by determination of this Court, in an action for declaratory relief by the citizen against the State, unless the Executive Government of the State has, at least, invoked legal process against the particular citizen to enforce the criminal law.[31]

This case also dealt with the issue of standing and will be considered further in that context. It highlights, however, the central importance of the concept of 'matter' in the judicial application of limitations to the activity of federal courts.

3 Advisory Opinions

One of the consequences of the approach to the definition of 'matter' in Chapter III of the Constitution is that it is not possible to confer on the High Court or other federal courts the power to give advisory opinions. This was established by the decision of the High Court in

---

[31] Ibid 136.

Re Judiciary and Navigation Acts.[32] There, the majority found Part
XII of the *Judiciary Act* to be invalid on the basis that it purported
to confer power on the High Court to determine in an authoritative
way questions of law referred by the Governor-General without the
right or duty of any body or person being involved. It is clear from
this case that under Chapter III of the Constitution no abstract determinations of law can occur. What was left open—at least by the
joint judgment of Knox CJ, Gavan Duffy, Powers, Rich and Starke JJ
—was whether non-judicial functions, such as providing opinions
rather than authoritative declarations of the law, could be conferred
on the Court or its members outside Chapter III.[33] The decision of
the High Court and Privy Council in *R v Kirby; Ex parte Boilermakers' Society of Australia (Boilermakers' Case)*[34] would now
appear to leave no room for such a conferral on the Court. More
recent decisions such as *Grollo v Palmer*[35] and *Wilson v Minister for
Aboriginal and Torres Strait Islander Affairs*[36] also suggest that it
is probably incompatible with judicial power to confer any such
'opinion' function on judges as designated persons.

In his dissent in *Re Judiciary and Navigation Acts*, Higgins J
preferred the Canadian and Imperial practice whereby questions
could be put before the Supreme Court or Privy Council for advice.
He distinguished as inapplicable to Australia the United States practice, which since 1793 has involved the Supreme Court refusing to
provide opinions to the President[37] as resulting from a request for
advice on questions pertaining to treaties, and hence political questions.[38] Professor Stewart Jay has recently reasserted the view that
the 1793 refusal of the Supreme Court to advise the President was
the result of political and ideological circumstances at the time and

---

[32] (1921) 29 CLR 257.

[33] Ibid 264.

[34] (1956) 94 CLR 254 and (1957) 95 CLR 529 respectively.

[35] (1995) 184 CLR 348.

[36] (1996) 189 CLR 1. In that case, one of the specific matters relied on to find that the
function conferred on the judge in her personal capacity was incompatible with her
position as a judge was the requirement to advise on legal issues.

[37] Tribe (1988) 73–7.

[38] *Re Judiciary and Navigation Acts* (1921) 29 CLR 257, 275.

not the necessary result of evolution of constitutional structure.[39] However, the prohibition remains firmly established in the United States.[40] Whatever the original rationale, the refusal of federal courts to provide advisory opinions has become paradigmatic in both American and Australian constitutional law.

The requirement that there be a relevant judgment, decree or order for the purposes of an appeal to the High Court has continued to raise difficulties when the decision appealed from has the character of an advisory opinion. As recently as 1991 the High Court was still coming to terms with its power to hear appeals from state courts which had given decisions on references or stated cases made to them by the relevant Attorney-General for the state. Such provisions are common in relation to completed criminal trials.[41] Yet such provisions have characteristics more akin to the provision of advisory opinions than the resolution of justiciable controversies.

In *Mellifont v Attorney-General (Q) (Mellifont's Case)*,[42] six judges of the High Court, with Brennan J dissenting, held that the opinion of a state Supreme Court on a point of law referred by a state Attorney-General after the acquittal or discharge of a person was a judgment, decree or order within s 73 of the Constitution from which an appeal to the High Court might be brought. This situation was distinguished from that which arose in *Re Judiciary and Navigation Acts* on the basis that the decision on the reference was sought in order to determine the correctness of the trial judge's rulings. It was not, therefore, an abstract question, and hypothetical in the sense that it was unrelated to any actual controversy between the parties.[43] This decision overruled an earlier and more restrictive view that answers to questions in a stated case could not be appealed to

---

[39] Jay (1997).

[40] Tribe (1988) 73–7; Chemerinsky (1994) 47–53.

[41] For examples, see s 669A of the *Criminal Code* (Qld) and s 474D of the *Crimes Act 1900* (NSW). For trials of federal criminal matters, these provisions are picked up by s 68 of the *Judiciary Act*, but this can only be to the extent that where state courts are given functions under these provisions for the purposes of federal law, they must be functions falling within federal judicial power.

[42] (1991) 173 CLR 289.

[43] Ibid 304–5.

the High Court unless the answers finally determined the rights of the parties in a suit.[44] The Court saw the second of the two passages quoted earlier from *Re Judiciary and Navigation Acts* as containing 'two critical concepts'. These were, first, the notion of an abstract question of law and, second, the declaration of law divorced from any attempt to administer it.[45] It is the Court's attempt to apply these concepts to various appellate matters brought before it that has led to differences of view and some changes of judicial direction.

In *Mellifont's Case* the Court explained why the answers to the questions of law did not infringe the requirements for a matter:

> Answers given by the full court of a court to questions reserved for its consideration in the course of proceedings in a 'matter' pending in that court do not constitute an advisory opinion or abstract declaration of the kind dealt with in *In Re Judiciary and Navigation Acts* whether or not those answers, of themselves, determine the rights of the parties. Such answers are not given in circumstances divorced from an attempt to administer the law as stated by the answers; they are given as an integral part of the process of determining the rights and obligations of the parties which are at stake in the proceedings in which the questions are reserved. Once this is accepted, as indeed it must be, it follows inevitably that the giving of the answers is an exercise of judicial power because the seeking and the giving of the answers constitutes an important and influential, if not decisive, step in the judicial determination of the rights and liabilities in issue in the litigation. Viewed in this context, it matters not whether the giving of the answers is, as a matter of legal theory, a binding determination.[46]

This is not an altogether compelling conclusion. It can be best understood in light of remarks later in the judgment that the statutory procedure there under consideration, with counterparts in other jurisdictions, is

---

[44] *Fisher v Fisher* (1986) 161 CLR 438; *Swiss Aluminium Australia Ltd v Federal Commissioner of Taxation* (1987) 163 CLR 421. See also *Saffron v The Queen* (1953) 88 CLR 523.

[45] *Mellifont v Attorney-General (Q)* (1991) 173 CLR 289, 303.

[46] Ibid 303.

a standard procedure for correcting error of law in criminal proceedings without exposing the accused to double jeopardy . . . the fundamental point . . . is that s. 669A(2) enables the Court of Criminal Appeal to correct an error of law at the trial. It is that characteristic of the proceedings that stamps them as an exercise of judicial power and the decision as a judgment or order within the meaning of s. 73.[47]

However, there are still limits on the right of appeal from a reference or case stated. In *Director of Public Prosecutions (SA) v B*,[48] where the questions reserved were not related to a particular trial, the critical requirement for the conclusion in *Mellifont's Case* was missing. What was being sought in *Director of Public Prosecutions (SA) v B*, particularly given the generality of the questions, was an advisory opinion.[49] In the context of a statutory provision similar to that considered in *Mellifont's Case*, and on the basis of prudential rather than constitutional considerations, the House of Lords has also emphasised the limits that exist in relation to the proper judicial role in providing answers to academic questions referred to a court after an acquittal.[50]

The full implications of the decision in *Mellifont's Case* for pronouncements by the federal courts on legal questions raised in other contexts remain somewhat controversial, as is illustrated by the decision in *North Ganalanja Aboriginal Corporation v Queensland (Waanyi Case)*.[51] In that case six judges refused to consider the issue of the effectiveness of the grant of a pastoral lease to extinguish native title on the ground that once one issue concerning the statutory duties of the Registrar of the Native Title Tribunal was determined in a certain way there were no properly constituted proceedings in which the issues concerning native title could arise. To pronounce on such issues would be to deliver an advisory opinion. The law 'is not judicially administered by judicial declarations of its

---

[47] Ibid 305.
[48] (1998) 194 CLR 566.
[49] Ibid 576–7.
[50] *Attorney-General's Reference (No 3 of 1994)* [1998] AC 245, 265.
[51] (1996) 185 CLR 595.

content "divorced from any attempt to administer that law" '.[52] As McHugh J put it:

> If the Court had also granted special leave and purported to give an opinion on the extinguishment issue, it would have given an opinion which it had no constitutional jurisdiction to give. The opinion of the Court would have been an advisory opinion. It would have been giving an opinion on a matter that did not arise because, ex hypothesi, the order of the Court on the procedural issue would direct the Tribunal to accept the application. The Constitution gives this Court no jurisdiction to give advisory opinions in either its original or its appellate jurisdiction. Once the Court directed the Tribunal to accept the application of the Waanyi People, a decision by the Court on extinguishment would be binding on nobody, just as the opinion of the Federal Court that the title of the Waanyi People has been extinguished is now binding on nobody.[53]

Kirby J wrote a very strong dissent in relation to this approach, concluding:

> The current rather narrow state of authority on the Court's original jurisdiction to provide advisory opinions may one day require reconsideration as the Court adapts its process to a modern understanding of its constitutional and judicial functions. Since *In re Judiciary and Navigation Acts* was decided in 1921 there has been a substantial development in the understanding of what the judiciary in Australia may properly do in discharging its proper functions. For example, the scope of the availability of the beneficial remedy of a declaration, to deal with an apprehended threat of invasion of rights, has expanded greatly, overcoming in the process some of the same resistance as lay behind the refusal to provide advisory opinions ... I would resist any attempt to expand the principle against the giving of 'advisory opinions' to a new doctrine which would deprive this Court of jurisdiction to deal with issues potentially critical to the rights of the parties properly before it in an appeal. To do so would impose on the Court a rigidity which its past practice and authority negate.[54]

---

[52] Ibid 612.
[53] Ibid 642.
[54] Ibid 666–7.

Similar views were repeated by Kirby J in relation to appellate matters in *Director of Public Prosecutions (SA) v B*. In that case, however, Kirby J acknowledged that the requirement that the Court not make declarations of the law divorced from its administration 'is grounded in the constitutional text itself'.[55] He pointed to the nature of the judicial power referred to in s 71 of the Constitution; the nature of appeals from judgments, decrees, orders and sentences in s 73; the nature of 'matters' as referred to in ss 75, 76, 77 and 78; and 'the implications derived from the language, structure and purposes of Ch III of the Constitution with its establishment of an independent judiciary'.[56] This passage would be likely to be supported by all other members of the Court. However, Kirby J takes a much broader view of what is related to the administration of the law than other members of the Court. The Court as a whole emphasises the limits on its ability to decide legal issues not necessary to the resolution of an actual controversy and that it is not a judicial role to provide guidance. This was emphasised in *Bass v Permanent Trustee Co Ltd*.[57] There, the majority of the Court said it was incompatible with the efficient administration of justice for courts to provide answers to hypothetical questions. The trial judge, without any agreed or found facts, had answered certain questions and made a declaration. Kirby J again disagreed with the rest of the Court, regarding the issue of law as neither hypothetical nor abstract.[58] Individual judges do not, however, always resist the temptation to provide advice or to express their views on issues not necessary to the decision.[59]

In Canada, by contrast, the Supreme Court finds no difficulty in providing advisory opinions, even on sensitive political issues. This is evident from the 1998 decision in *Reference Re: Secession of Quebec*.[60] The Supreme Court said that in the absence of a strict separation of powers in the Canadian Constitution there is no

---

[55] (1998) 194 CLR 566, 594.
[56] Ibid 593–4.
[57] (1999) 161 ALR 399, 413–18.
[58] Ibid 425–7.
[59] For the United States position, see Katyal (1998) and Mikva (1998).
[60] (1998) 161 DLR (4th) 385.

constitutional bar to that Court's receipt of jurisdiction to undertake an advisory role in tandem with its other duties.

There is no doubt that the refusal to provide an advisory opinion can be inconvenient at times when an opinion could provide useful guidance to a legislature in an uncertain area. This explains repeated support for amendment of the Constitution to enable advisory opinions to be given by the High Court.[61] The 1929 Royal Commission on the Constitution recommended inserting a provision empowering the Parliament to make laws authorising the High Court to advise as to the validity of any Commonwealth or state law. In 1978 the Australian Constitutional Convention supported the insertion of a provision in the Constitution authorising the Governor-General or Governor in Council to refer respectively the validity of a Commonwealth or state enactment or proposed law to the High Court. In 1977 a Senate Committee reported in favour of conferral of advisory jurisdiction on the High Court. This led to further consideration and a revised proposal being adopted by the Australian Constitutional Convention in 1983 which was then reflected in a proposal to alter the Constitution passed by both Houses of the Parliament in 1983 (Constitution Alteration (Advisory Jurisdiction of the High Court) 1983). At the insistence of the Senate, this did not extend to proposed laws. The proposal was never submitted to a referendum.

The Constitutional Commission revisited this issue. Its Advisory Committee on the Australian Judicial System recommended against conferring any advisory jurisdiction on the High Court. It was concerned to avoid drawing the courts into the legislative process. The Commission itself in its 1988 Report recommended a very limited advisory jurisdiction significantly confined to making a declaration on a question of law relating to the manner and form of enacting any proposed law including any proposed alteration to the Constitution. This was designed to cover questions concerning the operation of s 57 (the double dissolution provision) and s 128 (the amendment provision), but did not support any conferral of general advisory opinion jurisdiction.[62]

[61] For a review of various proposals see Australian Constitutional Commission (1988) 415–16.

[62] Ibid 414.

It is necessary to consider in greater detail the attraction of some advisory opinion mechanism and the strengths and weaknesses of the various models. Despite enthusiasm for the idea, particularly in the 1970s and 1980s, there appears to be little support or pressure at present to revive any of the earlier proposals.

The wide support for advisory jurisdiction was explained by the Constitutional Commission as 'principally motivated by a desire to make the governmental and legislative process work more smoothly, efficiently and speedily. The reports of the bodies concerned emphasised difficulties for government and the waste of resources that can occur as a result of having to await the challenge to legislation a considerable time after its enactment'.[63] It also said:

> The main reason for conferring on the High Court jurisdiction to give authoritative answers to constitutional questions asked by prescribed authorities is the inconvenience and confusion that can arise from a cloud of doubt hanging over the validity of legislation. The legislation may involve the setting up of costly administrative machinery, such as the creation of statutory bodies with staff and equipment. If the legislation is declared invalid after a period of time a great deal of money and resources may be wasted. Even if the legislation is eventually upheld, threats or rumours of challenges to it can sap the vitality of those administering the scheme.[64]

In response to this it stated the arguments against as follows:

(a) It would undermine the principle of the separation of the judiciary from the legislative and executive arms of government. It puts the judges into the position of advisers to the Government. Alternatively, it empowers the Court to interfere with executive and legislative processes.

(b) A reference for an advisory opinion results in the Court having to determine legal questions in the abstract instead of in a factual setting. Many issues can only be seen when facts are presented which bring them to light. Parties who will be affected by the legislation or Executive action, if it is upheld, may be denied an opportunity to present arguments.

---

[63] Ibid 417.
[64] Ibid 414–15.

(c) An advisory jurisdiction will encourage governments to refer many matters to the Court, so increasing the work of the High Court at the expense of other important functions, including its function as a final court of appeal laying down the general law for Australia.[65]

The Commission recommended against any general advisory power. Once a law is enacted, the very generous standing rules, particularly for states, avoid many of the earlier perceived problems in relation to enacted laws. Separation of powers reasons strongly suggest that there should be no judicial role at an earlier stage of a proposed law. Arguments that an advisory opinion jurisdiction would allow the law to be 'open and clear' and would therefore help to promote the rule of law[66] need to be balanced against the considerable weight of the counter arguments.

One can contrast the debate in Australia with the established Canadian practice of providing advisory opinions. Interestingly, many of the opinions provided in Canada concern not proposed laws but issues concerned with underlying constitutional principle, such as the *Reference Re: Amendment of the Constitution of Canada (Nos 1, 2 and 3)*[67] or, more recently, questions relating to the secession of Quebec.[68] None of the Australian proposals for advisory opinions contemplates such references, doubtless reflecting the accepted importance of the separation of powers and a concern to avoid embroiling the courts in political controversy. In Canada, however, the Supreme Court retains a discretion not to give an opinion if a matter is considered not to be within its area of expertise, namely, the interpretation of law, or the question is too imprecise or ambiguous to permit a complete answer. It seems unlikely that the Australian judicial or political system is ready to embrace conferral of a similar broad advisory role on Australian courts. Rather, as indicated by the recent decisions in *Director of Public Prosecutions (SA) v B*[69] and

---

[65] Ibid 415; see also Crawshaw (1977) 119–25.
[66] J. Williams (1996).
[67] (1982) 125 DLR (3rd) 1.
[68] *Reference Re: Secession of Quebec* (1998) 161 DLR (4th) 385.
[69] (1998) 194 CLR 566.

Bass v Permanent Trustee Co Ltd[70] the High Court is emphasising a purer and more limited judicial role.

4 Standing

The limited judicial role in relation to advisory opinions can be contrasted with the approach taken to the issue of standing. This is an issue related to the definition of 'matter'. Standing is concerned with the issue of access to the courts and the appropriateness of the plaintiff. In this sense it is separate from the issue of justiciability, which is concerned with the subject matter of the case. Nevertheless, it is a mistake to view standing in complete isolation from the nature of the action before the court.

This was illustrated in *Croome v Tasmania*[71] in which Tasmania conceded that the plaintiffs had standing but sought to argue that there was no 'matter' the Court could decide. The High Court rejected this attempt to separate the two issues. In an action challenging the validity of a law, whether a person seeking a declaration of invalidity has a sufficient interest may determine, or significantly influence, whether there is a 'matter'. In *Croome v Tasmania* the Court was not prepared to consider the argument that there was only a hypothetical or abstract question of law for determination in isolation from the particular interest of the plaintiffs. The fact that the plaintiffs had engaged in conduct which they contended was no longer illegal as a result of a federal law overriding an inconsistent state law was considered by three judges to confer sufficient standing.[72] For the remaining three it was enough that the plaintiffs 'faced possible criminal prosecution'.[73] In circumstances where a declaration of invalidity was sought, this standing was sufficient to constitute a justiciable controversy. Brennan CJ, Dawson and Toohey JJ said that a sufficient interest was necessary for a justiciable controversy. As to what was a sufficient interest, they said:

---

[70] (1999) 161 ALR 399.

[71] (1997) 191 CLR 119. For more detailed consideration of standing in a constitutional context, see Burmester (1992).

[72] (1997) 191 CLR 119, 127 (Brennan CJ, Dawson and Toohey JJ).

[73] Ibid 138 (Gaudron, McHugh and Gummow JJ).

We do not wish now to assent to the broad proposition that any person who desires or intends to act in contravention of a law has, by reason merely of that desire or intention a cause of action to seek a declaration of invalidity of the law. It may be that the curial discretion to refuse relief warrants acceptance of that broad proposition but, in the present case, it is not necessary to decide the question.[74]

Gaudron, McHugh and Gummow JJ indicated that questions of standing are subsumed in the issue of whether jurisdiction has been invoked with respect to a matter.[75] The notions of standing and matter are interdependent. Reference was made to a number of United States cases which highlighted that standing was an essential element of the 'cases and controversies' concept contained in Article III of the United States Constitution. For these judges the position is the same in Australia in relation to the concept of 'matter'.[76] Their emphasis on the constitutional foundation suggests that there is less scope for a discretionary approach to standing than suggested by the other three judges.

The High Court has required a member of the public challenging the validity of a law or executive act to have a 'special interest' establishing that they are affected more particularly than is the public at large. This is, however, a flexible requirement, as is evident from *Shop Distributive & Allied Employees Association v Minister for Industrial Affairs (SA)*.[77] There it was held that the union had standing to apply for orders concerning the validity of certain exemptions from shop trading hours on the basis that members of the union were shop assistants who had a special interest in the trading hours of shops in which they were employed. In a five-member joint judgment, the High Court said that the generally accepted rule remains that stated in *Australian Conservation Foundation v Commonwealth* and *Onus v Alcoa of Australia Ltd*,[78] namely, that a

---

[74] Ibid 127. See also *Davis v Commonwealth* (1988) 166 CLR 79, 96 which also left the issue open.

[75] *Croome v Tasmania* (1997) 191 CLR 119, 132–3.

[76] Ibid 133.

[77] (1995) 183 CLR 552.

[78] (1980) 146 CLR 493 and (1981) 149 CLR 27, 35–6 respectively.

plaintiff has no standing to bring an action to prevent the violation of a public right if they have no interest in the subject matter beyond that of any other member of the public. However, the Court stated that 'the rule is flexible and the nature and subject matter of the litigation will dictate what amounts to a special interest'.[79]

The High Court's reluctance to allow standing requirements to preclude the use of appropriate judicial remedies in preventing breaches of the law is illustrated in *Bateman's Bay Local Aboriginal Land Council v Aboriginal Community Benefit Fund Pty Ltd* (*Bateman's Bay Case*).[80] There the appellants proposed to establish a contributory funeral benefit scheme. The respondent operated such a business catering for the New South Wales Aboriginal community. The High Court, applying the 'special interest' test, found that the likely detriment to the respondent's business was sufficient to confer standing. However, the Court went on to make wider observations about the roles of the courts and the Attorney-General in ensuring observance of the law. In separate judgments, McHugh and Hayne JJ recognised that the enforcement of the law as a general proposition was often appropriately left to be resolved by the political process. This explained the traditional reluctance of the courts to accord standing to an individual to seek enforcement of the law where they could establish no special interest of their own.

In a joint judgment Gaudron, Gummow and Kirby JJ identified a public interest in the maintenance of due administration and in restraining the apprehended misapplication of public funds. In these areas, equitable intervention by declaration or injunction is not designed to protect any particular proprietary or other rights of a plaintiff. The joint judgment rejected the English view that it was for the Attorney-General and not a private individual to protect the public in the assertion of public rights. This view was rejected as reflecting 'a view of standing which sees administrative review as concerned with the vindication of private not public rights'.[81] The special position of the Attorney-General in this area was rejected as

---

[79] *Shop Distributive & Allied Employees Association v Minister for Industrial Affairs (SA)* (1995) 183 CLR 552, 558.

[80] (1998) 194 CLR 247.

[81] Ibid 262.

inappropriate in the Australian context. The joint judgment also drew attention to the fact that in federal jurisdiction 'questions of "standing", when they arise, are subsumed within the constitutional requirement of a "matter"'.[82]

The joint judgment makes it clear that in areas such as due administration of public bodies with recourse to public revenues, the issue of standing is unlikely to be an insurmountable hurdle if the cause of action is otherwise justiciable and is not otherwise an abuse of process. Given the basis on which the case was argued, the joint judgment did not proceed according to a new approach to standing. It applied the established test and found a sufficient special interest in the likely detriment to the respondent's business, emphasising the flexible nature of this requirement, which should be construed as 'an enabling, not a restrictive, procedural stipulation'.[83] The judgment appears to adopt a view similar to Professor Peter Cane's—that the public interest in governmental observance of basic constitutional principles justifies the courts granting standing to individuals in cases designed to ensure the protection of the interests of citizens against the government.[84] This decision suggests that in an appropriate case a taxpayer or individual who can point to no special interest of their own may be accorded standing. Instead of rejecting such a possibility, the High Court has in earlier cases left the issue open.[85]

The relaxed approach to standing of private individuals has also been reflected in the willingness of the High Court to allow the states to challenge Commonwealth laws on the ground that they infringe the Constitution, whether or not any state law or direct state interest is affected.[86] In the United States, the attitude to the standing of states to bring constitutional challenges is much more restrictive than in Australia. Much frustration at the inability to obtain advisory opinions has been overcome in Australia by the High Court's willingness to determine challenges by the states to the validity of Com-

---

[82] Ibid 262.

[83] Ibid 267.

[84] Cane (1995a) 142–4.

[85] *Croome v Tasmania* (1997) 191 CLR 119; *Davis v Commonwealth* (1988) 166 CLR 79, 96; Burmester (1992) 168–71; Taylor (1979).

[86] See Burmester (1992) 172–4; Johnston (1979).

monwealth laws that have been enacted but have not yet come into force.[87]

This generous approach to standing evident in recent High Court decisions is reflected in a number of cases in the Federal Court dealing with administrative law issues which have applied the 'special interest' criterion or other statutory tests in the context of challenges to decisions under various statutory schemes. For instance, under the *Administrative Decisions (Judicial Review) Act 1977* (Cth) (*ADJR Act*), standing to apply for review under its provisions is accorded to 'a person who is aggrieved by' a decision made under certain federal enactments.[88] In an overview of these decisions, Justice Kevin Lindgren, writing extra-judicially in 1996, said:

> Starting from the position that the AD(JR) Act requires something more than that an applicant should sincerely *claim* to be aggrieved or objectively *feel* aggrieved, the Federal Court at first interpreted the statutory criterion as if its terms posed a test indistinguishable from the 'special interest' test of the general law. Arguably, it has construed the statutory test of a 'person who is aggrieved' more expansively in recent times.[89]

Here I am concerned with the constitutional limitations that may be imposed in relation to the rules of standing. This is not the place to attempt a detailed overview of the considerable number of cases dealing with standing in a judicial review context. However, what seems clear from examining those cases is that the courts take a broad view of what constitutes a special interest. Thus, associational or representative standing has been accorded to conservation groups because of their active involvement in an issue.[90] By contrast, there will be no interest where the actual outcome of the review will

---

[87] *Attorney-General (Vict) v Commonwealth (Marriage Act Case)* (1962) 107 CLR 529; *New South Wales v Commonwealth (Incorporation Case)* (1990) 169 CLR 482. See also Crawshaw (1977) 114–16.

[88] Mack (1987); Allars (1991).

[89] Lindgren (1996) 277 (emphasis in original). For a general survey, see Aronson and Dyer (1996) ch. 12.

[90] *North Coast Environment Council Inc v Minister for Resources* (1994) 127 ALR 617. For discussion of representational standing see Cane (1995b).

not affect the applicant.[91] Trade rivals have not fared so well in achieving standing.[92]

There remains the question of whether a statutory conferral of standing on 'any person' for purposes of enforcing a particular statutory regime is within power. Such provisions will be upheld provided they do not require the court to adjudicate in a situation that cannot properly be described as a 'matter', having regard to the subject matter and context in which the suit arises.[93] In the United States, however, in *Lujan, Secretary of the Interior v Defenders of Wildlife*,[94] the Supreme Court held that a right of standing statutorily conferred on all persons could not overcome the constitutional requirement to allege and establish some concrete and particularised invasion of a legally protected interest—what is referred to as an 'injury in fact'. A generalised grievance about government did not constitute an Article III case or controversy. The present High Court has rejected such a restrictive approach,[95] although questions of discretion may still operate to limit any relief unless the circumstances warrant judicial intervention.

Despite the relaxed attitude to standing demonstrated by the federal courts, there continue to be demands for further relaxation of the rules of standing. Thus, there have been a number of reports and reviews on this issue by Law Reform Commission bodies, including a major report in 1985 by the Australian Law Reform

---

[91] *Transurban City Link Ltd v Allan* (1999) 168 ALR 687.

[92] *Alphapharm Pty Ltd v Smithkline Beecham (Aust) Pty Ltd* (1994) 49 FCR 250. In *Bateman's Bay Local Aboriginal Land Council v Aboriginal Community Benefit Fund Pty Ltd* (1998) 194 CLR 247, 266, the High Court explained the decisions in that case, and in *Right to Life Association (NSW) Inc v Secretary, Department of Human Services and Health* (1995) 56 FCR 50, to be the result of the subject, scope and purpose of the particular statutory regime under which the particular decisions were made.

[93] See, for example, s 80 of the *Trade Practices Act 1974* (Cth), the validity of which was upheld in *Truth About Motorways Pty Ltd v Macquarie Infrastructure Investment Management Ltd* [2000] HCA 11.

[94] 504 US 555 (1992).

[95] *Truth About Motorways Pty Ltd v Macquarie Infrastructure Investment Management Ltd* [2000] HCA 11.

Commission (ALRC).[96] More recently the ALRC has revisited the issue and in 1996 released a further report proposing a new test for standing.[97] The approach of the ALRC in both reports was to advocate a very broad test for standing, as one element that facilitates access to justice. It recommends a new test for standing in public law proceedings, defined as matters arising under the Constitution or involving its interpretation, matters involving federal legislation, or suits against the Commonwealth. Instead of requiring a special interest the ALRC recommends that any person should be able to commence public law proceedings unless the relevant legislation provides otherwise or the litigation would unreasonably interfere with the ability of a person having a private interest in a matter to deal with it as he or she wishes. This new test replaces the earlier recommendation which was similarly broad, allowing any person to have standing unless it was shown that the person was 'merely meddling'. These would require courts to concentrate attention on the issue in dispute divorced from any consideration of what interest the plaintiff has in resolving the particular matter.

The latest ALRC report reaffirms the view expressed in the earlier report that 'there is no constitutional requirement for a plaintiff to possess a personal or special interest in order to commence public law proceedings'.[98] In one sense this is correct, and the *Bateman's Bay Case* reinforces this. At the same time, in that case Gaudron, Gummow and Kirby JJ pointed to the link between standing and the constitutional requirement of a 'matter'.[99] This link emphasised 'the general consideration that the principles by which standing is assessed are concerned to "mark out the boundaries of judicial power" whether in federal jurisdiction or otherwise'.[100] In

---

[96] Australian Law Reform Commission (1985). For a discussion of this report, and those by other Law Reform Commissions, see Lindgren (1996) 280–5. For a critique of the report, see Burmester (1992) 159–60.

[97] Australian Law Reform Commission (1996).

[98] Ibid 47.

[99] *Bateman's Bay Local Aboriginal Land Council v Aboriginal Community Benefit Fund Pty Ltd* (1998) 194 CLR 247, 262; see also *Croome v Tasmania* (1997) 191 CLR 119.

[100] (1998) 194 CLR 247, 262.

light of these remarks and those discussed earlier with reference to *Croome v Tasmania*, it does not seem possible to dismiss the relevance of standing to whether there is a 'matter' as easily as the ALRC appears to do.

The issue that ultimately lies behind the approach to be adopted on standing is determining the appropriate role for the courts in relation to matters of public interest. The constitutional requirement for there to be a 'matter' reflects underlying prudential considerations as to the suitability of courts to deal with certain issues. While the ALRC complains that the 'special interest' test is 'uncertain, complicated, inconsistent and overly dependent on subjective value judgments',[101] recent cases demonstrate the considerable breadth of that test. The alleged defects with the present test cannot be considered without also balancing other considerations related to the role of courts in relation to decisions of the executive or Parliament. This is recognised by all five judges in the *Bateman's Bay Case*. The three judges who wrote a joint judgment in that case are attracted to a more robust judicial role than are McHugh and Hayne JJ. Where the balance is struck looks set to be further debated but a restrictive approach to standing appears to have less judicial support than previously. At the same time, other prudential or discretionary doctrines such as justiciability or abuse of process remain relevant to the overall consideration of whether there is a 'matter' appropriate for judicial determination. Arguments for broad standing rules grounded in 'democratic theory of government'[102] need to give proper regard to the limited role of the judiciary in a democratic system, particularly one with a strong separation of powers.

While Australia adopts a more relaxed approach to standing a narrower approach seems to be gaining favour in the United States Supreme Court. In recent decisions the Court appears to have retreated from some of its earlier decisions which adopted a broad approach to standing. There is now emphasis on the onus on a plaintiff to establish a concrete interest of their own. A generalised grievance against allegedly illegal government conduct is not regarded as

[101] Australian Law Reform Commission (1996) 5.
[102] Fisher and Kirk (1997).

sufficient to confer standing.[103] The tenor of the recent judgments emphasise that vindicating the public interest in government observance of the Constitution and law is not a judicial function, at least unless the legislative arm has clearly conferred broad standing rights for the purposes of enforcing a particular statutory scheme. Even then, sufficient 'interest' needs to be shown by the person bringing the action. By contrast, the most recent Australian position reflects a reluctance to erect standing as a barrier if to do so would be to prevent the adjudication of an otherwise justiciable issue involving compliance by the executive with statutory or constitutional imperatives.

Interestingly, recent Canadian cases also indicate a trend back to some limitations on standing. There is no constitutional peg in Canada confining the federal courts to 'matters' in the Australian sense. Advisory opinions are regularly provided and very liberal rules of standing have previously been adopted.[104] The incorporation into the Canadian Constitution of a Bill of Rights and attempts to use the courts to agitate generalised grievances on the basis of the Bill of Rights appears to have led to the erection of at least some discretionary barriers to universal standing. Thus in *Canadian Council of Churches v The Queen*,[105] the Council was denied standing to challenge provisions of the *Immigration Act 1976*. The Supreme Court, while emphasising that the reason for allowing public interest standing is to ensure that legislation is not immune from challenge, recognised that it was still legitimate to consider whether there was a reasonable and effective way to bring the issue before the court. Where there were alternative potential plaintiffs this may provide a reason to decline to grant standing to a public interest plaintiff. While the Canadian courts continue to apply broader standing rules than in Australia or the United States, they do recognise that a balance still needs to be struck between available judicial resources and access to the courts by anyone with a grievance. To

---

[103] *Lujan, Secretary of the Interior v Defenders of Wildlife*, 504 US 555 (1992); *United States v Hays*, 515 US 737 (1995); *Federal Election Commission v Akins*, 524 US 11 (1998).

[104] *Minister for Justice of Canada v Borowski* (1981) 130 DLR (3rd) 588; *Thorson v Attorney-General of Canada (No 2)* (1974) 43 DLR (3rd) 1.

[105] (1992) 88 DLR (4th) 193.

allow marginal cases to be brought by well-meaning organisations pursuing their own causes could be 'detrimental, if not devastating, to our system of justice and unfair to private litigants'.[106] One of the justifications given in Canada for precluding public interest standing is that an interested organisation may be able to put its views in the form of an intervener in other proceedings. This remains a less developed area in Australia.

5 Justiciability

In addition to standing and the existence of an actual controversy, the third broad issue which the courts have identified as providing a basis for them to decline to adjudicate a dispute is the 'justiciability' of the matter before them. Justiciability is 'not a legal concept with a fixed content or susceptible of scientific verification'.[107] As Geoffrey Lindell reminds us, the terms 'justiciability' and 'non-justiciable' have a number of different meanings.[108] The first is that the court lacks jurisdiction because the subject matter or relief sought falls outside the competence of the court. An example is the intra-mural proceedings of the Parliament. The second is that as a matter of discretion the court will decline to determine the issues. An example might be where the issue is to be judged by standards that are not judicially manageable. A third meaning is that the question or issue raised need not be determined as the relevant legal principles do not depend on the determination of the question in issue. This is more a situation where an issue does not arise rather than an example of non-justiciability. The problem is that the cases do not clearly distinguish between these different meanings. Whatever meaning is adopted, the consequence is the same—the court does not adjudicate on a particular matter. The inherent uncertainty of the concept has led to calls for greater clarity, but it seems unlikely and even inappropriate to expect too many clear boundaries.[109] As with standing, the

---

[106] Ibid 204.
[107] *Poe v Ullman, State's Attorney*, 367 US 497, 508 (1961).
[108] Lindell (1992) 183.
[109] Ibid 190–1; Castles (1979) 209.

quest for precise rules ignores the reason for the limitations—namely, whether constitutionally based or not, they are prudential tools available to the judiciary to allow it to declare certain issues off-limits as circumstances warrant.

To some extent the issue of justiciability, as with standing, is subsumed within, or is an aspect of, the definition of 'matters' over which a federal court has jurisdiction. This was the approach taken in 1911 in relation to disputes between states, a subject matter included as part of the original jurisdiction of the High Court in s 75(iv) of the Constitution.[110] As Griffith CJ said: 'A matter between States, in order to be justiciable, must be such that a controversy of like nature could arise between individual persons, and must be such that it can be determined upon principles of law. This definition includes all controversies relating to the ownership of property or arising out of contracts'.[111]

Gummow J recognised this in *Re Ditfort; Ex parte Deputy Commissioner of Taxation*.[112] He referred to the case of *Minister for Arts, Heritage and Environment v Peko-Wallsend Ltd*[113] where a mining company complained about a Cabinet decision to nominate an area for inclusion on the World Heritage list established under the World Heritage Convention. The Court in that case held that the company had standing to seek judicial review on the ground of want of procedural fairness but held the complaint non-justiciable. Gummow J explained this decision as follows:

> The decision of the Full Court in the *Peko-Wallsend* case, that nevertheless the complaints made were 'non-justiciable', reflects another element in the constitutional concept of a 'matter'. This is that, even if the plaintiff has standing in respect of the complaint sought to be agitated before a court exercising federal jurisdiction, nevertheless there will be no 'matter' if the plaintiff seeks an extension of the court's true function into a domain that does not belong to it, namely the consideration of undertakings and obligations depending entirely

---

[110] *South Australia v Victoria* (1911) 12 CLR 667, 675.
[111] Ibid 675; Campbell (1971).
[112] (1988) 19 FCR 347, 370.
[113] (1987) 15 FCR 274.

on political sanctions. Such non-justiciable issues include agreements and understandings between governments within the federation (*South Australia v Commonwealth* (1962) 108 CLR 130 at 141) and between the Australian and foreign governments: *Gerhardy v Brown* (1985) 159 CLR 70 at 138–139. Those issues do not give rise to 'matters' in the sense necessary for the exercise of federal jurisdiction.[114]

Thus, the conclusion that this type of issue is non-justiciable is constitutionally mandated on the basis that the issues are not suitable for judicial determination.

The classic statement of the rationale for the doctrine in this area is drawn from the United States Supreme Court decision in *Baker v Carr*, where the Court said:

> Prominent on the surface of any case held to involve a political question is found a textually demonstrable constitutional commitment of the issue to a coordinate political department; or a lack of judicially discoverable and manageable standards for resolving it; or the impossibility of deciding without an initial policy determination of a kind clearly for nonjudicial discretion; or the impossibility of a court's undertaking independent resolution without expressing lack of the respect due coordinate branches of the government; or an unusual need for unquestioning adherence to a political decision already made; or the potentiality of embarrassment from multifarious pronouncements by various departments on one question.[115]

Two particular areas where issues of justiciability arise can be noted. One is where the Constitution confers competence over certain matters on the Parliament rather than the judiciary. The other area is where it is argued that there is a conferral of competence over certain matters on the executive and not the judiciary. In relation to the former there has been recognition that certain areas of parliamentary procedure and the internal workings of Parliament are immune from judicial scrutiny. Thus, for instance, s 53 of the Constitution deals with the powers of the Senate to amend certain proposed laws and makes clear that the Senate may not amend a

---

[114] *Re Ditfort; Ex parte Deputy Commissioner of Taxation* (1988) 19 FCR 347, 370.
[115] 369 US 186, 217 (1962).

proposed law so as to increase any charge or burden on the people. Traditionally, 'a procedural provision governing the intra-mural activities of the Parliament' is not justiciable. Section 53 of the Constitution is in this class.[116] The reference in the section to 'proposed' laws has been taken to indicate that the matters are not appropriate for judicial consideration.

A contrast can be found in the attitude of the courts to s 57 of the Constitution which deals with the requirements for a double dissolution. It sets out procedures to be followed in relation to 'proposed laws'. However, in this area the High Court considers that issues of compliance with the constitutional requirements are justiciable on the basis that a challenge to the validity of a law enacted in reliance on that section does not relate to the parliamentary process as such but to whether there has been compliance with a constitutionally prescribed method for enacting a law where there is disagreement between the two Houses of Parliament.[117] Despite some judicial support for a broad concept of non-justiciability in this area, it has not gained majority support.[118]

However, the convening of, and deliberations on, a bill in a joint sitting convened pursuant to s 57 are proceedings in Parliament and the Court appears reluctant to intervene at that preliminary stage prior to the enactment of the law.[119] As indicated, it may later consider the validity of a law passed at such a joint sitting in terms of compliance with the conditions imposed by s 57 including requirements at stages prior to the joint sitting. This is one reason to avoid any earlier intervention. Until completed, the legislative process is not an appropriate subject for judicial review. While there is some discussion in *Cormack v Cope* that suggests this abstention

---

[116] *Western Australia v Commonwealth (Native Title Act Case)* (1995) 183 CLR 373, 482; *Northern Suburbs General Cemetery Reserve Trust v Commonwealth* (1993) 176 CLR 555, 578; *Osborne v Commonwealth* (1911) 12 CLR 321, 326, 352, 355. See also *Victoria v Commonwealth and Connor* (1975) 134 CLR 81, 161 (Gibbs J).

[117] *Cormack v Cope* (1974) 131 CLR 432, 454; *Victoria v Commonwealth and Connor* (1975) 134 CLR 81, 184; compare *Clayton v Heffron* (1960) 105 CLR 214.

[118] For a review of individual judgments which have proposed that this area should be non-justiciable, see Saunders (1984) 42–5. See also Zines (1977) 227–30 and Reid (1977) 240–3.

[119] *Cormack v Cope* (1974) 131 CLR 432, 465, 472.

occurs as a matter of discretion, the better view is that it is a constitutional bar.[120]

One other parliamentary area where the issue of justiciability arises relates to the extent to which the courts will scrutinise or control the exercise by Parliament of its privileges. In *R v Richards; Ex parte Fitzpatrick and Browne (Fitzpatrick's Case)*,[121] the High Court refused to adjudicate on the occasion and manner of exercise by a House of Parliament of a privilege, although it said it is for the courts to judge the existence of the privilege.[122] This remains an area in which there are many unanswered questions.

This was highlighted in the recent decision in *Egan v Willis*[123] in which the High Court recognised the continuing relevance of the approach in *Fitzpatrick's Case*.[124] In a joint judgment, Gaudron, Gummow and Hayne JJ considered the extent of the powers and privileges of the Legislative Council of New South Wales to call for the production of documents. They expressed doubt as to the propriety of a bare declaration as to the validity of the Council proceedings unrelated to determination of the private rights of the plaintiff.[125] In *Egan v Willis* the original action involved a claim of trespass to the person. Kirby J rejected any broad scope for nonjusticiability in the parliamentary context. While appearing to accept *Fitzpatrick's Case* as relevant to this issue, he signalled that the regarding of parliamentary privilege as beyond the reach of Chapter III of the Constitution may one day need reconsideration.[126] Callinan J said nothing on the subject of justiciability and simply considered the powers of the Council to call for documents. Only McHugh J decided the case by taking a narrow approach to the issue of justiciability. He said that the issue should have been dealt with on the basis that the Council has power to suspend a member and it is for the Council alone to determine the facts and whether

---

[120] Saunders (1984) 45–6.

[121] (1955) 92 CLR 157.

[122] See now *Parliamentary Privileges Act 1987* (Cth).

[123] (1998) 158 ALR 527.

[124] Ibid 535–6 (Gaudron, Gummow and Hayne JJ), 551–2 (McHugh J), 571–3 (Kirby J).

[125] Ibid 529–30.

[126] Ibid 571–4.

they amounted to obstruction justifying suspension.[127] Given the way in which the issue was argued, he went on to express his views as to the powers of the Council. The decision in *Egan v Willis* highlights the problems that arise when a court is asked to determine the validity of parliamentary proceedings. These difficulties were further considered in a subsequent action arising out of a call by the Legislative Council for documents where legal and public interest privilege was claimed by the executive.[128]

In relation to the executive, non-justiciability has been invoked on the basis that certain matters fall within the peculiar knowledge or responsibility of the executive and should not be subject to judicial review. These include matters of foreign relations, particularly issues related to recognition of foreign governments or the extent of territory claimed by the Crown.[129] The courts no longer consider prerogative exercises of power to be beyond judicial scrutiny in all cases. There remains, however, a recognition that certain executive decisions may be non-justiciable. Examples include 'national security, the making of treaties, the defence of the country; the prerogative of mercy, the grant of honours, the dissolution of Parliament and the appointment of Ministers'.[130]

In his judgment in *Re Citizen Limbo*,[131] a case concerning the legality of Australia's controls on certain military exports which it was contended were contrary to a number of international agreements, Brennan J said:

> It is essential to understand that courts perform one function and the political branches of government perform another. One can readily understand that there may be disappointment in the performance by one branch or another of government of the functions which are allocated to it under our division of powers. But it would be a mistake for one branch of government to assume the functions of another in

---

[127] Ibid 551–2.

[128] *Egan v Chadwick* (1999) 46 NSWLR 563.

[129] *Shaw Savill & Albion Co Ltd v Commonwealth* (1940) 66 CLR 344, 364; *Ffrost v Stevenson* (1937) 58 CLR 528, 549; *Horta v Commonwealth* (1994) 181 CLR 183.

[130] *Minister for Arts, Heritage and Environment v Peko-Wallsend Ltd* (1987) 15 FCR 274, 277 (Bowen CJ).

[131] (1989) 92 ALR 81.

the hope that thereby what is perceived to be an injustice can be corrected. Unless one observes the separation of powers and unless the courts are restricted to the application of the domestic law of this country, there would be a state of confusion and chaos which would be antipathetic not only to the aspirations of peace but of the enforcement of any human rights.[132]

Kirby J adopted a similar approach in *Lindon v Commonwealth (No 2)*, a case involving the legality of the use of nuclear weapons.[133]

However, even where matters are suitable for only limited judicial review, the courts are reluctant to give the executive too much immunity from scrutiny. Thus, the courts will not allow the executive to compel an interpretation of statutory words by issue of any conclusive or non-justiciable certificate, even in relation to a matter traditionally within the particular responsibility of the executive.[134] In this context a certificate by the executive or communication to a court of information on foreign relations issues may be 'helpful and relevant' but no more.[135] Nor is it likely that the courts will allow the executive 'to determine conclusively the existence of facts by certificate where they are disputed constitutional facts' as this would raise a fundamental question of consistency with the role of the courts in interpreting the Constitution.[136] In *Horta v Commonwealth* the High Court indicated that 'nothing in this judgment should be understood as lending any support at all for the proposition that, in the absence of some real question of sham or circuitous device to attract legislative power, the propriety of the recognition by the Commonwealth Executive of the sovereignty of a foreign nation over foreign territory can be raised in the courts'.[137] It was not, therefore, open to the Court to review the legality of Indonesia's annexation of East Timor and its ability to conclude the Joint Development Zone Treaty with Australia dealing with the maritime

---

[132] Ibid 82–3.

[133] (1996) 136 ALR 251; *Thorpe v Commonwealth (No 3)* (1997) 144 ALR 677, 690–2.

[134] *Attorney-General (Cth) v Tse Chu-Fai* (1998) 193 CLR 128; Lindell (1997) 195–7.

[135] *Attorney-General (Cth) v Tse Chu-Fai* (1998) 193 CLR 128, 149.

[136] Ibid 149.

[137] (1994) 181 CLR 183, 195–6; see also *Chow Hung Ching v The King* (1948) 77 CLR 449, 467.

area between Australia and East Timor. In that case, the validity of the legislation implementing the treaty did not depend on the validity of the recognition of Indonesia's sovereignty over East Timor. The legislation operated in the maritime area and came within the geographically external aspect of the external affairs power.

The case highlights the reluctance of the courts to adjudicate on the validity of acts of state related to territory. The same attitude applies to legal proceedings that seek to challenge the acts of state by which British sovereignty was established over Australia.[138]

An examination of Australian decisions on justiciability suggests, as Lindell says, that 'more work needs to be done in Australia and elsewhere to elucidate in what circumstances the political nature of certain issues renders them unfit or inappropriate for judicial determination'.[139] As with standing, the doctrine of justiciability is in many respects linked to the meaning of 'matter'. As with other limits on adjudication, the courts assume the ultimate responsibility in deciding where to draw the line between an issue that is justiciable and one that is non-justiciable. In some areas there seems a consensus that a judicial role does not exist as the issues are not suitable for judicial determination. However, the fact that an issue is 'political' provides little guidance or explanation.[140] In the constitutional area, there has been much less unanimity as to whether issues such as the validity of appropriations[141] or double dissolution procedures[142] are ultimately matters for judicial determination. It seems unlikely at present that much judicial abstention will occur where interpretation of the Constitution arises.

6 Conclusion

In the absence of a Bill of Rights, Australian courts have been free of much of the 'public interest' litigation that has arisen in the United

---

[138] *Coe v Commonwealth* (1979) 53 ALJR 403, 408, 410; *Walker v New South Wales* (1994) 182 CLR 45; *Thorpe v Commonwealth (No 3)* (1997) 144 ALR 677; see also Lindell (1997) 188–90.

[139] Lindell (1992) 250.

[140] Henkin (1976); Lindell (1992).

[141] *Victoria v Commonwealth (AAP Case)* (1975) 134 CLR 338.

[142] *Victoria v Commonwealth and Connor* (1975) 134 CLR 81.

States. One consequence may be that the High Court and other federal courts have to date had less need to invoke barriers to avoid dealing with controversies brought before them. There has not been the same avoidance of adjudication of constitutional issues that has to some extent been evident in the United States. Thus, on occasions, the court will deal with a case on its merits, regardless of whether standing is clearly made out. This may occur because the defendant party, which is often governmental, is happy to defend the matter on the merits or the court can dispose of the case on its merits without reaching any view on standing.[143] There is also a willingness to allow declaratory judgments at the instigation of a state to determine the validity of federal law divorced from any factual context.[144] Protestations that the High Court does not give advisory opinions sit uncomfortably with this approach.

In the United States the last decade has certainly seen a greater emphasis on the constitutional constraints imposed on judicial review. This reflects a renewed preference for viewing federal courts as existing primarily to resolve concrete disputes brought by individual litigants and not to provide coherent interpretations of the Constitution (or the law generally) for the purpose of resolving generalised grievances. Thus, there has been a re-emphasis in the United States on the need for standing.

The approach to the interpretation of the 'case' requirement in the United States Constitution continues to be criticised as fragmented and incoherent. In a major critique, Professor Susan Bandes has argued that the private rights model should be abandoned and replaced with a normative principle from which the interpretation of the 'case' limitation can begin. That principle is 'to preserve the Court as the primary guardian of the Constitution'.[145] Bandes is correct in asserting that the process of defining a 'case' or a 'matter' 'cannot properly occur free of value judgments about the proper

---

[143] See, for example, *Horta v Commonwealth* (1994) 181 CLR 183, 193.

[144] *Attorney-General (Vict) v Commonwealth (Marriage Act Case)* (1962) 107 CLR 529; *New South Wales v Commonwealth (Incorporation Case)* (1990) 169 CLR 482.

[145] Bandes (1990) 319.

role of the federal judicial power'.[146] The Australian High Court explicitly recognised this in the *Bateman's Bay Case*.[147] However, it is not self-evident that courts are necessarily the only or even the primary guardians of the Constitution in relation to every matter.[148] They are certainly not the appropriate body to resolve generalised grievances.

Our democratic polity cannot expect, nor should it, that the courts will provide the answer to the multitude of 'public interest' disputes that arise between government and citizen. The private rights model of adjudication may be unfashionable, but it is suggested that its core components of a concrete dispute between two parties involving the application of the law to individualised facts continues to provide a valuable indication of the types of 'case' or 'matter' suitable for judicial adjudication. The requirements for standing may be relaxed in order to enable breaches of the law not to go without a remedy if the circumstances otherwise make relief appropriate. But this does not require standing to be accorded to any person. The courts need to remain conscious that not all public law disputes can be suitably addressed judicially. The Parliament remains an important if neglected institution in ensuring accountability. The executive arm of government itself has a responsibility to put accountability mechanisms in place and to ensure they operate effectively.

Harlan J in *Flast v Cohen*, in dissent, concluded that 'The powers of the federal judiciary will be adequate for the great burdens placed upon them only if they are employed prudently, with recognition of the strengths as well as the hazards that go with our kind of representative government'.[149] This is indeed the case.

The Australian federal courts have for the most part recognised this in their approach to limitations on adjudication. Changes to

---

[146] Ibid 276.

[147] *Bateman's Bay Local Aboriginal Land Council v Aboriginal Community Benefit Fund Pty Ltd* (1998) 194 CLR 247.

[148] Gageler (1987).

[149] 392 US 83, 131 (1967).

judicial process to facilitate better access to justice may require a re-examination of some of the limitations. However, they remain fundamentally relevant and important indications that the federal courts recognise their own important but limited role in the constitutional structure. To the extent that the limitations are identified as constitutionally based, this emphasises that the judicial arm has a limited and particular role in a system of government that is based on a separation of powers between the judiciary and the other arms of government. The balance to be struck between the different roles of the different arms remains, however, an important area of legal debate.

9

Federal, Associated and Accrued Jurisdiction

Leslie Zines

1 Constitutional Framework and Design

The United States Constitution provided the guiding light in respect of a number of features of the Australian Constitution, including the division of legislative powers between the Commonwealth and the states, the separate provisions and chapters relating to the legislative, executive and judicial powers of the Commonwealth, and many of the detailed provisions (set out in Appendix 1) of the content of federal judicial power in Chapter III.

The Australian founders, however, did not take the federal concept of a distribution of separate powers and institutions between the central polity and the states to the same length as did the Americans. Whereas the Australians readily accepted that in their legislative and executive fields the Commonwealth and states were separate and, largely, co-ordinate, the federal judiciary was not seen as competing with the judicial power of the states or as a threat to state 'sovereignty'. There was ready agreement that, unlike the position in the United States, the Federal Supreme Court (expressly provided for in s 71 and titled 'The High Court of Australia') should be an appellate court in respect of all matters, whether federal or state. There was thus created the only institution in the Constitution—apart from the Sovereign—which could be described as 'national'.

The other provision that cut across an otherwise co-ordinate federal design was the power of Parliament, conferred by s 77, to invest jurisdiction (and thus impose powers and duties) on state courts and so require them to act as judicial agents of the Commonwealth.[1] No one appears to have argued that s 77 represented an unwarranted intrusion into state affairs.

Lawyers of a later generation argued that the concept of 'federal jurisdiction' in our Constitution was a great mistake and that the provision for investing it in state courts had resulted in unnecessary complication.[2]

Until the enactment of the *Judiciary Act 1903* (Cth) and the establishment of the High Court in October 1903, the state courts had little difficulty in applying the Constitution and Acts of the Commonwealth Parliament under their general ('state') jurisdiction and in accordance with their duty to enforce the law of the land from whatever source it derived. So far as constitutional and federal law were concerned this was reinforced by covering clause 5 of the Constitution under which the Constitution and laws of the Commonwealth are binding on the courts, judges and people of every state. There were said to be two exceptions to this principle, namely, cases where the Commonwealth was a defendant and where a writ of mandamus or other writ was sought to command or prohibit a federal officer.[3]

It was argued in the early days of the Commonwealth, with some reason, that s 77(iii) should not be interpreted to empower the Commonwealth to invest the state courts with the jurisdiction, referred to in ss 75 and 76, that those courts already had. The seeming absurdity and complexity of such an interpretation was made clear by the provisions of s 39 of the *Judiciary Act*. Sub-section (1) (made in reliance on s 77(ii)) declared that all the High Court's jurisdiction was exclusive. This had the immediate result of depriving the state

---

[1] In s 120 the Constitution imposes a duty on state governments to detain a person accused or convicted of federal offences and empowers Parliament to make laws to give effect to that provision.

[2] Sir Owen Dixon (1935) 606.

[3] *Ex parte Goldring* (1903) 3 SR (NSW) 260.

courts of all their state jurisdiction in those matters. Sub-section (2) (made under s 77(iii)) then invested the state courts with federal jurisdiction in those matters. That provision also invested further federal jurisdiction in respect of all other matters included in s 76 of the Constitution, that is, matters in respect of which the High Court did not have jurisdiction. The most important of these was 'matters arising under any laws made by the Parliament' in s 76(ii). All the federal jurisdiction was made subject to conditions.

The Commonwealth is not empowered to deprive state courts of state jurisdiction except by the indirect method of making the jurisdiction of a federal court exclusive. For many decades, therefore, there appeared to be an extraordinary situation where, in respect of matters within s 76 where the High Court did not have jurisdiction, the state courts retained their 'state' jurisdiction and also had federal jurisdiction to determine the same matters, but subject to conditions. The High Court put an end to this ridiculous and confusing situation by holding that any concurrent state jurisdiction was excluded by the operation of s 109, which renders state laws inoperative if inconsistent with Commonwealth law.[4]

To a non-lawyer the Court's interpretation of s 77 of the Constitution and the enactment of the provisions of s 39 of the *Judiciary Act* must appear bizarre; but the primary motive of the Court and of Parliament in each case was, so far as possible, to prevent appeals from state courts to the Privy Council. One of the conditions of federal jurisdiction, prescribed in s 39(2)(a), was that every decision of a Supreme Court was final and conclusive except for an appeal to the High Court.[5] As Dixon J put it: 'An acknowledged purpose [of s 39(2)] was to exclude appeals as of right to the Privy Council, and it was intended to exclude them over the whole field of Federal jurisdiction'.[6]

---

[4] *Felton v Mulligan* (1971) 124 CLR 367; Cowen and Zines (1978) 224–8.

[5] In 1968 the paragraph was amended to provide that a decision of any state court shall not be subject to appeal to the Privy Council, whether by special leave or otherwise. Other conditions relate to appeals to the High Court and to ensuring that only magistrates, and not justices of the peace, shall exercise federal jurisdiction in courts of summary jurisdiction.

[6] *Minister for Army v Parbury Henty & Co* (1945) 70 CLR 459, 505.

2 The Heads of Jurisdiction

To the modern mind the method by which the areas of federal juris-diction were set out is strange. They are primarily dealt with as sub-jects or possible subjects of original jurisdiction of the High Court. The power to define the jurisdiction of other federal courts and invest jurisdiction in state courts is treated as consequential on the earlier provisions. For many decades much of the jurisdiction in ss 75 and 76 has been regarded as quite unsuitable original jurisdiction for the highest court in the land, burdened with the duty of a final court of appeal and constitutional interpreter.

Section 75 vests the High Court with original jurisdiction that cannot be divested by Parliament. Some of the paragraphs of s 75 comprise matters that are appropriate to the Court because of the status of the parties, such as suits between states (included in s 75(iv)) and between a state and the Commonwealth (s 75(iii)). Indeed, in these matters, jurisdiction is exclusive to the High Court under s 38 of the *Judiciary Act* (unless remitted by the High Court under s 44 of that Act).[7]

(a) The Constitution, the Commonwealth and states, and federal officers

Section 75(iii) confers jurisdiction in matters 'in which the Common-wealth, or a person suing or being sued on behalf of the Common-wealth, is a party'. Section 75(v) refers to matters 'in which a writ of Mandamus or prohibition or an injunction is sought against an officer of the Commonwealth'. These two heads of jurisdiction ensure, inter alia, that there is an entrenched jurisdiction in which the Commonwealth and its officers can be made accountable for observance of the law. In *Bank of NSW v Commonwealth* (*Bank Nationalisation Case*), Dixon J said that s 75(iii) was designed to ensure that the Commonwealth 'fell in every way within a juris-diction in which it could be impleaded and which it could invoke'. He went on to say that it should be read with s 75(v) 'which, it is apparent, was written into the instrument to make it constitution-

---

[7] *Johnstone v Commonwealth* (1979) 143 CLR 398.

ally certain that there would be a jurisdiction capable of restraining officers of the Commonwealth from exceeding Federal power'.[8]

From the viewpoint of upholding the Constitution, the great importance of the entrenched jurisdiction in these paragraphs is reinforced by the strange fact that the original jurisdiction of the High Court to determine matters 'arising under the Constitution or involving its interpretation' is conferred by s 30(a) of the *Judiciary Act*. Section 76(i) of the Constitution left to the discretion of Parliament whether the High Court should be invested with that jurisdiction. Section 75(iii) and (v) therefore guarantee (among other things) that there is an entrenched jurisdiction to deal with the validity of Commonwealth legislation and executive action.

Despite the absence of entrenched general jurisdiction to determine constitutional questions, it has always been accepted that this is one of the most important functions of the High Court. This is not obvious from the face of the Constitution. If s 30(a) were repealed, the only general jurisdiction of the High Court in respect of the Constitution would be by way of appeal under s 73 of the Constitution. The issue would then be whether all or any such appeals could be removed from the High Court's appellate jurisdiction. The appellate jurisdiction from state Supreme Courts would remain because of the provision in s 73 which provides against preventing appeals from those courts in any matter in which an appeal lay to the Queen in Council at the establishment of the Commonwealth. The issue whether constitutional appeals from federal courts may be removed or restricted depends on the meaning of the phrase 'with such exceptions and subject to such regulations as the Parliament prescribes'. (Under s 77(ii), constitutional jurisdiction of federal courts could be made exclusive of state courts, thus avoiding the guarantee of appeals to the High Court from Supreme Courts, referred to above.)

In *Cockle v Isaksen*[9] the Court upheld the validity of a provision which precluded an appeal to the High Court from a judgment from which an appeal lay to the Commonwealth Industrial Court. It was emphasised that the provision did not destroy the general rule. In an earlier case the Court had said that 'after all it is only

---

[8] (1948) 76 CLR 1, 363.
[9] (1957) 99 CLR 155, 165–6.

a power of making exceptions' and that 'it would be surprising if it extended to excluding altogether one of the heads specifically mentioned by s 73'.[10] The exclusion of some or all constitutional questions would not fall within that category. However, in *Re McJannet; Ex parte Minister for Employment, Training and Industrial Relations (Q)*,[11] Toohey, McHugh and Gummow JJ suggested that the exclusion of an appeal from a judgment of the Federal Court on a constitutional issue might not constitute an 'exception' from the general rule in s 73. If that were so, it is certainly not because of any express provisions in the Constitution but rather a conclusion derived from a perceived object of Chapter III taken as a whole.[12]

The lack of entrenchment of the High Court's original jurisdiction under s 30(a) of the *Judiciary Act* makes it difficult to understand statements by some High Court judges that it is the only court that can make conclusive determinations on constitutional questions. While the High Court has been described as the primary custodian of the Constitution, it could not have been intended to be the only one. Not only is the Court's general constitutional jurisdiction in s 76(i) left to Parliament's discretion, but s 77 makes it clear that that head of jurisdiction may be vested in other courts. Yet a number of judges have said that no other court can conclusively determine a constitutional question.

In *R v Federal Court of Australia; Ex parte WA National Football League*[13] a majority (Barwick CJ, Gibbs, Stephen, Murphy and Aickin JJ) seemed to hold that it was not possible for Parliament to confer on the Federal Court jurisdiction to determine conclusively whether a body was a 'trading corporation' within the meaning of s 51(xx) of the Constitution when determining a matter arising under the *Trade Practices Act 1974* (Cth). It was held that the Federal Court's determination of that question was subject to review by the High Court by means of a writ of prohibition.[14] Mason and

---

[10] *Collins v Charles Marshall Pty Ltd* (1955) 92 CLR 529, 544.

[11] (1995) 184 CLR 620, 651.

[12] See Wynes (1976) 506–7.

[13] (1979) 143 CLR 190.

[14] The Court was possibly referring to the Federal Court's statutory jurisdiction, but the language of the majority seems to go further. See Zines (1997) 243–8.

Jacobs JJ dissented. Barwick CJ said that 'the Parliament has no constitutional power to confer on a court or tribunal a power to make orders requiring a corporation which is not within the constitutional language of s. 51(xx) to observe the terms of a statute depending for its validity upon that paragraph of s. 51'.[15] Similarly, Gibbs J said if Parliament purported to invest the Federal Court with jurisdiction to determine conclusively that a person is a trading corporation within s 51(xx), then 'the investiture of jurisdiction on that Court would be pro tanto invalid'.[16]

These comments clearly ignore the provisions of s 76(i) and s 77(i) under which the Parliament may invest a federal court with jurisdiction in matters arising under the Constitution. It is true that a law made under s 51(xx) may depend for its valid application on 'the actual existence' of a trading corporation, but a law conferring jurisdiction on a court under s 76(i) and s 77(i) depends merely on the actual existence of a matter falling within s 76(i). This criticism was recognised by Mason J (with whom Jacobs J agreed). He said that there was 'no embargo against the Federal Court hearing and deciding constitutional questions in the course of exercising its jurisdiction'. He qualified that view, however, by saying that the validity of the investiture depended on whether an appeal to the High Court was possible.[17] It is difficult to read that qualification into s 76(i), combined with s 77(i). If the views referred to above are correct it would be impossible to exclude the High Court's appellate jurisdiction in respect of constitutional questions. While that conclusion is not blindingly obvious from a study of the detailed provisions of Chapter III, it is consistent with the views expressed from the very beginning that it is the High Court which is the ultimate 'guardian of the Constitution'. For example, in the second reading speech on the first Judiciary Bill in 1902, Alfred Deakin declared that 'the High Court exists to protect the Constitution against assaults'.[18] In 1997 the Commonwealth amended s 39B of the *Judiciary Act* by conferring on the Federal Court the jurisdiction in s 76(i).

---

[15] (1979) 143 CLR 190, 203.

[16] Ibid 215.

[17] Ibid 225, 228.

[18] *Commonwealth Parliamentary Debates*, House of Representatives, 18 March 1902, 10 967. See also Bennett (1980) ch. 1; Galligan (1987) ch. 2.

(i) Commonwealth and states as parties
In the *Bank Nationalisation Case* Dixon J said of s 75(iii) that its purpose

> of providing a jurisdiction which might be invoked by or against the Commonwealth could not, in modern times, be adequately attained and secured against colourable evasion, unless it was expressed so as to cover the enforcement of actionable rights and liabilities of officers and agencies in their official and governmental capacity, when in substance they formed part of or represented the Commonwealth.[19]

This broad object has ensured that a statutory corporation may fall within the terms of s 75(iii) even though it does not fall within 'the shield of the Crown'.[20] The fact, therefore, that a body does not enjoy the immunity of the Commonwealth under its prerogative or under constitutional doctrines relating to inter-governmental immunity does not answer whether it is 'the Commonwealth or a person suing or being sued on behalf of the Commonwealth' for the purposes of s 75(iii).

Jacobs J in *Maguire v Simpson*[21] said that s 75(iii) should be given a wide construction and effect for the reason given by Dixon J, while the same considerations did not apply to the prerogative. This statement was followed by McHugh and Gummow JJ in declaring that there was a distinction between the bodies included in the words of s 75(iii) and those entitled to the benefit of the *Cigamatic* doctrine.[22]

Another reason for this distinction is that the issue of whether a statutory body shares Crown immunity and privilege is to a considerable extent one of legislative intention. If, however, the purpose of s 75(iii) is to secure jurisdiction in relation to the Commonwealth government against 'colourable evasion', parliamentary intention cannot be conclusive.[23]

---

[19] *Bank of NSW v Commonwealth* (1948) 76 CLR 1, 367.
[20] Ibid; *Inglis v Commonwealth Trading Bank of Australia* (1969) 119 CLR 334.
[21] (1977) 139 CLR 362, 406.
[22] *Re Residential Tenancies Tribunal (NSW); Ex parte Defence Housing Authority* (1997) 190 CLR 410, 458, 463–4.
[23] Cowen and Zines (1978) 41.

One difference between ss 75(iii) and (iv) is that the latter provision refers only to 'States' and not to a person 'suing or being sued
on behalf of' a state. The jurisdiction extends, inter alia, to matters
'between States' or 'between a State and a resident of another State'.
In the cases holding an entity to be within s 75(iii) there have been
some differences of opinion as to whether the body is the Commonwealth or is a person suing or being sued on its behalf. In *Inglis
v Commonwealth Trading Bank of Australia*,[24] for example, Barwick
CJ placed the bank in the former category and Kitto J put it in the
latter. In *Maguire v Simpson*[25] Barwick CJ changed his mind, but
Mason J agreed with Barwick CJ's earlier view. For the purposes of
s 75(iii) that disagreement does not matter, but it became important
in arguing whether a body was the 'State' within s 75(iv).

In *Crouch v Commissioner for Railways (Q)*[26] and *State Bank
of NSW v Commonwealth Savings Bank of Australia (State Bank
Case)*,[27] the High Court seems to have regarded the concept of
'State' in s 75(iv) as having a similar breadth to the more extended
wording in s 75(iii). That interpretation is justified on two grounds.
First, the issue of what is a 'matter' in s 75 is one of substance and
not to be determined merely by the form of the proceedings. If the
party sued is an instrumentality through which the state government
discharges its functions, even though it is a separate corporation, the
matter is 'in substance' one involving the state.[28] Second, s 75(iii)
refers to the Commonwealth as a 'party'. The equivalent United
States provision refers to 'controversies to which the United States
shall be a party', but does not contain the added phrase in s 75(iii),
and there was a tendency in the United States to determine the question whether the United States was a party by reference to the party
named on the record. This was motivated by the desire to avoid the
immunity from suit of the United States. It was therefore thought
necessary, in light of the American cases, to add the phrase in

---

[24] (1969) 119 CLR 334.
[25] (1977) 139 CLR 362.
[26] (1985) 159 CLR 22.
[27] (1986) 161 CLR 639.
[28] *Crouch v Commissioner for Railways (Q)* (1985) 159 CLR 22, 33, 37–9.

s 75(iii) so as to prevent a technical interpretation. The High Court pointed out, however, that in s 75(iv) the word 'party' is not used.[29]

In applying these two provisions, therefore, the same policy governs, namely the prevention of 'colourable evasion' of the jurisdiction by the Commonwealth or a state.[30] However, the question of how one determines whether a separate entity is an instrumentality or agency of the Commonwealth or a state for the purposes of s 75 has not been clearly answered by the Court. In the *State Bank Case* the bank was not under the direct control of the executive government. In holding that the bank could sue under s 75(iv), the Court relied on a number of factors in combination, including the absence of corporators, the power of the Governor to appoint nearly all the directors (indicating a measure of control), the public character of its policy objectives, the guarantee of payments by the government, the payment of profits into consolidated revenue, scrutiny by the auditor-general, and (a somewhat narrow) power to make by-laws.

In my view, any public corporation, whether commercial or otherwise, should come within the scope of s 75(iii) or (iv). For example, in *Australian Coastal Shipping Commission v O'Reilly*[31] the Court upheld the power of the Commonwealth to exempt the national shipping line from all state taxes. It was referred to as a 'corporate agency of the Crown in right of the Commonwealth having for its purpose the carrying on of shipping services under the legislative control of the Parliament for the public advantage and not for private profit and subject only to ministerial directions given in pursuance of the statute'.[32] Such agencies should, in my opinion, come within s 75(iii).

In the *State Bank Case* the Court said that the issue of executive control was 'obviously an issue of central importance',[33] but found the degree of control sufficient. In fact, the control over the bank

---

[29] Ibid 33, 40–2.

[30] *State Bank of NSW v Commonwealth Savings Bank of Australia* (1986) 161 CLR 639, 648–9.

[31] (1962) 107 CLR 46.

[32] Ibid 54.

[33] *State Bank of NSW v Commonwealth Savings Bank of Australia* (1986) 161 CLR 639, 648.

was largely indirect, being that which was reflected in the power of appointing members of the governing body. As the Commonwealth or a state might choose to conduct an activity or exercise a function by means of an independent statutory body, it is suggested that the degree of control over it by the executive government should not be regarded as an important factor, provided other indicia of a 'public body' exercising 'public functions' are present.

(ii) Officers of the Commonwealth: s 75(v)

Section 75(v) entrenches a jurisdiction in which federal officers may be ordered to carry out their duties or be restrained from acting beyond their constitutional and statutory powers. It had been held by the Supreme Court of New South Wales before the *Judiciary Act* that it had no power to grant a mandamus against a federal officer. Stephen ACJ said: 'we cannot compel a federal officer to discharge a duty which he owes to the Federal Government'.[34] Although that case followed United States authority it seems inconsistent with the duty placed on state judges by covering clause 5 of the Constitution. However that may be, s 75(v) provides a jurisdiction to deal with acts of federal officers, tribunals and courts. Judges were held from an early date to be officers of the Commonwealth for this purpose.

There is a considerable overlap between ss 75(iii) and (v) because of the broad interpretation given to the former. Some persons coming within s 75(iii), such as the Commissioner of Taxation, may, therefore, also be officers of the Commonwealth.[35] If so, the Court's power to issue remedies will not be limited to those mentioned in s 75(v). However, while judges of the Federal Court and the Family Court are officers of the Commonwealth,[36] it is unlikely that they would be regarded as 'the Commonwealth' or persons 'suing or being sued on behalf of the Commonwealth'.

The Parliament cannot, of course, deprive the High Court of the jurisdiction in s 75(v), but it can alter the substantive law that

---

[34] *Ex parte Goldring* (1903) 3 SR (NSW) 260, 262.

[35] *Deputy Commissioner of Taxation v Richard Walter Pty Ltd* (1995) 183 CLR 168, 179, 204, 221, 231.

[36] *R v Federal Court of Australia; Ex parte WA National Football League* (1979) 143 CLR 190; *R v Commonwealth Court of Conciliation and Arbitration; Ex parte Brisbane Tramways Co* (1914) 18 CLR 54.

the Court has to apply in the course of exercising that jurisdiction. To do so would 'merely alter the substantive law in a way which produced the consequence that, while the jurisdiction and the right to invoke it were unaffected, the particular ground for the grant of injunctive or other relief was removed'.[37]

A privative clause providing, for example, that the decisions of a statutory body 'shall not be subject to prohibition, mandamus or injunction' seems to fly in the face of s 75(v). It would be possible, however, to interpret it so as to enlarge the powers of the body concerned so that there is no occasion to grant the application for the writ or injunction. That is, the decision would be treated as within power. Such a provision could not, of course, apply where the authority that the Act purports to give would be beyond the Commonwealth's constitutional power. The Court has instead adopted an intermediate approach to the interpretation of these clauses. The problem is said to be that the restricted power in the Act 'contradicts' what is regarded as unlimited power conferred as a result of the privative clause. This is a curious way of looking at it. Nevertheless, the classic formulation is that of Dixon J in *R v Hickman; Ex parte Fox and Clinton*. He said that such a clause means that no decision of a body is invalid

> on the ground that it has not conformed to the requirements governing its proceedings or the exercise of its authority or has not confined its acts within the limits laid down ... provided always that its decision is a bona fide attempt to exercise its power, that it relates to the subject matter of the legislation, and that it is reasonably capable of reference to the power given to the body.[38]

This interpretation has been followed in many cases and is applicable to both federal and state privative clauses.[39] In *Darling*

---

[37] *Deputy Commissioner of Taxation v Richard Walter Pty Ltd* (1995) 183 CLR 168, 207 (Deane and Gaudron JJ).

[38] (1945) 70 CLR 598, 615.

[39] *Deputy Commissioner of Taxation v Richard Walter Pty Ltd* (1995) 183 CLR 168; *O'Toole v Charles David Pty Ltd* (1990) 171 CLR 232; *Darling Casino Ltd v NSW Casino Control Authority* (1997) 191 CLR 602.

Casino Ltd v NSW Casino Control Authority,[40] Gaudron and Gummow JJ said that because of s 75(v) the considerations that apply to state privative clauses are somewhat different from those applicable to federal clauses. However, in view of the power of both Parliaments to prescribe the authority of officers and tribunals (subject to constitutional restrictions), there would seem to be no need for different treatment. In fact, the application of the interpretation in *R v Hickman; Ex parte Fox and Clinton* seems to have been much the same in each case. There could only be a relevant distinction between the federal and state use of these clauses if s 75(v) impliedly restricted the power of the Commonwealth to alter the substantive law in some way. That has not, as yet, been suggested in the cases.[41] What the Commonwealth cannot do, which a state, theoretically, can do, is to prevent a court from prohibiting or restraining an act of an officer that is unlawful. A privative clause is, however, in each case relevant to the issue of whether the act is unlawful.

Section 75(v) does not refer to the writ of certiorari. This remedy can, of course, be issued by the Court if relevant to some matter arising under another head of jurisdiction, such as s 30(a) of the *Judiciary Act*, dealing with constitutional matters.[42] In *Pitfield v Franki*,[43] an application was made for prohibition and certiorari. The Court ordered certiorari to issue. There was no discussion of the source of jurisdiction to grant the writ. Mason J later attempted to rationalise the decision by suggesting that it was a matter involving interpretation of the Constitution 'and that this circumstance, possibly taken in conjunction with a bona fide claim for prohibition, gave the Court jurisdiction, despite the absence of any reference to certiorari in s. 75(v) of the Constitution'.[44] This statement proved fruitful.

---

[40] (1997) 191 CLR 602, 633.

[41] But see Zines (1998); Creyke (1997).

[42] *Re McJannet; Ex parte Minister for Employment, Training and Industrial Relations (Q)* (1995) 184 CLR 620, 651–2.

[43] (1970) 123 CLR 448.

[44] *R v Marshall; Ex parte Federated Clerks Union of Australia* (1975) 132 CLR 595, 609.

A problem has arisen where s 75(v) seems to be the only possible source of jurisdiction and where (a) a purported order of a court or tribunal has been held to be beyond its jurisdiction, (b) prohibition will prevent it being enforced, but (c) only certiorari can result in the quashing of the order. In a number of cases it has been said that certiorari can issue in those circumstances. Aickin J described as the narrowest basis for such action that the writ will be available where prohibition could properly issue and the application is not 'merely colourable', and certiorari is an adjunct to making the order for prohibition effective. He said that it was merely a procedural issue whether prohibition should be granted as well.[45] Gibbs and Stephen JJ relied on similar reasoning, but thought the matter remained open for future examination.[46] In *Philip Morris Inc v Adam P Brown Male Fashions Pty Ltd* (*Philip Morris Case*), Barwick CJ described *Pitfield v Franki* as a case where the Court had jurisdiction to grant prohibition and 'the writ of certiorari was a convenient, indeed a more convenient, mode of exercising the jurisdiction'.[47] Later cases have followed that view.[48]

The Federal Court and the Family Court are each a 'superior court of record' under their respective constitutive Acts. It has been accepted for a long time in Australia that a writ of prohibition can issue against such a court in respect of an order in excess of jurisdiction. In *R v Ross-Jones; Ex parte Green*[49] a writ of certiorari was issued to the Family Court, when an application had been made for prohibition and certiorari. That decision was questioned by Deane J in *R v Gray; Ex parte Marsh*.[50] He did not deny that s 75(v) was available as a source of jurisdiction, and that in a proper case certiorari could issue. But he said that the substantive law, which included the common law, prevented the issue of certiorari to a

[45] *R v Cook; Ex parte Twigg* (1980) 147 CLR 15, 31.
[46] Ibid 26.
[47] (1981) 148 CLR 457, 477.
[48] *R v Ross-Jones; Ex parte Green* (1984) 156 CLR 185; *R v Gray; Ex parte Marsh* (1985) 157 CLR 351; *Re Keely; Ex parte Kingham* (1995) 129 ALR 255, 279. See P. H. Lane (1997) 587–8 for cases in which mandamus and certiorari have been granted.
[49] (1984) 156 CLR 185.
[50] (1985) 157 CLR 351, 383.

superior court. Section 75(v), being merely a conferral of jurisdiction, did not affect that position. Deane J said that the scope of certiorari was different from prohibition. It notionally removed the record of the lower court into the High Court and it extended to errors of law on the face of the record that were committed within jurisdiction. Prohibition was available against a superior court because it was confined to excesses of jurisdiction.

Ultimately, Deane J recognised that earlier cases ran contrary to his view and, in any case, he did not have to decide the issue. He added, however, that if he were constrained to follow earlier decisions they should be regarded as going no further than making certiorari available for excess of jurisdiction. Dawson J expressed doubts similar to those of Deane J. Mason J thought there was a question whether certiorari could issue for error of law on the face of the record.[51]

There has been criticism of the Court in respect of the issue of certiorari in s 75(v) cases. It might be said that in many of them the grant of certiorari to quash seems to go beyond what is merely incidental to an application for prohibition. If, for example, s 75(v) had extended to all remedies for judicial review, the appropriate action on some occasions might have been simply to apply for certiorari. Indeed, in some of the cases, such as *R v Cook; Ex parte Twigg*, certiorari was granted and not prohibition. This makes the application for prohibition look contrived (even though that is not a sufficient reason to regard it as not bona fide, provided there is a 'proper' case for prohibition).[52]

In my view, the High Court should continue to follow those cases where certiorari has been granted in respect of a matter coming within s 75(v). While cognisance must be taken of the technical differences between the remedies because of the specification of the three remedies, the heads of jurisdiction in Chapter III should be interpreted bearing in mind their place in a constitution and with regard to their purpose. The purpose divined by Dixon J in the *Bank Nationalisation Case* has been accepted for fifty years and, in any case, is a likely one.

---

[51] Ibid 377 (Mason J), 397 (Dawson J).

[52] Aitken (1986).

There, Dixon J said that the purpose of s 75(v) was to make it 'constitutionally certain that there would be a jurisdiction capable of restraining officers of the Commonwealth from exceeding Federal power'.[53] The mischief is excess of power or jurisdiction. In those circumstances a liberal interpretation of what remedies are ancillary and appropriate for determining matters within s 75(v) is as appropriate as the broad interpretation given to the words of s 75(iii). Both are designed (in part in the case of s 75(iii)) to subject the Commonwealth, its agencies and officers to the Constitution and to laws prescribing power, authority and jurisdiction. Such a consideration, however, also supports the view that while the issue of a writ of certiorari should be regarded, in appropriate circumstances, as ancillary to prohibition or mandamus, it should be limited to the ground of excess of jurisdiction.

The Constitutional Commission (following its Advisory Committee) recommended that s 75(v) be amended to read: 'In which there is sought an order (including a declaratory order) for ensuring that the powers or duties of an officer of the Commonwealth (other than a Justice of a superior court) are exercised or performed in accordance with law'.[54] The Commission saw no reason why review of administrative action should include some writs and remedies and not others. The Advisory Committee recommended the exclusion of superior court justices because, in its view, ordinary appellate processes should be the only means of review. The Commission agreed, and added that if those courts were not excluded from the new clause it would be possible to review a judgment for error of law on the face of the record. Where the issue related to the Constitution, under the Commission's recommendations the High Court would have had entrenched jurisdiction and would have been able to grant any appropriate remedy. It should be pointed out, however, that the recommendation was made in the context of other recommendations under which the High Court would be guaranteed power to grant special leave to appeal from any court in Australia.[55]

---

[53] *Bank of NSW v Commonwealth* (1948) 76 CLR 1, 363.

[54] Australian Constitutional Commission (1988) 377.

[55] Ibid 385.

(b) Matters 'arising under' Commonwealth law

As mentioned earlier, the heads of jurisdiction in s 76 are not vested in the High Court by the Constitution, but require legislation. The subject of s 76(ii)—matters 'arising under any laws made by the Parliament'—is not a general area of jurisdiction conferred on that court. Section 30(c) of the *Judiciary Act* vests the High Court with jurisdiction in respect of trials of indictable offences against laws of the Commonwealth. (It may be that this jurisdiction is included in the High Court's entrenched jurisdiction in s 75(iii).)[56]

As a result of statutory reforms in the 1970s, provisions vesting original jurisdiction in the High Court under many particular statutes pursuant to s 76(ii) were repealed (see Chapter 4).[57] Most of the jurisdiction of the Federal Court is in respect of matters arising under specific Acts of Parliament, including legislation on the subjects of bankruptcy, trade practices, judicial review of administrative action, admiralty, the corporations law, and intellectual property. Under s 39B of the *Judiciary Act*, the Court has the jurisdiction referable to s 75(v). It also has jurisdiction to determine matters remitted to it by the High Court, such as those in which the Commonwealth is a party. In 1997 s 39B of the *Judiciary Act* was amended to vest in the Federal Court all the jurisdiction in s 76(i) and s 76(ii). The prime jurisdiction of the Family Court is, of course, also referable to s 76(ii).

At times, the High Court has emphasised that s 76(ii), unlike s 76(i), does not include the words 'or involving its interpretation'.[58] The standard formulation of 'a matter arising under' a federal law was stated by Latham CJ to be one in which 'the right or duty in question in the matter owes its existence to Federal law or depends

---

[56] *R v Kidman* (1915) 20 CLR 425; Cowen and Zines (1978) 7–8.

[57] The High Court retains jurisdiction as a Court of Disputed Returns under the *Commonwealth Electoral Act 1918* (Cth) and has jurisdiction in respect of trials of federal indictable offences, and matters removed from other courts: s 30(c) and s 40(3) respectively of the *Judiciary Act*.

[58] *Felton v Mulligan* (1971) 124 CLR 367, 374 (Barwick CJ); *Collins v Charles Marshall Pty Ltd* (1955) 92 CLR 529, 540; *R v Commonwealth Court of Conciliation and Arbitration; Ex parte Barrett* (1945) 70 CLR 141, 154 (Latham CJ).

on Federal law for its enforcement'.[59] In *Collins v Charles Marshall Pty Ltd* the Court said that a matter may involve the interpretation of an Act even though it does not arise under the Act, and that 'it may be said that almost always it will be so when the Act . . . is relevant only to some matter of defence to a proceeding based on some cause of action or ground which is prima facie independent of the Act'.[60]

In *Felton v Mulligan*,[61] however, it was held that if the defence is based on Commonwealth law and is an issue for decision, the matter comes within the terms of s 76(ii). This means, of course, that a court may not know whether it is exercising federal jurisdiction (or, on some occasions, whether it has, as a result, lost all jurisdiction) until the defence or answer to the defence.

The substantive issue behind the technical arguments in a number of these cases was whether before 1986 an appeal lay to the Privy Council from a state Supreme Court. The appeal could be sought in respect of state jurisdiction only. In *Felton v Mulligan* all the judges agreed that a matter could arise under federal law if it was the source of a right or immunity upon which the defence was based. They disagreed on whether that principle was satisfied in the instant case. The plaintiff sought a declaration as to her rights under a maintenance covenant against her former husband's executor. The defendant argued that the covenant was void as contrary to public policy, in that it attempted to oust the court's jurisdiction under the *Matrimonial Causes Act 1959* (Cth) to make a maintenance order. The Supreme Court had upheld that contention.

All agreed that in determining the defence some regard had to be made to the Act, but Menzies, Owen and Gibbs JJ considered that the defence arose under the common law. The majority (Barwick CJ, McTiernan, Windeyer and Walsh JJ) held that it arose under the Act. The decision makes somewhat fine the distinction between 'arising under' an Act and 'involving its interpretation'.

---

[59] *R v Commonwealth Court of Conciliation and Arbitration; Ex parte Barrett* (1945) 70 CLR 141, 154.

[60] (1955) 92 CLR 529, 540.

[61] (1971) 124 CLR 367.

The meaning of 'arising under' was taken a stage further in *LNC Industries Ltd v BMW (Australia) Ltd.*[62] The plaintiff sued on a contract with the defendant under which, it was alleged, the defendant held rights to import goods under customs legislation on trust for the plaintiff. The defendant succeeded in the Supreme Court on the ground that the contract was subject to unfulfilled conditions. The High Court held that the matter arose under federal law and therefore there could be no appeal to the Privy Council. Although the claim was for specific performance or damages for breach of contract (being a cause of action and remedies under general law), it was also in respect of property or of a right created by federal law and, therefore, was a 'matter arising under' that law. In that case neither the interpretation nor application of the Commonwealth legislation seemed to be in dispute, but the Court held that in substance 'the very subject of the issue between the parties is an entitlement under the Regulations'.[63]

This increase in the area of federal jurisdiction by judicial decision was part of a long tradition, going back to the early days of the Court, of interpreting the Constitution and legislation so as to further statutory attempts to prevent appeals to the Privy Council and the bypassing of the High Court. With the enactment of the *Australia Acts 1986* (UK and Cth) that was no longer an issue. The tendency of the Court to favour expansion of the content of federal jurisdiction continued, however, as new social issues and policy choices arose.

Of course, one reason for an increase in the proportion of cases involving federal jurisdiction was simply the increase in areas on which the Parliament legislated and the litigation that occurred in respect of those laws. To a large extent this flow of federal law into new areas was a result of, or was supported by, High Court decisions on the extent of the external affairs power (s 51(xxix)), the corporations power (s 51(xx)) and the creation of joint Commonwealth–state authorities.[64] These decisions upheld or paved the way for legislation relating to trade practices, consumer protection, family

---

[62] (1983) 151 CLR 575.

[63] Ibid 582.

[64] *Re Cram; Ex parte NSW Colliery Proprietors' Association Ltd* (1987) 163 CLR 117.

law, racial and sex discrimination, the environment, Aboriginal rights, and so on. All this new legislation gave rise to much litigation and therefore to an increase in the proportion of matters 'arising under any laws made by the Parliament'.

(c) Other jurisdiction in sections 75 and 76(iii) and (iv)

Apart from those matters dealt with above, many of the areas of jurisdiction in s 75 (and also s 76(iv)) have been regarded by most lawyers as useless, meaningless or inappropriate.

(i) Diversity jurisdiction

The jurisdiction referred to in s 75(iv) in respect of matters between residents of different states has long been regarded as inappropriate for the High Court or for federal jurisdiction generally. Elsewhere, Sir Zelman Cowen and I set out our reasons for deploring the existence of diversity jurisdiction, including unthinking copying of the United States Constitution, the absence in Australia of fear that state courts might be biased against residents of other states, and the placing of an unnecessary burden on the High Court.[65]

As early as 1922 this jurisdiction was questioned by two High Court judges.[66] It was criticised by Owen Dixon KC in 1927 in evidence to the Royal Commission on the Constitution.[67] Even earlier, the jurisdiction puzzled W. Harrison Moore.[68] Inglis Clark (who had been Chairman of the Judiciary Committee at the 1891 Convention, which recommended it) was driven to suggest that a reason for this jurisdiction was that it ensured that court process and judgments were effective throughout Australia.[69] Having regard to the powers conferred on the Commonwealth in that respect by s 51(xxiv), that rationalisation is not very convincing. It is totally irrelevant today as a result of the *Service and Execution of Process Act 1992* (Cth).

---

[65] Cowen and Zines (1978) Chapter 2.
[66] *Australasian Temperance and General Mutual Life Assurance Society Ltd v Howe* (1922) 31 CLR 290, 330 (Higgins J), 339 (Starke J).
[67] Cowen and Zines (1978) 84–5.
[68] Harrison Moore (1910) 492.
[69] Inglis Clark (1905) 157–8.

The High Court has succeeded in reducing the scope of the jurisdiction in a number of ways. It has held that a corporation was not a 'resident' for purposes of s 75(iv);[70] that the jurisdiction did not arise where there was a person on each side of the proceedings who was a resident of the same state;[71] and that there was no jurisdiction whenever a corporation was a party, even though an individual was a co-party and diversity of parties was satisfied.[72] It has also threatened not to allow costs, or to allow only reduced costs, where the jurisdiction was invoked,[73] and since 1976 has remitted such cases to other courts under s 44 of the *Judiciary Act.*

The reasoning in *Australasian Temperance and General Mutual Life Assurance Society Ltd v Howe* (*Howe's Case*) has always been recognised as unsatisfactory in the light of a long history of cases where courts had ascribed residence to corporations. The Court was, it is suspected, motivated by a desire to reduce the scope of an absurd jurisdiction. That was in effect argued sixty years later in *Crouch v Commissioner for Railways (Q).*[74] In that case the judges seemed to agree with the force of the argument, but refused to overrule the earlier cases because there was nothing to be said for the jurisdiction and, therefore, the result of *Howe's Case* was desirable.

The Constitutional Convention recommended that the jurisdiction be repealed.[75] The only body that has in several decades had a good word to say for it as a head of federal jurisdiction was the Judicial Advisory Committee of the Constitutional Commission. They recommended that it be retained (though not as entrenched High Court jurisdiction) but that it should remain confined to natural persons. The Constitutional Commission rejected that view and recommended repeal of the jurisdiction.[76]

---

[70] *Australasian Temperance and General Mutual Life Assurance Society Ltd v Howe* (1922) 31 CLR 290, 330–1 (Higgins J), 337–8 (Starke J).

[71] *Watson v Cameron* (1928) 40 CLR 446.

[72] *Union Steamship Co of New Zealand Ltd v Ferguson* (1969) 119 CLR 191.

[73] See Cowen and Zines (1978) 76. Regarding appellate jurisdiction compare *Ritter v North Side Enterprises Pty Ltd* (1975) 132 CLR 301, 305.

[74] (1985) 159 CLR 22.

[75] Australian Constitutional Convention (1978) 204–5.

[76] Australian Constitutional Commission (1988) 381.

(ii) Treaties

Section 75(i) vests jurisdiction in matters 'arising under any treaty'. The problem here is not so much inappropriateness as lack of apparent denotation in view of the fact that a treaty cannot, as such, change domestic law. If the treaty is the cause of legal change it will have occurred through an Act of Parliament. In that case, if (as is usual) it is a federal Act, the matter would arise under an Act and come within s 76(ii). Puzzlement is further compounded by the enactment of s 38(a) of the *Judiciary Act* which makes exclusive to the High Court jurisdiction in matters arising directly under any treaty. Again, this is a case of copying in an unreflective manner from the United States Constitution under which treaties have direct legal effect if self-executing. The Australian Constitutional Convention recommended that this paragraph be repealed.[77]

The Constitutional Commission's Advisory Committee on the Australian Judicial System recommended that this paragraph be retained, but not as entrenched High Court jurisdiction. The Committee argued that s 75(i) could acquire some meaning as a result of a broader interpretation of the meaning of the words 'arising under' in relation to cases on s 76(ii).[78] The only authority it referred to was *LNC Industries Ltd v BMW (Australia) Ltd.*[79] It argued that the reasoning there employed by the Court could 'support the conclusion that a matter may arise under a treaty even though the treaty itself was not self-executing as a matter of Australian law'. It is difficult to know what to make of this. The case referred to held that a claim based on a contract which had as its subject property or a right created by federal law was one which arose under that law. The Constitutional Commission said it was unable to see that the reasoning employed in those cases assisted in understanding the meaning of s 75(i).[80]

The Advisory Committee, however, had additionally recommended that this head of jurisdiction be extended to matters in-

[77] Australian Constitutional Convention (1978) 204.
[78] Australian Constitutional Commission Advisory Committee on the Australian Judicial System (1987) 59.
[79] (1983) 151 CLR 575, 581.
[80] Australian Constitutional Commission (1988) 380.

volving the interpretation of a treaty. The Commission agreed that that was a suitable subject of federal jurisdiction and had a clearer meaning. They agreed, as well, to recommend the retention as federal jurisdiction of matters arising under a treaty because of 'the possibility of a matter arising under a treaty in a manner that is beyond our present conception'.[81] That statement of course does not help to understand the meaning of the existing provision.

So far as the interpretation of a treaty is concerned it was held in *Bluett v Fadden*[82] by McLelland J in the Supreme Court of New South Wales that s 75(i) must refer to cases where the decision depends on the interpretation of a treaty. He added that, if that were not so, it was difficult to ascertain any subject matter in that paragraph. A number of judges have, in a different context, pointed to the distinction between 'arising under' and 'involving the interpretation' as indicated by the inclusion of the latter phrase in s 76(i) and its absence from s 76(ii). The distinction is increasingly hard to ascertain in recent cases.

On the other hand, on the basis that a provision of the Constitution should be construed to give it some meaning, it is possible that it will be regarded as covering any matter that arises under a law which implements a treaty.[83] If so, the only matters within s 75(i) that do not come within s 76(ii) will be those that arise under a state Act which implements a treaty, such as the *Sale of Goods (Vienna Convention) Act 1989* (Vic). It is difficult to see this head of jurisdiction performing any useful service.

(iii) Consuls

Section 75(ii) refers to matters 'affecting consuls or other representatives of other countries'. There is some question whether ambassadors and high commissioners are included because 'consuls'—a lower rank—is the prime category. The reason they are not included is, of course, that Australia as a colony did not in 1900 have ambassadors. It is highly likely, however, that the Court in interpreting s 75(ii) will have regard to the evolution of Australian sovereignty.

---

[81] Ibid 380.
[82] (1956) 56 SR (NSW) 254.
[83] See P. H. Lane (1997) 556–7.

There are other difficulties of interpretation such as the meaning of 'affecting' and whether it must affect the consul in his or her public (as distinct from private) capacity. The Australian Constitutional Convention and the Advisory Committee to the Constitutional Commission recommended that the head of jurisdiction read 'Affecting ambassadors, high commissioners, consuls or other representatives of other countries'. The Constitutional Commission agreed and also took the view that because of the status of the parties it was an appropriate subject of federal jurisdiction.[84]

If the international status of the parties is what makes this a suitable subject, any new wording should, perhaps, be extended to the representatives of international bodies, such as the United Nations, or supra-national groups, such as the European Union, which would not be regarded as 'countries'.

(iv) Claims under different laws

Section 76(iv) authorises Parliament to invest jurisdiction in matters 'relating to the same subject-matter claimed under the laws of different States'. Of this provision Owen Dixon said to the Royal Commission in 1927 that 'so far, the meaning of this and the application of it has been elucidated by no one'. The Constitutional Convention recommended its repeal. The Advisory Committee of the Constitutional Commission recommended that it be preserved because it might be of use in resolving matters of conflict of laws (including statutes) among the states. The Constitutional Commission, somewhat unenthusiastically, said that was a 'possible interpretation' because the High Court was required to give it 'some meaning'.[85] Leslie Katz has examined the sources of s 76(iv) in American and Australian history. He shows, persuasively, that the intention was probably to create a jurisdiction that was similar to, but more extensive than, the United States jurisdiction which is 'Controversies ... between Citizens of the same State claiming Lands under Grants of different States'. Katz deduced that it was intended to cover 'all matters in which the resolution of conflicting claims of interests in

[84] Australian Constitutional Commission (1988) 376–7.
[85] Ibid 382.

or in relation to land or waters depended upon the determination of the respective boundaries of States'.[86] The jurisdiction (which is conferred on state courts under s 39(2) of the *Judiciary Act*) has never been used.

(v) Admiralty and maritime jurisdiction

Admiralty and maritime jurisdiction is the subject of s 76(iii). No one denies its appropriateness as a matter of federal jurisdiction. Until recently this area of law raised many difficulties, partly because of the operation of Imperial law.[87] The matter is now governed solely by the *Admiralty Act 1988* (Cth).

There has for years been doubt as to the scope of this subject—particularly as to the meaning of the word 'maritime'. To some extent the difficulty arose from the different approaches in Britain and the United States to this matter. In Britain there had been a struggle between the Courts of Admiralty and the common law courts which narrowed the admiralty jurisdiction. This was widened somewhat in the nineteenth century by legislation operating throughout the Empire. The *Colonial Courts of Admiralty Act 1890* (Imp) governed the jurisdiction of courts of British possessions. The issue in respect of s 76(iii) was the extent to which it went beyond those matters that came within the Imperial legislation at 1900. In the United States there was a very broad conception of admiralty and maritime jurisdiction and s 76(iii) was borrowed from the United States Constitution. From the first half of the nineteenth century the American courts had declared that the jurisdiction was to be determined, not by English law, but by principles of maritime law followed by the maritime courts of Europe.[88]

The High Court has taken the broader approach, consistent with familiar principles relating to the interpretation of constitutional power. The Court held that 'maritime' extended beyond 'Admiralty' jurisdiction as at 1900 to matters generally accepted by maritime nations as falling within a special jurisdiction. Central to the concept were controversies relating to maritime commerce and

---

[86] Katz (1991) 239.

[87] Cowen and Zines (1978) 63–72, 228–33.

[88] Ibid 64–5.

navigation. The Court showed a preference for United States decisions, although it left open whether some decisions were too narrow. These were cases which had held that contracts on land for the construction or sale of ships did not come within the jurisdiction.[89]

3 Accrued and Associated Jurisdiction

(a) Accrued jurisdiction

The expansion of federal jurisdiction was given a further boost by the development of accrued jurisdiction. This time the context was not appeals to the Privy Council, but the exclusive jurisdiction of the Federal Court. The key concept used to craft accrued jurisdiction was 'matter' in Chapter III. The conflicting social interests involved were the status and viability of the state courts and the interest of litigants.

The early cases had made it clear that if an issue is raised which brings the matter within a head of federal jurisdiction a federal court does not necessarily lose jurisdiction if that issue is decided against the party raising it. The court can determine other issues involved in the matter.[90] The High Court, however, distinguished matters where the plaintiff alleged two or more distinct and 'entirely severable' claims, and only one of them came within federal jurisdiction.[91]

These issues arose mainly in cases in the original jurisdiction of the High Court in respect of constitutional matters. The justification for the Court deciding the non-federal claims was that they formed part of the one 'matter' being litigated. The questions arose more frequently and had greater impact after the creation of the Federal Court of Australia with jurisdiction under the *Trade Practices Act* and, in particular, under s 86. That provision vested exclusive jurisdiction in the Court in proceedings related to restrictive practices and monopolies, and, until 1987, actions in respect of breach of s 52 prohibiting misleading or deceptive conduct in trade or commerce.

---

[89] *Owners of 'Shin Kobe Maru' v Empire Shipping Co Inc* (1994) 181 CLR 404.

[90] Cowen and Zines (1978) 72–5.

[91] *Carter v Egg and Egg Pulp Marketing Board (Vict)* (1942) 66 CLR 557, 580, 602; *Airlines of NSW Pty Ltd v New South Wales (No 1)* (1964) 113 CLR 1.

The problem was examined in the *Philip Morris Case*,[92] where applications were made to the Federal Court arising under Part VI of the *Trade Practices Act* (where the Court's jurisdiction was exclusive) and also for relief not based on federal law, namely, passing-off. A majority of the High Court held that the Federal Court had jurisdiction to determine the 'non-severable' claims not based on federal law. The judges differed on the principle applicable, but the circumstance that the facts on which the statutory and common law claims were based were 'identical' or 'almost wholly' identical was the deciding factor.[93]

Mason J expressly adverted to the underlying conflicting interests in the Australian court system and the practical aspects of decision-making in this area. He said:

> Lurking beneath the surface of the arguments presented in this case are competing policy considerations affecting the role and status of the Federal Court and the Supreme Courts of the States. There is on the one hand the desirability of enabling the Federal Court to deal with attached claims so as to resolve the entirety of the parties' controversy. There is on the other hand an apprehension that if it be held that the Federal Court has jurisdiction to deal with attached claims, State courts will lose to the Federal Court a proportion of the important work which they have hitherto discharged, work which the Federal Court has no jurisdiction to determine if it be not attached to a federal claim. Added force is given to this apprehension by the vesting of exclusive federal jurisdiction in the Federal Court, for example, by s. 86 of the *Trade Practices Act*.[94]

It was argued that the difficulty for litigants could be avoided by making the jurisdiction of the Federal Court concurrent with the state courts. Wilson J, although 'burdened' by the difficulty of litigants, pointed to s 77(iii) of the Constitution enabling federal jurisdiction to be vested in state courts. Mason J replied that the Constitution had empowered the Commonwealth to create federal

---

[92] *Philip Morris Inc v Adam P Brown Male Fashions Pty Ltd* (1981) 148 CLR 457.

[93] Ibid 499 (Gibbs J), 516 (Mason J). See also 480 (Barwick CJ).

[94] Ibid 513.

courts and to give them exclusive jurisdiction. The Court must assume that Parliament decided the way it did for good reason. For him, the predominant interest was 'the speedier determination of entire controversies between parties without undue duplication of proceedings'. On the other hand, for Wilson J the adverse effects on state courts of a broad interpretation of 'matter' would 'diminish [the Constitution's] effectiveness in maintaining a viable federation'. Mason J's reply was that the consequences for state courts were 'secondary to the interests of litigants'.[95]

In *Fencott v Muller*,[96] a majority (Mason, Murphy, Brennan and Deane JJ) adopted an approach that went beyond that in the *Philip Morris Case*. They did not express any clear principle or formula for distinguishing between a severable and non-severable state claim, but they said that it might be necessary to examine the conduct of the proceedings and the pleadings. In the end, however, it was 'a matter of impression and of practical judgment'.[97] Where they differed from the opposing view was mainly in respect of the object of s 76(ii) which, they said, was not to ensure the correct application of federal law, but to determine the dispute and quell controversy. The restrictive approach would lead to 'arid jurisdictional disputes' and possibly different findings of fact in the federal and state courts. They said that the test of 'common transactions or facts' was a sound guide for distinguishing non-severable claims.

How far the High Court was prepared to go in favour of regarding separate claims and remedies as part of one matter is illustrated by the decision in *Fencott v Muller*. All the claims were held to be part of the matter within jurisdiction, although they included allegations by one party of a breach of s 52 of the *Trade Practices Act*, and of fraud, negligent misrepresentations and breach of contract, claims by another party for compensation for breach of fiduciary relations by its directors, and a claim under an indemnity against a trustee company. The elements of these different causes of action varied as did the parties and the remedies sought. Nevertheless, they were all part of the one matter because they 'all arise

---

[95] Ibid 514 (Mason J), 548 (Wilson J).
[96] (1983) 152 CLR 570.
[97] Ibid 608.

out of common transactions and facts, namely, the negotiations for sale, contract of sale and performance of the contract of sale of O'Connors Wine Bar and Restaurant'.[98]

The dissents of Wilson and Dawson JJ were motivated by different objects and possible consequences. They held that the Federal Court had no jurisdiction over any of the non-federal claims because the facts on which they were based were not identical to the federal ones. Dawson J attacked the majority view by reference to the text of the Constitution and past decisions. The avoidance of inconvenience to litigants, which Mason J had regarded as the paramount purpose, was for Dawson J 'no explanation in legal or constitutional terms'. He then pointed out that the majority's approach 'is to create problems at the other end'. If the whole 'matter' before the court included claims arising under state law and the court had exclusive jurisdiction to determine the matter, the jurisdiction in respect of those state claims might be excluded from state court jurisdiction, whether or not the jurisdiction of the Federal Court was invoked.[99]

That difficulty in fact arose in *Stack v Coast Securities (No 9) Pty Ltd (Stack's Case).*[100] There, four corporations applied to the Queensland Supreme Court for specific performance of contracts for the sale of home units. In each case the defendants applied to the Federal Court, in respect of the same transactions, for orders under s 52 of the *Trade Practices Act.* In some of the latter cases the corporations delivered defences and cross claims for a declaration that the contract was valid and for specific performance. Applicants in the Federal Court applied for injunctions to restrain the proceedings in the Supreme Court. In one case the corporation applied to the Supreme Court for an injunction restraining proceedings in the Federal Court.

In the High Court all the judges accepted that, on the basis of previous decisions, all the issues in these cases were part of matters arising under the *Trade Practices Act* and, therefore, within the jurisdiction of the Federal Court. As s 86 provided that that jurisdiction was exclusive, it was argued that the Supreme Court had no

---

[98] Ibid 610.
[99] Ibid 629.
[100] (1983) 154 CLR 261.

jurisdiction in the actions for specific performance. This raised the possibility of some bizarre consequences, such as a defendant in the Supreme Court leaving it to the last minute to raise the federal issue and then not pursuing the matter in the Federal Court.

The solution adopted was to declare that s 86 made exclusive only actions under Part VI of the Act, but not the accrued jurisdiction. The Federal Court, therefore, had a discretion whether or not to exercise the accrued jurisdiction, a possibility suggested by Barwick CJ in the *Philip Morris Case*.[101] The principle that there is a duty to exercise jurisdiction was offset by the consequences of its application here, which could hardly have been intended by Parliament. Wilson and Dawson JJ, while accepting the earlier decisions, added that 'until there is an opportunity for reconsideration, the Court may find itself committed to a course of reasoning which involves artificiality and error'.[102]

As already mentioned, the court does not lose its accrued jurisdiction merely because the federal claim is decided against the person raising it. It would seem to be clear, however, that if it is held that there is no federal jurisdiction, there can be no accrued jurisdiction, because the state claim is not 'inseverable' from any federal claim. Six judges in *Carlton & United Breweries Ltd v Castlemaine Tooheys Ltd*[103] said it was obvious 'that there can be no accrued jurisdiction unless there are federal issues which that Court has jurisdiction to entertain'. This raises the continuing problem in administrative law of when an issue goes to jurisdiction and when to merits.

This is illustrated by four decisions of single judges of the Federal Court where it was found that the Court could not give relief under the *Administrative Decisions (Judicial Review) Act 1977* (Cth) (*ADJR Act*). That Act seems to limit the jurisdiction of the Court to the review of administrative decisions made under an enactment. In each of three cases it was found that the action the Court was asked to review did not come within the *ADJR Act* and

---

[101] *Philip Morris Inc v Adam P Brown Male Fashions Pty Ltd* (1981) 148 CLR 457, 475.

[102] *Stack v Coast Securities (No 9) Pty Ltd* (1983) 154 CLR 261, 302.

[103] (1986) 161 CLR 543, 553.

the judges went on to consider 'accrued' common law claims and remedies.

In the first case, *Post Office Agents Association Ltd v Australian Postal Commission*, Davies J dismissed quite shortly the argument that if there could be no review under the Act, there could be no accrued jurisdiction, saying that:

> the court has jurisdiction. The jurisdiction of the court under the ADJR Act has been invoked. The application is brought thereunder as a matter of substance, not as a matter of artificiality or subterfuge. The court has jurisdiction to deal with the claim and jurisdiction to deal with all other claims not otherwise within its jurisdiction arising out of the subject matter of the dispute.[104]

This decision was followed as a matter of comity by Hodgson J[105] and Finn J.[106] Hodgson J tried to explain Davies J's brief remarks to mean that the determination by the Court as to whether the application came within the *ADJR Act* was within the statutory jurisdiction of the Court. If so, presumably it is a conclusive determination and not subject to prohibition or mandamus under s 75(v) of the Constitution. If that is the case, it is arguable that there was 'accrued jurisdiction' in the circumstances.

On the other hand, the Federal Court in determining that question may simply be exercising the function which of necessity all courts and tribunals must have, namely, of deciding (but not conclusively) whether it has any statutory jurisdiction. If it has no statutory jurisdiction, it cannot have accrued jurisdiction. The decision, either way, in those circumstances could be subject to review in the High Court. In *Vietnam Veterans' Affairs Association of Australia New South Wales Branch Inc v Cohen*,[107] Tamberlin J rejected the view of Davies J and held that the Court had no jurisdiction under the *ADJR Act* where the actions involved were of a legislative rather than an administrative nature. It followed that there was no accrued jurisdiction.

---

[104] (1988) 84 ALR 563, 565.
[105] *Standard Chartered Bank of Australia Ltd v Antico* (1995) 131 ALR 1.
[106] *Buck v Comcare* (1996) 137 ALR 335. See also Aitken (1986).
[107] (1996) 46 ALD 290.

(b) Associated jurisdiction

In *Stack's Case*[108] Mason, Brennan and Deane JJ, in determining that under s 86 of the *Trade Practices Act* the primary (and not accrued) jurisdiction was exclusive, said that the drafter may have intended to achieve that result by a different route, namely by means of s 32 of the *Federal Court of Australia Act 1976* (Cth). That section provides: 'To the extent that the Constitution permits, jurisdiction is conferred on the Court in respect of matters not otherwise within its jurisdiction that are associated with matters in which the jurisdiction of the Court is invoked'.

It was the view of some at the time that actions now held to be within 'accrued jurisdiction' would instead be upheld as within s 32.[109] This would have meant in relation to the *Trade Practices Act* that they would not have been within 'exclusive jurisdiction' because not included in s 86. As we have seen, however, the High Court preferred to use the concept of 'matter' and 'accrued jurisdiction' for this purpose.

Section 32 refers to matters which are subjects of federal jurisdiction (that is, they are matters referred to in ss 75 and 76) which (a) do not otherwise come within the Court's jurisdiction, but (b) are 'associated' with it. In the *Philip Morris Case*[110] it was held that the Court had jurisdiction in respect of a claim for breach of copyright as 'associated' with an action alleging breach of ss 52 and 53 of the *Trade Practices Act*. No clear test or principle has emerged as to the meaning of 'associated'. There is no reason in principle why the 'matter' within associated jurisdiction should not include 'accrued' claims.

(c) 'Matters' in appellate jurisdiction

It has been long settled that the power to define the jurisdiction of federal courts in s 77(i) extends to appellate jurisdiction.[111] The legislation creating the federal courts has provision for the exercise of original and appellate jurisdiction. In relation to some matters the

---

[108] *Stack v Coast Securities (No 9) Pty Ltd* (1983) 154 CLR 261, 296.
[109] Gummow (1979).
[110] *Philip Morris Inc v Adam P Brown Male Fashions Pty Ltd* (1981) 148 CLR 457.
[111] *Ah Yick v Lehmert* (1905) 2 CLR 593.

Federal Court has jurisdiction to determine appeals from state Supreme Courts, such as in matters of intellectual property and bankruptcy. This was the case with taxation matters until 1987 when the Federal Court was given exclusive original as well as appellate jurisdiction.

In *Collins v Charles Marshall Pty Ltd*,[112] the High Court said that in the case of the appellate jurisdiction of a federal court or a state court exercising federal jurisdiction, the matter arising on the appeal must come within s 75 or s 76. It is not enough that it is an appeal from a judgment determining a matter that at first instance was within federal jurisdiction. This view was affirmed in *Cockle v Isaksen*.[113] While the Court in those cases was concerned with an appeal from judgments of state courts to the Commonwealth Industrial Court, it would seem to be applicable also to appeals from judgments determined in the original jurisdiction of a federal court. Section 77, which concerns 'matters', is to be contrasted with the appellate jurisdiction of the High Court in s 73, which refers to appeals from 'judgments' of specified courts or justices.

This view creates problems when the matter heard and determined in original jurisdiction includes a federal claim and an accrued non-federal claim and the only issue on appeal from the judgment concerns the non-federal claim. It would seem to follow that in those circumstances the federal courts do not have federal jurisdiction to hear the appeal, whether the judgment appealed against is that of its own court or a state court exercising federal jurisdiction.

This approach creates unnecessary complexity and is inconsistent with the otherwise liberal attitude taken to the interpretation of Chapter III, where there has usually been an emphasis on practical solutions and an avoidance, so far as possible, of difficulty for litigants. The principle dictated by these cases is unnecessary because it is not the only interpretation that can be given to s 77. Section 77 is prefaced with the words 'With respect to any of the matters mentioned in the last two sections the Parliament may make laws'. In defining or investing appellate jurisdiction under s 77(i) or (iii),

---

[112] (1955) 92 CLR 529.
[113] (1957) 99 CLR 155, 164.

appeals from judgments determining matters referred to in ss 75 and 76 can reasonably be described as 'with respect to' those matters. This is particularly so when it is noted that 'with respect to' has always been regarded in Australian constitutional law as a phrase of broad connotation requiring 'a relevance to or connection with the subject'.[114] It seems to me that a conferral of appellate jurisdiction in respect of judgments determining matters mentioned in s 75 and s 76 is a law that has a close relevance or connection with those matters.

4 Cross-vesting

The extension of the concept of accrued jurisdiction had a consider-able effect on avoidance of a multiplicity of proceedings, and to a lesser degree that may have also been true of associated jurisdiction. Nevertheless, in many circumstances jurisdictional conflicts and dif-ficulties remained.[115] The cross-vesting legislation, which came into force on 1 July 1988, solved many of those problems. However, in 1999 the High Court invalidated an important part of the cross-vesting scheme (see Chapter 10). In the light of this development many of the matters referred to above, such as accrued jurisdiction, will have renewed impact. In any case these issues have not gone away because the scheme does not apply to the scope of jurisdiction of the High Court, and, except in certain cases, lower state courts. Also, the Federal and Family Courts are not vested with all the fed-eral jurisdiction exercisable by state courts under s 39(2) of the *Judiciary Act*.

---

[114] *Grannall v Marrickville Margarine Pty Ltd* (1955) 93 CLR 55, 77 (Dixon CJ, McTiernan, Webb and Kitto JJ). The judges were referring to ss 51 and 52, but their remarks seem relevant to s 77.

[115] See Opeskin (1995) 805–6.

10

Cross-vesting of Jurisdiction and the Federal Judicial System

*Brian Opeskin**

ON 1 JULY 1988, a national scheme for cross-vesting jurisdiction between Australian superior courts commenced operation. At the time of its commencement, the scheme was hailed as a significant landmark on the road towards the creation of a unitary judicial system in Australia. Its supporters celebrated it as a peerless example of intergovernmental co-operation between the six states, the two internal territories, and the Commonwealth. Many lawyers lauded it as a practical and effective solution to jurisdictional difficulties that previously beset the federal judicial system. And an official review of the scheme, conducted after four years of operation, concluded that the scheme had had, even at that early stage, a 'profound and largely beneficial impact on the Australian judicial system'.[1]

However, two High Court decisions have unsettled the constitutional foundations of the scheme. The central issue in each case

---

[1] Moloney and McMaster (1992) 147.

* I am grateful to Justice Leslie Katz and Fiona Wheeler for valuable comments on a draft of this chapter. I also wish to thank Chief Justice Michael Black for making available his Memorandum of April 1999 to Federal Court judges on the corporations jurisdiction of the Federal Court, and for providing valuable information on the role of the Chief Justices in monitoring the operation of the cross-vesting scheme.

was the validity of legislation conferring, or consenting to the conferral of, state jurisdiction on federal courts. In the first of the two
cases, *Gould v Brown*, an evenly divided High Court led to the
result that the scheme was upheld, though in circumstances that
made further challenge to the scheme inevitable.[2] In the second of
the two cases, *Re Wakim; Ex parte McNally* (*Re Wakim*) a significant change in the composition of the bench led to a different
result.[3] By a majority of six to one the High Court held that the
legislative scheme was invalid in so far as it purported to confer state
jurisdiction on federal courts. The dust from the decision has yet to
settle, and it may be unclear for some time what steps will be taken
to repair the structural damage caused by the High Court's decision.

The purpose of this chapter is to trace the development of the
cross-vesting scheme and assess its significance for the Australian
federal judicial system. That significance lies not only in the unique-
ness of the scheme in the evolution of a unified judicial system in
Australia, but in the continued relevance of the substantial parts of
the scheme that survived the decision in *Re Wakim*. The scheme
comprises nine complementary pieces of short but rather technical
legislation. This chapter is not intended as a detailed account of the
technical operation of the scheme, for that can be found elsewhere.[4]
Rather, the intention is to place the scheme in the context of the
development of the federal judicial system as a whole, and examine
it as an institutional response to a significant institutional problem.

To this end, Part 1 considers some questions of institutional
design of the judiciary in federal systems, and Australia's early
answers to those questions. Part 2 discusses both the problems that
emerged in the 1970s and 1980s as a result of the establishment of
two new federal courts, and the strains that this placed on the Australian judicial system as a whole. Part 3 discusses the partial solutions to these problems, which arose from the development of the
judicial doctrine of accrued jurisdiction and the reference of certain
family law matters by the states to the Commonwealth under
s 51(xxxvii) of the Constitution. Part 4 examines the origins of the

---

[2] (1998) 193 CLR 346.

[3] (1999) 163 ALR 270.

[4] See *Practice and Procedure: High Court and Federal Court of Australia*, Butterworths
(looseleaf).

scheme for cross-vesting jurisdiction and its realisation in the legislative package that we have today. Parts 5 and 6 examine structural and operational aspects of the cross-vesting scheme, including the provisions for the transfer of proceedings between participating courts. Part 7 discusses special federal features of the scheme, which are designed to privilege the jurisdiction of federal courts in certain types of matters. And, finally, Part 8 considers possible futures for the cross-vesting scheme, and the federal judicial system as a whole, in the wake of the High Court's decision in *Re Wakim*.

1 Institutional Design of Courts in Federal Systems

(a) Universal questions

The distribution of power between organs within the state is the hallmark of a federal system.[5] Yet, while this distribution of power is usually well pronounced in the executive and legislative branches of government, the judicial branch of government is often more ambiguous (and potentially less federal) in its arrangements. The method of organising courts in federations cannot be easily stereotyped.[6]

The drafters of any federal constitution must address several fundamental questions of design when formulating the state, federal and national elements of their judicial system. The first is the institutional question whether central and regional governments should establish separate and parallel systems of courts. In his influential 1947 study, K. C. Wheare observed that if the 'federal principle' were to be strictly applied, one would expect a dual court system to be established in every federation—one set of courts to apply and interpret the law of the central government, and another to apply and interpret the law of each regional government.[7] Some federations adopt this model—amongst them the United States, Brazil and Mexico—but it is not especially common. Others take the view that disputes can be satisfactorily resolved within a system of courts that is wholly centralised (as in South Africa, Venezuela and

---

[5] Elazar (1966) 2.

[6] Wheare (1947) 71.

[7] Ibid 70–1.

Malaysia). Still others are organised in a highly regionalised fashion, there being no federal courts other than the highest court, as in Germany and Switzerland.[8]

The second question of design is the jurisdictional one of whether the constitution should distinguish between different classes of legal disputes for certain purposes. The constitutions of the United States and Australia, for example, distinguish matters of federal jurisdiction from residual state matters by reference to the subject matter of the action or the identity of the parties. Amongst the heads of federal jurisdiction in ss 75 and 76 of the Australian Constitution are matters arising under the Constitution, matters arising under federal law, suits in which the Commonwealth is a party, and prerogative writs against Commonwealth officers. These are, for the most part, matters in which the federal polity has a special interest.

The third design question is that of the relationship between the previous two. It is natural to assume that if a distinction is drawn between matters of federal and state jurisdiction, the former ought to be adjudicated in federal courts and the latter in state courts. This assumption was evident in the design of the United States judicial system. By way of example, the inclusion of 'Controversies to which the United States shall be a Party' as a head of federal jurisdiction in Article III of the United States Constitution was based on the view that the United States government ought to have the facility of suing or being sued in a neutral federal forum, free from potential state biases. To hold otherwise would 'compel the national government to become a supplicant for justice before the judicature of those who were by other parts of the Constitution placed in subordination to it'.[9] The idea was thus that only federal courts should decide matters of federal jurisdiction. But this was not to be the case in Australia, where the two streams of jurisdiction, federal and state, were in many cases administered concurrently by the state courts.

(b) Australian answers

The central elements of the Australian judicial system have been dealt with at length in other chapters in this book (see especially

---

[8] Duchacek (1970) 252–5; Watts (1966) 226–8.
[9] Story Commentaries, s 1674, cited in Cowen (1959) 33–4.

Chapter 2). At federation, the essential institutional features of the system were the obligation of federal Parliament to create the High Court; the capacity of federal Parliament to create additional federal courts; and the recognition of a continuing role for state courts.[10] The essential jurisdictional feature was the creation of separate classes of federal jurisdiction and residual state jurisdiction. And the essential relational features were the conferral of some but not all original federal jurisdiction on the High Court; the capacity of the federal Parliament to confer federal jurisdiction on federal courts (including the High Court); the capacity of the federal Parliament to invest federal jurisdiction in state courts without their consent; and the right of appeal from state courts to the High Court in matters of state as well as federal jurisdiction.

Many writers have commented on the last two relational features as important points of departure from the judicature article of the United States Constitution, and so they were.[11] The capacity of federal Parliament to confer federal jurisdiction on state courts, in particular, created a confusion of design that placed the Australian judicature in uncharted waters somewhere between the dual court system of the United States and the regionalised systems now found in Germany and Switzerland. The problem, as Zelman Cowen explained it, was not simply that it was irrational to establish two separate channels of jurisdiction (federal and state) and then administer them within the same set of courts. It was that there was no need in Australian circumstances to divide jurisdiction into state and federal matters in the first place.[12] The reason for this frolic was the 'hypnotic fascination' of the drafters with the United States Constitution, a fascination which, according to Sir Owen Dixon, 'damped the smoldering fires of their originality'.[13]

Many of the problems generated by this flawed constitutional design remained dormant for over seventy years. This was because, as Quick and Garran predicted in 1901, the judicial power of the

---

[10] See now *Kable v Director of Public Prosecutions (NSW)* (1996) 189 CLR 51.

[11] In the United States there had been doubt as to whether state courts could be compelled to enforce federal law. See Congressional Research Service (1992) 795–7.

[12] Cowen (1959) x, xi.

[13] Sir Owen Dixon (1935) 597.

Commonwealth was for some considerable period exercised entirely by the High Court and by state courts invested with federal jurisdiction.[14] The authority of state courts in exercising the judicial power of the Commonwealth was left basically unchallenged until the 1970s. The increasing volume of federal legislation around this period, covering many aspects of commercial and private life, brought about a corresponding rise in the range of matters falling within federal jurisdiction, and with it questions about the appropriate allocation of the new jurisdiction within the federation. Specialised federal courts had earlier been created in respect of bankruptcy and labour law (see Chapter 5). But the establishment of the Family Court in 1975 and the Federal Court in 1976 posed a new and direct challenge to the traditional position of state courts, in so far as state courts were invested with federal jurisdiction.

2 Emerging Problems

Three chief difficulties were generated by the creation of new federal courts in the 1970s. These difficulties were the problems of split jurisdiction, the perceived decline in status of state courts, and forum shopping.

(a) Split jurisdiction

A dual court system may present a serious threat to the laudable goal of having one court adjudicate all disputed issues between the parties.[15] If one court is able to resolve only some of the relevant issues because of limitations on its jurisdiction, the parties may be forced to pursue the remainder of their claim in another court, with consequent expense and delay. Split jurisdictional problems such as these became a common feature of federal–state court relations during the 1980s, particularly in relation to trade practices and family law matters.

Consider, for example, the jurisdictional problems experienced in relation to the custody of children. The *Family Law Act 1975*

---

[14] Quick and Garran (1901) 726.

[15] Street (1978) 435; Rogers (1980) 288.

(Cth) provides a nationwide scheme with respect to divorce, child custody, maintenance and property settlement. However, as the Act rests principally on the marriage power in s 51(xxi) of the Constitution, there are constraints on its scope of operation. In relation to child custody it was held early on that the *Family Law Act* could deal validly only with the natural or adopted children of both parties to the marriage.[16] Accordingly, the Act could not regulate the custody of ex-nuptial children of the husband or wife, or the custody of a child of other parents, such as a foster child.

The limitations on the scope of the marriage power translated directly into jurisdictional difficulties for the courts and practical difficulties for families. If a family comprised both children of a marriage and ex-nuptial children, a dispute over custody would have to be determined in two different courts: the former in the Family Court and the latter in a state court. Commenting on this discreditable situation in 1983, a government committee expressed 'its most serious concern and dismay regarding the effect which the present distribution of family law powers has had on the personal lives of ordinary members of the community'.[17] Understandably, split jurisdictional problems brought the legal system into disrepute and gave rise to considerable pressure for reform.

(b) Court status

Another problem that arose in the 1980s was the perception that the prestige and status of the state Supreme Courts was deteriorating. Before the growth of federal jurisdiction in the 1970s, the community and the profession generally regarded the Supreme Courts of the states as courts of high standard. Yet, as social regulation by federal law increased over the years, a wider range of matters fell within the scope of federal jurisdiction. So long as this jurisdiction was invested in state courts pursuant to s 77(iii) of the Constitution, state courts had little to lose from the expansion of federal law. However, to the extent that this jurisdiction was vested in federal

---

[16] *Russell v Russell* (1976) 134 CLR 495; *In the Marriage of Cormick* (1984) 156 CLR 170.

[17] Australian Constitutional Commission Advisory Committee on the Distribution of Powers (1987) 53.

courts rather than state courts, there was said to be a corresponding decline in the role and function of state courts.[18] This gave rise to a concern for the future that 'much of the variety [in state courts' work] might go, leading to a decline in the quality of appointees to State courts and a consequent, if gradual, loss of prestige'.[19]

(c) Forum shopping

Federations provide litigants with a golden opportunity for forum shopping. Australian cases in which the issue of forum shopping has been raised have generally involved a choice between state and territorial forums.[20] However, the conferral of concurrent jurisdiction on state and federal courts raises an additional possibility for forum shopping.

During the 1980s, concurrent jurisdiction of state and federal courts was not widespread, so that problems of federal–state forum shopping were not acute. The inhospitable environment for federal–state forum shopping was, and still is, supported by three factors. First, many matters of federal jurisdiction are matters arising under laws made by the federal Parliament, so that the federal law itself provides the relevant rule of decision. Second, s 79 of the *Judiciary Act 1903* (Cth) requires all courts exercising federal jurisdiction to apply the laws of the state or territory in which they sit, unless alternative provision is made. This minimises the incentive to engage in forum shopping between state and federal courts within a state (see Chapter 11). And third, parties may sometimes be subject to adverse costs rulings if they bring suit in an inappropriate forum.[21]

Yet, despite the absence of formal differences between litigating in state and federal courts, there are less tangible disparities that incline litigants to favour one court system over the other. It is often said, for example, that the Federal Court can offer parties a speedier trial than state courts in certain matters due to its method of active

---

[18] Australian Constitutional Convention Judicature Sub-Committee (1984) 6–7.

[19] Australian Constitutional Commission Advisory Committee on the Australian Judicial System (1987) 28.

[20] For example, *Stevens v Head* (1993) 176 CLR 433; *McKain v RW Miller & Co (SA) Pty Ltd* (1991) 174 CLR 1; *Breavington v Godleman* (1988) 169 CLR 41.

[21] See, for example, Federal Court Rules, O 62, r 36A(2).

case management. There may also be some cost incentive to litigate small claims in state courts.[22] And, rightly or wrongly, litigants may have greater confidence in the quality of decisions of federal courts.

These considerations fuelled the concerns of some observers of the judicial system during this period, since they thought it might lead to a drift towards litigants choosing federal courts over state courts in important litigation.[23] At the very least, the problem of federal–state forum shopping often hovered in the background as a relevant factor in any proposed reconfiguration of the jurisdiction of state and federal courts. As a former Commonwealth Attorney-General once observed, extending the concurrent jurisdiction of federal and state courts on a wide scale was likely to introduce new problems of forum shopping in place of the old problems of jurisdictional uncertainty.[24]

3 Partial Solutions

The difficulties that arose from the expansion of federal courts and federal jurisdiction in the 1970s and 1980s engendered a number of significant developments in the federal judicial system. This part briefly reviews two of them—the evolution of accrued jurisdiction and the reference of legislative power from the states to the Commonwealth in relation to child custody. The proposal for a third solution—the establishment of a scheme for cross-vesting jurisdiction of state and federal courts—was in its infancy at this time, but later became a central plank in addressing the concerns raised by a federal judicial system.

(a) Accrued jurisdiction

The doctrine of accrued jurisdiction is surveyed in detail in Chapter 9. For present purposes it may be noted that the purpose of the doctrine is to bring within the scope of an existing federal claim another claim that is otherwise non-federal in character and which a federal

---

[22] Ibid O 62, r 36A(1).
[23] Australian Constitutional Commission Advisory Committee on the Australian Judicial System (1987) 42.
[24] Durack (1981) 782.

court could not otherwise adjudicate. The High Court has embraced a broad notion of accrued jurisdiction, using the constitutional notion of a 'matter' as its vehicle (see Chapter 8).[25] Thus, it is now clear that a federal court has jurisdiction to adjudicate an entire matter, including federal claims and claims that would otherwise be non-federal, but which are transmuted into federal claims by virtue of their adjudication by a federal court. However, the 'non-federal' claims must be attached to and not severable from the federal claims for the doctrine to be successfully invoked.[26] Once a federal court is properly seized of a matter, it has jurisdiction to determine the 'non-federal' claim even if the federal claim is rejected or is considered unnecessary to resolve.[27]

Yet, despite the benefits of accrued jurisdiction in avoiding multiplicity and duplication of proceedings, the doctrine has been more an anodyne than a panacea for the jurisdictional ills of federal courts. Even when the doctrine was at its zenith, split jurisdictional problems persisted in cases in which federal and non-federal claims arose in the course of one dispute, but were nonetheless regarded as severable.[28] It had also been held that the federal claim must be a substantial aspect of the controversy,[29] thus limiting the application of the doctrine in some circumstances. And the doctrine was never applied with full vigour to the jurisdiction of the Family Court.[30]

Accrued jurisdiction has enjoyed a renaissance since the High Court invalidated the exercise by federal courts of cross-vested state jurisdiction in *Re Wakim*.[31] For some judges, this resurgence has come with an understandable sense of regret that litigants are required to 'dust off old arguments and invoke old learning that could

[25] *Philip Morris Inc v Adam P Brown Male Fashions Pty Ltd* (1981) 148 CLR 457; *Fencott v Muller* (1983) 152 CLR 570; *Stack v Coast Securities (No 9) Pty Ltd* (1983) 154 CLR 261.

[26] *Fencott v Muller* (1983) 152 CLR 570, 606.

[27] *Moorgate Tobacco Co Ltd v Philip Morris Ltd* (1980) 145 CLR 457, 476; *Philip Morris Inc v Adam P Brown Male Fashions Pty Ltd* (1981) 148 CLR 457, 474.

[28] *Obacelo Pty Ltd v Taveraft Pty Ltd* (1985) 5 FCR 210.

[29] *Fencott v Muller* (1983) 152 CLR 570, 609–10.

[30] *Smith v Smith* (1986) 161 CLR 217; Opeskin (1995) 804–5.

[31] (1999) 163 ALR 270.

be more usefully applied as doorstop material than to the workings of a modern judicial system'.[32]

(b) Reference of power to the Commonwealth

A second solution has been limited use of the reference power in s 51(xxxvii) of the Constitution. This section empowers the federal legislature to make laws with respect to matters referred to it by the Parliament of any state. The purpose of this grant was evidently to provide a means by which states might bring about federal action without the need to amend the Constitution. It is thus one of several means by which state and federal governments may co-operate to solve problems arising from limitations on federal legislative power.

Although the section has been used sparingly over the course of this century, in the 1980s it was employed for the purpose of referring to the Commonwealth matters relating to child custody. A principal objective of the reference was to avoid the jurisdictional difficulties that the Family Court had faced in dealing with the custody of ex-nuptial children, as described above. Between 1986 and 1990 five states referred to the Commonwealth the matters of (a) child maintenance and (b) custody and guardianship of, and access to, children.[33] The sixth state, Western Australia, gave no reference because the establishment of a state family court in that state circumvented the jurisdictional difficulties experienced elsewhere in Australia.

In 1987, the Commonwealth enacted a law in reliance on the reference, inserting a substantially new Part VII into the *Family Law Act 1975* (Cth).[34] The practical significance of the reference is that the Commonwealth is no longer required to enact child custody laws that bear a nexus to the marriage relationship, as it was previously required to do when it relied on the 'marriage' power.[35]

---

[32] *Cambridge Gulf Investments Pty Ltd v Dandoe Pty Ltd* [1999] FCA 1142, 18 August 1999 (French J).

[33] See, for example, *Commonwealth Powers (Family Law—Children) Act 1986* (NSW) and cognate legislation.

[34] *Family Law Amendment Act 1987* (Cth).

[35] See now s 63 *Family Law Act 1975* (Cth).

Although the cross-vesting scheme temporarily removed the necessity for this reference of power, the invalidity of part of that scheme has made reliance on the reference important once again in family law matters.

4 The Evolution of an Idea

The extent to which the above mechanisms were effective in solving the difficulties experienced in the Australian judicial system in the late 1970s and early 1980s is a matter of debate. They clearly went some way towards meeting these problems, but the case law on accrued jurisdiction did not settle into a stable pattern until the mid-1980s, and state references of power in relation to family law were spread out over several years from 1986 to 1990. In these circumstances it is not surprising that other proposals continued to be discussed during this period. This part examines the evolution of the cross-vesting scheme, and focuses in particular on the institutions that helped shape its final form.

(a) The Australian Constitutional Convention

The idea of cross-vesting jurisdiction was born in the Australian Constitutional Convention (ACC) in the 1970s.[36] During its relatively brief life (1973–1985), the ACC provided an important forum for discussion of constitutional change and renewal. The topic of the judicial system was placed on the agenda of the ACC at its first meeting in 1973, and re-emerged regularly thereafter. In 1977 the Judicature Sub-Committee recommended a partial forerunner of the cross-vesting scheme by proposing that the Constitution be amended to empower the states to vest jurisdiction in federal courts (other than the High Court) in matters arising under state law.[37] The proposal was endorsed by the Plenary Session at Perth in 1978 but was not further acted on.

The issue was agitated again at the Adelaide session of the ACC in 1983, which recommended that the Constitution be amended to provide for the integration of federal and state courts (of Supreme

---

[36] For a brief history, see *Gould v Brown* (1998) 193 CLR 346, 469–71 (Kirby J).

[37] See C. Baker (1987) 121–2.

Court level or above) into a single system of Australian courts. The implementation of that proposal was referred to a Standing Committee and from there to the Judicature Sub-Committee, which reported in 1984.[38] The report endorsed two proposals, though neither fulfilled the promise of wholesale reform to the structure of the judicial system hinted at by the Adelaide resolution.

The first proposal was for the cross-vesting of jurisdiction at trial level between state Supreme Courts, the Federal Court and the Family Court. Under the proposal, at trial level, the Federal Court was to have, in addition to its federal jurisdiction, all the jurisdiction of the state Supreme Courts, in order to enable it to determine all issues before it. Likewise, each state Supreme Court was to have, in addition to its state jurisdiction, all the jurisdiction of the Federal Court and of all other state Supreme Courts, in order to enable it to determine all issues before it. The Family Court was likewise to be brought into the scheme. Since such a dramatic expansion of concurrent jurisdiction might give rise to forum shopping, it was thought necessary to introduce a procedure whereby matters could be transferred to another court if they had been commenced in an inappropriate court.

The second proposal complemented the first but was not necessarily tied to it. Instead of recommending that the cross-vesting scheme be extended to appeals, the Sub-Committee proposed the creation of a new federal court—the Australian Court of Appeals—to act as an intermediate appellate court from state, territory and federal courts. This proposal did not have widespread support, and when the matter was considered at the Brisbane session of the ACC in 1985 only the first of the two proposals was successful. Support for cross-vesting varied, however, from its enthusiastic endorsement as a 'sensible, practical, rational, logical solution to a problem' to a grudging acceptance of it as a third best solution.[39]

(b) Drafting and enactment

Soon after the ACC endorsed the proposal for the cross-vesting of jurisdiction, the Standing Committee of Attorneys-General (SCAG)

---

[38] Australian Constitutional Convention Judicature Sub-Committee (1984).
[39] Australian Constitutional Convention (1985) 151, 143.

met in Brisbane to consider the matter. Most of the Attorneys had been present as delegates to the ACC, so that the issues had already been well aired. SCAG has been credited with moving with the speed of cold molasses,[40] but on this occasion the Committee quickly referred the matter of cross-vesting to the Standing Committee of Solicitors-General (SCSG) to draft appropriate legislation. That legislation, discussed further below, was unanimously agreed in 1986. Its essential components are the *Jurisdiction of Courts (Cross-vesting) Act 1987* (Cth) (the Commonwealth Act), and the eponymous Acts for each state and territory (the State Acts).

The process of implementing a national legislative scheme can be tortuous. It is remarkable, therefore, that the package of cross-vesting legislation was enacted by nearly every Australian jurisdiction in almost identical terms and within the space of approximately one year. (The Australian Capital Territory enacted legislation in 1993, after it had been granted self-government.) Provision was made in each piece of legislation for its operative sections to commence on a day fixed by proclamation. The legislation in all jurisdictions was proclaimed to commence on 1 July 1988. The legislation was also supported by the establishment of a committee of judges of the participating courts. The committee's function is to monitor the continued operation of the scheme and report regularly to the Council of Chief Justices, which may in turn release the reports to SCAG. This institutional feature is not mentioned in the legislation, but was said by the Commonwealth Attorney-General to be an important factor in the Commonwealth's agreement to participate in the scheme.[41]

(c) The Australian Constitutional Commission

Contemporaneously with the drafting and enactment of the cross-vesting legislation, reforms to the Australian judicial system were under consideration in another forum. The Australian Constitutional Commission was established in 1985 for the purpose of undertaking a fundamental review of the Australian Constitution. An Advisory Committee on the Australian Judicial System was also established 'to consider the provisions of Chapter III of the Consti-

---

[40] Ibid 151.

[41] *Commonwealth Parliamentary Debates*, House of Representatives, 22 October 1986, 2556.

tution dealing with the structure of the Australian judicial system, and to advise on the desirable future structure of that system'.

At the time of the Advisory Committee's report (22 May 1987), the terms of the proposed cross-vesting legislation had been settled by the SCSG, and legislation had been introduced or passed in some, but not all, Australian parliaments. The existence of the nascent scheme appears to have been a powerful factor in the Advisory Committee's Report.[42] They rejected the idea that there should be an alteration to the basic structure of the Australian judicial system. In their view, persistent problems should be dealt with by attacking them at the point at which they arose, and the cross-vesting scheme would considerably reduce the remaining difficulties in the judicial system, if not remove those difficulties altogether. However, the Advisory Committee was concerned that the scheme be put on a sound constitutional footing, and so recommended a constitutional amendment to empower the states to vest state jurisdiction in federal courts. In its *Final Report*, the Constitutional Commission agreed that the cross-vesting scheme was 'highly desirable', and that any move towards the constitutional restructuring of the judicial system ought to be stayed pending an examination of experience under the new cross-vesting arrangements.[43] Displaying the same caution as its Advisory Committee, the Commission also recommended a constitutional amendment to ensure that this important matter was not left in a state of uncertainty.

The work of the Constitutional Commission and its Advisory Committee came too late to be influential in shaping the general contours or details of the cross-vesting scheme. In particular, its preference for a transparent constitutional foundation for the scheme had already been rejected by the ACC, which had opted to proceed with a legislative scheme whose validity could be tested in the High Court. Nevertheless, the Constitutional Commission's strong endorsement of the cross-vesting scheme provided valuable support at an early stage, and validated the scheme as a sound alternative to more radical proposals to restructure the judicial system.

---

[42] Australian Constitutional Commission Advisory Committee on the Australian Judicial System (1987) 39.

[43] Australian Constitutional Commission (1988) 371–3.

(d) A proliferation of schemes

In addition to the general cross-vesting scheme described above, specialised cross-vesting schemes were subsequently established in particular areas such as corporations law, family law, admiralty, trade practices, competition policy, and agricultural chemicals.[44] The co-existence of general and specialised cross-vesting schemes undoubtedly adds a degree of complexity to the operation of the cross-vesting legislation, and some have rightly described the justification for separate schemes as unconvincing.[45]

The reasons for the multiplicity of schemes vary from one context to another, but are amply illustrated by the corporations law provisions. The general cross-vesting scheme extended to most corporate law matters from its commencement in 1988 until 1 January 1991. From that date, Part 9 of the *Corporations Act 1989* (Cth) and cognate state and territory legislation made separate provision for cross-vesting of civil matters arising under the Corporations Law, to the exclusion of the general scheme.[46] The motivation for the separate treatment of corporate law matters was not a deficiency in the general scheme but an apparent desire to make the Corporations Law a single and complete national code in all matters affecting companies and securities, without the need to have recourse to other legislation. A preference was thereby demonstrated for unity of corporations law over unity of the cross-vesting scheme itself.

5 Structural Aspects—Cross-Vesting Jurisdiction

(a) Structural aspects described

The cross-vesting scheme was developed to solve the problems of institutional design outlined in Part 1 of this chapter. It addresses the jurisdictional question, not by abolishing the distinction between federal and state jurisdiction, but by seeking to make the distinction

---

[44] Moloney (1993) 51–67; *Competition Policy Reform Act 1995* (Cth), s 26; *Agricultural and Veterinary Chemicals Act 1994* (Cth), s 20.

[45] Moloney (1993) 58.

[46] See *BP Australia Ltd v Amann Aviation Pty Ltd* (1996) 62 FCR 451, 482–4 (Lindgren J).

irrelevant.[47] It also preserves the institutional structures of state and federal courts, but purports to allow each court to administer the law without regard to whether it is applying state or federal law. Commenting on these changes when introducing the legislation into federal Parliament, the Attorney-General stated that the various Australian governments thereby hoped to bring about a situation in which 'no action will fail in a court through lack of jurisdiction, and ... no court will have to determine the boundaries between Federal, State and Territory jurisdictions'.[48]

The cross-vesting scheme has been described as 'simple in concept, imperious and breathtaking in its amplitude'.[49] A radical change to the Australian judicial system is effected through two features, which operate independently but are nonetheless related. The first—and structural—part of the scheme cross-vests the subject matter jurisdiction of participating courts.[50] The second—and operational—part of the scheme provides for the transfer of proceedings between those courts (see Part 6 below). The courts participating in the scheme are two federal courts (the Federal Court and the Family Court), the Supreme Courts of the six states, the Supreme Courts of the two internal territories (the Northern Territory and the Australian Capital Territory) and the Family Court of Western Australia. Importantly, the scheme excludes from its ambit the High Court and all criminal proceedings.[51] It also excludes the lower state courts from the structural provisions that relate to jurisdiction, although it does encompass these courts in the transfer provisions.

So far as the structural aspect of the scheme is concerned, the pivotal provisions are those vesting the subject matter jurisdiction of participating courts in other participating courts, subject to certain

---

[47] In a practical but not a formal sense, the legislation might be seen to create a third classification—cross-vested jurisdiction—with its own choice of law rules (see Chapter 11).

[48] *Commonwealth Parliamentary Debates*, House of Representatives, 22 October 1986, 2556.

[49] Fryberg (1987) 113.

[50] Whether the legislation also cross-vests the personal jurisdiction has been the subject of debate. See Mason and Crawford (1988) 335; Griffith, Rose, and Gageler (1988) 1022.

[51] Section 3(1) Commonwealth Act (definition of 'proceeding').

exceptions. To take a central example, s 4 of the Commonwealth Act invests the jurisdiction of the Federal Court and the Family Court in each of the state Supreme Courts and, reciprocally, s 4 of the State Acts confer jurisdiction in 'state matters' on the Federal Court and the Family Court.[52] Likewise, the jurisdiction of each state and territory Supreme Court is cross-vested in all the other state and territory Supreme Courts. However, the jurisdiction of the Federal Court and of the Family Court is not cross-vested as between themselves. There was no need to do so because the doctrine of associated jurisdiction ensured that split jurisdictional problems did not arise between these courts (see Chapter 9).

The cross-vesting legislation also provides for appropriate channels of appeal. The general rule, embodied in s 7 of the Commonwealth and State Acts, is that an appeal must not be brought outside the appellate system of the court in which the primary decision was made. This solution to the problem of appeals differs from the one proposed by the ACC in 1984, which had recommended the establishment of a new intermediate appellate court to hear appeals from state, territory and federal courts. By contrast, the legislation prevents an appeal being taken from a single judge of a state court to a full federal court, or from a single judge of a federal court to a state Court of Appeal or Full Supreme Court. This provision is premised on the understanding that the cross-vesting of jurisdiction effected by s 4 applies to both original and appellate jurisdiction, so that, but for s 7, an appeal might have been taken to any other court encompassed by the scheme.[53]

(b) Constitutional validity

From its inception, the cross-vesting scheme rested on unsettled constitutional foundations. Some aspects of the scheme have a clear constitutional mandate and give rise to no difficulty. The Commonwealth can clearly invest state courts with additional federal jurisdiction under s 77(iii) of the Constitution, and can invest state courts with territory jurisdiction under s 122. Similarly, states can cross-vest their state jurisdiction in each other pursuant to their

---

[52] 'State matter' is defined in s 3(1) Commonwealth Act.
[53] K. Mason (1987) 21; Fryberg (1987) 114; Moloney and McMaster (1992) 28–9.

plenary legislative powers. The principal points of difficulty relate to the power of state Parliaments to confer state jurisdiction on federal courts, and of the Commonwealth Parliament to authorise the receipt of state jurisdiction. The legislative scheme proceeds on the basis that federal courts can exercise judicial power from sources outside Chapter III of the Constitution. On this view, Chapter III exhaustively specifies only the federal jurisdiction of federal courts, and says nothing about the jurisdiction that federal courts may exercise from other sources. A competing view is that this is not permissible because the comprehensive language of ss 75 and 76 of the Constitution specifies exhaustively the scope of the original jurisdiction that may be exercised by federal courts from any source.

From the time the cross-vesting proposal was first debated, the tension between these conflicting conceptions of Chapter III has been evident in the writings of independent commissions, academics and judges. For example, in 1984 the Judicature Sub-Committee of the ACC recommended implementation of a cross-vesting scheme without an express constitutional amendment, after obtaining an opinion to that effect from Professor Zines.[54] By contrast, as noted in Part 4 above, the Australian Constitutional Commission's Advisory Committee on the Judicial System, and the Constitutional Commission itself, thought that the constitutionality of the cross-vesting scheme was sufficiently doubtful to warrant constitutional amendment.[55]

Early skirmishes in the courts revealed that judges too held disparate views on the question.[56] Surprisingly, however, it took ten years for the validity of the scheme to be challenged directly in the High Court—despite early predictions that the legislation would be tested before it was proclaimed to take effect.[57] The challenges arose

[54] Australian Constitutional Convention Judicature Sub-Committee (1984) Appendix, 27–32.
[55] Australian Constitutional Commission Advisory Committee on the Australian Judicial System (1987) 43–4, 118; Australian Constitutional Commission (1988) vol. 1, 371–3, vol. 2, 1013–15.
[56] *Grace Bros Pty Ltd v Magistrates of the Local Courts of New South Wales* (1989) ATPR 40–921; *West Australian Psychiatric Nurses' Association (Union of Workers) v Australian Nursing Federation* (1991) 102 ALR 265, 274–80. For opposing views, see *Re T* [1990] 1 Qd R 196.
[57] Australian Constitutional Convention Judicature Sub-Committee (1984) 14.

in two cases in quick succession. Both cases concerned the corporations cross-vesting scheme, but they had clear implications for the validity of the general scheme as well. The first of the cases, *Gould v Brown*,[58] was decided in February 1998, and led to a very unsatisfactory outcome. The six-member bench was evenly divided—with Brennan CJ, Toohey and Kirby JJ upholding the Federal Court's competence to exercise jurisdiction that had been cross-vested from the states, and Gaudron, McHugh and Gummow JJ opposing that conclusion. As a result, the decision of the Full Federal Court appealed from was affirmed.[59] Since the Federal Court had unanimously endorsed the scheme as a valid co-operative arrangement between the Commonwealth, states and territories, the corporations cross-vesting scheme narrowly survived challenge.[60]

The circumstances surrounding the decision in *Gould v Brown* made it certain that its influence would be short-lived. In the first place, a decision of a statutory majority of the High Court has no force as precedent—it does no more than resolve the case between the particular parties to it.[61] In the second place, there was a significant change in the composition of the bench soon after the decision in *Gould v Brown*. Two of the three justices in the statutory majority (Brennan CJ and Toohey J) retired from the High Court, leaving only one justice (Kirby J) who had ruled in favour of the scheme. The views of three new justices (Gleeson CJ, Hayne and Callinan JJ) had yet to be tested, but all three would have had to side with Kirby J for the scheme to be saved.

The second of the two cases, *Re Wakim*, was decided in June 1999, and actually comprised a constellation of four proceedings.[62] Two of these—*Re Wakim; Ex parte McNally* and *Re Wakim; Ex parte Darvall*—raised the question whether the Federal Court could exercise state jurisdiction vested in it by the New South Wales Parliament. A third proceeding—*Re Brown; Ex parte Amann*—

---

[58] (1998) 193 CLR 346.
[59] *Judiciary Act 1903* (Cth), s 23(2)(a).
[60] *BP Australia Ltd v Amann Aviation Pty Ltd* (1996) 62 FCR 451.
[61] *Federal Commissioner of Taxation v St Helens Farm (ACT) Pty Ltd* (1981) 146 CLR 336; *Re Wakim; Ex parte McNally* (1999) 163 ALR 270, 275, 282, 300–1, cf 322.
[62] (1999) 163 ALR 270.

concerned the application of the doctrines of res judicata and issue estoppel to a person who was implicated in the decision in *Gould v Brown*, though not actually a party to it. This issue is of no relevance here and need not be further considered. The fourth proceeding—*Spinks v Prentice*—raised the question whether the Federal Court could exercise jurisdiction in civil matters arising under the Corporations Law of the Australian Capital Territory, which was a law enacted for the Territory by the Commonwealth Parliament. This question was answered affirmatively by a unanimous High Court, following the decision in *Northern Territory v GPAO*.[63]

In *Re Wakim; Ex parte McNally* and *Re Wakim; Ex parte Darvall*, the High Court reversed its *Gould v Brown* position. By a majority of six to one it decided that state jurisdiction could not be vested in federal courts. Kirby J, in dissent, maintained his earlier position in stating that the 'rare (if not unique) governmental and legislative unity on the issue over an extended period of time' was a strong reason for hesitating before adopting a view of the Constitution that would destroy the legislation.[64] The majority justices did not dispute the value of co-operation as a principle underlying the Constitution, but denied that it provided a criterion of constitutional validity. Thus, for McHugh J, 'cooperative federalism' was a 'political slogan' rather than a constitutional term, and recorded a result reached as a result of the states and the Commonwealth legislating within the powers conferred on them by the Constitution. Similarly, for Gummow and Hayne JJ, no amount of co-operation could supply power where none existed.[65] Why, then, was there an absence of constitutional power to vest state jurisdiction in federal courts?

Central to the reasoning of Gummow and Hayne JJ (with whom Gleeson CJ and Gaudron J agreed) was s 9(2) of the *Jurisdiction of Courts (Cross-vesting) Act 1987* (Cth).[66] That provision authorised the Federal Court (and certain other courts) to exercise

---

[63] (1999) 161 ALR 318.

[64] (1999) 163 ALR 270, 323.

[65] Ibid 288 (McHugh J), 305 (Gummow and Hayne JJ).

[66] For the corporations law equivalent see s 56(2) *Corporations Act 1989* (Cth).

jurisdiction conferred on it by a state law relating to cross-vesting of jurisdiction. In their Honours' opinion, two views might be taken of s 9(2). If the section purported to do no more than grant federal consent to the exercise of a jurisdiction conferred on federal courts by state legislation, then there was no constitutional power in the Commonwealth to grant that consent. In particular, the incidental power in s 51(xxxix) did not support such a law because the conferral of state jurisdiction on federal courts could not be said to be 'necessary or proper' to render effective the exercise of federal (as opposed to state) judicial power. If, however, s 9(2) had a substantive operation and actually conferred state jurisdiction on federal courts (which is the construction their Honours preferred), it was still ineffective. This was because, according to long-standing principle and authority, ss 75 and 76 of the Constitution provided an exhaustive statement of the circumstances in which the Commonwealth Parliament could confer jurisdiction on federal courts. The affirmative language of those sections gave rise to a negative implication that excluded the possibility of conferring additional jurisdiction on federal courts.[67] As a result, the Commonwealth legislation that purported to consent to the conferral of state jurisdiction on federal courts (on one view), or to confer state jurisdiction on federal courts (on the other), was invalid.

(c) Rescue package

Following the decision in *Re Wakim*, uniform state legislation was drafted for the purpose of validating those Federal Court and Family Court decisions that were rendered invalid by the High Court's decision. The legislation was drafted through the Standing Committee of Attorneys-General, in conjunction with the Special Committee of Solicitors-General and the Parliamentary Counsel's Committee. The *Federal Courts (State Jurisdiction) Act 1999* (NSW) and similarly titled legislation in other states is to be enacted throughout Australia. Each Act purports to make the rights and liabilities of all persons the same as if the ineffective judgment of the Federal Court or Family Court had been a valid judgment of the

---

[67] *Re Wakim; Ex parte McNally* (1999) 163 ALR 270, 303–8.

Supreme Court in its original or appellate jurisdiction, as the case may be.

However, the validity of the remedial legislation may be open to question. One week after the South Australian version of the Act commenced operation, a challenge to its validity was announced, and notices under s 78B of the *Judiciary Act 1903* (Cth) were duly issued.[68] The basis of the challenge is that the Act imposes a decision of the Federal Court on the South Australian Supreme Court in a manner that compromises the latter's integrity and independence as an institution exercising the judicial power of the Commonwealth. The removal of this challenge to the High Court may prolong the uncertainty surrounding the cross-vesting scheme.

The uniform legislation is not intended to do more than validate past decisions of the Federal and Family Courts and provide for the transfer of pending matters to Supreme Courts. It does not address the problems caused by *Re Wakim* for the future, for which a permanent solution is both urgent and desirable. Some options for change are considered in Part 9 below.

6 Operational Aspects—Transfer of Proceedings

(a) The importance of the transfer provisions

The second central feature of the cross-vesting scheme relates to the transfer of proceedings between participating courts. As a result of the cross-vesting of jurisdiction, it is possible for a litigant to commence most proceedings in any of the participating courts without regard to the subject matter of the action (subject to the question of constitutional validity, discussed in Part 5). However, it was always intended that federal and state courts keep within their traditional jurisdictional fields. To this end, the legislation provides for the transfer of proceedings between participating courts, at the initiative of a party to the proceeding, an Attorney-General, or the court of its own motion.[69]

---

[68] *Macks v Saint, Re Emanuel Investments Pty Ltd (in liq)*, Sup Ct SA, Matter No. 1021 of 1995.

[69] Section 5 Commonwealth Act, s 5 State Acts.

The transfer provisions are of continuing importance, despite the decision in *Re Wakim*. This is because significant parts of the cross-vesting scheme survive that decision, and because the transfer provisions operate independently of the provisions with respect to the cross-vesting of jurisdiction. As a result, a matter may be transferred between participating courts irrespective of whether cross-vested jurisdiction is being exercised. It is clear, however, that both the transferor court and the transferee court must have jurisdiction from some source in order to effectuate a transfer.

One interesting feature of the transfer provisions is their ability to reach down to the lower courts and tribunals of the states and territories, despite the fact that such bodies are not expressly included in the structural cross-vesting arrangements. Section 8 of the Commonwealth and State Acts allows a Supreme Court to make an order removing into that court a proceeding that is pending in a lower court or tribunal. Once uplifted in this way, the Supreme Court may then transfer the proceeding, in accordance with s 5, to another participating court in which a related proceeding is pending. The receiving court may then deal with the proceeding in accordance with local case management practices, and this might include remitting the matter to a lower court within that state. Through this three-step process of removal, transfer and remittal, a proceeding might be translocated from a lower court in one state to a lower court in another. In view of the liberalisation of the monetary limits on the jurisdiction of District and County Courts, the s 8 procedure is potentially an important mechanism for expanding the net of the cross-vesting scheme.[70]

To a very large extent the transfer provisions are the lynchpin of the cross-vesting scheme. Unless proceedings are transferred in such a way that each participating court keeps within its 'proper' jurisdictional fields, there is the potential for a most dramatic redistribution of jurisdiction between state and federal courts in Australia. The Attorney-General, Lionel Bowen, recognised this when introducing the cross-vesting legislation into Parliament:

---

[70] Moloney and McMaster (1992) 119–20. Matters arising under Part V of the *Trade Practices Act 1974* (Cth) may also be transferred to lower state courts pursuant to s 10 Commonwealth Act and s 10 State Acts.

Courts will need to be ruthless in the exercise of their transferral powers to ensure that litigants do not engage in 'forum shopping' by commencing proceedings in inappropriate courts or resort to other tactical manoeuvres that would otherwise be available to them by reason of the fact that State courts would have all the jurisdiction of the Federal Courts and vice versa. The courts themselves would also be expected not to take advantage of the legislation to aggregate business to their own courts in matters that would not otherwise have been within their respective jurisdiction.[71]

Of equal concern is the danger that 'some judges at least will view the power to transfer as a welcome affirmation of their "superior" status by sloughing off menial, unwanted or financially insignificant litigation'.[72] At the end of the day the success of the scheme depends on a sense of judicial comity, as well as oversight by the Committee of Chief Justices, to ensure that it is implemented in a way that enhances the administration of justice throughout Australia.

(b) Criteria for transfer

Section 5 of the Commonwealth Act and the State Acts places an obligation on a court to transfer a pending matter to another participating court where it would be more appropriate for the other court to hear the matter, having regard to a number of factors. The factors relevant to the exercise of the discretion are articulated in a complex way, but in essence they include the following:

- the existence of related proceedings in another court;
- whether the chosen forum would have had jurisdiction in the absence of the cross-vesting scheme;
- whether the interpretation of a Commonwealth law or state law of another jurisdiction is in issue;
- the interests of justice.

While it is clear that any decision to transfer a matter to another participating court must be made in accordance with the

---

[71] *Commonwealth Parliamentary Debates*, House of Representatives, 22 October 1986, 2557.

[72] K. Mason (1987) 22.

statutory criteria, the breadth of the discretion and the inability to appeal a transfer decision have given rise to some persistent difficulties of application. If one seeks guidance as to how a broad discretion of this nature might be exercised, analogies might be found in a number of fields. These include the power of the High Court to remit matters in its original jurisdiction to other courts, the power of the Federal Court to transfer matters between its different registries, the statutory criteria relevant to a lower court's decision to stay a proceeding in favour of another Australian forum, and the principles of private international law relating to forum non conveniens.[73] The relevance of the latter has been a particular source of uncertainty.

Australian courts have applied two fundamentally different approaches to the issue of a transfer of proceedings under s 5.[74] The New South Wales Court of Appeal articulated the most widely accepted approach in *Bankinvest AG v Seabrook*.[75] This case treats a transfer decision as a matter of judicial management, which should be undertaken without excessive legalism. Street CJ stated that a decision to transfer a proceeding called for:

> a 'nuts and bolts' management decision as to which court, in the pursuit of the interests of justice, is the more appropriate to hear and determine the substantive dispute. Consideration of textured principle and deep learning—in particular principles of international law such as forum non conveniens—have no place in a cross-vesting adjudication.

Similarly, Rogers AJA stated that the interests of justice was the only lodestar that a judge may steer by and that principles of forum non conveniens had no role to play in the resolution of applications made under the legislation.[76] Accordingly, there could be no pre-

---

[73] See s 44 *Judiciary Act 1903* (Cth); s 48 *Federal Court of Australia Act 1976* (Cth) and *National Mutual Holdings Pty Ltd v Sentry Corp* (1988) 19 FCR 155; s 20(4) *Service and Execution of Process Act 1992* (Cth); *Voth v Manildra Flour Mills Pty Ltd* (1990) 171 CLR 538.

[74] See generally Moloney and McMaster (1992) 81–103.

[75] (1988) 14 NSWLR 711.

[76] Ibid 714 (Street CJ), 726–7 (Rogers AJA).

sumption that a court ought to exercise jurisdiction that had been regularly invoked by the plaintiff, nor that a defendant should bear an onus of proving that the criteria for transfer had been satisfied.

An alternative approach to the problem, which has been adopted by courts in the Australian Capital Territory and Western Australia, is to exercise the discretion to transfer in the light of pre-existing principles of private international law.[77] Under these principles, a plaintiff's initial choice of forum has significant bearing on the disposition of a defendant's transfer application because of the presumption that a court ought to exercise jurisdiction that has been regularly invoked by the plaintiff. As a corollary, if a defendant seeks to have the proceedings transferred to another court, he or she bears the onus of proving that the grounds for a transfer are satisfied.

Several commentators have remarked on the inappropriateness of interpreting the transfer provisions by reference to the common law principles of private international law.[78] The common law principles are not necessarily appropriate to a statutory scheme established for the purpose of remedying problems in the Australian judicial system. Moreover, the High Court has developed those principles in the context of international cases, without regard to considerations relevant to a federal system. Additionally, some aspects of the more restrictive approach—such as whether anyone bears an onus of proof—are difficult to reconcile with the ability of a court to transfer a proceeding of its own motion.

For a national scheme that is intended to operate with a fair degree of uniformity, the development of a 'wilderness of conflicting and unappellable decisions' under s 5 is a source of considerable concern.[79] To this end, a 1992 report on the scheme recommended that the major interpretational questions be referred to SCAG with

---

[77] *Waterhouse v Australian Broadcasting Corp* (1989) 86 ACTR 1; *Mullins Investments Pty Ltd v Elliott* (1990) 1 WAR 531.
[78] See, for example, Nygh (1995) 91–2. Difficult questions arise when applications for a stay (at common law) or a transfer (under the legislation) are sought concurrently: *McEntee v Connor* (1994) 4 Tas R 18; *Pegasus Leasing Ltd v Balescope Pty Ltd* (1994) 63 SASR 51; *Schmidt v Won* [1998] 3 VR 435.
[79] *Re Chapman and Jansen* (1990) 13 Fam LR 853, 869 (Fogarty J).

a view to resolving them by legislative means.[80] However, no changes have yet been made.

7 Special Federal Features

It has been remarked that a proper understanding of the cross-vesting legislation can only be acquired through an appreciation of the profound significance and distinctive qualities of federal jurisdiction.[81] The comment is a salutary reminder that the cross-vesting scheme is implemented within a federal judicial system, which is itself founded on significant asymmetries between the power of federal and state legislatures, and between the jurisdiction of their courts. This part examines some special federal features of the cross-vesting scheme and the reasons underlying them.

(a) Exclusion of the High Court

In 1976 the Commonwealth Attorney-General made the following observations on the special role of the High Court in the Australian judicial system:

> The High Court occupies a position of special importance under our constitutional framework. Not only is it the final interpreter of the Constitution, but it has a significant role as the court of appeal from State supreme courts and other federal courts. In this role, it has achieved recognition throughout the common law world as one of the great common law courts. It is vital to the working of the High Court that it should be left free to concentrate on constitutional issues and on the fundamental issues of law that come before it in the exercise of its appellate jurisdiction.[82]

Similar policies underlie the exclusion of the High Court from the cross-vesting scheme. If the High Court is to be preserved as the 'keystone of the federal arch'[83] it would be inappropriate to burden

---

[80] Moloney and McMaster (1992) 103.

[81] *NEC Information Systems Australia Ltd v Lockhart* (1992) 108 ALR 561, 565.

[82] *Commonwealth Parliamentary Debates*, House of Representatives, 3 June 1976, 2944.

[83] Ibid 18 March 1902, 10967 (Deakin). See also Bennett (1980) 12–20.

it with original jurisdiction in state matters, even if this were done with the consent of the federal legislature. But even apart from questions of propriety, it has been suggested that it is constitutionally impermissible for state law to vest additional original jurisdiction in the High Court. In *Gould v Brown*, Brennan CJ and Toohey J rejected the view that the original jurisdiction of the High Court could be altered by state law, despite their willingness to uphold the conferral of state jurisdiction on other federal courts. The principal reason for their exceptional treatment of the High Court was that the original jurisdiction of the Court was closely defined by s 75 and 76 of the Constitution itself—a conclusion supported by consideration of the scope of the Court's appellate jurisdiction.[84]

(b) Exclusion of certain Commonwealth legislation

A second area of federal privilege arises in relation to the exclusion of certain federal legislation from the reach of the cross-vesting scheme. As we saw in Part 5 of this Chapter, s 4 of the federal Act cross-vests the jurisdiction of the Federal Court and the Family Court in the Supreme Courts of the states and territories.

However s 4(4) exempts matters arising under four named federal Acts.[85] The majority of these matters relate to federal industrial matters and their separate treatment stems from a clear desire to keep sensitive matters of industrial relations within the exclusive jurisdiction of the Federal Court.[86] In this vein, it is worth recalling that under the Keating Labor government, and at several other times over the course of this century, industrial jurisdiction was regarded as sufficiently specialised to warrant its own federal court.

(c) Guaranteed appeals to federal courts

In Part 5, reference was made to s 7 of the cross-vesting legislation, which seeks to prevent cross-jurisdictional appeals. This provision

---

[84] (1998) 193 CLR 346, 383–4.

[85] *Conciliation and Arbitration Act 1977* (Cth), *Workplace Relations Act 1996* (Cth), *Native Title Act 1993* (Cth), and certain provisions of the *Trade Practices Act 1974* (Cth).

[86] C. Baker (1987) 128; *NEC Information Systems Australia Pty Ltd v Lockhart* (1992) 108 ALR 561, 567.

was necessary because s 4 of the legislation cross-vests both original and appellate jurisdiction, so that without further regulation it would have been possible, for example, to appeal a decision of a single judge of the Federal Court to a state Court of Appeal. The architects of the cross-vesting scheme thought that cross-jurisdictional appeals were generally undesirable.

However, s 7 provides that in certain classes of matters, an appeal from a single judge of a state or territory Supreme Court cannot be taken to an appellate court within the same judicial hierarchy. In these cases, appeals must go to a Full Federal Court, a Full Family Court or the High Court, as appropriate.[87] Several purposes might be served by preserving the jurisdiction of federal courts to hear appeals from primary decisions of state court judges, but the most compelling of them is the need to achieve uniform interpretation of federal law. This purpose has been evident in the jurisdictional arrangements applicable to intellectual property disputes since the 1980s, where it has been the norm to have state court decisions at the trial level and federal court decisions on appeal.[88]

There are currently thirteen federal Acts given special appellate treatment, as listed in a Schedule to the federal legislation. A significant number of these relate to matters of intellectual property (copyright, designs, patents, and trade marks), but other scheduled Acts relate to family law, bankruptcy, electoral law, shipping registration, and other sundry matters.

(d) Special federal matters

A fourth situation of federal privilege arises in relation to 'special federal matters', which have been described as fundamental to the operation of the cross-vesting scheme.[89] A special federal matter is defined in s 3(1) of the Commonwealth legislation to include, inter alia, certain matters arising under Part IV of the *Trade Practices Act 1974* (Cth), under the Competition Code, or from judicial review of federal administrative action.

Where a special federal matter is pending in a state Supreme Court, the Court must transfer the matter to the Federal Court (or

---

[87] K. Mason (1987) 22; C. Baker (1987) 133.

[88] Opeskin (1995) 776–8.

[89] *NEC Information Systems Australia Pty Ltd v Lockhart* (1992) 108 ALR 561, 570.

other specified court) unless the Supreme Court makes an order to retain the matter. In making a retention order, the Supreme Court must be satisfied that there are special reasons for doing so unrelated to the convenience of the parties. The Court must also have regard to the general rule that the Federal Court should hear special federal matters, and it must take into account any submission made by the Commonwealth Attorney-General.[90] The practical effect of these provisions is that, notwithstanding that state Supreme Courts generally have cross-vested jurisdiction in relation to special federal matters, it is rare for a Supreme Court to determine such a matter.[91]

The provisions relating to special federal matters were introduced to recognise the special expertise of the Federal Court in matters in which it had exclusive original jurisdiction prior to the commencement of the cross-vesting scheme. In addition, it was thought desirable that matters of particular concern to the Commonwealth should be determined in a court of its choice.[92] Interestingly, when the cross-vesting legislation was being debated in the House of Representatives, the Opposition spokesperson on legal affairs moved to have the category of special federal matters abolished on the basis that cross-vesting should be general and that no special privilege should be given to the Federal Court.[93] Far from taking that course, the participating legislatures have sought to strengthen the position of the Federal Court. In 1992–93 amendments were enacted in all jurisdictions to make it more difficult for a state court to retain a special federal matter, in recognition of the special role of the Federal Court.[94]

8 The Future

This chapter has charted aspects of the evolution of the Australian judicial system since the establishment of the Federal Court and the Family Court in the mid-1970s. A notable feature of the system has been its dynamism, and its ability to respond to changing

---

[90] Section 6 Commonwealth Act.
[91] Moloney and McMaster (1992) 103–4.
[92] *Metroplaza Pty Ltd v Girvan NSW Pty Ltd (in liq)* (1991) 24 NSWLR 718, 722.
[93] Fryberg (1987) 114.
[94] See, for example, *Law and Justice Amendment Act (No 3) 1992 (Cth)*.

circumstances. The High Court's decision in *Re Wakim* must be seen in this context, and as an opportunity (perhaps not welcomed by some) for new development. Three areas have been particularly hard-hit by that decision—resolution by the Federal Court of disputes arising under state corporations law, resolution by the Family Court of financial disputes between de facto couples, and resolution by the Family Court of claims for damages arising from intra-family violence. This part considers possible futures for the judicial system in light of the inroads made by the High Court to the cross-vesting scheme.

(a) Limited scope of operation

One option is to persevere with the cross-vesting scheme but accept limitations on its scope of operation. There appears to be no constitutional impediment to state courts cross-vesting their state jurisdiction in each other. Nor is there any impediment to the Commonwealth Parliament conferring federal or territory jurisdiction on state courts, pursuant to s 77(iii) and s 122 of the Constitution respectively. All that is required to avoid constitutional challenge is to excise that part of the scheme that seeks to confer state jurisdiction on federal courts.

However, the effect of this should not be minimised, particularly as the Federal Court and Family Court have been major beneficiaries of the scheme.[95] For example, through cross-vesting, the Federal Court has assumed a leading role in developing modern corporations and securities law, although these are matters arising under state law. One measure of the Federal Court's pre-eminence in this field is that, although it is only one of nine superior courts that exercise concurrent jurisdiction in corporations law matters, its decisions consistently account for nearly one-third of all reported corporations law cases.[96] Yet the loss of this role may be the price to be paid for ensuring constitutional compliance with the dictates of Chapter III. In this scenario, state courts would be left to adjudicate matters formerly cross-vested in the federal courts, such as those mentioned above.

---

[95] O'Brien (1989) 313–14.
[96] Black (1999).

(b) Federalise existing state laws

A second option is to use relevant constitutional powers to federalise those areas of state law that will give rise to the greatest jurisdictional difficulty in the period following *Re Wakim*. Making these areas subject to Commonwealth law would enable federal jurisdiction in these matters to be conferred concurrently on state courts under s 77(iii) and on federal courts under s 77(i) of the Constitution, with provision made for the transfer of proceedings between them. Clearly, the potential for federalising any field of law depends on the scope of the legislative powers granted to the Commonwealth by the Constitution. For example, the limited federal legislative powers over 'marriage' and 'divorce' in s 51(xxi) and (xxii) present substantial difficulties for Commonwealth legislation aimed more generally at children and families.

Similarly, the federalisation of corporations law—by enacting legislation under s 51(xx)—has been limited by the High Court's 1990 decision on the scope of that power in *New South Wales v Commonwealth (Incorporation Case)*.[97] But that decision does not impinge on the ability of the Commonwealth to make laws with respect to most post-incorporation matters affecting corporations—such as receiver and manager issues, administrations, takeovers, and breaches of the substantial shareholding provisions. These formed the core of the corporations law matters dealt with by the Federal Court immediately prior to the *Re Wakim* decision. It is thus not surprising that the Chief Justice of the Federal Court has favoured this approach as providing an immediate solution to the pressing problems presented by jurisdiction over corporate law matters.[98]

(c) Reference of power

There are other ways in which an area of law might be federalised, while still invoking the co-operative spirit of the original scheme. Section 51(xxxvii) of the Constitution—the reference power—enables the Commonwealth Parliament to make laws on matters referred to it by the states. State references to the Commonwealth on the subject matter of 'corporations' and 'financial settlement

---

[97] (1990) 169 CLR 482.

[98] Black (1999).

between de facto couples' would provide a constitutional basis for federal regulation of the entire area, and a corresponding solution to inter-jurisdictional problems.[99] The New South Wales Attorney-General, Jeff Shaw, has promoted the idea of a reference of power to solve the jurisdictional difficulties that have left company and family law cases languishing in the state courts. However, there may be practical difficulties with this approach. Some states are understandably reluctant to cede additional powers to the Commonwealth in light of their revenues from incorporation fees, as well as the history of steady federal encroachment into areas of traditional state concern. It may also be difficult to secure the simultaneous agreement of the states, in circumstances where a uniform approach is clearly desirable even though not strictly necessary under the s 51(xxxvii) mechanism.

While this option may provide a solution to the specific jurisdictional problems arising in particular subject areas, such as under the Corporations Law, it cannot provide a practical solution to cross-vesting problems across all areas of law. The prospect of the states referring to the Commonwealth the substantive subject matter of all state law is too unrealistic to contemplate. Moreover, state references on the subject of cross-vesting itself would be ineffective in achieving a solution. The grant of power in s 51(xxxvii), like all those in s 51, is 'subject to this Constitution' and hence conditioned by any limitation that might be implied from Chapter III.

(d) Constitutional amendment

Another option is to attempt to secure constitutional change by referendum. As we saw in Part 4, in 1987 the Australian Constitutional Commission's Advisory Committee on the Australian Judicial System thought that the cross-vesting scheme warranted constitutional amendment, and the Constitutional Commission agreed. This proposal has not been put to the people and it is difficult to speculate on the likely result if it were. On the one hand, commentators are keen to remind us that the Australian people have been notoriously reluctant to endorse constitutional change by referendum—only 8 of 44 proposals have succeeded, none since 1977. On the other hand, the jurisdictional changes might be seen to be technical in nature and

---

[99] *Gould v Brown* (1998) 193 CLR 346, 443, 453 (Gummow J), 468–9 (Kirby J).

are unlikely to attract opposition from any government or major political party. In these circumstances it might be possible to sell such a change as a rationalisation of a dual court system that is otherwise prone to duplication and inefficiency. Whatever the electoral outcome of such a proposal, it would seem unassailable that any major structural change in the judicial system away from the founders' federal conception ought to rest on the legitimacy of popular referendum. That solution has been favoured by the Law Council of Australia and several Attorneys-General. It is a solution further buoyed by doubts about the constitutional validity of the state saving legislation, as discussed in Part 5.

(e) A unified judicial system

It is also possible that the inroads to the cross-vesting scheme will reignite calls for a major restructuring of the judicial system through the establishment of a unitary court system. As eminent an authority as Sir Owen Dixon made this plea in 1935 when he claimed that 'neither from the point of view of juristic principle nor from that of the practical and efficient administration of justice can the division of the Courts into state and federal be regarded as sound'.[100] In his view, courts should be established as an independent organ that is neither Commonwealth nor state. Similar views attracted minority support in the Constitutional Commission's Advisory Committee on the Judicial System in 1987.[101] However, the extent of restructuring required to implement such a solution makes it a constitutional fantasy. There appears to be a strong political commitment to retaining something approximating the existing court structure for the foreseeable future, and for good reason.[102] Even if radical change were possible, it is undesirable to establish a court system that divides political responsibility for its administration between several executives and parliaments, no matter how attractive the idea of avoiding sterile jurisdictional disputes between state and federal courts.[103]

---

[100] Sir Owen Dixon (1935) 606.

[101] Australian Constitutional Commission Advisory Committee on the Australian Judicial System (1987) 37–43.

[102] K. Mason (1987) 19.

[103] Australian Constitutional Commission Advisory Committee on the Australian Judicial System (1987) 37–8.

(f) Conclusion

Since 1988, the unique scheme for cross-vesting the civil jurisdiction of Australian superior courts has received the benediction of politicians, judges and commentators alike. For more than a decade it has provided a pragmatic solution to some very practical problems that attend our federal judicial system. In these circumstances it is not surprising that the High Court's invalidation of one part of the scheme has met with criticism that has ranged from disappointment to vitriolic condemnation. There is no doubt that the consequence of the decision in *Re Wakim* is the subversion of the integrity of the co-operative scheme as originally envisaged.

Yet blame, if warranted at all, cannot be placed at the doors of the High Court. As Gummow and Hayne JJ remind us in *Re Wakim*, the drafters of the Australian Constitution created a federal judicial system, not a unitary one. In retrospect, the choice may not have been a particularly wise one, and may have followed from the founders' hypnotic fascination with the United States Constitution. But we should not expect the High Court to repair, through judicial decision, the perceived structural flaws of a dual court system. In a constitutional democracy, such change is best initiated and executed through other channels.

The greatest problems of the Australian federal judicial system did not become apparent until the great expansion of federal courts and federal jurisdiction in the 1970s. Since that time, there has been much discussion of the prospects and possibilities for change. The judicial system has been reasonably responsive to the transformative pressures exerted through all arms of government—legislative, executive and judicial. The current concerns about the future of cross-vesting, and the future of the federal judicial system as a whole, must be seen as part of a dynamic and evolutionary process. There is little doubt that in time *Re Wakim* will come to be regarded not as the epilogue of a gothic novel but as the prologue of its engaging sequel.

11

Choice of Law in Federal and Cross-vested Jurisdiction

Peter Nygh

1 The Rationale for Special Choice of Law Rules

Federal jurisdiction comprises the jurisdiction of the High Court and other federal courts and the jurisdiction in matters arising out of the application or interpretation of federal statutes with which state and territorial courts have been invested, other than the general investment of state and territorial courts with federal jurisdiction under the cross-vesting legislation.[1] This definition of federal jurisdiction excludes the jurisdiction of territorial courts of self-governing territories in matters arising out of the application of the common law or statutes enacted by the territorial legislature which, for the sake of conciseness, will be included in the general description of state jurisdiction.[2] But it does include the jurisdiction conferred upon a state court when the High Court remits a matter to it under s 44(1) of the *Judiciary Act 1903* (Cth).[3]

---

[1] *Jurisdiction of Courts (Cross-vesting) Act 1987* (Cth) and complementary state and territorial legislation, and see *Kruger v Commonwealth* (1997) 190 CLR 1, 108–9 (Gaudron J).

[2] See *Capital TV & Appliances Pty Ltd v Falconer* (1971) 125 CLR 591.

[3] *Johnstone v Commonwealth* (1979) 143 CLR 398, 408 (Aickin J); *Dinnison v Commonwealth* (1997) 143 ALR 635.

Cross-vested jurisdiction is federal, state and territorial jurisdiction with which the Federal Court and Family Court and the superior courts of the states and territories are invested only by reason of the joint federal and state cross-vesting legislation (see Chapter 10). It includes the federal jurisdiction with which state and territorial Supreme Courts have been invested under s 4 of the *Jurisdiction of Courts (Cross-vesting) Act 1987* (Cth), that is to say, federal jurisdiction which, but for that section, the invested court would not have possessed. It excludes any federal jurisdiction with which state courts may have been invested under other legislation, such as s 39(2) of the *Judiciary Act*.

Choice of law issues can arise in either type of jurisdiction. They arise in the course of federal jurisdiction because federal law does not, and cannot, deal with all issues that may arise in the exercise of federal jurisdiction. Indeed, a federal court in the exercise of federal jurisdiction may have to determine a matter that arises solely by reference to non-federal law.[4] That gap must be filled by reference to the common law or state or territorial statutory law. If the matter before the court involves states with different laws, that conflict must also be resolved. It arises in the course of cross-vested jurisdiction because by definition the court is exercising a jurisdiction that does not normally belong to it. The question then arises of whether it should apply its own law, that of the law area from which the jurisdiction is taken, or, in the case of a matter having connections with yet another law area, the law of that place.

Since state and territorial statutes cannot by their own force apply in the federal sphere, a mechanism is needed to 'pick them up' and translate them into federal surrogate rules. This is the function of ss 79 and 80 of the *Judiciary Act* in the exercise of federal jurisdiction. In cross-vested jurisdiction the problem is broader: in so far as the court is exercising cross-vested federal jurisdiction, no doubt ss 79 and 80 might have been used. But, in so far as it is exercising state jurisdiction, the relevance of those sections is dubious to say the least. Different 'picking up' rules might have been applicable

---

[4] This is the case in 'diversity jurisdiction' under s 75(iv) of the Constitution, or in 'accrued jurisdiction' as adumbrated in *Philip Morris Inc v Adam P Brown Male Fashions Pty Ltd* (1981) 148 CLR 457.

depending on the nature of the cross-vested jurisdiction. In order to avoid such an inelegant outcome, s 11(1) of the Commonwealth and state cross-vesting legislation provides its own choice of law rules.

One solution is to seek uniformity of outcome as between state, federal and cross-vested jurisdiction whereby the court exercising federal or cross-vested jurisdiction adapts its decision on issues of state law as much as possible to that which would have been reached by a court exercising state jurisdiction in the same place. The advantage is uniformity of outcome as between courts operating in the same law area. The disadvantage is that the outcome of the litigation may differ depending on the state or territory in which the court sits.

A second option would be to enact, or develop by judicial methods, separate choice of law rules for use in federal and cross-vested jurisdiction. This could only be justified if one was aiming to unify outcomes in those jurisdictions. The court exercising federal jurisdiction in that case would not adapt itself to the law of the place of sitting (including its choice of law rules), but be directly referred by its own choice of law rule to the internal law of the place with the most relevant connection to the subject matter of the litigation. In *Commonwealth v Mewett*,[5] Gaudron J proposed a common law choice of law rule aiming at uniformity of outcome in the exercise of federal jurisdiction. The idea of achieving uniformity of outcome through choice of law rules in cross-vested jurisdiction also underlies s 11(1)(b) of the Commonwealth and state cross-vesting legislation. But by solving one problem, another is ignored. While there will no longer be the scandal of different outcomes in different registries of the same court, there will be different outcomes depending on whether the jurisdiction of state or federal courts is invoked or whether one proceeds by way of cross-vested jurisdiction.

The third solution is to have uniform choice of law rules operating at state, federal and cross-vested levels. This can be brought about by discerning a constitutional mandate in s 118 of the Constitution,[6] or through the use by the federal Parliament of its

---

[5] (1997) 191 CLR 471, 522–8; see also 554–5 (Gummow and Kirby JJ).
[6] *Breavington v Godleman* (1988) 169 CLR 41, 135–7 (Deane J); see also 98–9 (Wilson and Gaudron JJ).

powers under s 51(xxv) of the Constitution,[7] or, as proposed by the Australian Law Reform Commission, by joint legislative action on the part of the Commonwealth, the states and the self-governing territories.[8] The High Court has rejected the first method[9] and the second method might be seen as a gross interference with the legislative competence of the states. Only the third method remains as a feasible option.

Australia is currently at a crossroad as regards choice of law in federal and cross-vested jurisdiction. The traditional assumption that the court exercising federal jurisdiction should in matters of state law conform to the law of the place in which it sits is being challenged in favour of greater emphasis on unity of outcome. This chapter will explore the implications of such a change, and how it can be justified.

2 Sections 79 and 80 of the *Judiciary Act*

(a) The traditional interpretation

Where a court is exercising federal jurisdiction, be it a federal court, a state or territorial court (other than a state or territorial court exercising federal cross-vested jurisdiction), or the High Court in the exercise of its original jurisdiction,[10] it must consider the directions given by ss 79 and 80 of the *Judiciary Act*:

> 79 The laws of each State or Territory, including the laws relating to procedure, evidence, and the competency of witnesses, shall, except as otherwise provided by the Constitution or the laws of the Commonwealth, be binding on all Courts exercising federal jurisdiction in that State or Territory in all cases to which they are applicable.
>
> 80 So far as the laws of the Commonwealth are not applicable or so far as their provisions are insufficient to carry them into effect, or

---

[7] Ibid 83 (Mason CJ). For an argument that the Commonwealth Parliament lacks this power, see Wynes (1976) 174.

[8] Australian Law Reform Commission (1992).

[9] *McKain v R W Miller & Co (SA) Pty Ltd* (1991) 174 CLR 1, 36 (Brennan, Dawson, Toohey and McHugh JJ).

[10] *Musgrave v Commonwealth* (1937) 57 CLR 514, 532 (Latham CJ).

to provide adequate remedies or punishment, the common law in Australia as modified by the Constitution and by the statute law in force in the State or Territory in which the Court in which the jurisdiction is exercised is held shall, so far as it is applicable and not inconsistent with the Constitution and the laws of the Commonwealth, govern all Courts exercising federal jurisdiction in the exercise of their jurisdiction in civil and criminal matters.

The traditional view places the emphasis on s 79, as summarised by Dixon J in *Commissioner of Stamp Duties v Owens (No 2)*: 'The purpose of [s 79] is to adopt the law of the State where federal jurisdiction is exercised as the law by which, except as the Constitution or federal law may otherwise provide, the rights of the parties to the *lis* are to be ascertained and matters of procedure are to be regulated'.[11] A number of points can be made about this statement. First, s 79 is interpreted as determining the choice of law as regards both substance ('the rights of the parties to the *lis*') and procedure. Second, the place where the court exercises federal jurisdiction is seen as a surrogate forum whose body of law, consisting of its common law and statute law, applies unless the Constitution or federal statute provides otherwise.[12] As Windeyer J said in *Suehle v Commonwealth*, when a federal court 'exercises jurisdiction in a State in a matter which might have been litigated in a court of that State, the law which it is to apply should be the same law as the State court would apply in a like case'.[13] This body of state law includes its rules of private international law,[14] which may refer the resolution of the dispute to the law of a second state or even a foreign country.

The question then arises whether under this interpretation s 80 adds anything to s 79. This depends on two issues: first, whether s 79 is designed to 'pick up' any laws other than those within the category specifically named therein, that is to say, 'the laws relating

---

[11] (1953) 88 CLR 168, 170.

[12] As is done, for instance, in the *Evidence Act 1995* (Cth).

[13] (1967) 116 CLR 353, 356.

[14] *Musgrave v Commonwealth* (1937) 57 CLR 514, 532 (Latham CJ). This view was not necessarily shared by the other justices. See 547–8 (Dixon J) and 550–1 (Evatt and McTiernan JJ).

to procedure, evidence, and the competency of witnesses' or, to put it in more general terms, matters of procedure; and, second, on the meaning of the words 'the common law in Australia'.

(b) Section 79 and procedural law

Is s 79 of the *Judiciary Act* primarily concerned with procedural law? At first sight the answer would be negative. After all, the relevant reference is preceded by the word 'including', which normally means that the words are intended as non-exhaustive. However, in *Commonwealth v Mewett* Brennan CJ said:

> Section 79 picks up the State's laws relating to procedure, evidence and the competency of witnesses, whether those laws be statutory or common law. So the common law relating to procedure, evidence and the competency of witnesses is picked up by s 79 as modified by local statutory laws relating to those subjects. Section 80, on the other hand, picks up the general common law in the circumstances which it states.[15]

This distinction does not have general support.[16] It is inconsistent with the hitherto accepted basis that it is s 79 that primarily does the 'picking up' of state laws whether procedural or not. It was not accepted by other members of the Court in *Commonwealth v Mewett*. Thus, Gaudron J clearly took the view that s 80 was relevant to procedural laws as well, which would have the effect of reversing the traditional situation with the emphasis on s 80 instead of s 79.[17]

Yet the view propounded by Brennan CJ has the obvious advantage of giving each section a distinct role. Although the examples given in s 79 can not be read as exhaustive, they all refer to examples of the genus 'procedure'. Clearly that must be read in a wider sense so as to include statutes of limitation[18] and statutes capping the damages recoverable in a common law action.[19] But they do

---

[15] (1997) 191 CLR 471, 492.

[16] But see Phillips (1962) 184–6, who, for somewhat different reasons, argues that the scope of s 79 is confined to procedural laws.

[17] (1997) 191 CLR 471, 528.

[18] *McKain v R W Miller & Co (SA) Pty Ltd* (1991) 174 CLR 1.

[19] *Stevens v Head* (1993) 176 CLR 433.

not go beyond that genus. If the gap occurs in 'substantive law', s 80 must be considered.

There is another justification for this approach. The traditional view proceeds on the conflicts analogy whereby the state in which the court exercises jurisdiction is regarded as the forum. However, this analogy is inappropriate. As Gaudron J pointed out in *Commonwealth v Mewett*, a federal court's forum is Australia as a whole.[20] A state court which exercises jurisdiction pursuant to a federal statute, such as the *Family Law Act 1975* (Cth), exercises that jurisdiction by reference to nationwide criteria, such as domicile or residence in Australia, or Australian citizenship.[21] It has rightly been said that s 79, in 'picking up' state law, transforms it into 'surrogate Commonwealth laws'.[22] In other words, s 79 does not transform federal jurisdiction into state jurisdiction, but quite the reverse.

To summarise, s 79 does not give a federal court a 'state forum' or make applicable state common law rules of choice of law. Because the forum is Australia as a whole, and federal law may not provide all the procedural laws that state law offers, s 79 has adopted the quite arbitrary solution of 'picking up' the statutes dealing with such matters in the state where the court is exercising jurisdiction. But that is all it does: it does not 'pick up' the common law or the general law of torts and contracts. That is the function of s 80.

(c) Several common laws or one?

There are six states and two self-governing territories in the Commonwealth of Australia. Does each, plus the Commonwealth itself, proudly possess a common law? Section 80, as amended in 1988, speaks of 'the common law in Australia', rather than 'the common law of Australia'.[23] This formula appears to leave open the issue of

---

[20] (1997) 191 CLR 471, 524–5.

[21] *Family Law Act 1975* (Cth) s 39(3) and (4).

[22] *Commonwealth v Mewett* (1997) 191 CLR 471, 554 (Gummow and Kirby JJ, adapting the words used by Murphy J in *Maguire v Simpson* (1977) 139 CLR 362, 408 to describe the effect of s 64 of the *Judiciary Act 1903* (Cth)).

[23] *Law and Justice Legislation Amendment Act 1988* (Cth) s 41, which replaced the words 'the common law of England' with the present text.

whether there is one common law in Australia, or whether each state and territory and even the Commonwealth has its own common law, albeit one which is identical.[24] In the United States, where a common court of appeal on matters of state law is lacking, there is no doubt that each state has its own common law which may differ from state to state. It is also accepted in that country that there is a federal common law, albeit one which is not as extensive as was once thought.[25] In Australia, on the other hand, the High Court has recently pointed out in *Lange v Australian Broadcasting Corporation* that:

> There is but one common law in Australia which is declared by this Court as the final court of appeal. In contrast to the position in the United States, the common law as it exists throughout the Australian States and Territories is not fragmented into different systems of jurisprudence, possessing different content and subject to different authoritative interpretations.[26]

This challenges the traditional approach to ss 79 and 80, according to which it does not matter much whether one proceeds by way of s 79 or s 80. As Dawson J said in *Commonwealth v Mewett*: 'The effect of those two sections is to apply to each proceeding the whole body of law in the relevant State, except to the extent to which it is inconsistent with Commonwealth laws'.[27] This approach treats the common law as part of the 'whole body of law' of each state rather than as part of the whole body of Australian law. The reference in both ss 79 and 80 is to that 'whole body of law in the relevant State', whether described as 'the laws of each State', as in s 79, or as 'the common law in Australia as modified by . . . the statute law in force in the State', as in s 80. On that view s 80 repeats s 79 and hence becomes superfluous. If s 80 were deleted, the law would remain the same. But, if the common law in Australia is part

[24] See Priestley (1995), who inclines to the view—increasingly challenged in the High Court—that each state has its own common law.
[25] Leflar, McDougall and Felix (1986) 198–201.
[26] (1997) 189 CLR 520, 563 (Brennan CJ, Dawson, Toohey, Gaudron, McHugh, Gummow and Kirby JJ).
[27] (1997) 191 CLR 471, 506.

of an undivided Australian law, there is no need to refer to state law in cases where no issue of statutory law arises. Thus, in *Commonwealth v Mewett* Gaudron J made the following remarks:

> In my view, there is one common law, the common law in Australia, which may be modified in its operation in the States and Territories by Commonwealth, State or Territory legislation. On that view, it is the common law in Australia, not that of Victoria or New South Wales, which is determinative of the Commonwealth's liability in tort in these cases. And because the contracts involved in these cases are contracts with the Commonwealth, it may well be that it is Australian contract law that determines liability in the claims based on contract.[28]

A similar statement is found in the joint judgment of Gummow and Kirby JJ in the same case. There they state that

> there is much to be said for the view that regard is to be had to s 80, and to the common law in Australia, before turning to s 79 to ascertain whether a State or Territory law is to be picked up in the case at hand. In particular, that common law may be developed so as to provide choice of law rules applicable in federal jurisdiction.[29]

One would agree with much of that statement except that, in the case of non-procedural laws, s 79 would not be applicable, should the common law have been amended or abrogated in any relevant state. In that case reference should be made to s 80 to determine to what extent the statute law of the state in which the court is held is applicable. In most cases this will depend on the common law in Australia including its choice of law rules, unless they have been changed or overridden by the law of the state in which the court is held. If that state statute is not applicable, the common law choice of law rules will determine which one is. Section 79 only deals with the selection of the procedural law which the common law conflict rules would refer to the law of the forum. As has been demonstrated, since a court exercising federal jurisdiction has no state forum, s 79 is required to produce a similar effect.[30]

---

[28] Ibid 526.
[29] Ibid 554.
[30] See Priestley (1995) 223; Phillips (1962) 176.

What is the effect of such an interpretation of ss 79 and 80? A number of propositions can be advanced. First, if the issue before the court exercising federal jurisdiction arises solely out of the common law, such as an issue of tortious liability, s 80 permits the court to resolve that issue by reference to the common law. There is no need to 'pick up' any state law. If more than one state is involved, but the common law in each is unaffected by statute, no issue of choice of law or conflict arises: the court is dealing with a domestic tort subject to the same law. Second, if the common law has been amended or altered by statute, the answer depends on whether the issue is one of procedure or substance. Third, in the former case, s 79 applies to 'pick up' any statute regulating procedure of the state in which the court is exercising jurisdiction. If the local statute has the effect of referring the court to the law of another jurisdiction, as happened in the *Choice of Law (Limitation Periods) Act 1993* (NSW) and similar legislation in other states and territories, the court must apply the law so indicated.[31] Fourth, if the issue is one of substantive law, s 80 refers the court in the first place to the common law, including its choice of law rules. Those rules will indicate the law that is applicable, unless the choice of law rules themselves have been changed by the state in which the court is held or that state makes its own law applicable by a mandatory rule notwithstanding any common law choice of law rule.[32]

The actual operation of these principles will not differ much from the application of the traditional rules. It matters little in outcome whether one regards the common law choice of law rules as part of the body of state law or as common property of both states and the federation. But this assumes that the choice of law rules for use by state courts exercising state jurisdiction on the one hand, and for courts exercising federal jurisdiction on the other, are the same. They need not be. In the first place, the Commonwealth Parliament may exercise its power under s 51(xxv) of the Constitution to replace the common law rules as operating in the federal sphere with statutory rules. It was proposed by the Australian Law Reform

---

[31] See *Commonwealth v Mewett* (1997) 191 CLR 471.

[32] See *Kay's Leasing Corporation Pty Ltd v Fletcher* (1964) 116 CLR 124, 143 (Kitto J); see also the *Credit Act 1984* (NSW) s 3(1)(a).

Commission in its report on choice of law to insert a Division 2A following s 80 of the *Judiciary Act* setting out statutory choice of law rules applicable in courts exercising federal jurisdiction.[33] Assuming this to be a valid exercise of legislative power, those rules would have replaced the common law rules referred to in s 80.

Alternatively, there may be different common law rules depending on the nature of the court exercising jurisdiction. In *Commonwealth v Mewett* Gaudron J pointed out the incongruity of speaking of a federal court exercising jurisdiction in a state or territory. In her view the High Court and Federal Court exercise jurisdiction in Australia as a whole.[34] Hence s 79 is inappropriate and a common law rule should be developed based on the unity of Australian law and 'the need to ensure that the one set of facts occurring in Australia gives rise to only one possible legal consequence, regardless of the location of the court in which proceedings are brought'.[35] As far as choice of law in tort is concerned, this points to the application of the law of the place where the tort occurred without reference to, or input from, the law of the forum. In their joint judgment Gummow and Kirby JJ said that there was 'much to recommend this approach', but chose not to apply it because it had not been the subject of submissions.[36]

This would mean that the common law choice of law rule applicable in the exercise of federal jurisdiction would be different from that applicable in the exercise of state jurisdiction. Gaudron J acknowledged that she was bound by the decision of the High Court in *McKain v R W Miller & Co (SA) Pty Ltd* which reasserted a double liability test which gives the law of the forum a determinative, if not pre-eminent, role in liability for foreign torts.[37] However, on the principles outlined above, reference to a federal forum would be meaningless under s 80. A court exercising federal jurisdiction does not adopt as its forum the place in which it exercises that federal jurisdiction; it only adopts its procedural statutes as 'surrogate

[33] Australian Law Reform Commission (1992) Appendix A.
[34] (1997) 191 CLR 471, 524–5.
[35] Ibid 527.
[36] Ibid 554.
[37] (1991) 174 CLR 1, 38–40 (Brennan, Dawson, Toohey and McHugh JJ).

Commonwealth law' under s 79. Hence, the forum test becomes inapplicable and the second test, referring to the law of the place of the wrong, is solely indicative under s 80.

This point was made as early as 1937 in the joint judgment of Evatt and McTiernan JJ in *Musgrave v Commonwealth*. Speaking of a suit for defamation instituted in the Sydney Registry of the High Court in respect of a libel committed in Queensland, they said:

> Whatever may be the precise limits to be assigned to sec.79 of the *Judiciary Act*, it does not introduce, for the purpose of determining the lawfulness of the publication complained of, the general body of New South Wales law, merely because the action, being instituted in the High Court, happens to have been heard at Sydney. Therefore, in our opinion, the principle embodied in such cases as *Machado v Fontes* . . . has no application to the present case. The result is that the law of Queensland and it alone must determine the lawfulness of the defendant's publication.[38]

Two qualifications can be made to that statement. First, as has already been argued, where the issue is one of substantive law, as in the case of the lawfulness of an act, it is s 80 and not s 79 which is relevant. Second, in so far as their Honours' views proceeded on an interpretation of s 56 of the *Judiciary Act* as containing an implied choice of law direction, they were mistaken (as discussed later). But the essence of the statement is that by exercising jurisdiction in a particular place, the court does not 'pick up' any body of state law as the law of the forum.

3 The Laws 'Picked Up' by Section 79 of the *Judiciary Act*

(a) Distinguishing 'picking up' and the choice of law technique

From the above discussion it will have appeared that 'picking up' is largely a feature of s 79 and to a much more limited extent of s 80. Once again, the question arises whether the traditional conflicts analogy is relevant.

---

[38] (1937) 57 CLR 514, 551.

The main distinction between 'picking up' a state law under s 79 and incorporating such a law in the law of the forum by virtue of a choice of law rule as 'a rule of decision' is that in the first case the statute 'picked up' becomes a 'surrogate Commonwealth law'[39] which must be applied with its meaning and ambit[40] unaltered as if it had been enacted by the Commonwealth Parliament for the purposes of the case at hand. A conflicts approach, on the other hand, treats the foreign rule in quite a different fashion on the basis that it is and remains a foreign rule of decision, albeit incorporated into the law of the forum.

The distinction is best illustrated by the approach taken by the majority in *Commonwealth v Mewett*. The main issue for determination was whether the cause of action by the plaintiff against the Commonwealth which had arisen in 1979 had been barred or extinguished at the time when s 44 of the *Safety Rehabilitation and Compensation Act 1988* (Cth) came into effect on 1 December 1988.[41] The matter came before the Federal Court sitting in Sydney. Section 14 of the *Limitation Act 1969* (NSW) barred the action after the expiry of six years in traditional statute of limitation fashion, while s 63(1) of the same Act extinguished the right and title to the cause of action. On a conflicts approach the plaintiff's right of action would appear to have been extinguished by 1988. Notwithstanding that the alleged tort occurred on the high seas, it was assumed that it had occurred in New South Wales, and under the *Limitation Act* of that state, no civil liability existed at the relevant time. A conflicts approach would have regarded the wrong as a local tort and consequently the issue would have been whether at the time in question a New South Wales court would have recognised an existing right.

---

[39] *Maguire v Simpson* (1977) 139 CLR 362, 408 (Murphy J).

[40] See *Pedersen v Young* (1964) 110 CLR 162.

[41] Section 44 bars all common law actions for damages against the Commonwealth whether the injury occurred before or after 1 December 1988. But in *Georgiades v Australian and Overseas Telecommunications Corporation* (1994) 179 CLR 297, the High Court held that the provision could not deprive a plaintiff of a right of action which existed as at 1 December 1988. At issue in *Commonwealth v Mewett* was whether the cause of action was still in existence as at 1 December 1988.

The joint judgment of Gummow and Kirby JJ, with whom Brennan CJ and Gaudron J agreed on this point, took a different approach.[42] On their view, s 79 did not operate to 'pick up' the New South Wales statute until and unless that section was engaged by the plaintiff instituting his action in 1994. There being no federal statute of limitations, his action was not barred or extinguished by federal law in 1988. Thus, what is applied under s 79 is not a foreign rule of decision but a federal rule, albeit one borrowed for the particular purpose of the litigation and activated only when s 79 is engaged. This does not occur when the proceedings are instituted, but when and where the substantive hearing takes place. Of course, once the local statute is 'activated', it must be applied as it stands and the plaintiff could not argue that the limitation period only commenced from 1994, but had to accept that under s 14 of the *Limitation Act*, the period started to run when his cause of action accrued in 1979.

(b) State laws expressed to apply to state courts

In *Pedersen v Young* Kitto J said that s 79 'does not purport to do more than pick up State laws with their meaning unchanged'.[43] That statement, read literally, would mean that no state statute which was expressed to apply to the courts of that state could ever be applicable in a court exercising federal jurisdiction. In *John Robertson & Co Ltd v Ferguson Transformers Pty Ltd* Mason J made the following suggestion:

> To ensure that State laws dealing with the particular topics mentioned in the section are applied in the exercise of federal jurisdiction by courts other than State courts, it is necessary that State laws be applied according to the hypothesis that federal courts do not necessarily lie outside their field of application. Section 79 requires the assumption to be made that federal courts lie within the field of application of State laws on the topics to which it refers, at least in those cases in which the State laws are expressed to apply to courts generally.[44]

---

[42] (1997) 191 CLR 471, 553–8 (Gummow and Kirby JJ); 491–2 (Brennan CJ); 530 (Gaudron J).

[43] (1964) 110 CLR 162, 165.

[44] (1973) 129 CLR 65, 93–5.

Although the remarks were obiter, this test has been applied by the Federal Court on a number of occasions.[45] But is it logical to make the outcome depend on the choice of the words used? According to the Mason test, if the local statute confers power to award interest in respect of damages only on the Supreme Court, the Federal Court cannot avail itself of that power.[46] But if that power is given to all courts in the state, the Federal Court could do so.[47] Such a mechanical test ignores the purpose of the legislation. As Gaudron J remarked in *Kruger v Commonwealth*, there may be functions given by state statute to state courts, either in general terms or in respect of a specific court, which cannot effectively be translated into a 'surrogate Commonwealth law'.[48] An example was the *Suitors' Fund Act 1951* (NSW) which provided for a form of financial assistance by the New South Wales authorities to litigants in appellate proceedings.[49] One could hardly expect that state to extend its largesse to litigants in the Federal Court. Furthermore, it was probably not a law in contemplation of s 79. But the power to award interest on damages is in quite a different position: it goes to the quantum of the damages awarded and it regulates the proceedings as between the parties. It can be translated into the federal sphere.

4 The Effect of a Change of Venue on the Applicable Law

A change of venue may occur in a number of situations: a matter filed in a particular registry of a federal court may be heard in another state or territory, or judgment may be delivered in another state or territory, or the case having been filed in the original jurisdiction of the High Court may be remitted by that Court pursuant to s 44 of the *Judiciary Act* to the Federal Court or a state court.

---

[45] *Bond Corp Pty Ltd v Thiess Contractors Pty Ltd* (1987) 71 ALR 125; *Davis v Federal Commissioner of Taxation* (1989) 86 ALR 195; *Trade Practices Commission v Manfal Pty Ltd* (1990) 97 ALR 231, 243 (Wilcox J).

[46] *Australian National Airlines v Commonwealth* (1975) 6 ALR 433, 435–6 (Mason J).

[47] *Neilsen v Hempstead Holdings Pty Ltd* (1984) 65 ALR 302, 311 (Pincus J).

[48] (1997) 190 CLR 1, 140–1.

[49] See *Commissioner of Stamp Duties (NSW) v Owens [No 2]* (1953) 88 CLR 168.

When is a court 'exercising federal jurisdiction in that State or Territory' within the meaning of s 79? In *Parker v Commonwealth* Windeyer J addressed this issue:

> In the present case I sat in Victoria. I heard evidence and argument there and at the conclusion stated my opinion on the legal matters involved, thus assuming and exercising jurisdiction in the case. But I reserved my decision so that I might put my reasons fully in writing and because I wished to consider submissions that had been made as to the amount of damages to be awarded. Adjudication is no doubt an essential part of the exercise of jurisdiction; but, with the assent of counsel for both parties, I am delivering my judgment in New South Wales to avoid keeping the parties waiting until the Court next sits in Melbourne; and I do so on the view, which both parties urge, that jurisdiction in the case is to be taken as having been exercised in Victoria.[50]

The submission of counsel in this case was undoubtedly correct. It would be both absurd and inconvenient if the applicable law depended on where judgment was delivered and, even worse, if the hitherto applicable law on the basis of which the case was argued was changed because it suited the convenience of the judge to deliver judgment in the state in which he or she resided. Nor should the applicable law change because the court moves to another state in order to receive local evidence. As Gaudron J pointed out in *Kruger v Commonwealth*, pragmatic considerations require 'that s 79 be applied to pick up the law of the State or Territory in which the court first sits to hear the substance of the matter, unless it is clear that the court will later sit in a State or Territory more closely connected with the matter'.[51] The effect of this is that neither the registry where the initiating process is filed nor the place where the judgment is delivered should be applicable per se.

(a) The filing of proceedings and statutes of limitation

A particular problem has arisen in relation to statutes of limitation. If proceedings are first filed four years after the occurrence of the tort in a state where the relevant period of limitation is six years, but

[50] (1965) 112 CLR 295, 305–6.
[51] (1997) 190 CLR 1, 139.

the substantive hearing is conducted in another state where the relevant period is three years, a question arises as to which state's law is applicable. The matter was first considered by the High Court in *Pedersen v Young*.[52] In that case of diversity jurisdiction in the High Court, the plaintiff issued the writ against a resident of Queensland out of the Sydney registry of the Court. Under the law of New South Wales at the time the limitation period was six years, but under Queensland law it was three years. The plaintiff was within time in New South Wales, but out of time in Queensland. The point was raised by way of demurrer by the plaintiff to the defendant's plea that the plaintiff's action was statute barred under Queensland law because the tort sued upon was committed in Queensland. The demurrer was upheld for the simple reason that whatever s 79 did, it did not make a Queensland statute applicable to an action commenced out of that state.

This made it unnecessary to decide what the position would be if the matter was heard and determined in Queensland. Kitto J took the view that since the action was commenced outside Queensland, its statute of limitations would have no application even if the substantive hearing took place in Queensland.[53] But Menzies J confined himself to the proposition 'that the Queensland statute pleaded cannot apply if the action is heard in the registry in which it now is'.[54] That, indeed, is the ratio decidendi of *Pedersen v Young*.

Nevertheless, single justices of the High Court for a time accepted as good law Kitto J's view that once the action is commenced in a High Court registry outside the state with a restrictive limitation period, the action is not restrained by the law of that state, even if the venue is changed with the effect that the substantive hearing takes place in that state.[55] This proposition is not free of doubt. In *Gardner v Wallace* Dawson J expressed himself very cautiously on this point.[56]

---

[52] (1964) 110 CLR 162.

[53] Ibid 165–6.

[54] Ibid 168.

[55] *Bargen v State Government Insurance Office (Q)* (1982) 154 CLR 318 (Stephen J); *Fielding v Doran* (1984) 60 ALR 342 (Dawson J).

[56] (1995) 184 CLR 95, 97. See also *Bowtell v Commonwealth* (1989) 86 ALR 31, 32 (Toohey J).

Arguably, the view expressed by Kitto J in *Pedersen v Young* is incorrect. In that case the outcome of the demurrer was inevitable because the place of hearing had not yet been determined. But in *Kruger v Commonwealth* Gaudron J considered the limitation statute of the Australian Capital Territory relevant, not because the action was commenced there, but because it was going to be heard there.[57] It is not the commencement of the proceedings, but the exercise of the jurisdiction that attracts s 79.

(b) Remitter under section 44 of the *Judiciary Act*

Pursuant to s 44(1) of the *Judiciary Act*, the High Court may remit a matter arising in its diversity jurisdiction to 'any federal court, court of a State or court of a Territory, that has jurisdiction with respect to the subject-matter and the parties'. By virtue of s 44(3)(a), upon remitter to any state court that court is invested with federal jurisdiction.

Leaving aside the specific problem of the application of statutes of limitation, the general assumption has been that upon remitter the non-federal law applicable will be the law of the state in which the recipient court is exercising jurisdiction. This assumption certainly underlies the exercise of choice by the High Court which, for that reason, has favoured remitting the matter to a court in the place where the cause of action arose, rather than remitting the matter to suit the convenience of one of the parties in cases where there were material differences in the applicable law as between the competing states.[58]

However, s 79 only starts to operate once federal jurisdiction is being exercised. Although the High Court under s 44 may give directions in relation to the conduct of the further proceedings, it is now clear that those directions can only relate to the method of proceeding in the court, not as regards the applicable law.[59] This must be read, of course, subject to the comments made earlier. Although the remitter may change the venue from the place of filing to the

---

[57] (1997) 190 CLR 1, 139–41.

[58] *Pozniak v Smith* (1982) 151 CLR 38.

[59] Ibid 44 (Gibbs, Wilson and Brennan JJ). See also *Dinnison v Commonwealth* (1997) 143 ALR 635.

place of hearing, the matter remains within federal jurisdiction. There is no change of forum in the conflictual sense.

If s 79 is applicable because the issue is one of procedure, it is not engaged until the federal jurisdiction is exercised at the substantive hearing. Consequently there is no change of the applicable law for the simple reason that there was no previously applicable law. But, if s 80 is applicable because the issue is one of substantive law, then in the absence of a mandatory law of the place where jurisdiction is being exercised, a uniform common law choice of law rule will indicate, regardless of the place of sitting, what law should be applied. In each case there is no change of any previously applicable law, but rather a determination of it.

5 Choice of Law in Suits Against the Commonwealth

There has been a strong body of High Court opinion expressed on various occasions over the last sixty years that in relation to suits against the Commonwealth, the *Judiciary Act* provides a specific choice of law rule by way of exception to the rules found in ss 79 and 80. This argument is based on ss 56(1) and 64 of the *Judiciary Act*.

Section 56(1) provides:

A person making a claim against the Commonwealth, whether in contract or in tort, may in respect of the claim bring a suit against the Commonwealth—

(a) in the High Court;

(b) if the claim arose in a State or Territory—in the Supreme Court of that State or Territory or in any other court of competent jurisdiction of that State or Territory; or

(c) if the claim did not arise in a State or Territory—in the Supreme Court of any State or Territory or in any court of competent jurisdiction of any State or Territory.

Section 64 provides:

In any suit to which the Commonwealth or a State is a party, the rights of the parties shall as nearly as possible be the same, and judgment may be given and costs awarded on either side, as in a suit between subject and subject.

At first sight s 56(1) does no more than define the courts in which suit may be brought against the Commonwealth. Section 64 undoubtedly has the effect of subjecting the Crown in right of the Commonwealth to the same law, including common law and state statutory law, as applies in suits between citizens, but, on the face of it, the section contains no direction as to what law shall be applied.

The suggestion that s 56 implies that the substantive liability of the Commonwealth in tort 'should be that otherwise flowing from the law of the State or territory in which the wrongful act or omission is committed or made' appears in the judgment of Dixon J in *Musgrave v Commonwealth*[60] and has the support of the joint judgment of Evatt and McTiernan JJ in the same case.[61] But it was not necessary to reach a conclusion on the matter.

In fact, the implication based on s 56 has been applied only once. In *Suehle v Commonwealth*[62] an action in respect of a tort committed in South Australia was filed in the Canberra Registry of the High Court but heard in Sydney. A defence of contributory negligence was raised. At the relevant time this would have been a plea barring the plaintiff's action in New South Wales, but both the Australian Capital Territory and South Australia had amended the common law by introducing apportionment legislation. Relying on the suggested implication in s 56 and treating this as an exception to the provisions of ss 79 and 80 which would otherwise have been applicable, Windeyer J applied the law of South Australia as the law of the place where the claim arose. Despite several obiter dicta in support of the proposition,[63] there has not been any further decision based on the suggested implication.

As regards the operation of s 64, reference has been made to the decision of the High Court in *Maguire v Simpson*[64] as supporting the proposition that it subjects the Commonwealth to the liability in tort which is imposed by the law of the state in which the tort was

[60] (1937) 57 CLR 514, 547–8.

[61] Ibid 550–1.

[62] (1967) 116 CLR 353.

[63] See *Breavington v Godleman* (1988) 169 CLR 41, 118 (Brennan J), 151–2 (Dawson J); *Commonwealth v Dinnison* (1995) 129 ALR 239, 244–5 (Gummow and Cooper JJ).

[64] (1977) 139 CLR 362.

committed.[65] It is true that *Maguire v Simpson* is authority for the proposition that s 64 makes applicable to the Commonwealth as 'surrogate Commonwealth law' state statutes which would not otherwise be applicable to the Commonwealth. But in order to make the statute of a particular state applicable one must refer either to s 79 or, if the argument concerning s 56 is correct, to that section. Section 64 does not achieve a selection of law by itself. It was not necessary to determine that issue in *Maguire v Simpson* since all relevant factors pointed to New South Wales and the issue was whether s 63 of the *Limitation Act* was applicable to the Commonwealth Trading Bank as an emanation of the Crown in right of the Commonwealth. The only justice who referred to the issue was Gibbs J who remarked: 'The effect of s 64, stated more directly, is that the Limitation Act, which is to be applied in the proceedings by virtue of s 79, is rendered applicable to the Commonwealth as though it were a subject, and therefore binds the Bank'.[66]

Another possible effect of s 64 was proposed by Mahoney JA in *Commonwealth v Dixon*.[67] His Honour did not suggest that s 64 contained a selection of law rule, but took the view that s 64 determined the rights and liabilities of the parties, both as to substance and procedure, as at the time and place where the proceedings were instituted. Thus, if proceedings against the Commonwealth were instituted in the High Court Registry in Victoria, it was at that point that the respective rights and liabilities of the parties 'jelled' and s 64 prevented the normal operation of s 79 in making applicable the law of the jurisdiction to which the venue was changed.[68] Although his Honour did not address this specifically, presumably ss 79 and 80 would determine the selection of law at the stage of filing the writ.

It has been argued earlier that ss 79 and 80 do not necessarily apply by reference to the place in which proceedings are filed. If that is the case, s 79 does not operate to change the applicable law; it is

---

[65] *Commonwealth v Mewett* (1995) 140 ALR 99, 103 Cooper J (Full Court of the Federal Court).

[66] (1977) 139 CLR 362, 377.

[67] (1988) 13 NSWLR 601.

[68] Ibid 625–6.

only when the substantive hearing begins that those provisions are engaged. Accordingly, s 64 has nothing to say on this point.

The view that s 64, either by itself[69] or in conjunction with s 56,[70] has the effect of making the law of the place in which the tort was committed applicable in an action against the Commonwealth has found support in the Full Court of the Federal Court in *Commonwealth v Mewett*. However, it was not endorsed on appeal by the High Court.[71]

On appeal Brennan CJ would not ascribe any operation to s 64 in this regard.[72] Gaudron J subjected the proposition to the following devastating critique:

> Were s 56 concerned solely with actions in tort, it might be possible to treat s 56 as having the effect ascribed to it by Windeyer J. However, it also applies to actions in contract which, by the general law, are governed by the proper law of the contract in question, not the law of the place of its breach ... Moreover, s 56 leaves it to the common law or, perhaps, to s 79 of the *Judiciary Act* to determine the law to be applied in actions that do not arise in a State or Territory. These considerations present real obstacles in the path of an implication that s 56 directs the law to be applied in an action arising out of events in a State or Territory. And that is so even if the implication is confined to actions in tort.[73]

It may be remarked that even Brennan CJ, Dawson and Gummow JJ, who on previous occasions had expressed some sympathy for the implication, proceeded in the appeal on the basis that ss 79 and 80 were the provisions relevant to the application of state law. It may therefore safely be concluded that implications based on either s 56 or s 64 alone do not have the support of the current High Court.

---

[69] *Commonwealth v Mewett* (1995) 140 ALR 99, 103 (Cooper J, with whose reasons Spender J agreed).

[70] Ibid 122 (Lindgren J).

[71] *Commonwealth v Mewett* (1997) 191 CLR 471.

[72] Ibid 492.

[73] Ibid 523.

6 Choice of Law in Cross-vested Jurisdiction

(a) Distinguishing federal and cross-vested jurisdiction

The Commonwealth, state and territory cross-vesting legislation contains in s 11(1) its own choice of law rules that apply when 'it appears to a court that the court will, or will be likely to' be exercising cross-vested jurisdiction. Since the provisions of s 11(1) differ markedly from those of ss 79 and 80 of the *Judiciary Act*, it is important to determine whether a court is exercising cross-vested or federal jurisdiction.

Under its so-called 'accrued jurisdiction', the Federal Court of Australia, in the course of exercising its 'proper' federal jurisdiction, can deal with any related state matters that might arise, including causes of action arising solely under state law, provided they arise out of the same sub-stratum of facts.[74] This 'accrued' jurisdiction is federal, not cross-vested, jurisdiction to which ss 79 and 80 are applicable. Similarly, the jurisdiction with which state courts have been invested under s 39(2) of the *Judiciary Act* is federal jurisdiction outside the purview of s 11(1) of the cross-vesting legislation.

There appear to be three situations in which cross-vested jurisdiction will be exercised: first, where a state court exercises a jurisdiction under a federal statute or a statute of another state which, but for the cross-vesting legislation, it would not have possessed; second, where a federal court exercises state jurisdiction which, but for the cross-vesting legislation, it would not have possessed;[75] and, third, where one of the courts within the cross-vesting scheme exercises jurisdiction in respect of a proceeding which has been transferred to it from another such court pursuant to s 5 of the cross-vesting legislation. In respect of the last group it does not matter whether the proceeding was originally commenced in the cross-vested jurisdiction or not. Nor does it matter that the transferred proceeding could have been instituted in the 'proper' jurisdiction of the court to which transfer was made, had the plaintiff

---

[74] See *Philip Morris Inc v Adam P Brown Male Fashions Pty Ltd* (1981) 148 CLR 457; *Fencott v Muller* (1983) 152 CLR 570.

[75] But see now *Re Wakim; Ex parte McNally* (1999) 163 ALR 270.

chosen to do so.[76] It is the method whereby the proceeding comes before the second court that gives it its cross-vested character.[77]

(b) Section 11 of the Cross-vesting legislation

Section 11(1) sets out three choice of law rules. The first is the primary rule: the court shall 'apply the law in force in the State or Territory in which the court is sitting (including choice of law rules)'.[78] This formula bears a resemblance to the traditional interpretation of s 79 of the *Judiciary Act* which has increasingly come under challenge. It assumes that the place where the court is sitting acts as a forum and that it will apply choice of law rules, which are predominantly derived from the common law, as part of the common law of the state. Furthermore, the definition of the place where the court is sitting in s 11(2) as the place 'in which any matter for determination in the proceedings was first commenced in or transferred to that court' gives credence to the assumption that it is the law of the place of filing (or first receipt of the transmitted file) that becomes applicable, rather than that of the place where the substantive jurisdiction is exercised.

However, the first rule does not apply in cases where 'that matter is a right of action arising under a written law of another State or Territory',[79] in other words, where the claim arises under a statute of another state. Nor does it apply to questions of evidence and procedure which are the subject of the third rule.[80] If, as Gummow J suggested in *David Syme & Co Ltd v Grey*,[81] a right of action can be so described even if it only partly depends on statutory law, or

---

[76] *Australian Broadcasting Corporation v Waterhouse* (1991) 25 NSWLR 519.

[77] For that reason it is submitted that Branson J was mistaken in *Abrook v Paterson* (1995) 136 ALR 753 when she held that s 11(1) was not applicable to a proceeding transferred from the Supreme Court of South Australia to the Federal Court, because that proceeding could have been instituted independently in the Federal Court. See *Australian Broadcasting Corporation v Waterhouse* (1991) 25 NSWLR 519.

[78] *Jurisdiction of Courts (Cross-vesting) Act 1987* (Cth) s 11(1)(a).

[79] Section 11(1)(b).

[80] Section 11(1)(c).

[81] (1993) 115 ALR 247, 260.

where a statutory defence is raised against a common law liability, the operation of the first rule will not be inconsistent with the proposition that the common law in Australia applicable to questions of substance applies as an undivided whole.

The second rule provides that where 'the matter is a right of action arising under a written law of another State or Territory, the court shall, in determining that matter, apply the written and unwritten law of that other State or Territory'.[82] This is a radical departure from both the traditional interpretation of ss 79 and 80 and the interpretation advocated here.

As we have seen, the traditional interpretation of ss 79 and 80 jointly 'picks up' the law of the place where the court is exercising jurisdiction. My interpretation of s 80 refers the issue to the law indicated by the choice of law rules of the common law in Australia. But the second rule makes applicable any interstate statute which a party seeks to have applied, provided it validly applies on its own terms to the case before the court. This need not be the law indicated by the common law choice of law rules, nor the law of the place in which the court is sitting. It could be a statute that provided for relief in respect of contracts made within a particular state, even though the proper law of the contract in question was that of another state and the court exercising cross-vested jurisdiction sat in that state.

This is not to say that the solution adopted in the second rule is wrong. Like the interpretation of s 80 that I support, it presents a rule which is 'federally' neutral and does not adopt the 'forum analogy'. It is quite respectable to adopt a solution which makes the question of whether state law applies to a given situation depend on whether that law on its proper construction applies to that situation.[83] It may on odd occasions lead to a conflict when more than one state statute claims application, but this no doubt could be avoided through judicious interpretation. What is undesirable is a

---

[82] *Jurisdiction of Courts (Cross-vesting) Act 1987* (Cth) s 11(1)(b).

[83] See Phillips (1962) 360–1, arguing for a somewhat similar proposition as an interpretation of s 80 of the *Judiciary Act 1903* (Cth).

divergence of solutions depending on the type of jurisdiction the court is exercising.

The third rule is equally unorthodox. It provides that 'the rules of evidence and procedure to be applied ... shall be such as the court considers appropriate in the circumstances, being rules that are applied in a superior court in Australia or in an external Territory'.[84]

Once again this differs radically from s 79, which is not necessarily a criticism of the rule itself. There is much to be said for a rule that renders applicable the procedural law of the state which is appropriate in the sense that, in so far as it affects the outcome of the proceedings, it is the same law as should govern the substance of the litigation. This can be illustrated by the decision of Anderson J in *Reidy v Trustee of Christian Brothers*.[85]

That case concerned an action in tort instituted in the Supreme Court of Victoria and transferred under s 5(2) of the cross-vesting legislation to the Supreme Court of Western Australia. The cause of action had arisen entirely in Western Australia some thirty years prior to the commencement of the action. The limitation statute of Western Australia would have barred the action with little chance of obtaining an extension of time. Victorian law might have permitted an extension in the circumstances of the case. When Anderson J was urged by the plaintiff to apply the Victorian statute as 'appropriate', he declined, pointing out that the 'gist of the actions is in this State',[86] it being the jurisdiction in which the tort was committed and in which both parties were resident at the time. There was no Victorian element. 'Appropriateness' does not mean merely applying the law of the place in which the court sits, nor does it mean applying the 'better law' or the law that might give the plaintiff a remedy. It means the law most relevant to the issue before the court. This is in essence the solution now adopted by the *Choice of Law (Limitation Periods) Act 1993* (NSW) and similar legislation in other states and territories.

---

[84] *Jurisdiction of Courts (Cross-vesting) Act 1987* (Cth) s 11(1)(c).

[85] (1995) 12 WAR 583. This decision was followed by Mullane J in *In Marriage of Wilton and Jarvis* (1996) 133 FLR 355.

[86] *Reidy v Trustee of Christian Brothers* (1995) 12 WAR 583, 586.

7 The Proposals of the Australian Law Reform Commission

As mentioned earlier, the Australian Law Reform Commission has accepted the proposition which underlies the approach to s 80 of the *Judiciary Act* advocated here, namely, that the federal Parliament can legislate to replace the common law choice of law rules with rules of its own making.[87] Since the Commission has not proposed a codification of the choice of law rules, it envisages that ss 79 and 80 will remain in place, but will be supplemented by a new Division 2A of Part XI of the *Judiciary Act* containing specific rules, primarily in the areas of tort, contract, and procedure. It also proposes that s 11(1)(b) of the Commonwealth cross-vesting legislation be deleted.[88] This legislation would be complemented by uniform legislation passed in every state and self-governing territory.[89]

---

[87] For a view that the federal Parliament lacks the power to determine what law is applicable under s 80 (but not under s 79), see Phillips (1962) 348–9.

[88] Australian Law Reform Commission (1992) Appendix A.

[89] Ibid Appendix B.

PART IV
Federal Judges

12

A Profile of the Federal Judiciary

Andrew J. Goldsmith *

1 Introduction

Australian judges are increasingly the subjects of media attention and public commentary. For example, the press and other news media widely reported comments made by then Deputy Prime Minister Tim Fischer in 1997 about the need to appoint 'capital C' conservatives to the High Court. Recent appointments to that Court, in particular the appointment of Justice Ian Callinan, have been the subject of greater scrutiny. Much of the commentary in recent years relating to the High Court has focused upon particular decisions by that Court, the most obvious examples being the decisions in *Mabo v Queensland [No 2]*[1] and *Wik Peoples v Queensland*.[2] The trend under Chief Justice Mason, especially during the early 1990s, towards an 'implied rights' constitutional

[1] (1992) 175 CLR 1.
[2] (1996) 187 CLR 1.

* For assistance in the preparation of this paper I would like to thank: Michelle Sutcliffe and Trish Mitchell; Georgia Livissianos and Jack Nicholson; Dr Roger Douglas; Jane Turner Goldsmith; and the editors of this book.

jurisprudence[3] has also served to promote discussion, and even vigorous debate, about the proper functions of Australia's highest courts. Public recognition of the creative role played by appellate level judges has inevitably led to the politicisation of the judiciary especially in the federal sphere, where judges must confront questions about the exercise of public power and important constitutional and other issues. Judges, it seems, and especially federal judges, are more likely now to be seen widely as political as well as legal actors.

Questions about judicial function increasingly seem to be linked to questions about the appointment and training of judges. As the impersonal and disinterested exercise of judicial power is exposed to greater examination and indeed scepticism, curiosity about those who exercise this power has grown. In this vein, the representativeness of the judiciary has become a matter for public discussion, following the suggestion in some quarters that the judiciary should fairly reflect its society.[4] In general terms, the political motives, actual or attributed, of our most senior judges are more frequently in the spotlight now than in past generations. While the belief that politics and judging are distinct activities that need to be kept separate was once widely held, or at least not commonly challenged, judges now face a less credulous media and public. And even though judges continue to insist upon a separation between their professional judgments and their personal opinions, concerned as they rightly are about public confidence in the judiciary,[5] it is no longer the case that their observers, critics, or indeed in some instances supporters, will accept the previous tendency towards mystery and ignorance about the judicial role and those who exercise it. Judicial institutions, like other public institutions, are being subjected to unprecedented levels of surveillance.

In struggling to identify and understand the political or indeed other motivations of our judges, it is not uncommon, and indeed is understandable, to want to know more about just who our judges

---

[3] See *Australian Capital Television Pty Ltd v Commonwealth* (1992) 177 CLR 106; *Theophanous v Herald & Weekly Times Ltd* (1994) 182 CLR 104.

[4] This proposal—Commonwealth Attorney-General's Department (1993)—is critically discussed in King (1995) 14–15. See also Sir Anthony Mason (1997) 7–9.

[5] See Handsley (1998).

are. Generally speaking, apart from obvious conclusions about the dominance of the judiciary by men, information of this kind in Australia has not been readily or systematically available. I will endeavour here to provide a profile of the social and professional backgrounds of federal judges in Australia, focusing upon the members of the High Court, the Federal Court and the Family Court.[6] The purpose of this empirical examination lies in the widely presumed relationship between the prior socialisation of judicial members and their judicial behaviour. Few people today would see judicial decision-making behaviour as simply the product of the mechanical interpretation of legal principles and rules (the literalist approach). Indeed, many judges themselves have contributed to the re-examination of this traditional approach.[7] Besides the judges, many ordinary citizens have become increasingly aware of, and have started to participate in, discussions of policy issues at the heart of judicial decisions. Increased scepticism towards the literalist approach and claims of judicial neutrality has also been promoted by elements within the academic community.[8]

Underlying this interest, explicitly or implicitly, is a focus upon the notion of judicial legitimacy. Doubts about judicial motives or techniques throw public estimation of the judiciary into question. Some legal academics have played a part in this, raising questions about the social influences upon judges under a variety of theoretical banners: sociological jurisprudence, legal realism, critical legal studies, and the sociology of law, to name the main contenders.[9] But from a more practical point of view, the indisputable power and influence of judges in public affairs, and especially the administration of justice, makes the quest to find and fathom those principles governing the exercise of their influence both foreseeable and sensible.

---

[6] The Industrial Relations Court of Australia has now effectively been abolished (see Chapter 5). It was not included as a separate court for the purposes of the present study as all remaining judges of the Court hold concurrent commissions as judges of the Federal Court.

[7] The contribution of Sir Anthony Mason, former Chief Justice of the High Court, is notable in this respect.

[8] See, for example, Sexton and Maher (1982) ch. 1.

[9] On these movements see Freeman (1994).

2 The Backgrounds of Judges—the Theory

As Lawrence Baum points out, 'most studies of the impact of justices' personal attributes or social background characteristics rest on the premise that these characteristics shape policy preferences, which in turn determine justices' positions in cases'.[10] In the American literature, there has been an attempt among some political scientists to produce predictive models of judicial behaviour, explaining variation in judicial positions along a spectrum between liberal and conservative stances on controversial issues. In the United Kingdom, the work of public lawyer John Griffith on the judiciary of England and Wales has been devoted to explaining the relative homogeneity of viewpoints he finds among the judiciary when they are confronted by cases with strong political connotations. For American scholars, examining the social backgrounds of United States judges is one way of seeking to explain variations in decision-making process and outcomes, while for Griffith, it becomes a means of understanding the rather unitary outlook and approach of the Law Lords. He writes of the highest levels of the judiciary in England and Wales: 'These judges have by their education and training and the pursuit of their profession as barristers, acquired a strikingly homogenous collection of attitudes, beliefs and principles, which to them represent the public interest. They do not always express it as such. But it is the lodestar by which they navigate'.[11]

A range of personal attributes have been considered by the (mainly American) literature dealing with judges' social and professional backgrounds. Gerard Gryski and Elenor Main have posited four personal attribute models: demographic (looking at circumstances at birth, upbringing, and education); prior experience (previous kinds of appointment); age and tenure (length of time as a judge, impact of age); and partisanship and ascension to the bench (party affiliation, method of appointment).[12] I examine a range of factors suggested by each of these models (but mainly the first three), making allowances for variations between Australian and

---

[10] Baum (1997) 26.
[11] Griffith (1997) 295.
[12] Gryski and Main (1986) 529–30.

United States judicial practice and the available data.[13] It is worth noting that there has been very little scholarship of this kind in Australia, and none at all in recent decades.[14]

How much reliance can be placed upon inferences of judicial behaviour from examinations of social background is controversial and problematic. Socialisation is undoubtedly relevant to explaining and understanding variations in any practice, judicial or otherwise. However, what is less clear in the judicial arena is how often pre-dispositions acquired through socialisation are reflected in particular decisions. Attitudes acquired through individual social experiences may not always be reflected in behaviour, especially when that behaviour occurs within professional contexts. The profession of judging, like other professions, carries with it various standards, traditions, and conventions of practice which influence and, presumably in many cases, restrict the exercise of judicial power. In other words, judges as a group may well affect how an individual judge acts. Moreover, the very public nature of most judicial functions would seem likely to make it at least more difficult for a judge to follow a legally irrelevant predisposition from his or her background in reaching a professional judgment. Apart then from a few profound sceptics, few knowledgeable observers of judicial practice would accept the view of judging reflected in the hoary chestnut—a crude reduction of the Legal Realist position—that a judge's decision often simply depends upon what he or she had for breakfast that morning.[15] Most informed commentators would accept that the law constrains the influence of non-legal factors upon judicial decision-making and case outcomes.[16] At this point then, we are a long way short of having strongly predictive models connecting judges'

---

[13] Political appointments of judges are relatively infrequent in Australia, and tend not to be acknowledged as such when they occur. Thus, it is more difficult in a study of this kind in Australia to find data on partisanship.

[14] For a study of High Court judges from 1903 to 1972, see Neumann (1973). See also Blackshield (1972); Blackshield (1978); Schubert (1968a); Schubert (1968b); Schubert (1969a); Schubert (1969b).

[15] On realism, see Freeman (1994).

[16] In criminal sentencing it is clear that legal variables such as offence severity and criminal history are, independently of other variables, strongly predictive of case outcomes. See, for example, J. Dixon (1995) 1157–98.

background characteristics with their decision-making behaviour. Two leading theorists in the area, Sidney Ulmer and James Gibson, separately have called for more work to be done on the processes linking backgrounds to behaviour.[17]

However, the scholarly caution in this area in no way diminishes the legitimate interest in the social attributes of our most senior and influential judges. The quest for greater understanding of judicial backgrounds seems set to continue. While we cannot yet be sure when or to what degree background attitudes and attributes will influence specific case decisions, there is sufficient empirical knowledge as well as common sense that indicates there is a likelihood that judges will, under certain (though still not wholly known) conditions, allow their backgrounds to influence their decision-making function. This is not to impute impropriety to individual judges or to judges as a group, but rather to admit that socialisation can influence subsequent conduct, even when we are talking about professional judges acting under the mediating influence of law. As Benjamin Cardozo remarked:

> The spirit of the age, as it is revealed to each of us, is too often only the spirit of the group in which the accidents of birth or education or occupation or fellowship have given us a place. No effort or revolution of the mind will overthrow utterly and at all times the empire of these subconscious loyalties.[18]

As the political quality of much judicial work becomes more visible, especially through discussion of particular decisions in the public arena, it is only natural that we should want to know more about those in high judicial office.

3 The Study

This empirical examination of the social backgrounds of Australia's federal judges seeks mainly to reveal information on a variety of specific background characteristics of members of the three principal courts constituting the federal judiciary: the High Court, the

---

[17] Gibson (1983) 26; Ulmer (1986) 965.
[18] Cardozo (1949) 174–5.

Federal Court of Australia and the Family Court of Australia. It does not presume to go so far as to draw firm inferences about judicial attitudes or values from the findings. However, it does seek to map shifts in social and professional background between 1978 and 1998 by comparing features of the membership of the three courts in each of these years. The attributes considered for the most part emerge from the personal attribute models discussed earlier. Thus, age, age at appointment, gender, place of birth, type of schooling, type of university education, place of university education, religious affiliations and recreational interests are examined. Aspects of professional career background prior to judicial appointment are also considered, in particular experience as a Queen's Counsel (or, as they are now referred to in New South Wales, 'Senior Counsel'),[19] practice as a barrister, practice as a solicitor, academic experience, involvement in politics and the military, and contributions to professional associations. In this way, an attempt is made to identify a variety of potential background characteristics that may define paths to appointment as a federal judge.

By making comparisons across time, as well as between the constituent courts of the federal judiciary, internal differences between the courts should emerge where they exist and some sense of historical trajectory regarding the social composition of the judiciary can be identified. Consequently, the study deals with the composition of the courts as at June 1998 (including Chief Justice Gleeson and Justice Callinan on the High Court), and the composition in 1978 as determined by the lists of judges for the three courts published in volumes of the *Federal Law Reports* and the *Family Law Reports* for that year.

The data is derived from two principal sources: the 1978 and 1998 volumes of *Who's Who in Australia*, and *Biographies of Federal Judges*, a publication of the Commonwealth Attorney-General's Department. In particular respects, information has been supplemented from other sources, including newspaper articles, published biographies and website addresses of the relevant courts.

---

[19] For convenience and consistency with practice in most Australian states, this group is referred to simply as 'QCs'.

Supplementation of data has occurred mainly in the case of High Court judges where it was suspected other sources would readily reveal information relevant to the study. It should therefore be clear that the data collected is publicly available, and also, for the most part, limited to the kind of information available from official biographies and self-reported information in *Who's Who in Australia*. The fact that so much of the information relied upon was self-reported means that there was often variation between judges on the amount of information available. This consideration affected the counting procedures as well as the interpretations of the data, as a failure to report on a particular background characteristic had to be counted as 'missing' rather than as a negative on the particular feature. For this reason, for interpretive purposes, it should be noted that the study focuses upon numbers of reports of specific background characteristics, rather than absolute incidences of those characteristics.

There are doubtless limitations in relying on such a database. In a number of instances, judges have provided little or no information on particular social background characteristics. Religious affiliation is one example, so discussion of this point is not based upon data provided by the present study. Another social characteristic, parental background, was also inadequately covered by the data chosen for the study and so has not been discussed here. The sample sizes therefore vary for different characteristics. The method adopted was commensurate with the available time and resources. In contrast to the earlier study of members of the High Court by Eddy Neumann which looked into the backgrounds of 26 members of the High Court,[20] this study deals with a much larger group of federal judges. This study draws upon data relating to 100 of the 107 federal judges listed in 1998, and 70 of the 71 listed federal judges in 1978. In this sense, it is not as complete as Neumann's study of the High Court, which considered all High Court justices appointed between 1903 and 1972. Despite variations in response numbers, the study draws upon a fairly comprehensive data set in terms of the number of judges for whom data is held. One must be careful, however, in interpreting the statistics from such a database. This is why I have

---

[20] Neumann (1973).

tended to refer to 'reports' of particular characteristics, rather than implying or suggesting that the sample is complete, and have sought to be careful in drawing inferences.

4 Age

The conservatism of the bench is associated for many people with the relatively advanced age of judges. Former legal scholar and United States Supreme Court justice, Oliver Wendell Holmes, who himself continued to sit on the Supreme Court into his early nineties, observed that 'judges commonly are elderly men, and are more likely to hate at sight any analysis to which they are not accustomed, and which disturbs repose of mind, than to fall in love with novelties'.[21] Given the typical career trajectory of judges in common law countries in which judicial appointment has followed often extensive careers in legal practice, the fact that Australian judges are at least middle-aged at the time of their appointment should surprise relatively few. It hardly needs pointing out that we know more now than twenty years ago about the effects of advancing age upon mental capacities and attitudinal characteristics. This knowledge has enabled some scholars to explore the relationship between age and judicial character.[22]

The present study reveals that in 1978 the average age of federal judges was 53 years, whereas in 1998 it was 58 years. This apparent increase is in spite of the introduction of the restriction upon holding federal judicial office beyond the age of 70 years, introduced for new appointees by constitutional amendment in 1977.[23] What is apparent, however, is that this change means that there are now fewer serving judges in their seventies or above than just a few decades ago.[24] Interestingly, in 1998 the average age for each of the three federal courts was virtually identical, at 58 years,

---

[21] Oliver Wendell Holmes (1920) 61.

[22] Schubert (1983).

[23] Prior to 1992, Family Court judges were required under s 23A of the *Family Law Act 1975* (Cth) to retire at 65. This section was repealed by the *Family Law Amendment Act (No 2) 1991* (Cth), s 3. Family Court judges are now appointed to the age of 70.

[24] Among Sir Owen Dixon's generation, it was not unusual for High Court judges to continue serving until well into their eighties. See Barwick (1995) 208.

whereas two decades earlier, as might have been predicted, the average age for judges in the three courts varied from 60 years (High Court) to 56 years (Federal Court) to 49 years (Family Court). As many High Court judges held judicial office prior to their appointment to the High Court, in several instances in the Federal Court, the 1998 figures, in contrast to the earlier figures, are counter-intuitive. This seems to suggest that the present federal judiciary is characterised by a significant band of judges in their sixties. This concentration would make sense in terms of other aspects of the current picture, namely compulsory retirement at 70 years, and a trend towards younger appointees.

When we look at age at time of appointment, we see that, across the three courts, the average age in 1998 was 48 years, three years younger than the average age in 1978. While age at appointment to the High Court has continued to average 54 years, the average age of appointment for Federal Court judges has dropped significantly from 55 to 49 years, and in the Family Court it has fallen from 48 to 45 years. The Family Court has continued to appoint the youngest judges, appointing them as early as 37 years of age, while the Federal Court in recent years has received judges in their late thirties (39), a shift from two decades ago when the youngest appointment was made at 43 years of age. The tendency to younger appointments is even reflected in the High Court. Whereas in 1978 the age of the youngest appointment to the High Court was 47 years, by 1998 it had fallen to 44 years. So in all, while the present average age of federal judges is higher than it was twenty years ago, changes in the law meant that there are fewer judges in their seventies, while there is an apparent trend towards appointing judges at a younger age in each of the three courts.

5 Gender

While in the past decade there has been a profound increase in the number of women studying law and qualifying for admission to practise, men continue to dominate the upper echelons of the profession and the judiciary.[25] But things are changing. Whereas twenty

---

[25] In 1996, women constituted 53 per cent of Australian law students: see Centre for Legal Education (1997) 29.

years ago there were very few women judges and they were to be found in the Family Court, by 1998 we find a significant increase in female representation across the three federal courts. Comparing the figures of the present study, only the Family Court had female judges in 1978 (3 judges, representing nearly 8 per cent of the sample), but by 1998 there were four women appointed to the Federal Court and one to the High Court, an increase from 4 per cent to 17 per cent of overall appointments. The Family Court remains the federal court with highest female representation, a quarter of its judges being women (25 per cent).[26] In the Federal Court, the figure is closer to 1 in 10 judges (9 per cent),[27] while just 1 of the 7 High Court justices (14 per cent) is female (see Table 1).

Table 1   Gender composition of the three courts in 1978 and 1998

Court	1978				1998			
	Male		Female		Male		Female	
	No.	%	No.	%	No.	%	No.	%
High Court	7	100	0	–	6	86	1	14
Federal Court	26	100	0	–	43	91	4	9
Family Court	35	92	3	8	40	75	13	25

Thus, the Family Court continues to be the federal court of greatest opportunity for aspiring women judges. There have, however, been modest improvements in gender balance across the board. The stronger representation of women among Family Court judges is hardly surprising, given the stereotypes about women practitioners that have long existed within the profession,[28] and the fact that

---

[26] According to statistics kept by the Australian Institute of Judicial Administration, as at 28 April 1998, 11 of the 53 Family Court judges were women. The difference in these figures compared with those obtained from Who's Who and the published court lists in the relevant law reports is somewhat puzzling. It may be explicable in terms of different sampling moments for the two sources. However, given the present study's general reliance upon these sources, no specific attempt was made to reconcile the figures obtained from them with the figures from the Australian Institute of Judicial Administration.

[27] According to the Australian Institute of Judicial Administration, at the same date only 4 of the 46 Federal Court judges (8.7 per cent) were female, a smaller percentage than was indicated by the sample.

[28] Thornton (1996).

in comparison to other areas of practice many family law practitioners have been women. Family law itself is widely viewed within the legal profession as a highly specialised area, such that those whose experience has been in other areas of legal work are unlikely to be suitable for appointment to the Family Court.[29] The irony, of course, is that so long as female lawyers continue to find better opportunities in this area of practice, it is likely that the representation of women on the Family Court will continue to be greater than in the other federal courts.

6   Ethnicity and Place of Birth

Neumann's study revealed that until 1972 at least, there had only been one appointee to the High Court whose antecedents did not derive wholly from the British Isles. That exception was Sir Isaac Isaacs, whose father was a Polish Jew, and whose mother was an English Jew.[30] In terms of the present study however, there was relatively little available data on this issue. Of the handful of federal judges in 1978 for whom this information existed, all were born in Australia. In 1998, of the 44 judges for whom this information was available, only 4 reported being born outside Australia, while the other 40 were Australian-born. Of those born overseas, two were Family Court judges and two were Federal Court judges. No High Court justice fell into this category. Three of the 4 judges had been born in the United Kingdom, while one (Justice Finkelstein) was born in Germany. While a number of other federal judges have family names suggestive of ethnic backgrounds, the available data did not permit a closer examination of ethnic backgrounds or place of birth. Firm conclusions on shifts in this area are therefore virtually impossible. However, it might be noted that the apparent absence in 1998 of federal judges with non-European birth or ethnic back-

---

[29] A review of the biographical material for this study indicates that most appointments to the Family Court since its formation have been of persons who have had extensive, and sometimes exclusive, practices in family law. In many cases, the appointees have held positions in the family law sections of their legal professional bodies, as well as having extracurricular involvement in issues such as marriage guidance and child protection.

[30] Neumann (1973) 16.

grounds is arguably consistent with post-World War II patterns of migration, in which migrants were principally European in origin, at least until the 1970s. It is still unlikely that migrants from more recent intakes from Asia and other parts of the world will have had sufficient time to achieve the qualifications and general level of practical experience—not less than fifteen, and typically twenty years—which characterise appointments to either the Federal or Family Court. However, given the greater diversity of immigration intakes in the past two decades, it can only be a matter of time before this picture starts to change.

7 Secondary Education

Education is generally treated by social commentators as a fairly strong indicator of socioeconomic background, though there are undoubtedly significant numbers of individual cases in which it is less indicative of significant family wealth. A few years ago, Justice Peter Heerey of the Federal Court of Australia expressed the view that 'educational background is one of the few objective criteria that the public can look to in assessing the worth of current criticism of the Australian judiciary'.[31] As one might have predicted, the present study found an overwhelming number of judges had undertaken their secondary education in Australia, and that a substantial majority attended private rather than government schools. Less than a handful of federal judges were educated at secondary level anywhere else but Australia, a finding broadly similar to the position two decades ago.

Regarding the type of secondary school attended, Justice Heerey produced his own calculations of schools attended by members of the High and Federal Courts in his closing remarks to the 1993 Australian Legal Convention. He sought to draw a distinction within the private school category between elite 'APS/GPS'[32] (mainly non-Catholic) schools, and 'Catholic etc', the latter comprising those schools, principally Catholic, 'which would not be regarded as

---

[31] Heerey (1993) 67.

[32] These terms refer to 'Associated Public Schools' and 'Greater Public Schools', associations or groupings of independent or private schools.

particularly privileged'.[33] On these categories, he found that for the High Court, the figures were: APS/GPS 2 (28 per cent); government 2 (28 per cent); and Catholic 3 (43 per cent). For the Federal Court, his figures were: APS/GPS 38 per cent; government 41 per cent; and Catholic 21 per cent. His conclusion was that in both courts, a substantial majority of judges came from what he termed 'non-privileged educational backgrounds'.[34]

The survey material from the present study on type of secondary education was limited, so caution is necessary in using and interpreting the figures obtained. However, in terms of type of school attended, less than a quarter (23 per cent) of federal judges in 1978 (44 of 57 reports) had attended a government school. In other words, an average of more than 3 in 4 (77 per cent) federal judges for whom data existed had attended some kind of non-government school. Little seems to have changed in the intervening years. Of the 76 judges for whom data was available in 1998, still only one-quarter (26 per cent) had attended government schools. To lend these figures some perspective, it is worth noting that in 1996, government schools accounted for 71 per cent of the total school population.[35] While we know that some federal judges did not have elite private secondary educations, the combined picture provided by this and Justice Heerey's study indicates that federal judges as a group still appear to be unrepresentative of the community at large, in the sense of being more likely to have gone to non-government, rather than government, schools.

Interestingly, the Federal Court seems to contain the highest percentage of government school graduates: 41 per cent (14 of the 34 for whom this information was available), an increase from 26 per cent (5 of 19) in 1978. The 1998 figures of the present study are

---

[33] Heerey (1993) 67.

[34] Ibid 67. Clearly, it makes sense to try to find meaningful distinctions within the category of private schools, particularly as this category seems to be becoming increasingly diverse. Doubtless there are differences between elite Catholic and some other Catholic secondary schools. Some of these schools charge fees comparable to the elite non-Catholic schools, while many others charge only nominal fees. Justice Heerey's figures do not tell us how many judges attended Catholic schools of any kind, in contrast to government or other kinds of school.

[35] Australian Bureau of Statistics homepage: http://www.statistics.gov.au

in this regard virtually identical to Justice Heerey's findings. In the High Court in 1998, the data indicates that only Justices Kirby and McHugh attended government schools (29 per cent). Twenty years ago 2 High Court justices could similarly claim not to have attended private schools. Justice Murphy attended Sydney Boys High School,[36] while former Chief Justice Barwick spent his secondary years at Cleveland Street Intermediate High School, followed by Fort Street High School.[37] Justice Kirby was also a student at Fort Street High.[38] In respect of the Family Court, the relatively small number of reports make it difficult to say whether there has been any shift away from non-government schools. The overall trend reported above and the figures obtained specifically for the Family Court do not suggest any such movement among its appointees.[39]

One of the interesting changes in patterns of secondary schooling between 1978 and 1998 is the diminished contribution made to the ranks of the federal judiciary by certain elite (and principally Anglican) private schools. The federal judiciary in 1998 is drawn from a wider range of schools, proportionately, than twenty years earlier. In 1978, three private schools stood out: Melbourne Grammar School, Sydney Grammar School, and St Peter's College (Adelaide), each of which contributed 5 members to the ranks of the federal judiciary. Contributions per school then fell away quite markedly; St Patrick's Melbourne (Catholic) contributed 3, followed by a number of private (mainly Catholic) schools and a few government high schools which could claim 2 members each: Xavier College (Melbourne), Rostrevor College (Adelaide), Scotch College (Melbourne), Melbourne High School, and North Sydney Boys High School.

In 1998, by comparison, only one school had contributed more than 3 members of the federal judiciary—Sydney Boys High School could claim 6 old scholars among the ranks of the federal judiciary, all of them appointed to the Federal Court. The range of schools

---

[36] Hocking (1997) 12.

[37] Marr (1980) 5–6.

[38] Kirby (1997) 521.

[39] If anything, the figures point the other way. However, the incomplete response set makes any firm conclusions either way unreliable.

with 3 old scholars among the federal judiciary shows some notice-
able diversification from 1978. The schools contributing 3 federal
judges each were: Scotch College (Melbourne), Sydney Church of
England Grammar School, St Peter's College (Adelaide), Fort Street
High School (Sydney), and Melbourne High School. The significant
representation of a number of government high schools among this
group is indeed striking. A number of private schools and one
government school can now claim to have 2 old scholars on the federal benches: Sydney Grammar School, Brisbane Grammar, Wesley
College (Melbourne), North Sydney High School, St Virgil's (Tasmania), Perth Modern School, Hale School (Perth), Scots College
(Sydney), and Melbourne Grammar School.

8 Tertiary Education

I have examined the incidence of university education among members of the federal judiciary, as well as the type of university education undertaken. The significant entry by university law schools
into the field of professional legal education after World War II has
meant that lawyers of senior standing today are more likely than
earlier generations of lawyers to have attended university in order to
study law and qualify for admission to practise. As well as looking
at whether federal judges studied law at university, I examined the
kind of degrees taken (honours, postgraduate), whether degrees in
other disciplines were also taken, where the tertiary education
occurred, and the university from which the law degree was taken.
As tertiary education has become a more common attribute of
lawyers, it is interesting to explore the extent to which membership
of the judiciary is characterised by particular educational paths or
attributes, and the degree to which our judges are pursuing
advanced degrees, education in other, non-legal, disciplines or both.

(a) Undergraduate degrees
Except for Justice McHugh of the present High Court, who
obtained his admission to practise through the New South Wales
Barristers Admission Board (now known as the Legal Practitioners
Admission Board), all judges in the 1978 and 1998 samples for
whom data was available had graduated from university. In the vast

majority of cases, it is clear that the degree was in law. Over-whelmingly, the university education undertaken by members of the federal judiciary occurred in Australia. In 1998, only 2 Family Court judges, less than 3 per cent of the sample, attended overseas universities for their basic university education. There were no such instances in the other two courts. More federal judges are now reporting having completed honours degrees in law; 14 judges in 1998, as opposed to only 1 in 1978. In the absence of better information on this point, it is difficult to infer too much about the significance of this variable.

There has been an interesting measurable shift in terms of the university law schools attended. In 1978, two university law schools (Sydney and Melbourne) accounted for nearly three-quarters (73 per cent) of the federal judiciary. At that time, the University of Adelaide could claim 8 federal judges, and the University of Queensland 6 (see Figure 1).

Figure 1   Universities attended by 1978 federal judiciary

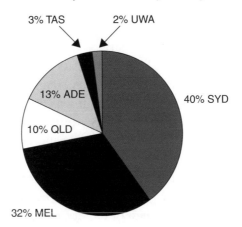

By 1998, the Sydney/Melbourne dominance had fallen to just over half the federal judges (54 per cent) for whom information was available (see Figure 2). The University of Adelaide could only claim 6 federal judges, while Queensland could now claim that its graduates held 14 judicial positions. The University of Sydney continues to dominate the High Court, with 4 of the 7 present justices as graduates (Gleeson, Gaudron, Gummow and Kirby).

Figure 2   Universities attended by 1998 federal judiciary

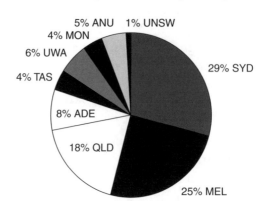

What is particularly interesting about the 1998 position is the not insignificant number of federal judicial posts held by graduates of 'second generation' universities, in particular Monash, the Australian National University, and the University of New South Wales. While none of these universities can yet claim a High Court judge among their graduates (nor can Adelaide or Tasmania), Monash can now claim 2 Federal Court judges and 1 Family Court judge, the Australian National University 3 Federal Court positions and 1 Family Court judge, and the University of New South Wales a Federal Court judge. In explaining this trend, we can consider as an example Monash law school, which was founded in the early 1960s and did not graduate its first class until the late 1960s. Given that the average age of appointment to first judicial office (late forties) is some twenty-five or so years after many law graduates finish university, one would not have predicted the appointment of judges from law schools such as Monash until the early 1990s. As more law schools reach their twentieth or twenty-fifth anniversaries, one would predict a further spread of appointments to the federal benches. It will be interesting to see what proportion of future appointments are from non-sandstone universities, and in particular, the extent to which the pre-eminence of Sydney and Melbourne suffers by the growth in the number of law schools.[40]

---

[40] Since 1987, the number of Australian law schools has more than doubled, from 13 to 29.

In terms of university education other than in law, there appears to be an upward trend—from 30 per cent of the 1978 sample to 39 per cent in 1998—in the number of federal judges with degrees in other disciplines as well as in law. This trend corresponds with the development of the 'joint' degree structure at many universities in the 1960s. Thus, those federal judges with degrees in other disciplines would also have completed law degrees. Australian judges, at least in recent decades, do not appear to have observed the once quite common practice among the senior judiciary of England and Wales of taking a degree in another discipline before completing professional training in law through the Inns of Court or in another non-university setting.[41]

(b) Postgraduate degrees

Another factor considered in the data was the incidence and type of postgraduate study, especially in law. As university education has become far more prevalent among lawyers in the past four decades, the number of those preparing for professional legal practice has risen dramatically, particularly in the last decade or so.[42] Postgraduate study has become one means of distinguishing oneself professionally. One might therefore predict that recent appointees to the federal judiciary are more likely than judges of an earlier era to have undertaken postgraduate study, either in Australia or overseas. The data indeed points in this direction. Whereas, in 1978, 10 members of the federal judiciary reported holding higher degrees of some kind, 20 federal judges made this claim by 1998. Putting to one side the 3 members of the current High Court with higher degrees, the remaining federal judges holding higher degrees were all members of the Federal Court. There were no reported higher degrees among members of the Family Court. In other words, approximately 40 per cent of both the High Court and Federal Court benches report having higher degrees of some kind.

---

[41] Weisbrot (1990) 121, 157.

[42] There are currently around 20 000 law students in Australia and around 30 000 lawyers in practice.

Overwhelmingly, these higher degrees are in law. Three of the federal judges held MAs, that is, degrees not clearly in law,[43] but in each case, the judge concerned also held a higher degree in law. The majority of judges (60 per cent) holding higher degrees had obtained them from overseas institutions (see Figure 3). Among the 9 judges holding LLM degrees in law from Australian universities, 5 had taken their degrees at the University of Sydney, 3 at the University of Melbourne, and 1 at the University of Queensland. Justices Gummow and Kirby of the High Court both hold LLMs from the University of Sydney. The universities attended and the relative proportions in this aspect bear a resemblance to the pattern described above with respect to undergraduate education.

Most judges who had taken degrees from overseas universities had taken the LLM degree, although 4 Federal Court judges also reported holding doctorates.[44] The overwhelming number of postgraduate degrees in law, unsurprisingly, were from London, Oxford,[45] Cambridge, Yale, and Harvard universities. The distribution among these universities was surprisingly even. Among those holding doctorates, Justice Lindgren holds a PhD from the University of London, while Justice Paul Finn holds a PhD from Cambridge University.[46] Somewhat unusually against this 'Ivy League' background, Justice Einfeld holds two doctoral degrees from lesser-known American universities: a PhD from Pacific Western University and an LLD from Century University (USA).

Looking at these figures by individual court, the striking contrast between the Federal and Family Courts bears further consideration. Why Family Court judges by background should have been less likely to undertake postgraduate study is not obvious, and warrants further examination. The relatively specialised nature of family law practice, in comparison to the broader fields of commercial

---

[43] It was not possible from the database to determine in which discipline the degree had been conferred.

[44] Honorary doctorates were not included for the purposes of these calculations.

[45] Justices Hayne (High Court) and Sundberg (Federal Court) hold the Oxford Bachelor of Civil Laws (BCL) degree. As this degree is widely equated with the LLM degree from other universities, I have not sought to distinguish it.

[46] While Justice Sundberg also holds a PhD, the available data did not disclose from which institution it was awarded.

Figure 3   Place of postgraduate study by court

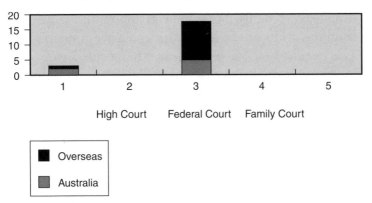

litigation or regulatory matters, may disincline those interested in family law from taking the typical LLM degree, involving four or more courses from different areas of law. This aside, the distinctive character of the Federal Court is further underlined by the incidence (albeit in only a handful of cases) of doctorates among its members, in contrast to both the High and Family Courts. This may well be attributable to the greater number of former full-time academics appointed to the Federal Court. Certainly, both Justices Finn and Lindgren spent considerable periods as legal academics prior to their appointment to the Federal Court. While former Justice Nygh of the Family Court was a full-time academic with a doctorate prior to his appointment to the Family Court, his case appears to be unusual for that jurisdiction.[47] Exploration of the reasons for such a concentration of postgraduate degrees among members of the Federal Court must be left for others. Given current demographic trends in this area, however, one might readily predict the further growth of postgraduate studies among members of the federal judiciary as a whole.[48] Especially given the recent growth of specialised LLM degrees in fields such as family law, it seems unlikely that the present pattern among Family Court judges will continue for much longer.

---

[47] In 1978, there were two higher degrees reported among members of the Family Court.

[48] The growth in the range of postgraduate courses in law and related areas in recent years has been quite striking. In 1996, there were nearly 4000 postgraduate law students: see Centre for Legal Education (1997) 52.

9 Professional Career Paths

It has long been recognised that judicial appointments are typically
made from the ranks of barristers with extensive courtroom experience. The justification for this practice has tended to be the perceived necessity for judges to have extensive exposure to the rules of
evidence and procedure, areas of professional knowledge and experience less commonly associated with solicitors' work or academic
life. Consequently, those appointed to judicial office have often
received prior recognition of their abilities as advocates through the
award of professional honours such as Queen's Counsel or (in New
South Wales) Senior Counsel. Professional distinction among lawyers can also be measured by achievement of high office within
relevant professional bodies, in particular the barristers' professional associations. Alternatively, appointees to the federal bench
are likely to have first served as a judge of a state (usually superior)
court. Another line of professional advancement to the federal judiciary may be through government service, for example, as Solicitor-
General, or following occupation of high political office, perhaps as
Attorney-General. These career possibilities were considered in relation to the available data on the federal judiciary in 1978 and
1998.

(a) How many federal judges were Queen's Counsel?

Not surprisingly, a substantial number of appointments to the federal judiciary are made from the ranks of Queen's Counsel. This
would seem to be particularly true of the High and Federal Courts.
Nearly half (47 per cent) of the 1978 sample reported being made
QCs at an earlier stage of their career, while 41 per cent of the 1998
group fell into this category. Given the data limitations, this difference is unlikely to be significant. However, once again, the contrast
between the Family and the other federal courts is quite striking. In
1998, while some 28 Federal Court judges (66 per cent) reported
having been appointed QCs, only 6 of 50 Family Court judges (12
per cent) reported being QCs prior to appointment. The situation
was broadly similar in this regard in 1978, when 80 per cent of
Federal Court judges, as opposed to 15 per cent of Family Court
judges indicated prior appointment as a QC. One apparent consistency in appointment practice is reflected in the prevalence of QCs on

the High Court. In both 1978 and 1998, all 7 High Court justices had been QCs prior to taking up their present positions. Justice Mary Gaudron, to date the only female justice on the High Court, was also the first woman QC appointed to the Sydney Bar.[49]

(b) How many have been solicitors?

As a general proposition, it is probably true to say that persons are less likely in Australia than in the United Kingdom to become barristers or judges without having also spent some time in solicitors' practice. In the United Kingdom, there is a longstanding tradition of election at the professional training stage between qualifying for barristers' or solicitors' admission, with the result that many barristers in England and Wales practise as barristers with no previous experience as a solicitor.[50] Of course in Western Australia, South Australia and, technically at least, Victoria, lawyers receive a common admission to practise as barristers and solicitors of the Supreme Court of their respective states. This has tended to have the effect of promoting a career path for the overwhelming majority of lawyers at least initially through solicitor practice, however brief the period. Even with the growth of separate bars in the so-called 'unified profession' states, there is a higher probability that judges from those states will have had at least some background as solicitors.

More federal judges now report prior experience as solicitors. In 1978, only 14 per cent indicated experience as solicitors, whereas this had risen to 48 per cent in 1998. Perhaps not surprisingly, this was most evident among Family Court judges (54 per cent), though 42 per cent of Federal Court judges also indicated prior experience as solicitors, a substantial rise from the 8 per cent reported two decades earlier. It would seem that even members of the High Court are more likely to have worked as solicitors at some time. While in 1978 only 1 appeared to have previous experience as a solicitor, 4 of the 1998 High Court so reported. The database for this study did not enable the determination in sufficient numbers of the extent or type of solicitor practice undertaken by federal judges. However, many individual biographies for Family Court judges suggested a

---

[49] Davies and Smark, *Sydney Morning Herald*, 10 July 1993, 42.
[50] See Lord Chancellor's Advisory Committee on Legal Education and Conduct (1996).

strong background in family law practice, as solicitors as well as barristers. A future study of Australian judges would do well to look more closely at the kinds of practice that have led to judicial appointment. Nevertheless, some further insight into judicial career paths is available through considering the appointments held by federal judges prior to their present positions.

(c) Position immediately prior to current appointment

In 1998, a significant number of federal judges (around 1 in 4) were appointed to their current positions from judicial positions on state Supreme Courts. In 1978, nearly 30 per cent of appointees to federal courts were from Supreme Court positions. This pattern has been particularly true of the High Court, where 50 per cent or more of appointments have been from these state courts. It is also true, though to a lesser extent, of the Federal Court (approximately 1 in 3), but only rarely so in the case of the Family Court (around 1 in 20 appointments). The latter finding is not really surprising, given the predominant federal responsibility for family-related matters since 1975. As most family law work takes place before the Family Court, there is less opportunity within this field of practice to obtain experience relevant to appointment as a state judge. After previous appointment to state Supreme Courts, the next most likely category of prior position is that of barrister, followed in 1998 by judicial service at the County/District Court level, and government legal service.

Of the present High Court, 3 members (Gleeson, Kirby and McHugh) came from the Supreme Court of New South Wales,[51] while Justice Hayne was appointed from the Supreme Court of Victoria. Justice Gummow previously served on the Federal Court. Of the 2 justices appointed from non-judicial backgrounds, Justice Gaudron previously served as New South Wales Solicitor-General, while Justice Callinan was appointed from the Queensland Bar.

(d) Earlier professional positions

In order to explore career paths further, the study also examined the position held prior to that from which the appointment to the federal judiciary was made. Here perhaps there were few surprises.

---

[51] Justices Kirby and McHugh came from the New South Wales Court of Appeal.

Nearly half (47 per cent) of the 1998 sample were practising as barristers, and approximately half of those as QCs. Twenty-two per cent were working as solicitors, while 18 per cent reported working in some other kind of judicial office. This pattern is broadly consistent with that revealed by the 1978 sample. In 1998, 4 members of the High Court (57 per cent) reported working as barristers at this stage of their career. Federal Court judges were almost as likely to report working as barristers (49 per cent), or in some kind of judicial office (23 per cent). Among Family Court judges, by comparison, nearly half the sample (47 per cent) reported working as barristers, though only 1 as a QC. Family judges were most likely to indicate working as solicitors at this stage of their careers (33 per cent), in contrast with Federal Court judges (10 per cent) and no High Court judges.

(e) Other work experience

When looking at other work experience, two factors were considered. One was prior involvement in academic work, and the other was participation in non-legal work of some kind. In view of limitations in the data set as well as issues raised by the social background literature, non-legal experience was confined to holding a political office, such as minister of government or member of parliament, and previous military experience.[52] The apparent political inclinations and backgrounds of judges inevitably raise questions about their reliability in terms of acting neutrally in the adjudication of disputes. In the United States, the notion of political appointment to judicial office is relatively commonplace, and it is hardly unknown either in Australia or in the United Kingdom.[53] Perhaps the most recent, and notorious, example in the Australian context was the appointment of former Labor Attorney-General, Lionel Murphy, to the High Court by the Whitlam government in 1975.[54] Finally, it was decided to include previous military experience as one indicator

---

[52] Some federal judges have achieved prominence and recognition in other fields of work, such as law reform (Justice Kirby) and Aboriginal land rights (former Justice Toohey).

[53] On changing attitudes to this issue among Lord Chancellors, see Griffith (1997) 16.

[54] Hocking (1997) 220–2.

of social background, given the availability of data on this factor. It is at least plausible that military service is indicative of conventional social values.

Undoubtedly, previous academic experience can vary in form significantly, from full-time academic teaching and research, perhaps over an extensive period, to a part-time position which is combined with full-time practise of law. Schmidhauser's study of the United States Supreme Court found that four justices (10 per cent of the sample) had worked principally in academic pursuits prior to appointment, while Neumann found no such career pattern among High Court justices.[55] It was decided nonetheless in the present study to examine whether there are any discernible patterns on this issue. It is sometimes said that the group from which judges are appointed needs to be broadened to include others with relevant legal skills. Legal academics are an obvious group for consideration, although many have had very limited or no prior experience in legal practice.

There has been an increase in the percentage of federal judges reporting some university teaching experience. Whereas in 1978, 14 per cent (10 cases) indicated such experience, by 1998, this had risen slightly to just 19 per cent (19 cases). Given the relatively small numbers involved, it is once again difficult to know how much significance to attach to these figures. However, as between courts (leaving aside the High Court), the figures suggest that Federal Court judges are more likely to have had teaching experience than Family Court judges. In 1978, 6 of the 10 judges reporting teaching experience came from the Federal Court, while two-thirds of the reported instances in 1998 (21 in total) were again Federal Court judges. As noted earlier, there may be some kind of correlation between higher degrees in law (greater in the case of the Federal Court) and previous academic teaching experience. Certainly, the Federal Court stands out in both these respects.

In relation to prior political involvement or military service, the political activities of two members of the High Court in 1978 are too well known to ignore. Before his appointment to the High Court, Justice Lionel Murphy had been a longstanding member of

---

[55] For both studies, see Neumann (1973) 72.

the Australian Labor Party as well as an Attorney-General in the Whitlam government.[56] Chief Justice Barwick had served in the Menzies government between 1958 and 1964, until 1963 as Attorney-General.[57] Barwick's autobiography indeed revealed that as a Cabinet Minister and former Attorney-General, he had proposed to then Prime Minister Menzies that only himself and Menzies had the appropriate administrative skills to fill the Chief Justice's position on the High Court following Sir Owen Dixon's retirement.[58] However, in contrast to the position in 1978, there are currently no former government ministers serving on the High Court, and indeed in the present study, no federal judge in 1998 reported party political involvements. In terms of military service, there has been a decline in the number of reports, from 26 cases (37 per cent) in 1978 to only 7 cases (7 per cent) in 1998. This might have been predicted, at least to some extent, given the different generations of judges in the federal courts in 1978 and 1998. A federal judge aged sixty in 1978 would have been twenty-one years old at the outbreak of World War II, whereas a judge of sixty in 1998 would have only been a year old at that time, and barely a teenager at the outbreak of the Korean War. In other words, a federal judge in 1978 is much more likely to have faced the prospect of military service than a judge twenty years later. It would take greater numbers of judges and a different kind of study to consider whether a judge with a military background during relatively peaceful times is inclined to have quite different attitudes and values to one whose military service coincided with large-scale war and the enlistment of large numbers of people.

(f) Office bearers in professional associations

Achieving high office within a particular professional body is widely seen as a substantial sign of recognition within that profession. It presumably also indicates a relatively high level of commitment to the traditions and values of that profession. Legal orthodoxy, historically speaking, has tended to sit well with ability as criteria for

---

[56] See Hocking (1997).

[57] Marr (1980) chs 12–15.

[58] Barwick (1995) 209.

appointment to the highest judicial ranks.[59] Thus, it would scarcely be surprising to find that former bar association presidents and other office holders of legal professional bodies featured conspicuously among the ranks of the federal judiciary. There is some data to support this proposition. In 1978, 1 in 5 federal judges (20 per cent) indicated previous responsibilities either as president or other office holder in relevant professional bodies such as bar associations and law societies. Two decades later, a slightly higher proportion (23 per cent) reported having previously occupied such positions. There are occasions where the commonality of interests between leaders of the practising profession and the judiciary becomes quite obvious. At times, for example, leaders of the legal profession have found it necessary to speak out in support of the judiciary after judges have been exposed to criticism from non-lawyers including politicians, or when there is a question regarding the adequacy of court resources.[60]

(g) Knighthoods, honours awards

When Murray Gleeson replaced Sir Gerard Brennan as Chief Justice of the High Court in 1998, the High Court ceased to contain members with knighthoods. In 1978, by contrast, only Justice Murphy did not hold a knighthood. Prior to the election of the Hawke government in 1983, there had existed a convention of appointments to the nation's highest court being offered knighthoods. With that government's abolition of federal Imperial honours, only those High Court justices appointed prior to the early 1980s were likely to be knighted. Four members of the present High Court have the AC (Companion of the Order of Australia), while three members (Callinan, Gaudron and Hayne) appear not to hold any such awards. Justice Kirby would seem to be the only member of the Court holding an Imperial honour, the award of CMG (Companion of the Order of St Michael and St George).

---

[59] Griffith makes this point in relation to the higher judiciary of England and Wales: Griffith (1997) 338.

[60] The Law Council of Australia, the umbrella body for Australian legal professional bodies, has played a significant role in this regard. The backlog of work in the Family Court has also seen representatives of the profession call for more resources for the Family Court.

Among the other federal benches, there are 3 holders of AOs (Officer of the Order of Australia) on the Federal Court, and a number of honours among Family Court judges, including 3 AOs, 2 AMs (Member of the Order of Australia), and 1 OBE (Officer of the Order of the British Empire). Among the Federal Court of 1978, there were a number of holders of Imperial honours, including 2 knighthoods, 2 OBEs, 2 CBEs (Commander of the Order of the British Empire), and 1 OStJ (Officer of the Order of St John of Jerusalem). For the Family Court in that year, only 1 honour, an OBE, was reported.

10 Religious Affiliation

A person's religious beliefs and affiliations tend to be highly personal matters. Perhaps for this reason, the database did not provide much significant information on the question of religious affiliation.[61] Either judges have less reason to self-report on such matters, or fewer of them maintain active religious involvements.[62] It is possible however to look not simply at current religious affiliations but also at past religious affiliations. In this regard there is other material available to interested researchers, particularly in respect of the type of secondary school attended. It is certainly possible to trace the religious affiliations of some federal judges, mainly High Court justices, through a variety of disparate sources, including biographies and newspaper articles. From a historical perspective, Neumann's study remains useful in this regard.[63]

Neumann's study, which concludes with the High Court bench in 1972, revealed the dominance of the Anglican denomination throughout the history of the Court.[64] Eleven of the 26 High Court

---

[61] In 1978, information was available for 26 of the 70 federal judges, while in 1998 it was available for only 20 of the 100 judges surveyed.

[62] Since 1990, the publishers of *Who's Who in Australia* have not solicited information on religious affiliation. In addition, data from the 1996 Census showed that some 16.6 per cent of Australians claimed 'no religion', an increase from the 12.9 per cent in the same category in the 1991 Census: Australian Bureau of Statistics homepage: http://www.statistics.gov.au

[63] Neumann (1973).

[64] Ibid 19.

justices to 1972 (42 per cent) had had some connection with the Anglican Church, while the next largest group, 5 justices (19 per cent), had Roman Catholic affiliations. Only 2 acknowledged no religion. There had only been 1 justice with Jewish affiliations (Sir Isaac Isaacs), while the remainder were either from Methodist (3 justices) or Presbyterian (4 justices) backgrounds. In 1978, the bench was under the direction of Sir Garfield Barwick, a man with a strong Protestant background, mainly in Methodism.[65]

By the 1990s, the High Court had become far more Catholic in its acknowledged religious affiliations. An article in 1993 by Davies and Smark on the High Court revealed a bench consisting almost entirely of either active Catholics or persons of Catholic background, with only Sir Daryl Dawson claiming a Protestant background.[66] This has continued to be true of the more recent High Court benches. When one considers the stewardship of the Court, the two previous Chief Justices (Mason and Brennan) as well as the current Chief Justice (Gleeson) have come to that position from Catholic backgrounds, measured in terms of either their current or past religious involvements or the nature of their secondary schooling.

The growth in numbers of judges with Catholic backgrounds on the High Court must, of course, be put in perspective by reference to figures on the general population. According to Australian Bureau of Statistics data from the 1996 Census, Catholics constitute 27 per cent of the Australian population, while Anglicans constitute 22 per cent. Other Christian denominations constitute 21.9 per cent, among which Uniting (7.5 per cent) Presbyterian and Reformed (3.8 per cent), and Orthodox (2.8 per cent) are the largest groups.[67] The increase in High Court judges with Catholic backgrounds is interesting for several reasons. While these figures show that currently and in recent times Catholics have constituted slightly more than 1 in 4 members of the general population, we have witnessed over the past two decades a shift to a striking predominance of High Court justices with Catholic backgrounds. This change is also

---

[65] See Marr (1980) chs 1 and 2.
[66] Davies and Smark, *Sydney Morning Herald*, 10 July 1993, 42. A former High Court justice, Sir Ronald Wilson, who retired in 1989, was (and remains) well known for his association with the Uniting Church.
[67] See Australian Bureau of Statistics homepage: http://www.statistics.gov.au

marked by the significant decline in the numbers of High Court justices with Anglican backgrounds since the period covered by Neumann's study. The decline in Anglican influence parallels the decline in Anglican numbers as reported by recent census data.[68]

It was more difficult to reach firm conclusions on the religious backgrounds of members of the Federal and Family Courts. Nonetheless, the available data, while far from complete, is suggestive of a significant representation of judges with Catholic backgrounds across the federal judiciary. Here, the data used pertained to the religious affiliation of secondary schools attended.[69] It was noted earlier, for example, that Justice Heerey's figures suggest that at least 21 per cent of federal judges attended Catholic schools, but his figures do not tell us, additionally, how many of the judges included within his elite category attended Catholic schools. From the present survey, we know that a number of elite Catholic schools have made significant contributions to the federal judiciary, including Xavier College and St Patrick's College, Melbourne, and Rostrevor College, Adelaide. As a second indicator of significant Catholic representation, among the far from complete samples of federal judges for whom this information was available both in 1978 and 1998, there was a substantial representation of judges with Catholic school backgrounds: 54 per cent in 1978, and 40 per cent in 1998.[70] This apparent over-representation of judges with Catholic school backgrounds may simply reflect a greater propensity by such people to disclose to *Who's Who* matters of religious background, though this seems unlikely. However, it cannot pass unnoticed that in both

---

[68] Between 1991 and 1996, the percentage of Anglicans fell from 23.8 per cent to 22 per cent; the percentage of Catholics fell only slightly, from 27.3 per cent to 27.0 per cent over the same period: Australian Bureau of Statistics homepage: http://www.statistics.gov.au

[69] Some might wish to distinguish between attending a religiously affiliated school and being a practising member of a denomination or religion. Partly due to unavailable relevant data, I have chosen to talk about religious school backgrounds in many instances, rather than limiting 'religious background' to current membership of religious groups. While not all students attending religious schools will adhere to that faith or practise it later in life, it still makes some sense to take into consideration exposure to particular religious beliefs at school.

[70] That is, in 1978, 14 of the 26 for whom this information was available. For 44 of the 70 judges surveyed, this information was not disclosed. In 1998 this figure represents 8 of the 20 for whom this information was available. In the cases of 80 judges, data was not available.

survey years, whatever the data source limitations, persons with Catholic school backgrounds were substantially over-represented in comparison to the Census picture of the proportion of Catholics—27 per cent in the general population in 1996.

11 Clubs and Recreational Interests

Only limited information was available under this heading, as federal judges in 1998 revealed relatively few club memberships, and permitted only fairly modest insight into their recreational interests. Among members of the High Court, justices continue to belong to clubs, but there would seem to be fewer memberships of establishment men's clubs (such as the Australian, Union, Melbourne, Savage clubs) than previously. In some cases, justices appear to have sporting club memberships (including Rugby Union and Australian Jockey Club) in lieu of the older style men's clubs, whereas in 1978, justices of the High Court would often report both kinds of memberships. Multiple memberships of establishment type clubs seems also to have diminished. Members of the Family and Federal Courts reported comparatively few club memberships, and those memberships reported were often likely to be of sporting clubs rather than establishment type clubs.

In terms of recreational interests, federal judges in 1998 appear as a whole still to be interested in sports of different kinds (54 per cent), a slight drop from the 64 per cent reporting this interest twenty years earlier. This seems particularly so in the case of judges of the Federal and Family Courts. Tennis, golf, sailing and cricket feature among the more popular judicial sporting pursuits. After sport, 1 in 5 judges (20 per cent) admits to enjoying music, and around 1 in 10 (11 per cent) lists reading as a pastime. A variety of other activities was reported, though typically not more than once each. Among the more idiosyncratic interests listed were poker, tai chi, and 'child management', while Justice Kirby of the High Court listed 'work' as his hobby.

12 Conclusion

This study has attempted to explore the nature of the backgrounds and career achievements of Australia's federal judges. As Australia has become home to people from a greater variety of social backgrounds, one can detect changes in the kinds of people appointed as federal judges in recent years. However, there are some clear limitations upon the extent of the changes and hence the representativeness of the judiciary. The Australian federal judiciary continues not to be representative of the population at large. It still does not, for example, have at least half its membership drawn from the female population, nor does it reflect the ethnic, religious or educational profile of Australia as a whole. However, in considering such questions it is sensible to remember that judges in common law countries such as Australia, unlike in civil law countries, are typically appointed in mid-life, after extensive careers as advocates before various courts. This is one reason why it is important to assess the backgrounds of judges not simply on demographic grounds such as age, birth and education, but also in terms of professional career paths. The fact that they are appointed in mid-life also means that current changes in some social background characteristics of the population as a whole, such as place of birth and school attended, will inevitably take some time, perhaps as long as fifty years, to filter through to the ranks of the various federal courts.

It therefore remains true overall, though less so now than in 1978, that federal judges are likely to be male, middle-aged, white, from a Christian (and quite likely Catholic rather than Protestant) background, educated at private rather than government schools, and to have spent significant periods of time prior to their appointment as barristers in private practice. While federal judges are still members of various clubs, these are less likely to be establishment type clubs than previously, and ever more likely to be sporting clubs. In 1998, members of the High Court are highly likely to come from Catholic backgrounds, if not also to be practising Catholics. Federal judges in 1998 are more likely to have been appointed in their late forties or early fifties, to have undertaken further study, more likely than not overseas, and to have spent time as solicitors or maybe in some kind of academic post. They are less likely to report strong political or religious affiliations than two decades ago. A significant change in the past twenty years has been the almost total disappearance from the federal judiciary of judges with Imperial honours; rather, today judges tend to hold Australian honours where they hold honours at all.

There are some interesting differences between the courts. Twenty years ago, both the Family and Federal Courts were relatively new entities. In the past two decades, they have tended to develop distinctive profiles. Family Court judges, in comparison with their fellow judges on the Federal Court, are more likely to have worked as solicitors, are less likely to have become QCs prior to appointment to the Family Court, and are less likely to have undertaken further academic study or to have worked in an academic position. They are also more likely than members of the other federal courts to be female and to have been appointed at a younger age than Federal Court judges. Although the federal judiciary is still dominated by judges educated at private schools, Federal Court judges today are more likely than judges of the other federal courts to have been educated at government secondary schools, in particular select high schools such as Sydney Boys High School.

What these patterns suggest about judicial attitudes and behaviour remains moot. The lack of recent local scholarship in this area may well reflect in part the considerable methodological difficulties of studying the relationship between individual attributes and professional behaviour. Judges also self-consciously continue to distance their personal opinions from their professional judgments, making the drawing of inferences in this area very difficult. As well as individual characteristics, we need to know more about the interactive effects upon individual behaviour of membership of particular professional communities such as judges and lawyers. For all the solitude of much of their work, judges remain social beings, so that understanding more about the contexts in which they operate is important.

The question of the representativeness of the judiciary will continue to be debated, as issues of inclusiveness and diversity play a larger part in discussions of fairness in the administration of justice. In this regard, we might well see more pressure for a wider range of appointments than has been the case in the past. Current as well as future moves to reduce the emphasis upon adversarial-type proceedings within the federal courts may well have an impact upon the kinds of persons seen as appropriate for appointment. The differences found between the Federal and Family Courts in this study may in fact indicate that changes of this kind are beginning to take effect.[71] However, a policy decision to change the mix of judges, determined by reference to their backgrounds, may not necessarily translate into significant changes of judicial outlook. As Griffith has argued, the effects of years in practice and middle-aged affluence might be expected to eliminate many, if not all, unorthodox political or social viewpoints among those considered for appointment.[72] Without greater transparency of appointment criteria, further changes to the litigation culture, and more public discussion of, and influence over, these issues, the nature of appointments to Australia's federal courts is likely to evolve gradually rather than shift radically in the coming years, much as it has done in the past twenty or so years.

---

[71] The Family Court's longstanding commitment to the provision of counselling services, and its more recent investment in family mediation are examples of procedural features which are at odds with the traditional litigation approach which relies substantially upon lawyer intervention and third party adjudication.

[72] Griffith (1997) 338.

13

The Appointment and Removal of Federal Judges

A. R. Blackshield*

1 The American Constitutional Provisions

For the framers of the United States Constitution, meeting at Phila-
delphia in 1787, the appointment of Supreme Court justices posed a
dilemma. Despite its novel federal features, their bicameral Congress
was essentially to inherit the powers of the British Parliament, and
their Presidency those of the British Crown. But to which institution
should judicial appointments be entrusted? James Wilson (Pennsyl-
vania) preferred the executive; John Rutledge (South Carolina) preferred the legislature, as had most of the states.[1]

In the end the Convention chose both. By Article II s 2 of the
United States Constitution, the President 'shall nominate, and by
and with the Advice and Consent of the Senate, shall appoint Ambassadors, other public Ministers and Consuls, Judges of the supreme
Court'.

The removal of Supreme Court justices attracted less attention.
Article III s 1 affirmed that 'the Judges, both of the supreme and
inferior Courts, shall hold their Offices during good Behaviour'; and

---

[1] Benton (1986) vol. 2, 1228, 1229–44.

* With research assistance from Belinda Baker.

that affirmation was understood (as in England) as ensuring irremovability while good behaviour continued. But, as Isaac Isaacs pointed out at the Australasian Federal Convention in 1898, no clear procedure for removal was specified: 'No mode of removing them is mentioned, except that by a construction of the Constitution they are held as civil officers to be liable to impeachment'.[2] That is, by the debatable construction of treating them as 'civil Officers', judges were brought within the general provision in Article II s 4. This section provided that 'The President, Vice President and all civil Officers of the United States, shall be removed from Office on Impeachment for, and Conviction of, Treason, Bribery, or other high Crimes and Misdemeanors'.

The only grounds for impeachment were 'Treason, Bribery, or other high Crimes and Misdemeanors'. Yet judicial tenure 'during good Behaviour' under Article III s 1 had a positive and a negative import: a judge maintaining standards of 'good Behaviour' could not be removed, but one who failed to do so could be removed. Did that mean that the executive branch retained an independent discretion to terminate a judicial appointment for want of 'good Behaviour'? Or did it mean that the formula 'high Crimes and Misdemeanors' must be stretched to encompass misbehaviour?

Such questions reproduced the position then obtaining in England under s 3 of the *Act of Settlement 1701*,[3] which provided that (after 1714) 'Judges Commissions be made *Quandiu se bene gessirint* [during good behaviour] . . . but upon the Address of both Houses of Parliament it may be lawful to remove them'. Was such an address the only means of enforcing the 'good behaviour' condition? Or were there in England two modes for removal of judges —a parliamentary address (on unspecified and hence unlimited grounds), and a continuing power, vested in the Crown, of removal for misbehaviour? In England, that ambiguity was resolved by s 5 of the *Supreme Court of Judicature Act 1875* (UK),[4] which expressed the 'good behaviour' condition to be 'subject to a power of removal by Her Majesty, on an address presented to Her Majesty by both

---

[2] Craven (1986) (1898 Convention, Melbourne) 311.
[3] 12 & 13 Will III c 2.
[4] 38 & 39 Vic c 77.

Houses of Parliament'.[5] This seemed to make removal on address the only permissible option. Yet in 1892 Sir William Anson continued to insist that a royal power of removal for misbehaviour had survived as an independent alternative; and in 1897 Isaac Isaacs insisted that this was still the position.[6]

In practice, by 1787, it seems to have been accepted in England that parliamentary address was the only mode of removal: any remaining ambiguity was a matter for academic debate.[7] Similarly, in the United States, it seemed to be accepted from the outset that removal was by impeachment alone. But that meant that the limits of the formula 'high Crimes and Misdemeanors' would be tested by a wide and unpredictable range of allegations.

Whatever the criteria under Article II s 4, the inclusion of judges among 'civil Officers' brought into play the clearly defined procedure in Article I. In that Article 'the sole Power of Impeachment' (that is, of framing articles of impeachment) is vested in the House of Representatives (s 2 cl 5) and 'the sole Power to try all Impeachments' is vested in the Senate, with a two-thirds majority required for conviction (s 3 cl 6). The effect of a successful impeachment (without excluding collateral criminal prosecution where appropriate) is confined to 'removal from Office, and disqualification to hold and enjoy any Office of honor, Trust, or Profit under the United States' (s 3 cl 7).

Effectively, therefore, the power of appointment of judges in the United States is shared between President and Senate. The power of removal is entrusted exclusively to the Senate, in response to articles of impeachment framed by the House of Representatives.

2 The American Experience of Appointment

Whether the American provisions have worked out as the framers intended is open to debate.[8] That Presidents (in making nominations) and senators (in giving or withholding consent) might be

---

[5] See now s 11(3) of the *Supreme Court Act 1981* (UK).

[6] Anson (1907) vol. 2, pt 1, 222–3; Craven (1986) (1897 Convention, Adelaide) 947–9.

[7] Shetreet (1976) 93–103; Hood Phillips and Jackson (1987) 387–8; Wade and Bradley (1993) 377.

[8] See generally Abraham (1974); Mitzner (1989); Tribe (1985); Frank (1941).

influenced by political factors directly affecting judicial performance was probably inevitable. But the influence of other political factors, having nothing to do with judicial performance, had already become dramatically clear by 1795. In that year the Senate rejected George Washington's nomination of John Rutledge as Chief Justice because of Rutledge's public opposition to the Jay Treaty.[9] The rejection in 1811 of James Madison's nomination of Alexander Wolcott was arguably a simple case of insufficient professional merit;[10] but the 1824 presidential election set the scene for twenty years of conflict, as supporters of successive Presidents contended in the Senate with supporters of Henry Clay. In the 1850s the nomination process was engulfed by the looming tensions between North and South over slavery; and once the Civil War was over, the conflict within the Senate resumed.

A protracted controversy in 1880 over Stanley Matthews' nomination introduced a new ingredient: Matthews' involvement with 'corporate financial and railroad interests' provoked 'perhaps the first clear instance' of opposition based on 'economic affiliation'.[11] Perhaps it was Matthews' previous membership of the Senate that saved him; yet in 1882 that was not enough to save Senator Roscoe Conkling, who declined the nomination after an outcry in the press.[12] And in 1894, attempts by President Grover Cleveland to fill the Supreme Court's 'New York seat' led to two spectacular examples of 'senatorial courtesy'—the convention by which the Senate will reject a nominee if a senator of the President's party opposes the nomination of a resident of the senator's state.[13]

In short, throughout the nineteenth century, the politicisation of Supreme Court appointments had been a normal feature of American political life. And, almost invariably, the conflict was a by-product of other tensions within the Senate, or between it and the President.

---

[9] Which by healing the rift with Britain was perceived by its opponents as offensive to France. See Tribe (1985) 80; Mitzner (1989) 398–9.

[10] Abraham (1974) 80.

[11] Ibid 127. Other issues were Matthews' chequered political alliances and cronyism with Hayes.

[12] Ibid 129.

[13] Ibid 17–19.

3 The American Experience of Removal

By contrast, the most significant attempt to politicise the removal process had established such a negative precedent as to make it unlikely that any Supreme Court justice would ever be impeached again. Samuel Chase, appointed to the Court by Washington in 1796, had been a hero of the Revolution and a former Chief Justice of Maryland. But, immediately on appointment to the Supreme Court, he began to use it as a platform for intemperate attacks on the emergent Republican party, and especially on Thomas Jefferson. When Chase continued his campaign after Jefferson became President, the House of Representatives framed articles of impeachment. The main charges related to his 'indecent solicitude', as a trial judge in 1800, to procure the conviction of a defendant accused of having libelled President John Adams; and to his misuse of a charge to a Baltimore grand jury in 1803 for 'an intemperate and inflammatory political harangue ... tending to prostitute [his] high judicial character ... to the low purpose of an electioneering partisan'.[14]

However injudicious Chase's conduct had been, the impeachment proceedings were clearly a step in the ongoing Republican campaign against 'Federalist judges' that began with *Marbury v Madison*.[15] Indeed, the prospect that Chief Justice John Marshall might be next in line may well have operated as a deterrent against the conviction of Chase, since there was a view that the Chief Justice ought never to be impeached.[16] When Chase's Senate trial ended on 1 March 1805, five of the articles of impeachment were rejected, and the 'guilty' findings on the other three articles failed to reach the requisite two-thirds majority. The nine Federalist senators had voted 'Not guilty' on every article; but so had six of the Republican senators. The votes of these six sent a powerful signal that political differences are not a ground for impeachment.

Since then, Supreme Court justices have rarely been threatened. In 1868 some indiscreet remarks by an unnamed Supreme Court

---

[14] Rehnquist (1992) 58–115; Bushnell (1992) 57–88; US Congress (1974) 411–73; Haw (1980).
[15] 5 US 137 (1803).
[16] Benton (1986) vol. 2, 1282.

justice, reported in the Washington *Evening Express*, were referred
to the House Judiciary Committee; but that Committee took no
action and four months later was quietly discharged from further
consideration of the matter.[17] More recently, the possible impeachment of Justice William O. Douglas was debated in the House of
Representatives on three occasions—in 1953 when he granted a stay
of execution to Julius and Ethel Rosenberg;[18] in 1957 when he mar-
ried for the fourth time; and (most seriously) in 1970 in a bitter
sequel to the resignation of Justice Abe Fortas,[19] ending only when
the House Judiciary Committee, after full investigation, found all
charges to be without substance.[20] The investigation had 'exposed
and perhaps even diffused the personal or partisan motivations for
[the] attempted impeachment'.[21] Again, in the firestorm of resistance
to the Supreme Court's authority after *Brown v Board of Education
of Topeka*,[22] demands for the impeachment of Chief Justice Earl
Warren blossomed on billboards across the South, but with no congressional action. In general, the very intensity of the political process surrounding appointments has seemed to help ensure that, once
appointed, Supreme Court justices are secure for life.

No such inhibition has been felt against the impeachment of
other federal judges. In 1804, a year before the unsuccessful move
against Chase, a judge of the United States District Court for New
Hampshire, John Pickering, had been successfully removed from
office. (He was said to be an alcoholic and mentally deranged.)[23] By
the 1890s three more cases involving United States District Court
judges had progressed as far as formal impeachment proceedings
in the Senate. In 1831 James Peck (from the District Court for
Missouri) was acquitted (of abusing the power of contempt of

---

[17] US Congress (1974) 713.

[18] Douglas (1980) 78–82, 84–8.

[19] Fortas's resignation on 15 May 1969 did not result from impeachment, but from public controversy after President Johnson tried to nominate him as Chief Justice. See
Abraham (1974) 265–6.

[20] Douglas (1980) 355–77.

[21] Gerhardt (1996) 29.

[22] 347 US 483 (1954).

[23] Bushnell (1992) 43–55; US Congress (1974) 381–409.

court),[24] but in 1862 West Humphreys (from the District Court for Tennessee) was successfully impeached and removed from office (for supporting secession and purporting to exercise Confederate judicial power).[25] In 1873 Mark Delahay (from the District Court for Kansas) was the subject of an impeachment motion in the Senate, but resigned before articles of impeachment were drafted.[26]

In addition, by 1897, the House of Representatives had considered possible impeachment action against at least fifteen other United States District Court judges, as well as one Circuit Court judge.[27] At least five of these cases were abandoned only because the judge in question resigned. And in two cases where the House Judiciary Committee did recommend impeachment, a significant reason for the ensuing inaction was that the Committee had given the judge no opportunity to defend himself or to cross-examine witnesses. In later years this procedural concern led increasingly to a regular practice of allowing impugned judges to give evidence to the Committee and be represented by counsel.

In the twentieth century, seven proceedings against United States District Court judges have progressed to a full Senate hearing. Two judges were acquitted and one resigned. In one case in 1936 and three in the 1980s, the proceedings resulted in impeachment and removal from office. In many other cases considered by the House Judiciary Committee, no further action was taken.[28] In at least two cases the Committee's investigations had cleared the judge of any impropriety; and in several cases the Committee concluded that its disapproval of the judge's conduct stopped short of grounds for impeachment. In at least three cases proceedings were discontinued because the impugned judge resigned.

4 The Australian Constitutional Provisions

In delineating the categories of federal jurisdiction, the framers of the Australian Constitution followed the United States model closely.

---

[24] Bushnell (1992) 91–113; US Congress (1974) 475–507.

[25] Bushnell (1992) 115–24; US Congress (1974) 509–24.

[26] Bushnell (1992) 1–2; US Congress (1974) 713–16.

[27] US Congress (1974) 687–740.

[28] See, generally, ibid 851–900.

Initially, however, the possibility that appointment and removal procedures might incorporate elements of the American model seems not to have been considered. The 1891 draft had simply assumed a continuation of the British practice, as it had evolved by that time.

The first questionings in 1897 arose as a by-product of debate over the number of judges to comprise the High Court, now specified in s 71 of the Constitution. Dividing the delegates to the Convention was the ambiguity in s 3 of the *Act of Settlement*. How exactly did its assurance of tenure during good behaviour fit in with the Parliament's power to pray for removal by address? Were the two conceptions complementary, with the 'good behaviour' provision defining the only possible grounds for removal, but parliamentary address providing the procedure for adducing such grounds? Or were they independent alternatives, so that the Crown could remove a judge for misbehaviour (independently of parliamentary action), but alternatively a judge could be removed at the instance of Parliament (on any ground that it deemed sufficient)? Isaacs in particular pressed the latter view.[29]

In clause 70 of the 1891 Bill (now s 72), paragraph (i) had asserted the principle of tenure during good behaviour, while paragraph (iii) had asserted that federal judges 'May be removed by the Governor-General with [Executive Council] advice, but only upon an Address from both Houses of the Parliament in the same Session praying for such removal'. If Edmund Barton was correct in asserting that these two provisions must be read together, then the power of removal under paragraph (iii) was limited by paragraph (i). For those like Isaacs who wanted no limit on the sovereignty of Parliament, that was an unacceptable reading. If Isaacs was correct in asserting that paragraph (iii) should be read independently, then a judge could be removed on any grounds at all that the Parliament considered appropriate. But for those like Charles Kingston who wanted 'to protect the judges as far as ever I possibly can', that was an unacceptable reading.[30]

It was Kingston who broke the impasse by proposing the insertion of the words 'shall only be removed for misconduct, unfitness

---

[29] Craven (1986) (1897 Convention, Adelaide) 947. See also Thomson (1984).
[30] Craven (1986) (1897 Convention, Adelaide) 946.

or incapacity'. After further debate 'misbehaviour' was substituted for 'misconduct', and the reference to 'unfitness' was deleted. Misbehaviour and incapacity, said Symon, 'are exhaustive of the conditions under which the Parliament should exercise its power of removal, otherwise we would place the High Court . . . entirely under the dominance of the legislature for the time being, and that would be fatal to that independence of the High Court, which we all desire to secure'.[31]

Clearly, those who urged the inclusion of the words 'misbehaviour' and 'incapacity' were seeking to limit Parliament's power to procure the removal of a judge. On the other hand, Isaacs was induced to accept the amendment only because he was satisfied that the words would impose no real limit on parliamentary power at all.[32] H. B. Higgins was unpersuaded. Initially he appeared to accept the same assurance as Isaacs; but ultimately he would have been satisfied only if a judge could be removed whenever 'both Houses are of opinion that he has been guilty of misconduct or misbehavior'.[33]

Only Higgins appeared to think that the specification of grounds for removal would require the Parliament to establish them by proof in a court of law. Other delegates, however, were concerned either to insist that the Parliament itself should conduct a full formal trial, or to protest that any Parliament in the British tradition obviously would conduct such a trial. On the other hand Adye Douglas appeared to think that the facts would be sufficiently obvious that no elaborate trial would be needed.[34]

It was in this context that some delegates began to invoke the American model.[35] It was Patrick Glynn who first raised directly the possibility that the American impeachment model be followed. Reading at length from Woodrow Wilson's study of *Congressional Government*, he noted that 'even with this safeguard in America, attempts have been made to influence the court, and, therefore, it is

---

[31] Ibid 951.

[32] Ibid 952.

[33] Ibid 953–4.

[34] Ibid 955.

[35] Ibid 936, 942 (Symon), 939 (Peacock), 940 (Trenwith).

necessary to have this as a protection'.[36] On the other hand, Bernhard Wise argued that the cumbrous and unfamiliar impeachment model would 'raise difficulties out of all proportion to [its] value',[37] and in the end these arguments prevailed. The clause agreed to at the Adelaide session, though slightly more emphatic than the eventual s 72(ii), was apparently no different in effect. Yet echoes of the impeachment option lingered. Higgins, though still advocating the British practice, seemed finally convinced that there was little practical difference between address and impeachment, a view that Joseph Carruthers shared.[38]

Kingston thought that no procedures need be specified at all. Whether the two Houses should have distinct functions, and how to initiate the process, could all be left to the Parliament.[39] Only Sir John Downer was thoroughly persuaded by the arguments in favour of impeachment. Convinced of the need for a definite finding 'of misbehavior, or unfitness, or something else', and hence for some form of trial, he was further convinced that the 'method' of trial must be clearly prescribed:

> We ought to surround the removal of the judge ... with all sorts of precautions. We ought to ensure him a trial, and not act upon the loose talk of the two popular Houses in a mere debate, to which he has no possible opportunity of replying ... this the Americans understood, for they prescribed accordingly, and in doing that they did well.[40]

Perceiving that there was no majority support for impeachment, Downer did not force the issue, and he never availed himself of the opportunity to raise the matter again before the Convention was over.[41]

---

[36] Wilson (1885); Craven (1986) (1897 Convention, Adelaide) 944–5.

[37] Craven (1986) (1897 Convention, Adelaide) 945.

[38] Ibid 953, 958.

[39] Ibid 959.

[40] Ibid 956–7.

[41] Ibid 960.

5 The Australian Experience of Removal

(a) The Murphy affair

The uncertainty as to how exactly 'proved misbehaviour or incapacity' might be established remained unexplored until the 'Murphy affair' of 1984–86; but throughout the turbulent two-and-a-half years of that unhappy ordeal, the procedural uncertainties were exacerbated by a seemingly endless torrent of allegations, ambiguities and innuendoes. Effectively the story began on 2 February 1984, when the Melbourne *Age* published a front page story headlined 'Secret Tapes of Judge'.

The reference was to a series of transcripts allegedly derived from police tape recordings of telephone conversations with the Sydney solicitor Morgan Ryan.[42] Lionel Murphy, then a justice of the High Court, was named as the judge in question in the New South Wales Parliament on 21 February 1984, and again in the Queensland Parliament on 6 March 1984. The ensuing unsuccessful search for a satisfactory way of testing the allegations involved two Senate inquiries, two criminal trials and a Parliamentary Commission of Inquiry.

The sheer profusion of the allegations, and the jumble of sophistries and apocrypha on which many of them depended, make any brief summary impossible. An objective impartial summary is impossible in any event. I have elsewhere attempted a detailed summary which, while striving for objectivity, depends on interpretations of the evidence obviously coloured by my personal belief in his Honour's innocence.[43] For his part Justice J. B. Thomas of the Supreme Court of Queensland has attempted a detailed summary which, while similarly striving for objectivity, depends on interpretations of the evidence obviously coloured by his personal belief in his Honour's guilt.[44] That such diverse interpretations are possible may simply reflect the impossibility of meeting any acceptable probative standard either way.

---

[42] The transcripts were ultimately found to be unreliable. See Royal Commission of Inquiry into Alleged Telephone Interceptions (1986); Blackshield (1987) 233–4.

[43] Blackshield (1987).

[44] Thomas (1997) 178–88.

The first Senate Committee[45] cleared Justice Murphy of any allegations arising from the '*Age* tapes'; but in evidence before the Committee Clarrie Briese (the Chief Stipendiary Magistrate for New South Wales) made a new allegation on which the Committee could not agree. That became the focus for a second Senate Committee in which four senators were assisted by two retired judges, John Wickham QC and Xavier Connor QC. This time it was Paul Flannery (a New South Wales District Court judge) whose evidence yielded a new allegation, lending possible corroborative support to the 'Briese allegation', and leaving the second Committee more hopelessly divided than the first. Four of the six participants in the second Senate Committee found that Justice Murphy could not be guilty of any criminal offence; but five of the six found that it was open to the Parliament to take the view he was guilty of 'misbehaviour' in the constitutional sense.[46]

Of all the allegations, those by Briese and Flannery perhaps were the ones bearing most directly upon Murphy's judicial role. Both allegations related to the prosecution of the Sydney solicitor Morgan Ryan for alleged conspiracy in immigration matters.[47] Ryan's relationship with Murphy had been a principal focus of the '*Age* tapes'.

The 'Briese allegation' related to a dinner which Murphy had attended at Briese's home on 6 January 1982, while Ryan's committal for trial was pending before Kevin Jones SM. During the dinner conversation the Ryan matter had been referred to, and Briese had said (on his version) that he would 'make some inquiries', or (on Murphy's version) that he would 'have a look to see how it's going'. Although Briese had volunteered this statement without direct prompting from Murphy, he had come to believe in retrospect that Murphy was inviting him to put pressure on Jones SM to decide that Ryan should not be committed for trial. In short, the allegation was that Murphy had attempted to pervert the course of justice.[48]

---

[45] Senate Select Committee on the Conduct of a Judge (1984) (appointed 28 March 1984, reported 24 August 1984). See Blackshield (1987) 235–40.

[46] Senate Select Committee on Allegations Concerning a Judge (1984) (appointed 6 September 1984, reported 31 October 1984). See Blackshield (1987) 245–8.

[47] See *R v Ryan* (1984) 55 ALR 408; Blackshield (1987) 240.

[48] Blackshield (1987) 240–5; Thomas (1997) 180–1.

The 'Flannery allegation' related to a dinner which Flannery had attended at Murphy's Darling Point home on Saturday 9 July 1983. By that time Ryan had been committed for trial, and his trial (with Judge Flannery presiding) was to commence the following Monday. Again, the allegation was that Murphy had attempted to pervert the course of justice. The dinner conversation on this occasion had made no direct reference to the Ryan case, but during a general discussion of the dangers of conspiracy charges, Murphy had referred to his judgment in *R v Hoar*.[49] Two days later, Ryan's counsel had cited that case in his opening argument.[50]

It was after the fiasco of the second Senate Committee that Ian Temby QC, then Commonwealth Director of Public Prosecutions, recommended on 21 November 1984 that Murphy be prosecuted on charges (the Briese and Flannery allegations) of attempting to pervert the course of justice. Two weeks earlier Temby had argued in a seminar paper that in such a case criminal prosecution would help to 'clear the air'; and when his opinion in the Murphy matter was later released to the press, it confirmed that that had been his intention.[51]

On 5 July 1985, the jury at Murphy's first trial (presided over by Justice Henry Cantor) acquitted him of the 'Flannery allegation' but convicted him of the 'Briese allegation'.[52] On 28 November 1985, a specially constituted five-judge bench of the New South Wales Supreme Court quashed this conviction and ordered a new trial.[53] On Monday 28 April 1986, the jury at the second trial (presided over by Justice David Hunt) acquitted on the 'Briese allegation' as well.

The finding that Murphy was innocent of any criminal conduct did not necessarily negate 'misbehaviour', which may well be constituted by conduct falling short of criminality. But in the week following the jury acquittal, politicians of all parties made it plain that

---

[49] (1981) 148 CLR 32.

[50] Blackshield (1987) 246.

[51] Temby (1985) 199–200; Blackshield (1987) 248–9; *Sydney Morning Herald*, 4 August 1986, 4.

[52] For the aftermath of that verdict see Blackshield (1987) 251–2; Blackshield (1985).

[53] *R v Murphy* (1985) 4 NSWLR 42.

for them the matter was over. By Friday 2 May, however, it was clear that a fresh crisis was brewing;[54] and by Wednesday 7 May the Hawke government had announced a new Parliamentary Commission of Inquiry, to be constituted by three retired judges (Sir George Lush, Sir Richard Blackburn and Andrew Wells QC). The Commission was not to reconsider the Briese and Flannery allegations ('except to the extent that the Commission considers necessary for the proper examination of other issues'), and was limited to 'specific allegations made in precise terms'. But within those limits it was to consider 'any conduct' by Justice Murphy which in its opinion might amount to 'proved misbehaviour'.[55]

By 31 July 1986 the Commission had assembled 42 allegations; had determined that 28 of them were wholly lacking in substance; and was poised to consider the remaining 14.[56] But on that day Justice Murphy announced that he was dying of incurable cancer, and intended to return to the Court for as long as he could. The work of the Commission was immediately halted, its constituent statute repealed, and Commission documents containing 'material relating to the conduct of the Honourable Lionel Keith Murphy' embargoed for thirty years.[57]

Murphy returned to the Court for one week of sittings, and died on 21 October 1986. How the Commission would have dealt with the remaining 14 allegations will never be known.

(b) Procedural lessons

Perhaps the most obvious lesson of this deeply distressing history is that the hope expressed by Temby QC, that a criminal prosecution would 'clear the air', was tragically misplaced. For Murphy's supporters, the detour into the criminal courts had only prolonged the agony. For his detractors, it was equally unsatisfactory: although his jury acquittal did not exclude the possibility of 'misbehaviour', it did as a matter of political reality preclude any further parliamentary action, at least on the Briese and Flannery charges. The

---

[54] Blackshield (1986).
[55] *Parliamentary Commission of Inquiry Act 1986* (Cth), ss 5(4), 5(2), 8(1)(b).
[56] Parliamentary Commission of Inquiry (1986).
[57] *Parliamentary Commission of Inquiry (Repeal) Act 1986* (Cth), s 6.

relationship in the United States between the impeachment of judges and their prosecution on criminal charges has been deeply problematic; and the Murphy affair exposed similar problems. For one thing, the attempt in the criminal proceedings to use evidence from the Senate inquiries raised questions of parliamentary privilege.[58] For another thing, whatever standard of proof is implied by the words 'proved misbehaviour',[59] it ought surely to be determined on the merits of the constitutional issue. Yet a parliamentary finding that 'misbehaviour' was proved beyond a reasonable doubt would so obviously be prejudicial to subsequent criminal proceedings that members of Parliament might be led for that reason to adopt a lesser standard; while, conversely, a prior acquittal on criminal charges might unduly inhibit a parliamentary finding of misbehaviour, even where that was appropriate.[60]

Whether the use of Senate committees could have worked more effectively than it did in the 'Murphy affair' is a difficult question, complicated by the limited extent to which Murphy himself participated in both the Senate inquiries. In particular, the first Senate Committee, which effectively disposed of the '*Age* tapes' allegations, might also have disposed of the 'Briese allegation' if Murphy had appeared before the Committee and submitted to interrogation by it. But this he refused to do. He had given the Committee a written statement in response to the '*Age* tapes' materials, and after Briese's evidence he submitted another (confirming Briese's general account of their conversations, but denying the use of particular phrases and the inferences of impropriety which Briese appeared to have drawn). He refused, however, to submit to questioning, for three distinct reasons.

First, he maintained that any such hearing would violate the rules of natural justice unless his counsel were permitted to cross-examine Briese. Under Senate Standing Order 304, this was not permissible. (One member of the Committee, Senator Chipp, was

---

[58] *R v Murphy* (1986) 5 NSWLR 18—apparently a trigger for the *Parliamentary Privileges Act 1987* (Cth).

[59] An analogy might be found in *Briginshaw v Briginshaw* (1938) 60 CLR 336, 362 (Dixon J).

[60] Evans (1987) 24.

willing to cut through this impasse by suspending the Standing Order; but the majority rejected this course.) Second, Murphy maintained that for a High Court judge to submit to questioning by a Senate Committee would infringe the separation of powers.

Third, he maintained that what the Committee called its 'investigative' function was being taken too far. In his view, the decision whether grounds exist for a judge's removal from office is entrusted by s 72(ii) exclusively to the Parliament. Consistently with this it may be possible for Parliament (or either House) to seek preliminary advice and guidance from a delegated committee, or even from an external body which remains under Parliament's control. But any such inquiry must stop short of anything approaching an adjudicative role. For the Senate Committee to contemplate summoning or interrogating a High Court judge was not only an attempt by a legislative body to assert coercive power against the judicial branch of government, but a misconception of any role that could possibly be delegated to a committee consistently with s 72. What the Senate was doing through its Committees was to develop ways of subjecting a judge to interrogation, outside of the formal machinery of s 72. It was thus undermining the protection for federal judges, which the section was meant to confer.

To a large extent the force of these arguments was conceded when the second Senate Committee was established, since its rules of procedure were carefully formulated to meet Murphy's objections. Elaborate evidentiary rules were devised with a view to ensuring fairness to Murphy if he chose to give evidence. The new procedures specifically authorised cross-examination of witnesses, and stipulated that 'Justice Murphy shall not be summoned to give evidence', though after all other evidence had been heard he could be invited to do so.

Again, however, when that invitation was extended, Murphy declined it; and, again, his refusal may well have been determinative of the outcome. Under the evidentiary rules of the second Committee, Murphy's written statement was not accepted, leaving the Committee to assess the allegations as if they stood uncontested. This time, however, his refusal reflected an immediate political context. By the time of the Committee's invitation to Murphy, the Hawke government had called an early election. On 26 October

1984 the Parliament was to be dissolved. In that situation, Murphy's counsel (T. E. F. Hughes QC) informed the Committee on 12 October that the judge would refuse to appear, adducing two principal reasons. The first was that, in the time frame now remaining, there was no possibility that any proceedings under s 72 could be completed before the Parliament rose. Any further inquiry could therefore 'be seen as a futile step taken solely for political reasons', and as 'an unjustifiable attempt based upon political considerations to pre-empt the proper role of the new Parliament'. The second reason was that the Committee proceedings were now being conducted 'in a highly politicised environment . . . as a factor in the opening stages of an election campaign. If the judge gives evidence, it is virtually inevitable that he may become a political football in the election. This would be intolerable'.

These reasons for refusal to give evidence were politically compelling, and graphically highlight the need for inquiries under s 72(ii) to be divorced as far as possible from any immediate political context. The three reasons given for his Honour's refusal to submit to questioning by the first Committee, however, raise wider issues of principle. Each of them helps to bring into focus the difficulties of devising an acceptable procedure for handling such sensitive issues. Yet each of them also must be assessed in the light of the broad power assigned to each House by s 50(i) of the Constitution, to determine for itself 'the mode in which its powers, privileges, and immunities may be exercised and upheld'. And on each of them, the American impeachment experience offers useful guidance.

On the first point, as to whether natural justice requires that a person accused of 'misbehaviour' be able to cross-examine witnesses, the legal answer is inconclusive: it depends 'on the circumstances of the case, the nature of the inquiry, the rules under which the tribunal was acting and the subject-matter being dealt with'.[61] In this instance, the fact that cross-examination was excluded by Senate standing orders may well have been conclusive. Yet, in any event, a question relating to the internal procedures of a House of Parliament may not be amenable to strictly legal analysis either way. It seems better to approach the matter not from a legalistic view-

---

[61] *O'Rourke v Miller* (1985) 156 CLR 342, 353 (Gibbs CJ).

point, but simply with an intuitive sense of what standards of fairness and probative value seem reasonably to require. On that basis, the right to be represented by counsel and (through counsel) to cross-examine witnesses seems an elementary minimal safeguard. In the United States, the House Judiciary Committee, after some initial vacillation, has invariably adopted that course.

The second point about separation of powers is more paradoxical. Murphy's position appeared to reflect his characteristic dogmatic adherence to conceptions derived from American constitutional law. Yet in that context the separation of powers is not an impermeable barrier—as Madison insisted in *The Federalist* (No 47), it does not mean that the various departments of government can have 'no *partial agency* in, or no *control* over', each other. On the contrary, a significant purpose is precisely to create a system of checks and balances, of which the power of the legislative branch to procure the removal of judges (whether by impeachment or by address) is itself a significant example. The vesting of that power in the legislature should be seen as a safeguard of judicial independence, not as a threat to it.

Murphy's argument did not necessarily conflict with that general principle, since it focused on the more specific point that a member of the judicial branch ought not to submit to interrogation by the legislative branch. That, too, however, is debatable. Harry Evans[62] has pointed out that British parliamentary history offers ample precedents for the summoning of judges by the House of Commons; and that even if the Australian separation of powers makes those precedents inapplicable, inquiries under s 72 present special problems. Murphy's argument is at its strongest on the even more limited point that a judge should not be compelled to appear. But that was not in issue at either Senate Committee; and for Evans even that is debatable.

As for Murphy's third point, that the crucial functions of the Houses of Parliament under s 72(ii) are non-delegable, the fundamental principle thus asserted seems undoubtedly correct. While a House may be entitled to seek assistance in preliminary fact-finding

---

[62] Evans (1987) 25–6.

processes, the extent to which those processes can pre-empt the responsibilities of the House must be strictly limited. Where the fact-finding task is assigned to an external body, such as the 1986 'Parliamentary Commission of Inquiry', this may be an issue of acute concern.[63] Yet the reference of investigative and advisory tasks to a committee of the House itself is in a different position. The broad authority of each House under s 50(i) to regulate the exercise of its constitutional powers must surely extend to some delegation of fact-finding tasks to committees, so long as the final judgment is reserved for the full House itself. Moreover, the use of a committee system has much to commend it. Whatever the practical difficulties in establishing and interpreting the factual and other considerations relevant to an issue of 'proved misbehaviour', it seems easier to deal with the problem initially in the context of a small committee. In particular, this is likely to be a less dramatic (and therefore less damaging) course in those cases where no sufficient foundation emerges for a finding of 'proved misbehaviour'.

Again, the experience of the United States Congress is reassuring. While the House of Representatives retains full responsibility for determining whether articles of impeachment are warranted, the preliminary functions of gathering and hearing evidence, and making recommendations have regularly been assigned to the House Judiciary Committee. Both in those cases where the Committee has recommended impeachment, and in the much larger number of cases where it has not, the Committee appears to have exercised its functions conscientiously and responsibly. In fact, the smaller committee procedure appears to have worked in favour of judges facing possible impeachment, in that members of the House who have participated in the committee process are more likely to vote against impeachment than those who have not.[64] Nor is there any evidence that Committee recommendations have precluded full consideration de novo by the full House.

Indeed, the experience of the 'Murphy affair' leads Evans to conclude that perhaps Sir John Downer was right in 1897, and that

---

[63] Its designation as a 'Parliamentary Commission' was clearly intended to signify responsibility to and control by the Parliament itself.

[64] Volcansek (1993) 165–6.

the American impeachment model should receive further consideration.[65] No doubt, as Evans concedes, its acceptable working may
depend on the greater capacity of members of Congress, as compared with Australian politicians, for 'devotion to constitutional
principles and a willingness to perform their constitutional duties
without allowing their activities to be distorted by partisan considerations'. Under 'the intense party discipline ... of an Australian
Parliament', the impeachment model might work less well. Yet, of
course, this is also a cause for concern in relation to the existing
procedure.

The essential features of the procedure required by s 72(ii) are,
first, that each House of Parliament must adopt an address praying
for removal; and, second, that the two Houses must consider the
matter separately (albeit in the same session). A closer approxi-
mation of the American model would require, first, that the presence
or absence of grounds for removal should invariably be considered
first in the House of Representatives, and only thereafter by the
Senate. Second, it would require that the deliberations in the lower
House should be predicated on preliminary inquiry by a committee
of that House. Third, it would require that if the lower House thereupon adopted a formal address praying for removal, it should formulate a precise statement of the grounds on which removal was
sought. That statement of grounds would then provide the basis for
the Senate's response.

A significant aspect of such a procedure would be that the two
Houses consider the matter separately and sequentially. Yet, as Evans
argues, that may be implied by the text of s 72(ii) in any event.[66] In
Australia, the idea of initiation by the House of Representatives
might appear to exacerbate the danger of partisan distortion, since
party discipline normally runs stronger and deeper in that House.
Yet, in so far as allegations against judges (or at least against High
Court judges) may themselves be politically inspired or encouraged,
or reflect Opposition resentment of a controversial appointment, it
might even be an additional safeguard against political distortion if
serious pressure for removal were dependent on the initiative of the

---

[65] Evans (1987) 28–9.
[66] Ibid 21.

House effectively controlled by the appointing government. In any functional differentiation between the two Houses, it would clearly be appropriate that the lower House (more directly representative of the people) should have the accusatory role, and the Senate (less dominated by party politics) the determinative or judgmental role; and the ascription of these roles might itself have a clarifying and sobering value.

6 Proved Misbehaviour

(a) A legal or political concept?

No procedural model can avoid the fundamental problem of knowing what is meant by 'proved misbehaviour or incapacity'—or by any other verbal formula that might be adopted, since the answer does not depend on legalistic exegesis of a textual formula, but on judgment of what constitute sufficient grounds for removal. That the latter is the decisive question was itself among the significant lessons of the 'Murphy affair'.

The earlier authorities[67] had repeated ad nauseam the summation by Alpheus Todd[68] of the traditional English meaning of 'misbehaviour': 'Misbehaviour includes, firstly, the improper exercise of judicial functions; secondly, wilful neglect of duty, or non-attendance; and, thirdly, a conviction for any infamous offence, by which, although it be not connected with the duties of his office, the offender is rendered unfit to exercise any office or public franchise'.

Before the first Senate Committee, Murphy's lawyers argued that 'misbehaviour' should thus be restricted; and as early as 24 February 1984, an opinion by the Commonwealth Solicitor-General, Gavan Griffith QC, had taken a similar view. But a later opinion given to the Committee by C. W. Pincus QC on 14 May 1984 took a wider view: 'I think it is for Parliament to decide whether any conduct alleged against a judge constitutes misbehaviour sufficient to justify removal from office. There is no "technical" relevant meaning of misbehaviour and in particular it is not necessary . . . that an offence be proved'.

---

[67] For example Quick and Garran (1901) 731.
[68] Todd (1869) 727.

The only significant pronouncement of the Parliamentary Commission of Inquiry also took this view. In a ruling on the meaning of 'misbehaviour' on 5 August 1986 (tabled in Parliament on 21 August 1986), all three Commissioners seemed inclined to accept a submission that Todd's enumeration never had been an accurate reflection of the British position. But in any event, all three of them convincingly held that the Australian provision should not be regarded as perpetuating the British position, but as a distinctive fresh start.

In considering the wider and narrower views of 'misbehaviour', the wider view seems clearly correct.[69] Its only deficiency, in the version expounded by Pincus QC and the three Parliamentary Commissioners, is a logical paradox. The essential point, as Pincus observes, is that there is no relevant 'technical' meaning of 'misbehaviour'; but what this really means is that Parliament's power of removal cannot legally be defined at all. Yet inevitably, as Pincus and the Commissioners set out their views, they were in the position of legal authorities expounding a legal opinion. They were simultaneously informing us of the section's legal meaning, and asserting that it has no legal meaning.

In the Pincus opinion, this self-negation was perhaps only latent. The three Commissioners, however, met the paradox head on, insisting that their wide definition of 'misbehaviour' involved legal propositions, to be arrived at by legal construction. Andrew Wells QC spoke of s 72 as a 'code', and sought to emulate 'the approach that a Court should adopt' to 'construing' such a code. Commissioner Blackburn also spoke of 'solving this problem of construction'. All three of them sought to avoid the problem of self-invalidation by insisting that, though the concept of 'misbehaviour' was wide, it was not unlimited; and that the limits they sought to articulate were legal limits.

This, however, is precisely the problem. Assume that the crucial words 'proved misbehaviour' do have a legal meaning. Then, if the Governor-General did in fact remove a judge in response to an address by both Houses, the judge would be entitled to appeal to the High Court of Australia, arguing that the Parliament (and the

---

[69] Blackshield (1987) 254–5; Blackshield (1986).

Governor-General) had not correctly understood or applied their legally circumscribed powers. Commissioner Lush tentatively suggested that, in 'the present state of Australian jurisprudence', such an issue was justiciable. Yet in 1897 the possibility that the phrase 'proved misbehaviour or incapacity' might open the way to judicial intervention was the very reason why Higgins and others resisted the inclusion of any such limiting phrase at all, since it was common ground that the process should not be so exposed. The 1897 debate had a double purpose: to ensure that no one but Parliament can remove a judge from office, but also to ensure that Parliament can, and that its decision should be final.

Accordingly, my own position throughout the 'Murphy affair' was that the meaning of 'proved misbehaviour' must rest solely on the Parliament's judgment in any given case, and that its potential meaning thus has no legal limits at all. No doubt this proposition is itself a legal proposition, and the High Court could be asked to say whether this proposition is correct. But, if it did so decide, it could then have nothing further to say.

This does not mean that there are no limits on the Parliament's scope for removal of judges. But it means that the limits are essentially political, not legal, in nature. To say this is not to dispute the good sense of the various suggestions and cautions advanced by the three Commissioners as to what might or might not be sufficiently serious to warrant removal. It is simply to stress that their comments were valid as political advice which each member of Parliament was free to accept or reject, not as legal instruction by which the Parliament or its members were in any way bound.

(b) The Callinan case

The inconclusive speculation which flared briefly in 1998 as to the position of Justice Ian Callinan is a good example of the profound indeterminacy of the issues which the Parliament may have to resolve, as well as the formidable difficulties of procedure and principle in any particular case. His Honour had been appointed to the High Court on 3 February that year. The relevant controversy arose four months later.

The issue arose out of litigation relating to a building contract, and formally commenced by statement of claim (signed by Callinan as senior counsel) on 23 December 1986. The plaintiff company alleged that the contract had been procured by fraud, and by contravention of s 52 of the *Trade Practices Act 1974* (Cth). The plaintiff company's action was dismissed on 18 August 1989; a cross-claim by the defendant was upheld on 6 April 1990. The defendant was awarded damages of over $5 million, plus costs.

By that time the plaintiff company was in liquidation. For-tuitously for the defendant, the liquidator allowed it to purchase a bundle of documents passing between the plaintiff company and its legal advisers, and normally protected by legal professional privi-lege. The documents disclosed that the allegation of fraud was known to be unfounded; that the statement of claim was filed in the knowledge that it could not succeed; and that its sole purpose was to delay or embarrass the defendant's claim on the contract.

On the basis of that apparent abuse of process, the defendant maintained that the plaintiff's solicitors should indemnify the defen-dant for its costs (since the plaintiff company was in liquidation). After some procedural uncertainty, the claim was formulated as a notice of motion. That the Federal Court could entertain such a motion was determined by a Full Federal Court on 22 September 1993;[70] the substantive claim against the solicitors was upheld by Justice Alan Goldberg on 14 July 1998.[71]

Justice Goldberg's judgment not only made strong adverse find-ings against the solicitors, on the basis that the sole purpose of the statement of claim was 'to gain a temporary bargaining stance and bargaining position', but specifically found that Callinan QC 'was privy to that purpose and at the least acquiesced in it and approved of it'.[72] At the least, an improper litigious strategy had been adopted with Callinan's knowledge and approval; and a possible inference left open by the evidence (and by Goldberg J in his judgment) was that the entire strategy had been his idea.

---

[70] *Caboolture Park Shopping Centre Pty Ltd (in liq) v White Industries (Qld) Pty Ltd* (1993) 117 ALR 253.

[71] *White Industries (Qld) Pty Ltd v Flower & Hart (a firm)* (1998) 156 ALR 169.

[72] Ibid 206.

On appeal,[73] a Full Federal Court held on 11 June 1999 that the findings against the solicitors were in no way dependent on any ascription of an improper purpose to Callinan, so that 'whether or not his Honour erred in making findings about Mr Callinan's purpose', that could not affect the result. Accordingly the Full Court expressed no opinion on whether the findings against Callinan were warranted.

In any consideration of whether this narrative gave rise to grounds for concern under s 72(ii), the preliminary questions would be myriad. Was the 1986 statement of claim, as a matter of law, an abuse of process? The finding to that effect depended on the High Court decision in *Williams v Spautz*;[74] yet dicta in that case were also relied on as supporting a contrary view. Was the issuance of a statement of claim for the purpose merely of delay and embarrassment a breach of professional ethics? It was common ground that litigious strategies are frequently adopted in part for such purposes, provided that the claim advanced has some slender prospect of success.[75] Given that virtually all legal arguments are inherently uncertain and contestable, what meaningful line can be drawn between a slender prospect of success, and none? Was a knowingly false allegation of fraud a breach of professional ethics? If in either respect there was a breach of professional ethics, how serious a breach was it? Were these questions to be judged by the general standards of the Australian legal profession, or the wider Australian community, or specifically by the ethical standards of the Queensland bar in the 1980s? In the latter event who should make the relevant judgment? Should it not be the Queensland bar?

All these were only preliminary questions. Even if we assume that all of them could be answered adversely to Callinan, the most difficult question would remain. It is generally accepted that, for conduct to be capable of amounting to 'misbehaviour', it need not occur in the actual exercise of judicial power, nor even contempor-

---

[73] *Flower & Hart (a firm) v White Industries (Qld) Pty Ltd* (1999) 163 ALR 744.

[74] (1992) 174 CLR 509.

[75] See, for example, *Nelungaloo Pty Ltd v Commonwealth* (1947) 75 CLR 495.

aneously with the holding of judicial office.[76] But it must at least bear in some ill-defined way upon fitness for judicial office. Would conduct by a practising barrister, assumed for this purpose to constitute an abuse of judicial process, be sufficiently relevant to his duties as a judge, or his attitude to the judicial process, to affect his fitness for office? In any event, could fitness for office in 1998 be impugned by reference to a transient occurrence in an entirely different context in 1986?

Perhaps the answer to this latter question might vary from case to case, since, even after a prolonged lapse of time, we might consider some past conduct so serious, or so directly relevant to fitness for judicial office, that it should provide grounds for removal whatever the time interval involved. But how serious the conduct must be, or how directly it must bear upon fitness for judicial office, are questions of degree; and it may be that the greater the lapse of time, the higher the level of seriousness or relevance needed to justify removal.

In the Callinan case the apparent outcome is that legal and professional guidelines for the conduct of litigation have now been tightened to make it clear that what seems to have happened in 1986 is no longer acceptable; but that any tentative questioning of Callinan's fitness for office has quietly been put to rest. The tacit implication is that this is one of those cases where our reappraisal of past events should lead us to make clearer rules for the future, but where the very recognition that clearer rules are needed necessarily implies that, at the time, the relevant standards were too ambiguous to permit retrospective condemnation. Even if the decisive questions were answered adversely to Callinan, this would mean only that he had the misfortune to be 'caught on the ebb-tide of a previously acceptable practice'.[77]

For the good of the Court and the community, that appears to be a desirable outcome. Yet the crucial point remains that, had the matter gone further, the questions outlined above could have been answered only by Parliament. To ask such questions is to suggest

---

[76] But compare *Capital TV & Appliances Pty Ltd v Falconer* (1971) 125 CLR 591, 691 (Windeyer J).

[77] Thomas (1997) 242.

considerations which members of Parliament might wish to address, but which they alone can resolve.

7 The Australian Appointment Procedure

(a) Overview

The requirement of s 72(i) that federal judges be appointed 'by the Governor-General in Council' means effectively that the appointment is within the gift of the federal executive government.[78] The normal practice is for the Attorney-General to take a recommendation to Cabinet. For High Court appointments, what happens then may depend on whether the Prime Minister of the day is himself a lawyer. If not, the Attorney's recommendation has usually been accepted; if so, the Prime Minister may have views of his own, which are likely to prevail.[79] Although in recent years each impending vacancy has given rise to some degree of public speculation (including the running of a 'book'), there is no public canvassing of the names officially being considered until an appointment is made. Perhaps for that reason, public criticism of appointments is usually non-existent or muted.

The exceptional cases that have generated public controversy have mostly involved appointments by a Labor government: Albert Piddington and Charles Powers in 1913;[80] H. V. Evatt and Edward McTiernan in 1930;[81] and Lionel Murphy in 1975.[82] Only in the case of Piddington did the controversy induce him to resign; only in the case of Powers was the controversy arguably focused on the appointee's lack of merit. In 1930, though the real objection was to Evatt, his indisputable academic and professional brilliance meant that McTiernan unfairly bore the brunt of the criticism.

---

[78] In relation to the Australian appointment procedure see generally Sir Anthony Mason (1997).
[79] Menzies' attempt to make Dixon Chief Justice in 1935 is a counter-example. See Fricke (1986) 106.
[80] Graham (1995); Fitzhardinge (1964) 271–83; Sawer (1956) 105–6.
[81] Sawer (1963) 34.
[82] Blackshield (1977) 118–19.

For both of them, as for Murphy, what was really at stake was conservative opposition to the appointment of a Labor politician.[83] For Evatt and McTiernan the controversy was so great (and the economic austerity of the time so exigent) that when another vacancy occurred a month later, the Scullin Labor government left it unfilled. The number of High Court judges was reduced to six, and the bench was not restored to its full strength of seven until 1946. Even then, the appointment of William Webb was primarily to allow him to preside with the status of a High Court judge at the International Military Tribunal for the Far East. It was not until 1948 that he actually sat in the High Court.

Though Webb, too, was a Labor appointment, his appointment was regarded as 'safe': the earlier controversies had made Labor governments cautious about whom they appointed. In most of those controversies, the ostensible objection was to 'political' appointments. Yet, as Geoffrey Sawer observed in 1967, 'the non-Labor parties do not have to make deliberately "political" appointments', since (at least in the earlier part of the century) appointees selected simply on the basis of professional success at the bar 'will nearly all be as a matter of course supporters of non-Labor parties or apolitical men with middle-of-the-road or conservative temperaments'. Barristers 'specifically socialist in active politics or in temperament' were not necessarily of lesser ability, but 'tend not to acquire an extensive practice in appellate courts and in . . . heavy commercial and property cases'.[84]

(b) Political appointments

Judicial appointments may be 'political' in at least three different senses. First, an appointing government may try to influence the court's future direction by finding candidates who are sympathetic (or at least not unsympathetic) to its own broad political outlook. To varying degrees all governments tend to do this, though most Australian Prime Ministers and Attorneys-General have seemed less driven in this regard than some American Presidents. The tendency

---

[83] McTiernan had been Attorney-General in the NSW Lang Labor government, though by the time of his appointment he had long fallen out with Lang.

[84] Sawer (1967) 64–5.

seems natural and unavoidable. Given a democratic electoral system in which government changes hands at regular intervals, it may even be beneficial, since a regular alternation of political influence might be one way of ensuring the diversity of viewpoints which a collegiate bench needs.

Second, an appointment might be 'political' in the sense that the appointee is 'political': a practising member of Parliament, or some other public figure well-known for current and active political involvement. In 1903 Sir Edmund Barton set a precedent yet to be repeated when, as Prime Minister, he appointed himself to the High Court; but his other appointees, Sir Samuel Griffith and R. E. O'Connor, had also been active in the federal movement and as politicians in their colonies. More commonly, the appointee might be a current or recent Attorney-General, as Isaac Isaacs, John Latham, Garfield Barwick and Lionel Murphy all were. Again, this seems not merely unobjectionable, but positively beneficial, especially at the High Court level. Just as the Court benefits, when it hears appeals in the equity jurisdiction, from having at least one member with specialised contextual expertise in equity (or in criminal appeals from having at least one member with practical contextual experience of the conduct of criminal trials), so in constitutional cases it benefits from having at least one member with practical contextual understanding of legislative and executive government. Again, this may help to produce the diversity of experience and outlook which a collegiate bench needs.

Third, a government's choice of candidates may be influenced (or even dictated) by political considerations, not merely with an eye to the long-term development and direction of judicial doctrine, but in the more immediate sense that the appointment is made (retrospectively) as a personal reward for political services rendered, or (prospectively) with a calculated eye to its impact on a pending election campaign, or particular pending litigation. It is only in this case that the inevitably political process of judicial appointment can be said to have been politically abused.

Even here, an objection to the government's political motivation for the appointment is not necessarily an objection to the appointee. When Sir Victor Windeyer was appointed to the High Court in 1958, and Sir William Owen in 1961, both appointments were perceived as rewards for services rendered to the Menzies government in the Petrov Commission. But while Owen served on the Court for almost ten years with no particular distinction, Windeyer quickly established himself among the Court's most outstanding judges.

One common reaction to the 'Murphy affair' was to blame the whole tragedy on the fact that prior to his appointment Murphy had been a politician (and a controversial one), and to infer that such appointments ought henceforth to be avoided. Thus Justice J. B. Thomas concludes 'that it is time to recognise that a significant political career should be a barrier to judicial appointment'.[85] Yet, with respect, this is both an overreaction and a misdiagnosis. The problem with the 'Murphy affair', as participants on both sides of the controversy recognised with increasing dismay, was the intense politicisation of the affair itself. Both Murphy and Barwick were controversial, and both displayed judicial faults as well as judicial virtues; but their practical experience of government and their determination to locate the development of legal doctrine contextually in the real world were among their strengths.

An analogous judgment can be made of their political predecessors. Looking back at the close of the century to the High Court's formative years, some of us nowadays are in greater sympathy with the constitutional views of the original Court (Griffith, Barton and O'Connor), and some with the contrary views which Isaac Isaacs had imposed by the 1920s. But, whichever view we prefer, we must recognise that the contributions of both were essentially those of men accustomed to working as judge-politicians. The time has not come to say that we no longer need such contributions; on the contrary, the danger is that more timid appointments may produce a more homogenous and inhibited bench.

Indeed, the danger of homogeneity and of inhibition is precisely what has haunted the High Court, and the Australian judiciary as a whole, throughout the last two centuries. If the danger has been averted from time to time, it is only through the capacity for personal growth and philosophical reflectiveness of individual judges. To some extent the tradition and culture of a separate professional

---

[85] Thomas (1997) 243.

bar have encouraged such individuality; but the same tradition and culture have also tended to produce in the bar as a whole a relatively narrow range of experience, conservativism of attitude, and homogeneity of outlook which, translated into judicial performance, have tended to hinder the ability of the courts to respond to community needs. While these contradictory pressures to individuality and to conformity are both significant features of life at the bar, the apparent tendency in recent years has been for the fostering of individuality to become less prominent, and the pressure of conformity more so. In any event, as Sawer hinted in 1967, it is in the higher echelons of successful barristers that a relative homogeneity of outlook is likely to be most pronounced.

Accordingly, the focus of recent proposals for reform of the judicial appointment process has not been primarily on the need to avoid 'political' appointments, but on the need to open up the existing process in terms both of inputs and outputs: to achieve a greater diversity of inputs into the selection process, and a greater diversity of appointees.

The call for a greater diversity of inputs into High Court appointments was traditionally bound up with the 'federal' issues of Commonwealth–state relations which had until recently dominated the Court's constitutional work. The effective monopoly of High Court appointments by the Commonwealth government was perceived by the states as producing a Court which unduly favoured the Commonwealth. In the heightened political atmosphere of 1975 this perception, too, was intensified by the appointment of Justice Murphy, and the New South Wales Parliament established a committee to consider the issue.[86]

The Committee noted with surprise that the Constitution specifies no qualifications for High Court appointment—not even a law degree. This apparent lacuna is, of course, encouraging to proponents of reform. On the one hand, if 'diversity' were ever carried so far as to include the appointment of non-lawyers, there would be no constitutional impediment to such a course. On the other hand, at least prima facie, whatever qualifications we do think appropriate

---

[86] Select Committee of the Legislative Assembly upon the Appointment of Judges to the High Court of Australia (1976).

can be varied from time to time by legislation, without constitutional amendment.

That, at least, was the view of Richard O'Connor at the 1898 Convention.[87] It is also the view which underlies the existing provision in s 7 of the *High Court of Australia Act 1979* (Cth), requiring that an appointee be a judge or legal practitioner of at least five years' standing.[88] (On the other hand, it is sometimes argued that this provision is itself invalid, in that any legislative limit on eligibility for appointment restricts the absolute discretion conferred on the executive government by s 72.)[89]

On the main point which had constituted its raison d'être, the New South Wales Parliamentary Committee recommended that High Court appointments 'be made by the Governor-General on the advice of the Federal Executive Council after considering the recommendation of a majority of a High Court Appointments Commission constituted by the Attorneys-General for all States and the Commonwealth Attorney-General. Such recommendation should be advisory only'.[90] In practice, this Commission was to be identical with the Standing Committee of Attorneys-General, 'sitting in the capacity as advisor on High Court appointments'.

The nomenclature of a 'High Court Appointments Commission' has never been adopted; nor has the idea of a collegiate recommendation by a majority of Attorneys-General. Since 1979, however, s 6 of the *High Court of Australia Act* has provided: 'Where there is a vacancy in an office of Justice, the Attorney-General shall, before an appointment is made to the vacant office, consult with the Attorneys-General of the States in relation to the appointment'. This statutory provision for 'consultation', and for that matter the New South Wales proposal for an advisory 'recommendation', are clearly constitutional since they would in no way fetter the Commonwealth's executive discretion to make any appointment it chooses.

---

[87] Craven (1986) (1898 Convention, Melbourne) 309.

[88] See also *Federal Court of Australia Act 1976* (Cth) s 6(2); *Family Law Act 1975* (Cth) s 22(2).

[89] Thomson (1992) 265–9.

[90] Select Committee of the Legislative Assembly upon the Appointment of Judges to the High Court of Australia (1976) 21.

(c) Representativeness

Another perennial issue rooted in the tensions of Australian federalism is the overwhelming dominance of the Sydney and Melbourne bars in appointments to the High Court. Queensland has had six High Court justices (Griffith, Powers, Webb, Gibbs, Brennan, Callinan), including three of the eleven Chief Justices. Western Australia has had only two (Wilson and Toohey). South Australia and Tasmania have had none.

More recently, this inequality of state participation has been overshadowed by demands for other kinds of 'representativeness', not merely in the High Court but in Australian courts as a whole. In particular, over the past three decades, the growing influence of successive waves of Australian feminism (including its influence upon judges themselves) has led to increasing concern at the continued under-representation of women among Australian judges at both state and federal levels.[91] But, while this concern has tended to dominate the debate, it is not the only concern. The increasingly multi-cultural and multi-ethnic demography of the population has led to demands for the appointment of judges from a wider range of ethnic backgrounds or origins: in particular, the High Court has remained overwhelmingly Anglo-Celtic. And from yet another perspective, as the boundaries between forms of legal practice are increasingly blurred or restructured, solicitors and lawyers in government service have joined academic lawyers in ruefulness (and sometimes even resentment) at the dominance, among judicial appointees, of those who have established their credentials through the traditional avenue of private practice at the bar.[92]

Each of these concerns raises its own distinct issues. In particular, the argument that selection processes should draw upon a wider and more diverse range of forms of legal experience is frequently met by members of the practising bar (and by judges appointed from the bar) with the counter-argument that thorough familiarity with courtroom procedure and practice is an indispensable prerequisite of competent judicial performance. Ironically, this argument becomes less compelling the further one progresses up the judicial hierarchy.

---

[91] See Cooney (1993); O'Sullivan (1996). Compare Perry (1991) 111–29.
[92] Commonwealth Attorney-General's Department (1993) 16–19.

For a judge presiding at a criminal trial, an experienced understanding of the rules and conventions of courtroom procedure and evidence may well be indispensable. For effective participation in an appellate bench primarily concerned with questions of legal principle, the same need is less apparent. The irony is that those Australian governments which have begun to appoint academic lawyers to the bench have done so primarily at the lower levels.

Fundamentally, however, the various demands for greater 'representativeness' raise the same issue: namely, whether any bench of judges can or should be 'representative' in any meaningful sense. As a practical matter, the larger benches (such as the Federal Court or the larger state Supreme Courts) are probably sufficiently numerous for approximate statistical replication of the distribution among the population at large of characteristics such as ethnicity or gender (including, in the case of the federal judiciary, 'State of Origin'). But the smaller the bench, the more unattainable such a replication becomes. In particular, a High Court composed at any one time of only seven individuals cannot be 'representative' in any meaningful sense. The most that could be envisaged would be a kind of serial representation over time.

The deeper question is whether courts or individual judges should in any sense be representative. The judiciary as a whole, or any one court as a whole, is not and cannot be a 'democratic' institution. To paraphrase Christian Bay,[93] where public decisions call for expert experience and specialised knowledge or technique, such decisions should be made by the relevant experts, and not by participatory or representative majoritarianism. Where public decisions primarily affect the fundamental human rights of a minority, with only a tangential or incidental effect on majority interests, a proper understanding of democracy itself requires that such decisions be based primarily on deference to the affected minority rights. And, finally, there are 'certain questions' affecting human rights to which there are simply 'right and wrong answers'. The work of the courts involves questions of all three kinds; and in all three respects, the appropriate answers are not to be tailored simply to prevailing majoritarian views. Principles of 'representative government', designed

---

[93] Bay (1958) 378–82.

at least to make it more likely that public decisions will reflect the prevailing majoritarian view, are simply out of place.

This, of course, does not mean that judicial efforts at interpreting legal doctrine or protecting minority rights can be wholly inadvertent to community views and values. But assessment of such views and values, and of the weight that they should receive in any individual case, is itself a task to be undertaken judicially and impartially on behalf of the people as a whole, rather than by accommodation of particular sectional interests.

In Australia, some High Court judgments in the 1990s have implied that the judicial arm of government, like its legislative and executive branches, should function in a certain sense as representative of 'the people'. For Deane and Toohey JJ in *Nationwide News Pty Ltd v Wills*,[94] 'the doctrine of representative government' extended to 'those entrusted . . . with the exercise of any part of the legislative, executive *or judicial* powers of government which are ultimately derived from the people themselves'. But this conception of judicial power as a public trust, to be exercised on behalf of 'the people', does not imply a decision-making process based on sectional representation. On the contrary, it emphasises that the responsibility of the courts, like that of the Crown, is to 'the people' as a whole.

This institutional responsibility is also the responsibility of each individual judge. A female judge of Italian descent may well have particular insights to contribute, drawn from her personal experience as a woman or as a member of an Italian community in an Australian multicultural setting. But her task is not to 'represent' the views and interests of women or Italians, but to make her own conscientious attempt at objective assessment of how the problem before the court can best be resolved, on the basis of the most persuasive response to the relevant legal materials. As Sir Gerard Brennan has observed, even in the areas of judicial decision where assessments of 'value' or 'policy' are most inescapably exigent, the task of the individual judge is to evaluate not what she should do, but what the court should do.[95]

---

[94] (1992) 177 CLR 1, 74 (emphasis added).

[95] Brennan (1979) 768–9.

Accordingly, any legitimate demand for more 'representative' judicial appointments is confined to more modest arguments. One is the point, well made by Deborah Cass and Kim Rubenstein,[96] that 'representation', in the case of women, means not only that they should be *represented by* government and *represented in* government, but also that they ought to appear in *representations of* government. Through the major public institutions by which a nation governs itself, it also depicts itself or shows itself forth: and if, in these public manifestations, any distinctive population group is unrepresented (or so minimally represented as to highlight its unequal status more starkly), the symbolic message of exclusion or impotence is itself discriminatory. This first argument applies as strongly to courts as to any other public institution.[97] The second is that the call for 'representativeness' is simply a call for diversity: that even if it is neither possible nor desirable for all experiences and viewpoints to be represented in a collective decision, the inclusion of a wider range of different experiences and viewpoints is more likely to lead to sound judgment. After all, it is just for this reason that appellate and constitutional tasks are assigned to collegiate benches. If all members of a bench share the same kind of background and outlook, the very purpose of a multi-judge bench may be defeated.

To demands for 'representativeness' in this limited sense, the appropriate response lies not in any mandatory system of proportional quotas or dedicated seats, as it might do in principle (subject to difficulties of practical implementation) for a legislative body whose legitimacy depends on representation of the electorate in a more literal sense. The appropriate response lies simply in a greater sensitivity of appointment procedures, first, to the general need for diversity, and second, to the needs or claims of particular demographic groups.

It follows that the real focus of any attempt to reform the appointment process should be not on diversity of output (though that may be the goal to be aimed at), but rather on diversity of input.

---

[96] Cass and Rubenstein (1995) 26.

[97] Compare the emergent 'principle of fair reflection of society by the judiciary' formulated by Shetreet (1987), and adopted by Commonwealth Attorney-General's Department (1993) 6–9.

How can the present appointment process be opened up to greater transparency, and a wider range of external criticism or public debate?

At this point comparisons with the American experience become somewhat paradoxical. In relation to the possible removal of judges, our experience with the 'Murphy affair' proved so intensely and destructively 'political' that we may well have cause to look again with envy at the seemingly more responsible and more solemn operation of the American impeachment process. In relation to the appointment process, the comparison is almost the reverse. For almost a century the Australian experience has been one of relatively smooth and uncontroversial appointments; for over two centuries the American experience has erupted periodically into scarifying and sensational crisis, immensely damaging to the nominees and perhaps to the whole body politic. In the past two decades the sensational hearings of the Senate Judiciary Committee in relation to the nominations of Robert Bork (rejected in 1987) and Clarence Thomas (confirmed in 1991, but only after the national trauma of Anita Hill's sensational allegations of sexual harassment) have convinced most Australians that any reform of Australia's appointment process should not involve anything resembling the American system of Senate confirmation hearings.

Perhaps this reaction underestimates the extent to which the American crises have been by-products of periodic tensions arising for other reasons between President and Congress—as well as the extent to which those tensions in turn reflect the Washington version of the separation of powers, which has no Australian equivalent. In our own political context of closer links between legislative and executive government, a system of Senate confirmation hearings conceivably might prove less colourful than it has in the United States. Yet, even allowing for this possibility, what appears to be needed in Australia is a process which would offer some greater transparency, with more opportunity for professional and public assessment of candidates prior to any decision on appointment, while avoiding the full degree of public exposure and controversy involved in the American system.

While the opportunities for comment in any such process ought not to be limited to the judiciary and the legal profession, each of these bodies would seem to have a special contribution to make. In the United States, the American Bar Association is now regularly expected to offer a formal assessment of nominees,[98] and (less formally) sitting Supreme Court justices have exerted a consistent influence.[99] In India, the constitutional requirement that the Chief Justice of India must always be 'consulted'[100] has been interpreted as meaning that his view must be accepted as binding.[101] By contrast, the anecdotal evidence suggests that although successive Australian Chief Justices have tried to influence the selection process, their efforts have always been in vain.[102] That may be a matter for regret. Yet, in the Australian context, judicial control of judicial appointments would heighten the very danger that has most to be avoided: that is, the danger that the judiciary may become a self-perpetuating homogenous elite.

8 Conclusion: A Judicial Commission?

As it happens, there already exists in Australia a number of institutional avenues through which a collective judicial assessment could be formed and communicated, including the Australian Institute of Judicial Administration, the Judicial Conference of Australia, and the Council of Chief Justices. There has also been considerable interest (most recently from the Australian Law Reform Commission) in establishing, on a more formal institutional basis, an Australian Judicial Commission.[103] Yet again, the intuitive conception is borrowed from an American model, and specifically from the Judicial Commissions now established in a very large number of American states.[104]

---

[98] For all federal judges since 1945, and for the Supreme Court since 1956. See Abraham (1974) 22–31.

[99] Ibid 19–22.

[100] Constitution of India, Art 124(2) (Supreme Court) and Art 217(1) (state High Courts).

[101] *Supreme Court Advocates-on-Record Association v Union of India*, AIR 1994 SC 268.

[102] For instance, it is said that Sir Owen Dixon sought unsuccessfully to have Sir Frederick Jordan appointed to the High Court.

[103] Australian Law Reform Commission (1999b) 75–6.

[104] See Thomas (1997) 247–52; Comisky and Patterson (1987) 10–17.

The composition of these American Judicial Commissions has been extremely diverse. In some cases they consist only of sitting judges, or of sitting and retired judges; in other cases the membership is a mixture of judges and other persons, including lay representatives. The Australian proposals, however, have mostly been for a Commission constituted by members of the judiciary itself. The one standing Commission of this kind in Australia, established in New South Wales by the *Judicial Officers Act 1986* (NSW), is generally seen as a model.

The functions envisaged for a Judicial Commission have also been diverse. Its primary day-to-day function is to oversee the work of the courts in its own jurisdiction; to facilitate efficient solutions to problems of case management and workload; and to receive and investigate complaints about judicial performance, at a level normally stopping far short of any question of removal from the bench.

In these day-to-day functions, Judicial Commissions may well serve a useful role (though even here the supporting argument may sometimes seem to smack unduly of managerialism). But the growing interest in Judicial Commissions appears to be prompted chiefly by the need for an innovative response to the issues discussed in this chapter. The establishment of a Commission, it is said, would provide an avenue for additional input to decisions on judicial appointment, but also (and perhaps primarily) for the orderly investigation and preliminary assessment of allegations potentially leading to a judge's removal from the bench.

As a means of input to appointment decisions, such proposals again encounter the problem that while consultation with judges themselves would be one valuable source of guidance, it ought not under Australian conditions to be the sole or dominant guidance. If the ultimate need is for greater diversity in the range of appointments, that can only be achieved by a greater diversity of consultative or critical opinion. Even if formal arrangements for consultation with a Judicial Commission were explicitly associated with similar consultative arrangements for other bodies, the Commission's institutional status might effectively ensure that its view had 'primacy'.

At least as a means of input to appointment decisions, a formal provision for consultation with a Judicial Commission would raise no constitutional problems, any more than the provision for consultation with state Attorneys-General has been thought to do. (In both cases, of course, the assumption is that mere consultation would in no way limit the ultimate executive discretion.) The use of a Commission to pave the way for consideration of a judge's removal from office is, however, fraught with constitutional problems. The case for Commission inquiry would be strongest in cases where it resulted in a finding of no grounds for removal. It would be weakest in cases where the inquiry resulted in a recommendation that a judge be removed, or simply in the transmission to Parliament of possible grounds for removal. The practical danger in such a case would be that the role of the Commission might pre-empt the constitutional role of the Parliament: that members of Parliament, faced with an onerous and unfamiliar duty, might simply accept at face value the apparent view of the Commission, without the independent assessment that the Constitution requires.

The limited Australian experience on this issue is inconclusive. In Queensland, in June 1989, Justice Angelo Vasta was removed from office on the basis of adverse findings by a Parliamentary Commission of Inquiry;[105] and although the Parliament allowed the judge to appear and speak in his own defence, the vote to remove him was taken late at night after what some members of the House considered to be insufficient debate.[106] The implication was that the House (and the government) had too readily accepted the findings of the Commission. In New South Wales, in June 1998, in the only Australian example of a case considered by a standing Judicial Commission, Justice Vince Bruce was not removed from office.[107] But the allegation against him was a novel and disturbing one not of 'misbehaviour', but of 'incapacity', allegedly demonstrated by extended and repeated delay in delivery of reserved judgments. The judge's defence was that the delay was due to clinical depression. Although it was clear that most members of Parliament, on both

---

[105] See *Parliamentary (Judges) Commission of Inquiry Act 1988* (Qld).

[106] *Queensland Parliamentary Debates*, 7 June 1989, 5273–4.

[107] Waugh (1998).

sides of the debate, had considered the issue for themselves,[108] it is arguable that this was only because the Conduct Division of the Judicial Commission had not itself been unanimous.

The potential constitutional issue is also one of pre-emption, and was illustrated graphically by the doubts surrounding the Parliamentary Commission of Inquiry in the final stages of the 'Murphy affair'. By s 8(1)(b) of its constituent statute the Commission was required to 'inquire and advise the Parliament whether any conduct of the Honourable Lionel Keith Murphy has been such as to amount, in its opinion, to proved misbehaviour within the meaning of section 72 of the Constitution'. In so far as its role was confined to advice, or preliminary fact-finding to prepare the way for a parliamentary debate, its validity was not in doubt. But if the Commission was being asked itself to reach conclusions or express opinions about whether there was 'proved misbehaviour', it was pre-empting the very job on which Parliament alone could venture. The statutory wording was capable of falling on either side of the line. Moreover, even if a form of words was adopted which made it clear that as a matter of law no pre-emption was intended, the possibility that a Commission report might in fact pre-empt full consideration de novo would be constitutionally troubling.

For Evans, though a delegation of preliminary findings to a body external to Parliament is in his view constitutionally possible, the idea that such a body should be constituted by members of the judicial branch is itself a cause for concern. In his view, the answer to the question 'Who judges the judges?' should not be the judges themselves. For judges literally to be judging themselves would clearly be contrary to natural justice;[109] and for judges to be judging a judicial colleague might potentially involve a risk of too sympathetic a view of some colleagues, and too harsh a view of others.

---

[108] Even then, some members felt bound to accept the majority view of the Conduct Division. See *New South Wales Parliamentary Debates*, Legislative Council, 25 June 1998, 6576.

[109] Compare Gerhardt (1996) 174.

In any event, the current fashion for supplementing existing administrative and institutional arrangements by a proliferation of satellite institutions and offices resembles the strategy of pre-Copernican cosmology, in which an inherently unsatisfactory system of explaining planetary orbits was eked out by adding more and more tangential 'epicycles', supposedly bringing each postulated orbit closer to accuracy. If existing procedures for appointment and removal of judges seem unsatisfactory, then, rather than devising additional institutional epicycles, we might do better to modify the central existing design.

14

Federal Judges as Holders of Non-judicial Office

Fiona Wheeler *

1 Introduction

Throughout our history, Australian governments have asked judges to perform a variety of non-judicial functions in addition to the responsibilities of judicial office. Many judges have acceded to these requests, accepting appointments as Royal Commissioners, tribunal members or heads of executive agencies. They have also agreed to conduct governmental inquiries and investigations, to serve on certain advisory bodies, and to issue warrants authorising telephone taps and the use of listening devices in criminal investigations. McHugh J recently observed that many state Chief Justices serve as Lieutenant-Governors and Acting Governors.[1] Most dramatically, Sir John Latham and Sir Owen Dixon, while retaining their commissions as justices of the High Court, served during World War II

---

[1] *Kable v Director of Public Prosecutions (NSW)* (1996) 189 CLR 51, 118.

* I am grateful for the comments of Sir Anthony Mason and Brian Opeskin on an earlier draft of this chapter. Professor Roy Mersky also provided valuable insights into United States law and practice in this area.

as Australian diplomatic representatives in Japan and the United States respectively.[2]

In the extensive literature on this subject, judicial 'skills' and 'authority' feature prominently in the reasons why executive governments have sought to retain the services of judges in these roles.[3] Persons appointed to the bench are leaders in their profession. Their many years of legal experience, usually at the bar, mean that they possess special expertise in analysing evidence and reaching conclusions of fact—skills which are further developed and refined in judicial office. Moreover, judges appointed to inquire into matters of public moment or to participate in the functions of an administrative tribunal not only bring to the task their fact-finding skills, but a detailed understanding of the legal framework within which the inquiry or tribunal is to operate, including the application of the rules of natural justice.[4] In addition, it is widely recognised that judges bring to non-judicial office the 'dignity and authority'[5] associated with the judicial branch. This authority flows in part from judicial expertise but is also intimately linked to the judicial characteristics of independence, impartiality and commitment to due process. Thus, the call for a 'judicial inquiry' into a matter is a call for an expert and impartial investigation by someone above party politics and beyond reproach.[6]

Judges have doubtless accepted these extra-judicial tasks for a variety of reasons; a sense of 'public duty',[7] the challenge of an

---

[2] For examples of the federal government's use of judges in non-judicial roles, see Brown (1992) 50–68. For a list of Royal Commissions undertaken by judges at the request of Australian governments (colonial, state and federal), see McInerney, Moloney and McGregor (1986) 70–87. See also *Wilson v Minister for Aboriginal and Torres Strait Islander Affairs* (1996) 189 CLR 1, 33–4, 42, 45–6 (Kirby J).

[3] Brown, for example, identifies judicial 'skills' and 'prestige' as the 'twofold attraction to Governments in search of people to appoint as Royal Commissioners': (1992) 54. See also McInerney, Moloney and McGregor (1986) 54–8 and *Wilson v Minister for Aboriginal and Torres Strait Islander Affairs* (1996) 189 CLR 1, 36 (Kirby J).

[4] See, for example, Brennan (1978) 4 and McInerney, Moloney and McGregor (1986) 54–5.

[5] Reid (1978) 92.

[6] Reid acutely observed that 'the Executive's need for the help of Judges cannot be divorced from the declining reputation of, and our increasing impatience with, politics and politicians': ibid 92.

[7] *Grollo v Palmer* (1995) 184 CLR 348, 384 (McHugh J).

interesting and novel assignment, and a break from the pressure and monotony of judicial life have all been suggested.[8] Many judges have the capacity to make a valuable contribution to public life outside their courtrooms. Indeed, involvement in at least some of these activities may make judges more effective in the courtroom. With this in mind, Chief Justice Spigelman of the New South Wales Supreme Court in his swearing-in speech urged 'all lawyers, especially judges, to participate in community life beyond the law. This is not a monastic order'. But, as his Honour acknowledged, 'there are restraints on such participation. It is not desirable for members of the judiciary to place themselves in situations where they seek favour from the executive, whether Commonwealth or State'.[9] This then is the well-recognised dilemma: by agreeing to perform the sort of non-judicial functions outlined above and thereby bringing to the task their judicial skills and authority (even if notionally acting in their capacity as private citizens), do judges risk their 'reputation for impartiality and nonpartisanship' upon which 'the legitimacy of the Judicial Branch ultimately depends'?[10] And, as a subsidiary consideration, do judges who accept non-judicial assignments unduly deprive their courts of judicial services at a time when many Australian benches are understaffed?

These questions (and hence the boundary between 'appropriate' and 'inappropriate' extra-judicial involvement in quasi-legislative or executive activities) raise ethical issues which all judges —state and federal—need to address as holders of public office and members of a professional community.[11] For federal judges, however, these ethical issues overlap with, and to a significant extent are subsumed by, important questions of law.[12] The Australian federal judicial system is characterised by a constitutionally entrenched doctrine of separation of powers. As one aspect of this doctrine, the

---

[8] Brown (1992) 87; see also McInerney, Moloney and McGregor (1986) 52–3.

[9] (1998) 44 NSWLR xxvii, xxxv.

[10] *Mistretta v United States*, 488 US 361, 407 (1989).

[11] Wheeler (1996b) 10. See also Thomas (1997) 160–9.

[12] See Thomas (1997) 146.

High Court has recognised that the Constitution sets legally enforceable limits on the non-judicial functions that can validly be exercised by persons who are federal judges. These limits are expressed in the 'designated person principle' (or persona designata doctrine)[13] which has been discussed and applied by the High Court in a series of recent cases. These cases provide considerable guidance as to the elements of the designated person principle, but leave unanswered many questions about its application. This is particularly the case in light of the possible extension of the principle to state judges who are members of courts invested with federal jurisdiction following the decision of the High Court in *Kable v Director of Public Prosecutions (NSW)*.[14]

The question of whether judges—both federal and state—should perform non-judicial functions has always prompted opposing views and the various arguments have been exhaustively surveyed elsewhere.[15] Rather than adopting a position, the purpose here is to trace the evolving role of federal judges as holders of non-judicial office and to examine the way in which the High Court has endeavoured to use the designated person principle to marry this practice with the Constitution's separation of federal judicial power from legislative and executive power.

Based on the actions of certain of its members, the High Court was long regarded as inclined to support the use of individual federal judges in a broad range of executive or quasi-legislative roles. In the last decade, however, the High Court's attitude has hardened and it has curtailed the range of non-judicial functions that can validly be conferred, either by statute or executive action, on a person who is a federal judge. The reasons for this change and the consequences for both the Commonwealth government and members of the federal judiciary will be examined. The position of state judges is also touched on.

---

[13] Except where the context indicates otherwise, 'designated person principle' refers to this constitutional doctrine. Compare the use of the expression in statutory interpretation: *Grollo v Palmer* (1995) 184 CLR 348, 363.

[14] (1996) 189 CLR 51.

[15] See, for example, McInerney, Moloney and McGregor (1986).

2 Historical Overview

To review the history of federal judges serving in non-judicial roles is a difficult task as there is no comprehensive list of such appointments. It is instead a matter of piecing together a generalised account from a disparate range of sources. For this reason, what follows is simply an overview and draws in large part on the compilations of others. The picture that emerges is one of longstanding involvement by members of the federal judiciary in executive and quasi-legislative functions. However, the level of this involvement has varied over time and between different courts.

For many years after federation, the only 'federal' judges in Australia were the members of the High Court and the Commonwealth Court of Conciliation and Arbitration. Section 12(1) of the *Commonwealth Conciliation and Arbitration Act 1904* (Cth) required the President of the Arbitration Court to be appointed 'from among the Justices of the High Court'. Thus, Justice O'Connor and Justice Higgins served in both capacities, Justice O'Connor from 1905 to 1907 and Justice Higgins from 1907 until 1921. In the early years of its existence the legal character of the Arbitration Court's functions was in dispute. Some saw it as an essentially judicial institution exercising the 'judicial' function of industrial arbitration.[16] However, following the 1918 High Court decision in *Waterside Workers' Federation of Australia v J W Alexander Ltd* (*Alexander's Case*)[17] it was accepted that industrial arbitration under s 51(xxxv) of the Constitution was non-judicial in nature as it involved the creation of new industrial rights and responsibilities. *Alexander's Case* also found that as the President of the Arbitration Court was appointed to that post for a term of seven years, the Court could not validly exercise judicial power, such as the enforcement of awards.

Despite these findings, Justice Higgins continued to discharge the arbitral functions of the Court until resigning its presidency in 1921. He was succeeded by Justice Powers, also a member of the

---

[16] See the judgments of Griffith CJ and Barton J in *Waterside Workers' Federation of Australia v J W Alexander Ltd* (1918) 25 CLR 434. See also Sawer (1961a) 73–4.

[17] (1918) 25 CLR 434.

High Court.[18] It was not until 1926 that the Arbitration Court was reconstituted and given a membership distinct from the High Court. As it was intended that the reconstituted court would exercise both arbitral and judicial functions its members were appointed for life in accordance with s 72 of the Constitution. This arrangement continued until 1956 when the High Court in *R v Kirby; Ex parte Boilermakers' Society of Australia (Boilermakers' Case)*[19] found that the Commonwealth Parliament cannot validly invest a body with both judicial and non-judicial power. Thereafter, the Conciliation and Arbitration Commission was established to exercise the function of industrial arbitration. The judicial functions associated with the federal arbitral system were conferred on a separate Commonwealth Industrial Court.

The participation of High Court judges in the functions of the original Arbitration Court is not commonly included among examples of federal judges as holders of non-judicial office, presumably because these appointments were to a 'court', albeit one which *Alexander's Case* found was not constituted as a Chapter III court and could not validly exercise judicial power. Turning to more conventional examples of federal judges in non-judicial roles, both Chief Justice Griffith and Justice Rich served as Royal Commissioners during World War I—Justice Rich on a 1915 Royal Commission into the Liverpool Military Camp and Sir Samuel Griffith on a 1918 Royal Commission into numbers in the Australian Imperial Force.[20] (Justice Rich also served as a delegate to the League of Nations in 1922.)[21] Although the High Court was subsequently approached several times to provide a judge for a Commonwealth Royal Commission, it thereafter adopted a policy of declining such requests.[22]

---

[18] Additionally, Justices Isaacs, Gavan Duffy, Powers, Rich and Starke all served as Deputy Presidents of the Arbitration Court at various times between 1914 and 1922.

[19] (1956) 94 CLR 254. The decision of the High Court was affirmed on appeal to the Privy Council in *Attorney-General of the Commonwealth of Australia v The Queen* (1957) 95 CLR 529.

[20] See McInerney, Moloney and McGregor (1986) 84. See also Bennett (1980) 44; *Australian Dictionary of Biography* vol. 9 (1983) 119 (Griffith); *Australian Dictionary of Biography* vol. 11 (1988) 372 (Rich).

[21] *Australian Dictionary of Biography* vol. 11 (1988) 372.

[22] J. D. Holmes (1955) 268, 272; Winterton (1987) 114–15; Bennett (1980) 44–5.

Despite the position adopted by the High Court, judges appointed to the post-1926 Arbitration Court and to the Federal Court of Bankruptcy conducted inquiries on behalf of the Commonwealth in 1931 and on three occasions during and in the immediate aftermath of World War II.[23] Several members of the High Court also held non-judicial office during the war. The diplomatic roles undertaken by Sir John Latham and Sir Owen Dixon have already been mentioned.[24] In addition, during this period Sir Owen Dixon served on the Central Wool Committee, the Australian Coastal Shipping Control Board, the Commonwealth Marine War Risks Insurance Board, the Salvage Board and the Allied Consultative Shipping Council.[25] Speaking of these appointments in 1955, Sir Owen revealed that in the early stages of the war he had felt 'very depressed' about its outcome:

> In those conditions, feeling very restless indeed and finding it difficult to accommodate myself to sitting on the Bench throughout the war, I agreed to do other work. Looking back from this point of view, I am not sure that it was right. I do not wish it to be thought that, looking in retrospect, I altogether approve of what I myself did.[26]

Justice McTiernan also undertook non-judicial work during World War II, engaging in a Commonwealth inquiry into a controversy over aircraft production.[27] During the initial period of his appointment to the High Court, Justice Webb served as President of the International Military Tribunal for the Far East (1946–48) (see Chapter 13).[28] In addition, Sir Owen Dixon was appointed by the United Nations Security Council in 1950 to mediate between India and Pakistan in relation to Kashmir. He produced a report on the issue.[29]

---

[23] McInerney, Moloney and McGregor (1986) 84–5.

[24] See further Brown (1992) 51–2.

[25] Ibid 51; McInerney, Moloney and McGregor (1986) 33; *Australian Dictionary of Biography* vol. 14 (1996) 8.

[26] J. D. Holmes (1955) 272.

[27] Kirby (1991) 177–8. It is unclear whether this is the same inquiry as the one Griffith and Kennett note is mentioned at 66 CLR iv. See Chapter 2.

[28] Official High Court website: http://www.hcourt.gov.au/: (1958) 32 ALJ 57.

[29] Stephen (1986) 35–6; *Australian Dictionary of Biography* vol. 14 (1996) 8–9.

There were two further federal inquiries presided over by Commonwealth Arbitration or Industrial Court judges in the 1950s and 1960s, including the Royal Commission into the 'Voyager' disaster.[30] It is the 1970s and 1980s, however, that in retrospect mark the highpoint of this type of extra-judicial activity by members of federal courts. With the creation of the Federal Court of Australia and the Family Court of Australia, the period witnessed a significant increase in the number of federal judges. There was also an increase in the number of such judges discharging executive functions, many of these associated with novel legislative initiatives introduced at the time.[31] Thus, members of federal courts—most prominently the Federal Court of Australia[32]—accepted appointment to the Administrative Appeals Tribunal, the Administrative Review Council, the Law Reform Commission and the Trade Practices Tribunal. Federal judges served as Aboriginal Land Commissioner and on various Royal Commissions and inquiries. A federal judge became an ambassador-at-large for nuclear non-proliferation and safeguards; another, Director-General of Security; and a third, Chair of the National Crime Authority.[33] On the application of law enforcement agencies, federal judges performed the non-judicial function of issuing warrants authorising the interception of telecommunications.[34]

The trend in recent years, however, although difficult to quantify, has been towards a declining role for persons who are federal judges in the performance of executive functions.[35] In part this is a

---

[30] McInerney, Moloney and McGregor (1986) 85–6.

[31] See Brown (1992) 58.

[32] Although comprehensive information is not readily available, it is apparent that members of the Family Court have not held non-judicial office to the same extent as members of the Federal Court. Moreover, I can find no record of a High Court judge in this period accepting appointment to undertake an executive or quasi-legislative task. However, Sir Garfield Barwick (Chief Justice 1964–81) was a judge of the International Court of Justice (1973–74) and Sir Daryl Dawson (a Justice 1982–97) served on the Australian Motor Sport Appeal Court (1974–87). Shortly before his retirement from the High Court in 1989, Sir Ronald Wilson became President of the Uniting Church of Australia. See official High Court website: http://www.hcourt.gov.au/. See also McInerney, Moloney and McGregor (1986) 32–4.

[33] Many of these appointments are discussed in Brown (1992) 58–65. See also McInerney, Moloney and McGregor (1986) 86–7. The last appointment mentioned was in 1990–91.

[34] See *Hilton v Wells* (1985) 157 CLR 57; *Grollo v Palmer* (1995) 184 CLR 348.

[35] See also Thomas (1997) 160.

reaction to recent High Court decisions dealing with the designated person principle which have imposed tighter constraints upon the ability of federal judges to perform non-judicial functions consistent with the constitutional separation of powers. These decisions are discussed later. In other respects, however, this trend (and the recent attitude of the High Court itself) may amount to a recognition that, with hindsight, judges in the 1970s and 1980s ventured too far from their courtrooms and that certain functions were, or would now be, incompatible with judicial office as liable to undermine public confidence in the institutional impartiality of the federal courts.[36] A changing social and political environment may also be at work. Thus, Justice J. B. Thomas cites the 'increased politicisation of society' as a reason why Australian judges should be more cautious than ever in deciding whether to undertake commissions of inquiry.[37]

The Federal Court of Australia's *Annual Report 1997–98* indicated that of the 48 members of the Court, 11 held presidential appointments to the Administrative Appeals Tribunal and 4 held such appointments to the National Native Title Tribunal. In addition, there were 7 appointments from among members of the Court to 4 other Commonwealth tribunals. Several persons were appointed to more than one tribunal.[38] Moreover, one member of the Federal Court served as Aboriginal Land Commissioner, another as a part-time Commissioner of the Australian Law Reform Commission, and a third as President of the Australian Industrial Relations Commission.[39] The official Family Court of Australia website indicates that of the 52 members of the Court, 2 are presidential members of the Administrative Appeals Tribunal, and 1 is a part-time Commissioner of the Australian Law Reform Commission.[40]

---

[36] See ibid 160, although framing the point differently: 'The increasing tendency of governments to use the reputation of judges to reduce the impact of controversial issues has led to a discernible movement in Australia against permitting the judiciary to be so used'.

[37] Ibid 164.

[38] For example, all the members of the Court who were appointed to the National Native Title Tribunal also held appointments to the Administrative Appeals Tribunal.

[39] Federal Court of Australia (1998) 2–7.

[40] http://www.familycourt.gov.au/court/html/body_list.html (14 April 1999). In the Family Court of Australia's most recent annual report, three members were listed at 30 June 1998 as presidential members of the Administrative Appeals Tribunal: see Family Court of Australia (1998) 9.

The Federal Court's *Annual Report 1997–98* also noted that 'some judges are identified as designated persons under various Acts, which means they may issue warrants authorising telephone interceptions and the use of listening devices'.[41] As will be seen later in this chapter, the High Court has twice upheld the ability of federal judges to issue interception warrants.[42] However, the practice seems unlikely to continue, at least to any great extent. In May 1997, the Commonwealth Attorney-General told Parliament that the Federal Court judges had decided to withdraw from this activity. According to the Attorney-General, the judges' decision was motivated by 'concern that the workload involved should not interfere with the performance of their judicial duties'.[43] He also referred to recent statements by the High Court that the performance of certain executive tasks by persons who are federal judges may imperil public confidence in judicial independence, but it is not clear whether this was a second reason given by the judges for their decision.[44] Members of the Family Court have apparently adopted the same position.[45] Thus, amendments to federal legislation effected by the *Telecommunications (Interception) and Listening Device Amendment Act 1997* (Cth) now provide for certain members of the Administrative Appeals Tribunal to issue warrants authorising electronic surveillance for the purposes of criminal investigation. The same Act, however, did not remove references to persons who are federal judges from existing legislation in case there was a shift in judicial attitude 'at some time in the future'.[46]

Before leaving this historical overview it remains to point out that individual state judges have performed executive functions at the request of the Commonwealth government, notably the conduct

---

[41] Federal Court of Australia (1998) 7.

[42] *Hilton v Wells* (1985) 157 CLR 57; *Grollo v Palmer* (1995) 184 CLR 348.

[43] *Commonwealth Parliamentary Debates*, House of Representatives, 14 May 1997, 3480 (Daryl Williams, Attorney-General).

[44] Ibid.

[45] Ibid 18 June 1997, 5658 (Daryl Williams, Attorney-General).

[46] Ibid 14 May 1997, 3481 (Daryl Williams, Attorney-General). It seems that some Federal Court and Family Court judges still issue interception warrants, though the majority do not: Attorney-General's Department (1999) 44–5. Whether this represents more than a transitional arrangement is unclear.

of Royal Commissions and other inquiries.[47] Practice at purely state level has varied: in New South Wales, state judges have historically performed a range of non-judicial functions at the request of the state government.[48] By contrast, the tradition in Victoria has been shaped by the 'Irvine Memorandum' of 1923 in which the Chief Justice of that state set out his reasons for declining to free a member of the Supreme Court to conduct a state Royal Commission. Victorian judges, at least of the Supreme Court, have traditionally declined extra-judicial roles.[49]

3 The Separation of Federal Judicial Power

The separation of federal judicial power from federal legislative and executive power enshrined in the text and structure of the Australian Constitution—notably the wording of ss 1, 61 and 71, and the framework of Chapters I, II and III—was discussed in Chapter 1. The stringency with which the High Court has applied the separation doctrine has varied over the years. However, a series of cases prior to 1920 established that federal judicial power can only be exercised by Chapter III courts and cannot be invested, for example, in federal tribunals whose members are not appointed in accordance with the tenure requirements set out in s 72 of the Constitution.[50] In 1956 in *R v Kirby; Ex parte Boilermakers' Society of Australia* (*Boilermakers' Case*) the separation doctrine was extended to embrace the further requirement that the Commonwealth Parliament cannot validly invest federal courts with non-judicial functions.[51] In this regard, s 71's exclusive vesting of the 'judicial power of the Commonwealth' in a series of 'courts' was read as an exhaustive statement of the functions that can validly be conferred on such

---

[47] McInerney, Moloney and McGregor (1986) 83–7.

[48] Ibid 19–31.

[49] Ibid 10–19. See also Thomas (1997) 160–1.

[50] *Huddart, Parker & Co Pty Ltd v Moorehead* (1909) 8 CLR 330; *New South Wales v Commonwealth* (*Wheat Case*) (1915) 20 CLR 54 and *Waterside Workers' Federation of Australia v J W Alexander Ltd* (1918) 25 CLR 434.

[51] (1956) 94 CLR 254 upheld on appeal to the Privy Council in *Attorney-General of the Commonwealth of Australia v The Queen* (1957) 95 CLR 529.

bodies by the Commonwealth. It follows, for example, that it would be contrary to Chapter III of the Constitution for the Commonwealth to add to the judicial responsibilities of the Federal Court the merits review function currently exercised by the Administrative Appeals Tribunal.

Although the High Court has traditionally justified the separation doctrine primarily in terms of textual factors, the doctrine serves to promote the rule of law and the impartial administration of justice.[52] These values should inform any system of government, but are widely regarded as particularly important in a federal system such as ours.[53] As the Privy Council observed in the *Boilermakers' Case*: 'in a federal system the absolute independence of the judiciary is the bulwark of the constitution against encroachment whether by the legislature or by the executive. To vest in the same body executive and judicial power is to remove a vital constitutional safeguard'.[54] The High Court majority in the *Boilermakers' Case* had earlier bolstered its textual arguments in favour of the separation doctrine by reference to a similar policy consideration.[55] Thus, it has long been acknowledged that the separation doctrine is a purposive one, or, at least, one that serves an important role in our constitutional system.[56]

But despite the consolidation of the separation doctrine in the above form by 1956, the question whether, or to what extent, federal judges can validly exercise legislative or executive functions in their personal capacities—the validity of 'personal mixtures of function'[57]—was not directly considered by the High Court until comparatively recently. Prior to the expansion in the 1970s of the

---

[52] *Wilson v Minister for Aboriginal and Torres Strait Islander Affairs* (1996) 189 CLR 1, 11–13 (Brennan CJ, Dawson, Toohey, McHugh and Gummow JJ).

[53] Ibid 12–13 (Brennan CJ, Dawson, Toohey, McHugh and Gummow JJ).

[54] *Attorney-General of the Commonwealth of Australia v The Queen* (1957) 95 CLR 529, 540–1.

[55] *R v Kirby; Ex parte Boilermakers' Society of Australia* (1956) 94 CLR 254, 276 (Dixon CJ, McTiernan, Fullagar and Kitto JJ). See also Hamilton, Jay and Madison (1787) No 78.

[56] See also *R v Davison* (1954) 90 CLR 353, 380–2 (Kitto J).

[57] Sawer (1967) 165.

number of federal judges serving in non-judicial roles, the issue was unlikely to generate litigation.[58] Nonetheless, the practical precedent provided by leading members of the High Court serving in ambassadorial-style positions in Tokyo and Washington doubtless fostered a belief among lawyers that such appointments were constitutionally valid, provided the judge was acting as a designated person.[59] In this context, the High Court had recognised in cases prior to the *Boilermakers' Case* (although none of these concerned federal judges in non-judicial roles) that it was possible to distinguish between a judge acting as a member of his or her court and a judge acting as a designated person, that is, as a person or tribunal separate from their court.[60] Although Dixon J in *Medical Board of Victoria v Meyer* criticised certain applications of this designated person device as possessing a 'metaphysical' quality, he did not reject the notion outright.[61] Thus, in the wake of the *Boilermakers' Case* it was possible to argue that if a federal judge agreed to perform a particular non-judicial task in a personal capacity, no violation of the separation of powers was involved because no function had been conferred on a federal court or on a judge as a member of a federal court.[62]

Clearly, this is a highly formalistic interpretation of the separation doctrine which ignores the values associated with the *Boilermakers'* rule: 'if contact with non-judicial functions is likely to undermine the impartiality and independence of the judiciary, that influence will be no less if the judge voluntarily undertakes the func-

---

[58] Sawer doubted whether the issue would ever be litigated: ibid 165. See also Sawer (1961b) 181.

[59] See Sawer (1961b) 181. See also Winterton (1987) 122.

[60] See *Holmes v Angwin* (1906) 4 CLR 297, 304–7 (Griffith CJ), 309 (Barton J); *Medical Board of Victoria v Meyer* (1937) 58 CLR 62, 71–2 (Latham CJ), 80–1 (Rich J), 105–6 (Evatt J); *Queen Victoria Memorial Hospital v Thornton* (1953) 87 CLR 144, 152 (Dixon CJ, McTiernan, Williams, Webb, Fullagar, Kitto and Taylor JJ). In relation to a similar distinction in the United States, see Calabresi and Larsen (1994) 1132.

[61] (1937) 58 CLR 62, 97.

[62] See, for example, Sawer (1967) 166.

tion in his "personal capacity" than if he does so ex officio'.[63] Nonetheless, this formalism was not inconsistent with the approach to
constitutional interpretation which prevailed in the High Court in
the 1950s and 1960s. Indeed, Webb J suggested in dissent in the
Boilermakers' Case that if he were wrong in upholding the conferral
of both arbitral and judicial functions on the Arbitration Court, this
arrangement could be maintained under the majority view by simply
conferring arbitral powers upon the judges of the Arbitration Court
as designated persons.[64]

The view that 'personal mixtures of function' were not necessarily inconsistent with the *Boilermakers' Case* gained further force
from the fact that when Australian lawyers in this period looked to
the United States—whose Constitution also embodies a binding
doctrine of separation of powers—they saw that federal judges had
historically accepted a range of non-judicial assignments.[65] This
'continuing, albeit controversial, practice' included members of
the Supreme Court.[66] For example, in 1941 Justice Roberts was
appointed by President Roosevelt to head an inquiry into the attack
on Pearl Harbor. In 1945 Justice Jackson accepted appointment as a
prosecutor at the Nuremberg War Trials and was absent from the
Court for a year. And in 1963, Chief Justice Warren agreed, with
well known reservations, to head the executive inquiry into the
assassination of President Kennedy.[67] In a more extreme example it
was revealed in the late 1960s that Justice Fortas had acted as an
informal adviser to President Johnson and had contributed to the

---

[63] Zines and Lindell (1982) 613. Zines and Lindell were specifically referring to the Federal Court decision in *Drake v Minister for Immigration and Ethnic Affairs* (1979) 24
ALR 577. However, they were responding to the same formalistic argument outlined
in the text. See also Sawer (1967) 165 and Winterton (1987) 124.

[64] *R v Kirby; Ex parte Boilermakers' Society of Australia* (1956) 94 CLR 254, 329–30.
His Honour observed that this 'might seem to circumvent the Constitution by observing its letter whilst violating its spirit. But it is sufficient for my purposes that Parliament could resort to it': 330. See also 281 (Dixon CJ, McTiernan, Fullagar and
Kitto JJ).

[65] Calabresi and Larsen (1994) 1131–41. See also Sawer (1961b) 181.

[66] *Mistretta v United States*, 488 US 361, 400 (1989) (Blackmun J for a majority of the
Court). For criticism of the practice see, for example, A. T. Mason (1953).

[67] See A. T. Mason (1953) 199, 209–13; Calabresi and Larsen (1994) 1136–7.

framing of a State of the Union Address and executive policy on the Vietnam War.[68] Justice Fortas' actions polarised opinion, resulting, in the view of one commentator, in a 'collective black eye for the federal judiciary'.[69]

4 The Designated Person Principle in the Courts

Ultimately, the designated person exception to the rule in the *Boilermakers' Case* was authoritatively recognised by the Australian courts in a series of cases beginning in 1979. In the 1980s, it seemed a broad and somewhat formalistic exception, untuned to the constitutional values which the rule in the *Boilermakers' Case* promotes. More recent cases, however, have sought to 'rein in' the designated person principle and to mould its substantive application to the object and purpose of the separation doctrine. The use of federal judges in non-judicial roles has thus been constrained, although not rejected.

(a) The cases: from *Drake* to *Wilson*

The first cases specifically to consider the performance of non-judicial functions by federal judges as designated persons were *Drake v Minister for Immigration and Ethnic Affairs* (*Drake's Case*), decided by the Federal Court in 1979, and *Hilton v Wells*,[70] decided by the High Court in 1985. Both arose from the expansion during this period of the use of federal judges in non-judicial roles.

Drake's Case was an 'appeal' to the Federal Court from a determination of the Administrative Appeals Tribunal affirming the

---

[68] See Calabresi and Larsen (1994) 1137; Krotoszynski (1997) 465.

[69] Krotoszynski (1997) 465. Compare Sir Garfield Barwick's decision as Chief Justice of the High Court to advise the Governor-General during the 1975 constitutional crisis: Marr (1992) ch. 19. Former federal politician Sir John Latham did not sever all political contacts while Chief Justice of the High Court. On several occasions he offered advice on a range of issues to leading figures on the conservative side of federal politics: Thomas (1997) 150–1. See also Thomas's discussion of the activities of Justice Evatt (151–2) while on the High Court, and his reference to Sir Owen Dixon (153–5). For an overview of the advisory activities of Sir Samuel Griffith while Chief Justice of the High Court, see *Australian Dictionary of Biography* vol. 9 (1983) 119.

[70] (1979) 24 ALR 577 and (1985) 157 CLR 57 respectively.

Minister's decision to deport Mr Drake. The Tribunal had been constituted by presidential member Davies who was also a member of the Federal Court. Section 7 of the *Administrative Appeals Tribunal Act 1975* (Cth) nominated membership of a court created by Parliament as one of the qualifications for appointment to the Tribunal as a presidential member. The Federal Court rejected an argument that Justice Davies' appointment to the Tribunal was constitutionally invalid. Without exploring the constitutional issues in detail, the joint judgment of Bowen CJ and Deane J (with whom Smithers J agreed on this aspect of the case) claimed that the argument:

> confuses the appointment of a person, who has the qualification of being a judge of a court created by the Parliament, to perform an administrative function with the purported investing of a court created under Ch III of the Constitution with functions which are properly administrative in their nature. Mr Justice Davies' appointment as a presidential member was a personal appointment.[71]

That is, the separation of powers was not infringed because no functions had been conferred on the Federal Court. This was so even though Justice Davies had been appointed to the Tribunal in his personal capacity on the basis that he met the statutory criterion of being a federal judge.

Although the issue was addressed only briefly, the Court's response to the separation of powers argument in *Drake's Case* suggested that the designated person exception to the rule in the *Boilermakers' Case* was a broad one, potentially sustaining a wide range of 'personal mixtures of function'. The approach of the High Court majority in *Hilton v Wells* supported this view. The case concerned the validity of s 20 of the *Telecommunications (Interception) Act 1979* (Cth) which empowered a 'Judge' upon application by a member of the federal police to issue a warrant authorising a telephone tap for the purpose of a criminal investigation. 'Judge' was defined to include 'a Judge of the Federal Court of Australia' and 'a Judge of the Supreme Court of a State' but, in the case of the latter, only where 'an appropriate arrangement' had been made in relation

---

[71] *Drake v Minister for Immigration and Ethnic Affairs* (1979) 24 ALR 577, 583–4.

to 'all or any' such persons with the state Governor. The interception warrants in question had been authorised by two members
of the Federal Court. The function was clearly a non-judicial one.

Gibbs CJ, Wilson and Dawson JJ upheld s 20 in the face of a
separation of powers challenge. With surprisingly little analysis, but
referring approvingly to *Drake's Case*, their Honours endorsed the
designated person exception to the rule in the *Boilermakers' Case*:
'Although the Parliament cannot confer non-judicial powers on a
federal court … there is no necessary constitutional impediment
which prevents it from conferring non-judicial power on a particular individual who happens to be a member of a court'.[72]

Thus, the critical question was one of statutory construction:
was the power in s 20 of the Act vested in the Federal Court or in its
judges considered as individuals? Despite the fact that s 20 was
directed to all judges of the Federal Court described as judges, their
Honours concluded that the power was conferred on designated
persons. Three reasons supported this outcome. First, as the power
was clearly conferred on judges of state Supreme Courts in their personal capacity, it could be assumed that Parliament meant to be consistent in this regard. Second, as the power to issue an interception
warrant was non-judicial in nature, 'it is likely that it is intended to
be exercised by the judge as a designated person'. Third, their
Honours noted that nothing in the *Federal Court of Australia Act
1976* (Cth) was expressly made relevant to performance of the s 20
function.[73]

By contrast, Mason and Deane JJ criticised this outcome as inconsistent with settled principles of statutory construction and fail-
ing to give substantive effect to the separation doctrine. Significantly,
their Honours did not reject the designated person exception to
the rule in the *Boilermakers' Case*. They spoke approvingly, for
example, of the outcome in *Drake's Case*.[74] However, they signalled
that the use of federal judges in non-judicial roles was subject to
restraints flowing from 'the underlying concept of the separation of

---

[72] *Hilton v Wells* (1985) 157 CLR 57, 68.
[73] Ibid 73.
[74] Ibid 81.

powers'.[75] Thus, they suggested that Parliament could not oblige a federal judge to undertake a particular legislative or executive activity as a designated person, and that such activities must not be 'inconsistent with the essence of the judicial function and the proper performance by the judiciary of its responsibilities for the exercise of judicial power'.[76] Admittedly, the majority also recognised this latter proposition, but included it as something of an afterthought to their decision, seemingly downplaying its significance.[77] Ultimately, Mason and Deane JJ did not explore these ideas because they found, as a matter of statutory construction, that the function of issuing interception warrants had been conferred upon Federal Court judges as such.[78] Nonetheless, their Honours declined to find s 20 invalid in the absence of argument on a submission foreshadowed by the Commonwealth that the *Boilermakers' Case* be reconsidered.[79]

When these issues returned to the High Court a decade later in *Grollo v Palmer*,[80] the approach of Mason and Deane JJ in *Hilton v Wells* formed the basis of a significant restatement of the way in which the exercise by federal judges of non-judicial functions was to be reconciled with the separation of powers. Whereas the majority in *Hilton v Wells* had not seemed unduly worried by federal judges serving in non-judicial roles, in *Grollo v Palmer* all members of the High Court showed concern about the practice, or at least aspects of it.[81] The issue in *Grollo v Palmer* was again the validity of provisions of the *Telecommunications (Interception) Act* enabling Federal Court judges to issue interception warrants. However, the

---

[75] Ibid 82.

[76] Ibid 82–3.

[77] Ibid 73–4.

[78] Ibid 84–6.

[79] Mason J had earlier suggested that he may be prepared to revisit the rule established in *R v Kirby; Ex parte Boilermakers' Society of Australia* (1956) 94 CLR 254: see *R v Joske; Ex parte Australian Building Construction Employees & Builders' Labourers' Federation* (1974) 130 CLR 87, 102. See also his criticisms of the *Boilermakers' Case*: Sir Anthony Mason (1996).

[80] (1995) 184 CLR 348. In *Jones v Commonwealth* (1987) 71 ALR 497 a majority of the High Court declined to reconsider *Hilton v Wells* (1985) 157 CLR 57.

[81] See the view of the Attorney-General: *Commonwealth Parliamentary Debates*, House of Representatives, 18 June 1997, 5658 (Daryl Williams).

Act had been amended since *Hilton v Wells* in order to emphasise that the function was given to judges as designated persons. Entwined with this was a mechanism which ensured that only those individual judges who consented were entrusted with authority under the Act. Thus, figures quoted by the High Court showed that in 1994, 30 of the 35 judges of the Federal Court had agreed to serve under the Act as 'eligible Judges'.[82]

Once again these provisions survived Chapter III challenge, but the joint majority judgment of Brennan CJ, Deane, Dawson and Toohey JJ specifically endorsed the limitations heralded by Mason and Deane JJ in *Hilton v Wells* upon the power 'to confer non-judicial functions on judges as designated persons':

> first, no non-judicial function that is not incidental to a judicial function can be conferred without the judge's consent; and, second, no function can be conferred that is incompatible either with the judge's performance of his or her judicial functions or with the proper discharge by the judiciary of its responsibilities as an institution exercising judicial power ('the incompatibility condition').[83]

Their Honours recognised that incompatibility 'may arise in a number of different ways', notably by the performance of non-judicial functions which 'prejudice' a judge's capacity to discharge his or her judicial duties with integrity or, alternatively, undermine public confidence in that capacity or public confidence in the integrity of the judiciary as a whole. In addition, incompatibility could flow from 'so permanent and complete a commitment to the performance of non-judicial functions by a judge that the further performance of substantial judicial functions by that judge is not practicable'.[84] Both the 'consent' and 'incompatibility' limitations were implied from the constitutional separation of powers and the nature of the judicial function.[85] In their separate judgments, McHugh J and Gummow J recognised a similar incompatibility limitation.[86]

---

[82] *Grollo v Palmer* (1995) 184 CLR 348, 357.

[83] Ibid 364–5.

[84] Ibid 365.

[85] Ibid 365.

[86] Ibid 376–7 (McHugh J), 389, 392, 398 (Gummow J).

It thus became necessary in *Grollo v Palmer* to determine whether the activities of individual federal judges under the Act infringed the incompatibility condition. Three features of service as an 'eligible Judge' suggested that it was liable to undermine public confidence in the Federal Court. First, the circumstances associated with the issue of a warrant could subsequently generate a 'matter' coming before the Federal Court for judicial resolution. Thus, an individual judge might need to disqualify him or herself, a situation complicated by the duty of confidentiality to which persons issuing interception warrants were subject. Second, the issue of a warrant was an intrusive aspect of the criminal investigative process. Third, the manner in which the power was exercised was contrary to the traditional judicial process, being discharged ex parte, in secret, and without the giving of reasons.[87] For McHugh J, in a forcefully argued dissent, these factors were sufficient to establish incompatibility based on a weakening of public confidence in judicial independence and impartiality.[88] For Brennan CJ, Deane, Dawson and Toohey JJ, however, two additional factors led to the opposite conclusion. Their Honours conceded the force of the incompatibility argument, but emphasised that in authorising telecommunications interceptions, judges fulfilled a valuable social function the objective of which was consistent with the traditional role of the courts:

> it is precisely because of the intrusive and clandestine nature of interception warrants and the necessity to use them in today's continuing battle against serious crime that some impartial authority, accustomed to the dispassionate assessment of evidence and sensitive to the common law's protection of privacy and property . . . be authorised to control the official interception of communications. In other words, the professional experience and cast of mind of a judge is a desirable guarantee that the appropriate balance will be kept between the law enforcement agencies on the one hand and criminal suspects or suspected sources of information about crime on the other. It is an eligible judge's function of deciding independently of the applicant agency whether an interception warrant should issue that separates

---

[87] Ibid 366–7.
[88] Ibid 378–83.

the eligible judge from the executive function of law enforcement. It is the recognition of that independent role that preserves public confidence in the judiciary as an institution.[89]

In addition, their Honours pointed out that similar reasoning had resulted in judges being invested with like powers in a number of other countries and in a majority of Australian states and territories.[90]

Despite this outcome in *Grollo v Palmer* certain passages in the joint judgment suggest that the finding of compatibility was a borderline one. This, in turn, may have contributed to the recent decision of members of the Federal Court to exit the field of telecommunications interceptions. Whether or not this is so, only a year after *Grollo v Palmer* the High Court's intensifying concern to shield the federal judiciary from the political branches of government was made manifest in *Wilson v Minister for Aboriginal and Torres Strait Islander Affairs* (*Wilson's Case*).[91] This is the first and, as yet, only decision in which the appointment of a federal judge as a designated person to perform a non-judicial function has been struck down by the High Court as contrary to the Constitution. The case was a challenge to the consensual appointment, in her personal capacity, of a Federal Court judge to serve as a 'reporter' under the *Aboriginal and Torres Strait Islander Heritage Protection Act 1984* (Cth). The function involved writing a report for the Minister as a prerequisite to the Minister's exercise of a statutory discretion to issue a protection order in relation to an area of significance to Aborigines. The Act required a report to deal with enumerated matters such as the nature of the prohibitions that should apply to the area, the impact of those prohibitions on persons holding proprietary or pecuniary interests in the area, and 'the extent to which the area is or may be protected by or under a law of a State or Territory'.

The joint majority judges (Brennan CJ, Dawson, Toohey, McHugh and Gummow JJ) found that service by an individual judge

---

[89] Ibid 367.
[90] Ibid 367–8.
[91] (1996) 189 CLR 1.

as a reporter was inconsistent with maintenance of public confidence in judicial independence from the executive branch.[92] In what looked like a conscious attempt further to limit the scope of the designated person principle, their Honours said that when asking whether performance of a function 'closely connected' with the legislature or the executive was liable to undermine public confidence in the judiciary or an individual judge, incompatibility would be established if the function was not 'required to be performed independently of any instruction, advice or wish of the Legislature or the Executive Government, other than a law', or involved the exercise of a 'political' discretion. This was described as a discretion exercisable on grounds 'not confined by factors expressly or impliedly prescribed by law'.[93]

Although a reporter was bound by the rules of natural justice (a consideration the High Court recognised would assist a finding of compatibility), the reporting function infringed both criteria: the Act did not insulate a reporter from the wishes of the Minister, but instead placed a reporter 'in a position equivalent to that of a ministerial adviser'. Moreover, in the absence of a policy directive from the Minister, a reporter acted politically in advising on such matters as the nature of an appropriate protective regime.[94] A further indication of incompatibility was the requirement that a reporter deal with the extent to which an area was protected under state law. This was said to be an advisory opinion, the rendering of which to the executive was 'alien to the exercise of the judicial power of the Commonwealth'.[95]

These 'criteria of incompatibility' were presented by the joint majority in *Wilson's Case* in such a way as to suggest that they henceforth govern the question whether 'public confidence incompatibility'[96] exists in any particular case. But if *Wilson's Case* now states the 'test' for this form of incompatibility, it seems an unduly

---

[92] Ibid 16–21. Gaudron J reached the same conclusion in a separate judgment: 26.
[93] Ibid 17.
[94] Ibid 19.
[95] Ibid 19–20.
[96] Walker (1997) 159.

rigid one. Significantly, towards the end of their judgment their Honours commented that 'it seems that the criteria of incompatibility above expressed have not always been observed in practice'.[97] Thus, it was recognised that certain non-judicial functions undertaken by federal judges in the past would not survive constitutional challenge today. (Possible examples of such functions are discussed at the end of the chapter.)

Kirby J dissented in *Wilson's Case*. Two factors, in particular, contributed to his Honour's finding against incompatibility.[98] First, he emphasised that Australian judges, including federal judges, had historically conducted inquiries on behalf of the Commonwealth. The utilisation of judges in these and many other non-judicial roles was 'incontestably to the benefit of good government'.[99] Second, his Honour took a more robust view than the majority of the provision made by statute for the independence of a reporter, observing that he or she was obliged 'to act with lawfulness, integrity and fairness' and in a manner 'wholly independent of the Minister and completely conformable to the conduct normal to a judge'.[100] In these circumstances, if the secretive function of authorising telephone taps was compatible with judicial office under Chapter III of the Constitution, then the appointment of a federal judge to serve as a reporter must be valid.[101]

(b) Application of the designated person principle

The treatment of the designated person principle in the courts from *Drake's Case* to *Wilson's Case* prompts several questions. Why has the High Court taken a progressively stricter approach to the ability of persons who are federal judges to discharge legislative and executive functions? In terms of the application of the incompatibility test, are the outcomes in *Grollo v Palmer* and *Wilson's Case* consistent or, as some commentators have argued, do those cases reveal the

---

[97] *Wilson v Minister for Aboriginal and Torres Strait Islander Affairs* (1996) 189 CLR 1, 20.

[98] See also Wheeler (1996b) 12.

[99] *Wilson v Minister for Aboriginal and Torres Strait Islander Affairs* (1996) 189 CLR 1, 42. See also 34, 49 (Kirby J).

[100] Ibid 38. See generally 37–8 (Kirby J).

[101] Ibid 49–50.

inherent uncertainty of the incompatibility notion?[102] What non-judicial functions can now validly be performed by federal judges in their personal capacity?

One explanation for the narrowing of the designated person exception to the rule in the *Boilermakers' Case* is the trend, apparent for over a decade, to substance over form in constitutional interpretation.[103] Although the more prominent examples of this trend are associated with ss 90, 92 and 117 of the Constitution, there are several recent cases in which members of the High Court have depicted the separation of federal judicial power from legislative and executive power as a purposive doctrine and endorsed a substantive approach to its application: the emergence of the curial due process implication[104] and the implied immunity of citizens from executive detention recognised by three judges in *Chu Kheng Lim v Minister for Immigration*[105] fall into this category. Seen in this light, the consent and incompatibility limitations to the designated person principle adopted in *Grollo v Palmer* and *Wilson's Case* were simply a belated reaction to the formalism of the generalised 'designated person' concept. As McHugh J said in *Grollo v Palmer* in a passage that was quoted approvingly by the joint majority in *Wilson's Case*:

> Clearly, a tension exists between complying with the principle of the separation of powers and vesting powers in federal judges as persona designata. If the separation of powers doctrine is to continue effectively as one of the bulwarks of liberty enacted by the Constitution, the incompatibility qualification on the persona designata doctrine is a necessity ... The constitutional wall that separates the exercise of judicial power and the exercise of executive power would be effectively breached if a federal judge could exercise any executive power invested in him or her as persona designata.[106]

The High Court in *Grollo v Palmer* and *Wilson's Case* was also influenced by United States authority, notably the 1989 decision of

---

[102] See, for example, Walker (1997).

[103] As to this trend, see generally Zines (1997) 444–9.

[104] Winterton (1994) 199–200 and Wheeler (1997) 249–55.

[105] (1992) 176 CLR 1, 27–9 (Brennan, Deane and Dawson JJ).

[106] *Grollo v Palmer* (1995) 184 CLR 348, 376. And see *Wilson v Minister for Aboriginal and Torres Strait Islander Affairs* (1996) 189 CLR 1, 13–14.

the Supreme Court in *Mistretta v United States*. There it was held that the separation of powers under the United States Constitution did not prevent federal judges, considered as individuals, from serving in non-judicial roles. Nonetheless, the Supreme Court found that Congress could not necessarily require federal judges to perform such non-judicial functions and that 'the ultimate inquiry remains whether a particular extrajudicial assignment undermines the integrity of the Judicial Branch'.[107] Somewhat surprisingly, by the Supreme Court's own admission, *Mistretta v United States* was the first occasion the Court had 'specifically addressed the constitutionality of extrajudicial service'.[108] The position it adopted clearly helped shape the High Court's response to the same issue.[109]

But, as foreshadowed earlier, other factors may also be at work. A reduced role for federal judges in the discharge of executive functions and the identification of the boundaries of constitutionally permissible extra-judicial activity primarily by reference to the needs of judicial independence and impartiality (as well as public confidence therein) signal a renewed emphasis by the High Court on the values implicit in Chapter III of the Constitution. This may in turn reflect a concern more vigorously to assert and maintain the independence of the judiciary in increasingly uncertain times. A multiplicity of interconnected factors may be fuelling such a concern, including the 'judicialisation of society' in the sense of the growth in the range of social issues which now come before the courts as justiciable controversies,[110] and the decline of 'legalism' as a method of judicial reasoning.[111] The past decade has also witnessed a weakening of the conventions and attitudes that traditionally shielded judges from personal criticism and political 'attacks' on judgments, particularly

---

[107] *Mistretta v United States*, 488 US 361, 404 (Blackmun J for a majority of the Court).

[108] Ibid 402 (Blackmun J for a majority of the Court).

[109] See, for example, *Grollo v Palmer* (1995) 184 CLR 348, 365 (Brennan CJ, Deane, Dawson and Toohey JJ) and *Wilson v Minister for Aboriginal and Torres Strait Islander Affairs* (1996) 189 CLR 1, 9 (Brennan CJ, Dawson, Toohey, McHugh and Gummow JJ). However, on the facts in *Mistretta v United States*, the Supreme Court found that federal judges, as individuals, could validly participate in the non-judicial functions of the United States Sentencing Commission.

[110] Sackville (1997) 152–3.

[111] Ibid 151–2.

from politicians.[112] At the same time, the Attorney-General's role as 'defender' of the federal judiciary has become more limited, with the prospect that the judges themselves must now publicly explain their responsibilities and functions in the face of unjustified attack. There have been tensions between the judiciary and Australian governments over the appropriate level of public funding for courts and the legal system generally,[113] as well as a decline in the tradition of 'judicial reticence' in Australia (see generally Chapter 3). The politicisation of certain recent inquiries conducted by retired judges is also a relevant factor.[114]

Whatever the exact reasons for this shift to a more stringent assertion of judicial independence under Chapter III of the Constitution, they are not confined to the federal courts as the decision in *Kable v Director of Public Prosecutions (NSW)* (*Kable's Case*)[115] demonstrates (see Chapters 1 and 2). There the High Court reasoned that the Constitution envisages the existence of an 'integrated system of State and federal courts'[116] for the exercise of the judicial power of the Commonwealth and therefore it is contrary to Chapter III for a state to confer functions on a state court 'incompatible with' or 'repugnant to' the exercise by that court of federal judicial power.[117] McHugh J accepted that this incompatibility limitation extended to the use of individual state judges in non-judicial roles, observing that 'although nothing in Ch III prevents a State from conferring executive government functions on a State court judge as persona designata, if the appointment . . . gave the appearance that the court as an institution was not independent of the executive

---

[112] Brennan (1998) 39–42. See also Kirby (1998).

[113] Aspects of this are touched on in Brennan (1998) 35–6.

[114] The 'Marks Inquiry' is a frequently cited example. See Sir Anthony Mason (1996) 7; Thomas (1997) 165; T. Sherman (1997) 8. Many of these factors are associated with the 'increased politicisation of society': Thomas (1997) 164. See the earlier discussion of this.

[115] (1996) 189 CLR 51.

[116] Ibid 114 (McHugh J).

[117] Ibid 103 (Gaudron J), 116 (McHugh J), 126–8 (Gummow J). This summary necessarily glosses over many subtleties. In particular, the approach of Toohey J (the fourth member of the majority of the six-member bench) was somewhat narrower than that of Gaudron, McHugh and Gummow JJ.

government of the State, it would be invalid'.[118] He suggested, however, that in relation to persons who are state judges, this incompatibility test will be applied more liberally and with greater deference to historical practice than is the case with persons who are federal judges.[119] The only other member of the majority in *Kable's Case* to address the designated person issue was Gaudron J. She denied that the incompatibility doctrine in *Kable's Case* applied to the conferral of non-judicial functions on state judges in their personal capacity.[120] Her Honour's view, however, seems a formalistic one, and McHugh J's view is likely to prevail.[121]

On its facts, *Kable's Case* concerned the validity of a New South Wales statute empowering the Supreme Court to issue a 'preventive detention order', but McHugh J described the doctrine in *Kable's Case* as limiting both Commonwealth and state power.[122] Thus, in the wake of *Kable's Case* the Commonwealth will not necessarily be able to look to state judges, even with the agreement of the state and judge concerned, to fill a quasi-legislative or executive post which *Grollo v Palmer* and *Wilson's Case* would deny to a federal judge.[123]

Returning to the designated person principle as an exception to the rule in the *Boilermakers' Case*, one might ask why the High Court has continued to recognise that exception at all. A substantive approach to the separation doctrine coupled with a renewed emphasis on judicial independence under the judicature provisions of the Constitution might lead to the conclusion that the rule in the *Boilermakers' Case* should be rigidly applied to prevent the conferral of legislative and executive functions on federal courts and federal judges, even when the latter are acting in their personal capacity. Kristen Walker has recently argued the case for this out-

---

[118] Ibid 117.

[119] Ibid 117–18.

[120] Ibid 104.

[121] See also Campbell (1997) 414 and Carney (1997) 186–7.

[122] *Kable v Director of Public Prosecutions (NSW)* (1996) 189 CLR 51, 116.

[123] See also Carney (1997) 182.

come.[124] While the rule in the *Boilermakers' Case* stands[125] it is difficult to accept that the designated person principle as it emerged from *Grollo v Palmer* and *Wilson's Case* is other than a pragmatic compromise which recognises both aspects of historical practice and the current role of federal judges on certain quasi-judicial bodies such as the Administrative Appeals Tribunal.[126] But if such non-judicial functions can in fact be performed by persons who are federal judges without undermining public confidence in judicial independence, or otherwise threatening judicial integrity, then maybe it is the rule in the *Boilermakers' Case* which should be overturned.[127]

Whichever course the High Court adopts, the current incompatibility condition is arguably no more inherently uncertain as a legal test than asking whether a function conferred on a federal court is 'judicial' or 'non-judicial' in nature.[128] The major difficulty with incompatibility is that the High Court in *Grollo v Palmer* and *Wilson's Case* has sent inconsistent messages about its application. In finding against 'public confidence incompatibility' in *Grollo v Palmer* the majority took into account the social role performed by judges in issuing interception warrants as well as the established pattern, both internationally and in other Australian jurisdictions, of judicial involvement in this function. In *Wilson's Case* the joint majority judgment did not invoke considerations of this type,[129] although they featured in the dissent of Kirby J.[130] Commentators

---

[124] Walker (1997) 163, 167. See also Winterton (1987) 125.

[125] There have long been arguments against the rule. See, for example, *R v Joske; Ex parte Australian Building Construction Employees & Builders' Labourers' Federation* (1974) 130 CLR 87, 90 (Barwick CJ); Sir Anthony Mason (1996) 5–6.

[126] See Chapter 2 and the reference by Griffith and Kennett in this context to 'the practical impossibility of "unwinding" years of judicial involvement' in the functions of the Administrative Appeals Tribunal.

[127] See generally Sir Anthony Mason (1996) 5–6.

[128] See *Brandy v Human Rights and Equal Opportunity Commission* (1995) 183 CLR 245, 267 (Deane, Dawson, Gaudron and McHugh JJ). Compare *R v Spicer; Ex parte Australian Builders' Labourers' Federation* (1957) 100 CLR 277 with *R v Commonwealth Industrial Court; Ex parte the Amalgamated Engineering Union, Australian Section* (1960) 103 CLR 368. See also Sir Anthony Mason (1996) 5–6.

[129] The majority thought such considerations were irrelevant: *Wilson v Minister for Aboriginal and Torres Strait Islander Affairs* (1996) 189 CLR 1, 9, 20.

[130] See Walker (1997) 160 and Handsley (1998) 199–201 where versions of this critique are put.

have pointed to other inconsistencies between the two cases.[131] The High Court needs to confront this uncertainty and identify the criteria of constitutional incompatibility more clearly, particularly the role of historical practice and social policy in the compatibility equation. As both 'history' and 'social policy' have played a major role in shaping our conception of judicial power under Chapter III of the Constitution,[132] it would seem odd to exclude these issues from consideration when asking whether a non-judicial function is compatible with the exercise of judicial power.[133]

5 The Future

As the cases stand, what type of non-judicial functions can validly be performed by federal judges acting in their personal capacities, and what non-judicial functions can no longer be discharged in this manner?

Wilson's Case compels the conclusion that a federal judge can no longer validly be appointed to a diplomatic post (assuming, that is, that such appointments were valid in the past). Applying the criteria governing 'public confidence incompatibility', such a post is 'closely connected' with the functions of the executive and its occupant would necessarily be subject to political 'instruction, advice or wish' and exercise a myriad 'political discretions'. Moreover, an ambassador acts as a 'ministerial adviser' and directly represents the interests of his or her government to other nations. Thus, if the much narrower function of acting as a 'reporter' in *Wilson's Case* was liable to undermine public confidence in the independence of the federal judiciary from the executive branch, then persons who are federal judges can no longer accept ambassadorial or other diplomatic office.

Likewise, the High Court would almost certainly find that a federal judge cannot validly be appointed to head an organisation

---

[131] See generally Walker (1997) and Handsley (1998).

[132] Zines (1997) 173.

[133] See *Wilson v Minister for Aboriginal and Torres Strait Islander Affairs* (1996) 189 CLR 1, 25 where Gaudron J accepts the relevance of these issues to assessing incompatibility.

such as the National Crime Authority. In *Grollo v Palmer*, the joint majority judges said that if the function of issuing interception warrants 'were reasonably to be regarded as a judicial participation in criminal investigation, it would be a function which could not be conferred on a judge without compromising the judiciary's essential separation from the executive government'.[134] On the facts of that case, the independent nature of the warrant issuing power militated against invalidity, but it follows that for a federal judge, albeit as a designated person, actually to head a criminal investigative agency must surely cross the boundary into incompatibility. Applying the criteria in *Wilson's Case*, whatever the independence of the Authority from the government of the day,[135] its 'chair', in directing the activities of the organisation, would necessarily be required to exercise 'political discretions' on a scale exceeding those involved in serving as a reporter. Thus, in light of *Grollo v Palmer* and *Wilson's Case*, a recent call in a parliamentary report for a return to the practice of appointing a 'judge' to chair the National Crime Authority must be rejected as unconstitutional to the extent that such a person is drawn from the federal judiciary.[136] Were such a person a state court judge, it is possible that *Kable's Case* would invalidate the appointment.[137]

On the other hand, the joint majority judges in *Wilson's Case* hinted strongly that for federal judges to serve in their personal capacities on the Administrative Appeals Tribunal did not violate the separation of powers. Their Honours emphasised that the Tribunal must exercise its review functions independently of the

---

[134] *Grollo v Palmer* (1995) 184 CLR 348, 366–7.

[135] See *National Crime Authority Act 1984* (Cth) s 18.

[136] T. Harris, 'Crime authority "needs more powers"', *Australian*, 7 April 1998. The same report 'strongly supported' the current non-judicial head of the Authority.

[137] Sir Laurence Street, then Chief Justice of the New South Wales Supreme Court, strongly opposed the appointment in 1984 of Justice Stewart, a member of the Court, as Chair of the National Crime Authority. Justice Stewart resigned from the Court several months after his appointment to the Authority. However, under special Commonwealth legislation he continued to hold the title of judge, although not a member of any court. For a full account, see McInerney, Moloney and McGregor (1986) 23–31.

legislature and the executive.[138] In his dissenting judgment in *Grollo v Palmer* McHugh J expressly endorsed the constitutionality of federal judges serving on the Administrative Appeals Tribunal as well as the appointment of a person who is a federal judge as President of the Industrial Relations Commission.[139] These views accord with the earlier suggestion of Mason and Deane JJ in *Hilton v Wells* that where a judge is appointed to a 'separately constituted tribunal', this will assist a finding of validity.[140]

Whether federal judges can now validly act as Royal Commissioners or conduct other governmental inquiries is more problematic. The joint judgment in *Wilson's Case* contains the following passage:

> A judge who conducts a Royal Commission may have a close working connection with the Executive Government yet will be required to act judicially in finding facts and applying the law and will deliver a report according to the judge's own conscience without regard to the wishes or advice of the Executive Government except where . . . given by way of submission for the judge's independent evaluation. The terms of reference of the particular Royal Commission and of any enabling legislation will be significant.[141]

Although this passage appears to accept that service as a Royal Commissioner can survive the 'public confidence incompatibility' test as applied in *Wilson's Case* the last part of the quote suggests that this may not be so in all cases. Even if a Royal Commissioner was shielded by legislation from any 'instruction, advice or wish' of the political branches and was bound by the rules of natural justice, could a Commission's recommendations amount to 'political decisions'? The question is more problematic in the context of the joint majority in *Wilson's Case* characterising as 'political' the recommendations of a reporter to the Minister about heritage protection.

---

[138] *Wilson v Minister for Aboriginal and Torres Strait Islander Affairs* (1996) 189 CLR 1, 17–18.

[139] *Grollo v Palmer* (1995) 184 CLR 348, 383.

[140] (1985) 157 CLR 57, 81.

[141] *Wilson v Minister for Aboriginal and Torres Strait Islander Affairs* (1996) 189 CLR 1, 17. See also 25–6 (Gaudron J).

And could a Royal Commissioner inquiring into allegations of corruption or responsibility for a major industrial disaster avoid 'the giving to the executive of advisory opinions on questions of law'?[142] On the assumption of freedom from political direction made above, it is possible that the greater independence of a Royal Commissioner could lead to different answers to these questions than in the case of the reporting function in *Wilson's Case*. Nonetheless, lingering uncertainty about the boundary of constitutional incompatibility in this area is likely to give the federal executive cause for thought before requesting a federal judge to serve in this capacity and a judge cause for thought before agreeing to accept.[143]

Notably, in 1997 the Australian Defence Force withdrew the publicly announced appointment of a member of the Family Court to conduct a review of the military inquiry into the 'Black Hawk' helicopter disaster. The concern was that the appointment of the judge may be unconstitutional. A Queen's Counsel filled the breach.[144]

6 Conclusion

For the foreseeable future it is evident that a conservative approach to the use of federal judges in non-judicial roles will prevail.[145] Putting aside the question whether the High Court has adopted too parsimonious an approach to the utilisation of judicial talent in our system of government—or has not gone far enough in enforcing the separation of powers—it is clear that there are other persons to whom the Commonwealth can look to fill non-judicial roles. Retired judges and Queen's Counsel can conduct Royal Commissions and other governmental inquiries; members of the Administrative Appeals Tribunal currently issue telecommunications interception

---

[142] Ibid 19–20.

[143] Sherman also predicts caution on the part of judges and the Commonwealth: T. Sherman (1997) 8.

[144] D. Greenlees, 'Judge to test conduct of Black Hawk inquiry', *Australian*, 16 September 1997; D. Greenlees, 'Black Hawk judge ditched', *Australian*, 24 September 1997; D. Greenlees, 'QC leads Black Hawk Review', *Australian*, 30 September 1997.

[145] Carney expresses the same view: (1997) 182. See also Chapter 1.

warrants.[146] The Department of Foreign Affairs and Trade seems able to fill diplomatic posts without calling on the federal judiciary. And it is noteworthy that the parliamentary committee that called for the head of the National Crime Authority to be a 'judge' was reported as expressing strong support for the Authority's then current non-judicial head.[147]

There is a distinct possibility, however, that the Commonwealth will no longer be able to look to state courts to fill positions now constitutionally barred to persons who are federal judges. Although the scope of the incompatibility doctrine in *Kable's Case* is unclear, were a member of a state court to be appointed, for example, to the National Crime Authority without resigning his or her judicial commission, the appointment would be open to challenge in the High Court. Although constitutional lawyers would welcome the opportunity to discover more about the doctrine in *Kable's Case*, it is unlikely that either the potential judicial appointee or the Commonwealth would relish this risk.

---

[146] Two members of the High Court in *Grollo v Palmer* suggested that this function might also be appropriately discharged by Commonwealth law officers or retired judges: (1995) 184 CLR 348, 384 (McHugh J), 391 (Gummow J).

[147] T. Harris, 'Crime authority "needs more powers"', *Australian*, 7 April 1998.

Appendix 1

Constitutional and Statutory Provisions

The Australian Constitution

Chapter III The Judicature

Judicial power and Courts

71 The judicial power of the Commonwealth shall be vested in a Federal Supreme Court, to be called the High Court of Australia, and in such other federal courts as the Parliament creates, and in such other courts as it invests with federal jurisdiction. The High Court shall consist of a Chief Justice, and so many other Justices, not less than two, as the Parliament prescribes.

Judges' appointment, tenure and remuneration

72 The Justices of the High Court and of the other courts created by the Parliament—

   (i) Shall be appointed by the Governor-General in Council:

   (ii) Shall not be removed except by the Governor-General in Council, on an address from both Houses of the Parliament in the same session, praying for such removal on the ground of proved mis-behaviour or incapacity:

   (iii) Shall receive such remuneration as the Parliament may fix; but the remuneration shall not be diminished during their continuance in office.

The appointment of a Justice of the High Court shall be for a term expiring upon his attaining the age of seventy years, and a person shall not be appointed as a Justice of the High Court if he has attained that age.

The appointment of a Justice of a court created by the Parliament shall be for a term expiring upon his attaining the age that is, at the time of his appointment, the maximum age for Justices of that court and a person shall not be appointed as a Justice of such a court if he has attained the age that is for the time being the maximum age for Justices of that court.

Subject to this section, the maximum age for Justices of any court created by the Parliament is seventy years.

The Parliament may make a law fixing an age that is less than seventy years as the maximum age for Justices of a court created by the Parliament and may at any time repeal or amend such a law, but any such repeal or amendment does not affect the term of office of a Justice under an appointment made before the repeal or amendment.

A Justice of the High Court or of a court created by the Parliament may resign his office by writing under his hand delivered to the Governor-General.

Nothing in the provisions added to this section by the *Constitution Alteration (Retirement of Judges)* 1977 affects the continuance of a person in office as a Justice of a court under an appointment made before the commencement of those provisions.

A reference in this section to the appointment of a Justice of the High Court or of a court created by the Parliament shall be read as including a reference to the appointment of a person who holds office as a Justice of the High Court or of a court created by the Parliament to another office of Justice of the same court having a different status or designation.

Appellate jurisdiction of High Court

73 The High Court shall have jurisdiction, with such exceptions and subject to such regulations as the Parliament prescribes, to hear and determine appeals from all judgments, decrees, orders, and sentences—

   (i) Of any Justice or Justices exercising the original jurisdiction of the High Court:

   (ii) Of any other federal court, or court exercising federal jurisdiction; or of the Supreme Court of any State, or of any other court of any State from which at the establishment of the Commonwealth an appeal lies to the Queen in Council:

(iii) Of the Inter-State Commission, but as to questions of law only: and the judgment of the High Court in all such cases shall be final and conclusive.

But no exception or regulation prescribed by the Parliament shall prevent the High Court from hearing and determining any appeal from the Supreme Court of a State in any matter in which at the establishment of the Commonwealth an appeal lies from such Supreme Court to the Queen in Council.

Until the Parliament otherwise provides, the conditions of and restrictions on appeals to the Queen in Council from the Supreme Courts of the several States shall be applicable to appeals from them to the High Court.

Appeal to Queen in Council

74 No appeal shall be permitted to the Queen in Council from a decision of the High Court upon any question, howsoever arising, as to the limits inter se of the Constitutional powers of the Commonwealth and those of any State or States, or as to the limits inter se of the Constitutional powers of any two or more States, unless the High Court shall certify that the question is one which ought to be determined by Her Majesty in Council.

The High Court may so certify if satisfied that for any special reason the certificate should be granted, and thereupon an appeal shall lie to Her Majesty in Council on the question without further leave.

Except as provided in this section, this Constitution shall not impair any right which the Queen may be pleased to exercise by virtue of Her Royal prerogative to grant special leave of appeal from the High Court to Her Majesty in Council. The Parliament may make laws limiting the matters in which such leave may be asked, but proposed laws containing any such limitation shall be reserved by the Governor-General for Her Majesty's pleasure.

Original jurisdiction of High Court

75 In all matters—
    (i)   Arising under any treaty:
    (ii) Affecting consuls or other representatives of other countries:
    (iii) In which the Commonwealth, or a person suing or being sued on behalf of the Commonwealth, is a party:
    (iv) Between States, or between residents of different States, or between a State and a resident of another State:

(v) In which a writ of Mandamus or prohibition or an injunction is sought against an officer of the Commonwealth:

the High Court shall have original jurisdiction.

Additional original jurisdiction

76 The Parliament may make laws conferring original jurisdiction on the High Court in any matter—
  (i) Arising under this Constitution, or involving its interpretation:
  (ii) Arising under any laws made by the Parliament:
  (iii) Of Admiralty and maritime jurisdiction:
  (iv) Relating to the same subject-matter claimed under the laws of different States.

Power to define jurisdiction

77 With respect to any of the matters mentioned in the last two sections the Parliament may make laws—
  (i) Defining the jurisdiction of any federal court other than the High Court:
  (ii) Defining the extent to which the jurisdiction of any federal court shall be exclusive of that which belongs to or is invested in the courts of the States:
  (iii) Investing any court of a State with federal jurisdiction.

Proceedings against Commonwealth or State

78 The Parliament may make laws conferring rights to proceed against the Commonwealth or a State in respect of matters within the limits of the judicial power.

Number of judges

79 The federal jurisdiction of any court may be exercised by such number of judges as the Parliament prescribes.

Trial by jury

80 The trial on indictment of any offence against any law of the Commonwealth shall be by jury, and every such trial shall be held in the State where the offence was committed, and if the offence was not committed within any State the trial shall be held at such place or places as the Parliament prescribes.

Judiciary Act 1903 (Cth)

Original jurisdiction conferred

30 In addition to the matters in which original jurisdiction is conferred on the High Court by the Constitution, the High Court shall have original jurisdiction:

(a) in all matters arising under the Constitution or involving its interpretation; and

(c) in trials of indictable offences against the laws of the Commonwealth.

Matters in which jurisdiction of High Court exclusive

38 Subject to section 44, the jurisdiction of the High Court shall be exclusive of the jurisdiction of the several Courts of the States in the following matters:

(a) matters arising directly under any treaty;

(b) suits between States, or between persons suing or being sued on behalf of different States, or between a State and a person suing or being sued on behalf of another State;

(c) suits by the Commonwealth, or any person suing on behalf of the Commonwealth, against a State, or any person being sued on behalf of a State;

(d) suits by a State, or any person suing on behalf of a State, against the Commonwealth or any person being sued on behalf of the Commonwealth;

(e) matters in which a writ of mandamus or prohibition is sought against an officer of the Commonwealth or a federal court.

Federal jurisdiction of State Courts in other matters

39 (1) The jurisdiction of the High Court, so far as it is not exclusive of the jurisdiction of any Court of a State by virtue of section 38, shall be exclusive of the jurisdiction of the several Courts of the States, except as provided in this section.

(2) The several Courts of the States shall within the limits of their several jurisdictions, whether such limits are as to locality, subject-matter, or otherwise, be invested with federal jurisdiction, in all matters in which the High Court has original jurisdiction or in which original jurisdiction can be conferred upon it, except as provided in section 38, and subject to the following conditions and restrictions:

(a) A decision of a Court of a State, whether in original or in appellate jurisdiction, shall not be subject to appeal to Her Majesty in Council, whether by special leave or otherwise.

Special leave to appeal from decisions of State Courts though State law prohibits appeal

(c) The High Court may grant special leave to appeal to the High Court from any decision of any Court or Judge of a State notwithstanding that the law of the State may prohibit any appeal from such Court or Judge.

Exercise of federal jurisdiction by State Courts of summary jurisdiction

(d) The federal jurisdiction of a Court of summary jurisdiction of a State shall not be judicially exercised except by a Stipendiary or Police or Special Magistrate, or some Magistrate of the State who is specially authorized by the Governor-General to exercise such jurisdiction, or an arbitrator on whom the jurisdiction, or part of the jurisdiction, of that Court is conferred by a prescribed law of the State, within the limits of the jurisdiction so conferred.

Original jurisdiction of Federal Court of Australia

39B (1) The original jurisdiction of the Federal Court of Australia includes jurisdiction with respect to any matter in which a writ of mandamus or prohibition or an injunction is sought against an officer or officers of the Commonwealth.

(1A) The original jurisdiction of the Federal Court of Australia also includes jurisdiction in any matter:

(a) in which the Commonwealth is seeking an injunction or a declaration; or

(b) arising under the Constitution, or involving its interpretation; or

(c) arising under any laws made by the Parliament.

(2) The reference in subsection (1) to an officer or officers of the Commonwealth does not include a reference to:

(a) a person holding office under the *Workplace Relations Act 1996* or the *Coal Industry Act 1946*; or

(b) a Judge or Judges of the Family Court of Australia.

Suits against the Commonwealth

56 (1) A person making a claim against the Commonwealth, whether in contract or in tort, may in respect of the claim bring a suit against the Commonwealth:

(a) in the High Court;

(b) if the claim arose in a State or Territory—in the Supreme Court of that State or Territory or in any other court of competent jurisdiction of that State or Territory; or

(c) if the claim did not arise in a State or Territory—in the Supreme Court of any State or Territory or in any other court of competent jurisdiction of any State or Territory.

Suits by a State against the Commonwealth

57 Any State making any claim against the Commonwealth, whether in contract or in tort, may in respect of the claim bring a suit against the Commonwealth in the High Court.

Suits against a State in matters of federal jurisdiction

58 Any person making any claim against a State, whether in contract or in tort, in respect of a matter in which the High Court has original jurisdiction or can have original jurisdiction conferred on it, may in respect of the claim bring a suit against the State in the Supreme Court of the State, or (if the High Court has original jurisdiction in the matter) in the High Court.

State or Territory laws to govern where applicable

79 The laws of each State or Territory, including the laws relating to procedure, evidence, and the competency of witnesses, shall, except as otherwise provided by the Constitution or the laws of the Commonwealth, be binding on all Courts exercising federal jurisdiction in that State or Territory in all cases to which they are applicable.

Common law to govern

80 So far as the laws of the Commonwealth are not applicable or so far as their provisions are insufficient to carry them into effect, or to provide adequate remedies or punishment, the common law in Australia as modified by the Constitution and by the statute law in force in the State or Territory in which the Court in which the jurisdiction is exercised is held shall, so far as it is applicable and not inconsistent with the Constitution and the laws of the Commonwealth, govern all Courts exercising federal jurisdiction in the exercise of their jurisdiction in civil and criminal matters.

Jurisdiction of Courts (Cross-vesting) Act 1987 (Cth)

Additional jurisdiction of certain courts

4   (1) Where:
   (a) the Federal Court or the Family Court has jurisdiction with respect
       to a civil matter, whether that jurisdiction was or is conferred
       before or after the commencement of this Act; and
   (b) the Supreme Court of a State or Territory would not, apart from
       this section, have jurisdiction with respect to that matter;
   then:
   (c) in the case of the Supreme Court of a State (other than the
       Supreme Court of the Australian Capital Territory and the Supreme
       Court of the Northern Territory)—that court is invested with fed-
       eral jurisdiction with respect to that matter; or
   (d) in the case of the Supreme Court of a Territory (including the
       Australian Capital Territory and the Northern Territory)—juris-
       diction is conferred on that court with respect to that matter.
   (2) Where:
   (a) the Supreme Court of a Territory has jurisdiction with respect to a
       civil matter, whether that jurisdiction was or is conferred before or
       after the commencement of this Act; and
   (b) the Federal Court, the Family Court or the Supreme Court of a
       State or of another Territory would not, apart from this section,
       have jurisdiction with respect to that matter;
   jurisdiction is conferred on the court referred to in paragraph (b) with
   respect to that matter.
   (3) Where a proceeding is transferred to the Federal Court, the Family
   Court or a State Family Court of a State, that court has, by virtue of
   this subsection, jurisdiction with respect to so many of the matters for
   determination in the proceeding as that court would not have apart
   from this subsection.
   (4) This section does not apply to a matter arising under:
   (a) the *Conciliation and Arbitration Act 1904*; or
   (b) the *Workplace Relations Act 1996*; or
   (ba) the *Native Title Act 1993*; or
   (c) section 46A, 155A or 155B of the *Trade Practices Act 1974*;
       or
   (d) a provision of Part VI or XII of the *Trade Practices Act 1974* so
       far as the provision relates to section 46A, 155A or 155B of that
       Act.

Transfer of proceedings

5 (1) Where:
   (a) a proceeding (in this subsection referred to as the 'relevant pro-
        ceeding') is pending in the Supreme Court of a State or Territory
        (in this subsection referred to as the 'first court'); and
   (b) it appears to the first court that:
        (i) the relevant proceeding arises out of, or is related to, another
             proceeding pending in the Federal Court or the Family Court
             and it is more appropriate that the relevant proceeding be
             determined by the Federal Court or the Family Court;
        (ii) having regard to:
              (A) whether, in the opinion of the first court, apart from this
                   Act and any law of a State relating to cross-vesting of
                   jurisdiction and apart from any accrued jurisdiction of
                   the Federal Court or the Family Court, the relevant pro-
                   ceeding or a substantial part of the relevant proceeding
                   would have been incapable of being instituted in the first
                   court and capable of being instituted in the Federal Court
                   or the Family Court;
              (B) the extent to which, in the opinion of the first court, the
                   matters for determination in the relevant proceeding are
                   matters arising under or involving questions as to
                   the application, interpretation or validity of a law of the
                   Commonwealth and not within the jurisdiction of the
                   first court apart from this Act and any law of a State
                   relating to cross-vesting of jurisdiction; and
              (C) the interests of justice;
              it is more appropriate that the relevant proceeding be deter-
              mined by the Federal Court or the Family Court, as the case
              may be; or
        (iii) it is otherwise in the interests of justice that the relevant pro-
               ceeding be determined by the Federal Court or the Family
               Court;
   the first court shall transfer the relevant proceeding to the Federal Court or
   the Family Court, as the case may be.
   [Subsequent subsections authorise a transfer of proceedings between one
   state or territory Supreme Court and another (s 5(2)); between a state
   Supreme Court and a state Family Court (s 5(3)); between the Federal
   Court or Family Court and a state or territory Supreme Court (s 5(4)); and
   between the Federal Court and the Family Court (s 5(5)).]

Conduct of proceedings

11 (1) Where it appears to a court that the court will, or will be likely to, in determining a matter for determination in a proceeding, be exercising jurisdiction conferred by this Act or by a law of a State relating to cross-vesting of jurisdiction:

   (a) subject to paragraphs (b) and (c), the court shall, in determining that matter, apply the law in force in the State or Territory in which the court is sitting (including choice of law rules);

   (b) subject to paragraph (c), if that matter is a right of action arising under a written law of another State or Territory, the court shall, in determining that matter, apply the written and unwritten law of that other State or Territory; and

   (c) the rules of evidence and procedure to be applied in dealing with that matter shall be such as the court considers appropriate in the circumstances, being rules that are applied in a superior court in Australia or in an external Territory.

(2) The reference in paragraph (1)(a) to the State or Territory in which the court is sitting is, in relation to the Federal Court or the Family Court, a reference to the State or Territory in which any matter for determination in the proceeding was first commenced in or transferred to that court.

(3) Where a proceeding is transferred or removed to a court (in this subsection referred to as the 'transferee court') from another court (in this subsection referred to as the 'transferor court'), the transferee court shall deal with the proceeding as if, subject to any order of the transferee court, the steps that had been taken for the purposes of the proceeding in the transferor court (including the making of an order), or similar steps, had been taken in the transferee court.

Appendix 2
Table of Cases

*Re Ranger Uranium Mines Pty Ltd; Ex parte Federated Miscellaneous
    Workers' Union of Australia* (1987) 163 CLR 656, 136, 200
*Re Residential Tenancies Tribunal (NSW); Ex parte Defence Housing Auth-
    ority* (1997) 190 CLR 410, 272
Re T [1990] 1 Qd R 196, 317
Re Tracey; Ex parte Ryan (1989) 166 CLR 518, 9
Re Usines de Melle's Patent (1954) 91 CLR 42, 107
Re Wakim; Ex parte Darvall (1999) 163 ALR 270, 319
Re Wakim; Ex parte McNally (1999) 163 ALR 270, 24, 41, 57, 58, 131,
    300, 301, 308, 318, 319, 320, 321, 322, 331, 334, 357
Rees v Crane [1994] 2 AC 173, 90
Reference Re: Amendment of the Constitution of Canada (Nos 1, 2 and 3)
    (1982) 125 DLR (3rd) 1, 244
Reference Re: Secession of Quebec (1998) 161 DLR (4th) 385, 241, 244
Reidy v Trustee of Christian Brothers (1995) 12 WAR 583, 360
Richardson v Forestry Commission (1988) 164 CLR 261, 118
*Right to Life Association (NSW) Inc v Secretary, Department of Human
    Services and Health* (1995) 56 FCR 50, 250
Ritter v North Side Enterprises Pty Ltd (1975) 132 CLR 301, 255
Romeo v Conservation Commission (NT) (1998) 192 CLR 431, 117
Rose Holdings Pty Ltd v Carlton Shuttlecocks Ltd (1957) 98 CLR 444,
    107
Russell v Russell (1976) 134 CLR 495, 142, 305
Ryan v Great Lakes Council (1998) 154 ALR 584, 188
Rylands v Fletcher (1868) LR 3 HL 330, 117
Sachter v Attorney-General (Commonwealth) (1954) 94 CLR 86, 140
Saffron v The Queen (1953) 88 CLR 523, 238
Sali v SPC Ltd (1993) 116 ALR 625, 166, 167, 168
Schmidt v Won [1998] 3 VR 435, 325
Seamen's Union of Australia v Matthews (1957) 96 CLR 529, 134
Shaw Savill & Albion Co Ltd v Commonwealth (1940) 66 CLR 344,
    259
Shell Co of Australia Ltd v Federal Commissioner of Taxation [1931] AC
    275, 15, 200
*Shop Distributive & Allied Employees Association v Minister for Indus-
    trial Affairs (SA)* (1995) 183 CLR 552, 246, 247
Slater v Miles (unreported, Federal Court, Finn J, 16 October 1998), 40
Smith v Smith (1986) 161 CLR 217, 143, 308
Smith Kline & French Laboratories (Aust) Ltd v Commonwealth (1991)
    173 CLR 194, 112
South Australia v Commonwealth (1962) 108 CLR 130, 256
South Australia v Victoria (1911) 12 CLR 667, 231, 255
Southern Centre of Theosophy Inc v South Australia (1979) 145 CLR
    246, 101

UK Practice Statement (Commercial Cases: Alternative Dispute Resolution) (No 2) [1996] 1 WLR 1024, 187

Union Steamship Co of New Zealand Ltd v Ferguson (1969) 119 CLR 191, 285

United States v Hays, 515 US 737 (1995), 253

United States v Will, 449 US 200 (1980), 78

Valente v The Queen (1985) 24 DLR (4th) 161, 80

Victoria v Commonwealth (AAP Case) (1975) 134 CLR 338, 261

Victoria v Commonwealth and Connor (1975) 134 CLR 81, 257, 261

Victorian Stevedoring & General Contracting Co Pty Ltd v Dignan (1931) 46 CLR 73, 6, 7, 199

Vietnam Veterans' Affairs Association of Australia New South Wales Branch Inc v Cohen (1996) 46 ALD 290, 295

Voth v Manildra Flour Mills Pty Ltd (1990) 171 CLR 538, 324

W J D v T E K (1998) 19(9) Leg Rep SL4, 188

Wakeley v The Queen (1990) 93 ALR 79, 172

Walker v New South Wales (1994) 182 CLR 45, 261

Walton v The Queen (1989) 166 CLR 283, 116

Waterhouse v Australian Broadcasting Corp (1989) 86 ACTR 1, 325

Waterside Workers' Federation of Australia v J W Alexander Ltd (1918) 25 CLR 434, 11, 14, 66, 73, 132, 199, 200, 446, 452

Watson v Cameron (1928) 40 CLR 446, 285

Watson v Federal Commissioner of Taxation (1953) 87 CLR 353, 106

Webb v Outtrim (1906) 4 CLR 356, 99

West Australian Psychiatric Nurses' Association (Union of Workers) v Australian Nursing Federation (1991) 102 ALR 265, 131, 317

Western Australia v Commonwealth (Native Title Act Case) (1995) 183 CLR 373, 134, 257

White Industries (Qld) Pty Ltd v Flower & Hart (a firm) (1998) 156 ALR 169, 423

Wik Peoples v Queensland (1996) 187 CLR 1, 85, 365

Williams v Spautz (1992) 174 CLR 509, 424

Williams v The Queen (1986) 161 CLR 278, 116

Wilson v Minister for Aboriginal and Torres Strait Islander Affairs (1996) 189 CLR 1, 17, 18, 26, 51, 52, 66, 158, 202, 203, 204, 224, 236, 443, 453, 462, 463, 464, 465, 466, 468, 469, 470, 471, 472, 473

Zecevic v Director of Public Prosecutions (Vict) (1987) 162 CLR 645, 116

Appendix 3
Table of Acts and Bills

Australia

Australian Constitution

6, 8, 36, 39, 128, 266, 275
Ch I, 10, 227, 452
Ch II, 452
Ch III, xi, xii, 8, 9, 10, 11, 12, 20, 22, 28, 29, 34, 36, 40, 46, 47, 58, 59, 61, 114, 128, 129, 131, 132, 133, 140, 145, 147, 158, 227, 235, 241, 265, 271, 317, 332, 447, 452, 466
s 1, 8
s 44, vi
s 50, 416
s 51, 9, 12, 24, 49, 141, 142, 271, 283, 284, 300, 305, 309, 320, 331, 332, 338, 344, 446
s 53, 256, 257
s 57, 242, 257
s 61, 452
s 64, 199
s 71, 8, 9, 18, 22, 39, 41, 42, 46, 50, 73, 74, 75, 110, 125, 128, 133, 231, 241, 265, 407, 452
s 72, v, 9, 12, 22, 24, 39, 41, 72, 73, 74, 77, 78, 89, 124, 129, 133, 407, 409, 415, 416, 417, 419, 421, 426, 431, 440, 447, 452
s 73, 9, 22, 24, 39, 40, 41, 97, 102, 103, 110, 124, 130, 132, 230, 234, 237, 241, 269, 270, 297
s 74, 44, 97, 99, 101, 230

Commonwealth

Bibliography

Abel, R. L. (ed.) (1982). *The Politics of Informal Justice*, Academic Books, New York.

Abraham, H. J. (1974). *Justices and Presidents*, Oxford University Press, New York.

Administrative Review Council (1983). *Review of Pension Decisions Under Repatriation Legislation*, Report No. 20, AGPS, Canberra.

—— (1984). *The Structure and Form of Social Security Appeals*, Report No. 21, AGPS, Canberra.

—— (1986). *Review of Migration Decisions*, Report No. 25, AGPS, Canberra.

—— (1995). *Better Decisions: Review of Commonwealth Merits Review Tribunals*, Report No. 39, AGPS, Canberra.

—— (1997). *Appeals from the Administrative Appeals Tribunal to the Federal Court*, Report No. 41, AGPS, Canberra.

Aitken, L. J. W. (1986). 'The High Court's Power to Grant Certiorari—The Unsolved Question', 16 *Federal Law Review* 370.

Allan, T. R. S. (1993). *Law, Liberty and Justice*, Clarendon Press, Oxford.

Allars, Margaret (1991). 'Standing: The Role and Evolution of the Test', 20 *Federal Law Review* 83.

—— (1996a). 'Reputation, Power and Fairness: A Review of the Impact of Judicial Review upon Investigative Tribunals', 24 *Federal Law Review* 235.

—— (1996b). 'Theory and Administrative Law: Law as Form and Theory as Substance', 79 *Canberra Bulletin of Public Administration* 20.

American Bar Association (1997). *An Independent Judiciary: Report of the Commission on Separation of Powers and Judicial Independence.*

Andrews, N. H. (1988). 'The Passive Court and Legal Argument', 7 *Civil Justice Quarterly* 125.

Anson, W. R. (1907). *The Law and Custom of the Constitution*, 3rd edn, Clarendon Press, Oxford.

Aronson, M. and Dyer, B. (1996). *Judicial Review of Administrative Action*, Law Book Company, Sydney.

Arthur Robinson & Hedderwicks (1998). *Submission of Arthur Robinson & Hedderwicks to the Australian Law Reform Commission*, May.

Arthurs, H. (1985). *Without the Law: Administrative Justice and Legal Pluralism in Nineteenth-Century England*, University of Toronto Press, Toronto.

Atiyah, P. S. (1978). *From Principles to Pragmatism: Changes in the Function of the Judicial Process and the Law*, Clarendon Press, Oxford.

—— (1987). *Pragmatism and Theory in English Law*, Stevens and Sons, London.

Attorney-General's Department (1999). *Telecommunications (Interception) Act 1979: Report for the Year Ending 30 June 1998*, Canberra.

Australian Constitutional Commission (1988). *Final Report of the Constitutional Commission*, AGPS, Canberra.

Australian Constitutional Commission Advisory Committee on the Australian Judicial System (1987). *Report*, AGPS, Canberra.

Australian Constitutional Commission Advisory Committee on the Distribution of Powers (1987). *Report*, AGPS, Canberra.

Australian Constitutional Convention (1978). *Proceedings of the Australian Constitutional Convention*, Perth 26–28 July.

—— (1983). *Proceedings of the Australian Constitutional Convention*, Adelaide 26–29 April, vol. 1 (Official Record of Debates etc) and vol. 2 (Standing Committee D Reports).

—— (1985). *Proceedings of the Australian Constitutional Convention*, Brisbane 29 July–1 August, vol. 1 (Official Record of Debates etc) and vol. 2 (Sub-Committee Reports).

Australian Constitutional Convention Judicature Sub-Committee (1984). *Report to Standing Committee on an Integrated Court System*, October.

Australian Dictionary of Biography (1983, 1988, 1996). Vols 9, 11, 13, Melbourne University Press, Melbourne.

Australian Institute of Judicial Administration (1983). *An Integrated Court System for Australia*, AIJA, Melbourne.

Australian Law Reform Commission (1985). *Standing in Public Interest Litigation*, Report No. 27.

—— (1992). *Choice of Law*, Report No. 58.

—— (1996). *Beyond the Door-keeper: Standing to Sue for Public Remedies*, Report No. 78.

—— (1997a). *Review of the Adversarial System of Litigation: Rethinking the Federal Civil Litigation System*, Issues Paper No. 20.

—— (1997b). *Seen and Heard—Priority for Children in the Legal Process*, Report No. 84.

—— (1999a). *Managing Justice: A Review of the Federal Civil Justice System*, Report No. 89.

—— (1999b). *Review of the Federal Civil Justice System*, Discussion Paper No. 62.

Baker, C. (1987). 'Cross-vesting of Jurisdiction between State and Federal Courts', 14 *University of Queensland Law Journal* 118.

Baker, Thomas (1994). *Rationing Justice on Appeal: The Problems With the United States Courts of Appeals*, West Publishing Company, St Pauls.

Bandes, Susan (1990). 'The Idea of a Case', 42 *Stanford Law Review* 227.

Barker, I. and Beaumont, B. A. (1992). 'Trans-Tasman Legal Relations—Some Recent and Future Developments', 66 *Australian Law Journal* 566.

Barwick, Sir Garfield (1964). 'The Australian Judicial System: The Proposed New Federal Superior Court', 1 *Federal Law Review* 1.

—— (1977). 'The State of the Australian Judicature', 51 *Australian Law Journal* 480.

—— (1995). *A Radical Tory: Garfield Barwick's Reflections and Recollections*, Federation Press, Sydney.

Baum, Laurence (1997). *The Puzzle of Judicial Behavior*, University of Michigan Press, Ann Arbor.

Baur, Fritz (1976). 'The Active Role of the Judge', 13 *Law and State* 31.

Bay, Christian (1958). *The Structure of Freedom*, Stanford University Press, Stanford.

Beardsley, James (1986). 'Proof of Fact in French Civil Proceedings', 34 *American Journal of Comparative Law* 459.

Bell, John (1992). *French Constitutional Law*, Oxford University Press, Oxford.

Bennett, J. M. (1980). *Keystone of the Federal Arch*, AGPS, Canberra.

Benton, W. E. (ed.) (1986). *1787: Drafting the US Constitution*, Texas A & M University Press.

Black, M. E. J. (1996). 'The Courts, Tribunals, and ADR—Assisted Dispute Resolution in the Federal Court of Australia', 7 *Australian Dispute Resolution Journal* 138.

—— (1999). Corporations Jurisdiction: Memorandum to Federal Court Judges, unpublished manuscript.

Blackshield, A. R. (1972). 'Quantitative Analysis: The High Court of Australia 1964–1969', 3 *Lawasia* 3.

—— (1977). 'Judges and the Court System', in Gareth Evans (ed.), *Labor and the Constitution 1972–1975*, Heinemann, Melbourne.

—— (1978). 'X/Y/Z/N Scales: The High Court of Australia 1972–1976', in R. Tomasic (ed.), *Understanding Lawyers: Perspectives on the Legal Profession in Australia*, Law Foundation of New South Wales/Allen & Unwin, Sydney.

—— (1985). 'After the Trial: The Free Speech Verdict', 59 *Law Institute Journal* 1187.

—— (1986). 'Lionel Murphy: Return to the Court', 76 *Arena* 28.

—— (1987). 'The "Murphy Affair"', in J. A. Scutt (ed.), *Lionel Murphy: A Radical Judge*, McCulloch Publishing, Melbourne.

Blackstone, William (1765). *Commentaries on the Laws of England*, republished in Adam Lively and Jack Lively, *Democracy in Britain*, Blackwell, Oxford, 1994.

Bland Committee (1973a). *Final Report of the Committee on Administrative Discretions*, AGPS, Canberra.

—— (1973b). *Interim Report of the Committee on Administrative Discretions*, AGPS, Canberra.

Bowen, N. H. (1967). 'Some Aspects of the Commonwealth Superior Court Proposal', 41 *Australian Law Journal* 336.

—— (1985). 'The Anatomy of a Federal Court', 1 *Australian Bar Review* 190.

Bowman, Sir Jeffery (1997). *Review of the English Court of Appeal—Civil Division* (Bowman Report).

Brennan, Sir Gerard (1978). 'Limits on the Use of Judges', 9 *Federal Law Review* 1.

—— (1979). 'Judging the Judges', 53 *Australian Law Journal* 767.

—— (1996). Judicial Independence, Opening Address to the Annual Symposium of the Australian Judicial Conference, Canberra.

—— (1997). 'Key Issues in Judicial Administration', 6 *Journal of Judicial Administration* 142.

—— (1998). 'The State of the Judicature', 72 *Australian Law Journal* 33.

Bright, S. B. (1997). 'Political Attacks on the Judiciary', 80 *Judicature* 165.

Brooke, Lord Justice (1997). 'Judicial Independence: Its History in England and Wales', in H. Cunningham (ed.), *Fragile Bastion: Judicial Independence in the Nineties*, Judicial Commission of New South Wales, Sydney.

Brown, A. J. (1992). 'The Wig or the Sword? Separation of Powers and the Plight of the Australian Judge', 21 *Federal Law Review* 48.

Burmester, H. (1992). 'Locus Standi in Constitutional Litigation', in H. P. Lee and George Winterton, *Australian Constitutional Perspectives*, Law Book Company, Sydney.

—— (1996). 'Commentary', 24 *Federal Law Review* 387.

Burt, Francis (1982). 'An Australian Judicature', 56 *Australian Law Journal* 509.

Bushnell, Eleanore (1992). *Crimes, Follies, and Misfortunes: The Federal Impeachment Trials*, University of Illinois Press, Urbana.

Byers, M. H. and Toose, P. B. (1963). 'The Necessity for a New Federal Court: A Survey of the Federal Court System in Australia', 36 *Australian Law Journal* 308.

Byrne, David (1994). 'Special References—A Renaissance?', 12 *The Arbitrator* 207.

Cairns, B. (1997). 'Lord Woolf's Report on Access to Justice', 16 *Civil Justice Quarterly* 98.

Calabresi, S. G. and Larsen, J. L. (1994). 'One Person, One Office: Separation of Powers or Separation of Personnel?', 79 *Cornell Law Review* 1045.

Campbell, Enid (1971). 'Suits Between the Governments of a Federation', 6 *Sydney Law Review* 309.

—— (1997). 'Constitutional Protection of State Courts and Judges', 23 *Monash University Law Review* 397.

Cane, Peter (1995a). 'Standing, Representation and Environment', in Ian Loveland (ed.), *A Special Relationship?: American Influences on Public Law in the UK*, Clarendon Press, Oxford.

—— (1995b). 'Standing Up for the Public', *Public Law* 276.

Cappelletti, Mauro (1989). *The Judicial Process in Comparative Perspective*, Clarendon Press, Oxford.

Capra, Fritjof (1988). *Uncommon Wisdom*, Bantam, Toronto.

Cardozo, Benjamin (1949). *The Nature of the Judicial Process*, Yale University Press, New Haven.

Carney, G. (1997). '*Wilson* and *Kable*: The Doctrine of Incompatibility— An Alternative to Separation of Powers?', 13 *Queensland University of Technology Law Journal* 175.

Casper, Gerhard (1997). *Separating Power*, Harvard University Press, Cambridge, Mass.

Cass, Deborah and Rubenstein, Kim (1995). 'Representation/s of Women in the Australian Constitutional System, 17 *Adelaide Law Review* 3.

Castles, A. C. (1979). 'Justiciability: Political Questions', in L. Stein (ed.), *Locus Standi*, Law Book Company, Sydney.

Centre for Legal Education (1997). *The Australasian Legal Education Yearbook 1996*, Law Foundation of New South Wales, Sydney.

Chemerinsky, E. (1994). *Federal Jurisdiction*, 2nd edn, Little, Brown & Company, Boston.

Chief Justices of the States and Territories (1997). 'Declaration of Principles on Judicial Independence', 8 *Public Law Review* 114.

Clark, Bryan and Mays, Richard (1997). 'The Development of ADR in Scotland', 16 *Civil Justice Quarterly* 26.

Collins, H. (1997). 'The Sanctimony of Contract', in R. Rawlings (ed.), *Law, Society, and Economy*, Clarendon Press, Oxford.

Comisky, Marvin and Patterson, P. C. (1987). *The Judiciary—Selection, Compensation, Ethics, and Discipline*, Quorum Books, New York.

Committee of Review into Australian Industrial Relations Law and Systems (1985). *Report of the Committee of Review into Australian Industrial Relations Law and Systems*, AGPS, Canberra.

Commonwealth Attorney-General's Department (1993). *Judicial Appointments—Procedure and Criteria*, Discussion Paper, September.

Commonwealth Remuneration Tribunal (1989). *Special Report on Judicial Remuneration*.

Congressional Research Service (1992). *The Constitution of the United States of America: Analysis and Interpretation*, United States Government Printing Office, Washington, DC.

Cooney, S. (1993). 'Gender and Judicial Selection: Should There Be More Women on the Courts?', 19 *Melbourne University Law Review* 20.

Cooper, R. E. (1998). 'Federal Court Expert Usage Guidelines', 16 *Australian Bar Review* 203.

Coper, M. (1990). *The Second Coming of the Fourth Arm: The Present Role and Future Potential of the Inter-State Commission*, Discussion Paper No. 2, Legislative Research Service, Department of the Parliamentary Library, Canberra.

Cowen, Z. (1959). *Federal Jurisdiction in Australia*, Oxford University Press, Melbourne.

Cowen, Sir Zelman and Zines, Leslie (1978). *Federal Jurisdiction in Australia*, 2nd edn, Oxford University Press, Melbourne.

Cox, Archibald (1996). 'The Independence of the Judiciary: History and Purposes', 21 *Dayton Law Review* 566.

Craig, P. P. (1990). *Public Law and Democracy in the United Kingdom and the United States of America*, Clarendon Press, Oxford.

Cranston, Ross (1995). 'Social Research and Access to Justice', in A. A. S. Zuckerman and Ross Cranston (eds), *Reform of Civil Procedure— Essays on Access to Justice*, Clarendon Press, Oxford.

Craven, G. (ed.) (1986). *Official Record of the Debates of the Australasian Federal Convention*, Legal Books, Sydney (facsimile of Convention Debates, 1897–1898).

Crawford, James (1993). *Australian Courts of Law*, 3rd edn, Oxford University Press, Melbourne.

Crawshaw, Stephen (1977). 'The High Court of Australia and Advisory Opinions', 51 *Australian Law Journal* 112.

Creyke, Robin (1992). 'Interpreting Veterans' Legislation: Lore or Law?', in John McMillan (ed.), *Administrative Law: Does the Public Benefit?*, Australian Institute of Administrative Law, Canberra.

—— (1997). 'Restricting Judicial Review', 15 *AIAL Forum* 22.

Dahl, R. (1982). *Dilemmas of Pluralist Democracy: Autonomy Versus Control*, Yale University Press, New Haven.

Davies, G. (1997). Judicial Reticence, Address to the Annual Symposium of The Judicial Conference of Australia, Sydney.

De Garis, Annesley H. (1994). 'The Role of Federal Court Judges in the Settlement of Disputes', 13 *University of Tasmania Law Review* 217.

de Meyrick, John (1995a). 'Whatever Happened to Boilermakers? Part I', 69 *Australian Law Journal* 106.

—— (1995b). 'Whatever Happened to Boilermakers? Part II', 69 *Australian Law Journal* 189.

Deakin, Alfred (1944). *The Federal Story: The Inner History of the Federal Cause 1880–1900*, Robertson & Mullens, Melbourne.

Dixon, Jo (1995). 'The Organisational Context of Criminal Sentencing', 100 *American Journal of Sociology* 1157.

Dixon, Sir Owen (1965). 'Science and Judicial Proceedings', in Woinarski (ed.), *Jesting Pilate and Other Papers and Addresses*, Law Book Company, Sydney.

—— (1935). 'The Law and the Constitution', 51 *Law Quarterly Review* 590.

Dockray, M. S. (1997). 'The Inherent Jurisdiction to Regulate Civil Proceedings', 113 *Law Quarterly Review* 120.

Douglas, William O. (1980). *The Court Years: 1939–1975*, Random House, New York.

Downes, Garry (1999). 'Changing Roles and Skills for Advocates', in C. Sampford, S. Blencowe and S. Condlln (eds), *Educating Lawyers for a Less Adversarial System*, Federation Press, Sydney.

Doyle, J. (1997). 'The Well-Tuned Cymbal', in H. Cunningham (ed.), *Fragile Bastion: Judicial Independence in the Nineties*, Judicial Commission of New South Wales, Sydney.

Duchacek, I. D. (1970). *Comparative Federalism: The Territorial Dimension of Politics*, reprinted by Holt, Rinehart and Winston, New York, 1987.

Dunleavy, P. and O'Leary, B. (1987). *Theories of the State: The Politics of Liberal Democracy*, Macmillan, London.

Durack, P. (1981). 'The Special Role of the Federal Court of Australia', 55 *Australian Law Journal* 778.

Elazar, D. J. (1966). *American Federalism: A View From the States*, Thomas Y. Crowell, New York.

Ellicott Committee (1973). *Prerogative Writ Procedures—Report of the Committee of Review*, Parliamentary Paper No. 56 of 1973, AGPS, Canberra.

Elliott, E. Donald (1986). 'Managerial Judging and the Evolution of Procedure', 53 *University of Chicago Law Review* 306.

Else-Mitchell, R. (1969). 'Burying the Autochthonous Expedient?', 3 *Federal Law Review* 187.

Elster, J. (1989) *Solomonic Judgments: Studies in the Limits of Rationality*, Cambridge University Press, New York.

Evans, Harry (1987). 'Parliament and the Judges: The Removal of Federal Judges under Section 72 of the Constitution', 2 *Legislative Studies*, No. 2, 17.

Evatt, Elizabeth (1985). 'Foreword to Family Law Special Issue', 8 *University of New South Wales Law Review* vi.

Family Court of Australia (1997). *Annual Report 1996–97.*

—— (1998). *Annual Report 1997–98.*

Family Law Council (1995). *Magistrates in Family Law: An Evaluation of the Exercise of Summary Jurisdiction to Improve Access to Family Law*, AGPS, Canberra.

Federal Court of Australia (1998). *Annual Report 1997–98.*

Fitzhardinge, L. (1964). *William Morris Hughes: A Political Biography*, vol. 1, Angus & Robertson, Sydney.

Finnis, J. M. (1968). 'Separation of Powers in the Australian Constitution', 3 *Adelaide Law Review* 159.

Fisher, Elizabeth and Kirk, Jeremy (1997). 'Still Standing: An Argument for Open Standing in Australia and England', 71 *Australian Law Journal* 370.

Flanders, S. (1998). 'Case Management: Failure in America? Success in England and Wales?', 17 *Civil Justice Quarterly* 308.

Forsyth, Christopher (1998). 'Characterisation Revisited: An Essay in the Theory and Practice of the English Conflict of Laws', 114 *Law Quarterly Review* 141.

Frank, J. P. (1941). 'The Appointment of Supreme Court Justices', *Wisconsin Law Review* 172, 343, 461.

Freeman, Michael (1994). *Lloyd's Introduction to Jurisprudence*, 6th edn, Sweet and Maxwell, London.

French, R. S. (1989a). 'The Law of Torts and Part V of the Trade Practices Act', in P. D. Finn (ed.), *Essays on Torts*, Law Book Company, Sydney.

—— (1989b). 'A Lawyer's Guide to Misleading or Deceptive Conduct', 63 *Australian Law Journal* 250.

—— (1993). 'Manner and Form in Western Australia: An Historical Note', 23 *University of Western Australia Law Review* 335.

—— (1996). 'The Action for Misleading and Deceptive Conduct: Future Directions', in Colin Lockhart (ed.), *Misleading or Deceptive Conduct: Issues and Trends*, Federation Press, Sydney.

Fricke, Graham (1986). *Judges of the High Court*, Hutchinson, Melbourne.

Friedland, M. L. (1995). *A Place Apart: Judicial Independence and Accountability in Canada*, Canadian Judicial Council.

Fryberg, H. G. (1987). 'Cross-vesting of Jurisdiction', 17 *Queensland Law Society Journal* 113.

Fuller, Lon L. (1978). 'The Forms and Limits of Adjudication', 92 *Harvard Law Review* 353.

Gageler, Stephen (1987). 'Foundations of Australian Federalism and the Role of Judicial Review', 17 *Federal Law Review* 162.

Galligan, B. (1987). *Politics of the High Court*, University of Queensland Press, St Lucia.

Gerhardt, M. J. (1996). *The Federal Impeachment Process*, Princeton University Press, Princeton.

Gibbs, Sir Harry (1981). 'The State of the Australian Judicature', 55 *Australian Law Journal* 677.

—— (1983). 'Comment: The High Court Today', 10 *Sydney Law Review* 1.

—— (1985). 'State of the Australian Judicature', 59 *Australian Law Journal* 522.

—— (1987). 'The Separation of Powers—A Comparison', 17 *Federal Law Review* 151.

Gibson, James L. (1983). 'From Simplicity to Complexity: The Development of Theory in the Study of Judicial Behaviour', 5 *Political Behaviour* 7.

Giles, R. D. (1996). 'The Supreme Court Reference Out System', 12 *Building and Construction Law* 85.

Gleeson, M. (1998). The Role of a Judge and Becoming a Judge, Address to the National Judicial Orientation Program, 16 August.

Goldschmidt, J., Mahoney, B., Solomon, H. and Green, J. (1998). *Meeting the Challenge of Pro Se Litigation*, American Judicature Society, Michigan.

Gould, Nicholas and Cohen, Michael (1998). 'ADR: Appropriate Dispute Resolution in the UK Construction Industry', 17 *Civil Justice Quarterly* 103.

Graham, Morris (1995). *A. B. Piddington: The Last Radical Liberal*, UNSW Press, Sydney.

Griffith, G., Rose, D. and Gageler, S. (1988). 'Further Aspects of the Cross-vesting Scheme', 62 *Australian Law Journal* 1016.

Griffith, J. A. G. (1997). *The Politics of the Judiciary*, 5th edn, Fontana Press, London.

Gryski, Gerard and Main, Elenor (1986). 'Social Background as Predictors of Votes on State Courts of Last Resort: The Case of Sex Discrimination', 39 *Western Political Quarterly* 528.

Gummow, W. M. C. (1979). 'Pendent Jurisdiction in Australia—Section 32 of the Federal Court of Australia Act', 10 *Federal Law Review* 211.

Gunther, G. (1994). *Learned Hand: The Man and the Judge*, Knopf, New York.

Hamilton, A., Jay, J. and Madison, J. (1787). *The Federalist*, reprint E. M. Earle (ed.), Modern Library, New York, 1937.

Hand, Learned (1901). 'Historical and Practical Considerations Regarding Expert Testimony', 15 *Harvard Law Review* 40.

Handsley, Elizabeth (1998). 'Public Confidence in the Judiciary: A Red Herring for the Separation of Judicial Power', 20 *Sydney Law Review* 183.

Harrison Moore, W. (1910). *The Constitution of the Commonwealth of Australia*, 2nd edn, reprint, Legal Books, Sydney, 1997.

Haw, James (1980). *Stormy Patriot: The Life of Samuel Chase*, Maryland Historical Society, Baltimore.

Hawke, R. J. (1956). 'The Commonwealth Arbitration Court—Legal Tribunal or Economic Legislature?', 3 *University of Western Australia Annual Law Review* 422.

Hay, D., Linebaugh, P., Rule, J. G., Thompson, E. P. and Winslow, Cal (1977). *Albion's Fatal Tree: Crime and Society in Eighteenth-Century England*, Penguin, Harmondsworth.

Heard, Jim and Edwards, Sue (1998). Managing Electronic Information— A Litigation Perspective, AGS Law Group, CLE Seminar, Sydney, 4 June.

Heerey, Peter (1993). 'Justice for All?', 87 *Victorian Bar News* 65.

Henkin, Louis (1976). 'Is There a Political Question Doctrine?', 85 *Yale Law Journal* 597.

Hill, G. (1998). 'The Impact of Federal Court Appeals on the AAT: A View from the Court', in John McMillan (ed.), *The AAT—Twenty Years Forward*, Australian Institute of Administrative Law, Canberra.

Hocking, Jenny (1997). *Lionel Murphy: A Political Biography*, Cambridge University Press, Cambridge.

Holmes, J. D. (1955). 'Royal Commissions', 29 *Australian Law Journal* 253.

Holmes, Oliver Wendell (1920). 'Law in Science and Science in Law', in David Pannick (ed.), *Judges*, Oxford University Press, Oxford, 1987.

Hood Phillips, O. and Jackson, Paul (1987). *O. Hood Phillips' Constitutional and Administrative Law*, 7th edn, Sweet & Maxwell, London.

Hope, Janet (1996). 'A Constitutional Right to a Fair Trial? Implications for the Reform of the Australian Criminal Justice System', 24 *Federal Law Review* 173.

Independent Committee of Inquiry (1993). *National Competition Policy* (Hilmer Report), AGPS, Canberra.

Industrial Property Advisory Committee (1992). *Practice and Procedures for Enforcement of Industrial Property Rights in Australia*, Report to the Honourable Ross Free, 12 March.

Industrial Relations Court of Australia (1995). *Annual Report 1994–1995*.

Inglis Clark, A. (1901). *Studies in Australian Constitutional Law*, reprinted by Legal Books, Sydney, 1997.

—— (1905). *Studies in Australian Constitutional Law*, 2nd edn, Maxwell, Melbourne.

Jacob, J. (1998). 'The Bowman Review of the Court of Appeal', 61 *Modern Law Review* 390.

Jay, Stewart (1997). *Most Humble Servants: The Advisory Role of Early Judges*, Yale University Press, New Haven.

Johnson, Herbert A. (1993). 'Historical and Constitutional Perspectives on Cross-vesting of Court Jurisdiction', 19 *Melbourne University Law Review* 45.

Johnston, P. W. (1979). 'Governmental Standing Under the Constitution', in L. Stein (ed.), *Locus Standi*, Law Book Company, Sydney.

Joint Select Committee on Certain Aspects of the Operation and Interpretation of the Family Law Act (1992). *The Family Law Act 1975: Aspects of Its Operation and Interpretation*, AGPS, Canberra.

Joint Select Committee on Certain Family Law Issues (1995). *Funding and Administration of the Family Court of Australia*, AGPS, Canberra.

Joint Select Committee on the Family Law Act (1980). *Family Law in Australia*, AGPS, Canberra.

Joint Standing Committee on Migration (1994). *The Immigration Review Tribunal Appointments Process*, AGPS, Canberra.

Joyce, Roger B. (1984). *Samuel Walker Griffith*, University of Queensland Press, St Lucia.

Judicial Conference of Australia (1996). 'Abolition of Courts: Guidelines'.

Justice Society Committee on the Judiciary (1992). *The Judiciary in England and Wales: A Report*, Justice Society, London.

Katyal, N. K. (1998). 'Judges as Advicegivers', 50 *Stanford Law Review* 1709.

Katz, L. (1991). 'The History of the Inclusion in the Commonwealth Constitution of Section 76(iv)', 2 *Public Law Review* 228.

Kenny, Susan (1998). 'Interveners and Amici Curiae in the High Court', 20 *Adelaide Law Review* 159.

Kerr Committee (1971). *Report of the Commonwealth Administrative Review Committee*, AGPS, Canberra (Parliamentary Paper No. 144/1971).

King, Len (1995). 'The Separation of Powers', in Australian Institute of Judicial Administration, *Courts in a Representative Democracy*, AIJA, Melbourne.

Kirby, Michael (1991). 'Sir Edward McTiernan—A Centenary Reflection', 20 *Federal Law Review* 165.

—— (1995). 'Abolition of Courts and Non-reappointment of Judicial Officers', 12 *Australian Bar Review* 181.

—— (1997). 'What is it Really Like to be a Justice of the High Court?', 19 *Sydney Law Review* 514.

—— (1998). 'Attacks on Judges—A Universal Phenomenon', 72 *Australian Law Journal* 599.

Kommers, Donald P. and Finn, John E. (1998). *American Constitutional Law*, Wadsworth Publishing Company, Belmont.

Krotoszynski, R. J. (1997). 'On the Danger of Wearing Two Hats: *Mistretta* and *Morrison* Revisited', 38 *William and Mary Law Review* 417.

La Nauze, J. A. (ed.) (1968). *Federated Australia: Selections from Letters to the* Morning Post *1900–1910*, Melbourne University Press, Melbourne.

Lane, Patricia (1993). 'The AIJA Court Management Information Project: A Summary', 67 *Australian Law Journal* 527.

Lane, P. H. (1969). 'The Commonwealth Superior Court', 43 *Australian Law Journal* 148.

—— (1997). *Lane's Commentary on the Australian Constitution*, 2nd edn, Law Book Company, North Ryde.

Larivière, D. S. (1996). Overview of the Problems of French Civil Procedure, unpublished manuscript, Joint Law Courts Library, Sydney.

Lasser, Mitchel (1995). 'Judicial (Self) Portraits: Judicial Discourse in the French Legal System', 104 *Yale Law Journal* 1325.

Law Council of Australia (1951). 'Law Council Report', 25 *Australian Law Journal* 381.

—— (1997). *Submission to the Australian Law Reform Commission: Review of the Adversarial System of Litigation*.

Leflar, R. A., McDougal, L. L. III and Felix, R. L. (1986). *American Conflicts Law*, 4th edn, Michie Company, Charlottesville.

Leon, R. (1998). Tribunal Reform: The Government's Position, Address to the National Administrative Law Forum, Australian Institute of Administrative Law, Melbourne, 18–19 June.

Lindell, Geoffrey (1992). 'The Justiciability of Political Questions: Recent Developments', in H. P. Lee and George Winterton (eds), *Australian Constitutional Perspectives*, Law Book Company, Sydney.

—— (1997). 'Judicial Review of International Affairs', in Brian R. Opeskin and Donald R. Rothwell (eds), *International Law and Australian Federalism*, Melbourne University Press, Melbourne.

Lindgren, K. E. (1996). 'Standing and the State' in P. D. Finn (ed.), *Essays on Law and Government*, vol. 2, LBC Information Services, Sydney.

Lindgren, K. E. and Branson, C. M. (eds) (1998). *Federal Court Litigation Precedents*, Butterworths, Sydney.

Locke, John (1690). *Two Treatises of Civil Government*, reprinted by JM Dent & Sons, London, 1924.

Lord Chancellor's Advisory Committee on Legal Education and Conduct (1996). *First Report on Legal Education and Training*, Lord Chancellor's Office, London.

Ludeke, J. T. (1994). 'The Structural Features of the New System', 7 *Australian Journal of Labour Law* 133.

McCallum, Ronald (1992). 'A Modern Renaissance: Industrial Law and

Relations Under Federal Wigs 1977–1992', 14 *Sydney Law Review* 401.

MacCormick, N. (1978). *Legal Reasoning and Legal Theory*, Clarendon Press, Oxford.

McGarvie, R. E. (1996). 'Equality, Justice and Confidence', 5 *Journal of Judicial Administration* 141.

McHugh, M. H. (1999). 'The Judicial Method', 73 *Australian Law Journal* 37.

McInerney, M., Moloney, G. J. and McGregor, D. G. (1986). *Judges as Royal Commissioners and Chairmen of Non-Judicial Tribunals*, Australian Institute of Judicial Administration, Canberra.

Mack, Kathleen M. (1987). 'Standing to Sue Under Federal Administrative Law', 16 *Federal Law Review* 319.

Mackay, Lord (1994). *The Administration of Justice*, Stevens & Sons, London.

McKillop, Bron (1995). 'A French Judgment Through Common Law Eyes', 4 *Journal of Judicial Administration* 245.

—— (1997). 'ALRC's Issues Paper on the Federal Civil Litigation System: Contesting the Adversarial', 8 *Public Law Review* 139.

Mahoney, D. (1996). Procedural Fairness and Due Process, Address to the Local Court Annual Conference, 31 July.

Markesinis, Basil S. (1990). 'Litigation Mania in England, Germany and the USA: Are We So Very Different?, 49 *Cambridge Law Journal* 233.

—— (1995). 'The Comparatist (or a Plea for Broader Legal Education)', 15 *Yearbook of European Law* 261.

Marr, D. (1980). *Barwick*, Allen & Unwin, Sydney.

—— (1992). *Barwick*, 2nd edn, Allen & Unwin, Sydney.

Martineau, Robert J. (1990). *Appellate Justice in England and the United States: A Comparative Analysis*, William S Hein & Company, Buffalo.

Mason, A. T. (1953). 'Extra-Judicial Work for Judges: The Views of Chief Justice Stone', 67 *Harvard Law Review* 193.

Mason, Sir Anthony (1984). 'The Role of Counsel and Appellate Advocacy', 58 *Australian Law Journal* 357.

—— (1996). 'A New Perspective on Separation of Powers', 82 *Canberra Bulletin of Public Administration* 1.

—— (1997). 'The Appointment and Removal of Judges', in H. Cunningham (ed.), *Fragile Bastion: Judicial Independence in the Nineties*, Judicial Commission of New South Wales, Sydney.

—— (1998). 'A Comment', 20 *Adelaide Law Review* 173.

Mason, K. (1987). 'Cross-vesting and Other Proposals for Cooperative Arrangements by the Advisory Committee on the Australian Judicial System', in *Papers Presented at the Sixth Annual AIJA Seminar*, Australian Institute of Judicial Administration, Melbourne.

—— (1989). 'Prospective Overruling', 63 *Australian Law Journal* 526.

—— (1995). 'The Rule of Law', in P. D. Finn (ed.), *Essays on Law and Government*, vol. 1, Law Book Company, Sydney.

Mason, Keith and Crawford, James (1988). 'The Cross-vesting Scheme', 62 *Australian Law Journal* 328.

Mathew, T. (1902). *The Practice of the Commercial Court*, Butterworth & Company, London.

Mikva, Abner J. (1998). 'Why Judges Should Not be Advicegivers', 50 *Stanford Law Review* 1825.

Ministry of Attorney-General (Ontario) (1995). *Civil Justice Review*, First Report, Ontario.

Mitzner, Adam (1989). 'The Evolving Role of the Senate in Judicial Nominations', 5 *Journal of Law and Politics* 387.

Moloney, G. (1993). 'AIJA's Report on the Operation of the National Scheme of Cross-vesting of Jurisdiction', 67 *Australian Law Journal* 289.

Moloney, Garrie J. and McMaster, Susan (1992). *Cross-vesting of Jurisdiction: A Review of the Operation of the National Scheme*, Australian Institute of Judicial Administration, Melbourne.

Montesquieu, Charles-Louis de Secondat (1748). *L'Esprit des Lois, Book XI*, in Michael Curtis (ed.), *The Great Political Theories*, vol. 1, Avon Books, New York, 1981.

Murphy, W. T. (1991). 'The Oldest Social Science? The Epistemic Properties of the Common Law Tradition', 54 *Modern Law Review* 182.

—— (1998). 'Review of Richard A. Posner's *Law and Legal Theory in England and America*', 61 *Modern Law Review* 291.

Nand, Janice (1997). 'Judicial Power and Administrative Tribunals: The Decision in *Brandy v HREOC*', 14 *AIAL Forum* 15.

Neumann, Eddy (1973). *The High Court of Australia—A Collective Portrait (1903–1972)*, 2nd edn, University of Sydney, Sydney.

Nicholson, Alistair (1988). 'Separate Family Court Seen By CJ as Disaster', 23 *Australian Law News* 20.

Nygh, P. (1995). *Conflict of Laws in Australia*, 6th edn, Butterworths, Sydney.

O'Brien, B. (1989). 'The Constitutional Validity of the Cross-vesting Legislation', 17 *Melbourne University Law Review* 307.

Ohlinger, Theo (1998). 'Constitutional Review: The Austrian Experience as Seen From a Comparative Perspective', 53 *Zeitschrift für öffentliches Recht* 421.

Oliver, Lord (1992). 'The Appeal Process', 2 *Journal of Judicial Administration* 63.

Opeskin, Brian (1995). 'Federal Jurisdiction in Australian Courts: Policies and Prospects', 46 *South Carolina Law Review* 765.

Ormrod, Sir Roger (1968). 'Scientific Evidence in Court', *Criminal Law Review* 240.

520 Bibliography

O'Sullivan, Dominic (1996). 'Gender and Judicial Appoinment', 19 *University of Queensland Law Journal* 107.

Parker, Stephen (1998). *Courts and the Public*, Australian Institute of Judicial Administration, Melbourne.

Parliamentary Commission of Inquiry (1986). *Special Report*, Parliamentary Paper 443/1986.

Pengilley, Warren (1987). 'Section 52 of the Trade Practices Act—A Plaintiff's New Exocet', 15 *Australian Business Law Review* 247.

Perry, Barbara (1991). *A 'Representative' Supreme Court? The Impact of Race, Religion, and Gender on Appointments*, Greenwood Press, New York.

Phillips, P. D. (1962). 'Choice of Law in Federal Jurisdiction', 3 *Melbourne University Law Review* 170.

Posner, Richard (1995). *Overcoming Law*, Harvard University Press, Cambridge, Mass.

—— (1996). *Law and Legal Theory in England and America*, Clarendon Press, Oxford.

Pound, Roscoe (1913). 'The Causes of Popular Dissatisfaction with the Administration of Justice', Address to the Annual Convention of the American Bar Association 1906, in *Journal of the American Judicature Society* 1.

—— (1923). *Interpretations of Legal History*, Macmillan, New York.

Priestley, L. J. (1995). 'A Federal Common Law in Australia?', 6 *Public Law Review* 221.

Quick, J. and Garran, R. R. (1901). *The Annotated Constitution of the Australian Commonwealth*, reprinted by Legal Books, Sydney, 1976.

Quick, J. and Groom, L. E. (1904). *The Judicial Power of the Commonwealth*, Charles F. Maxwell, Melbourne.

Rehnquist, W. H. (1992). *Grand Inquests: The Historic Impeachments of Justice Samuel Chase and President Andrew Johnson*, William Morrow & Co, New York.

Reid, G. S. (1977). 'Commentaries', in Gareth Evans (ed.), *Labor and the Constitution 1972–1975*, Heinemann, Melbourne.

—— (1978). 'The Changing Political Framework', in T. van Dugteren (ed.), *The Political Process: Can it Cope?*, Hodder & Stoughton, Sydney.

Review of the Federal Court of Australia (1990). Review of the Resources of the Federal Court of Australia, 23 November.

Rogers, Andrew (1980). 'Federal/State Courts—The Need to Restructure to Avoid Jurisdictional Conflicts', 54 *Australian Law Journal* 285.

Royal Commission of Inquiry into Alleged Telephone Interceptions (1986). *Report*, AGPS, Canberra (Parliamentary Paper No. 155/1986).

Royal Commission on Australian Government Administration (1976). *Report*, AGPS, Canberra.

Ruddock, P. (1997). 'The Broad Implications for Administrative Law Under the Coalition Government with Particular Reference to Migration Matters', in John McMillan (ed.), *Administrative Law Under the Coalition Government*, Australian Institute of Administrative Law, Canberra.

Sackville, R. (1997). 'Continuity and Judicial Creativity: Some Observations', 20 *University of New South Wales Law Journal* 145.

Saunders, Cheryl (1984). 'Non-Justiciability in Australian Constitutional Law', in D. Galligan (ed.), *Essays in Legal Theory*, Melbourne University Press, Melbourne.

—— (1993). 'Appeal or Review: The Experience of Administrative Appeals in Australia', *Acta Juridica* 88.

Sawer, Geoffrey (1956). *Australian Federal Politics and Law 1901–1929*, Melbourne University Press, Melbourne.

—— (1961a). 'Judicial Power Under the Constitution', in R. Else-Mitchell (ed.), *Essays on the Australian Constitution*, 2nd edn, Law Book Company, Sydney.

—— (1961b). 'Separation of Powers in Australian Federalism', 35 *Australian Law Journal* 177.

—— (1963). *Australian Federal Politics and Law 1929–1949*, Melbourne University Press, Melbourne.

—— (1965). 'Judicial Administration: The Subject and Some Applications', 8 *Journal of the Society of Public Teachers of Law* 301.

—— (1967). *Australian Federalism in the Courts*, Melbourne University Press, Melbourne.

Schubert, G. (1968a). 'Opinion Agreement Among High Court Justices in Australia', 4 *ANZ Journal of Sociology* 2.

—— (1968b). 'Political Ideology on the High Court', 3 *Politics* 21.

—— (1969a). 'Judicial Attitudes and Policy-making in the Dixon Court', 7 *Osgoode Hall Law Journal* 1.

—— (1969b). 'Two Causal Models of Decision Making by the High Court of Australia', in G. Schubert and D. Danelski (eds), *Comparative Judicial Behavior*, Oxford University Press, New York.

—— (1983). 'Aging, Conservatism and Judicial Behavior', 3 *Micropolitics* 135.

Schwarzer, W. (1996). 'Case Management in the Federal Courts', 15 *Civil Justice Quarterly* 141.

Scott, I. R. (1995). 'Caseflow Management in the Trial Court', in A. A. S. Zuckerman and Ross Cranston (eds), *Reform of Civil Procedure— Essays on Access to Justice*, Clarendon Press, Oxford.

—— (1996). 'Access to Justice: Lord Woolf's Final Report', 15 *Civil Justice Quarterly* 273.

Scott, Sir Richard (1997). Regional Scenarios Affecting Courts and the Legal Profession in the 21st Century, Address to the AIJA/Asia Pacific Courts Conference, August.

Select Committee of the Legislative Assembly upon the Appointment of Judges to the High Court of Australia (1976). *Report*, Government Printer, Sydney (Parliamentary Paper No. 53/1975).

Senate Select Committee on Allegations Concerning a Judge (1984). *Report to the Senate*, Commonwealth Government Printer, Canberra, (Parliamentary Paper No. 271/1984).

Senate Select Committee on the Conduct of a Judge (1984). *Report to the Senate*, Commonwealth Government Printer, Canberra (Parliamentary Paper No. 168/1984).

Senate Standing Committee on Constitutional and Legal Affairs (1974). *Report on the Law and Administration of Divorce and Related Matters and the Clauses of the Family Law Bill 1974*, AGPS, Canberra.

Sexton, Michael and Maher, Laurence (1982). *The Legal Mystique: The Role of Lawyers in Australian Society*, Angus & Robertson, Sydney.

Shapiro, M. (1981). *Courts: A Comparative and Political Analysis*, University of Chicago Press, Chicago.

Shaw, Geoffrey (1994). 'The Industrial Relations Court of Australia', 71 *Current Affairs Bulletin* 17.

Sheppard, I. F. (1999). 'The Issue of the Inquisitorial System of Justice', 31 *Australian Journal of Forensic Sciences* 19.

Sherman, Jo and Stanfield, Allison (1998). *Final Report to Council of Chief Justices of Australia and New Zealand on Electronic Appeals Project*, Queensland Law Foundation Technology Services.

Sherman, T. (1997). 'Should Judges Conduct Royal Commissions?', 8 *Public Law Review* 5.

Shetreet, S. (1976). *Judges on Trial*, North-Holland, Amsterdam.

—— (1987). 'Who Will Judge: Reflections on the Process and Standards of Judicial Selection', 61 *Australian Law Journal* 766.

Star, Leonie (1996). *Counsel of Perfection—The Family Court of Australia*, Oxford University Press, Melbourne.

Stephen, Sir Ninian (1986). *Sir Owen Dixon—A Celebration*, Melbourne University Press, Melbourne.

—— (1989). *Judicial Independence*, Australian Institute of Judicial Administration, Melbourne.

—— (1998). Address to the Law Institute of Victoria, 19 August.

Stevens, Robert (1993). *The Independence of the Judiciary: The View from the Lord Chancellor's Office*, Clarendon Press, Oxford.

Stone, Julius (1981). 'From Principles to Principles', 97 *Law Quarterly Review* 224.

Stoner, James R. Jnr (1992). *Common Law and Liberal Theory: Coke, Hobbes, and the Origins of American Constitutionalism*, University of Kansas Press, Lawrence.

Story, Joseph (1891). *Commentaries on the Constitution of the United States*, Little, Brown & Company, Boston.

Street, Laurence (1978). 'The Consequences of a Dual System of State and Federal Courts', 52 *Australian Law Journal* 434.

—— (1982). 'Towards an Australian Judicial System', 56 *Australian Law Journal* 515.

Sullivan, A. M. (1928). 'The Last Forty Years of the Irish Bar', 3 *Cambridge Law Journal* 365.

Sunstein, C. R. (1996). *Legal Reasoning and Political Conflict*, Oxford University Press, New York.

Supreme Court of New South Wales (1997). *Annual Review 1997*, Supreme Court of New South Wales, Sydney.

Supreme Court of Victoria (1988). *Annual Report 1988*.

Susskind, Richard (1996). *The Future of Law: Facing the Challenges of Information Technology*, Clarendon Press, Oxford.

Taylor, G. D. S. (1979). 'Standing to Challenge the Constitutionality of Legislation', in L. Stein (ed.), *Locus Standi*, Law Book Company, Sydney.

Temby, Ian (1985). 'Prosecution Discretions and the Director of Public Prosecutions Act 1983', 59 *Australian Law Journal* 197.

Thomas, J. B. (1997). *Judicial Ethics in Australia*, 2nd edn, LBC Information Services, Sydney.

Thomson, J. A. (1984). 'Removal of High Court and Federal Judges: Some Observations Concerning Section 72(ii) of the Australian Constitution', *Australian Current Law* 36 033, 36 055.

—— (1992). 'Appointing Australian High Court Justices: Some Constitutional Conundrums', in H. P. Lee and George Winterton (eds), *Australian Constitutional Perspectives*, Law Book Co, Sydney.

—— (1997). 'Non-Justiciability and the Australian Constitution', in Michael Coper and George Williams (eds), *Power, Parliament and the People*, Federation Press, Sydney.

Thornton, Margaret (1996). *Dissonance and Distrust: Women in the Legal Profession*, Oxford University Press, Melbourne.

Todd, Alpheus (1869). *On Parliamentary Government in England: Its Origin, Development, and Practical Operation*, vol. 2, Longmans, Green & Co, London.

Toose, P. B. (1975). *Independent Enquiry into the Repatriation System: Report*, vol. 1, AGPS, Canberra.

Tribe, L. H. (1985). *God Save This Honorable Court*, Random House, New York.

—— (1988). *American Constitutional Law*, 2nd edn, Foundation Press, New York.

Twomey, Anne (1997). 'Reconciling Parliament's Contempt Powers with the Constitutional Separation of Powers', 8 *Public Law Review* 88.

Ulmer, Sidney (1986). 'Are Social Background Models Time-Bound?', 80 *American Political Science Review* 957.

US Congress (1974). House of Representatives Judiciary Committee, *Impeachment: Selected Materials on Procedure*, US Government Printing Office.

Victorian Legal and Constitutional Committee (1990). *Report to Parliament Upon the Constitution Act 1975*, Government Printer, Melbourne.

Vile, M. J. C. (1967). *Constitutionalism and the Separation of Powers*, Clarendon Press, Oxford.

Volcansek, Mary (1993). *Judicial Impeachment*, University of Illinois Press, Urbana.

Wade, E. C. S. and Bradley, A. W. (1993). *Constitutional and Administrative Law*, 11th edn by A. W. Bradley and K. D. Ewing, Longman, London.

Wald, Patricia M. (1983). 'The Problem With the Courts: Black-Robed Bureaucracy or Collegiality Under Challenge?', 42 *Maryland Law Review* 766.

Walker, Kristen (1997). 'Persona Designata, Incompatibility and the Separation of Powers', 8 *Public Law Review* 153.

Watts, R. L. (1966). *New Federations: Experiments in the Commonwealth*, Clarendon Press, Oxford.

Waugh, J. (1998). 'A Question of Capacity: The Case of Justice Bruce', 9 *Public Law Review* 223.

Weis, Joseph F. (1995). 'The Case for Appellate Court Revision', 93 *Michigan Law Review* 1266.

Weisbrot, David (1990). *Australian Lawyers*, Longman, Melbourne.

Wheare, K. (1947). *Federal Government*, Oxford University Press, New York.

Wheeler, Fiona (1996a). 'Original Intent and the Doctrine of the Separation of Powers in Australia', 7 *Public Law Review* 96.

—— (1996b). 'The Use of Federal Judges to Discharge Executive Functions: The Justice Mathews Case', 82 *Canberra Bulletin of Public Administration* 10.

—— (1997). 'The Doctrine of Separation of Powers and Constitutionally Entrenched Due Process in Australia', 23 *Monash University Law Review* 248.

Wilcox, Murray (1997). 'Representative Proceedings in the Federal Court of Australia: A Progress Report', 8(5) *Australian Product Liability Reporter* 77.

Williams, Daryl (1996). 'The Australian Parliament and High Court: Determination of Constitutional Questions', in Charles Sampford and Kim Preston (eds), *Interpreting Constitutions: Theories, Principles and Institutions*, Federation Press, Sydney.

—— (1998). 'Judicial Independence', 36 *Law Society Journal* 50.

Williams, John (1996). 'Rethinking Advisory Opinions', 7 *Public Law Review* 205.

Williams, P., Fry, T., Hyde, C. and Scheelings, R. (1998). *Report of the Review of Scales of Legal Professional Fees in Federal Jurisdictions*, Attorney-General's Department, Canberra.

Wilson, Woodrow (1885). *Congressional Government: A Study in American Politics*, Houghton Mifflin, Boston.

Winterton, George (1983). *Parliament, the Executive and the Governor-General: A Constitutional Analysis*, Melbourne University Press, Melbourne.

—— (1987). 'Judges as Royal Commissioners', 10 *University of New South Wales Law Journal* 108.

—— (1994). 'Separation of Judicial Power as an Implied Bill of Rights', in G. Lindell (ed.), *Future Directions in Australian Constitutional Law*, Federation Press, Sydney.

—— (1995). *Judicial Remuneration in Australia*, Australian Institute of Judicial Administration, Melbourne.

Wood, Gordon S. (1972). *The Creation of the American Republic, 1776–1787*, W W Norton & Co, New York.

Woolf, Harry (1952). 'The Proposed Commonwealth Divorce Law', 26 *Australian Law Journal* 307.

Woolf, Lord (1996a). *Draft Civil Proceedings Rules*.

—— (1996b). *Final Report to the Lord Chancellor on the Civil Justice System in England and Wales*, HMSO.

—— (1997). 'Medics, Lawyers and the Courts', 16 *Civil Justice Quarterly* 302.

Wright, C. (1994). *Law of Federal Courts*, 5th edn, West Publishing Company, St Pauls.

Wynes, W. A. (1976). *Legislative, Executive and Judicial Powers in Australia*, 5th edn, Law Book Company, Sydney.

Zeitz, S. (1998). 'Security of Tenure and Judicial Independence', 7 *Journal of Judicial Administration* 159.

Zines, Leslie (1966). '"Laws for the Government of Any Territory": Section 122 of the Constitution', 2 *Federal Law Review* 72.

—— (1977). 'The Double Dissolutions and Joint Sitting', in Gareth Evans (ed.), *Labor and the Constitution 1972–1975*, Heinemann, Melbourne.

—— (1997). *The High Court and the Constitution*, 4th edn, Butterworths, Sydney.

—— (1998). 'Constitutional Aspects of Judicial Review of Administrative Action', 1 *Constitutional Law and Policy Review* 50.

Zines, L. and Lindell, G. J. (1982). *Sawer's Australian Constitutional Cases*, 4th edn, Law Book Company, Sydney.

Zoller, Elizabeth (1999). *Droit Constitutionnel*, 2nd edn, Presses Univer-
    sitaires de France, Paris.
Zuckerman, A. A. S. (1994). 'Quality and Economy in Civil Procedure', 14
    Oxford Journal of Legal Studies 353.
—— (1996). 'Lord Woolf's Access to Justice: Plus ça change ...', 59
    Modern Law Review 773.
Zuckerman, A. A. S. and Cranston, Ross (eds) (1995). *Reform of Civil
    Procedure—Essays on Access to Justice*, Clarendon Press, Oxford.

Index

Compiled by Kingsley Siebel